A New
Fiedler
Reader

D0048563

A New Fiedler Reader

Leslie Fiedler

Prometheus Books

59 John Glenn Drive
Amherst, New York 14228-2197

Published 1999 by Prometheus Books

Inquiries should be addressed to
Prometheus Books, 59 John Glenn Drive, Amherst, New York 14228–2197.
VOICE: 716–691–0133, ext. 207.
FAX: 716–564–2711.
WWW.PROMETHEUSBOOKS.COM

03 02 01 00 99   5 4 3 2 1

Library of Congress Cataloging-in-Publication Data

Fiedler, Leslie A.
    [Selections. 1999]
    A new Fiedler reader / Leslie Fiedler.
        p.   cm.
    ISBN 1–57392–746–5 (pa. : alk. paper)
    I. Title.
PS3556.I34A6   1999   99–37952
810.9—dc21   CIP

Printed in the United States of America on acid-free paper

To Sally

Acknowledgments

The author wishes to thank the editors and publishers of the following firms and periodicals under whose imprints parts of this book originally appeared:

From *An End to Innocence*
> Come Back to the Raft Ag'in, Huck Honey!—originally published in *Partisan Review* (June 1948).
> Montana; or The End of Jean-Jacques Rousseau—originally published in *Partisan Review* (December 1949).
> Afterthoughts on the Rosenbergs—originally published in *Encounter* (October 1953).
> Roman Holiday

From *No! In Thunder*
> Archetype and Signature—originally published in *The Sewanee Review* (spring 1952).
> Dante: Green Thoughts in a Green Shade—originally published in *The Kenyon Review* (spring 1956).
> In the Beginning Was the Word—originally published in *The Sewanee Review* (summer 1958).

From *Love and Death in the American Novel*
> The Novel in America

From *Waiting for the End*
> Traitor or Laureate: The Two Trials of the Poet
> The Death of the Old Men

From *The Return of the Vanishing American*
> The Higher Sentimentality
> Boxing the Compass

From *Being Busted*
> Exhibit A: On Being Busted at Fifty—originally published in *The New York Review of Books* (July 1967).

From *To the Gentiles*
> Negro and Jew—originally published in *Encounter* (summer 1956).
> Saul Bellow—originally published in *Prairie Schooner* (summer 1957).

vii

Contents

NONFICTION

POETRY

FICTION

Preface to 1999 Edition

WHEN I ORIGINALLY contemplated a second edition of *A Fiedler Reader*, I planned to add nothing to it. Consequently, it seemed appropriate to call it *A Fiedler Re-Reader*, but since I finally did add four essays, a short story, and a narrative poem, I have entitled it instead *A New Fiedler Reader*. To be sure, there is nothing absolutely new in it. Not only had all the newly included items previously appeared in print, but so, too, had those included from the very start. Nearly all of both, moreover, before becoming words on the page had preexisted as sounds in the air, because, as is my habit, I had rehearsed them in speech before fixing them in writing.

When I can, I do this to a living audience in the classroom or auditorium and on radio or TV. When no such public forum is available (as it typically was *not* at the beginning of my career), I do so in the privacy of my study or bedroom. Such interior monologues, however, leave me unsatisfied, since I am always aware that to become a *real* writer one must cease talking to oneself and open a dialogue with others. But this, I also realize, requires publishing a substantial book, suitable for sale over the counter and permanent storage in libraries.

For many years, however, I was able to make it into print not in hardbound books but only in ephemeral publications with a small, narrow, readership. These sometimes were scholarly journals—but more often they were the sort of political periodicals which reserve a few back pages for discussions of the arts; and most often *avant-garde* "little mags," like the *Kenyon Review* and the *Partisan Review*. Improbably enough, it was the latter, which never had more than ten thousand subscribers, that introduced my work to a larger, more heterogeneous audience. But this did not happen until a poem of mine called "Dumb Dick," which had first appeared in its pages, was reprinted in a scurrilous pamphlet, distributed by the thousands to the citizens of Montana as evidence that I was a pornographer as well as a Commie-Jew-Easterner and therefore should be fired forthwith from the state university.

Ironically, however, not only was I not fired, but—thanks to the unsolicited publicity—I was read by a larger audience than I had ever reached before or, indeed, would again, until, many years later, the editors of mass circulation magazines like *Esquire* and *Playboy*, decided, for reasons I have never quite understood, that I had become saleable.

Long before that, shorter pieces of mine had begun to be published in perfectly respectable hard-cover books, most of which were anthologies intended for use in Freshman Composition courses. In them my name appeared only in the table of contents and the indexes, where it was lost among those of the many other equally unknown and undistinguished contributors. In order to move it to more visible spots on the title page and the spine, I would have to plan, sell and edit, I realized, rather than merely contribute to such an anthology; and finally I did so—twice over in fact. But even top billing as editor-in-chief did not satisfy me; since I could never forget that most of the material in the volume which I had, as it were, signed, sealed and delivered was not written by me.

I did not actually publish *An End to Innocence*, the first book I could proudly claim was mine, all mine until I was nearly forty; at which point I was so delighted that I failed utterly to perceive that though it was the work of a single author (and that author *me*), it was still an anthology in form—not composed but compiled by selecting and rearranging previously published pieces. Like all such arbitrarily ordered compilations, it had no real beginning, middle and end, and therefore tended to fall apart into the separate pieces out of which it had been assembled.

It is, in any case, one or another of those pieces rather than the patchwork whole that its readers are most likely to remember. The piece of *An End to Innocence* such readers thus recall is "Come Back to the Raft Ag'in, Huck Honey." I am pleased that even now, fifty years after its first appearance, I continue to be bombarded with requests to reprint it, usually from official academic sources. But what moves me more are personal responses like the one which lies on my desk at this very moment. In it, a correspondent hitherto quite unknown to me, after expressing her gratitude, asks me to autograph an enclosed mint first edition of *An End to Innocence.* She does so, she goes on to explain, because reading and arguing about its contents with her young man of the moment started a relationship that ended in a lifelong happy marriage to him, who in the interim, had become a football coach famous enough to send me an autographed photo of himself in return.

Soon after its publication my first book had begun to receive enough responses of both kinds to persuade me (and my publisher) to make my second, *No! In Thunder*, a first-person-singular anthology, too.

Nor have I ever abandoned that form. In fact, my two latest books, *Fiedler on the Roof* and *Tyranny of the Normal*, make a matching pair with the two earliest. Moreover, in the years between, I compiled three others and then combined all five in a two-volume super-anthology called simply *Collected Essays*. I thought of this originally as the ultimate rearrangement of these already much-rearranged essays, but it turned out to be only the penultimate one; since shortly after finishing it, I was impelled to do one more, which would not only be more inclusive than its predecessors—but absolutely the last.

This meta-anthology, which I eventually called by the modest name of *A Fiedler Reader*, I began to make by selecting from the *Collected Essays*, a considerably reduced number of short prose pieces that I then eked out with a few of my stories originally published under the title of *Nude Croquet* and a handful of poems that had only appeared before in periodicals.

The significance of thus juxtaposing my creative and critical words, I have dealt with sufficiently in the Preface to the first edition of the *Reader*. But somehow I failed even to mention that I had also included in it brief extracts from a genre to which I came later but over which I have lingered long: booklength critical narratives like *Love and Death in the American Novel*, *The Return of the Vanishing American*, and *The Stranger in Shakespeare*.

There are critics who believe that it is always an abomination to cut up into patches suitable for quilting what a writer has woven into a seamless whole cloth; and there is something in me which responds sympathetically to that belief. Yet something else responds even more strongly to those who contend that only by thus snipping and stitching can one discover the hidden fragmentary in the whole and hidden whole in the fragmentary. Certainly, it was only after such disassembling and reassembling of my own work that I perceived the underlying unit of it all: the sense in which everything I have written, no matter how different in genre and subject, scale and scope, is a variation on one or another of the same themes: the fear of the Other; the death of love; the love of death; the dream of interethnic male bonding.

By merely flipping a few pages ahead in this book, any reader can learn this half of the truth; and then by flipping them backward become a re-reader and learn the other half. This is that the unity I always seek and sometimes find is not the monotonous, bland uniformity of black and white, but a *discordia concors*, the simultaneous clash and confluence of the garish colors of a crazy quilt in which there is always room for one more suitably inappropriate patch.

LESLIE A. FIEDLER
Buffalo, New York
8 March 1999

Preface

MOST OF THE WORKS that I have included in this collection originally appeared in contexts which falsified them. Written in loneliness, which is to say, in the context of what survived in my head at the moment of composition of other things I had written (some half forgotten, some abandoned in manuscript) or planned to write (some not yet completed, some perhaps never to be begun), they were edited by men and women who, as often as not, did not quite understand them, and published side by side with the work of other writers whom, even more often, I found unsympathetic. In the glossier magazines, they appeared in the midst of nude fold-outs, panel cartoons and ads for beer, cigarettes, men's clothing, women's underwear: alien landscapes irrelevant to the ones in which they had been imagined or which they tried to evoke—libraries, classrooms, and the vanished streets of Newark, Missoula, Rome, or Buffalo. In the grimmer quarterlies and monthlies, it was the explicit politics which framed them that suggested relevances and resonances that they themselves sought to resist or subvert or ironize. But the effect was much the same in either case.

All stories, poems, and essays are, I know, altered by unforeseen, anonymous collaborators when they make it into print at all—a fate, I suppose, they do not escape even in such a one-man show as I have assembled here. But at least this time around compositions signed with my name (which itself has changed over 30 or 35 years from Leslie A. Fiedler to Leslie Fiedler for reasons I do not completely understand) appear only with others signed with one or another of those names. And this seems to me good. To be sure, I have published other collections of my own work, but these have been exclusively of short fictions or critical essays; and they are shelved in libraries as if they were of exactly the same kind as the essays or stories of authors who end up beside them by the accident of alphabetization. Another kind of falsification—falsification by genre.

This seems especially inappropriate to a writer like me whose poems have continued to rhyme when rhyme is unfashionable and whose criticism was ecstatic and autobiographical when the objective, impersonal, formalist criticism was all the vogue. Moreover, I have never managed to remember—indeed, I never quite understood—the differences between making stories and criticizing them, asking my readers to respond to both with the same act of poetic faith. In all my writing, it is images I pursue in the name of passion, sentiment, titillation, though I sometimes suspect that I love a joke, good or bad, better than anything else. I have, in short, sought to enlighten, amuse, and provoke without ever betraying either the cadences of ordinary speech or the aspiration to song that lives in the hearts of the most tone-deaf among us.

I like to think, therefore, that there is no passage in this volume that cannot be read aloud with profit and pleasure. And it is partly to make my readers aware of this fact that I have decided for the first time to publish in book form some of the verse which over the years has appeared in journals only to be forgotten as ephemeral poetry tends always to be forgotten. Yet I was first published as a poet; and many of the "porn" essays I like most out of all I have written seem to me to be really crypto-poems, whose nature it is high time I reveal.

Recently, therefore, I gave a reading in which I recited side by side with some of the verses that follow, the lyric heart of my perhaps best-known essay, "Come Back to the Raft Ag'in Huck Honey"—and was pleased to discover that in performance it *sang:* sang a true song about, as we used to say in the symposia of the fifties, Our Country and Our Culture. A true song about me.

It was an odd occasion, however, in which I found myself performing in a space as undefined and unfocussed as a dream—with lights shining into my eyes and the audience invisible in the dark, so that I was unsure how many, if indeed any, sat before me or listened. True, there was a murmur of approbation or assent from time to time, but chiefly my performance was greeted with silence (polite? bored? respectful? bemused?), quite as if I were back at my own desk, inside the loneliness of my own head, which is to say, without a living audience or the guarantee that one would ever exist. Yet I was all the more aware that I must continue to speak and write as I have done always *as if* to everyone: to the Great Dead, to readers not yet born, and especially to those among whom I pass daily (touching or not touching, eyes meeting or averted)—men and women who will never read any book ever, and could not care less (but I care).

Leslie Fiedler

Buffalo, New York
March 8, 1977

Nonfiction

Come Back to the Raft Ag'in, Huck Honey!

It is perhaps to be expected that the Negro and the homosexual should become stock literary themes in a period when the exploration of responsibility and failure has become again a primary concern of our literature. It is the discrepancy they represent that haunts us, that moral discrepancy before which we are helpless, having no resources (no tradition of courtesy, no honored mode of cynicism) for dealing with a conflict of principle and practice. It used once to be fashionable to think of puritanism as a force in our lives encouraging hypocrisy; quite the contrary, its emphasis upon the singleness of belief and action, its turning of the most prosaic areas of life into arenas where one's state of grace is tested, confuse the outer and the inner and make hypocrisy among us, perhaps more strikingly than ever elsewhere, *visible,* visibly detestable, the cardinal sin. It is not without significance that the shrug of the shoulders (the acceptance of circumstance as a sufficient excuse, the sign of self-pardon before the inevitable lapse) seems in America an unfamiliar, an alien gesture.

And yet before the continued existence of physical homosexual love (our crudest epithets notoriously evoke the mechanics of such affairs), before the blatant ghettos in which the Negro conspicuously creates the gaudiness and stench that offend him, the white American must make a choice between coming to terms with institutionalized discrepancy or formulating radically new ideologies. There are, to be sure, stopgap devices, evasions of that final choice; not the least interesting

3

is the special night club: the "queer" café, the black-and-tan joint, in which fairy or Negro exhibit their fairy-ness, their Negro-ness as if they were mere divertissements, gags thought up for the laughs and having no reality once the lights go out and the chairs are piled on the tables by the cleaning women. In the earlier minstrel show, a Negro performer was required to put on with grease paint and burnt cork the formalized mask of blackness; while the queer must exaggerate flounce and flutter into the convention of his condition.

The situations of the Negro and the homosexual in our society pose quite opposite problems, or at least problems suggesting quite opposite solutions. Our laws on homosexuality and the context of prejudice they objectify must apparently be changed to accord with a stubborn social fact; whereas it is the social fact, our overt behavior toward the Negro, that must be modified to accord with our laws and the, at least official, morality they objectify. It is not, of course, quite so simple. There is another sense in which the fact of homosexual passion contradicts a national myth of masculine love, just as our real relationship with the Negro contradicts a myth of that relationship; and those two myths with their betrayals are, as we shall see, one.

The existence of overt homosexuality threatens to compromise an essential aspect of American sentimental life: the camaraderie of the locker room and ball park, the good fellowship of the poker game and fishing trip, a kind of passionless passion, at once gross and delicate, homoerotic in the boy's sense, possessing an innocence above suspicion. To doubt for a moment this innocence, which can survive only as *assumed*, would destroy our stubborn belief in a relationship simple, utterly satisfying, yet immune to lust; physical as the handshake is physical, this side of copulation. The nineteenth-century myth of the Immaculate Young Girl has failed to survive in any *felt* way into our time. Rather, in the dirty jokes shared among men in the smoking car, the barracks, or the dormitory, there is a common male revenge against women for having flagrantly betrayed that myth; and under the revenge, the rather smug assumption of the chastity of the revenging group, in so far as it is a purely male society. From what other source could arise that unexpected air of good clean fun which overhangs such sessions? It is this self-congratulatory buddy-buddiness, its astonishing naïveté that breed at once endless opportunities for inversion and the terrible reluctance to admit its existence, to surrender the last believed-in stronghold of love without passion.

It is, after all, what we know from a hundred other sources that is here verified: the regressiveness, in a technical sense, of American life, its implacable nostalgia for the infantile, at once wrong-headed and somehow admirable. The mythic America is boyhood — and who would dare be startled to realize that the two most popular, most *absorbed*, I am sure, of the handful of great books in our native heritage are customarily to be found, illustrated, on the shelves of the children's library. I am referring, of course, to *Moby Dick* and *Huckleberry Finn*, so different in technique and language, but alike children's books or, more precisely, *boys'* books.

There are the Leatherstocking Tales of Cooper, too, as well as Dana's *Two Years Before the Mast* and a good deal of Stephen Crane, books whose continuing favor depends more and more on the taste of boys; and one begins to foresee a similar improbable fate for Ernest Hemingway. Among the most distinguished novelists of the American past, only Henry James completely escapes classification as a writer of juvenile classics; even Hawthorne, who did write sometimes for children, must in his most adult novels endure, though not as Mark Twain and Melville submit to, the child's perusal. A child's version of *The Scarlet Letter* would seem a rather far-fetched joke if it were not a part of our common experience. Finding in the children's department of the local library what Hawthorne liked to call his "hell-fired book," and remembering that *Moby Dick* itself has as its secret motto *"Ego te baptizo in nomine diaboli,"* one can only bow in awed silence before the mysteries of public morality, the American idea of "innocence." Everything goes except the frank description of adult heterosexual love. After all, boys will be boys!

What, then, do all these books have in common? As boys' books we should expect them shyly, guiltlessly as it were, to proffer a chaste male love as the ultimate emotional experience

— and this is spectacularly the case. In Dana, it is the narrator's melancholy love for the *kanaka*, Hope; in Cooper, the lifelong affection of Natty Bumppo and Chingachgook; in Melville, Ishmael's love for Queequeg; in Twain, Huck's feeling for Nigger Jim. At the focus of emotion, where we are accustomed to find in the world's great novels some heterosexual passion, be it "platonic" love or adultery, seduction, rape, or long-drawn-out flirtation, we come instead on the fugitive slave and the no-account boy lying side by side on a raft borne by the endless river toward an impossible escape, or the pariah sailor waking in the tattooed arms of the brown harpooner on the verge of their impossible quest. *"Aloha, aikane, aloha nui,"* Hope cries to the lover who prefers him to all his fellow-whites; and Ishmael in utter frankness tells us: "I found Queequeg's arm thrown over me in the most loving and affectionate manner. You had almost thought I had been his wife . . . he still hugged me tightly, as though naught but death should part us twain . . . Thus, then, in our heart's honeymoon, lay I and Queequeg — a cosy, loving pair . . . he pressed his forehead against mine, clasped me around the waist, and said that henceforth we were married."

In Melville, the ambiguous relationship is most explicitly rendered; almost, indeed, openly explained. Not by a chance phrase or camouflaged symbol (the dressing of Jim in a woman's gown in *Huck Finn*, for instance, which can mean anything or nothing at all), but in a step-by-step exposition, the Pure Marriage of Ishmael and Queequeg is set before us: the initial going to bed together and the first shyness overcome, that great hot tomahawk-pipe accepted in a familiarity that dispels fear; next, the wedding ceremony itself (for in this marriage like so many others the ceremonial follows the deflowering), with the ritual touching of foreheads; then, the queasiness and guilt the morning after the *official* First Night, the suspicion that one has joined himself irrevocably to his own worst nightmare; finally, a symbolic portrayal of the continuing state of marriage through the image of the "monkey rope" which binds the lovers fast waist to waist (for the sake of this symbolism, Melville changes a *fact* of whaling practice — the only time in the book), a permanent alliance that provides mutual protection but also threatens mutual death.

Physical it all is, certainly, yet somehow ultimately innocent. There lies between the lovers no naked sword but a
childlike ignorance, as if the possibility of a fall to the carnal
had not yet been discovered. Even in the *Vita Nuova* of Dante,
there is no vision of love less offensively, more unremittingly
chaste; that it is not adult seems beside the point. Ishmael's
sensations as he wakes under the pressure of Queequeg's arm,
the tenderness of Huck's repeated loss and refinding of Jim,
the role of almost Edenic helpmate played for Bumppo by
the Indian — these shape us from childhood: we have no
sense of first discovering them or of having been once without them.

Of the infantile, the homoerotic aspects of these stories we
are, though vaguely, aware; but it is only with an effort that
we can wake to a consciousness of how, among us who at the
level of adulthood find a difference in color sufficient provoca-
tion for distrust and hatred, they celebrate, all of them, the
mutual love of *a white man and a colored*. So buried at a
level of acceptance which does not touch reason, so desperately repressed from overt recognition, so contrary to what
is usually thought of as our ultimate level of taboo — the
sense of that love can survive only in the obliquity of a symbol,
persistent, obsessive, in short, an archetype: the boy's homoerotic crush, the love of the black fused at this level into a
single thing.

I hope I have been using here a hopelessly abused word
with some precision; by "archetype" I mean a coherent pattern
of beliefs and feelings so widely shared at a level beneath consciousness that there exists no abstract vocabulary for representing it, and so "sacred" that unexamined, irrational re-
straints inhibit any explicit analysis. Such a complex finds a
formula or pattern story, which serves both to embody it, and,
at first at least, to conceal its full implications. Later, the
secret may be revealed, the archetype "analyzed" or "allegorically" interpreted according to the language of the day.

I find the complex we have been examining genuinely
mythic; certainly it has the invisible character of the true archetype, eluding the wary pounce of Howells or Mrs. Twain, who

excised from *Huckleberry Finn* the cussing as unfit for children, but who left, unperceived, a conventionally abhorrent
doctrine of ideal love. Even the writers in whom we find it
attained it, in a sense, dreaming. The felt difference between
Huckleberry Finn and Twain's other books must lie in part
in the release from conscious restraint inherent in the author's
assumption of the character of Huck; the passage in and out
of darkness and river mist, the constant confusion of identities
(Huck's ten or twelve names; the question of who is the real
uncle, who the true Tom), the sudden intrusions into alien
violences without past or future, give the whole work, for all
its carefully observed detail, the texture of a dream. For *Moby
Dick* such a point need scarcely be made. Even Cooper,
despite his insufferable gentlemanliness, his tedium, cannot
conceal from the kids who continue to read him the secret
behind his overconscious prose: the childish, impossible
dream. D. H. Lawrence saw in him clearly the boy's Utopia:
the absolute wilderness in which the stuffiness of home yields
to the wigwam, and "My Wife" to Chingachgook.

I do not recall ever having seen in the commentaries of the
social anthropologist or psychologist an awareness of the role
of this profound child's dream of love in our relation to the
Negro. (I say Negro, though the beloved in the books I have
mentioned is variously Indian and Polynesian, because the
Negro has become more and more exclusively for us *the*
colored man, the colored man *par excellence*.) Trapped in
what have by now become shackling clichés — the concept
of the white man's sexual envy of the Negro male, the ambivalent horror of miscegenation — they do not sufficiently note
the complementary factor of physical attraction, the archetypal love of white male and black. But either the horror or
the attraction is meaningless alone; only together do they
make sense. Just as the pure love of man and man is in
general set off against the ignoble passion of man for woman,
so more specifically (and more vividly) the dark desire which
leads to miscegenation is contrasted with the ennobling love
of a white man and a colored one. James Fenimore Cooper
is our first poet of this ambivalence; indeed, miscegenation is
the secret theme of the Leatherstocking novels, especially of

The Last of the Mohicans. Natty Bumppo, the man who boasts always of having "no cross" in *his* blood, flees by nature from the defilement of all women, but never with so absolute a revulsion as he displays toward the *squaw* with whom at one point he seems at the point of being forced to cohabit; and the threat of the dark-skinned rapist sends pale woman after pale woman skittering through Cooper's imagined wilderness. Even poor Cora, who already has a fatal drop of alien blood that cuts her off from any marriage with a white man, in so far as she is white cannot be mated with Uncas, the noblest of redmen. Only in death can they be joined in an embrace as chaste as that of males. There's no good woman but a dead woman! Yet Chingachgook and the Deerslayer are permitted to sit night after night over their campfire in the purest domestic bliss. So long as there is no mingling of blood, soul may couple with soul in God's undefiled forest.

Nature undefiled — this is the inevitable setting of the Sacred Marriage of males. Ishmael and Queequeg, arm in arm, about to ship out, Huck and Jim swimming beside the raft in the peaceful flux of the Mississippi — here it is the motion of water which completes the syndrome, the American dream of isolation afloat. The notion of the Negro as the unblemished bride blends with the myth of running away to sea, of running the great river down to the sea. The immensity of water defines a loneliness that demands love; its strangeness symbolizes the disavowal of the conventional that makes possible all versions of love. In *Two Years Before the Mast,* in *Moby Dick,* in *Huckleberry Finn* the water is there, is the very texture of the novel; the Leatherstocking Tales propose another symbol for the same meaning: the virgin forest. Notice the adjectives — the virgin forest and the forever inviolable sea. It is well to remember, too, what surely must be more than a coincidence, that Cooper, who could dream this myth, also invented for us the novel of the sea, wrote for the first time in history the sea story proper.

The rude pederasty of the forecastle and the captain's cabin, celebrated in a thousand jokes, is the profanation of a dream; yet Melville, who must have known such blasphemies, refers to them only once and indirectly, for it was *his* dream that they threatened. And still the dream survives; in a recent book by Gore Vidal, an incipient homosexual, not yet aware of the implications of his feelings, indulges in the reverie of running off to sea with his dearest friend. The buggery of sailors is taken for granted everywhere, yet is thought of usually as an inversion forced on men by their isolation from women; though the opposite case may well be true: the isolation sought more or less consciously as an occasion for male encounters. At any rate, there is a context in which the legend of the sea as escape and solace, the fixated sexuality of boys, the myth of the dark beloved, are one. In Melville and Twain at the center of our tradition, in the lesser writers at the periphery, the archetype is at once formalized and perpetuated. Nigger Jim and Queequeg make concrete for us what was without them a vague pressure on the threshold of our consciousness; the proper existence of the archetype is in the realized character, who waits, as it were, only to be asked his secret. Think of Oedipus biding in silence from Sophocles to Freud!

Unwittingly, we are possessed in childhood by these characters and their undiscriminated meaning, and it is difficult for us to dissociate them without a sense of disbelief. What — these household figures clues to our subtlest passions! The foreigner finds it easier to perceive the significances too deep within us to be brought into focus. D. H. Lawrence discovered in our classics a linked mythos of escape and immaculate male love; Lorca in *The Poet in New York* grasped instinctively (he could not even read English) the kinship of Harlem and Walt Whitman, the fairy as bard. But of course we do not have to be conscious of what possesses us; in every generation of our own writers the archetype reappears, refracted, half-understood, but *there*. In the gothic reverie of Capote's *Other Voices, Other Rooms,* both elements of the syndrome are presented, though disjunctively: the boy moving between the love of a Negro maidservant and his inverted cousin. In Carson McCullers' *Member of the Wedding,* another variant is invented: a *female* homosexual romance between the boy-girl Frankie and a Negro cook. This time the Father-Slave-Beloved is converted into the figure of a Mother-Sweetheart-Servant, but remains still, of course, satisfactorily black.

It is not strange, after all, to find this archetypal complex in latter-day writers of a frankly homosexual sensibility; but it recurs, too, in such resolutely masculine writers as Faulkner, who evokes the myth in the persons of the Negro and the boy of *Intruder in the Dust*.

In the myth, one notes finally, it is typically in the role of outcast, ragged woodsman, or despised sailor ("Call me Ishmael!"), or unregenerate boy (Huck before the prospect of being "sivilized" cries out, "I been there before!") that we turn to the love of a colored man. But how, we cannot help asking, does the vision of the white American as a pariah correspond with our long-held public status: the world's beloved, the success? It is perhaps only the artist's portrayal of *himself*, the notoriously alienated writer in America, at home with such images, child of the town drunk, the hapless survivor. But no, Ishmael is in all of us, our unconfessed universal fear objectified in the writer's status as in the outcast sailor's: that compelling anxiety, which every foreigner notes, that we may not be loved, that we are loved for our possessions and not our selves, that we are really — *alone*. It is that underlying terror which explains our incredulity in the face of adulation or favor, what is called (once more the happy adjective) our "boyish modesty."

Our dark-skinned beloved will take us in, we assure ourselves, when we have been cut off, or have cut ourselves off, from all others, without rancor or the insult of forgiveness. He will fold us in his arms saying, "Honey" or "Aikane"; he will comfort us, as if our offense against him were long ago remitted, were never truly *real*. And yet we cannot ever really forget our guilt; the stories that embody the myth dramatize as if compulsively the role of the colored man as the victim. Dana's Hope is shown dying of the white man's syphilis; Queequeg is portrayed as racked by fever, a pointless episode except in the light of this necessity; Crane's Negro is disfigured to the point of monstrosity; Cooper's Indian smolders to a hopeless old age conscious of the imminent disappearance of his race; Jim is shown loaded down with chains, weakened by the hundred torments dreamed up by Tom in the name of bulliness. The immense gulf of guilt must not be mitigated any more than the disparity of color (Queequeg is not merely brown but monstrously tattooed; Chingachgook is horrid with paint; Jim is portrayed as the sick A-rab died blue), so that the final reconciliation may seem more unbelievable and tender. The archetype makes no attempt to deny our outrage as fact; it portrays it as meaningless in the face of love.

There would be something insufferable, I think, in that final vision of remission if it were not for the presence of a motivating anxiety, the sense always of a last chance. Behind the white American's nightmare that someday, no longer tourist, inheritor, or liberator, he will be rejected, refused, he dreams of his acceptance at the breast he has most utterly offended. It is a dream so sentimental, so outrageous, so desperate, that it redeems our concept of boyhood from nostalgia to tragedy.

In each generation we *play out* the impossible mythos, and we live to see our children play it: the white boy and the black we can discover wrestling affectionately on any American sidewalk, along which they will walk in adulthood, eyes averted from each other, unwilling to touch even by accident. The dream recedes; the immaculate passion and the astonishing reconciliation become a memory, and less, a regret, at last the unrecognized motifs of a child's book. "It's too good to be true, Honey," Jim says to Huck. "It's too good to be true."

Montana; or The End of
Jean-Jacques Rousseau

Hier oder nirgends ist Amerika.
GOETHE

There is a sense, disturbing to good Montanans, in which Montana is a by-product of European letters, an invention of the Romantic movement in literature. In 1743 a white man penetrated Montana for the first time, but there was then simply nothing to *do* with it: nothing yet to do economically in the first place, but also no way of assimilating the land to the imagination. Before the secure establishment of the categories of the *interessant* and the "picturesque," how could one have come to terms with the inhumanly virginal landscape: the atrocious magnificence of the mountains, the illimitable brute fact of the prairies? A new setting for hell, perhaps, but no background for any human feeling discovered up to that point; even *Sturm und Drang* was yet to come.

And what of the Indians? The redskin had been part of daily life in America and a display piece in Europe for a couple of hundred years, but he had not yet made the leap from a fact of existence to one of culture. *The Spirit of Christianity* of Chateaubriand and the expedition of Lewis and Clark that decisively opened Montana to the East were almost exactly contemporary, and both had to await the turn of the nineteenth century. Sacajawea, the Indian girl guide of Captain Clark (the legendary Sacajawea, of course, shorn of such dissonant realistic details as a husband, etc.), is as much a product of a

13

new sensibility as Atala — and neither would have been possible without Rousseau and the beautiful lie of the Noble
Savage. By the time the trapper had followed the explorer,
and had been in turn followed by the priest and the prospector,
George Catlin in paint and James Fenimore Cooper in the
novel had fixed for the American imagination the fictive Indian
and the legend of the ennobling wilderness: the primitive as
Utopia. Montana was psychologically possible.

One knows generally that, behind the thin neo-Classical
façade of Virginia and Philadelphia and Boston, the mythical
meanings of America have traditionally been sustained by the
Romantic sensibility (the hero of the first American novel died
a suicide, a copy of *Werther* lying on the table beside him);
that America had been unremittingly dreamed from East to
West as a testament to the original goodness of man: from
England and the Continent to the Atlantic seaboard; from the
Atlantic seaboard to the Midwest; from the Midwest to the
Rocky Mountains and the Pacific. And the margin where the
Dream has encountered the resistance of fact, where the Noble
Savage has confronted Original Sin (the edge of hysteria: of
the twitching revivals, ritual drunkenness, "shooting up the
town," of the rape of nature and the almost compulsive slaugh-
ter of beasts) we call simply: the Frontier.

Guilt and the Frontier are coupled from the first; but the inhabitants of a Primary Frontier, struggling for existence under
marginal conditions, have neither the time nor energy to feel
consciously the contradiction between their actuality and their
dream. Survival is for them a sufficient victory. The contradiction remains largely unrealized, geographically sundered;
for those who continue to dream the Dream are in their safe
East (Cooper in Westchester or New York City), and those who
live the fact have become total Westerners, deliberately cut off
from history and myth, immune even to the implications of
their own landscape. On into the second stage of the Frontier,
it is dangerous for anyone who wants to *live* in a Western community to admire the scenery openly (it evokes the Dream);
such sentiments are legitimate only for "dudes," that is to say,
visitors and barnstorming politicians.

But the schoolmarm, pushing out before her the whore,

symbol of the denial of romance, moves in from the East to marry the rancher or the mining engineer (a critical cultural event intuitively preserved as a convention of the Western movie); and the Dream and the fact confront each other openly. The schoolteacher brings with her the sentimentalized Frontier novel, and on all levels a demand begins to grow for some kind of art to nurture the myth, to turn a way of life into a culture. The legend is ready-made and waiting, and speedily finds forms in the pulps, the movies, the Western story, the fake cowboy song — manufactured at first by absentee dudes, but later ground out on the spot by cultural "compradors." The Secondary Frontier moves from naïveté to an elementary consciousness of history and discrepancy; on the one hand, it falsifies history, idealizing even the recent past into the image of the myth, while, on the other hand, it is driven to lay bare the failures of its founders to live up to the Rousseauistic ideal. The West is reinvented!

At the present moment, Montana is in some respects such a Secondary Frontier, torn between an idolatrous regard for its refurbished past (the naïve culture it holds up defiantly against the sophistication of the East, not realizing that the East *requires* of it precisely such a contemporary role), and a vague feeling of guilt at the confrontation of the legend of its past with the real history that keeps breaking through. But in other respects, Montana has gone on to the next stage: the Tertiary or pseudo-Frontier, a past artificially contrived for commercial purposes, the Frontier as bread and butter.

In the last few years, Montana has seen an efflorescence of "Sheriff's Posses"; dude ranches; chamber of commerce rodeos, hiring professional riders; and large-scale "Pioneer Days," during which the bank clerk and the auto salesman grow beards and "go Western" to keep the tourist-crammed coaches of the Northern Pacific and the Great Northern rolling. The East has come to see its ancient dream in action — and they demand it on the line, available for the two-week vacationer. What the Easterner expects, the Montanan is prepared to give him, a sham mounted half in cynicism, half with the sense that this is, after all, what the West really means, merely made visible, vivid. There is, too, a good deal of "play" involved, a not wholly unsympathetic boyish pleasure in dressing up and pulling the leg of the outlander, which overlays and to some degree mitigates the cruder motives of "going Western." But in Montana's larger cities and towns a new kind of entrepreneur has appeared: the Rodeo and Pioneer Days Manager, to whom the West is strictly business. There is scarcely a Montanan who does not at one remove or another share in the hoax and in the take; who has not, like the nightclub Negro or the stage Irishman, become the pimp of his particularity, of the landscape and legend of his state.

Astonishingly ignorant of all this, I came from the East in 1941 to live in Montana, possessing only what might be called the standard Eastern equipment: the name of the state capital (mispronounced); dim memories of a rather absurd poem that had appeared, I believe, in *The Nation,* and that began: "Hot afternoons have been in Montana"; some information about Burton K. Wheeler; and the impression that Montana (or was it Idaho?) served Ernest Hemingway as a sort of alternative Green Hills of Africa. I had, in short, inherited a shabby remnant of the Romantic myth; and, trembling on an even more remote periphery of remembering, I was aware of visions of the Indian (out of Cooper and "The Vanishing American") and the Cowboy, looking very much like Tom Mix. I was prepared not to call cattle "cows," and resolutely to face down any student who came to argue about his grades armed with a six-shooter.

I was met unexpectedly by the Montana Face.* What I had been expecting I do not clearly know; zest, I suppose, naïveté,

---

*Natives of Montana, it is only fair to say, don't believe in, don't *see* the Montana Face, though of course they can describe the Eastern Face, black, harried, neurotic. It takes a long time before newcomers dare confide in each other what they all see, discover that they have not been enduring a lonely hallucination; but the unwary outlander who sets down for public consumption an account of what he has noticed before he forgets it or comes to find it irrelevant must endure scorn and even hatred. Since the first publication of this essay, I have been reviled for putting in print my (I had supposed) quite unmalicious remarks on the "Montana Face" by men who have never read the *Partisan Review* — indeed by some who, I suspect, do not read at all. Yet some of those most exercised have been quite willing to admit the inarticulateness, the starvation of sensibility and inhibition of expression, of which "the Face" is an outward symbol. To criticize the soul is one thing, to insult the body quite another!

a ruddy and straightforward kind of vigor — perhaps even honest brutality. What I found seemed, at first glance, reticent, sullen, weary — full of self-sufficient stupidity; a little later it appeared simply inarticulate, with all the dumb pathos of what cannot declare itself: a face developed not for sociability or feeling, but for facing into the weather. It said friendly things to be sure, and meant them; but it had no adequate physical expressions even for friendliness, and the muscles around the mouth and eyes were obviously unprepared to cope with the demands of any more complicated emotion. I felt a kind of innocence behind it, but an innocence difficult to distinguish from simple ignorance. In a way, there was something heartening in dealing with people who had never seen, for instance, a Negro or a Jew or a Servant, and were immune to all their bitter meanings; but the same people, I knew, had never seen an art museum or a ballet or even a movie in any language but their own, and the poverty of experience had left the possibilities of the human face in them incompletely realized.

"Healthy!" I was tempted to think contemptuously, missing the conventional stigmata of neurosis I had grown up thinking the inevitable concomitants of intelligence. It was true, certainly, that neither the uses nor the abuses of conversation, the intellectual play to which I was accustomed, flourished here; in that sense the faces didn't lie. They were conditioned by a mean, a parsimonious culture; but they were by no means mentally incurious — certainly not "healthy," rather pricked invisibly by insecurity and guilt. To believe anything else was to submit to a kind of parody of the Noble Savage, the Healthy Savage — stupidity as mental health. Indeed there was, in their very inadequacy at expressing their inwardness, the possibility of pathos at least — perhaps even tragedy. Such a face to stand at the focus of reality and myth, and in the midst of all the grandiloquence of the mountains! One reads behind it a challenge that demands a great, liberating art, a ritual of expression — and there is, of course, the movies.

The seediest moving-picture theater in town, I soon discovered, showed every Saturday the same kind of Western picture at which I had yelled and squirmed as a kid, clutching my box of jujubes; but in this context it was different. The children still eagerly attended, to be sure — but also the cowhands. In their run-over-at-the-heels boots and dirty jeans, they were apparently willing to invest a good part of their day off watching Gene and Roy, in carefully tailored togs, get the rustlers, save the ranch, and secure the Right; meanwhile making their own jobs, their everyday work into a symbol of the Natural Gentleman at home.

They *believed it all* — not only that the Good triumphs in the end, but that the authentic hero is the man who herds cattle. Unlike, for instance, the soldier at the war picture, they never snickered, but cheered at all the right places; and yet, going out from contemplating their idealized selves to get drunk or laid, they must somehow have felt the discrepancy, as failure or irony or God knows what. Certainly for the bystander watching the cowboy, a comic book under his arm, lounging beneath the bright poster of the latest Roy Rogers film, there is the sense of a joke on someone — and no one to laugh. It is nothing less than the total myth of the goodness of man in a state of nature that is at stake every Saturday after the show at the Rialto; and, though there is scarcely anyone who sees the issue clearly or as a whole, most Montanans are driven instinctively to try to close the gap.

The real cowpuncher begins to emulate his Hollywood version; and the run-of-the-mill professional rodeo rider, who has turned a community work-festival into paying entertainment, is an intermediary between life and the screen, the poor man's Gene Autry. A strange set of circumstances has preserved in the cowboy of the horse opera the Child of Nature, Natty Bumppo become Roy Rogers (the simple soul ennobled by intimacy with beasts and a virginal landscape), and has transformed his saga into the national myth. The boyhood of most living Americans does not go back beyond the first movie cowpuncher, and these days the kid without a cowboy outfit is a second-class citizen anywhere in America. Uncle Sam still survives as our public symbol; but actually America has come to picture itself in chaps rather than striped pants.*

*The myth of the Cowboy has recently begun to decline in popular favor, crowded out of the pulps by the Private Eye and the Space Pilot; and is being "secularized," like all archetypes that are dying, in a host of more or less highbrow reworkings of the archetypal theme: *Shane, High Noon,* etc.

Since we are comparatively historyless and culturally dependent, our claim to moral supremacy rests upon a belief that a
high civilization is at a maximum distance from goodness; the
cowboy is more noble than the earl.

But, on the last frontiers of Montana, the noble lie of Rousseau is simply a lie; the face on the screen is debunked by the
watcher. The tourist, of course, can always go to the better
theaters, drink at the more elegant bars beside the local property owner, dressed up for Pioneer Days. The cowhands go to
the shabby movie house off the main drag and do their drinking
in their own dismal places. And when the resident Easterner
or the visitor attempts to pursue the cowpuncher to his authentic dive, the owner gets rich, chases out the older whores, puts
in neon lights and linoleum — which, I suppose, serves everybody right.

But the better-educated Montanan does not go to the Westerns. He discounts in advance the vulgar myth of the Cowboy,
where the audience gives the fable the lie, and moves the
Dream, the locus of innocence, back into a remoter past; the
surviving Cowboy is surrendered for the irrecoverable Pioneer.
It is the Frontiersman, the Guide who are proposed as symbols
of original nobility: Jim Bridger or John Colter, who outran
half a tribe of Indians, barefoot over brambles. But this means
giving up to begin with the possibilities that the discovery of
a New World had seemed to promise: a present past, a primitive *now*, America as a contemporary Golden Age.

When the point of irreconcilable conflict between fact and
fiction had been reached earlier, the Dream had been projected
westward toward a new Frontier — but Montana is a *last
Frontier;* there is no more ultimate West. Here the myth of
the Noble Woodsman can no longer be maintained in space
(the dream of Rousseau reaches a cul-de-sac at the Lions Club
luncheon in Two Dot, Montana); it retreats from geography
into time, from a discoverable West into the realm of an irrecoverable past. But even the past is not really safe.

Under the compulsion to examine his past (and there have
been recently several investigations, culminating in the Rocke-
feller Foundation-sponsored Montana Study), the contemporary Montanan, pledged to history though nostalgic for myth,

becomes willy-nilly an iconoclast. Beside a John Colter he
discovers a Henry Plummer, the sheriff who was for years
secretly a bandit; and the lynch "justice" to which Plummer
was brought seems to the modern point of view as ambiguous
as his career. The figure of the Pioneer becomes ever more
narrow, crude, brutal; his law is revealed as arbitrary force, his
motive power as — greed. The Montanan poring over his past
comes to seem like those dance-hall girls, of whom a local
story tells, panning the ashes of a road agent who had been
lynched and burned, for the gold it had been rumored he was
carrying. Perhaps there had never been any gold in the first
place. . . .

It is in his relations with the Indian that the Pioneer shows
to worst advantage. The record of those relations is one of
aggression and deceit and, more remotely, the smug assumption that anything goes with "Savages." There are honorable
exceptions among the early missionaries, but it is hard for a
Protestant culture to make a Jesuit its hero. For many years
the famous painting of Custer's Last Stand hung in the state
university, where the students of history were being taught
facts that kept them from taking Custer for the innocent Victim, the symbolic figure of the white man betrayed by crafty
redskins that he is elsewhere. In Montana it is difficult to see
the slaughter at Little Big Horn as anything but the result of
a tactical error in a long warfare with whose motives one can
no longer sympathize.

Driving across Montana, the conscientious sightseer who
slows up for the signs saying "Historic Point 1000 Feet" can
read the roadside marker beside US 2 at Chinook, which
memorializes "The usual fork-tongued methods of the white
which had deprived these Indians of their hereditary lands,"
"One of the blackest records of our dealings with the Indians
. . ." Or at Poplar he can learn how the Assiniboines "are
now waiting passively for the fulfillment of treaties made with
'The Great White Father.' "*

---

*I have since been told that these signs were composed by a self-conscious
"rebel," who later accommodated to the ruling powers and grew rich; but
such an account is itself an American Legend — and anyway the words of
the "rebel" have never seemed inappropriate to legislator, road commis-
sioner, or traveler on the highways.

It is at first thoroughly disconcerting to discover such confessions of shame blessed by the state legislature and blazoned on the main roads where travelers are enjoined to stop and notice. What motives can underlie such declarations: The feeling that simple confession is enough for absolution? A compulsion to blurt out one's utmost indignity? A shallow show of regret that protects a basic indifference? It is not only the road markers that keep alive the memory of the repeated betrayals and acts of immoral appropriation that brought Montana into existence; there are books to document the story, and community pageants to present it in dramatic form. The recollection of a common guilt comes to be almost a patriotic duty.

What is primarily involved is, I think, an attempt to *identify* with the Indian. Notice in the sentences quoted from highway signs the use of Indian terminology, "fork-tongued," "Great White Father" — the attempt to get *inside* the Indian's predicament. If the Pioneer seems an ignoble figure beside the Indian, it is perhaps because he was, as a Noble Savage, not quite savage enough; as close as he was to nature, the White Pioneer, already corrupted by Europe and civilization, could not achieve the saving closeness. "Civilization," a road sign between Hysham and Forsyth ironically comments, "is a wonderful thing, according to some people." The corpse of Rousseau is still twitching.

At the beginnings of American literature, Cooper had suggested two avatars of primeval goodness: Pioneer and Indian, the alternative nobility of Natty Bumppo and Chingachgook; and the Montanan, struggling to hang on to the Romantic denial of Original Sin, turns to the latter, makes the injured Chief Joseph or Sitting Bull the Natural Gentleman in place of the deposed Frontiersman.

But the sentimentalized Indian will not stand up under scrutiny either. "The only good Indian is a dead Indian," the old folk saying asserts; and indeed the Montanan who is busy keeping the living Indian in the ghetto of the reservation cannot afford to believe too sincerely in his nobility. The cruelest aspect of social life in Montana is the exclusion of the Indian; deprived of his best land, forbidden access to the upper levels of white society, kept out of any job involving prestige, even in some churches confined to the back rows, but of course protected from whisky and comforted with hot lunches and free hospitals — the actual Indian is a constant reproach to the Montanan, who feels himself Nature's own democrat, and scorns the South for its treatment of the Negro, the East for its attitude toward the Jews. To justify the continuing exclusion of the Indian, the local white has evolved the theory that the redskin is *naturally* dirty, lazy, dishonest, incapable of assuming responsibility — a troublesome child; and this theory confronts dumbly any attempt at reasserting the myth of the Noble Savage.

The trick is, of course, to *keep* the Indian what he is, so that he may be pointed out, his present state held up as a justification for what has been done to him. And the trick works; the Indian acts as he is expected to; confirmed in indolence and filth, sustained by an occasional smuggled bout of drunkenness, he does not seem even to have clung to his original resentment, lapsing rather into apathy and a certain self-contempt. The only thing white civilization had brought to the Indian that might be judged a good was a new religion; but one hears tales now of the rise of dope-cults, of "Indian Christianity," in which Jesus and Mary and the drug *peyote* are equally adored. Once I traveled for two days with an Indian boy on his way to be inducted into the Army; and, when he opened the one paper satchel he carried, it contained: a single extra suit of long underwear and forty comic books — all the goods, material and spiritual, with which our culture had endowed him.

On the side of the whites, there is, I think, a constantly nagging though unconfessed sense of guilt, perhaps the chief terror that struggles to be registered on the baffled Montana Face. It is a struggle much more difficult for the Montana "liberal" to deal with than those other conflicts between the desired and the actual to which he turns almost with relief: the fight with the Power Company or the Anaconda Copper Mining Company for the instruments of communication and the possibilities of freedom. The latter struggles tend to pre-empt the liberal's imagination, because on them he can take an unequivocal stand; but in respect to the Indian he is torn with inner feelings of guilt, the knowledge of his own complicity in perpetuating the stereotypes of prejudice and discrimination. In that relationship he cannot wholly dissociate himself from the oppressors; by his color, he is born into the camp of the Enemy.

There is, of course, no easy solution to the Indian problem; but so long as the Montanan fails to come to terms with the Indian, despised and outcast in his open-air ghettos, just so long will he be incapable of coming to terms with his own real past, of making the adjustment between myth and reality upon which a successful culture depends. When he admits that the Noble Savage is a lie; when he has learned that his state is where the myth comes to die (it is here, one is reminded, that the original of Huck Finn ended his days, a respected citizen), the Montanan may find the possibilities of tragedy and poetry for which so far he has searched his life in vain.

Archetype and Signature

The Relationship of Poet and Poem

I

A central dogma of much recent criticism asserts that biographical information is irrelevant to the understanding and evaluation of poems, and that conversely, poems cannot legitimately be used as material for biography. This double contention is part of a larger position which holds that history is history and art is art, and that to talk about one in terms of the other is to court disaster. Insofar as this position rests upon the immortal platitude that it is good to know what one is talking about, it is unexceptionable; insofar as it is a reaction based upon the procedures of pre-Freudian critics, it is hopelessly outdated; and insofar as it depends upon the extreme nominalist definition of a work of art, held by many "formalists" quite unawares, it is metaphysically reprehensible. It has the further inconvenience of being quite unusable in the practical sphere (all of its proponents, in proportion as they are sensitive critics, immediately betray it when speaking of specific works, and particularly of large bodies of work); and, as if that were not enough, it is in blatant contradiction with the assumptions of most serious practicing writers.

That the anti-biographical position was once "useful," whatever its truth, cannot be denied; it was even once, what is considerably rarer in the field of criticism, amusing; but for a long time now it has been threatening to turn into one of those annoying clichés of the intellectually middle-aged, proffered with all the air of a stimulating heresy. The position was born in dual protest against an excess of Romantic criticism and one of "scien-

24

tific scholarship." Romantic aesthetics appeared bent on dissolving the formally realized "objective" elements in works of art into "expression of personality"; while the "scholars," in revolt against Romantic subjectivity, seemed set on casting out all the more shifty questions of value and *gestalt* as "subjective," and concentrating on the kind of "facts" amenable to scientific verification. Needless to say, it was not the newer psychological sciences that the "scholars" had in mind, but such purer disciplines as physics and biology. It was at this point that it became fashionable to talk about literary study as "research," and graphs and tables began to appear in analyses of works of art.

Both the "scholarly" and the Romantic approaches struck the anti-biographists as "reductive"—attempts to prove that the work of art was *nothing but* the personality of the Genius behind it, or the sum total of its genetic factors. In answer to both heresies of attack, the anti-biographist offered what he came to call the "intrinsic" approach, which turned out, alas, to be another *nothing but* under its show of righteous indignation— namely, the contention that a poem was *nothing but* "words," and its analysis therefore properly *nothing but* a study of syntax and semantics. An attempt to illuminate a poem by reference to its author's life came therefore to be regarded with horror, unless it confined itself to an examination of his "idiosyncratic use of words"! This is not parody, but direct quotation.

By this time a generation of critics has grown up, of whom I am one, to whom the contention that biographical material is irrelevant to the essential "experience" of a poem was taught as the basic doctrine of all right-thinking readers. The word "experience" is important; it comes out of I. A. Richards at his most scientizing, and along with the "extrinsic-intrinsic" metaphor is a key to the anti-biographist point of view. It must be understood for what the word "experience" is being substituted: as an "experience," a poem is no longer regarded as an "imitation," in any of the received senses of the word; nor even as an "expression" in the Crocean sense; and above all not as a "communication." All three possible substitute terms imply a necessary interconnectedness between the art object and some *other* area of experience—or at least an essentially intended pointing outward or inward toward some independently existent *otherness*. This is distasteful to the anti-biographist, who shows the ordinary nominalist uneasiness at any suggestion that there are realities more comprehensive than particulars, to which words only refer.

An odd phenomenon is the support of a position to which nominalism is logically necessary, by many confirmed anti-scientizers and realists; they are betrayed into their ill-advised fellow-traveling, I think, by an excess of anti-Romanticism. It is no longer as fashionable as it once was to publicly anathematize Shelley and Swinburne, but the bias persists as a real force in current critical practice, and cuts off many, to whom the position would be temperamentally and metaphysically attractive, from Expressionism. What the modern sensibility finds particularly unsympathetic in some Romantic writing has been misleadingly called, I think, "the exploitation of personality"; it is rather a tendency toward the excessively "programmatic." Just as music and painting can be too "literary," so literature itself can be too "literary." In reaction against the programmatic, there are two possible paths: more deeply into and through the personalism of Romanticism to Expressionism; or outward and away toward the sort of "abstraction" achieved in cubist painting. As a matter of fact, there has been at work all along in our period an underground, and probably harmful, analogy between poetry and the plastic arts. A poem, the feeling has been, should be as "palpable and mute" not merely as an actual fruit, but as the fruit become pure color and texture of Picasso or Matisse. As pictures have become frankly paint, so should poems be frankly words. "A poem should not mean but be." There is the slogan of the movement!

It is a rather nice phrase in the limited context of MacLeish's little poem, but a dangerous full-blown aesthetic position. The notion that a work of art is, or should be, absolutely self-contained, a discrete set of mutually interrelated references, needs only to be stated clearly to seem the *reductio ad absurdum* which it is. Yet this belief in the poem as a closed system, "cut off" in ideal isolation, descends from the realm of theoretical criticism to practical criticism and classroom pedagogy (if not in practice, at least as an institutionalized hypocrisy) to become the leitmotif of the New Teacher: "Stay *inside* the poem!"

The narrative and dramatic poem, finally poetic drama itself, is assimilated to a formulation, even *apparently* applicable only to a lyric of the most absolute purity—and it becomes heretical to treat the work as anything but "words," to ask those questions which attest our conviction that the work of art is "real"; that in the poem, the whole is greater than the sum of its parts; that certain created actions and characters exist, in some sense, *outside* of their formalizations. How long was Hamlet in Wittemberg? How many children did Lady Macbeth have? In what sense does Prospero speak for Shakespeare? What developing sensibility can be inferred from the Shakespearian corpus and be called (what *else?*) Shakespeare? We cannot ask these questions in the dewy innocence with which they were first posed; we restate them on the second convolution, aware of all the arguments against them, and the more convinced that they are essential, and cannot be shelved any more than those questions about the ends and origins of existence which have also been recently declared "unreal."

Closely associated with the Richardsian experiential-semantic approach in the total, eclectic position of the anti-biographist, is the psychological notion of the poem as the "objective correlative" or a complex of "objective correlatives" of emotional responses to the given world. Mr. Eliot's term is as elusive as it is appealing; but I am concerned here (Mr. Eliseo Vivas has elsewhere criticized it as containing some "non-intrinsic" contradictions) only with the adjective "objective" in one of its possible implications. Whatever its origins, Mr. Eliot seems to be asserting, a poem succeeds, as a poem, insofar as it is detached from the subjectivity of its maker. The poem is achieved by a process of objectification, and can be legitimately examined and understood only as an "object." This formulation leaves a somewhat second-best use for the biographical approach, as a way of explaining the particular badness of certain kinds of bad poems, *e.g.,* Romantic verse and Shakespeare's *Hamlet*.

From this presumed insight follows the deprivation of the

poet's right to explain his own poem, or at least the challenging
of his claim to speak with final authority about his own work.
Once realized, the argument runs, the successful poem is detached; and the author no longer has any property rights in what
now belongs to the tradition rather than to him. And if, benight-
edly, he protests against some critical analysis or interpretation
which seems to him wrong on the basis of his special biographical
knowledge, he reveals that either his poem is not truly "successful," or even worse, that he has never read "Tradition and the
Individual Talent."

There are, in fact, two quite different contentions, one valid,
one invalid, confused in most statements about the poet as com-
mentator on his own work. First it is asserted (and with real
truth) that a poem may contain more meanings than the maker
is ever aware of; and second (this is false, of course) that
nothing the poet can tell us about his own work is of any *decisive*
importance, because the poet cannot help falling into the trap
of talking about his "intentions." But the notion of "intention"
implies the belief that there is a somehow existent something
against which the achieved work of art can be measured; and
although this has been for all recorded time the point of view
of the practicing writer, every graduate student who has read
Wimsatt and Beardsley's ponderous tract on the Intentional
Fallacy knows that we are all now to believe that there is no
poem except the poem of "words."

The fact that all recognized critics have consistently spoken
of intention shows merely that in the unfortunate past the writer
about literature has often (unfortunately!) spoken more like
the poet than the scientific semanticist. This regrettable loose-
ness of expression we can only hope will be amended in the
future, now that we have been duly warned. It is difficult not
to be tempted by analogy. Why, we want to ask, can we properly
laugh at the visiting dignitary in the high hat when he slips on
the steps to the platform, because of the disparity between the
entrance he *intended* and the one he achieved; and still not
speak of a bathetic disparity between what a poem obviously
aims at and what it does? On what respectable grounds can it
be maintained that a poem is all act and no potentiality?

It is difficult to understand the success of the anti-biographist tendency in more respectable critical circles and in the schools, in light of its own internal contradictions. The explanation lies, I suppose, in its comparative newness, and in the failure of its opponents to arrive at any *coherent* theory of the relationship between the life of the poet and his work; so long as biographers are content merely to place side by side undigested biographical data and uninspired paraphrases of poems—linking them together mechanically or pseudo-genetically: "Wordsworth lived in the country and therefore wrote Nature poetry," or even worse, so long as notes proving that Milton was born in one house rather than another continue to be printed in magazines devoted to the study of literature, people will be tempted into opposite though equal idiocies, which have at least not been for so long proved utterly bankrupt.

A recent phenomenon of some interest in this regard is the astonishing popularity of such texts as Thomas and Brown's classroom anthology called *Reading Poems*—the very title reveals the dogma behind the book; in a world of discrete, individual "experiences," of "close reading" (a cant phrase of the anti-biographist) as an ideal, one cannot even talk of so large an abstraction as poetry. It is only "poems" to which the student must be exposed, poems printed out of chronological order and without the names of the authors attached, lest the young reader be led astray by what (necessarily irrelevant) information he may have concerning the biography or social background of any of the poets. It is all something of a hoax, of course; the teacher realizes that the chances of any student knowing too much for his own good about such matters are slight indeed; and besides, there is an index in which the names are revealed, so that unless one is very virtuous, he can scarcely help looking up the anthologized pieces. In addition, the good teacher is himself aware to begin with of the contexts, social and biographical, of a large number of the pieces. Frankly, that is why they make sense to him; and even when he admonishes the young to "stay *inside*" the poems, he is bootlegging all kinds of rich relevancies which he possesses because he is capable of connecting.

I cannot help feeling that the chief problem of teaching

anything in our atomized period lies precisely in the fact that the ordinary student cannot or will not connect the few facts he knows, the slim insights he has previously attained, the chance extensions of sensibility into which he has been once or twice tempted, into a large enough context to make sense of the world he inhabits, or the works of art he encounters. It is because the old-line biographist fails to connect his facts with the works they presumably illuminate, and not because he does connect them, that he is a poor critic. And the doctrinaire anti-biographist, like the doctrinaire biographist before him, secure in pride and ignorance of the newer psychologies, makes worse the endemic disease of our era—the failure to connect. There is no "work itself," no independent formal entity which is its own sole context; the poem is the sum total of many contexts, all of which must be known to know it and evaluate it. "Only connect!" should be the motto of all critics and teachers—and the connective link between the poem on the page and most of its rewarding contexts is precisely—biography.

The poet's life is the focusing glass through which pass the determinants of the shape of his work: the tradition available to him, his understanding of "kinds," the impact of special experiences (travel, love, etc.). But the poet's life is more than a burning glass; with his work, it makes up his total meaning. I do not intend to say, of course, that some meanings of works of art, satisfactory and as far as they go sufficient, are not available in the single work itself (only a really *bad* work depends for all substantial meaning on a knowledge of the life-style of its author); but a whole body of work will contain larger meanings, and, where it is available, a sense of the life of the writer will raise that meaning to a still higher power. The latter two kinds of meaning fade into each other; for as soon as two works by a single author are considered side by side, one has begun to deal with biography—that is, with an interconnectedness fully explicable only in terms of a personality, inferred or discovered.

One of the essential functions of the poet is the assertion and creation of a personality, in a profunder sense than any nonartist can attain. We ask of the poet a definition of man, at once particular and abstract, stated and acted out. It is impossible to draw a line between the work the poet writes and the work he lives, between the life he lives and the life he writes. And the agile critic, therefore, must be prepared to move constantly back and forth between life and poem, not in a pointless circle, but in a meaningful spiraling toward the absolute point.

To pursue this matter further, we will have to abandon at this point the nominalist notion of the poem as "words" or "only words." We have the best of excuses, that such terminology gets in the way of truth. We will not, however, return to the older notions of the poem as a "document" or the embodiment of an "idea," for these older conceptions are equally inimical to the essential concept of the "marvelous"; and they have the further difficulty of raising political and moral criteria of "truth" as relevant to works of art. To redeem the sense of what words are all the time pointing *to* and what cannot be adequately explained by syntactical analysis or semantics, I shall speak of the poem as Archetype and Signature, suggesting that the key to analysis is *symbolics;* and I shall not forget that the poet's life is also capable of being analyzed in those terms. We have been rather ridiculously overemphasizing *medium* as a differentiating factor; I take it that we can now safely assume no one will confuse a life with a poem, and dwell on the elements common to the two, remembering that a pattern of social behavior can be quite as much a symbol as a word, chanted or spoken or printed. In deed as in word, the poet composes himself as maker and mask, in accordance with some contemporaneous *mythos* of the artist. And as we all know, in our day, it is even possible to be a writer without having written anything. When we talk therefore of the importance of the biography of the poet, we do not mean the importance of every trivial detail, but all that goes into making his particular life-style, whether he concentrate on re-creating himself, like Shelley, in some obvious image of the Poet, or, like Wallace Stevens, in some witty anti-mask of the Poet. Who could contend that even the *faces* of Shelley and Stevens are not typical products of their quite different kinds of art!

The word "Archetype" is the more familiar of my terms; I use it instead of the word "myth," which I have employed in

the past but which becomes increasingly ambiguous, to mean
any of the immemorial patterns of response to the human situation in its most permanent aspects: death, love, the biological
family, the relationship with the Unknown, etc., whether those
patterns be considered to reside in the Jungian Collective Unconscious or the Platonic world of Ideas. The archetypal belongs
to the infra- or meta-personal, to what Freudians call the id or
the unconscious; that is, it belongs to the Community at its
deepest, pre-conscious levels of acceptance.

I use "Signature" to mean the sum total of individuating
factors in a work, the sign of the Persona or Personality through
which an Archetype is rendered, and which itself tends to become
a subject as well as a means of the poem. Literature, properly
speaking, can be said to come into existence at the moment a
Signature is imposed upon the Archetype. The purely archetypal,
without signature elements, is the myth. Perhaps a pair of examples are in order (with thanks to Mr. C. S. Lewis). The story
of Baldur the Beautiful and Shakespeare's *Tempest* deal with
somewhat similar archetypal material of immersion and resurrection; but we recall *The Tempest* only in all its specificity: the
diction, meter, patterns of imagery, the heard voice of Shakespeare (the Signature as Means); as well as the scarcely motivated speech on pre-marital chastity, the breaking of the fictional
frame by the unconventional religious *plaudite* (the Signature
as Subject). Without these elements, *The Tempest* is simply not
The Tempest; but *Baldur* can be retold in any diction, any style,
just so long as faith is kept with the bare plot—and it is itself,
for it is pure myth. Other examples are provided by certain
children's stories, retold and reillustrated without losing their
essential identity, whether they be "folk" creations like *Cinderella*
or art products "captured" by the folk imagination, like Southey's
Three Bears.

In our own time, we have seen the arts (first music, then
painting, last of all literature) attempting to become "pure," or
"abstract"—that is to say, attempting to slough off all remnants
of the archetypal in a drive toward becoming unadulterated
Signature. It should be noticed that the *theory* of abstract art
is completely misleading in this regard, speaking as it does about

pure forms, and mathematics, and the disavowal of personality. The abstract painter, for instance, does not, as he sometimes claims, really "paint paint," but signs his name. So-called abstract art is the ultimate expression of personality; so that the spectator says of a contemporary painting, not what one would have said in the anonymous Middle Ages, "There's a *Tree of Jesse* or a *Crucifixion!*" or not even what is said of Renaissance art, "There's a Michelangelo *Last Judgment* or a Raphael *Madonna!*" but quite simply, "There's a Mondriaan or a Jackson Pollock!" Analogously, in literature we recognize a poem immediately as "a Marianne Moore" or "an Ezra Pound" long before we understand, if ever, any of its essential meanings.

The theory of "realism" or "naturalism" denies both the Archetype and the Signature, advocating, in its extreme forms, that art merely "describes nature or reality" in a neutral style, based on the case report of the scientist. Art which really achieves such aims becomes, of course, something less than "poetry" as I have used the term here, becoming an "imitation" in the lowest Platonic sense, "thrice removed from the truth." Fortunately, the great "realists" consistently betray their principles, creating Archetypes and symbols willy-nilly, though setting them in a Signature distinguished by what James called "solidity of specification." The chief value of "realism" as a theory is that it helps create in the more sophisticated writer a kind of blessed stupidity in regard to what he is really doing, so that the archetypal material can well up into his work uninhibited by his intent; and in a complementary way, it makes acceptance of that archetypal material possible for an audience which thinks of itself as "science-minded" and inimical to the demonic and mythic. It constantly startles and pleases me to come across references to such creators of grotesque Archetypes as Dostoevsky and Dickens and Faulkner as "realists."

A pair of caveats are necessary before we proceed. The distinction between Archetype and Signature, it should be noted, does not correspond to the ancient dichotomy of Content and Form. Such "forms" as the structures of Greek Tragedy (*cf.* Gilbert Murray), New Comedy and Pastoral Elegy are themselves *versunkene* Archetypes, capable of being rerealized in the great work of art. (Elsewhere I have called these "structural myths.")

Nor does the present distinction cut quite the same way as that between "impersonal" (or even "nonpersonal") and "personal." For the Signature, which is rooted in the ego and super-ego, belongs, as the twofold Freudian division implies, to the social collectivity as well as to the individual writer. The Signature is the joint product of "rules" and "conventions," of the expectations of a community and the idiosyncratic responses of the individual poet, who adds a personal idiom or voice to a received style. The difference between the communal element in the Signature and that in the Archetype is that the former is *conscious*—that is, associated with the superego rather than the id. The relevant, archetypal metaphor would make the personal element the Son, the conscious-communal the Father and the unconscious-communal the Mother (or the Sister, an image which occurs often as a symbolic euphemism for the Mother)—in the biological Trinity.

It is not irrelevant that the Romantic movement, which combined a deliberate return to the archetypal with a contempt for the conscious communal elements in the Signature, made one of the leitmotifs of the lives of its poets, as well as of their poems, the flight of the Sister from the threat of rape by the Father (Shelley's *Cenci*, for instance) and the complementary desperate love of Brother and Sister (anywhere from Chateaubriand and Wordsworth to Byron and Melville).

Even the most orthodox anti-biographist is prepared to grant the importance of biographical information in the *understanding* of certain ego elements in the Signature—this is what the intrinsicist calls the study of an author's "idiosyncratic use of words." But they deny vehemently the possibility of using biographical material for the purposes of *evaluation*. Let us consider some examples. For instance, the line in one of John Donne's poems, "A Hymne to God the Father," which runs, "When thou hast done, thou hast not done . . ." would be incomprehensible in such a collection without author's names as the Thomas and Brown *Reading Poems*. Without the minimum biographical datum of the name of the poet, the reader could not realize that a pun was involved, and he could not therefore even ask himself the evaluative question most important to the poem, namely, what is the value of the pun in a serious, even a religious, piece of verse? This is the simplest use of biography, referring us for only an instant outside of the poem, and letting us remain there once we have returned with the information. Other similar examples are plentiful in Shakespeare's sonnets: the references to his own first name, for instance, or the troublesome phrase "all *hewes* in his controlling."

A second example which looks much like the first to a superficial glance, but which opens up in quite a different way, would be the verse "they'are but *Mummy*, possest," from Donne's "Loves Alchymie." Let us consider whether we can sustain the contention that there is a pun on *Mummy*, whether deliberately planned or unconsciously fallen into. Can we read the line as having the two meanings: women, so fair in the desiring, turn out to be only dried-out corpses after the having; and women, once possessed, turn out to be substitutes for the Mother, who is the real end of our desiring? An analysis of the mere *word* does not take us very far; we discover that the *lallwort* "mummy" meaning "mother" is not recorded until 1830 in that precise spelling, but that there are attested uses of it in the form "mammy" (we remember, perhaps, that "mammy-apple" and "mummy-apple" are interchangeable forms meaning "papaya") well back into Donne's period, and that the related form "mome" goes back into Middle English. Inevitably, such evidence is inconclusive, establishing possibilities at best, and never really bearing on the question of probability, for which we must turn to his life itself, to Donne's actual relations with his mother; and beyond that to the science of such relationships.

When we have discovered that John Donne did, indeed, live in an especially intimate relationship with his mother throughout her long life (she actually outlived her son); and when we have set the possible pun in a context of other literary uses of a mythic situation in which the long-desired possessed turns at the moment of possession into a shriveled hag who is also a mother (Rider Haggard's *She*, Hilton's *Lost Horizon*, and, most explicitly, Flaubert's *L'Education Sentimentale*), we realize that our original contention is highly probable, for it is motivated by a traditional version of what the psychologists have taught us to call the Oedipus Archetype. It should be noticed in passing that the archetypal critic is delivered from the bondage of time, speaking of "confluences" rather than "influences," and finding the explication of a given work in things written later as well as earlier than the original piece. Following the lead opened up by "*Mummy*, possest," we can move still further toward an understanding of Donne, continuing to shuttle between life and work with our new clue, and examining, for instance, Donne's ambivalent relations to the greater Mother, the Roman Church, which his actual mother represented not only metaphorically but in her own allegiance and descent. This sort of analysis which at once unifies and opens up (one could do something equally provocative and rich, for instance, with the fact that in two of Melville's tales ships symbolic of innocence are called *The Jolly Bachelor* and *The Bachelor's Delight*) is condemned in some quarters as "failing to stay close to the actual meaning of the work itself"—as if the work were a tight little island instead of a focus opening on an inexhaustible totality.

The intrinsicist is completely unnerved by any reference to the role of the Archetype in literature, fearing such references as strategies to restore the criterion of the "marvelous" to respectable currency as a standard of literary excellence; for not only is the notion of the "marvelous" pre-scientific but it is annoyingly immune to "close analysis." Certainly, the contemplation of the Archetype pushes the critic beyond semantics, and beyond the kind of analysis that considers it has done all when it assures us (once again!) that the parts and whole of a poem cohere. The critic in pursuit of the Archetype finds himself involved in anthropology and depth psychology (not because these are New Gospels, but because they provide useful tools); and if he is not too embarrassed at finding himself in such company to look about him, he discovers that he has come upon a way of binding together our fractured world, of uniting literature and nonliterature *without the reduction of the poem.*

It is sometimes objected that though the archetypal critic can move convincingly between worlds ordinarily cut off from each other, he sacrifices for this privilege the ability to distinguish the essential qualities of literary works, and especially that of evaluating them. Far from being irrelevant to evaluation, the consideration of the archetypal content of works of art is essential to it! One of the earlier critics of Dante says someplace that poetry, as distinguished from rhetoric (which treats of the credible as credible), treats of the "marvelous" as credible. Much contemporary criticism has cut itself off from this insight—that is, from the realization of what poetry on its deepest levels *is*. It is just as ridiculous to attempt the evaluation of a work of art *purely* in formal terms (considering only the Signature as Means), as it would be to evaluate it *purely* in terms of the "marvelous," or the archetypal. The question, for instance, of whether *Mona Lisa* is just a bourgeoise or whether she "as Leda, was the mother of Helen of Troy, and, as St. Anne, was the mother of Mary" is just as vital to a final estimate of the picture's worth as any matter of control of the medium or handling of light and shadow.

The Romantics seem to have realized this, and to have reached, in their distinction between Fancy and Imagination, for rubrics to distinguish between the poetic method that touches the archetypal deeply and that which merely skirts it. Even the Arnoldian description of Pope as "a classic of our prose," right or wrong, was feeling toward a similar standard of discrimination. It is typical and ironic that Arnold in a moralizing age should have felt obliged to call the daemonic power of evoking the Archetype "High Seriousness." Certainly, the complete abandonment of any such criterion by the intrinsicist leaves him baffled before certain strong mythopoeic talents like Dickens or Stevenson; and it is the same lack in his system which prevents his understanding of the complementary relationship of the life and work of the poet.

II

The Archetype which makes literature itself possible in the first instance is the Archetype of the Poet. At the moment when myth is uncertainly becoming literature—that is, reaching tentatively toward a Signature—the poet is conceived of passively, as a mere vehicle. It is the Muse who is mythically bodied forth, the unconscious, collective source of the Archetypes, imagined as more than human, and, of course, female; it is she who mounts the Poet, as it were, in that position of feminine supremacy preferred in matriarchal societies. The Poet is still conceived more as Persona than Personality; the few characteristics with which he is endowed are borrowed from the prophet: he is a blind old man, impotent in his own right. That blindness (impotence as power, what Keats much later would call "negative capability") is the earliest version of the blessing-curse, without which the popular mind cannot conceive of the poet. His flaw is, in the early stages, at once the result and the pre-condition of his submitting himself to the dark powers of inspiration for the sake of the whole people.

But very soon the poet begins to assume a more individualized life-style, the lived Signature imposed on the Archetype, and we have no longer the featureless poet born in seven cities, his face a Mask through which a voice not his is heard, but Aeschylus, the Athenian citizen-poet; Sophocles, the spoiled darling of fate; or Euripides, the crowd-contemner in his Grotto. The mass mind, dimly resentful as the *Vates* becomes *Poeta*, the Seer a Maker, the Persona a Personality, composes a new Archetype, an image to punish the poet for detaching himself from the collective id—and the Poet, amused and baffled, accepts and elaborates the new image. The legend asserts that Euripides (the first completely self-conscious alienated artist?) dies torn to pieces by dogs or, even more to the point, by *women*. And behind the new, personalized application looms the more ancient *mythos* of the ritually dismembered Orpheus, ripped by the Maenads when he had withdrawn for lonely contemplation. The older myth suggests that a sacrifice is involved as well as a punishment—the casting-out and rending of the poet being reinterpreted as a death suffered for the group, by one who has dared make the first forays out of collectivity toward personality and has endured the consequent revenge of the group as devotees of the unconscious.

In light of this, it is no longer possible to think of the *poète maudit* as an unfortunate invention of the Romantics, or of the Alienated Artist as a by-product of mass communications. These are reinventions, as our archetypal history repeats itself before the breakdown of Christianity. Our newer names name only recent exacerbations of a situation as old as literature itself which in turn is coeval with the rise of personality. Only the conventional stigmata of the poet as Scape-Hero have changed with time: the Blind Man becomes the disreputable Player, the Atheist, the incestuous Lover, the Homosexual or (especially in America) the Drunkard; though, indeed, none of the older versions ever die, even the Homer-*typus* reasserting itself in Milton and James Joyce. Perhaps in recent times the poet has come to collaborate somewhat more enthusiastically in his own defamation and destruction, whether by drowning or tuberculosis or dissipation—or by a token suicide in the work (*cf.* Werther). And he helps ever more consciously to compose himself and his fellow poets—Byron, for instance, the poet par excellence of the mid-nineteenth century, being the joint product of Byron and Goethe—and, though most of us forget, Harriet Beecher Stowel Some dramatic version of the poet seems necessary to every age, and the people do not care whether the poet creates himself in his life or work or both. One thinks right now of Fitzgerald, of course, *our* popular image of the artist.

The contemporary critic is likely to become very impatient with the lay indifference to the poetizing of life and the "biographizing" of poetry; for he proceeds on the false assumption that the poet's life is primarily "given" and only illegitimately "made," while his work is essentially "made" and scarcely "given" at all. This is the source of endless confusion.

In perhaps the greatest periods of world literature, the "given" element in poetry is made clear by the custom of supplying or, more precisely, of *imposing* on the poet certain traditional bodies of story. The poet in such periods can think of himself only as "working with" materials belonging to the whole community, emending by a dozen or sixteen lines the inherited plot. Greek myths, the fairy tales and *novelle* of the Elizabethans, the Christian body of legend available to Dante are examples of such material. (In our world a traditionally restricted body of story is found only in subart: the pulp Western, or the movie horse opera.) In such situations, Archetype and "story" are synonymous; one remembers that for Aristotle *mythos* was the word for "plot," and plot was, he insisted, the most important element in tragedy. That Aristotle makes his assertions on rationalistic grounds, with no apparent awareness of the importance of the Archetype as such, does not matter; it does not even matter whether the poet himself is aware of the implications of his material. As long as he works with such an inherited gift, he can provide the ritual satisfaction necessary to great art without self-consciousness.

A Shakespeare, a Dante or a Sophocles, coming at a moment when the Archetypes of a period are still understood as "given," and yet are not considered too "sacred" for rendering through the individual Signature, possesses immense initial advantages over the poet who comes earlier or later in the process. But the great poet is not simply the mechanical result of such an occasion; he must be able to rise to it, to be capable (like Shakespeare) at once of realizing utterly the archetypal implications of his material and of formally embodying it in a lucid and unmistakable Signature. But the balance is delicate and incapable of being long maintained. The brief history of Athenian tragedy provides the classic instance. After the successes of Sophocles come the attempts of Euripides; and in Euripides one begins to feel the encounter of Signature and Archetype as a *conflict*—the poet and the collectivity have begun to lose touch with each other and with their common pre-conscious sources of value and behavior. Euripides seems to feel his inherited material as a burden, tucking it away in prologue and epilogue, so that he can get on with his proper business—the imitation of particulars. The poem begins to come apart; the acute critic finds it, however "tragic," sloppy, technically inept; and the audience raises the familiar cry of "incomprehensible and blasphemous!" Even the poet himself begins to distrust his own impulses, and writes, as Euripides did in his *Bacchae,* a mythic criticism of his own sacrilege. The poetry of the struggle against the Archetype is especially moving and poignant, but to prefer it to the poetry of the moment of balance is to commit a gross lapse of taste.

After the Euripidean crisis, the Archetypes survive only in fallen form: as inherited and scarcely understood structures (the seeds of the genres which are structural Archetypes become structural platitudes); as type characters, less complex than the masks that indicate them; as "popular" stock plots. The "Happy Ending" arises as a kind of ersatz of the true reconciliation of society and individual in Sophoclean tragedy; and the audience which can no longer find essential reassurance in its poetry that the superego and the id can live at peace with each other content themselves with the demonstration that at least Jack has his Jill, despite the comic opposition of the Old Man. Still later, even the tension in Euripidean tragedy and New Comedy is lost, and the Signature comes to be disregarded completely; poetry becomes either completely "realistic," rendering the struggle between ego and superego in terms of the imitation of particulars; or it strives to be "pure" in the contemporary sense—that is, to make the Signature its sole subject as well as its means.

Can the Archetype be redeemed after such a fall? There are various possibilities (short of the emergence of a new, ordered myth system): the writer can, like Graham Greene or Robert Penn Warren, capture for serious purposes—that is, rerender through complex and subtle Signatures—debased "popular" Archetypes: the thriller, the detective story, the Western or science fiction; or the poet can ironically manipulate the shreds and patches of outlived mythologies, fragments shored against our ruins. Eliot, Joyce, Ezra Pound and Thomas Mann have all made attempts of the latter sort, writing finally not archetypal poetry but poetry *about* Archetypes, in which plot (anciently, *mythos* itself) founders under the burden of overt explication or disappears completely. Or the poet can, like Blake or Yeats or Hart Crane, invent a private myth system of his own. Neither of the last two expedients can reach the popular audience, which prefers its Archetypes rendered without self-consciousness of so intrusive a sort.

A final way back into the world of the Archetypes, available even in our atomized culture, is an extension of the way instinctively sought by the Romantics, down through the personality of the poet, past his particular foibles and eccentricities, to his unconscious core, where he becomes one with us all in the presence of our ancient Gods, the protagonists of fables we think we no longer believe. In fantasy and terror, we can return to our common source. It is a process to delight a Hegelian, the triple swing from a naïve communal to a personal to a sophisticated communal.

We must be aware of the differences between the thesis and the synthesis in our series. What cannot be re-created as Plot is reborn as Character—ultimately the character of the poet (what else is available to him?), whether directly or in projection. In the Mask of his life and the manifold masks of his work, the poet expresses for a whole society the ritual meaning of its inarticulate selves; the artist goes forth not to "re-create the conscience of his race," but to redeem its unconscious. We cannot get back into the primal Garden of the unfallen Archetypes, but we can yield ourselves to the dreams and images that mean paradise regained. For the critic, who cannot only yield but must also *understand*, there are available new methods of exploration. To understand the Archetypes of Athenian drama, he needs (above and beyond semantics) anthropology; to understand those of recent poetry, he needs (beyond "close analysis") depth analysis, as defined by Freud and, particularly, by Jung.

The biographical approach, tempered by such findings, is just now coming into its own. We are achieving new ways of connecting (or, more precisely, of understanding a connection which has always existed) the Poet and the poem, the lived and the made, the Signature and the Archetype. It is in the focus of the poetic personality that *Dichtung und Wahrheit* become one; and it is incumbent upon us, without surrendering our right to make useful distinctions, to seize the principle of that unity. "Only connect!"

Afterthoughts on the Rosenbergs

Since the execution of the Rosenbergs, it has become possible to see clearly what was for a long time obscured: that there were *two* Rosenberg cases, quite distinct though referred to by a single name; and that this ambiguity made it difficult for the pro- and anti-Rosenberg forces ever to engage in a real dialogue. How often we were talking about quite different things under the same label!

The first Rosenberg case, which reached its climax with their trial in March 1951, involved certain questions of fact about the transmission of secrets to the Soviet Union, culminating in the handing over of sketches for the detonating device of the atom bomb. Implicated in this first case were: the brother of Ethel Rosenberg, David Greenglass, who made a full confession; Morton Sobell; Anatoli Yacovlev, the Russian vice-consul who had got safely out of the United States in December of 1946; and the notorious Communist "drop," Harry Gold. Through Gold, the Rosenberg case was linked with those of the confessed espionage agents, Klaus Fuchs and Allan Nunn May, woven inextricably into a context against which their guilt appeared clear beyond doubt. The denials of the Rosenbergs seemed merely the mendacious pleas of two people fighting for their lives in the face of overwhelming evidence.

In this initial open-and-shut case, scarcely anyone was very interested. In the United States, it did not stir up nearly as much discussion as the Hiss-Chambers affair, or even the trivial business of Judith Coplon. In Europe, it was ignored or meagerly reported, so that the European defenders of the

Rosenbergs tended to be happily ignorant of the first or factual case in its real interconnections; and this ignorance in many cases they fought desperately to preserve. The Communists themselves maintained a strange official silence about the Rosenbergs for more than a year after their arraignment, wary, presumably, about identifying themselves with a pair at once so central to their whole espionage effort and so flagrantly guilty; and baffled, no doubt, at how to defend two comrades who had been underground for six years and who refused to admit their party membership in court.

The second, or legendary, Rosenberg case was invented, along with the Committee to Secure Justice in the Rosenberg Case, at the end of October 1951 in Knickerbocker Village, a housing settlement in New York City. The place of the double birth seems almost too apt; the Rosenbergs themselves had once inhabited that melancholy block of identical dwelling units that seem the visible manifestation of the Stalinized petty-bourgeois mind: rigid, conventional, hopelessly self-righteous — the mind which dreamed the odd parody of the martyr which was the role of the Rosenbergs in their second case.*

The Rosenbergs stood alone in the new version of their plight — alone except for certain honorable ghosts. Gone were the real accomplices: Yacovlev and Sobell, Harry Gold, Klaus Fuchs and Allan Nunn May, though "Davy" Greenglass, recruited to the Movement at the age of twelve by his nineteen-year-old sister, remained to play the shadowy villain — replaced by the evoked figures of Sacco and Vanzetti, Tom Mooney, the Scottsboro Boys, and, especially, Dreyfus. The cue had been given by the "progressive" *National Guardian*, which had opened the defense campaign with a story head-lined: "Is the Rosenberg Case the Dreyfus Case of America's Cold War?" The revised Rosenbergs were no longer spies, but "political prisoners" in the European sense, victims of the class struggle and the Cold War, defenders of the peace, a perse-

---

*The Rosenbergs of the second case possess a certain kind of immortality; that is, they will continue to live in the official history and art of the Communist Movement, until, for one reason or another, their particular segment of history is forgotten or refalsified. But not yet! In 1954, the hit of the season on the Warsaw stage was a play called *Ethel and Julius*.

cuted minority — these very people, it must be remembered, who would not confess their political allegiance in court, and who for six years had been under instructions not even to appear "progressive."

The long-drawn-out process of appeal in the American courts had made it possible to set up the symbolic Rosenbergs in place of the real ones; between the first exposure of two spies and the appeal of the "framed up victims before the bar of world opinion" came the year (soon two, and three) of separation and imprisonment and real suffering. The Communists banked on this stretch of time to screen their sleight-of-hand; and it worked. Even those who had followed the first trial carefully found it difficult to keep it in mind; and the maintenance of the anti-Rosenberg position soon fell largely into the hands of those who countered liberaloid sentimentality and rancor not with facts but with their own even more wretched "Down with the Communist Rats — God Bless America" sentimentality and rancor. The second, the legendary, Rosenberg case possessed the imagination of the world.

It is that second case which I wish to discuss. There is no point in rehearsing the first; as far as I am concerned, the legal guilt of the Rosenbergs was clearly established at their trial, and it is from an assumption of that guilt that I begin. What I want to examine (and this, after all, is the enduring point of the matter) is why the Rosenbergs, for all their palpable guilt, won their second case before the world; why there arose such a universal condemnation of their sentence; and why so many, in the teeth of the evidence, even believed in their innocence.

One can say in a general way that in the second case the Rosenbergs were not tried at all, but that by a bit of prestidigitation they, too, disappeared along with Gold, Yacovlev, and the rest; and that we were called upon to judge in their places Sacco and Vanzetti or Dreyfus. And how did they get in? Through the evocation of these almost traditional victims, a kind of moral blackmail was practiced on us; the flags of the gallant old causes were unfurled, and we were expected to respond by revivifying the battered belief that the political dissident (but in what sense is the present-day flag-waving Communist a dissident?), the proud rebel (but in what sense were the Rosenbergs, peering slyly out from behind the Fifth Amendment, rebellious or proud?), the Jew (but in what sense were the Rosenbergs Jews?) is always framed, that the guilt is always on the other side.

What a relief to be able to reassert that simple-minded article of faith after Fuchs and Nunn May and Hiss, and after the thousand betrayals of the Soviet Union. The fact that the Rosenbergs were remarkable chiefly for their difference from the older martyrs, that the whole point of their affair lay in that difference, was hardly remarked; scarcely anyone wanted to see them as they were, but merely to *use* them for self-exculpation — for joining together once more the ranks that had marched unbroken for Vanzetti, but had since fallen hopelessly apart.

And yet the question remains. Why this occasion rather than another; why this improbable pair; and why (outside of the United States itself) so nearly unanimous a response to their plight? To disentangle the motives that found a focus in the pro-Rosenberg movement is to write a thumbnail moral history of our time.

One must begin, I suppose, by separating out the absolute cynics, the Communist bureaucrats who used the case coldly when it was convenient to use it, as they had ignored it calmly when it was convenient to ignore it; and who knew that they could not lose in any event. For if the freeing of the Rosenbergs would have been for them a minor victory, their death was a major one in the struggle against the United States. After a certain point, the energies of such functionaries were patently directed at insuring that clemency would not be granted. I do not want to seem to make master-minds out of shabby Communist bureaucrats, but surely a certain elementary cunning rather than mere stupidity led them to do everything that would infuriate official American opinion, make any revision of the death sentence seem an admission of a judicial error.

It is no accident, I think, that the only plea which came near saving the Rosenbergs was prompted by an outsider who had been expelled from both the Communist party and the Communist-controlled defense committee. The suffering and death of the Rosenbergs were *willed* by the makers of Communist opinion and relished by them, as every new lynching in America, every bit of violence against the Jews, is willed and relished as further evidence that they are right! These are the professional accomplices of calamity; and if they cried "innocent," it was because they thought that the greatest possibility of disaster lay in such an assertion.

These conscious exploiters of the case were a tiny minority, yet one which had ready to hand a mass of naïve communicants already trained to believe, sincerely and even fervently, what that minority decided they should believe. In this sense, one can think of the bacterial-warfare campaign and the various "peace" petitions as preparations for the Rosenberg case, as the Rosenberg case in turn is no end in itself but a rehearsal for the next real or manufactured issue on the Communist agenda. This prefabricated public is made up not only of the naïver party members, activists to whom ideas are unknown and the mute attenders of meetings, but also of fellow-travelers and the "innocents" who read nothing but the Communist press, or even only the Communist posters (knowing, of course, that all other sources of information are "bought"). For such believers an event does not even *exist*, much less have a significance, until it is recognized by their journals; and so for them there had simply been *no* Rosenberg case until the party had given the go-ahead signal after months of discreet silence. For them, only the legendary case was real.

The Communists have long controlled in Europe large numbers of "advanced" workers, peasants, and petty bourgeois by manipulating a mythology inherited from a hundred years of political struggle: the belief that the state and its courts are always wrong; that the bourgeoisie is always wrong; and especially that the United States, the bastion of capitalism, is always wrong* — with the corollaries that no Negro, Jew, or "progressive" (i.e., Communist or sympathizer) can ever be anything but innocent. This group was joined by an even larger periphery, stalinized to the extent of not believing its own

---

*Only the notion that priests are always wrong could not be exploited in the Rosenberg case; otherwise it was a perfect ritual expression of the sub-Marxist catechism.

press and of accepting in critical instances the opinions screamed in the piazzas by those whom they consider more "devoted" and "unselfish" than themselves, because they are louder and more assured. Together these formed a sizable public which appears really to have believed that the Rosenbergs were innocent in the basic sense of the word, guiltless of the crime with which they were charged. This they knew, not from scrutinizing the record, but from consulting the opinions of those who had always defined for them the truth. They would have believed it quite as firmly if there had been no such people as the Rosenbergs — as, in a sense, there were not.

Such a rank and file, stalinized at second and third remove, did not exist in the United States, which possesses in their place a mass of people politically innocent and merely indifferent to such affairs in a way no European can understand. To this oppositely corresponding American group, the *second* Rosenberg case had no existence; so that between them and their European opposite numbers there was not even ground enough for real disagreement.

In both Europe and America, however, a substantial minority of intellectuals shared a third position which asserted the innocence of the Rosenbergs, or at least maintained the final irrelevance of their guilt. This position combined in varying proportions two complementary attitudes: the *wish* that the Rosenbergs might actually be innocent; and the conviction that they were *symbolically* guiltless whatever action they may have committed. The first feeling led to an incantatory declaration of the Rosenbergs' guiltlessness, based on the belief that what these intellectuals repeated with truly unselfish fervor could not help but prove true; and, in any event, the Rosenbergs *couldn't* have done it, couldn't have committed treason — or these intellectuals, too, might have been guilty of as sordid a crime when in their own heedless youth they also had been Communists or had at least defended in perfect self-righteousness their Communist friends against the "Red-baiters."

But, even if the Rosenbergs *had* performed the act, this line of argument continues, treason was not what they had meant; they had been acting for a better world, for all Humanity (i.e., for the Soviet Union, whose interests all the more enlightened had once known were identical with those of mankind); and, anyhow, Russia had been our ally when the Rosenbergs gave them a helping hand, standing with us side by side against the Nazis; and, after all, Russia had not yet used the Bomb, will never use it, never, never, *never* (to stop believing this would mean having to rethink their whole lives), so that sharing the atomic secret in this somewhat unorthodox fashion was really a blow for world peace: just look at the present *détente*, etc., etc. In light of all which, isn't it better simply to declare that the Rosenbergs are "innocent," as a kind of shorthand for an analysis too complicated to explain to the uninitiated without re-educating them completely.

How near the conscious surface such reasoning was carried on must have varied from case to case; but in almost every instance it led to the by-now-customary double bookkeeping of the Communists' friends, the exploitation of a vocabulary which makes it possible to say, at one and the same time, "They didn't do it at all; it's a frame-up!" and, "After all, they had a right; their hearts were pure!" This is a fantastic enough position in any event, but when held by the accused themselves (and it *was* held by the Rosenbergs, as I shall show), it becomes utterly fantastic, the obverse of those equally absurd "symbolic" declarations of guilt in the rigged Russian trials.

Finally,* one is left with those who cried only for mercy, for the conversion of the death sentence, "even if they were guilty as charged." It is difficult to disentangle the position itself from those who maintained it; to redeem it from the scandalous way it was used by the Communists, who sought to confuse hopelessly the two kinds of protest, to make every cry for grace seem an assertion of innocence, and more: a condemnation of the United States, the Atlantic Pact, the European Army, and God knows what else. One is so ap-

---

*I am relegating to this footnote the "diplomatic" advocates of mercy — those who urged a revision of the sentence in order to "placate world opinion" or in order "not to give the Communists a martyr." This was not an important group, and the point of the whole case is precisely that the Rosenbergs were *incapable* of becoming martyrs.

palled at the cynicism of many of the exploiters of "mercy," with their own record of political executions without appeal, without trials — and after the most ignominious of self-degradations — that he is tempted to discount the whole movement.

Even where the Communists played only a secondary role, there was evident in the shrillness of the cries of horror (rising from countries where only a little while before the lynching of political enemies was considered an act of virtue) a desire to celebrate the fall of America from innocence, to indulge in an orgy of self-righteousness at our expense. There is no political act (and the simplest cry for clemency was inevitably a political act) that is not marred these days by the obsessive envy and anguish of the Europeans in our regard. If the Europeans could only have believed as firmly as they pretended that we had utterly yielded to hysteria and persecution, the balance of guilt that tilts so annoyingly in their direction would have been righted; and they might have loved us more, not less. But they could only *want* to believe this, not really credit it — any more than they have been able to really accept the stories of germ warfare in Korea. In a Europe that tends to admire where it is horrified, and to be overwhelmed by the fascination of ruthlessness, even our approximate innocence, or the mere inefficiency at terror that is its equivalent, is a reproach.

Yet, allowing for all that was stage-managed or disingenuous in the pleas for clemency; discounting the rather professional nature of some of the ecclesiastical protests; allowing for the sob sisters who are ready to howl bitterly at the sentencing of the most sadistic wretch; setting aside the pleading based on a general condemnation of the death penalty, which does not bear precisely on this case; and discounting the almost mechanical reflex of those to whom since Hitler any threat to any Jew seems a recrudescence of the old horror, one comes to a residual protest that cannot be explained away, and in the face of which we must as Americans admit a real, a perhaps tragic, failure of the moral imagination.

The final protest that existed behind all the others based on stupidity or malice or official dogma was the humane one. Under their legendary role, there were, after all, *real* Rosenbergs, unattractive and vindictive but human; fond of each other and of their two children; concerned with operations for tonsillitis and family wrangles; isolated from each other during three years of not-quite-hope and deferred despair; at the end, prepared scientifically for the electrocution: Julius' mustache shaved off and the patch of hair from Ethel's dowdy head (and all this painfully documented by the morning papers in an America that can keep no secrets); finally capable of dying. This we had forgotten, thinking of the Rosenbergs as merely typical, seeing them in the context of a thousand other petty-bourgeois Stalinists we had known, each repeating the same shabby standard phrases. That they were individuals and would die they themselves had denied in every gesture — and we foolishly believed them. In the face of their own death, the Rosenbergs became, despite themselves and their official defenders, symbols of the conflict between the human and the political, the individual and the state, justice and mercy; and this symbolic conflict only those who knew they were guilty could fully appreciate.

It is, in the end, no mere matter of protesting an excessive sentence, but of realizing that they *count,* these people moved always like puppets from above, that they count as *human,* though they committed treason in disregard of all real human considerations in the name of an intolerably abstract "Humanity." It is wonderful in a way that two individuals did still count to so many people in a world as accustomed as ours to mass slaughter and injustice become mere routine.

There is no sense in becoming enraged at the fact that these two, our *only* two victims, should have stirred up the response that could not be brought to focus for the millions of victims of Soviet firing squads; that most of the world should have been crying out for the lives of two American spies, convicted by due process, at the very moment when Willy Goettling and a score of nameless others were being summarily shot in Soviet Berlin. We should rather be flattered that as a nation we continue to act on a plane where moral judgment is still possible; elsewhere assertions of human value seem merely pointless, and the only possible protest is silence, the resolve at least not to hail institutionalized murder as social justice.

Some Americans have, indeed, felt flattered at being among the last peoples to whom real protest is still conceivable, not merely permitted by law, but possible to the uncorrupted moral sense; and they have been willing to stop there, arguing that this very fact sanctions the execution of the Rosenbergs, by proving it the sort of exceptional act we can still morally afford when political considerations demand it. But the point is surely that clemency to the Rosenbergs was what we could *not* afford to deny. The world had turned to us (that part at least still not hopelessly stalinized) for a symbolic demonstration that somewhere a government existed willing to risk the loss of political face for the sake of establishing an unequivocal moral position. A minority at least understood that the Communists were doing everything in their power to make any concession on our part seem a cowardly retreat; but they hoped we would have the courage to seem in that sense cowardly. I cannot help feeling that even among the rank-and-file Stalinists there existed on some deeply buried level the shadowy desire for someone somewhere to assert that the political man was not all of man, that our humanity is neither fictional nor irrelevant.

This opportunity we let slip away from us, in part because of our political innocence, in part through a lack of moral imagination, but also through a certain incapacity to really believe in Communists as people. In the official declarations of Eisenhower, one senses behind the cold reasoning from cause to effect, and the shaky conclusion that the secrets transmitted by the Rosenbergs unleashed the Korean War, the failure of the military mind to see beyond a justice defined in codes. In the justifications of Judge Kaufman, on the other hand, one feels a personal hysteria — a fear of Communism magnified by the sense that in the United States, where so many Stalinists have been Jews, the acts of the Rosenbergs were an attainder of the whole Jewish population. But the Rosenbergs were not, after all, excessively punished merely because their fates happened to rest in the hands of a military man and a Jew, but because mass opinion in America, in so far as it took notice of them at all, *wanted* their deaths, as an example and token.

When counter-pickets to the Rosenberg defenders carried

placards demanding "Death to the Communist Rats!" there
was involved, beyond an old American metaphor for spies, a
wish to believe that the enemy is subhuman, an animal to
exterminate rather than a man to confront. Needless to say,
the Communists themselves need no lessons in this sort of
maneuver; we have only to remember the words of the Rosenbergs' lawyer before the White House on the eve of their
death: "I don't know what animals I am dealing with, but I
know that I am dealing with animals." Yet we have no right
to let ourselves be provoked into answering the Communists
with equivalent strategies; differently from them, we still have
much to lose; and in trying to dehumanize our opponents we
may end by dehumanizing ourselves.

When the news of the Rosenbergs' long-delayed execution
was announced before the White House, the counter-pickets
cheered. A critical episode in the moral and political coming
of age of America had reached its climax; the hopes for a
world of equity and peace that had moved the more sensitive
and intelligent in the 1920's and 1930's, had been used as
camouflage by a brutally imperialistic power and had ended
by leading two undistinguished people into a trap of lies and
espionage and death; and the counter-pickets *cheered!* One is
tempted to echo the words of Irwin Edelman* just before he
was chased out of Pershing Square by an irate crowd: "If you
are happy about the execution of the Rosenbergs, you are
rotten to the core!" But, if this reaction seems the final indignity, there is much worse to come.

Our failure placed in the hands of the Communists the

---

*Edelman is one of the most extraordinary figures in the whole affair.
Thrown out of the Communist party in Los Angeles in 1947 for advocating
more inner party democracy, and expelled from the official Rosenberg defense committee as a heretic, he nonetheless provided the nearest thing to
a legal out for the Rosenbergs. His pamphlet, *Freedom's Electrocution,*
inspired two rather eccentric lawyers to make the plea which brought into
special session the Supreme Court, which had recently reviewed a case
against Edelman himself on a charge of vagrancy. He enters and exits
from the affair in a style that provides a real contrast to the Rosenbergs'
sly, maddeningly mendacious conduct. He seems a survival of the old-
fashioned American radical, refreshingly honest beside the new "underground" models. One would bid those who think the Rosenbergs were killed
for being radicals to notice that in a presumably hysterical America it was
the real radical who was free to come to their aid.

advantage of being able to exploit the very human considerations that they were least capable of feeling. And there was an additional advantage in their cynicism itself, which left them able to *use* the Rosenberg children, the coincidence of the electrocution date with the fourteenth wedding anniversary of Ethel and Julius, their frustrated love, and the shocking physical details of their death with a complete lack of squeamishness. On the hoardings of the whole world, the embraces of the Rosenbergs and their approach to the Chair were turned into clichés, occasions for public orgies of sentiment. The Judaism of the condemned pair was played on tearfully by the same activists who had screamed for the death of the Russian Jewish doctors until the line was changed; and the believers that religion is the opium of the people cried out against executing the Rosenbergs on the Sabbath.

But all this, it must never be forgot, was not until the leaders of the party had decided it was *safe* to be sorry — safe for the party, of course, and not for the Rosenbergs. The disregard of the Stalinists for the individuals whose causes they support, their willingness to compromise their very lives for the sake of making propitious propaganda, has been known to everyone since the days of the Scottsboro boys. But unlike those boys, or Tom Mooney, or the other classic cases, the Rosenbergs were actual comrades. This did not mean, however, that there was any more real desire to save them; indeed, as enlightened and disciplined members they would be expected to approve the tactics that assured their deaths in order to blacken the United States in the eyes of the world. Their actual affiliation was, in fact, an embarrassment, something not to be played upon but concealed. The Manchester *Guardian* and other liberal journals might talk of "making martyrs for the Communists," but the Communists, victims of the frantic game of hide-and-seek they had been playing with themselves ever since the dawning of the Popular Front, expended a good deal of energy to hide the fact that these martyrs were "theirs."

"Death for the Rosenbergs Is a Victory for McCarthy!" the posters read, and who, in Europe, at least, remembered that McCarthy had never had anything to do with the affair? Surely the chief evil of McCarthyism consists in branding

honest men as Communists out of malice and stupidity. But
how does this concern calling a Communist a Communist, or
with deciding by legal process that a spy is a spy? These
creatures of Soviet foreign policy were labeled the defenders
of all "freedom-loving peoples," sacrificed to nothing less than
their love for "American Democracy."

There were no limits to the absurd masquerade. A hundred
marching Communists in London put flowers at the foot of a
statue of Franklin Roosevelt, with an attached card reading:
"That Roosevelt's Ideas May Live the Rosenbergs Must Not
Die!" Not Marx or Lenin's ideas, please note, but Roosevelt's. It is all of a piece. Julius draped after his death not
with a red flag but with the ritual prayer shawl of the Jews;
not "The Internationale" sung but "Go Down, Moses" and
the Psalms; the American flags flying brazenly over the cortege
and the rabbi to intone unbelieved-in prayers at the grave.
But the hoax would not quite hold to the end, for the crowd
at the funeral parlor booed when a rabbi invited for the sake
of camouflage, reminded them that the Jewish religion teaches
forgiveness of enemies. In an instant, the fake piety and
humanity had disappeared from the carefully prepared faces,
and those who had cried for mercy a little while before hooted
down the mention of its name.

But there was worse yet. I was in Rome when the news of
the Rosenbergs' death came through, and I can speak only of
what I actually witnessed; but there, at least on the faces of
the Communist crowds surging and screaming before the
American Embassy, I saw evidence of *joy*. They were glad,
these young activists, that the Rosenbergs were safely dead;
for a little while they had been afraid that some last-minute
reprieve might cheat them out of their victory celebration,
that they would be unable to go through the streets in their
Sunday best chalking up "Death to the Killers of the Rosenbergs!" and to sit afterwards over a bottle of wine content
with a good day's work. But even this is not the utterest obscenity.

That the American public should deny the humanity of their
enemies is terrible enough; that the Communists should deny
the humanity of their comrades much worse; but that two

people should deny their *own* humanity in the face of death is the ultimate horror, the final revelation of a universal moral calamity. For even at the end the Rosenbergs were not able to think of themselves as real people, only as "cases," very like the others for which they had helped fight, Scottsboro and Harry Bridges and the Trenton Ten, replaceable puppets in a manifestation that never ends. There is something touching in their own accounts of reading each issue of the *National Guardian* (not the frank *Daily Worker*, but the crypto-Communist sheet) to share in the ritualistic exploitation of themselves. But even before the "progressive" journal had begun to spread their story, they themselves had written to each other the foreseeable platitudes of the propaganda on their behalf. From the start, they had not been able to find any selves realer than those official clichés. If there is a tragedy of the Rosenbergs, this is it.

The persistently evoked image of Sacco and Vanzetti had led many to expect in the correspondence of the Rosenbergs some evidence of an underlying honesty, some frank and simple declaration of faith; but they could not hit upon any note that rang true. Reading the "death-house letters" of the Rosenbergs, one has the sense that not only the Marxist dream of social justice but the very possibilities of any heroism and martyrdom are being blasphemed. It is a parody of martyrdom they give us, too absurd to be truly tragic, too grim to be the joke it is always threatening to become.

Ethel's last appeal to President Eisenhower was the first of their letters I read; and it is surely among the most embarrassing, combining with Ethel's customary attempts at a "literary" style, and the constitutional inability to be frank which she shared with her husband, a deliberate and transparent craftiness. She, who had already been writing about Eisenhower in private as "our gnaedige Gauleiter," refers in a painfully adulatory beginning to that embarrassment "which the ordinary person feels in the presence of the great and famous" and which has kept her from writing to the President before. Only the example of Mrs. Oatis,* who "bared her

---

*The evocation of the Oatis case raises problems which demand another article: the prefabricated stalinoid public's celebration of Oatis' re-

heart to the head of a foreign state," has led Ethel, she explains, to look for "as much consideration from the head of her own." She has been unable to avoid the note of reproach in this comparison of mercy on either side of the Iron Curtain, but to take off the curse she hastens to protest her ignorance, in the typical gesture of the Communist who has felt obliged to praise, however mildly, something publicly identified with his real allegiance. "Of Czechoslovakia I know very little, of her President even less than that. . . ." This unconvincing avowal, however, does not satisfy even her, so she tries the alternative gambit of gratuitous flag-waving, announcing quite inconsequently that for America she "would be homesick anywhere in the world."

She then reminds Eisenhower that before he became President he was a "Liberator," but it is not really a congenial memory to her who has still ringing in her ear her own cry of "gauleiter" and the conventional Communist characterization of the American general staff as "heirs of the Nazis." The transition to this note is easy: her execution will be, she charges, "an act of vengeance," and not the first, she reminds Eisenhower, identifying herself and her husband with the 6,000,000 hounded Jews of Europe, and the President with the masters of Buchenwald — those "ghastly mass butchers, the obscene fascists," who are presently "graciously receiving the benefits of mercy," while "the great democratic United States is proposing the savage destruction of a small unoffending Jewish family. . . ."

At last she is at home. The hatred, the obvious irony, the ready-made epithets of the Communist press are released like a dog's saliva at the *ting* of a bell. How happily she forgets that she has been defending the concept of mercy, and using the word "democratic" of her own country without sarcasm. But "a small unoffending Jewish family" — it seems incredible that anyone could speak so about herself, her own children.

---

lease as an unparalleled act of generosity; his own attitude toward himself and his sentence; etc. Here I would like to note merely how neatly this reference joins together two problems that are really one. Why do the guiltless confess on the other side of the Curtain, while the guilty protest their innocence here? In both cases, "symbolic" truth-telling, a shorthand for the uninitiate, is at stake.

At last she is ready for the final series of elegantly unctuous appeals: in the name of "fealty to religious and democratic ideals," as "an offering to God," in the name of the President's wife who will "plead my cause with grace and felicity," or of "the province of the affectionate grandfather, the sensitive artist, the devoutly religious man." And the rhetoric reaches its high point with the reminder that "truly the stories of Christ, Moses and Gandhi hold more sheer wonderment and spiritual treasure than all the conquests of Napoleon." Against the shadow of these names the alternating venom and flattery seem especially evident; and we are left astonished at the self-righteousness that dared evoke them.

The letters which the Rosenbergs wrote to each other from their cells in Sing Sing seem at first glance superior at least to this. Ethel, to be sure, is still hopelessly the victim not only of her politics but of the painfully pretentious style that is its literary equivalent; but Julius, more the scientist in his view of himself, manages from time to time to seem sincere and touching. One is moved by his feeling for his wife, which is more than love — an almost frantic dependence and adulation; and by the tears that stand in his eyes after the visits of his children. But even these scenes, we remember, were, if not staged, at least edited for publication; published in a context of the most banal thumbnail editorials ("I was horrified to read . . . that our government is planning an accord with Spain . . . to ally ourselves with the most reactionary, feudal, and Fascist elements in order to defend democracy . . . something is very rotten in Denmark . . ."*) at the wish of the Rosenbergs themselves.

In part, their self-exposure was aimed, as they declared, at raising money for their children; but, in part, it must have been intended to make political capital out of their own misery and frustrated passion. Finally, the letters are incomprehensible either as genuine expressions of feeling or as partisan

---

*The reader checking these quotations against the English text of the letters will find certain discrepancies, for I am translating them back from the French text of the *Figaro Littéraire,* the only one available to me. There is however, a certain justice in this procedure; for the documents of the legendary Rosenberg case were intended primarily for Europe, and should be seen backward through Europe to be truly appreciated.

manifestoes, since they consist almost equally of intimacies which should never have been published, and lay sermons which should never have been written to each other by a husband and wife confronting their deaths. The line between the person and the case, between private and public, had been broken down for them long before and could not be redrawn even in the extremest of situations. A single logic connects the Communist hating on order the person he has never seen; the activist ignoring on the street yesterday's best friend who has become a deviationist; the wife leaving her husband the day after he is expelled from the party; the son informing on the father; the accused in Russia slavishly vilifying themselves in court — and the Rosenbergs exploiting their final intimacies to strike a blow in the Cold War.

It is in light of this failure to distinguish the person from the cause, the fact from its "dialectical" significance, that we must understand the lies (what are for us, at least, lies) of the letters. The most flagrant, of course, is the maintenance by the Rosenbergs of the pose of innocence to the very end and *to each other!* We have grown used to Communist spies lying in court with all the conviction and fervor of true victims; there was the recent example of Alger Hiss, to name only one; but we had always hoped that to their wives at least, in darkness and whispers, they spoke the truth. Yet the Rosenbergs played out their comedy to the end; and this we should have foreknown.

Some, I recall, advocated a conversion of their sentences on the tactical grounds that they might in the long run confess; and some have even been shaken by their consequent persistence in the cry, "We are innocent!" An occasional less-convinced Stalinist, bullied into complicity like David Greenglass, can be bullied out again into a frank admission; but the true believer believes above all in his own unimpeachable innocence. Precisely because the Rosenbergs could have committed espionage as they did, they could not ever confess it. A confession would, in a certain sense, have shed doubt on their complicity.

They were able to commit their kind of treason because they were incapable of telling treason from devotion, deceit from honesty. It was not even, though this would be easier to accept, that they chose deliberately between rival allegiances: the Soviet Union versus the United States. They did not know that such a choice existed; but believed in their own way what they continued to assert, that they had always loved and served "American Democracy." It is misleading to think of them as liars, though their relationship to everything, including themselves, was false. When Julius, who had stuck up in his cell a copy of the Declaration of Independence clipped out of the New York *Times,* refers to it as if in passing so that all the world will know he is really a misunderstood patriot, one is tempted to call him a poseur and a hypocrite; but he is something much more devious.

When he and his wife carefully observe the coming of each Jewish holiday and sentimentalize over their double heritage as Americans and Jews, they are not deliberately falsifying, though they neither know nor care what Judaism actually is about; they will use as much of it as they need, defining it as they go. "In two days," Julius writes, "it will be Passover, which recalls the search of our people for liberty. This cultural heritage has for us a special significance, because we are imprisoned . . . by the Pharaohs of today. . . ." And in another place he remarks that "the culture of my people, its fight to liberate itself from slavery in Egypt" is astonishingly like "the great traditions in the history of America" — and, one understands though it is left unsaid, like those of the Communist party.

Ethel, typically, insists on defining her enlightened position more clearly. Thrilled by the sound of the shofar, she thinks of the Jews everywhere hastening to the synagogues to pray for a Happy New Year, but hastens to remind them via her husband that "we must not use prayer to the Almighty as an excuse for avoiding our responsibilities to our neighbors . . . the daily struggle for social justice." And she concludes, astonishingly, with the appeal: "Jews and non-Jews, Black and White, we must all stand together, firm, solid, and strong." It is like the curtain line of an *agit-prop* choral production at the combined celebration of *Rosh Hashanah* and the anniversary of the Russian Revolution.

Judaism happens to lie closest to hand because of the accident of the Rosenbergs' birth, but any other tradition would have done as well — and does. Not only the Christ, Gandhi and Moses of Ethel's letter to the President, but Roosevelt and "Butch" LaGuardia in their letters to each other — the list might be extended indefinitely. For they have been told, and are prepared to believe a priori, that they are the heirs of all the ages: Lincoln, Washington, Jefferson, Isaiah, Confucius, Leonardo da Vinci, Ivan the Terrible, Charlie Chaplin, and Christopher Columbus have all contributed to their patrimony.

They even like to think of themselves as sharing in the peculiarly American mana of the Brooklyn Dodgers. "The victory of the Dodgers," Ethel writes, "over the Phillies quickly restored me to my customary good spirits," and one takes it for a relatively harmless example of the pursuit of the popular and folksy that led Ethel to sing folk songs in the death house. But she cannot leave it at that; the editorial follows the next day, between declarations of love: "It is the Dodgers' unconquerable spirit which makes people love them. But where they have especially covered themselves with glory is in making an important contribution to the rooting out of racial prejudice." We have moved from melodrama to comedy, but the point is always the same. What is involved is the system of moral double bookkeeping invented to fool the Examiners, but so successful that it has ended by bamboozling the bookkeeper himself.

Nothing is what it seems: the Communist parties advocate revolution, and they do not; the Communist International has been dissolved, but it exists; one commits crimes, but he is innocent. Anyone can call war peace, or lies the truth; but to believe such assertions so that one will face death for them requires a trained will and imagination. For such belief, the Rosenbergs had been in training ever since they had combined wooing with the study of Communist literature; and they had finally reached a degree of perfection which enabled them to attain the final stage of subterfuge, to go "underground."

To me, even more extraordinary (for it seems on the face of it *pointless*) than the assertion of their innocence is the Rosenbergs' stubborn silence about their political affiliations.

In court, they had refused to speak on constitutional grounds; in their letters to each other, these "martyrs of the Communist cause" never mention the word "Communism," unless in quotation marks as an example of the slander of their enemies; while the name of the Soviet Union is, needless to say, avoided like a dirty word.

The expurgation goes sometimes to fantastic lengths, of which the most amusing example occurs in a letter of Ethel's written on June 21, 1951. "My beloved husband," she begins, "I feel so discouraged by this unjustifiable attack on a legally constituted American party! The specter of Fascism looms up, enormous and menacing . . ." But she does not identify the party beyond labeling it "American"; and the explanatory note attached by the defense committee in the published volume is equally coy. "Seventeen men and women had been arrested and convicted in New York under the recently passed Smith Act." If one already knows that those otherwise unqualified "men and women" were the leaders of the Communist party, all well and good. If not, it is apparently better to persist in one's ignorance.

The upshot of the whole business is that the Rosenbergs were quite incapable of saying in their last letters just what it was for which they thought they were dying. Not only had they excluded themselves from the traditional procedure of the old-style radical, who rises up in court to declare that he has acted in the teeth of accepted morality and law for the sake of certain higher principles; they could not even tell the world for what beliefs they were being framed. Beyond the cry of frame-up, they could only speak in hints and evasions; so that they finished by seeming martyrs only to their own double talk, to a handful of banalities: "democracy and human dignity," "liberty and peace," "the greatest good of our own children, our family, and all families," and finally "the interests of American Democracy, of justice and fraternity, of peace and bread and roses and the laughter of children."

To believe that two innocents had been falsely condemned for favoring "roses and the laughter of children," one would have to believe the judges and public officials of the United States to be not merely the Fascists the Rosenbergs called them, but monsters, insensate beasts; and perhaps this was partly their point. But one must look deeper, realize that a code is involved, a substitution of equivalents whose true meaning can be read off immediately by the insider. "Peace, democracy, and liberty," like "roses and the laughter of children," are only conventional ciphers for the barely whispered word "Communism," and Communism itself only a secondary encoding of the completely unmentioned "Defense of the Soviet Union." The Defense of the Soviet Union — here is the sole principle and criterion of all value — and to this principle the Rosenbergs felt that they had been true; in this sense, they genuinely believed themselves innocent, more innocent than if they had never committed espionage.

The final pity was that they could not say even so much aloud — except in certain symbolic outcries of frame-up and persecution, and only through the most palpable lies. It is for this reason that they failed in the end to become martyrs or heroes, or even men. What was there left to die?

Yet despite all this, *because* of it, we should have granted them grace. The betrayal of their essential humanity by their comrades and themselves left the burden of its defense with us. This obligation we failed, and our failure must be faced up to. Before the eyes of the world we lost an opportunity concretely to assert what all our abstract declarations can never prove: that for us at least the suffering person is realer than the political moment that produces him or the political philosophy for which he stands. Surely it is not even a paradox to assert that it is our special duty to treat as persons, as real human beings, those who most blasphemously deny their own humanity.

Roman Holiday

It is difficult really to believe in Passover in Rome. By the time I had set out with my two older sons in search of matzos and a community Seder, Holy Week was at hand, and the streets were full of tourists: the Germans (back in force this year) carefully avoiding every eye and speaking only to each other; the seedy herds of Austrians following their guides from crowded bus to crowded bus; the Americans resting between churches at chic sidewalk cafés. It was no use to remind my boys that, after all, the Last Supper was a Seder, too; nothing could redeem the sense of moving in loneliness against the current that flowed toward the great basilicas, the celebration of the Tenebrae, the washing of the feet, and the final orgy of Easter Sunday when half a million foreigners and Romans would stand flank against flank, the visible body of Christendom awaiting the papal benediction.

It does not matter that scarcely any Roman will confess to a belief in religious dogma — that Rome is also a city of anti-clericalism, with a statue of Giordano Bruno presiding over its busiest market; what is *not* believed is always and everywhere the same. And into each house before Easter is past, the priest will come with holy water and a blessing (only the most ferocious Communist will bar his way) to wash believer and non-believer clean for the new year. The rhythms of the year, the rhythms of life itself, are the rhythms of the Church; and to be outside those rhythms as an American and a Jew is to be excluded as no one can ever be in America, where one's loneliness is what he shares with all his neighbors.

Yet the history and legend of Rome belong also to the Jews.

65

My sons and I travel down the Corso where the *ebrei* were once forced to race against asses; we skirt the Forum whose furthest limit is the Arch of Titus, with its image of the defeated Jordan borne on a stretcher; and my oldest boy asks me if it is true that no Jew is permitted to walk under that memorial to the fall of Jerusalem. I tell him that this was once a commonly held belief, and that, for all I know, the Orthodox may still hold it; and I go on to recount the legend of how the Golden Candlestick of the Temple fell from the hands of a triumphal Roman procession into the Tiber. My sons argue about whether it was an accident or an act of God, and they make up a story about finding it again, gold in the black mud.

But by this time the modern Roman Synagogue stands behind us, dignified and ugly, "built," as the guidebooks say, "in an imitation Assyro-Babylonian style" — and my mind has wandered off to the melancholy gossip I have heard lately about the former Chief Rabbi who has become a Catholic. I saw him once in the halls of the University where he now lectures, distrait and melancholy — or perhaps it is only that I expected, *wanted,* him to seem so.

An East European type, certain unofficial informants tell me, despised by the "old Roman" members of his congregation, he was left to bear the brunt when the Nazis came, to face the problem of raising the ransom they demanded. Almost all of the rich Jews were in hiding, my informants go on to explain, so that in the end it was the Pope who put up the money. Then, the war over, the aristocratic members of the congregation returned and began to conspire against their somewhat shabby leader, who therefore. . . . God knows whether any of it is true; but that the story itself should exist is enough to confirm my melancholy.

But today there are wreaths in front of the Synagogue, eight or ten of them draped with the Italian tricolor, their green leaves already dusty and turning brown, for they have been standing out since March 24, anniversary of the mass reprisals in the Ardeatine Caves, when sixty or seventy Jews, along with nearly three hundred other Romans, were killed by the Nazis. The monument to the dead, surmounted by the cross and the Jewish star, is brutally impressive (the Romans have never lost their flair for celebrating death); but more moving are the occasional small plaques on nondescript apartment houses — memorializing some individual victim who once lived there. His fellow-tenants, though they may have stolen his furniture once he was dead, will never forget him.

It is better to concentrate only on the dead. We stand beside the wreath and try to ignore the jaunty youngster who approaches us with a "Shalom" and offers to show us what is left of the "old synagogue" on a lower level. He speaks the sort of American a hep kid would have picked up from our soldiers, and his approach is precisely that of a street peddler offering to sell you something or change your money.

I try to tell my children something about the Ardeatine Caves, but I do not know the details they ask (What does the overhanging slab weigh? How old was the youngest victim?); and, anyhow, it is time to meet R. at the Portico of Octavia. More history. One part of the ancient portico has become the atrium of the church of Sant'Angelo, where for hundreds of years the Jews were forced on each Sabbath to hear a sermon urging conversion. Across the front of the church, in Hebrew and Latin, an inscription still thunders against the outcast and stiff-necked people. Beyond lies the old Ghetto; and, since R. has not yet arrived, we walk through the narrow, sodden streets, where my boys are impressed by the smell of filth and oppression. I do not tell them that all the poorer quarters of Rome share equally that ghetto smell.

In a little square that opens with typical suddenness around a fountain, a woman smiles at us hopefully and says, "Shalom." When we answer, "Shalom," we are surrounded by six or eight young men who appear out of nowhere. Each of them is the twin of the boy before the Synagogue; each has a genuine Swiss watch or Parker 51 pen to sell. My children haggle with them enthusiastically, and they ask us about America; until, even more suddenly than they materialized, they have all disappeared. We see only the soles of feet flashing down a twisting alley. Then we understand, for a cop is riding past, winking at us good-naturedly.

Meanwhile R. has come, and we discuss getting tickets for the community Seder. He knows, he says, a certain kosher

butcher shop where one can buy tickets from a man named
Polacco; he has this on excellent authority. So we go on to
the butcher shop, where no one will confess to having heard of
our Polacco. "Naturally," the butcher tells us, wiping more
blood off his hands onto an already sufficiently bloody apron,
"there are many Polaccos. Which one, is the question, and
what do we want him for anyway? Tickets for the community
Seder? Naturally, there are several Seders. Which one, is the
question? Right or left, or — "

Right or left? In our bewilderment, R. and I consult each
other in English; and someone taps me on the shoulder, draws
me aside: a middle-aged man with a loud, impatient voice,
who unexpectedly speaks excellent English. He is sure we
would only be interested in the most Orthodox celebration.
"Naturally, where you don't have to worry about the food!"
He turns aside to consult an elderly man with a beard who has
been pretending all along not to be with him; I think they are
speaking Yiddish, but they whisper and I can't be sure. "The
price will be only — " The tickets are already in his hand,
and he presses them enthusiastically into mine.

"But isn't there another?" I ask.

His face loses a little of its not quite plausible friendliness.
"Another Seder? Yes, there is one, not so kosher, for the
younger men, *very* young — " He looks me up and down
carefully, estimating my age. "Twenty-, twenty-five-year-olds.
If anyone wants such company!"

"But isn't there one," I insist, "officially sponsored by the
Synagogue?"

He regards me now with open contempt. "Officially sponsored? Children! A Seder sung by school children — " He
walks off, followed by his accomplice with the beard, who
looks back at us scornfully.

"Aha!" the butcher puts in at this point, "you want the
children. It's the Polacco *School* you want, not Polacco!"

But R. isn't satisfied. He turns suspiciously on the butcher.
"The *other* butcher, isn't he Polacco?" By this time, we do
not know how many real or imaginary Seders there are, or
what lies we may not be told in the interests of one faction
or another.

"Him? He's my brother. We're Terracini."

It had to be Terracini! Not that it isn't a common enough name among Italian Jews: Terracina, Terracini — there must be at least twenty-five in the Rome telephone book, including the dealer in Catholic church supplies; but R. and I are momentarily taken aback. Terracini is also the name of the Communist Senator who was one of the leaders of the recent rioting in the Parliament. That very day a session has ended with the Communists hurling inkbottles at the president of the Senate; and, the day before, R. watched Terracini himself banging his desk with a stick in concert with his colleagues, so that the roll call would not be heard. . . . And it was Terracini, too, who a couple of months before explained away at a meeting of Roman Jewish intellectuals the anti-Semitic trials in Prague, denouncing as a Nazi and hireling our friend Professor T., who rose to challenge his lies.

But at last we have found the Polacco School, a *yeshiva* across the Tiber from the Synagogue, and Terracini is forgotten. The tickets and the matzos are being sold next door to each other; and the children are so delighted at reaching the end of our quest that we are not even disturbed at the curtness with which the young women in charge treat us. Never have they been so busy, so important! "Speak up! Speak up!" They have no time to waste over our indecision.

While we try to figure out the difference between Swiss matzos and regular matzos, we are good-naturedly but efficiently mauled by the large crowd, which struggles for first place with elbow and knee in the approved Roman style. They even look just like Romans, my children insist sadly; they don't look like Jews at all. And the matzos are called *azzime,* and they, too, are different in texture and shape from what we are used to. Even the Pesach wine (we buy everything in sight, flour, meal, wine; there will be complaints when we get home, but who cares!) turns out to be the customary *vino bianco* from Frascati, not the syrupy red stuff to which the children have been looking forward. But later we are all relieved and happy, balancing the awkward packages in our arms; we smile with a new and perilous sense of having found a community as we pass others carrying similar packages.

Next door, the lady in charge is delighted to see us; there will be another American at the Seder, she tells us, a woman with a small child. We will be like manna to them, for neither of them can speak anything but English. The Seder will be wonderful, *wonderful!* If we listen we can hear the children practicing now. It is true; we can just make out their voices, faint and sweet. We are pleased to be so wanted; and as we depart enthusiastically, the friendly *signora* assures us that the rabbi himself will be there. It is to be the next night, and the children can hardly wait.

Perhaps the rabbi *was* there, after all: we could never find out. It is true that there was at the head table a fine-looking, white-bearded old man, very genteel; but he could equally well have been an Italian Senator (even Terracini!), and he seemed throughout the celebration as bored as everyone else. The "American" woman turned out to be a South African who did not have a child at all, and she regarded the R.'s and us with dim hostility from the start. We arrived too early, of course, though we had allowed a half-hour past the announced time; and so we began under the terrible burden of shame borne by the first guest. The children from the school were already at their prayers, dressed in the Italian student uniform; but the white-draped tables which formed a square around their long crowded one were empty; and the teacher who led them glanced up from his book to us with what seemed to me a look of annoyance.

It was hot, and I walked up and down outside with R., watching the arrival of the other paying guests. They turned out to be mostly very old ladies, who drove up in expensive cars and were helped trembling up the steps by their chauffeurs. If they participated at all in the Seder, beyond nibbling a little from each of the plates set before them, I certainly could not tell. They were quite obviously only performing an act of charity.

Three young men came in at the last minute, dark and reticent, but obviously more at home than we, though they confessed later to being Americans. They seemed quite familiar to me, the kind of good Jewish boys who refuse invitations to dinner because they have promised their mothers to keep kosher. After the Seder, they told us in horror about the heterodoxies of the Roman Synagogue, about which I can remember only the fact that it celebrates Bat Mitzvah, the equivalent of Bar Mitzvah but for girls. Imagine it!

The Seder service itself was badly cut and extremely dull, despite the real charm of the children (there was one girl with the black, ugly-beautiful face of a Bedouin) and the freshness of their voices. The only emotion I could sense was the anxiety of the teacher that they get through it all without too horrible a blunder. The sacrifice was just a bone on a plate, the egg only something to eat; and the earnestness of the performing children (even the littlest ones did not squirm noticeably until the end) was canceled out by the apathy of the paying guests. It was a relief when the voice of the young Bedouin broke and they all giggled; or when the pregnant young wife of the teacher, who sat at the head of the table, reached over to slap her own child, distinguished from the others by not wearing a smock.

Three buxom waitresses in pink uniforms trimmed with the shield of David dashed frantically about with bowls of water for washing, herbs for dipping, etc., but they never managed to get anything to us on time, chiefly because the old ladies took so long waving them away; and we were often passed by completely, to the distress of my boys.

The meal itself was served somewhat more efficiently, though, naturally, not until everything was satisfactorily cold. It was a completely Roman, non-Paschal meal: broth with *pasta*, slices of roast veal, and finally artichokes *alla giudea*, which is to say, Jewish style; for the Jews have long been famous as restaurateurs in Rome, and this is their most notable contribution to the local cuisine. It was somehow the last disconsolate touch. Whether the school children had the same fare or not was difficult to discern, for they did not eat off china, like the guests, but from a single metal bowl, like the setting in a prison or a Dickensian workhouse.

There was more singing after the meal, of course; and for this the parents of the children were let in, ruddy-faced working people, ruddier with washing and the excitement of seeing their offspring perform for the rich. They sat across from us on wooden benches against a farther wall, looking at the pale old ladies and parchment-yellowish rabbi-senator, not in hostility, but like representatives of a different species. Over their heads, a sign read in Hebrew: *With a strong hand!* And it would have taken a Strong Hand, indeed, to have brought us all out of Egypt together.

From this point on, the ceremony was speeded up until I could no longer follow it in the *Haggadah* I had brought along; the children had long since lost interest. Finally, the weary little students were permitted to sing one song in Italian and out of tune: the *"Chad gadya,"* into which they flung themselves with obvious relief, while their parents beamed in approval and the old ladies tried hard to smile. Only then the teacher, who had conducted and prompted in suppressed anguish all evening, rose to explain the symbolism of the egg, the herb, the bitters; but conversation was general on all sides, and the chairs of the children creaked. Only his wife listened to him, earnestly, one hand resting lightly on her swollen belly — poised for the quick slap if her own child grew restive.

Afterward, the old ladies and the bearded gentleman shook the hand of the teacher, who bowed gratefully like a superior servant, while the children trotted off, chattering, on the arms of their parents. I was ashamed to look at my wife or the R.'s, and I wanted even to apologize to my sons; but they were content, after all, for they had been able to wear their new skullcaps with the initials that their great-grandmother had sent them, and they had drunk two glasses of wine apiece. *Next year in Jerusalem!*

There was not a bus or streetcar in sight. The Communist trade unions had called a strike for that day in protest against the new election law passed by the Demo-Christians despite inkwell-throwing and desk-banging. When we had come down to the Seder, there had still been some transportation available; but now everyone had decided to enjoy the stoppage with that frightening good humor with which a Roman crowd greets any disorder. They stood in groups on the street corners joshing each other about getting home, or sat at the tables of sidewalk cafés cursing the government of the priests. All the old ladies had long since been whisked back to the fashionable quarters by their chauffeurs, and no one was left who knew it was Pesach.

We could not even find a taxi, and the R.'s decided to walk. *"Gut yontif,"* we called to each other as we parted, but we did not believe in it. After three-quarters of an hour, during which the children grew wearier and crankier, a bus came lumbering along which would carry us within a mile of our house. On the long ride home, my wife and I argued bitterly, chiefly because I, for some reason I can no longer recall, refused to admit how miserable the whole evening had been. Finally, I was yelling so loud that the two other passengers were watching me, delighted to be so entertained. Despite it all, the children had fallen asleep, and had to be awakened for the hike home; but they were surprisingly cheerful.

We had almost arrived, when someone hailed us. It was an American girl we knew and her Italian husband, both Jewish, both very young, and determinedly liberal.

"A big day," I said, thinking wearily of the holiday.

"The strike, you mean," he answered. "We really tied them up tight! This should be a lesson for De Gasperi and the Vatican, too." He seemed as enthusiastic about it as if he had arranged it all himself.

What was the use of arguing? "We're just coming from a Seder," I said to change the subject.

"A Seder! I'll bet." He laughed, hoping it was a joke.

"No — no — I'm serious. And tomorrow we're having another — a *real* one at home, so the kids will really understand it."

At that his wife could no longer bear it. "How can you do it?" she cried in horror, turning from me to my wife in search of an ally. "Do you mean to say that in this day and age you tell your children — " she could hardly manage to say it — "you teach them that we're the *Chosen People?*"

Dante: Green Thoughts
in a Green Shade

Reflections on the Stony Sestina of Dante Alighieri

I have dreamed for many years now of rescuing from silence and misunderstanding the sestina of Dante which begins *Al poco giorno e al gran cerchio d'ombra*. But each time I set to work, I am depressed by the impossibility of rendering even that deceptively simple first line with accuracy or grace; and I end by telling myself that it is all a boy's dream anyhow. What reason is there to think that I am the St. George picked out for the rescue? And even if I achieve it, what then? No one insists on a reward for redeeming Princesses from the powers of darkness, but one looks forward at least to a small crowd of cheering relatives and friends. It is unendurable to contemplate bringing the Maiden back to—nothing. From silence to silence. Yet what else can one reasonably expect?

The professional *dantista*, trained in the language and learned in bibliography, has already what he needs or deserves, an established text and studies ranging from the comically pointless to the poetically illuminating, the fruit of German-trained scholarship and Crocean insight. And the crumbs of this feast are available even to the beginning student. Who else is there? I am aware that we seem to be in the midst of a revival of amateur interest in Dante, a wave of translation and assimilation, which has now reached the grocery-store bookstands with paperback editions of the *Comedy*; but it is with the *Comedy* that the nonprofessional interest begins and ends.

In a way, this is fair enough. To pretend that much beyond the *Comedy* can deeply move one not intimate with the poet's language is to add a further self-deception to a relationship already compromised with fraud and snobbishness. There are enough architectonics, rhetoric and melodrama in the *Commedia* to survive any translation, no matter how breezily colloquial or piously high church. And even the *Vita Nuova* can be read by those who cannot define a *canzone;* for it is blessed with a plot of sorts, a continuous symbolism and an imposed order, which make it possible to ignore the meaning of the poem as the record of a revolution in technique: the perfecting of a new way of making love poetry.

The uncollected lyrics of Dante, however, the so-called *Rime,* are completely at the mercy of the translator; for their appeal is all in their texture and technique. What "story" they possess is at best some vaguely defined and half-ironic myth; and their attitudes the fashionable beliefs of a long-dead "school"; a group of poets who drew from common sources and shared a common metaphysics; who evolved cooperatively a style at once technically "serious" and yet a kind of elegant play; who exchanged compliments and insults and rhyme schemes and lived out their love affairs very largely in those exchanges. The fact that Dante's minor poems are in this sense "love songs" serves only to confuse us. It is hard for us to remember that they are not poems of love, but poems about love; speculations on what it is and demonstrations of how best to express it. Consequently, they are really directed not to the beloved, but to other poet-philosopher-lovers as entries in an endless contest, in which the competitors and judges are the same, and the prize is not love but fame, "*la gloria della lingua.*" Referring to this tradition as it has developed from Guido Guinicelli to Guido Cavalcanti to himself, Dante makes the point quite explicitly behind the barely veiled boast:

> *Così ha tolto l'uno all'altro Guido*
> *la gloria della lingua e forse è nato*
> *chi l'uno e l'altro caccerà di nido . . .*

There have been some recent attempts to find in Dante's love theory a still valid wisdom; but for most of us his Aristotelian (in a technical sense) and Platonic (in the vulgar one) version of the codes of Provence is not merely difficult but tedious and a little silly. It is, in fact, precisely the sort of farrago one would expect from a group of university intellectuals, ridden by homosexuality, possessed by the psychology of scholasticism and haunted by the anti-sexual bias of the Church; but determined to make a poetry based on Provençal models, which thought of love as the noblest subject for verse, and conceived of that love as heterosexual and adulterous.

It is not the *bontà* of Dante's lyric verse, its doctrinal excellence, but its *bellezza*, its adornment and sweet sound, upon which its survival depends. This *bellezza* he apparently conceived as self-sufficient, independent of the *ragione*, the prose meaning of the poem. "If you do not grasp my import fully," the envoy of one *canzone* runs, "at least reflect on how beautiful I am!" ("*Ponete mente almen com' io son bella.*") This essay is intended to be such a reflection on the *bellezza* of the sestina, for me the loveliest of all the minor poems. Unfortunately a mere translation will not suffice, for it does not translate enough; and so I have set my own version beside an earlier one and have accompanied both with a running commentary on the text.*

It is necessary first of all, I suppose, to say what a sestina is. From the point of view of a single stanza, it is a poem which rejects rhyme; and this in a rime-haunted language like Provençal or Italian seems not a relaxation but an effort of the will. From the point of view of the poem as a whole, however, the sestina makes use of monorhyme—that is, of the repetition of identical words in places where one would expect only partial echoes. This means finally that the resemblance-difference we have learned to expect from ordinary rhyming is separated out: the difference insisted upon locally from line to line; the resemblance, become identity, suggested only from stanza to stanza. Such

---

* In my explication, I have drawn on such general knowledge of the tradition as I have derived from De Sanctis, Grandgent, Croce, Vossler, etc.; and I am more specifically indebted to Gianfranco Contini, whose edition of the *Rime* I have used. The rendering I am setting beside my own is Dante Gabriel Rossetti's out of his volume *Dante and His Circle;* this version seems to me as characteristic of Rossetti's age and its uses of Dante as I have tried to make mine of our own. I also refer from time to time to Grandgent's English in his *Ladies of Dante's Lyrics.*

disjunction reinforces that sense of holding apart by sheer will what belongs together by nature which is essential to the sestina.

In addition, the sestina is presided over by a kind of cold mathematics that functions like fate. In each of six stanzas, the same six monorhymes must be repeated, the last one of the first stanza becoming the first of the next, the first becoming the second, the fifth the third, etc., until all the mathematical possibilities are exhausted. Then there is added a *commiato* or *congedo*, in which the six key words must be crowded into only three lines. There is scant room left for invention; what free will is permitted must survive between closely repeated limits, until, at the conclusion, there is scarcely space for it to function at all.

In the *commiato* of Dante, four syllables of each eleven-syllable line are committed in advance; and the poet is confined almost entirely to contriving a syntax to bind together his six obsessive terms. The sestina seems, in this sense, a dialogue of freedom and necessity, like, say, Bach's *Art of Fugue*; but it is one loaded heavily on the side of necessity—a predestinarian dialogue.

The great sestinas of literature—this one of Dante, for example, and its protype in Arnaut Daniel, which begins *Lo ferm voler qu'al cor m'intra*—remain faithful to the metaphysical implications of the form itself. It is only too easy to make the sestina an embodiment of ingenuity rather than necessity, to give the impression that the word at each line ending is sought and prepared for, a prize rather than a trap. On the contrary, the successful sestina must make it seem that each monorhyme is seven times fled and seven times submitted to; that the poet is ridden by a passion which forces him back on the six obsessive words, turn and twist as he may. The periphrasis which is natural to the form (Arnaut, for instance, calls his mother "the sister of my uncle") must never seem a mere device to save the word whose turn has been mathematically determined, but such a giveaway of the poet's hidden madness, such a betraying slip of the tongue as Freud delighted in. *Ubi morbus, ibi digitus.*

Finally, in the *commiato*, there must be the sense (and this only Dante eminently attained) that the key words have managed at last not merely to utter themselves once more, but to achieve their fated relationship, which the poet has desperately evaded through six stanzas. This means that the fulfillment of the *commiato* is likely to be a reversal, to stand in the same relationship to the rest of the poem as the concluding couplet of a Shakespearian sonnet to the first twelve lines.

To keep so complicated a piece of machinery from seeming *merely* a machine is in the power of only the most accomplished poets. Yet mere accomplishment is not enough. The sestina can be handled only by a master poet in a tradition which believes passionately in technique as a good in itself, at the point where the technique is mythicized and becomes the actual subject of the poem. This kind of poet Dante was (though he was more, too), as was Arnaut Daniel, who invented the form. To Arnaut, Dante makes acknowledgment in the *De Vulgari Eloquentia;* and it is, of course, Arnaut who is hailed in Canto XXVI of the *Purgatory* by Guido Guinicelli himself as *"il miglior fabbro,"* the greatest craftsman of language.

This compliment has been adapted by T. S. Eliot to pay his respects to Pound; and these two between them have made the figure of Arnaut a part of the mythology of twentieth-century poetry. The references in Eliot, however, lead only to the Provençal verse which Dante composed for the mouth of his beloved master. And even Pound has not translated (if that is the proper word for his efforts) Arnaut's sestina; so that this amazing poem remains as unknown to most contemporary readers as in the not very distant past, when Grandgent could still call Arnaut "one of the most laborious and tiresome of the Provençal versifiers."

From Arnaut, Dante learned not only the superficial devices of the form, but also the appropriate obsessed tone, the note of barely repressed hysteria, which alone can keep it from seeming a piece of highfalutin' tomfoolery. Love is the required subject, of course, but not the easy adoration or smooth sensuality of other Provençal poets—rather a difficult love come on hard times, an unworthy or hopeless but irrepressible infatuation. The season of Arnaut's suffering is typically winter, and his poems are likely to open in ice or snow among mute and frozen birds, rather than in the musical springtime of the *trobar leu.* The *trobar clus* of which Arnaut is the great representative is a mode which rejects lightness and openness not only in diction, but also in imagery and feeling. Its mythical world endures a perpetual December—and it is to this world that the opening of Dante's sestina belongs, though, characteristically, he specifies his season with a vast astronomical image rather than in terms of Arnaut's more circumscribed background of stripped bushes and trees.

It is not, of course, from Arnaut's sestina alone that Dante has learned to make a poetry at once bleak and complicated, shrill and adorned; and it is not in his own sestina alone that he applies the lesson. *Al poco giorno* belongs to a group of Dante's poems which the Italian commentators call the *"rime pietrose,"* the stony verses. The name is an extension of a pun central to the poems themselves and needs a little explanation. There have survived at least four poems of Dante, similar in tone, diction and technical ambition, all addressed to a certain Donna Pietra (Dante uses the older form "Petra"), and all playing obsessively on the second meaning of her name, which is, of course, "rock" or "stone."

Much vain though amusing speculation has been devoted to the identity of this lady by two opposing wings of Dante scholars, the biographically and the allegorically inclined. One group would have her either a certain Pietra degli Scrovegni or else Pietra di Donato di Bruncaccio, who was Dante's sister-in-law (which "would account for the note of wickedness" in the poems, Grandgent remarks, though he finally dismisses the hypothesis). The others would make her variously the Virgin Mary, whom St. Bernard had called *"pietra,"* or Divine Wisdom or the Church itself, since her name is the feminine form of the nickname of his disciple Simon, on which Jesus punned so disastrously.

The latter misinterpretations Dante has brought upon himself, using with great deliberateness for his monorhymes words of the broadest possible symbolic resonance; but the former interpretations are diseases of an age of biographical criticism—accidental rather than necessary. If one insists upon a historical identification, the dry observation of Boccaccio (a pretty girl from the hills with a goiter) seems far more convincing than the romantic fantasies of some courtly affair or quasi-incestuous entanglement. After all, Boccaccio's no more documented identification of the equally suspicious name of Beatrice (with its equally convenient pun) has had much better luck. The real point is, of course (and here contemporary Italian critical opinion as opposed to "scholarly" speculation has reached an agreement), that the "Donna Pietra" is a myth, a personification of a "moment of Dante's art."

After his shift from an earlier artificial and obscure style to the comparative lucidity of the *stil nuovo,* which is the prevailing mode of the *Vita Nuova,* Dante seems to have turned again, briefly at least, to a second period of *trobar clus.* This second hermetic phase is based directly on the example of Arnaut Daniel, and does not so much woo obscurity out of a contempt for the popular as endure it out of a sense that the pursuit of richness and difficulty and involution may lead to certain reaches of meaning unavailable to perspicuity. It is a useful and (I hope) forgivable anachronism to call this Dante's "symbolist phase."

At any rate, one must imagine his searching for a subject to justify a new style, rather than vice versa (if there is a "true love" behind the *rime pietrose,* it is the love of Arnaut Daniel); and finally projecting into the image of a kind of woman and a kind of love his passionate search for a farfetched and anti-rhetorical rhetoric—"of all things not impossible the most difficult." The Donna Pietra is, then, a symbol of a poetics, an obscure and stony *bellezza;* and if that *bellezza* itself stands for some remoter and larger beauty, this meaning is not stated but hinted. The biographical fact, real or supposed, does not finally matter, and even the symbolic extension of meaning is secondary. What counts is the natural history of the myth constructed in the poems themselves.

The poet finds himself in a frozen world and among limestone hills, confronting a girl, immune to passion, unmoved as stone. He can hope for no easing of his winter with the turning of the seasons, for it is the projection of an inner hopelessness and of advancing age. The youngness of the girl is insisted upon; she is *"nova," "giovane,"* a *"pargoletta";* and though the poet does not directly refer to the years between them, one feels that distance as a final complication, the capstone of the absurdity of the whole affair. The scholars have, as they will, calculated the date

of the poems by the (not quite certain) astrological data at the
beginning of one of them; and have decided that they were written around 1296. This would make Dante just past thirty, a little
young to be the counterpart of his poetic "I," though old enough
to feel such a fiction as not utterly alien to him.

At any rate, the poems turn on the paradox of a wintry lover
moved like the earth in spring, and a beloved frozen like winter
though in the springtime of her life. There seems no chance for
any consummation of such a love except a bloody one; for it is
by definition absurd, and has been so long baffled that desire has
changed to a hope for revenge (*"che bell'onor s'acquisita in far
vendetta"*). To tear the Donna Pietra as a bear tears his prey, to
grab her by the hair and stare her down, and only at the moment
of her greatest terror make peace with the rapist's kiss—these
are the lover's sadistic fancies, turned into a language as tortured
and feverish as those fancies themselves.

Occasionally, he yields to a more idyllic dream, a vision of
his beloved alone in a grassy field, imprisoned among lofty hills
and hot with desire for him. But such comparatively gentle
images give way to the harsh cry. "Ah, let her yap for me, as I
for her, in hell's hot soup!" And finally over all, the cries of
desire and the recriminations, and the images of the lover hoar
but ardent, the woman green but icy, there hovers a final coldness, the end of both hope and suffering. Each of the poems
closes with a prescience of death, half-fear and half-wish, the
knowledge that the only stone on which the poet will ever sleep
(it is the last and bitterest pun) is the *"poca petra"* of his tomb.

Around this fable, Dante has woven his stony rhymes,
though the resulting verses must not be thought of as narrative
poems. They are too sluggish on the one hand, too ejaculatory on
the other to "tell a story." Their movement is the movement of
an obsession, circular within their trap of despair—in their tiny
compass, not unlike the motion of Faulkner's *Absalom! Absalom!*
This is why the sestina seems so apt an embodiment for the
sentimento behind the fable of the Donna Pietra. Among the
four least-doubtful poems, there is, beside our sestina, a so-called
double sestina, which tops the thirty-nine lines on six monorhymes of the former by achieving sixty-six lines with only five

repeated words. Dante's double sestina is not without merit; but its coldly proportional inflation of difficulty (excluding the *commiato*, the single sestina is based on a ratio of $36:6 = 6:1$, the *sestina doppia* on one of $60:5 = 12:1$; with the *commiato*, the sum of all the lines of the sestina is thirty-nine, whose integers added give first twelve, then the magical three; the *sestina doppia* gives sixty-six, another twelve which becomes three, etc., etc.) exudes an iciness which is beyond the poet's power to transmute from mathematics to poetry.

Besides, the longer poem, though it clings as it must to the inevitable monorhymes *donna* and *pietra*, substitutes for the *ombra, verde, erba* and *colli* of the shorter one, *freddo, luce* and *tempo:* a movement toward abstraction and away from the objectivity of key words, for which Dante had found a cue in Arnaut, and which he, indeed, carried much further than his master. In *Al poco giorno*, the thematic terms are all substantives (only "green" ambiguously teeters between noun and adjective), all "things" real in terms of the senses; and yet they avoid both the exaggerated "thinginess" and the eccentricity of *oncle* and *ongla* ("uncle" and "fingernail") in Arnaut's most famous sestina. To find another example of a diction as absurd as the latter, as seemingly frivolous yet poetically fruitful, one has to descend to *Le monocle de mon oncle* of Wallace Stevens. Dante is not completely averse to unusual words and fantastic conjunctions, played off in a double dissonance of meaning and sound; indeed, there are sufficient examples in the stony poem which begins with the declaration:

> *Cosi nel mio parlar voglio esser aspro*
> *com' è ne li atti questa bella petra*

"I would be as harsh in my speech as is this lovely stone in her behavior."

But something in Dante's temperament keeps him from the boast of the Provençal poet: "I am Arnaut . . . who yoke the ox and hare, and swim against the stream." Even in paradox, Dante prefers a certain blandness; and he is content to let his main conceit carry the chief burden of absurdity, substituting for

Arnaut's yoked dissimilars a series of three rather obvious and not discordant contrasts: *donna-petra, erba-colli, verde-ombra.* In each case there is the same playing off of the warm and living against the cold and dead. It is worth noting, however, that at least one of the antinomies is not as obvious as it seems at first glance. The simplest opposite of "green" would be "white," the color of winter versus the color of spring; and inside the lines, this opposition is exploited, as is the other easy contrast of "light" and "shade."

Dante wants, however, to insist upon an opposition less lexical, more deeply symbolic. The typology of Medieval Christianity had linked the color green with the second of the Christian Virtues, hope; while the figure of "the valley of shadow" had made *ombra* a familiar, even homely metaphor for death. It is upon these extended meanings that the not-quite-obvious polarity *verde-ombra,* hope-death, forces our attention. And this, in turn, makes us aware that Dante has deliberately chosen all his monorhymes from words with the widest connotations, so that they may provide a contrast *in depth*—less spectacular but less easily exhausted than Arnaut's. *Petra* is, for instance, the name of a thing, substantial and solid, or rather of a series of things: a girl, a rock, a jewel; yet it also evokes overtones of the Church and of salvation ("on this rock I found my church") which join with the whole penumbra of significance in Donna (mistress—possessor—lady—Our Lady, etc.) to reinforce the sense of how sacred a thing is profaned in the rejection of love.

There are, moreover, three assonances on "o" and three on "e" to underline the threeness of the pattern; indeed, the importance of triplets in the architecture of the sestina has led some commentators on Dante to find in this form the germ of *terza rima* itself. But the sound resemblances are not precisely coincident with the symbolic categories. With *colli* and *ombra,* which belong to the side of cold, is linked *donna* (which assonates both vowels with *ombra*), though the latter stands for all that is most living and desirable; while with the fertile and hopeful *erba* and *verde,* the cruel *petra* is joined by its sound (again in double-assonance with *erba*). But, of course, the ambiguity of "stone" (which is also the name of the beloved) and "lady" is precisely the point of the poem; and this ambiguity the apparently displaced assonances underline.

I have found it impossible to maintain these subtle and important assonances in my translation, though "grass" and "green" yield easily enough an alliteration to replace the vowel coincidence of *erba* and *verde*. I have preferred this rendering to the "leaves" and "green" of Grandgent's translation, out of a sense that in English a marked consonantal music must bear part of the burden carried almost exclusively in Italian by vowel play. It is for this reason that I have not avoided, and indeed have sometimes shamelessly pursued, alliteration. In "green" and "queen," I have heretically introduced one full rime among the more fleeting resemblances. Their conjunction is so shifting and so much at the mercy of the sestina pattern that one is by turns surprised by their chiming and disappointed by its apparent failure; so that the feeling of frustration-satisfaction peculiar to the sestina is rather augmented than diminished by this unorthodoxy.

Besides, "queen" has finally seemed to me the only possible way to translate "*donna*" in this context of imagery and sound. "Lady" or "mistress" suggest themselves first; indeed, "mistress" is quite attractive, rendering very well not only the overtone of command implied by *donna*, but giving, too, some sense of the conventional use of the word for the Beloved and its most neutral significance as a formal title: Donna Pietra = Mistress Stone. It is, however, an awkward word, and one which seems to me out of tune with the other monorhymes; "lady" would harmonize much better, making a partial rhyme with "shade," and this is, of course, what Rossetti uses: "Of the Lady Pietra degli Scrovigni." But "Lady" demands the capital again; without it, it has lost for us any meaning more than "woman"—and with it, seeming a shade nostalgic.

There is capital trouble enough in the problem of rendering "Petra" as "stone" or "Stone." Unfortunately, it yields up no common given name in English (why could the poet not have had the good grace to pun on, say, Rose!); and though Stone is not impossible as a family name, it seems improbable that a reader will remain sufficiently aware of the play on words it suggests; yet that pun must be as evident as the one on "Will" in Shakespeare's sonnets, or on "Rose" in Henry Green's *Back*.

No, "queen" is the best rendering, after all, the last title for a woman which suggests in our society the fiction of an immense social distance between the lover and the beloved on which this whole tradition depends. Moreover, the word has only one syllable, and this English meter demands. In Italian, of course, the monorhymes are all bisyllabic and each closing cadence feminine. Though it would be possible with some strain to maintain this pattern in English: "shadow," "verdure," "herbage," "mountains," etc., the eleven-syllable line closing on the offbeat is for us a pointless affectation, which clamors to become a ten-syllable one ending on the stress.

To maintain such a rhythm for five rhymes and not the sixth seems to me intolerable. But what other monosyllabic honorific for woman is there? "Dame" is ridiculous, and to use "lass," as does Grandgent (or "maid" or "girl"), blurs an important point. It is true, I think, that we should be aware of the beloved as really a girl, so absurdly young that the hopeless passion of an aging man seems all the more degrading; but there is a tension in such phrases as "*la giovane donna*" between the lady's actual youth and her status for the poet, best rendered by the paradox in "little queen."

Indeed, the whole poem must be conceived of as a series of ironic contrasts, some subtle, some stark almost to the point of melodrama; and nothing must conceal its nature as a nest of Chinese boxes, paradox within paradox down to the vanishing point. This sense no translation I know renders with real success, yet without this it, the poem, loses its *raison d'être*. Not only the logic but also the music of the sestina depends upon the establishing of this pattern of duality against a background of tripleness. It is as if the right hand played in double time against the triple time of the left. Over all, there is the balancing off of the three-line *congedo* against the preceding thirty-six verses; inside of this, a contrast of stanza one with stanza two, and of five with six. Stanzas three and four make quite separate units, each containing a sharp clash between opening and conclusion. But this, of course, is merely the beginning.

Stanzas one and two are linked by the adverb "*similemente*," which the earlier translators ignore, but which is the hinge of the wriest joke and the most delightfully ironic transition of the poem. I have rendered it "just so constantly" (literally it is "similarly") to make the point as clearly as possible. He and his beloved (the poet boasts) are equally faithful and unchanging; for quite as he remains the sole note of spring in winter, she remains the last vestige of winter in the spring. It is no more possible to make her love than to make him cease from loving. Yet there is a hint from the start that her kind of stubbornness will outlast his. The basic antimony of spring and winter suggests others: sunlight and shadow, white and green, grass and hills. The final pair introduces a further reach of irony; for if grass by virtue of its color stands for hope, it is also the symbol of impermanence; while the hills (associated with darkness, constriction and cold) are the type of what abides forever.

Though the winter is one of a set of contraries, it contains within itself a further contradiction described in terms of *"poco giorno"* and *"gran cerchio d'ombra."* That this represents more than the simple-minded contrast of short days and long nights, already a commonplace by Dante's time, can be seen by comparing it with its Provençal counterparts: "Anigh short days and evenings long," "The longest night and the smallest day of all the year," etc. Only the Dantesque version evokes the cosmic image of the great globe itself beneath its inverted cone of dark, and the diminishing focus of daylight inside of which the tiny protagonist prepares to face an overwhelming destiny. From this vast background, the poem shrinks to the final foreground detail of the stone lost in grass. Simply to give up, as Rossetti does, this opening contrast of "small" and "great" is to risk losing the leitmotif of the poem. The sigh of "alas!" cannot be spared either; and to render the straightforward *"giunto"* as "clomb" rather than "come" is to submit to the sort of archaizing which takes the accidents of aging for the essence of poetic appeal.

That hopeless desire wear the color of hope when the grass has yielded it up before the cold is a further twist, compounded by the revelation that the fertility of that desire is based on its rooting not in rich soil but in *"dura petra,"* that strange stone as sentient as a woman. The second stanza, being the mirror image of the first, suggests no new images, presenting only the complements of those already established. The only real problem of translation is the phrase "*nova donna*," in which it is hard to know whether the adjective means "new" in the sense of "just discovered" or "unique" or whether it rather signifies "curious" or even just "young." This ambiguity is not resolved until the final stanza, where "*giovane donna*" establishes the last possibility beyond question. It would have been nice to find a similarly ambiguous word in English, but I discovered none. "Little" has, however, parallel possibilities of its own, and it is for that reason that I have chosen it over "youthful."

The third stanza stands by itself. For the first four lines, it is the least "stony" in technique of any of the verses; the lady with the leafy garland is a stock figure of Dante's imagination (Fioretta, too, is crowned in this way); and the expected references to the gold of her hair and to love's finding a resting place in her eyes are not redeemed from banality by Dante's stunt of substituting "curling gold" for "gold curls"—or by his periphrasis which speaks indirectly of love's traditional seat as the shade of the garland. To emphasize the conventional sweetness of this opening, I have tried to out-Rossetti Rossetti, building up for the shock of the concluding turn with a diction quite mannered and verging on the cliché.

Dante does not repeat the word "love" in launching his reversal, which turns the conventional personification of *Amor* into the warden of the prison of the hills. A simple relative pronoun suffices him; but I did not dare risk confusion. I am aware that "*calcina petra*" in the final line may be subject and object rather than a compound noun, in which case the translation ought to read "More stubbornly than mortar stone on stone"—but this image would rather disconcertingly make the lady "mortar," the poet "stone"; and besides I was reluctant to give up the satisfying ring of "calcareous stone."

In the fourth stanza, the ratio between conventional opening and ironical counterstatement is reversed. The first two lines draw upon stock again, with quite conventional references to the *vertù* of gems and the medical properties of herbs. The redeeming twist here arises from the suggestion, implicit in the fact that a single word means both "jewel" and "rock," that the magic of the lady, her essential power, is inseparable from the very stoniness which baffles her lover. These lines are a real trap for the translator; both "stone" and "grass" seem to me to demand qualifying adjectives to make them mean unequivocally "gem" and "herb"; while the word *vertù* almost defies a rendering succinct enough to stay inside the poem. Rossetti's "more bright than is a precious stone" is an abject surrender.

The four-line reversal links a new pair of paradoxes: that the lover in fear has fled from the "queen" he really desires to possess through a nightmare landscape of rise and hollow; and that he seeks to hide from the lady's light in that same nightmare world whose humps and frondage cast no shade. The final two lines, though intended merely to specify the horror of a queen whose very radiance is terror, reflect back on the whimpering poet, who has begun by complaining of the *"gran cerchio d'ombra"* but now begs for the small shadow of wall or tuffet, later of the lady's skirts. Having narrowly resisted the temptation to make *"cotal donna"* "so cruel a queen," I feel free to express my disdain for Rossetti's "so dangerous a lady." "This kind of queen" seems to me finally just right in its bare suggestiveness, an example of Dante's tactful reticence.

The fifth and sixth stanzas are linked like the first and second, but this time with a frank adversative conjunction, while elements of the third and fourth stanzas enter into the beginning of the passage, somewhat transmuted. The lady wreathed in green changes slightly into another recurrent shape of Dante's fantasy, the woman draped in green (one thinks of Beatrice in the *Purgatory*, *"sotto verde manto"*); and the nightmare of flight through a shadowless waste, which closes four, is converted into a dream of the beloved herself on fire with love and sealed off in a meadow surrounded by hills. Rossetti, misled by the verb *"chesta,"* which he apparently took to mean "wooed" instead of "wished for," translates into fact what should be presented as an unreal vision.

The elegant syntax of the conclusion of stanza five, more Latin really than Italian, with the adjectives deliberately displaced (*"chiuso,"* which modifies *"prato,"* huddles next to "*donna*"; while "*innamorata,*" which modifies the pronoun in the phrase "*l'ho chesta,*" is shifted close to "prato") has baffled me. The effect of the original is to blur lady and meadow into each other as in a dream, until the queen almost becomes the grassy field in the hollow of the hills. The confusion of reference I have been able to retain; but the simultaneous delicate sorting out depends on the agreement of the endings beyond the power of English to simulate.

The impress of Latin verse extends into the sixth stanza, with its vaguely Vergilian figure at the opening ("sooner will the rivers climb the hills"); but the stanza soon swings violently in a new direction. The point of the "but" (or as Rossetti would have it "yet") on which the counterstatement hinges is lost in his rendering. In my fantasy, Dante is saying, I have imagined the *Donna Pietra* in love, but in fact I know her to be incapable of being kindled. The figure in "*s'infiammi*" I have carried back into the previous stanza, making "*innamorata*" not merely "in love" but "fired with love."

The subtlest development in this section seems to me to come in the new meaning of *verde* exposed in the second line: the adjective green applied to the wreath and the garment, this time is attached to the lady herself; but here the word *verde* signifies neither springtime nor hope, only youth in all its cruelty. For a moment she is imagined not as a rock, hard and lifeless, but as *legno* (I have translated "sprig" rather than simply "wood" to emphasize the elusive note of youthfulness), which is *molle*, soft but also damp, and *verde*, living but also uninflammable. Stone or sprig, she is not a "*bella donna,*" "a fair and proper queen," but an unawakened child, still ignorant of that ultimate obligation of her sex, which Francesca remembers even in hell: "*Amor, ch'a nullo amato amar perdona.*"

And yet, the poet protests, the man whom she so ungraciously rejects is ready for any sacrifice, would consent even to wander about "*pascendo l'erba*" and for the rest of his days "*dormire in petra.*" There is, I suspect, a triple pun, wicked and complex, in that last phrase. If Dante did not desire it, the sestina did: the terms of the game he accepted demanded it, and I am delighted to preserve (or even introduce) it in my own version. The basic meaning of *"dormire in petra"* restated in the alternative figure *"gir pascendo l'erba"* is to live like a beast; yet one must, I think, resist the temptation to make this too explicit, as Rossetti does with "feed like beasts on grass." To sleep out in the open, on stony ground, is then the first significance of the phrase; but the poet does not say "ground." He says "stone" and "stone" is *"petra,"* which is also the lady's name. It is a tart and hopeless jest, reinforced by the ambiguity of *"per veder do'suoi panni fanno ombra"*—consent to sleep in Petra, indeed!

But there is another level, even beyond the sexual one, a final convolution. In the double sestina, the poet foresees the time when "this gentle Stone shall see me prone within a little stone," and the concluding phrase of that poem *"coricare in petra"* fades into the *"dormire in petra"* of this one, to introduce the note of death that intrudes near the close of all the *rime petrose*. To sleep, to possess and to die—the three significances mingle in a bitter music.

The *congedo* is both unorthodox and mysterious; a gnarled but haunting passage, obscure in syntax, but possessing an odd beauty and power of implication beyond anything else in the poem. In these three lines, the symbolic exponent of the whole sestina is raised. Each of the other attested *rime pietrose* ends with the conventional address to the song: *Canzone, io porto ne la mente donna; Canzon, vattene dritto a quella donna*, etc.; Arnaut's classic sestina itself has a comparable close: *Arnutz tramet sa chansson d'ongla e d'oncle*. But here Dante has rejected the merely formal close in order to deepen and complicate his series of paradoxes with a final reversal—graceful enough, though anything but the conventional curtsy to spell *finis*.

About my own interpretation, I have more to say below; for now, I want only to make the point that I have accepted the established text, the editor's punctuation, etc., of all recent Italian editions. I therefore read the last phrase *"com'uom petra sott' erba"* as if *"uom"* were the subject, *"petra"* the object and the verb *"fa sparire"* understood: literally then "as one [makes] a stone [disappear] beneath the grass." Just a couple of years ago it was argued that the whole passage could be reinterpreted in a new and fascinating (though finally unconvincing) way. In this new reading, "*uom petra*" would be understood as the compound "*uom-petra,*" and the whole passage would then read "as a stone man (or petrified man) [is buried] beneath grass." This would make a characteristically grim conclusion, blending death and despair as in the other *rime pietrose:* the man who loved a stone instead of a woman is himself turned to stone and buried beneath the sod. The hyphenated *uom-petra* strikes me, however, as a contrived monster; and the meaning as not worthy of the richness, the quiet melancholy that one feels in the *commiato.*

The end of stanza six has been a desperate declaration of the poet's fidelity to the unyielding beloved; no longer does he flee or moan, but offers himself in almost hopeless humility. The *congedo* moves naturally enough from this into a compliment to the "little queen," a piece of hyperbolic praise, carefully keyed so as to tone down toward gentle melancholy the bitterness that has come before. "Whenever the hills cast blackest shade," the final counterstatement begins, echoing not only the thematic noun, but this time also the verb of the preceding line: "*fanno ombra*" "*fanno . . . ombra.*" (This echo Rossetti sacrifices to pointless variation.) In the transition from stanza to stanza, however, the pleasant shade of the lady's skirts (with its suggestion of a *double-entendre*) has been transformed into the ultimate blackness "*più nera ombra*"; and the poet finds himself in the very Valley of Shadow.

The verb after *quandunque* ("whenever" not "howsoe'er") is the generalizing present, which we feel as a future until the repetition of the tense in the second verb, *la fa sparer,* shocks us into an awareness that "whenever" is now! Not only do the hills cast their blackest shadow now, but at this moment, too, the lady triumphs over their terror. "Yea, though I walk through the valley of shadow, my *donna* is with me." "No medicinal grass" can cure the wounds she inflicts; but she, who has more *vertù* than a jewel, can assuage suffering even as she bestows it, even perhaps raise again the one her cruelty has killed.

It is by virtue of her greenness that she has a power over the power of blackness, overwhelming it as hope triumphs over death and as the living grass covers insentient stone. The metaphor of "drown" is my own, not Dante's; but its evocation of a green tide and its connotations of disaster suit so well my reading of this passage that I have not been able to resist it. The ambiguity of *verde* here reaches a final rest; from the thesis of *"vestita in verde"* we have moved to the antithesis of *"molle e verde,"* from awakening of hope to its bafflement; the *bel verde* of the *commiato* announces the synthesis: the birth of a greater and more metaphysical hope and the defeat of the *ombra* which has lain over the poem since the first line, "my little queen annuls it—"

But we are not yet through: the confrontation of *ombra* and *verde* suggests the parallel matching of *petra* and *erba;* and the simile introduces a new ambiguity which seems to tilt the resolution once more toward despair "as a stone is drowned in grass." Grass, as we have already noticed, is not simply the emblem of springtime, it is also the symbol of mortality; and when it is *petra* (Petra!) which disappears *sott'erba*—the notion of a new life covering lifeless rock threatens to blur into the image of a dead girl committed to earth. The balance of the final phrase is so delicate, a hope which is despair and a resurrection which is an entombment, that no further synthesis is required, no answering statement possible. The poem has exhausted its paradoxes at the same moment that it has rung the final changes on its rhymes.

AL POCO GIORNO . . .

> Al poco giorno e al gran cerchio d'ombra
> son giunto, lasso, ed al bianchir de' colli,
> quando si perde lo color ne l'erba:
> e'l mio disio però non cangia il verde,
> sì è barbato ne la dura petra
> che parla e sente come fosse donna.
>
> Similemente questa nova donna
> si sta gelata come neve a l'ombra:
> ché non la move, se non come petra,
> il dolce tempo che rescalda i colli,
> e che li fa tornar di bianco in verde
> perché li copre di fioretti e d'erba.

Quand'ella ha in testa una ghirlanda d'erba,
trae de la mente nostra ogn'altra donna:
perché si mischia il crespo giallo e'l verde
sí bel, ch'Amor lí viene a stare a l'ombra,
che m'ha serrato intra piccioli colli
piú forte assai che la calcina petra.

La sua bellezza ha più vertú che petra,
e'l colpo suo no può sanar per erba:
ch'io son fuggito per piani e per colli,
per potere scampar da cotal donna;
e dal suo lume non mi può far ombra
poggio né muro né fronda verde.

Io l'ho veduta già vestita a verde,
sí fatta ch'ella evrebbe messo in petra
l'amor ch' io porto pur a la sua ombra:
ond'io l'ho chesta in un bel prato d'erba,
innamorata com'anco fu donna,
e chiuso intorno d'altissimi colli.

Ma ben ritorneranno i fiumi a' colli
prima che questo legno molle e verdè
s'infiammi, come suol far bella donna,
di me; che mi torrei dormire in petra
tutto il mio tempo e gir pascendo l'erba,
sol per veder do' suoi panni fanno ombra.

Quandunque i colli fanno piú nera ombra,
sotto un bel verde la giovane donna,
la fa sparer, com'uom petra sott'erba.

SESTINA: OF THE LADY PIETRA DEGLI SCROVIGNI
(translated by D. G. Rossetti)

To the dim light and the large circle of shade
I have clomb, and to the whitening of the hills,

There where we see no color in the grass.
Natheless my longing loses not its green,
It has so taken root in the hard stone
Which talks and hears as though it were a lady.

Utterly frozen in this youthful lady,
Even as the snow that lies within the shade;
For she is no more moved than is the stone
By the sweet season which makes warm the hills
And alters them afresh from white to green,
Covering their sides again with flowers and grass.

When on her hair she sets a crown of grass
The thought has no more room for other lady;
Because she weaves the yellow with the green
So well that Love sits down there in the shade,—
Love who has shut me in among low hills
Faster than between walls of granite-stone.

She is more bright than is a precious stone;
The wound she gives may not be healed with grass:
I therefore have fled o'er plains and hills
For refuge from so dangerous a lady;
But from her sunshine nothing can give shade,—
Not any hills, nor wall, nor summer-green.

A while ago, I saw her dressed in green,—
So fair, she might have wakened in a stone
This love which I do feel even for her shade;
And therefore, as one woos a graceful lady,
I wooed her in a field that was all grass
Girdled about with very lofty hills.

Yet shall the streams turn back and climb the hills
Before Love's flame in this damp wood and green
Burn, as it burns within a youthful lady,
For my sake, who would sleep away in stone
My life, or feed like beasts upon the grass,
Only to see her garments cast a shade.

How dark soe'er the hills throw out their shade,
Under her summer-green the beautiful lady
Covers it, like a stone covered in grass.

TO SMALL DAYLIGHT: THE STONY SESTINA
OF DANTE ALIGHIERI
(translated by L. A. Fiedler)

To small daylight and the great circle of shade,
I've come, alas, and to the blanching of the hills,
That season when the color leaves the grass
And only my desire keeps its green,
So rooted is it in the rigid stone
That speaks and harks as if it were a queen.

And just so constantly, my little queen
Lies frozen fast, a snowbank in the shade,
And is not stirred except as is the stone
By time's sweet turning that now warms the hills
And changes all their whiteness into green
With blossoms and a blanketing of grass.

When she is garlanded with plaited grass,
She lures our longing from each other queen;
So intertwined the curling gold and green,
Love loves to lounge there in its shade—
That Love which locks me here in little hills,
More stubborn even than calcareous stone.

Her beauty's magic mocks the precious stone;
Her blows are eased by no medicinal grass;
And I have fled through fens and over hills
To find my freedom from this kind of queen;
But from her light there is no sheltering shade,
Not wall or tuffet or the leafiest green.

Yet there was once I watched her dressed in green,
So winsome she might wake within a stone
That love which wracks me for her merest shade;
And then I dreamed her in a field of grass,
More fired with love than ever any queen,
And sealed there by an arc of alpine hills.

But sooner will the rivers climb the hills
Than for my sake this sprig, too moist and green,
Be kindled like a fair and proper queen,
For me, who would consent to sleep on stone
For all my days, and pasture me on grass,
So I might see where her skirts cast their shade.

Whatever time the hills cast blackest shade,
Beneath a lovely green, my little queen
Annuls it, as a stone is drowned in grass.

Negro and Jew

THIS IS A MOMENT for questions, new questions or old ones newly posed, a moment when answers seem impertinent—which is, perhaps, why fiction (a method of posing questions without troublesome question marks) seems the most promising method of attacking the problem of Negro-Jewish hostility. I am thinking of such books as Norman Mailer's *An American Dream*, Nat Hentoff's *Call the Keeper*, and Jay Neugeboren's *Big Man*, as well as (hopefully) my own *The Last Jew in America*. In a strange way it has now become incumbent on the Jewish writer to re-imagine the Negro in terms which will escape the old WASP clichés, sentimental and vicious, and the recent even more soupy and hysterical Spade ones. Eventually, of course, the Negro writer himself will have to invent the New Negro as Harriet Beecher Stowe, Mark Twain, D. W. Griffith and Faulkner have invented the Old Negro. But Jews will apparently have to deal with him in the moment of transition, since the current crop of Negro novelists is fumbling the job: Ellison remaining stubbornly old-fashioned on this score, Baldwin caught between the exigencies of his poetic talent and his political commitment, LeRoi Jones the victim of his own anguish and *mishigas*. But the Jewish writer's assumption of this task can prove in the end only one more possible source of misunderstanding and tension between the two groups.

Some relevant questions then—and all which follows is a series of questions even when passion or strategy leads me to omit the question marks. Would not the proper title for an article on this subject be "Thou shalt not honor the poor man in his cause"—to remind the present-day enlightened Jew of certain therapeutic anti-liberal elements in his own tradition: a priestly admonition that might have protected him in the thirties from illusions about the working class and its parties (but did not); and might now serve as an antidote against delusive hopes about Negroes and their organizations (but probably will not). Or maybe it would be better—in light of my own continuing concerns—to use the title *An End to (Another) Innocence;* since the liberal tradition in America—to which the Jewish intellectual has attached himself, which, indeed, he has all but pre-empted—insists on stumbling from one innocence to another with appropriate bouts of self-recrimination between. It is not mere "white backlash" (the very term is a buttress of naïveté on the defensive) but simple wisdom (what used to be called "good sense") to notice that, like all such movements, the Civil Rights Movement is becoming, had to become with the beginnings of success, self-seeking, self-deceiving, self-defeating—devoted not to a search for justice but to the pursuit of power. But the liberals (the *Jewish* liberals, as Negro critics like to say) will be the last to admit this; since the liberal is a man who can drown in the same river twice—which is, let me be clear, his glory as well as his folly, the function of an incredible generosity of spirit which fades imperceptibly into willful stupidity: a combination, mythologically speaking, of *yiddishe hertz* and *goyishe kop.*

Why not continue to speak mythologically then; for mythology seems the basic way into the problem of Jewish-Negro hostility—which turns out not to exist sociologically at all, i.e., not *consciously* (using the methods of the behavioral sciences, investigators keep discovering to their own satisfaction and the confusion of the rest of us, that Negroes really love, respect, and honor Jews) but only preconsciously, on the level of legend and nightmare.

What, in fact, are the mythologies at work, first in the minds of Negroes concerning Jews and then in the minds of Jews concerning Negroes? "Sub-minds" would be a more precise way of naming the locus of myths: and is it not well to remind ourselves in this regard of the differing weights of mind and submind, conscious and preconscious factors in the case of Negro and Jew? It is no secret, surely, that in America the Jewish Community has largely committed itself to a life of logos, a cultivation of the ego and the whole Gutenburg bit whose demise Marshall McLuhan has been quite un-Jewishly predicting; while the Negro community in large part continues to live (even to make its living) in the world of subliteracy, unrationalized impulse, and free fantasy.

Do not Negroes, in any event, tend to begin with the WASP racist mythology (endorsing it in self-hatred, or inverting it in impotent rebellion) which divides the world into two ethnic-mythic segments only: White and Colored; and which further assumes that the distinction is hierarchal, corresponding roughly to higher and lower. The deep Jewish ethnic-mythic division, on the other hand, is threefold, as the legend of the three sons of Noah reminds us. As descendants of Shem, we were once taught, we have *two* hostile and inferior brothers, Ham and Japheth. The Negro, committed to his simpler mythology, tends to regard the Jew either as a Colored Man who is deviously passing as White; or a goddamned White Man pretending, for reasons hard to fathom, to the fate of the excluded Colored Man. The Jew, meanwhile, is struggling with the vestigial sense of being a third thing, neither-either, however one says it; and he therefore thinks of himself (his kind of awareness driving him compulsively from feeling to thinking) as being free to "pass" in either direction, in a world which oddly insists that he identify himself with one group of strangers or another, Hamitic or Japhetic. And he knows that historically segments of his people have done both (some first pretending to be White, then becoming prisoners of their pretense; some following the opposite strategy): that in Israel, for instance, it is possible to observe these two groups, "Black Jews" and "White Jews," in open conflict. He is, therefore, baffled as well as resentful when he discovers himself denominated "White" without choice and made the victim in a Black-White race riot; just as he was once baffled as well as resentful to discover himself linked without choice to Negroes in being excluded from White clubs and hotels and restaurants. And he is doubly baffled and resentful when the Negro switches from hating him as White to despising him in a mode imitated from those earlier-arrived North European Americans who thought themselves so much Whiter than he.

How can the Jew help seeing Negro anti-Semitism as a kind of culture-climbing, an illegitimate attempt to emulate WASP style —and, inevitably, a belated and misguided attempt; since the

WASPs are abandoning the racist attitudes to which the Negro aspires at the very moment he is assimilating them. Even Hitler, certain more ignorant or frantic Negroes tend to think of as just another White Man—rather more efficient than most, though not quite efficient enough in eliminating his Jew-enemies—and thus they have not felt shamed out of their anti-Semitism by the rise and fall of Nazism, as their WASP opposite numbers (who cannot help feeling Hitler in some sense one of them) have tended to be. It is especially unassimilated, unassimilable Jews, Jews who do not even seem to want to look like all other Americans, who stir the fury of Negro hoods—say, Hasidim with their beards, *peyes* and gabardines.

At the deepest mythological level, is it not the Jewish religion, finally, as well as the Jewish ethnic inheritance which bugs the Negroes? Certainly this would be understandable enough; for insofar as they are Christians, fundamentalist, evangelical Protestants, do they not inherit the simple-minded anti-Jewish mythology of the Gospels (which Catholics long had the good grace to keep out of the hands of subliterates) with its simple-minded melodrama of "our" Christ killed by "the Jews"? And do not Negroes in particular possess the additional sentimental myth of Simon the Cyrenean —kindly Negro by the wayside—who helped Jesus bear his cross as the Jews hooted and howled for his blood? And insofar as they are becoming Muslim (Why could not the first attempt of the ill-fated founder of that movement to establish a Black Judaism have succeeded?), are they not obsessed by the legendary notion of the "Evil Jacob," Israel the Usurper—as well as the myth of Isaac before him doing poor Ishmael out of his heritage? And as Muslims, do not they (along with the members of other non-Mohammedan Afro organizations) identify themselves with an Arab-African anti-Jewish political mythology, which leads them to consider Jews, in America as well as Israel, even wickeder than the rest of the depraved "hoojis"? Are not both Christianity and Islam, finally, being offshoots of a more primitive Judaism, subject to spasms of a kind of collective sibling rivalry, which passes over on occasion into fratricidal strife? And is not the *shul*-goer or temple-attending Jew caught once more in the old bind between the Christian Negro for whom he is not (spiritually) White enough—not sufficiently washed in the Blood of the Lamb—and the Muslim Negro for whom he is not (mythologically) Black enough—not far enough removed from the White Man's God?

It is not, however, only the worshipers of Christ or the followers of Mohammed among the Negroes who are possessed by anti-Jewish mythologies. The hippiest and most advanced Negroes, secular as they may seem to themselves, are committed to a myth system—the Beat Religion, let's call it for the purposes of quick identification, most recent form of an old Romantic anti-Church. And does that Church not necessarily, in view of its archetypal antecedents, see the Negro as the embodiment of (admired) impulse and irrationality, the Jew as the incarnation of (despised) sublimation and rationality? About these matters I have written at some length before; and have thought about them long enough not to be surprised at recent efforts at expelling Allen Ginsberg from the True Church (a kind of apostle to the Beat Gentiles, or maybe better, a Trotsky of the Hip revolution—his position is more than a little anomalous). No one, at any rate, need pretend astonishment when he hears the cry from a Negro at the back of a room in which Robert Creeley is reading aloud, "This is a poem for Allen Ginsberg" —"Hey, man, when you going to stop talking about those Jew poets?" Is it not a rule of the mythological literary life in America that when the Negro is up, the Jew is down? What was true in the twenties is true once again as the Jewish thirties, forties, and early fifties recede from us. Who can serve two masters, after all? One must choose between Saul Bellow and LeRoi Jones, Jerusalem (well, the Northwest side of Chicago at any rate) and Harlem (well, let's make it Newark's Third Ward). Mythological as well as historical factors, that is to say, have determined the fact that certain Hippies at the present moment find themselves protesting a Jewish Literary Establishment ("Norman Podhoretz's floating ghetto," one in-group joke calls it) in the name of a movement whose reigning figures are archetypal *goyim* like Charles Olson, Norman O. Brown and Marshall McLuhan. Jewish writers, from Mailer to Nat Hentoff, may try to escape the mythological hang-up by redefining themselves as imaginary or "White Negroes" (the very term was, of course, invented by a Jew)—just as their more political brethren have tried to assimilate to a world which mythologically rejects them by linking arms with Negroes in protests and demonstrations. But though young Jews have an affinity not only for protest but for folksongs, jazz, and marijuana (how much more readily they assimilate to pot than to the Paleface medicine of whiskey), the whole syndrome, they have trouble making it across the legendary line—remain always in danger of being told that they cannot *really* commit themselves to the Movement, cannot *really* make authentic jazz, cannot *really* sing the blues. The point is that other mythological demands are being made on them—to play the false liberal, or "Mr. Goldberg" or, ultimately, the super-ego in one or another currently unfashionable form.

So much—for the moment—about the Negro or Negroizing mythologies of the Jew; though I suppose a word at least demands to be said about the "Black Socialism" (the term antedates its adoption by actual Blacks), that presumably revolutionary anti-Semitism which poor Negroes have inherited from White workers, *lumpen* proletarians, peasants and "red-necks." This view (to which Leo Frank was once a victim) sees the Jew as rich, powerful, devious, behind the scenes if not at the centers of power—a Boss, in short. But this view tends to become less and less influential as the leading elements of the Negro Movement become prosperous or mobile and educated enough to afford overt anti-Semitism. It is real enough, to be sure, but is it not finally a vestige, as old-fashioned, which is to say, as peripheral in the current situation as the remnants among the aging Jewish bourgeoisie of the simple-minded anti-Negroism appropriate to our social-climbing days: the contempt of the still insecure Jewish housewife for the *schwarze* who cleaned for her, or the Jewish marginal small businessman for his Negro janitor, or the underpaid Jewish salesman for his Negro instalment customer? Do we not enjoy rehashing such elementary prejudices, long after we have made it in a way which renders them irrelevant, precisely because they are no longer urgent; and leaving them, we would have to confront relationships much more difficult to analyze or confess?

Almost as familiar, and therefore quite as ritually satisfying to discuss yet one more time, are certain good old Freudian notions— long since lapsed into semi-popular mythology—about the Negro: the projection onto the Negro male, for instance, of the sadist nightmares about his own women dreamed by the white male, etc.,

etc. These have always been rather confused as far as Jews in America are concerned, by the fact that Jews themselves have played similar mythological-sexual roles in WASP erotic fantasies; and in Norman Mailer's last novel one can see enacted in the form of comic melodrama a kind of contest between his (half) Jewish hero and a particularly potent Spade to see which one will possess the blond all-American *shikse*—which, mythologically speaking, amounts, I suppose, to an argument about which one of us she is dreaming these days. More interesting, and more dangerous to broach, are questions about the role of homosexual rather than heterosexual fantasies in the earlier stages of the Civil Rights Movement. I am not referring to the fact that there has been a strange confluence of the Homosexual Rebellion (the emergence of queer America from underground to the daylight world) and the Negro Movement; but rather to the influence on that Movement of the old antifemale dream of a pure love between males, colored and white, so crucial to our classic literature in the United States. I myself can report having heard several times in various forms from young civil rights workers the cry, so authentically American it was hard at first to believe: "Oh, Christ, things were great when just us buddies Black and White were fighting it out together; but these White chicks are just down here to get laid."

It seems to me, however, that none of these sexual concerns, deep as they may go, are as important at the moment as certain political mythologies. What chiefly exacerbates relations between Negroes and Jews, as far as Jews are concerned, is the persistence among them of the mythology of Liberal Humanism. This troublesome myth system, derived in part from Old Testament sources, most highly developed in modern Anglo-Saxondom, and picked up again in that world by emancipated Jewish intellectuals, includes the following articles of faith: that all men desire freedom and full human status and deny that freedom and status to others only when it has been refused to them; that equality of opportunity leads to maximum self-fulfillment and social well-being; that the oppressed and the injured have been so ennobled by their oppression and injury that they are morally superior to their masters; that all men desire literacy and suffrage—and can exercise those privileges equally well when granted them; that all the foregoing are not the parochial belief of a tiny minority of mankind over a minute span of time, but what all men have always believed, or would have believed given the opportunity. Intertwined with this credo—though not as often avowed as that credo itself—is the Whig Myth of History which sees freedom slowly broadening down from precedent to precedent, country to country and ethnic group to ethnic group. The Jews have always (since their exit from the ghetto and entry into the West, at least) considered themselves more qualified than anyone, less compromised than anyone because of their historical situation certainly, to preach this doctrine. They have felt especially righteous in respect to the application of these principles to the Negroes in the United States, since they were not as a group involved in the enslavement of the Negro, and they know themselves to have long been involved in Civil Rights Movements in numbers all out of proportion to the percentage of the total population which they represent. No Negro ever died for a Jewish cause, Jews tell themselves; but some of our boys have died for Negro rights.

How utterly unprepared they have been, therefore, to find a growing number of Negroes rejecting not only their credo but them in particular as its messengers—spurning in short the whole body of "Jewish Liberalism." "Hear our message and be saved," they cry only a little condescendingly and are dismayed to hear in return: "All we want from you white mothers (or alternatively, Jew mothers) is to get off our backs and out of our road!" Yet worse, much worse, is the fact that the Negroes, whatever their avowed credo, challenge by their very existence a basic article of the Liberal Faith: equality of opportunity will not grant very many of them, brutalized by long brainwashing and bred by a kind of unnatural selection, a decent life or the possibility of prosperity. What they demand, not so much by what they say as by how they are, how they test, how they perform, is *special privilege* rather than equality if they are to make it at all in the very world in which the Jews have so preeminently flourished. And what a shame and embarrassment that some men (i.e., most Jews) have done so well under conditions in which certain fellow-humans seem bound to do ill. What can survive of liberal mythology in the face of this? Is "liberalism,"

then, only a camouflage for a special sort of privilege, a code by
which the peoples who alone have long lived with the alphabet can
triumph over all others?

Marxism, especially in its more brutal Bolshevik versions, has
long offered an alternative mythology to that of liberalism; but so
many intellectual Jews now sufficiently advanced into middle age to
have become its spokesmen have been there before. Some, indeed,
are alive and articulate at the moment who have lived through the
loss of three religions: first Orthodoxy itself, then Stalinism or
Trotskyism, finally enlightened liberalism; and for them, what lies
ahead but despair? But for the young, and the politically obtuse
who remember nothing and have learned nothing, it seems possible,
even imperative—in order to justify or explain black violence,
black know-nothingism, black racism—to fall back once more on
the mythology of an already once-discredited anti-liberal Bolshevik
"Humanism." Certainly, there is superficial reassurance at least in
the simple-minded theory that the whole vexed problem is "economic"—and that the last vestiges of Black Racism will disappear
(like anti-Semitism in the Soviet Union? a nagging voice demands)
only after the major means of production have been appropriated
by the People's State. But how can a thinking man live by the mythology of a God who died in the declining thirties? And how especially can a Jew come to terms with the fate of his own people by
applying a Marxist mythology which denies the Jewishness of the
Jews—as is, after all, appropriate to a secular religion invented in
large part by recusant Jews. To be sure, any and all "Jewish problems" immediately disappear when the real reference of the adjective is denied; but this is a semantic solution which cannot conceal
the fact that actual Jews are being harried and threatened. And if
proof is needed that this semantic strategy is not only a lie but an
offense, one need only see Peter Weiss' current play, *The Investigation,* that obscene parody of what happened at Auschwitz, from
which "the Jews" have been expunged, even as a name to be spoken aloud.

No, more attractive to me than yesterday's defunct mythology
—more valid for all the self-pity easily attached to it—is the more
ancient mythology which insists that the ultimate villains of history
define themselves finally and essentially by their attitude toward the

Jews; and that all enemies of the Jews (with whatever pious slogans and whatever history of suffering they begin) are enemies to the good of mankind, whether they be black, brown, yellow, or white —Haman or Hitler or the CORE leader rising to scream that Hitler should have done a better job of getting rid of us. "Not in one generation alone, but in every generation they have risen up to destroy us," the ritual phrase in the Passover Haggadah runs; and it continues on to reassure us that God has always delivered us out of the hands of our enemies. But what about the hands of our presumed, even our real, allies? And what can we expect anyhow in these dark days when God is dead and only the devil survives: the devil still identified by Ku Kluxers with Negroes, and by some Negroes with the Jews? What does the devil's devil do in a world without God, or even gods?

Despair? Make jokes? Pray to the void? Confess that nothing can be done? That by a joke of history the amends that *must* be made to the Negroes (for indignities for which the Jews bear little or no guilt) must, alas, necessarily do harm to the Jews? That it is our turn again, or really on this continent at long last? Sometimes I feel this way and am tempted toward desolation; until, looking out into the streets, the schoolyards, the coffeehouses, I find my heart leaping up at the sight of young couples linked arm in arm. And I think our daughters will save us, love (not big theoretical, but small sexual love) will save us. I remember a year or two ago riding a plane to Jerusalem and being told by the man seated beside me, who worked for a Jewish adoption agency, that the number of illegitimate Negro babies being produced by Jewish girls was mounting spectacularly. And were there also, I asked, legitimate ones, *even* legitimate ones? But I did not listen for the answer, knowing it was yes, and not quite sure why I needed confirmation. What sunders us may not be first of all but is last of all a sexual taboo; and that taboo is every day being broken, with or without benefit of clergy, Christian or Jewish; and its breaking is the beginning (though *only* the beginning) of the end.

So naturally a new mythology is being invented, appropriate to that new solution; though like all new myths this one, too, contains within it one very old, indeed, the myth of the Jewish Daughter, Hadassah (renamed Esther, which is to say, Ashtoreth) dancing

naked for our salvation before the Gentile King. I sat the other day
eavesdropping on the conversation of a group of very young white
girls—most of them pretty, blonde daughters of Jews with black
boyfriends, discussing what they would do when the first race riots
broke out in Buffalo. And one of them suggested that they march
between the two opposed packs, Black and White, carrying signs
which read: MAKE LOVE NOT WAR. It was elegant and vain as
the loveliest dream; and I am old and cynical enough, after all, to
know it; as I know how much there is dark and desperate even in
their young love, and as I realize how much in marriage itself (for
some few of them *will* marry their Negro boyfriends, I am sure) is
a problem rather than a solution. To make matters worse, I had
just been reading in the *East Village Other* a statement by a Negro
poet, who not so long before had been able to write that he had
"married a Jewish Lady to escape Bohemia," that Jewish girls only
married Negroes in order to emasculate them. And I was aware
that it was his paranoid and sinister mythology which operated in
the tensions that made headlines day after day; but I knew that the
counter-mythology of those young girls had power to move men,
too. I, at least, prefer to live in its hope rather than the Negro
poet's despair, convinced of its superiority to all the weary mythologies of mere politics. The disillusionment it will inevitably breed at
least still lies ahead, and (if I am lucky) I may not live so long.
—1966

Saul Bellow

With the publication of *Seize the Day,* Saul Bellow has become not merely a writer with whom it is possible to come to terms, but one with whom it is *necessary* to come to terms—perhaps of all our novelists the one we need most to understand if we are to understand what the novel is doing at the present moment. Bellow has endured the almost ritual indignities of the beginning fictionist: his first novel a little over-admired and read by scarcely anyone; his second novel once more critically acclaimed, though without quite the thrill of discovery, and still almost ignored by the larger public; his third novel, thick, popular, reprinted in the paperbacks and somewhat resented by the first discoverers, who hate seeing what was exclusively theirs pass into the public domain; and now a fourth book: a collection of stories, most of which have appeared earlier, a play, and a new novella.

Suddenly, the novelist whom we have not ceased calling a "young writer" (it is a habit hard to break and the final indignity) is established and forty, a part of our lives and something for the really young to define themselves against. But it has become clear that he will continue to write, that he is not merely the author of a novel or two, but a *novelist;* and this in itself is a triumph, a rarity in recent American literary history and especially among the writers with whom we associate Bellow. We think of the whole line of Jewish-American novelists, so like him in origin and aspiration, of Daniel Fuchs and Henry Roth and Nathanael West, those poets and annalists of the thirties who did not survive their age, succumbing to death or Hollywood or a sheer exhaustion of spirit and subject. Or we think of Bellow's own contemporaries, the *Partisan Review* group, urban Jews growing up under the threat of failure and terror, the Depression and Spain and the hopelessly foreseen coming of war. We remember, perhaps, Isaac Rosenfeld or H. J. Kaplan or Oscar Tarcov or Delmore Schwartz or even Lionel Trilling, who had also to be twice born, committed first to Stalinism and then to disenchantment, but who were capable of using imaginatively only the disenchantment. And remembering these, we recall beginnings not quite fulfilled, achievements which somehow betrayed initial promises. Certain short stories remain in our minds (flanked by all those essays, those explanations and rejoinders and demonstrations of wit): Kaplan's "The Mohammedans," Rosenfeld's "The Pyramids," Schwartz's "In Dreams Begin Responsibilities," Trilling's "The Other Margaret"; but where except in *The Dangling Man* and *The Victim* and *Augie March* do the themes and motifs of the group find full novelistic expression?

We must begin to see Bellow, then, as the inheritor of a long tradition of false starts and abject retreats and gray inconclusions. There is a sense in which he fulfills the often frustrated attempt to possess the American imagination and to enter the American cultural scene of a line of Jewish fictionists which goes back beyond the postwar generation through Ben Hecht and Ludwig Lewisohn to Abe Cahan. A hundred, a thousand one-shot novelists, ephemeral successes and baffled eccentrics stand behind him, defining a subject: the need of the Jew in America to make clear his relationship to that country in terms of belonging or protest—and a language: a speech enriched by the dialectic and joyful intellectual play of Jewish conversation.

Bellow's own story is, then, like the archetypal Jewish dream a success story since, like the standard characters in the tales of my grandfather (Socialist though he was!), the novelist, too, has "worked himself up in America." Bellow's success must not be understood, however, as exclusively his own; for he emerges at the moment when the Jews for the first time move into the center of American culture, and he must be seen in the larger context. The background is familiar enough: the gradual breaking up of the Anglo-Saxon domination of our imagination; the relentless urbanization which makes rural myths and images no longer central to our

experience; the exhaustion as vital themes of the Midwest and of
the movement from the provinces to New York or Chicago or
Paris; the turning again from West to East, from our own heartland
back to Europe; and the discovery in the Jews of a people essentially urban, essentially Europe-oriented, a ready-made image for
what the American longs to or fears he is being forced to become.

On all levels in the years since World War II, the Jewish-American writer feels imposed on him the role of being The American,
of registering his experience for his compatriots and for the world
as The American Experience. Not only his flirtation with Communism and his disengagement, but his very sense of exclusion, his most
intimate awareness of loneliness and flight are demanded of him as
public symbols. The Southerner and the Jew, the homosexual out of
the miasma of Mississippi and the ex-radical out of the iron landscape of Chicago and New York—these seem the exclusive alternatives, contrasting yet somehow twinned symbols of America at
mid-century. *Partisan Review* becomes for Europe and *Life* magazine the mouthpiece of intellectual America, not despite but because of its tiny readership and its specially determined contributors; and in Saul Bellow a writer emerges capable of transforming
its obsessions into myths.

He must not, however, be seen only in this context. His appearance as the first Jewish-American novelist to stand at the center of
American literature is flanked by a host of matching successes on
other levels of culture and subculture. What Saul Bellow is for
highbrow literature, Salinger is for upper middlebrow, Irwin Shaw
for middle middlebrow and Herman Wouk for lower middlebrow.
Even on the lowbrow levels, where there has been no such truce
with anti-Semitism as prosperity has brought to the middle classes,
two young Jews in contriving Superman have invented for the
comic books a new version of the Hero, the first purely urban incarnation of the most ancient of mythic figures. The acceptance of
Bellow as the leading novelist of his generation must be paired off
with the appearance of Marjorie Morningstar on the front cover of
Time. On all levels, the Jew is in the process of being mythicized
into the representative American.

There is a temptation in all this to a kind of assimilation with
the most insipid values of bourgeois life in the United States. It is to

Bellow's credit that he has at once accepted the full challenge implicit in the identification of Jew with American, and yet has not succumbed to the temptation; that he has been willing to accept the burden of success without which he might have been cut off from the central subject of his time; and that he has accomplished this without essential compromise. In *Augie March,* which is the heart of his work (though technically not as successful as *The Victim* or *Seize the Day),* he has risked the final absurdity: the footloose Jewish boy, harried by urban Machiavellians, the picaresque *schlimazl* out of Fuchs or Nathanael West, becomes Huck Finn; or, if you will, Huck is transformed into the foot-loose Jewish boy. It is hard to know which way of saying it gives a fuller sense of the absurdity and importance of the transaction. The point is, I think, that the identification saves both halves of the combination from sentimental falsification: Huck Finn, who has threatened for a long time to dissolve into the snub-nosed little rascal, barefoot and overalled, and the Jewish *schlimazl,* who becomes only too easily the liberals' insufferable victim, say, Noah Ackerman in Irwin Shaw's *The Young Lions.*

The themes of Saul Bellow are not, after all, very different from those of the middlebrow Jewish novelists in step with whom he has "worked himself up"; but in treatment they become transformed. Like Wouk or Shaw, he, too, has written a War Novel: a book about the uncertainty of intellectual and Jew face to face with a commitment to regimentation and violence. But unlike Wouk and Shaw, Bellow has not merely taken the World War I novel of protest and adulterated it with popular front pieties. His intellectual is not shown up like Wouk's Keefer; his Jew does not prove himself as brave and brutal as his anti-Semitic buddies like Shaw's Ackerman or Wouk's Greenspan, whose presumable triumphs are in fact abject surrenders. The longing to relinquish the stereotyped protest of the twenties, no longer quite believed in, is present in Bellow's *Dangling Man,* but present as a *subject:* a temptation to be confronted, not a value to be celebrated.

Dangling Man is not an entirely successful book; it is a little mannered, a little incoherent, obviously a first novel. But it is fresh beyond all expectation, unlike any American war book before or since; for Bellow has realized that for his generation the war itself is an anticlimax (too foreknown from a score of older novels to be really lived), that their real experience is the waiting, the dangling, the indecision before the draft. His book therefore ends, as it should, with its protagonist about to leave for camp and writing in his journal: "Hurray for regular hours! And for the supervision of the spirit! Long live regimentation!" In the purest of ironies, the slogans of accommodation are neither accepted nor rejected, but suspended.

Similarly, in *The Victim* Bellow takes up what is, perhaps, the theme *par excellence* of the liberaloid novel of the forties: anti-Semitism. In proletarian novels, though many were written by Jews, this was a subject only peripherally treated; for the Jew in the Communist movement, Judaism was the enemy, Zionism and the Jewish religion the proper butt of satire and dissent. But Hitler had made a difference, releasing a flood of pious protests against discrimination; from Arthur Miller's *Focus* to John Hersey's *The Wall*, via *Gentleman's Agreement. The Professor's Umbrella*, etc., Jew and Gentile alike took up the subject over and over. In a time when the Worker had been replaced by the Little Man as a focus for undiscriminating sympathy, the Little Jew took his place beside the Little Negro, the Little Chinese, the Little Paraplegic as a favorite victim. Even what passed for War Novels were often merely anti-anti-Semitic fictions in disguise, the war itself being treated only as an occasion for testing a Noble Young Jew under the pressure of ignorant hostility.

In the typical middlebrow novel, it was seldom a real Jew who was exposed to persecution; rather some innocent gentile who by putting on glasses mysteriously came to look Jewish or some high-minded reporter only pretending to be a Jew. In part what is involved is the commercial necessity for finding a gimmick to redeem an otherwise overworked subject; but in part what is at stake is surely a confusion in the liberal, middlebrow mind about what a Jew is anyhow: a sneaking suspicion that Jew-baiting is real but Jews are imaginary, just as, to the same mind, witch-hunting is real but witches only fictions.

In Bellow's book about anti-Semitism, *The Victim*, once more the confusion becomes the subject. It is Asa Leventhal, not the author, who is uncertain of what it means to be a Jew because he does not know yet what it is to be a man; and neither he nor his author will be content with the simple equation: the victim equals the Jew, the Jew the victim. In *The Victim,* Jew and anti-Semite are each other's prey as they are each other's beloved. At the moment when the Jew in general, when the author himself as well as his protagonist, have moved into situations of security, however tenuous, inflicting injury in their scramble to win that security, Bellow alone among our novelists has had the imagination and the sheer nerve to portray the Jew, the Little Jew, as victimizer as well as victim. Allbee may be mad, a pathological anti-Semite and a bum, but his charge that Leventhal's success was achieved somehow at his expense is not utter nonsense. It is the necessary antidote to the selfpity of the Jew, one part of a total ambiguous picture. In the slow, gray, low-keyed exposition of *The Victim,* Leventhal's violence and his patience, his desire to exculpate himself and his sense of guilt, his haunting by the anti-Semite he haunts, become for us truths, part of our awareness of our place as Jews in the American scene.

As *The Victim* is Bellow's most specifically Jewish book, *Augie March* (in this, as in all other respects, a reaction from the former) is his most generally American. Its milieu is Jewish-American, its speech patterns somehow molded by Yiddish, but its theme is the native theme of *Huckleberry Finn:* The rejection of power and commitment and success, the pursuit of a primal innocence. It is a strangely non-Jewish book in being concerned not with a man's rise but with his evasion of rising; and yet even in that respect it reminds us of *David Levinsky,* of the criticism of David implicit in the text and entrusted to the Socialist characters. It is as if David had been granted a son, a grandson, to try again—to seek a more genuine Americanism of noncommitment. Certainly, Bellow's character is granted a symbolic series of sexual successes to balance off the sexual failures of Cahan's protagonist. But the Socialism of Cahan does not move his descendant; it has become in the meanwhile Soviet Communism, an alternative image of material success, and has failed; so that there is left to Augie only the denial of the values of capitalism without a corresponding allegiance, a desire to flee success from scene to scene, from girl to girl, from father to father—in favor of what? The most bitter of Happy Endings as well as the most negative, the truly American Happy Ending: no reunion with the family, no ultimately happy marriage, no return to the native place—only a limitless disponibility guarded like a treasure. It is, of course, the ending of *Huckleberry Finn,* an ending which must be played out as comedy to be tolerable at all; but unlike Twain, Bellow, though he has found the proper tone for his episodes, cannot recapture it for his close. *Augie,* which begins with such rightness, such conviction, does not know how to end; shriller and shriller, wilder and wilder, it finally whirls apart in a frenzy of fake euphoria and exclamatory prose.

Seize the Day is a pendant and resolution to *Augie March.* Also a study of success and failure, this time it treats them in contemporary terms rather than classic ones, reworking directly a standard middlebrow theme. Call it *The Death of a Salesman* and think of Arthur Miller. It is the price of failure in a world dedicated to success that Bellow is dealing with now; or more precisely, the self-consciousness of failure in a world where it is not only shameful but rare; or most exactly of all, the bitterness of success and failure become pawns in the deadly game between father and son. Bellow is not very successful when he attempts to deal with the sentimental and erotic relations that are the staples of the great European novels; his women tend to be nympholeptic projections, fantasies based on girls one never had; and his husbands and wives seem convincing only at the moment of parting. But he comes into his own when he turns to the emotional transactions of males inside the family: brother and brother, son and father—or father-hating son and Machiavellian surrogate father. It is the muted rage of such relationships that is the emotional stuff of his best work; and in *Seize the Day,* it is the dialogues of Tommy and his old man, Tommy and the sharper Tamkin, that move us, prepare us for Tommy's bleakest encounter: with himself and the prescience of his own death.

But how, we are left asking, has Bellow made tragedy of a theme that remains in the hands of Arthur Miller sentimentality and "good theater"? It is just this magical transformation of the most travestied of middlebrow themes which is Bellow's greatest triumph. That transformation is in part the work of style, a function of language. Bellow is in no sense an experimental writer; the scraps of *avant-garde* technique which survive in *The Dangling Man* are purged away in *The Victim;* yet he has managed to resist the impulse to lifeless lucidity which elsewhere has taken over in a literature reacting to the linguistic experiments of the twenties. There is always the sense of a living voice in his prose, for his books are all dramatic; and though this sometimes means a deliberate muting of rhetoric for the sake of characterization, it just as often provides occasions for a release of full virtuosity. Muted or released, his language is never dull or merely expedient, but always moves under tension, toward or away from a kind of rich, crazy poetry, a juxtaposition of high and low style, elegance and slang, unlike anything else in English except *Moby Dick,* though at the same time not unrelated in range and variety to spoken Yiddish.

Since Bellow's style is based on a certain conversational ideal at once intellectual and informal, dialogue is for him necessarily a distillation of his strongest effects. Sometimes one feels his characters' speeches as the main events of the books in which they occur; certainly they have the impact of words exchanged among Jews, that is to say, the impact of actions, not merely overheard but *felt,* like kisses or blows. Implicit in the direction of his style is a desire to encompass a world larger, richer, more disorderly and untrammeled than that of any other writer of his generation; it is this which impels him toward the picaresque, the sprawling, episodic manner of *Augie March.* But there is a counterimpulse in him toward the tight, rigidly organized, underplayed style of *The Victim:* and at his best, I think, as in *Seize the Day,* an ability to balance the two tendencies against each other: hysteria and catalepsy, the centrifugal and the centripetal in a sort of perilous rest.

But the triumphs of Bellow are not mere triumphs of style; sometimes indeed they must survive the collapse of that style into mannerism, mechanical self-parody. Beyond an ear, Bellow possesses a fortunate negative talent: a constitutional inability to dissolve his characters into their representative types, to compromise their individuality for the sake of a point. It is not merely that his protagonists refuse to blur into the generalized Little People, the Victims of sentimental liberalism; but that they are themselves portrayed as being conscious of their struggle against such debasement. That struggle is, indeed, the essence of their self-consciousness, their self-definition. Their invariable loneliness is felt by them and by us not only as a function of urban life and the atomization of culture, but as something *willed:* the condition and result of their search to know what they are.

More, perhaps, than any other recent novelist, Bellow is aware that the collapse of the proletarian novel, which marks the starting place of his own art, has meant more than the disappearance of a convention in the history of fiction. With the disappearance of the proletarian novel as a form there has taken place the gradual dissolution of the last widely shared definition of man: man as the product of society. If man seems at the moment extraordinarily lonely, it is not only because he finds it hard to communicate with his fellows, but because he has lost touch with any overarching definition of himself.

This Bellow realizes, as he realizes that it is precisely in such loneliness, once man learns not to endure but to *become* that loneliness, that man can rediscover his identity and his fellowship with others. We recognize the Bellow character because he is openly what we are in secret, because he is us without our customary defenses. Such a protagonist lives nowhere except in the City; he camps temporarily in boardinghouses or lonely hotels, sits by himself at the corner table of some seedy restaurant or climbs backbreaking stairways in search of another whose existence no one will admit. He is the man whose wife is off visiting her mother or has just left him; the man who returns to find his house in disorder or inhabited by a squalid derelict; the man who flees his room to follow the funeral of someone he never knew.

He is essential man, man stripped of success and belongingness, even of failure; he is man disowned by his father, unrecognized by his son, man without woman, man face to face with himself, which means for Bellow face to face not with a fact but a question: "What am I?" To which the only answer is: "He who asks!" But such a man is at once the Jew in perpetual exile and Huck Finn in whom are blended with perfect irony the twin American beliefs that the answer to all questions is always over the next horizon and that there is no answer now or ever.

—1957

In the Beginning Was the Word

Logos or *Mythos*?

To learn what an age most deeply believes, it is enough to discover what the acolyte is asked to be able to recite before he understands; for our age and for the arts, what the graduate student declares to his fellow or to the professor he particularly trusts: *a poem is not its ideas; poetry is not idea; the history of ideas is not the history of poetry; a poem should not mean, but be!* Dangerous thoughts become dogma, dogma platitude; nothing fails like success. When the callowest doctoral candidate shuns the heresy of paraphrase, the orthodoxy of nonparaphrase becomes unbearable, and someone tacks up a declaration on the church doors; *a poem is its ideas; poetry is idea,* etc. Meanwhile, the survivors of the last orthodoxy begin to adjust their faces from sullenness to superciliousness, as if they had always been right, instead of being (disconcertingly!) right again.

But at the point where one age is not quite out and another not quite in, when neither side is sure whose turn it is to feel defensive, whose advanced, it is possible to ask a new question instead of advancing alternative answers to the old one. We must, I am sure, be done for a while with the queries: How do ideas get into poems, and what becomes of them thereafter? What is the status of the Great Chain of Being in Pope, of Grace and Free Will in Dante? It will not even do to modernize the old chestnuts by concerning ourselves with Viconian evolution in James Joyce or the Dark Night of the Soul in Gerard Manley Hopkins; for such questions imply that ideas are merely added to whatever is essential in a poem, as it used to be believed that metaphor was added.

Since I am convinced that what are commonly called "ideas"

represent in fallen form an essential aspect of poetry, I prefer to ask, "How do ideas ever get out of poems at all, and what is lost, what gained in the process?" I would not deny that some poets in more sophisticated societies find it desirable to refer to previously detached ideas, but even in such cases, the proper question is: how do ideas get *back* into poems?

I shall try, then, to describe how certain ideas (or, more precisely, perceptions later developed in terms of logic and evidence) exist or pre-exist in works of art; and I shall attempt, by the way, to indicate how these insights are reclaimed by the poet, who has merely to redeem from use to wonder what was in the first instance drafted from wonder to use. From remote antiquity, it has been a commonplace that poetry is the "mother tongue of the human race"; but of late (for quite honorable strategic reasons) we have banished commonplaces not only from poetry but even from the discussion of it. Nonetheless, the old insight continues to be bootlegged into the latest scientific descriptions, in the form of an assertion that science specifies the mythic perceptions of the poet. But there is a whole school of thought which assures us that the assertions of a poem are outside the realm of belief; and that, since the only true knowledge is that which can be believed or disbelieved (fantastic inversion!), the ideas of poetry are pseudo-ideas, therapeutically valuable, but epistemologically untrustworthy. Certainly, most of us, even when we repeat the ancient wisdom in our own jargon, do it with a sense of indulging in pious rhetoric in honor of a humane discipline which we would hesitate to disown, though we cannot say why. To deny poetry would be like striking our parents, and though as good relativists, we know there is nothing *absolutely* wrong with taking a whack at mama, still . . .

It is, however, no mere piety to the past which demands we acknowledge and remember the priority of the poetic inventor over the purveyor of prose; without such a realization, it is hard to talk sensibly about the most important literary problems. I have, for instance, heard at a score of literary meetings the protest that a certain interpretation of, let us say, Shakespeare based on Freud or Jung cannot possibly be relevant, because Shakespeare belonged, "let us remind our younger colleagues, to the

Elizabethan Period while Freud . . ." The assumption is, of course, that ideas even about man's nature are established outside of and prior to their poetic expression; and that therefore any reading of Shakespeare not verifiable in Renaissance Humor Theory or speculation on Melancholy can only illegitimately be applied to his text. I do not think that the men who raise such objections would be quite prepared to admit that the psychologists in the sixteenth or twentieth centuries are the true "inventors," but what else can be the meaning of the assertion that to understand Shakespeare we must understand the science contemporary with him?

Perhaps they are only trying to express thus obliquely their distaste for the ideas of Freud, but their avowed reasoning plays into the hands of the positivist theoreticians who would have us believe that we did not really learn to know ourselves until we moved into the laboratory and bought a microscope. Freud was much more modest, claiming only to translate out of Sophocles and Shakespeare what had always been there, to state, in ways more useful to him as a doctor, what the poet had seized in the act of simultaneous perception and expression that precedes reason.

To insist on the priority of poetry to science is, it need hardly be said, an uncertain way of claiming for it honor in a world where an important segment of the population (and an important part of all of us) is prepared to identify "before" with "outgrown." It is, perhaps, a sense of this fact which has convinced some that it is impolitic to insist on the priority of *mythos* to *logos*. Where theories of progress have penetrated even into the kingdom of culture, it is a little risky to boast of ancient lineage. Peacock's essay on the *Four Ages of Poetry* is familiar at least by reputation to everyone who reads English; and Hegel's similar though less witty contentions at the end of the *Aesthetics* have made familiar to most of Europe the argument that poetry belongs to the childhood of humanity, realizing imperfectly the wisdom later better embodied in philosophy or science. The theory of poetry as the baby talk of the human race has passed into the common store of our ideas; while the notion that we have outgrown or are about to outgrow poetic statement continues to obsess minds dominated by concepts of progress, rational or mystical; and against a host of misconceptions based upon this view of poetry begins the debate to which Matthew Arnold gave classical form in his lecture, *Science and Poetry*.

Wherever the past is distrusted, whether as Father or Mother, as immemorial authority or primitive impulse, poetry is hated or, more or less hypocritically, mourned. It is, therefore, incumbent on anyone who would revive the ancient veneration for poetry (it would be better, of course, if one could pretend poetry were invented only yesterday and is even more up-to-date than science) to demonstrate not merely that ideas emerge from poetic insights, but that they are degraded in the course of their development. It is impossible to begin, however, without stating the conflict correctly, and that is not as easy as it seems. We are tempted to speak of the opposition of poetry and science, but it is better to say with Plato "the ancient quarrel between poetry and philosophy," understanding philosophy in the older inclusive sense; and it is, perhaps, best of all to define the issue as the dispute of *logos* and *mythos* as to which was the primal Word.

Poetry, however, is the representative of *mythos* in a much less direct way than philosophy (or science, its heir) is of *logos*; philosophy invented *logos*, but *mythos* created poetry. Poetry is historically the mediator between *logos* and *mythos*, the attempt to find a rationale of the pre-rational (which is to say, form)— and if philosophy quarrels with poetry, it is not because it considers its own mode of perception superior to the mythic way, but because it considers that there is *no* mode except its own; that mediation is therefore a betrayal of the truth. There is a *hubris* of science for which science has no way of atoning; for it denies poetry which could alone become its conscience.

In the poetry of primitive societies, in which philosophy has not yet detached itself as a separate discipline, insights about experience and relationship are *mythos* because they are not yet *logos*; and even in the most sophisticated communities, *mythos* survives below the margin of consciousness, and must until that community dies; since all power, even that invested in rationalization, must come from below the reason. But in ages which fear the irrational and conventionally assume its exclusion, *mythos* must disguise itself as the very *logos* it must cease to be if it is to function poetically. At certain times, the reigning poets are quite sure that they are merely versifying ideas; and they become poets only insofar as they are deceived.

In a similar way, we experience the controlling perceptions of poetry as poetry only when we experience them as something closer to *mythos* than to *logos;* and this, too, is independent of what we think we are doing, or what we call the satisfaction we have found: wit or realism or the Sublime. Having said so much, I am obliged now in order to proceed to define *mythos*, that is, to define what is prior to definition. But there are strategies for defining even God . . . and at the worst, I will have made clear another way in which the job cannot be done.

I should like to propose a multiple definition of *mythos*. First of all, it is intuition in the Crocean sense, an immediate intuition of being, pure quality without the predicate of existence. Implicit in this first definition are the notions that *mythos* is neither logic nor thought, that it involves no question of belief (and is therefore knowledge as opposed to opinion); and that, being a category of value, it is incapable of being evaluated except in terms of whether it is itself. Another way of saying that poetry is intuition is to call it, as Croce does, *linguaggio*, that is, Language as opposed to languages, conceptual rather than verbal speech—in short, the Word which was in the beginning.

But it is never quite clear in Croce of what *mythos* is an intuition; its materials, he says when pressed, are *sentimenti* and *imagini*, feeling and images. I should like to suggest, and this is the second part of my definition, that the intuited in *mythos* are the Archetypes, those archaic and persisting clusters of image and emotion which at once define and attempt to solve what is most permanent in the human predicament. The Jungian term locates in the unconscious mind that source of the simple, enduring poetic subjects which Romanticism felt to exist but sought so vainly in peasants, children, lunatics, savages and other figures that psychology has revealed to us as typical projections of the unconscious itself. It further adds another dimension to intuition by suggesting that the Word lies not only beyond all external languages with which the community strives to unify itself, but also behind the symbolic idiom of dreams in which the rent personality attempts to come to terms with itself and its fate. The Jungian term makes clear finally the *function* of *mythos* as mediator between the community and the individual, the person and his fate, the given and achieved.

But Archetype is a term somehow too modern and abstract to encompass the total richness of *mythos;* and I am forced against my will to use a word hopelessly compromised by fashion; to call *mythos* by its poor, prostituted cognate, myth. It is a word I would willingly have surrendered, if I could have found another capable of suggesting the relationship of *mythos* to *the* Myths, those ancient Greek stories that are our Archetypes par excellence, preserving for us the assurance which belongs to ritual alone: that what is done below is done above, what is done here and now is done forever, what is repeated in time subsists unbroken in eternity.

There is something beyond symbolism in the sense that the ritual act or its story docs not stand for but *is* the archetypal fact; and as this ambivalence of the durative-punctual persists in poetry, it has been recognized as the Concrete Universal. The latter term, however, smacks of the University Chair rather than the altar or sacrificial fillets, and denies, with its connotations of a process moving from the particular to the universal, the primitive vision capable of perceiving most particularly what is most general. The word myth should remind us that the concept of an individual is not a beginning but an end, the last triumph of the power of abstraction; and that Achilles or Don Quixote are types, though, indeed, types not of the Warrior or of Misguided Chivalry, but of Achilles and Don Quixote.

Moreover, the word myth contains still what the more philosophical term has never possessed, overtones of the Marvelous; and no definition of *mythos* can end on any other note. *Mythos* is finally the Marvelous, or, as we say nowadays, the Absurd. I prefer the older word, grown unfamiliar enough to have lost its banality, while the newer has attained the status of a cliché without having got old. Besides, I have long been haunted by the suggestion of Jacopo Mazzoni in his *Defense of Dante* that poetry is the credible marvelous. In his explication of the term,

Mazzoni seems to me to have gone astray, opposing to Rhetoric, defined as the Credible as Credible, Poetry, defined as the Credible as Marvelous. This, it seems to me, is the error of a Virgil-ridden age, which takes wonder for an adornment of the rational, an accident rather than an essence; and which moves inevitably toward the rococo, initiating a process that can only end with— Truman Capote!

I should like to recast the classification a little, defining poetry as the Marvelous as Credible, and inserting it into an extended series: The Marvelous as Marvelous is *mythos;* the Marvelous as Credible, Poetry; the Credible as Credible, philosophy and science; the Credible as Marvelous, the ersatz of Poetry which appears in ages oppressed by philosophy or science: rhetoric, journalism, *kitsch* . . .

With the criterion of the Marvelous, I should like to complete my definition, in order to establish in general what is lost in the conversion of *mythos* to *logos,* and what we hunger for desperately today. The parodies and counterfeits of wonder which are peddled successfully on all sides testify to our awareness of a lack we are not usually prepared to admit. Certainly, it is in the power of scientific discourse to specify archetypal intuitions of man's relation to his own existence, his death and the universe around him, so that they are more viable for healing and social control and even the encouragement of civic virtue; so that, in short, they *work.* What is lost, however, is the sense of reverence and astonishment (another degraded name for what I am trying to describe is the Sublime) which alone breeds *pietas* —not religion, for even science can be a religion; but that natural piety without which we can approach the given world only as an enemy or a bore. The "neutralization of nature," of which we are tempted sometimes to boast, has made us aliens in the universe. The world has not abandoned us, but we it; for only as we love it can we know it, and the scientific knowing is a knowledge without love, a rape of nature. The world has not denied us, but we it; for only what we fear can we acknowledge, and scientific experiment is an experience without fear, an enlightened tolerance of nature.

In the light of these general remarks, I should like to examine one complex of myth, poetry and science, one fall from intuition to idea. Several possibilities tempted me in prospect, but I have had to abandon them for one reason or another: the Amphytrion *mythos,* so variously developed in poetry but so difficult to disentangle in philosophical or scientific thought; the *mythos* of the Trinity and its translation into the assumptions of modern physical science as demonstrated by Collingwood in his *Metaphysics;* the legend of Prometheus from Aeschylus to Karl Marx; Pandora, Eve and theories of human behavior. An ironic instance would have been I. A. Richards's translation into psychological terms of a view of contemporary sensibility expressed archetypally in Eliot's *The Waste Land,* in the midst of a proof that literature contains no ideas.

But I have chosen finally to deal with the Oedipus story, and I must begin by apologizing for the banality of my choice, though it is almost inescapable. On the practical side, there is the consideration that the major part of the materials for such an analysis have been gathered together by Patrick Mullahy (in an otherwise disappointing book called *Oedipus: Myth and Complex*); and further, the Oedipus myth is *our* myth, unriddled by our age, to which it has seemed an essential clue to the human situation.

The *mythos* itself, that essence which I have defined elsewhere as the Archetype without Signature, is almost irrecoverable in this instance; for us, the story exists always through, if not actually in, the formal rendering of Sophocles. The closest we can come to what the legend might have been before *our* Oedipus is in Homer's description of the "wives or daughters of princes" gathered around the dark pool of blood in Hades. "Then I met Oedipus' mother, the lovely Epicaste. She in her ignorance committed the sin of marrying her son. For Oedipus killed his father and took his mother to wife." How near bald statement the final verse comes, but it *is* a verse and lives in the remembered context. Some *mythoi* exist for us without individual coloring, the fables of half-familiar literatures, the plots of Saturday matinee movies made compulsively over and over; but the mythic Oedipus we know ordinarily only as the word made flesh in the trilogy of Sophocles.

Sophocles imposes not merely a Signature and the rationale

of form; he has already begun the fall from *mythos* to *logos,* and the moment of the expulsion from the Garden is the loveliest moment of poetry. Through his choruses, and especially those last words before which we do not tremble as we tremble before the naked fable, for they ask of us only belief, he interprets the legend of Oedipus in terms of "wisdom." "We must call no one happy who is of mortal race, until he hath crossed life's border, free from pain. . . ." "Great words of prideful men are ever punished with great blows, and in old age, teach the chastened to be wise. . . ." The absurd reduced to the commonplace, "interpreted" even by the greatest of poets, is already the stuff of rhetoric, capable of instruction or delight or persuasion, but not of transport, which inheres only in what transcends reason, what the poet himself does not "understand." The great works of art are those too untidy to fit the most elastic of explanations, no precise "objective correlatives," but constructs inadequate to what they must stand for, full of loose ends, buffoonery and mystery: *Hamlet, The Rape of the Lock, Don Quixote, Huckleberry Finn,* the *Antigone.* What the reasonable do not dare utterly to disown, they attempt to edit into rationality, cutting out of *Cymbeline,* for instance, the great speech of sexual disgust, or out of the *Antigone* the inviolably absurd passage beginning: "Never had I been the mother of children, or if a husband had been moldering in death. . . ."

But in Sophocles' time, at least the *Oedipus* was still acted in the presence of the god and before an altar, so that its mystery was implicit in the mode of presentation. It is interesting to compare the fate of the fable in a period that we call neo-classical —that is, one in which a sense persists that the old subjects contain a certain power that must be evoked, but where the magic of the Archetypal is hopelessly confused with concepts of decorum and rules. The Heroic Tragedy of a Dryden, acted under artificial light and to amuse the City, is a baroque tragedy, one which alternates the cool observance of rules with a hysterical shrillness over the fact that those rules do not guarantee the presence of power.

In Dryden's version of *Oedipus the King,* the original legend has been analyzed by common sense into morality (pride goeth before a fall), sensationalism (incest as titillation) and the "marvelous" (understood as make-believe). But though the central myth has been secularized into "entertainment," into precisely what is not *mythos*, the Archetypal re-enters unnoticed, in a subplot which seems the merest sop to the audience, the "love interest" an age demanded without knowing why. What is irrelevant to the mythic meanings of the Oedipus legend is paradoxically enough the story of Oedipus, whereas the father-son-girl triangle descended from New Comedy performs the function of myth for a public that can yield only unwittingly to its spell. We live, of course, still in the age of the comic Oedipus Archetype, fallen utterly now to a formula; but some of us begin at last to understand just why this trivial formula has moved us so deeply and for so long. Each age since Sophocles has read or retold his story in a way that profanes the myth; but in each there has been an unsuspected avatar of the same Archetype, in which Oedipus, Jocasta and Laios have become Youth, Girl and Father; Lover, Lady and Husband; Poet, Sister and Father. I am chiefly concerned here, however, only with the classicizing parodies, the re-evocations of the Periclean Oedipus.

Most recently our poets have learned to exploit the myth not in the interest of classicism, but in search of the mythic itself. We are students of legend, anthropologists rather than humanists; and our errors arise from too much knowledge of what the Archetypal is rather than too little. We have substituted irony for make-believe, but we have not quite recaptured wonder. When, for instance, the contemporary Italian poet, Cesare Pavese, treats the legend of Oedipus he approaches it not only obliquely (in the form of a dialogue between Tiresias and Oedipus before the archetypal events unfold) but also with an awareness of his obligations to the absurdity and multivalence of the legend. Both the ancient Greek writer and the modern Italian one play off our foreknowledge of the events against the ignorance of the protagonist; but in Sophocles what we foreknow is Oedipus' fate, in Pavese it is his myth. The older poet assumes in his audience the knowledge of a legend, the modern the knowledge of their own plight as revealed by science. The contemporary writer effects a rapprochement between the Oedipus

of Sophocles and that of Freud, rationalizing the figure of poetry
and remythifying that of reason. But to understand so modern
an instance, we must first glance at the actual interpretations of
our scientists.

The first science to emerge from the total mythic view is
philosophy; and the first interpreter of Oedipus is the first philosopher to find in poetry not merely a rival but a subject for
analysis. The attempt of Aristotle is a strange one, for he has
attempted to rationalize the myth as pure form; that is, prior to
analysis, he has abstracted from the dramatic poem only what is
already rational. Everyone realizes that *Oedipus the King* is
Aristotle's ideal play, but scarcely anyone is sufficiently aware
that his ideal play is only *Oedipus* stripped of its particularity.
The form toward which Aristotle finds tragedy to have been tending turns out to be the schema of Sophocles' play, primarily its
plot (this is, of course, what *mythos* has come to mean to that
most unmythical mind), restated without individuation or wonder: a man, neither impossibly noble or villainous, commits
against someone to whom he has the closest ties of blood, etc.,
etc. This is rather like what Kenneth Burke considers as establishing the essential meaning of a myth (*cf.* his treatment of the
Bellepherontic letter)—but this method of myth interpretation,
by formal abstraction, has few other followers.

All other derivations of *logos* from *mythos* follow one of the
two classic patterns of myth interpretation, euhemerization or
allegorization, reading fable as encoded history or personified
description of nature and man. I am not referring merely to
what are avowedly attempts at analyzing myths, the more or less
scientific interpretations of Max Mueller, for instance (to whom
the struggle of Oedipus and his father is a mythicization of the
alternation of day and night or of seasons), or of Frazer (who
finds in the Oedipus story traces of a matriarchal system in which
the male had to become by adoption the son-husband of the
Queen through whom the royal line descended); but to any
systematic science of man or nature. Scientific systems are constructed by testing and measurement and controlled statement,
but their informing assumptions and motivating "hunches" are
in the first instance *mythoi*. I suspect that there are simply no

other sources. The heart may have reasons that the reason knows nothing of, but reason has no reasons that the heart does not foreknow. From the myths of ether or four-dimensional space, from metaphors of the four elements and chaos, attraction and repulsion and Love, the science of mechanics is eternally reborn; from a poem of fifth-century Athens, the science of our age, psychoanalysis, is derived.

I shall not presume to discuss the interpretations of Oedipus found in Freud himself; even their vulgarizations do not belie the major insights of Freud and they are in the public domain. For my purposes, it is sufficient to remark that in the founder of depth psychology, we find both euhemerization and allegorization as typical modes of analysis. A prime example of the former is Freud's still half-mythical pre-history of the Old Man and the Pack, with the totemic eating of the father; and the latter is best exemplified in his treatment of the biological triangle and its effects on maturation. It can be objected, of course, that Freud found evidences of our universal hatred of the father and love for the mother in the facts of existence rather than those of literature; but we know that in no other culture did anyone ever find them, and that in our own they have been hinted at over and over by the poets before Freud. I suppose it is even possible to argue that the Oedipus complex has been as much made as discovered; and certainly one still finds in Freud that mythopoeic power which the Romantics called Imagination, and which they liked to understand as continuous with the great creative power of God.

In Jung, who is also something of a Romantic poet in a white jacket, there is further allegorization, the revelation that what Freud took to be final facts were still only symbols of a deeper lurking reality. The sexual basis of the Oedipus story, Jung asserted, is only a figure of speech; the relations to father and mother of the legend represent relations to the *pater imago* and *mater imago*, dreamlike projections of man, spirit, law and the state on the one hand—woman, feeling, family and the clan on the other: Laios and Jocasta, Antigone and Creon. The desire for incest with the mother symbolizes the desire to remain a child, to be unborn. The murder of the father signifies the rejection of fatherhood, of adult responsibility.

Once the process of interpretation has begun there is no end; an interpretation is no more immune to further interpretation than the story with which it started. To the essentially euhemeristic Otto Rank, Freud's Oedipus is exactly like Sophocles', a datum, revealing as much about Freud's age as it does about the remote hero of the legend. In every era, we struggle to come to terms with the essentially insoluble conflict that arises out of society's demand (called Fate in the older versions) that we be fathers and sons rather than selves. The Oedipus story reflects three major attempts to solve this problem. In the Heroic Age, when society was still essentially collective, Heroes (the superiors in whom the community saw the reflection of its ideal self) were granted the privilege of incest—that is, of becoming their own sons, of being reborn. In the Poetic Age, at the moment of the rise of the patriarchal family, such personal, representative immortality was renounced for immortality in children; but still an occasional heroic figure yearned to be his own son, like the "Oedipus" of pre-history. In our time, in the age of psychology and the anti-patriarchal family, the Oedipus wish, which began as a denial of fatherhood, has become its own opposite, the desire to be one's own father rather than one's own son.

In the depth psychologists of the first generation, the scientific reduction of the myth is not carried so far that the poetic overtones of the archetype are threatened; conditioned by nineteenth-century German literature, the founding fathers perpetuate something of the archaic and multilayered in their interpretations, though they are of course interested in use, in healing and self-illumination. But precisely for this reason they have seemed to their successors insufficiently "scientific." To some, indeed, the whole of psychoanalysis has appeared too "insightful" to be trusted, hopelessly involved in a compromise between *logos* and *mythos*, and they have disowned Freudianism in toto. Others who do not utterly deny the value of the Freudian approach but find it insufficiently detached from the mythic have tried to "neutralize" the archetypal overtones of Freud's work. To such revisionists the chief problem has seemed the irredeemably poetic concept of the Oedipus complex, which was for Freud himself the center of his theories. Karen Horney will do for the entire "scientizing" wing, with her doctrine that fixations do not arise from biological causes but from describable conditions in the family. Optimism, as well as rationality, demands the casting overboard of a myth which contains a kind of despair at its heart. Freud's formulation is "dangerous," Miss Horney teaches, for it obscures 'rather than underlines the important lesson to be learned: the need for "a real interest and respect for the child, the necessity of real warmth, reliability and sincerity by the parents. . . ."

Here is the final reduction to common sense and practical platitude, the inevitable end of demythification; for *logos*, where it does not find a formula and retreat to the laboratory and the sine tables, can confront the world only with the opposite of the archetype, the stereotype. That wife and daughter and mother of a Prince who rose beside the black pool of blood in Hell needed only to have read Miss Horney to have avoided trouble; and Oedipus need never have bawled his inarticulate cry or plucked out the eyes that had beheld the place which gave him birth. Some, indeed, may be healed by these platitudes as they have been healed by everything else, the laying on of hands, the rubbing of the soles of feet, the taking of chalk pills; but society cannot live by them. In the beginning was *mythos*, and each new beginning must draw again from that inexhaustible source.

The Novel and America

BETWEEN THE NOVEL and America there are peculiar and intimate connections. A new literary form and a new society, their beginnings coincide with the beginnings of the modern era and, indeed, help to define it. We are living not only in the Age of America but also in the Age of the Novel, at a moment when the literature of a country without a first-rate verse epic or a memorable verse tragedy has become the model of half the world.

We have known for a long time, of course, that our national literary reputation depends largely upon the achievement of our novelists. The classical poetic genres revived by the Renaissance had lost their relevance to contemporary life before America entered the cultural scene; and even the lyric has provided us with occasions for few, and limited, triumphs. Not only in the United States, though pre-eminently there, literature has become for most readers quite simply prose fiction; and our endemic fantasy of writing "the Great American Novel" is only a local instance of a more general obsession. The notions of greatness once associated with the heroic poem have been transferred to the novel; and the shift is a part of that "Americanization of culture" which some European intellectuals continue ritually to deplore.

But is there, as certain continental critics have insisted, an "American novel," a specific sub-variety of the form? If we turn to these critics for a definition, we come on such terms as "neo-realist," "hard-boiled," "naive," and "anti-traditional"—terms derived from a standard view of America as an "anti-culture," an eternally maintained preserve of primitivism. This view (notoriously exemplified by André Gide) ends by finding in Dashiell Hammett the same values as in William Faulkner, and is more a symptom of European cultural malaise than a useful critical distinction. It is tempting to insist on the pat rebuttal that, far from being an anti-culture, we are merely a branch of Western culture; and that there is no "American novel," only local variants of standard European kinds of fiction: American sentimental, American gothic, American historical romance, etc. Certainly no single subgenre of the novel was invented in the United States. Yet the peculiarities of our variants seem more interesting and important than their resemblances to the parent forms.

There is a real sense in which our prose fiction is immediately distinguishable from that of Europe, though this is a fact that is difficult for Americans to confess. In this sense, our novels seem not primitive, perhaps, but innocent, unfallen in a disturbing way, almost juvenile. The great works of American fiction are notoriously at home in the children's section of the library, their level of sentimentality precisely that of a pre-adolescent. This is part of what we mean when we talk about the incapacity of the American novelist to develop; in a compulsive way he returns to a limited world of experience, usually associated with his childhood, writing the same book over and over again until he lapses into silence or self-parody.

Merely finding a language, learning to talk in a land where there are no conventions of conversation, no special class idioms and no dialogue between classes, no continuing literary language—this exhausts the American writer. He is forever *beginning*, saying for the first time (without real tradition there can never be a second time) what it is like to stand alone before nature, or in a city as appallingly lonely as any virgin forest. He faces, moreover, another problem, which has resulted in a failure of feeling and imagination perceptible at the heart of even our most notable works. Our great novelists, though experts on indignity and assault, on loneliness and terror, tend to avoid treating the passionate encounter of a man and woman, which we expect at the center of a novel. Indeed, they rather shy away from permitting in their fictions the presence of any full-fledged, mature women, giving us instead monsters of virtue or bitchery, symbols of the rejection or fear of sexuality.

To be sure, the theme of "love" in so simple a sense is by no means necessary to all works of art. In the *Iliad,* for instance, and in much Greek tragedy, it is conspicuously absent; and in the heroic literature of the Middle Ages, it is peripheral where it exists at all. The *"belle Aude"* of the *Chanson de Roland* is a supernumerary, and the only female we remember from *Beowulf* is a terror emerging from the darkness at the bottom of the waters. The world of the epic is a world of war, and its reigning sentimental relationship is the loyalty of comrades in arms; but by the eighteenth century the notion of a heroic poem without romance had come to seem intolerable. The last pseudo-epics of the baroque had been obsessed with the subject of love, and the rococo had continued to elaborate that theme. Shakespeare himself appeared to the English Augustans too little concerned with the "reigning passion" to be quite interesting without revision. Why, after all, should Cordelia not survive to marry Edgar, they demanded of themselves—and they rewrote *King Lear* to prove that she should.

The novel, however, was precisely the product of the sentimentalizing taste of the eighteenth century; and a continuing tradition of prose fiction did not begin until the love affair of Lovelace and Clarissa (a demythicized Don Juan and a secularized goddess of Christian love) had been imagined. The subject par excellence of the novel is love or, more precisely—in its beginnings at least—seduction and marriage; and in France, Italy, Germany, and Russia, even in England, spiritually so close to America, love in one form or another has remained the novel's central theme, as necessary and as expected as battle in Homer or revenge in the Renaissance drama. But our great Romantic *Unroman,* our typical anti-novel, is the womanless *Moby Dick.*

Where is our *Madame Bovary,* our *Anna Karenina,* our *Pride and Prejudice* or *Vanity Fair?* Among our classic novels, at least those before Henry James, who stands so oddly between our own traditions and the European ones we rejected or recast, the best attempt at dealing with love is *The Scarlet Letter,* in which the physical consummation of adultery has occurred and all passion burned away before the novel proper begins. For the rest, there are *Moby Dick* and *Huckleberry Finn, The Last of the Mohicans, The Red Badge of Courage,* the stories of Edgar Allan Poe— books that turn from society to nature or nightmare out of a desperate need to avoid the facts of wooing, marriage, and child-bearing.

The figure of Rip Van Winkle presides over the birth of the

American imagination; and it is fitting that our first successful homegrown legend should memorialize, however playfully, the flight of the dreamer from the drab duties of home and town toward the good companions and the magic keg of Holland's gin. Ever since, the typical male protagonist of our fiction has been a man on the run, harried into the forest and out to sea, down the river or into combat—anywhere to avoid "civilization," which is to say, the confrontation of a man and woman which leads to the fall to sex, marriage, and responsibility.

Rip's world is not only asexual, however, it is terrible: a world of fear and loneliness, a haunted world; and the American novel is pre-eminently a novel of terror. To "light out for the territory" or seek refuge in the forest seems easy and tempting from the vantage point of a chafing and restrictive home; but civilization once disavowed and Christianity disowned, the bulwark of woman left behind, the wanderer feels himself without protection, more motherless child than free man. To be sure, there is a substitute for wife or mother presumably waiting in the green heart of nature: the natural man, the good companion, pagan and un-ashamed—Queequeg or Chingachgook or Nigger Jim. But the figure of the natural man is ambiguous, a dream and a nightmare at once. The other face of Chingachgook is Injun Joe, the killer in the graveyard and the haunter of caves; Nigger Jim is also the Babo of Melville's "Benito Cereno," the humble servant whose name means "papa" holding the razor to his master's throat; and finally the dark-skinned companion becomes the "Black Man," which is a traditional American name for the Devil himself.

The enemy of society on the run toward "freedom" is also the pariah in flight from his guilt, the guilt of that very flight; and new phantoms arise to haunt him at every step. American literature likes to pretend, of course, that its bugaboos are all finally jokes: the headless horseman a hoax, every manifestation of the super-natural capable of rational explanation on the last page—but we are never quite convinced. *Huckleberry Finn,* that euphoric boys' book, begins with its protagonist holding off at gun point his father driven half mad by the D.T.'s and ends (after a lynching, a dis-interment, and a series of violent deaths relieved by such humor-ous incidents as soaking a dog in kerosene and setting him on fire) with the revelation of that father's sordid death. Nothing is spared; Pap, horrible enough in life, is found murdered brutally, aban-doned to float down the river in a decaying house scrawled with obscenities. But it is all "humor," of course, a last desperate attempt to convince us of the innocence of violence, the good clean fun of horror. Our literature as a whole at times seems a chamber of horrors disguised as an amusement park "fun house," where we pay to play at terror and are confronted in the innermost chamber with a series of inter-reflecting mirrors which present us with a thousand versions of our own face.

In our most enduring books, the cheapjack machinery of the gothic novel is called on to represent the hidden blackness of the human soul and human society. No wonder our authors mock themselves as they use such devices; no wonder Mistress Hibbins in *The Scarlet Letter* and Fedallah in *Moby Dick* are treated half jocularly, half melodramatically, though each represents in his book the Faustian pact, the bargain with the Devil, which our authors have always felt as the essence of the American experience. However shoddily or ironically treated, horror is essential to our literature. It is not merely a matter of terror filling the vacuum left by the suppression of sex in our novels, of Thanatos standing in for Eros. Through these gothic images are projected certain obsessive concerns of our national life: the ambiguity of our relationship with Indian and Negro, the ambiguity of our encounter with nature, the guilt of the revolutionist who feels himself a parricide—and, not least of all, the uneasiness of the writer who cannot help believing that the very act of composing a book is Satanic revolt. "Hell-fired," Hawthorne called *The Scarlet Letter,* and Melville thought his own *Moby Dick* a "wicked book."

The American writer inhabits a country at once the dream of Europe and a fact of history; he lives on the last horizon of an endlessly retreating vision of innocence—on the "frontier," which is to say, the margin where the theory of original goodness and the fact of original sin come face to face. To express this "blackness ten times black" and to live by it in a society in which, since the decline of orthodox Puritanism, optimism has become the chief effective religion, is a complex and difficult task.

It was to the novel that the American writer turned most naturally, as the only *popular* form of sufficient magnitude for his vision. He was, perhaps, not sufficiently sophisticated to realize that such learned forms as epic and tragedy had already outlived their usefulness; but, working out of a cultural background at best sketchy and unsure, he felt insecure before them. His obligations urged him in the direction of tragedy, but traditional verse tragedy was forbidden him; indeed, a chief technical problem for American novelists has been the adaptation of nontragic forms to tragic ends. How could the dark vision of the American—his obsession with violence and his embarrassment before love—be expressed in the sentimental novel of analysis as developed by Samuel Richardson or the historical romance as practiced by Sir Walter Scott? These sub-genres of fiction, invented to satisfy the emotional needs of a merchant class in search of dignity or a Tory squirearchy consumed by nostalgia, could only by the most desperate expedients be tailored to fit American necessities. Throughout their writing lives, such writers as Charles Brockden Brown and James Fenimore Cooper devoted (with varying degrees of self-consciousness) all their ingenuity to this task, yet neither Brown nor Cooper finally proved capable of achieving high art; and the literary types invented by both have fallen since into the hands of mere entertainers—that is, novelists able and willing to attempt anything *except* the projection of the dark vision of America we have been describing. The Fielding novel, on the other hand, the pseudo-Shakespearean "comic epic" with its broad canvas, its emphasis upon reversals and recognitions, and its robust masculine sentimentality, turned out, oddly enough, to have no relevance to the American scene; in the United States it has remained an exotic, eternally being discovered by the widest audience and raised to best-sellerdom in its latest imported form, but seldom home-produced for home consumption.

It is the gothic form that has been most fruitful in the hands of our best writers: the gothic *symbolically* understood, its machinery and décor translated into metaphors for a terror psychological, social, and metaphysical. Yet even treated as symbols, the machinery and décor of the gothic have continued to seem vulgar and contrived; symbolic gothicism threatens always to dissolve into its components, abstract morality and shoddy theater. A recurrent problem of our fiction has been the need of our novelists to find a mode of projecting their conflicts which would contain all the dusky horror of gothic romance and yet be palatable to discriminating readers, palatable first of all to themselves.

Such a mode can, of course, not be subsumed among any of those called "realism." Our fiction is essentially and at its best nonrealistic, even anti-realistic; long before *symbolisme* had been invented in France and exported to America, there was a full-fledged native tradition of symbolism. That tradition was born of the profound contradictions of our national life and sustained by the inheritance from Puritanism of a "typical" (even allegorical) way of regarding the sensible world—not as an ultimate reality but as a system of signs to be deciphered. For too long, historians of American fiction have mistakenly tried to impose on the course of a brief literary history a notion of artistic "progress" imported from France or, more precisely perhaps, from certain French literary critics.

But the moment at which Flaubert was dreaming *Madame Bovary* was the moment when Melville was finding *Moby Dick,* and considered as a "realistic" novel the latter is a scandalous botch. To speak of a counter-tradition to the novel, of the tradition of "the romance" as a force in our literature, is merely to repeat the rationalizations of our writers themselves; it is certainly to fail to be *specific* enough for real understanding. Our fiction is not merely in flight from the physical data of the actual world, in search of a (sexless and dim) Ideal; from Charles Brockden Brown to William Faulkner or Eudora Welty, Paul Bowles or John Hawkes, it is, bewilderingly and embarrassingly, a gothic fiction, nonrealistic and negative, sadist and melodramatic—a literature of darkness and the grotesque in a land of light and affirmation.

Moreover—and the final paradox is necessary to the full complexity of the case—our classic literature is a literature of horror for boys. Truly shocking, frankly obscene authors we do not possess; Edgar Allan Poe is our closest approximation, a child playing at what Baudelaire was to live. A Baudelaire, a Marquis de Sade, a "Monk" Lewis, even a John Cleland was inconceivable in the United States.* Our flowers of evil are culled for the small girl's bouquet, our novels of terror (*Moby Dick, The Scarlet Letter, Huckleberry Finn,* the tales of Poe) are placed on the approved

* In recent years the situation appears to have altered radically—perhaps, in part, because the taste of boys has changed, as the "latency period," which Freud thought immutable, tends to be abolished. At any rate, the line between "pornography" and respectable literature has blurred; and certain traditional themes of American literature—the love of white and colored males, for instance, and the vilification of women—are rendered with explicit sexual detail. Indeed, such detail becomes required rather than forbidden as American puritanism learns to stand on its head. It is a long way from James Fenimore Cooper to James Baldwin, or from Herman Melville to Norman Mailer; but even if our dreams have become more frankly erotic, the American *eros* has not really changed. We continue to dream the female dead, and ourselves in the arms of our dusky male lovers.

book lists of Parents' Committees who nervously fuss over the latest comic books. If such censors do not flinch at necrophilia or shudder over the book whose secret motto is "I baptise you not in the name of the Father . . . but of the Devil," or fear the juvenile whose hero at his greatest moment cries out, "All right, I'll *go* to Hell," it is only another irony of life in a land where the writers believe in hell and the official guardians of morality do not.

Yet our authors are as responsible as the P.T.A.'s for the confusion about the true nature of their books; though they may have whispered their secret to friends, or confessed it in private letters, in their actual works they assumed what camouflage prudence dictated. They *wanted* to be misunderstood. *Huckleberry Finn* is only the supreme instance of a subterfuge typical of our classic novelists. To this very day, it is heresy in some quarters to insist that this is not finally the jolliest, the *cleanest* of books; Twain's ironical warning to significance hunters, posted just before the title page, is taken quite literally, and the irreverent critic who explicates the book's levels of terror and evasion is regarded as a busybody and scandalmonger. Why, one is driven to ask, why the distortion and why the ignorance?

Perhaps the whole odd shape of American fiction arises simply (as simplifying Europeans are always ready to assure us) because there is no real sexuality in American life and therefore there cannot very well be any in American art. What we cannot achieve in our relations with each other it would be vain to ask our writers to portray or even our critics to miss. Certainly many of our novelists have themselves believed, or pretended to believe, this. Through *The Scarlet Letter,* there is a constant mournful undercurrent, a series of asides in which Hawthorne deplores the sexual diminution of American women. Mark Twain in *1601* somewhat similarly contrasts the vigor of Elizabethan Englishwomen with their American descendants; contrasting the sexual utopia of precolonial England with a fallen America where the men copulate "but once in seven yeeres"; and his pornographic sketch ends on the comic-pathetic image of an old man's impotent lust that "would not stand again." Such pseudo-nostalgia cannot be taken too seriously, however; it may, indeed, be the projection of mere personal weakness and fantasy. Certainly, outside their books, Hawthorne and Twain seem to have fled rather than sought the imaginary full-breasted, fully sexed woman from whom American ladies had presumably declined. Both married, late in life, pale hypochondriac spinsters, intellectual invalids—as if to assert publicly that they sought in marriage not sex but culture.

Such considerations leave us trapped in the chicken-egg dilemma. How can one say whether the quality of passion in American life suffers because of a failure of the writer's imagination or vice versa? What is called "love" in literature is a rationalization, a way of coming to terms with the relationship between man and woman that does justice, on the one hand, to certain biological drives and, on the other, to certain generally accepted conventions of tenderness and courtesy; and literature, expressing and defining those conventions, tends to influence "real life" more than such life influences it. For better or for worse and for whatever reasons, the American novel is different from its European prototypes, and one of its essential differences arises from its chary treatment of woman and of sex.

To write, then, about the American novel is to write about the fate of certain European genres in a world of alien experience. It is not only a world where courtship and marriage have suffered a profound change, but also one in the process of losing the traditional distinctions of class; a world without a significant history or a substantial past; a world which had left behind the terror of Europe not for the innocence it dreamed of, but for new and special guilts associated with the rape of nature and the exploitation of dark-skinned people; a world doomed to play out the imaginary childhood of Europe. The American novel is only *finally* American; its appearance is an event in the history of the European spirit—as, indeed, is the very invention of America itself.

II

Though it is necessary, in understanding the fate of the American novel, to understand what European prototypes were available when American literature began, as well as which ones flourished and which ones disappeared on our soil, it is even more important to understand the meaning of that moment in the mid-eighteenth century which gave birth to Jeffersonian democracy and Richardsonian sentimentality alike: to the myth of revolution and the myth of seduction. When Charles Brockden Brown, the first professional American author, sent a copy of his *Wieland* to Thomas Jefferson in 1798, he must, beneath his modest disclaimers, have had some sense of his and the President's kinship as revolutionaries. "I am therefore obliged to hope," Brown wrote, "that . . . the train of eloquent and judicious reasoning . . . will be regarded by Thomas Jefferson with as much respect as . . . me." But if Jefferson ever found the time to read Brown's novel, he left no record; we know only that he expressed general approval of "works of the imagination" as being able, more than history, to "possess virtue in the best and vice in the worst forms possible." It is a chillingly rational approach to art and a perhaps sufficient indication of the hopelessness of Brown's attempting in those sensible years to live by his writing.

Yet despite the fact that no professional novelist of real seriousness was to find a supporting public in America for twenty-five or thirty years more, Brown's instincts had not deceived him. He and Jefferson *were* engaged in a common enterprise; the novel and America did not come into existence at the same time by accident. They are the two great inventions of the bourgeois, Protestant mind at the moment when it stood, on the one hand, between Rationalism and Sentimentalism, and on the other, between the drive for economic power and the need for cultural autonomy. The series of events which includes the American and the French Revolutions, the invention of the novel, the rise of modern psychology, and the triumph of the lyric in poetry, adds up to a psychic revolution as well as a social one. This revolution, viewed as an overturning of ideas and artistic forms, has traditionally been called "Romantic"; but the term is paralyzingly narrow, defining too little too precisely, and leading to further pointless distinctions between Romanticism proper, pre-Romanticism, *Sturm und Drang,* Sentimentalism, *Symbolisme,* etc. It seems preferable to call the whole continuing, complex event simply "the Break-through," thus emphasizing the dramatic entry of a new voice into the dialogue of Western man with his various selves.

The Break-through is characterized not only by the separation of psychology from philosophy, the displacement of the traditional leading genres by the personal lyric and analytic prose fiction (with the consequent subordination of plot to character); it is also marked by the promulgation of a theory of revolution as a good in itself and, most notably perhaps, by a new concept of inwardness. One is almost tempted to say, by the invention of a new kind of self, a new level of mind; for what has been happening since the eighteenth century seems more like the development of a new organ than the mere finding of a new way to describe old experience.

It was Diderot who represented a first real awareness that man is *double* to the final depths of his soul, the prey of conflicting psyches both equally himself. The conflict had, of course, always been felt, but had traditionally been described as occurring between man and devil, or flesh and spirit; that the parties to the dispute are both man and spirit was a revolutionary suggestion. In his demi-novel, *Rameau's Nephew,* Diderot projected the conflicting divisions within man's mind as the philosopher and the parasite, the rationalist and the underground man, debating endlessly the cause of the head versus that of the gut. And in his pornographic *Bijoux Indiscrets,* he proposed another version of the same dialogue: the enchanted (and indiscreet) genitals speak the truth which the mouth will not avow, thus comprising an allegorical defense of pornography in the guise of a pornographic work. In the same year in which Richardson's sentimental novel *Clarissa* was published, John Cleland's long-lived dirty book *The Memoirs of Fanny Hill* was making a stir. Pornography and obscenity are, indeed, hallmarks of the age of the Break-through. Not only pious novels but titillating ones show the emergence of the underground emotions (of what the period itself euphemistically called "the heart") into high culture. Quite as influential as Diderot (or Richardson or Rousseau) in the *bouleversement* of the eighteenth century is the Marquis de Sade, who stands almost emblematically at the crossroads of depth psychology and revolution.

Not only did de Sade shed new light on the ambivalence of the inner mind, revealing the true darkness and terror implicit in the drive which the neo-classical age (revolting against Christian notions of sin) had been content to celebrate as simple "pleasure" or polite "gallantry"; he may even have caused that symbolic storming of an almost empty prison with which the Fernch Revolution begins. Himself a prisoner in the *Tour de la liberté* of the Bastille, de Sade, through an improvised loudspeaker made of a tube and funnel, screamed to bystanders to rescue his fellow inmates who were having their throats cut—and scattered handwritten leaflets complaining about jail conditions to the crowd he attracted. On July 3, 1789, he was finally transferred elsewhere to insure "the safety of the building," but not before he had started to write *Justine, or the Misfortunes of Virtue,* that perverse offshoot of the Richardsonian novel, and had thus begun to create the first example of revolutionary pornography.

In the Marquis de Sade, the Break-through found its most stringent and spectacular spokesman: the condemned man judging his judges, the pervert mocking the normal, the advocate of destruction and death sneering at the defenders of love and life; but his *reductio* follows logically enough from assumptions shared by Jefferson and Rousseau, Richardson and Saint-Just. Whatever has been suspect, outcast, and denied is postulated as the source of good. Before the Break-through, no one, Christian or Humanist, had doubted the inferiority of passion to reason, of impulse to law; and though it is possible sophistically to justify all eighteenth-century reversals by quoting the verse which says the last shall be the first, Christianity is dead from the moment such a justification is made. The Break-through is profoundly anti-Christian though it is not always willing to appear so. There is a brief age of transition when the Enlightenment and Sentimentalism exist side by side, when it is still possible to pretend that true reason and true feeling, the urgings of passion and the dictates of virtue are identical—and that all are alike manifestations of the orthodox God. But Sentimentalism yields quickly to the full Romantic revolt; in a matter of months, Don Juan, enemy of Heaven and the family, has been transformed from villain to hero; and before the process is finished, audiences have learned to weep for Shylock rather than laugh him from the stage. The legendary rebels and outcasts, Prometheus and Cain, Judas and the Wandering Jew, Faust and Lucifer himself are one by one redeemed. The parricide becomes an object of veneration and tourists (among them that good American abroad, Herman Melville) carry home as an icon Guido's picture of Beatrice Cenci, slayer of her father!

The process is continuous and nearly universal. Even the values of language change: "gothic" passes from a term of contempt to one of description and then of praise, while "baroque" makes more slowly the same transition; meanwhile terms once used honorifically to describe desired traits—"condescension," for example—become indicators of disapproval. The child is glorified over the man, the peasant over the courtier, the dark man over the white, the rude ballad over the polished sonnet, the weeper over the thinker, colony over mother country; the commoner over the king—nature over culture. At first, all this is a game: the ladies of the court in pastoral dress swing high into the air to show their legs with a self-consciousness quite unlike the abandon of children to which they are pretending. But in a little while, Jean-Jacques Rousseau has fainted on the road to Vincennes and awakened to find his waistcoat soaked with tears; and it is suddenly all in earnest. Whatever was down is now up, as the undermind heaves up out of the darkness; barricades are erected and the novel becomes the reigning form; the Jew walks openly out of the ghetto, and otherwise sensible men hang on their walls pictures of trees and cattle. The conjunctions are comic in their unexpectedness and variety.

It is hard to say what was cause and what effect in the complex upheaval; everything seems the symptom of everything else. Yet deep within the nexus of causes (gods must die for new genres to be born) was that "death of God" that has not yet ceased to trouble our peace. Somewhere near the beginning of the eighteenth century, Christianity (more precisely, perhaps, that desperate compromise of the late Middle Ages and early Renaissance, Christian Humanism) began to wear out. It was not merely, or even primarily, a matter of the destruction of the political and social power of one Church or another, much less of the lapse of economic control by the priests. The divisions within Christendom surely contributed to the final collapse, but they are perhaps better regarded as manifestations than as causes of the insecurity over dogma that was at work deep within. Institutionalized Christianity at any rate began to crumble when its mythology no longer proved capable of controlling and revivifying the imagination of Europe.

The darker motive forces of the psyche refused any longer to accept the names and ranks by which they had been demeaned for almost two thousand years; once worshiped as "gods," they had been made demons by fiat, but now they stirred again in discontent. Especially the Great Mother—cast down by the most patriarchal of all religions (to the Hebrews, she was Lilith, the bride of darkness), ambiguously redeemed as the Blessed Virgin and denied once more by a Hebraizing Protestantism—clamored to be honored once more. The very distinction between God and Devil, on which the psychic balance of Europe had for so long been staked, was threatened. It did not matter that some people (chiefly women) continued to go to church, or even that there were revivals within the framework of surviving sects; fewer and fewer men lived by the legends of the church, and the images of saints represented not living myths but "mythology" in a literary sense.

The effect of the growing awareness (an awareness, to be sure, at first shared by only a handful of advanced thinkers) of this cosmic catastrophe was double: a sense of exhilaration and a spasm of terror, to which correspond the two initial and overlapping stages of the Break-through. There was first of all the conviction of the Age of Reason and its spokesmen, the *philosophes,* gravediggers of the Christian God, that they—and all of mankind—were at last *free,* free of the superstition and ignorance so long sponsored by the priests for their own selfish ends. Those demons into which the early Christian apologists had translated the gods of antiquity seemed to the *philosophes* idle inventions of the Church itself: bugaboos to scare the pious into unquestioning subservience. Even the Christian God seemed to them such a contrivance, demonic and irrational. In the imagined universe presided over by their own "Author of Creation," there could be no place for mystery or blackness. Once *"l'infâme,"* the scandalous Church, had been crushed, all monsters would be eliminated forever, and man could take up his long, baffled march toward perfection in a sweet, sunlit, orderly world. Just such a vision, however modified by circumstance, moved the Deist intellectuals who founded America, especially that Thomas Jefferson to whom C. B. Brown, himself a follower of the *philosophes,* proffered his gothic novel.

Insofar as America is legendary, a fact of the imagination as well as one of history, it has been shaped by the ideals of the Age of Reason. To be sure, the European mind had dreamed for centuries before the Enlightenment of an absolute West: Atlantis, Ultima Thule, the Western Isles—a place of refuge beyond the seas, to which the hero retreats to await rebirth, a source of new life in the direction of the setting sun which seems to stand for death. Dante, however, on the very brink of an age which was to turn the dream into the actualities of exploration, had prophetically sent to destruction in the West, Ulysses, the archetypal explorer. The direction of his westward journey through the great sea is identified with the sinister left hand; and Ulysses himself comes to stand for man's refusal to accept the simple limits of traditional duty; "not the sweetness of having a son, nor the pious claim of an old father, nor the licit love that should have made Penelope rejoice could quench in me the burning to become familiar with the vice of men and men's valor." It is a fitting enough epigraph to represent that lust for experience which made America. There is, indeed, something blasphemous in the very act by which America was established, a gesture of defiance that began with the symbolic breaching of the pillars of Hercules, long considered the divine signs of limit.

To be sure, the poets of later Catholicism made an effort to recast the dream of America in terms viable for their Counter-Reformation imaginations, to forge a myth that would subserve new political exigencies. It is, however, the Enlightenment's vision of America rather than that of the Church that was written into our documents and has become the substance of our deepest sense of ourselves and our destiny. If North America had remained Latin, the story might have been different; but Jefferson himself presided over the purchase of the Louisiana Territory, which settled that question once and for all. History sometimes provides suitable symbolic occasions, and surely one of them is the scene that finds Jefferson and Napoleon, twin heirs of the Age of Reason, preparing the way for Lewis and Clark, that is to say, for the first actors in our own drama of a perpetually retreating West. Napoleon, it must be remembered, was the sponsor of the painter David and Jefferson the planner of Monticello; good neo-classicists both, they place the American myth firmly in the classicizing, neo-Roman tradition of the late eighteenth century. The New World is, of course, in one sense an older one than Europe, a preserve of the primitive, last refuge of antique virtue; indeed, the writers and artists of the Empire period could never quite tell the difference between Americans, red or white, and the inhabitants of the Roman Republic. The face of Washington, as rendered in bronze by Houdon, is that of the noblest Roman of them all, or, in Byron's phrase (already a cliché), "the Cincinnatus of the West."

But America is not exclusively the product of Reason—not even in the area of legend. Behind its neo-classical façade, ours is a nation sustained by a sentimental and Romantic dream, the dream of an escape from culture and a renewal of youth. Beside the *philosophes,* with whom he seemed at first to accord so well that they scarcely knew he was their profoundest enemy, stands Rousseau. It is his compelling vision of a society uncompromised by culture that has left the deepest impress on the American mind. The heirs of Rousseau are Chateaubriand and Cooper, after whom the world of togas and marble brows and antique heroism is replaced by the sylvan scene, across which the melancholy refugee plods in search of the mysterious Niagara, or where Natty Bumppo, buckskinned savior, leans on his long rifle and listens for the sound of a cracking twig. The bronze face of a bewigged Washington gives way to the image of young Abe splitting logs in a Kentucky clearing.

The dream of the Republic is quite a different thing from that of the Revolution. The vision of blood and fire as ritual purification, the need to cast down what is up, to degrade the immemorial images of authority, to impose equality as the ultimate orthodoxy—these came from the *Encyclopédie,* perhaps, as abstract ideas; but the spirit in which they were lived was that of full-blown Romanticism. The Revolution of 1789 (for which ours was an ideological dress rehearsal) may have set up David as its official interpreter, but it left the world to Delacroix; and though it enthroned Reason as its goddess, it prepared for a more unruly Muse.

In Sentimentalism, the Age of Reason dissolves in a debauch of tearfulness; sensibility, seduction, and suicide haunt its art even before ghosts and graveyards take over—strange images of darkness to usher in an era of freedom from fear. And beneath them lurks the realization that the "tyranny of superstition," far from being the fabrication of a Machiavellian priesthood, was a projection of a profound inner insecurity and guilt, a hidden world of nightmare not abolished by manifestos or restrained by barricades. The final horrors, as modern society has come to realize, are neither gods nor demons, but intimate aspects of our own minds.

A Night with Mr. Teas

THE IMMORAL MR. TEAS was approaching the end of a nine-month run at the little movie house in Seattle where I first saw it. Paired with it was *The Mouse that Roared,* a film I had accidentally seen twice before and one for which I have small affection. I am dismayed at its sentimental-liberal clichés espousing Love and deploring the Bomb. Naturally, I arrived too early and had to endure once more the final cuteness of "The Mouse," its technicolor reassurance that our world would survive—and that its survival would be an unmitigated Happy Ending. It was technicolor I really hated, I told myself; nothing could be true or good or beautiful in those never quite convincing tones, just as nothing could be high, wide, or handsome on the nonscale of the wide screen. "Justify God's ways to man—in color and VistaVision," I imagined the modern muse telling some new Milton; and foresaw the miserable event: four stars in the *Daily News,* ennui for any sensitive beholder.

Mr. Teas, however, turned out to be in technicolor, too—its opening all the vulgar tints of urban Southern California: a sun-dazzled city bus stop and our hero, briefcase in hand, beside a street-corner bench endorsed with an ad for a Jewish funeral home. Los Angeles and the undertakers again. Another cliché, I found myself thinking, the by-now-not-quite-fresh-or-moving metaphor for Hell in Our Time. And I was not reassured by the Monsieur Hulot-type music of the score—tinkle-jangle-tinkle, the submelody of city life, as Mr. Teas switched from bus to bike, changed from mufti to a pair of cerise-terra cotta overalls, and began to pedal along his insipid round of work: delivering false teeth to dentists' offices.

This at least was an apt metaphor, I argued with the self that wanted to get the hell out—a quite unhackneyed figure for a setting and routine as glistening and meaningless as death: the detached smile fixed in a polished vise. But one part of me still kept asking what I was doing there anyhow.

The last erotic picture I had been to see—also after a nine-month run—had been "Ecstasy"; but that had been some twenty-five or thirty years before, in another world. How different a world became clear quite soon, as I found myself laughing at a spectacle so antiromantic that it verged, for me, at least, on the anaphrodisiac. In *Mr. Teas* there was not only no passion, but no contact, no flesh touching flesh, no consummation shown or suggested. I remembered from the earlier film the pearls slipping from Hedy Lamarr's throat, her face blurred in the ecstasy advertised by the title. For pornography the woman's angle of vision is necessary, but here were no women outside of Bill Teas's head; and Bill Teas was nobody's dreamed lover, only a dreamer, with his half-modest, half-comical beard, his sagging pectoral muscles, his little lump of a belly creased by baggy shorts or hidden by overalls.

And Mr. Teas could touch no one—not in lust or love or in the press of movement along a street. Once in the film he lays his hand on flesh, the shoulder of an eight-year-old girl working out with a hula hoop, and she beans him with a rock. Any really nubile, desirable female is doomed to disappear into the ladies' room or the arms of some lover whose face we never see—as unreal, finally, as the girl he embraces. Mr. Teas conducts his odd business and carries his frustrated dreams through a world of noncontact and noncommunication.

In his wanderings from office to office, from home to lunchroom, the violently overalled Mr. Teas finds occasional refreshment in staring down the more than half-revealed bosoms of receptionists, waitresses, and cashiers. In his otherwise quite arid world, all females are singularly and lushly *décolleté,* as if they existed chiefly to titillate his impotent desire, and as the plot unfolds with all the step-by-step deliberateness of a strip tease, Mr. Teas is shown developing a talent for imaginarily stripping ever closer to the buff the girls who torment him on his rounds. An injection in a dentist's chair from an assistant, whose breasts become in fantasy the headrest which supports him, helps Mr. Teas create the first of his visions; but awake and undrugged, he continues to fabricate them, finally comes to regard them as a disease from which he asks a psychiatrist to deliver him.

The visions of Mr. Teas are, however, strange in a way which at first we do not notice, because their strangeness is an accepted part of a world in which we all live. That is to say, the nudity he creates is never *complete* nudity. Sitting, for instance, in a café, gnawing on an obscenely large slab of watermelon, Mr. Teas finds that the waitress who serves him has become quite naked, except for the merest doily of an apron covering the meeting place of thighs and belly. Admiring the nonchalance of Mr. Teas as he gnaws his cool fruit and pretends to ignore the feast beside him, we realize that the joke has adapted to the conditions which make the showing of the film possible: there must be an apron; he must not touch her.

It is not finally just a matter of observing certain rules of the censors, but of making those very rules the subject of the picture, the butt of its jokes. For what we are shown when the rules are observed is not female flesh, but pin-up pictures—moving pictures of moving pin-up pictures, life twice removed; and this is why *Mr. Teas,* funny as it is (and it *is* funny—chiefly because of the discretion of its cameraman, Russ Meyers, and the skill with which Bill Teas projects the impassive, dogged, low-keyed lust of its *schlemiel*-hero), is also a quite serious film. It is not merely like the strip tease, the candy-box cover, the girlie calendar, and the fold-out magazine nude; it is about them.

In one sequence, during which he presumably searches for escape at the beach, Mr. Teas stumbles on a professional photographer who is running through her paces a model or hopeful starlet, first in an ultimate bikini, then stripped of her bra and finally clothed only in the surf. How icily the girl simulates the poses of lewd appeal, wild abandon, and sexual allure, though for the camera only and on cue as the camera clicks. Meanwhile, Mr. Teas, too, has a camera, a miniature Brownie that cannot compete with the equipment of the professional any more than the meager personal dreams of Mr. Teas can compete with those professionally produced. He inhabits a world of prefabricated fantasies, stumbling into one situation after another in which those fantasies are being manufactured for men powerless to evoke for themselves even the intangible shadow of sex.

We are, therefore, constantly being reminded of how we, too, live in a world where, whatever the natural bent of our desires, we are forced by billboards, night clubs, stage entertainments, cartoons, and photographs, by the very ads which assail us for brassieres and Kleenex and Pepsi-Cola, into playing the Peeping Tom; and of how we, too, are not only teased by the ten thousand commercially produced provocations, but become finally our own teasers—stripping but not possessing (not even in the deepest imagination), as we have been taught. There is one unforgettable scene, in which, as Mr. Teas aimlessly walks down a street, a window shade springs up and, plastered almost against the pane, a female body is revealed from just below the shoulders to just above the waist—a noseless face in which the nipples make wide eyes above the pursed, tiny mouth of the navel; a face which seems to stare back at the starer, as if all flesh (not only male flesh, as our convention demands) had become eyes and the only communication in either direction were peeping.

As the picture draws to a close, we follow Mr. Teas on a day's outing to a lake, where he is after the same game as always, though by now he has become terrified by his talent, thinks he flees what he seeks; and he finds it. This time there is not just a single girl, but four at once, who, quite naked, rock themselves on hammocks, dip and splash in the shallow water or swim where it is deeper, row boats, and toss a ball, while Mr. Teas ogles and spies, smiling his half-beatific, half-idiotic smile, and separated from them still, as if by the invisible glass pane of the TV toothpaste commercial.

So stylized, so indistinguishable from mass-produced fantasies in every premeditated, robotic gesture are the girls he watches that it is difficult to tell whether the whole episode is intended to be taken for an actual event or merely the most extended of Mr. Teas's dreams. Certainly what of the audience remained to the end the night I first saw the movie (several more clean-cut pairs of college sweethearts had walked out early in the game) argued about it vehemently from either side. But the point, I suppose, lies really in this ambiguity, this irreality. And just as the girls were, in their gestures, more the fabrications of mass culture than of nature, so they were also in their dimensions and their textures. It is impossible to remember, two days after leaving the theater, what color their hair was.

These girls do not quite seem to be women, adapted as they are to the mythical dimensions of pin-ups and to a more than mythical smoothness of texture. Nowhere is there pimple or blemish or sagging skin or untoward wrinkle or mottled flesh. The loving, patient camera (not really a moviemaker's camera at all, but that of the still photographer) that follows the play of light and shade on haunch and hollow finds no human imperfection, not even goose flesh or beads of sweat. Such girls seem more like fruit than flesh—hothouse fruit, serenely perfect and savorless, not to be touched or eaten. Only looked at. Unreal. Unreal. Unreal. This is the sadness of *Mr. Teas.*

As old restrictions crumble in our society, the naked flesh assumes its proper place among the possible subjects for movies, the place it has always held in the other, less public arts; but meanwhile, in the United States, we have been long corrupted by the pseudo-arts of tease and titillation, conditioned to a version of the flesh more appropriate for peeking than love or lust or admiration or even real disgust. In European films like *Room at the Top* or *Hiroshima, Mon Amour,* we have been offered newer versions of nudity appropriate to serious art, versions of a nudity not so much seen as felt, responded to in tenderness and desire. Whether equivalent versions will prove possible in American films seems to me doubtful; perhaps our way will have to be comic rather than passionate or even sentimental. If this is so, *Mr. Teas,* for all its lapses into the obvious, may someday seem a pioneering effort. Its makers have not attempted to surmount the difficulties which confront the American moviemaker who desires to make nakedness his theme; but they have, with absolute good humor, managed at once to bypass and to illuminate those difficulties. The end result is a kind of imperturbable comedy, with overtones of real pathos.

How especially stupid in light of all this are the cuts demanded by the censors of New York, who, in deleting some twenty minutes, have eliminated not only the nipples and buttocks they were obviously after but also the wit and pathos and point of *Mr. Teas.* To

New York moviegoers I am moved to say: Stay away from what will be called *The Immoral Mr. Teas* in your theaters. It will be a tease in the worst sense of the word, the merest leering hint, the dullest remnant of a once witty film—a joke of its own kind on public standards of decency. Decency! How hard it is to believe that the names of those involved in the production are not anticipatory jokes which this final one fulfills. But DeCenzie is apparently the actual name of the producer of the film, Bill Teas that of the chief actor, and Cantlay the real name of a real California street. It pays to be lucky!

I do not know whether the makers of *Mr. Teas* were merely lucky or really aware of the implications of the movie they were making; and New York viewers will have no way of deciding for themselves without a trip to Atlantic City, where an uncut version is being shown. Perhaps DeCenzie and Russ Meyers, the cameraman, are themselves only two more victims of the process which reduces sex in America to sex in the eye, and are critics of the process only inadvertently. I have been reading press releases about how Russ Meyers, who shot *Mr. Teas* in four days at the cost of only twenty-four thousand dollars and dreams of earning a million on it, has produced another film, another bareback quickie, called *Eve and the Handyman*. Maybe from the start he has just been cashing in on the new freedom which provides new ways of exploiting the mindless audience. I would like to believe that this is not so, that he knew all along not merely how funny but how sad *Mr. Teas* really was. In the end, it doesn't matter. The artist is entitled to whatever can be found in his work. I hope he makes the million.

—1959

An Almost Imaginary Interview:
Hemingway in Ketchum

But what a book they both agreed, would be
the real story of Hemingway, not those he
writes but the confessions of the real
Ernest Hemingway . . .

The Autobiography of Alice B. Toklas

I AM WRITING NOW the article which I have known for months I must someday write, not merely because he is dead but because there sits on the desk before me a telegram from a disturbed lady whom I can not quite remember or despise. "Your confiding reminiscences of Papa Hemingway," it reads, "reminiscent of Louella (Hearst)." The clichés of "Papa" and "Hearst" date but do not identify the sender; and the fact that she has wired her malice from Seattle only confuses me. Why Seattle? Surely the few cagey remarks I have made to a reporter about my experiences in Ketchum, Idaho do not constitute "confiding reminiscences"—dictated as they were as much by a desire to conceal as to reveal, and concerned as they were with my own dismay rather than the details of Hemingway's life. How did they get to Seattle? And in what form?

I am aware, of course, of having told over the past six months in at least as many states the story of my inconclusive encounter with Hemingway last November. I have never been able to tell it until after the third drink or the fourth, and then always to those who, I was convinced, would understand that I was talking about a

153

kind of terror which rather joined me to than separated me from a stranger whose voice I have known all my adult life—a stranger obviously flirting with despair, a stranger whose destruction I could not help feeling my own calamity, too. After all, I was only talking the way everyone talks all the time about American letters, the plight of the American writer. What could be more banal or harmless?

But I can tell from the poor conventional ironies of the telegram before me what I have come to suspect already from my need to say over and over precisely how it was in Ketchum: that what is at stake is an image by which we have all lived—surviving haters of Hearst, middlebrow adulators of *For Whom the Bell Tolls,* Jews who have managed somehow to feel closer to Jake Barnes than to Robert Cohn—the lady from Seattle, and I. That image I must do my best to shatter, though on one level I cannot help wishing that it will survive my onslaught.

I do not want ever to see the newspaper article that cued the wire. I am willing to accept responsibility for whatever the press in its inaccuracy and confusion made of my own inaccuracy and confusion; but I want to accept it without having read it. If amends are to be made for pieties offended, they must be made by setting down the best version of what I am able to remember, by my writing this piece which perhaps already is being misunderstood by those who have managed to get so far.

I went to see Hemingway just after Hallowe'en last year along with Seymour Betsky, a colleague from Montana State University, the university attended briefly by one of Hemingway's sons; and, much more importantly, the one from which Robert Jordan took off for the War in Spain in *For Whom the Bell Tolls.* From a place as much myth as fact, from Hemingway's mythical home (I am told that during his last trip to Spain he signed tourist autographs, "E. Hemingway, Red Lodge, Montana"), I set out across the three hundred miles to his last actual home near Sun Valley, a winter resort out of season. We were charged with persuading Hemingway to give a public lecture at our school, to make the kind of appearance he had resolutely refused to make, to permit—like a good American —a larger audience to look at him than would ever read him, even in *Life.* Actually, we felt ourselves, though we did not confess it aloud, neither professors nor promoters, but pilgrims—seeking the shrine of a God in whom we were not quite sure we believed.

I had long since put on record my only slightly begrudged acknowledgment of Hemingway's achievement: his invention of a major prose style viable in the whole Western world, his contrivance of the kind of short story young writers are not yet done imitating, his evocation in *The Sun Also Rises* of a peculiar terror and a special way of coming to terms with it that must seem to the future the very hallmark of our age. But I had also registered my sense of his mindlessness, his sentimentality, his failure to develop or grow. And I could not help recalling as I hurtled half-asleep beside the driver through the lucid air of not-yet winter, up and down the slopes of such mountains as haunted Hemingway, a symposium in Naples just ten years before. I had been arguing in a tongue not my own against what I took to be the uncritical Italian veneration of Hemingway; and I was shouting my protest to one of those young writers from Rome or Palermo or Milan who write in translated Hemingwayese about hunting and *grappa* and getting laid—but who have no sense of the nighttime religious anguish which makes Hemingway a more Catholic writer than most modern Italians. "Yes," I remembered saying, "yes—sometimes he puts down the closest thing to silence attainable in words, but often what he considers reticence is only the garrulousness of the inarticulate." This I hoped at least I was managing to say.

What really stirred in me on that long blue ride into dusk and the snowless valley (there was near dismay in the shops and cafés since the season was at hand and no snow had fallen) was an old resentment at those, chiefly but not exclusively Europeans, unable to understand that Hemingway was to be hated and loved not merely as a special American case, but more particularly as a Western writer, even as an imaginary Montanan. It seemed only fair that revolutions and illness and time bring him to Sun Valley to die, to the western slopes of America, rather than to Spain or Africa or Cuba; and it was scarcely ironical that his funeral be held in a tourists' haven, a place where the West sells itself to all comers.

Hemingway never wrote a book set in the Mountain West, but he wrote none in which innocence and nobility, heroism and cowardice, devotion and passion (not love but *aficion*) are not defined as they are in the T.V. Westerns which beguile a nation. The West he exploited is the West not of geography but of our dearest and most vulnerable dreams, not a locale but a fantasy, whose meanings do not change when it is called Spain or Africa or Cuba. As long as the hunting and fishing is good. And the women can be left behind. In Gary Cooper, all at which Hemingway merely hinted was made explicit; for Cooper was what Hemingway only longed to be, the West made flesh—his face, in its inarticulate blankness, a living equivalent of Hemingway's prose style.

It is not at all odd to find a dramatist and a favorite actor collaborating in the creation of character and image; what Tennessee Williams imagines, for instance, Marlon Brando is—or has obligingly become. But a similar collaboration between novelist and actor seems to me unparalleled in literary history— a little strange, though in this case inevitable. How aptly the paired deaths of Cooper and Hemingway, each greeted as a national calamity, climaxed and illuminated their relationship, their joint role in sustaining on upper cultural levels an image of our character and fate common enough in pulps, comic books and T.V. That they did not manage to see each other before Cooper died seemed to the press (and to me) a more than minor disaster, mitigated perhaps by the fact that the one did not long survive the other. And like everyone else, I was moved by Hemingway's telegram offering Cooper odds of two to one that he would "beat him to the barn."

Death had presided over their association from the start, since their strongest link was Robert Jordan, invented by one, played by the other: the Westerner as fighter for Loyalist Spain, the anti-Fascist cowboy, the Montana innocent in a West turned oddly political and complex, a land ravaged not by the conflict of outlaw and sheriff but by the struggle between Communist and Nazi. In such a West, what can the Western Hero do but—despite the example of his immortal prototypes—die? Unlike the War for the American West, the War in Spain was lost by Our Side; and finally only its dead seemed true heroes. Hemingway's vision in *For Whom the Bell Tolls* is something less than tragic; but his self-pity is perhaps more adequate than tragedy itself to an age unsure of who its heroes are or what it would like to do with them.

Only a comic view could have been truer to our times, and this Hemingway notoriously lacks. He never knew how funny the Westerner had come to seem in our world, whether played by Roy Rogers or Cooper or Hemingway himself—only how sad. Of all his male leads, Jake Barnes comes closest to being redeemed from self-pity by humor—the humor implicit in his comic wound. And consequently Jake could no more have been played by Cooper than could the Nick Adams of the earliest stories, or the old men of the last books. Never quite young, Cooper was not permitted to grow really old—only to betray his age and suffering through the noncommital Montana mask. He represents ideally the protagonists of Hemingway's middle novels, Lieutenant Henry and, of course, Jordan; but he will not do for anything in *To Have and Have Not,* a Depression book and, therefore, an ill-conceived sport sufficient unto Humphrey Bogart. The roles on either side of middle age, Hemingway was able to play himself, off the screen yet in the public eye: the beautiful young man of up to twenty-three with his two hundred and thirty-seven wounds, the old stud with his splendid beard and his guns chased in silver. We cannot even remember the face of his middle years (except as represented by Cooper), only the old-fashioned photographs of the youth who became the "Papa" of cover-stories in *Look* and *Life:* his own doomed father, his own remotest ancestor as well as ours.

At any rate, it was a pilgrimage we contemplated, my colleague and I, leaving Missoula some twenty-five years after the fictional departure of Robert Jordan. But it was also—hopefully—a raid: an expedition intended to bring Hemingway home to Montana, where he might perhaps succeed in saying what he had never been able to say to outlanders, speak the meanings of the place in which we had been born or had improbably chosen to live. It was, I suppose, *my* Western I hoped Hemingway would play out (becoming for me what Cooper had been for him); and there would have been something appropriately comic, after all, in casting the boy from Oak Park, Illinois in a script composed by the boy from Newark, New Jersey, both of them on location in the Great West. But, of course, the first words we exchanged with Hemingway made it clear that if he had ever been able to speak in public, he was unable to do so now; that if he did, indeed, possess a secret, he was not about to reveal it from the platform. And how insolent, how absurd the quest seems in retrospect—excused only by a retrospective sense that what impelled us was a need to identify with an image we thought we despised. If it was not an act of love we intended, it was a more typical American effort magically to establish something worthy of love. *Here or Nowhere is America.* Surely the phrase rang someplace in the back of my head as we approached Ketchum; but Here turned out to be Nowhere and Hemingway in the middle of it.

At first, however, we were elated, for we were able to reach quickly the young doctor we had been told was Hemingway's friend and hunting companion; and we were as much delighted as embarrassed (everything seemed to be composing itself more like a poem than a mere event) by the fact that he was called, symbolically, Dr. Saviers. They hunted together during the afternoons, Dr. Saviers told us, though Hemingway could no longer crouch in a blind, only walk in search of birds, his last game. Hemingway worked mornings, but perhaps he would adjust his routine, find some time for us the next day before noon . . . after all, we had driven three hundred miles . . . and even though he never made public appearances, still . . . .

We sat that night in a half-deserted bar, where the tourists had not yet come and the help waited on each other, making little ingroup jokes. No one noticed us nursing over our drinks the elation about which we scarcely dared speak. God knows what unworthy elements fed our joy: a desire for scraps of gossip or occasions for articles, a secret yearning to be disappointed, to find the world figure fatuous or comic or—No, surely there were motives less ignoble at its root: a genuine hope that emanating from greatness (the word came unbidden to our minds) there would be a *mana* we could share, a need somehow to verify the myth. We entered Hemingway's house through a back porch in character with the legend —limp ducks hanging from the rafters, a gun against the wall—the home of the hunter; but to step into the kitchen was to step out of the mythic world. There were the neatly wrapped trick-or-treat packages left over from the week before, loot unclaimed by kids; *The Readers Digest, The T.V. Guide* open on tables; and beyond, the nondescript furniture of a furnished house, a random selection of meaningless books on the half-empty shelves.

And the Hemingway who greeted us, framed by the huge blank television screen that dominated the living room, was an old man with spectacles slipping down his nose. An old man at sixty-one.

For an instant, I found myself thinking absurdly that this must be not the Hemingway we sought but his father, the ghost of that long-dead father—materialized at the age he would have been had he survived. Hemingway's handclasp I could scarcely feel; and I stood there baffled, a little ashamed of how I had braced myself involuntarily for a bone-crushing grip, how I must have yearned for some wordless preliminary test of strength. I had not known, I realized standing dumb before one even dumber, how completely I had been victimized by the legend Hemingway had worn himself out imagining, writing, living.

Why should he not, after all, inhabit a bourgeois house, sit before T.V. with a drink in his hand, while his wife passed out Hallowe'en packages to children? Why the hell not? But he dwindled so abruptly, so touchingly from the great red and white head to his spindly legs, accentuated by tapered pants, legs that seemed scarcely able to hold him up. Fragile, I found myself thinking, breakable and broken—one time too often broken, broken beyond repair. And I remembered the wicked sentence reported by Gertrude Stein, "Ernest is very fragile, whenever he does anything sporting something breaks, his arm, his leg, or his head." The scar of one more recent break was particularly evident on his forehead as he stood before us, inarticulately courteous: a scar just above the eyes that were the wrong color—not blue or grey as they should have been, not a hunter's eyes at all, but the eyes of a poet who dreamed of hunters, brown, soft, scared. . . .

These, at least, I knew could not have changed. Whatever had recently travestied him, whatever illness had ravaged his flesh, relaxed his handclasp, could not have changed his eyes. These must have been the same always, must always have tried to confess the secret he had perhaps more hoped than feared would be guessed. "But Jake Barnes is in some sense then a self-portrait," I almost said aloud. "And that's why *The Sun Also Rises* seems your truest book, the book of fear and fact, not bravado and bullshit." I did not speak the words, of course, and anyhow he was saying in a hesitant voice, after having listened politely to our names, "Fiedler? Leslie Fiedler. Do you still believe that st— st— stuff about Huck Finn?"

He did not stammer precisely but hesitated over the first sounds of certain words as if unsure he could handle them, or perhaps only a little doubtful that they were the ones he really wanted. And when I had confessed that yes, I did, did still think that most American writers, not only Twain but Hemingway, too (naturally, we did not either of us mention his name in this context), could imagine an ennobling or redemptive love only between males in flight from women and civilization, Hemingway tried to respond with an appropriate quotation. "I don't believe what you say," he tried to repeat, "but I will defend to the death your right to say it." He could not quite negotiate this platitude, however, breaking down somewhere in the neighborhood of "defend." Then—silence.

I knew the motives of my own silence though I could only speculate about his. I had been cast, I could see, in the role of The Critic, hopelessly typed; and I would be obliged to play out for the rest of our conversation not the Western I had imagined, but quite another fantasy: the tragicomic encounter of the writer and the mistrusted professional reader upon whom his reputation and his survival depend. That Hemingway was aware at all of what I had written about him somehow disconcerted me. He was, I wanted to protest, a character in my *Love and Death in the American Novel;* and how could a character have read the book in which he lived? One does not imagine Hamlet reading the play that bears his name. But I was also, I soon gathered, a semifictional character—generically, to be sure, rather than particularly—a Hemingway character, an actor in his imaginary world. So that finding me before him made flesh, he felt obliged to play out with me a private drama, for which he would, alas, never be able to frame quite appropriate sentences, an allegorical quarrel with posterity. At least, for an hour he could get the dialogue out of his haunted head.

He had read or glanced at, I could soon see, not only my essays but practically everything anyone had written on the modern novel in the United States. I fancied him flipping the pages, checking the indexes (or maybe he got it all out of book reviews in *Time),* searching out the most obscure references to himself, trying to find the final word that would allay his fears about how he stood; and discovering instead, imbedded in the praise that could never quite appease his anguish, qualifications, slights, downright condemnations. "T-tell Norman Mailer," he said at one point, "I never got his book. The mails in Cuba are— are— terrible." But who would have guessed that Hemingway had noticed the complaint in *Advertisements for Myself* about his never having acknowledged a presentation copy of *The Naked and the Dead*. And yet the comment was not out of character; for at another point he had said, really troubled, "These d-damn students. Call me up in the middle of the night to get something they can h-hang me with. So they can get a Ph.D." And most plaintively of all, "Sometimes when a man's in—when he can stand it least, they write just the things that—"

Between such observations, we would regard each other in the silence which seemed less painful than talk until Seymour Betsky would rescue us. I did not really want to be rescued, it seems to me now, finding silence the best, the only way of indicating that I knew what was racking the man I faced, knew his doubt and torment, his fear that he had done nothing of lasting worth, his conviction that he must die without adequate reassurance. It was not for Hemingway that I felt pity; I was not capable of such condescension. It was for myself, for all American writers. Who, *who,* I kept thinking, would ever know in these poor United States whether or not he had made it, if Hemingway did not. I may even have grown a little angry at his obtuseness and uncertainty.

"A whole lifetime of achievement," I wanted to shout at him, "a whole lifetime of praise, a whole lifetime of reveling in both. What do you want?" But I said nothing aloud, of course, only went on to myself. "Okay, so you've written those absurd and trivial pieces on Spain and published them in *Life*. Okay, you've turned into the original old dog returning to his vomit. But your weaknesses have never been a secret either from us, or, we've hoped at least, from you. We've had to come to terms with those weaknesses as well as with your even more disconcerting strengths—to know where we are and who, where we go from here and who we'll be when we get there. Don't we have the right to expect the same from you? Don't we have the right to—" But all the while he kept watching me warily, a little accusingly, like some youngster waiting for the reviews of his first book and trying desperately not to talk about it to one he suspects may be a reviewer.

And what could I have told him, I ask myself now, that might have helped, and what right did I really have anyhow, brought there by whim and chance? What could anyone have said to him that had not already been repeated endlessly and without avail by other critics or by sodden adulators at bars. The uncertainty that Hemingway betrayed was a function surely of the depression that was about to destroy him; but, in a deeper sense, that depression must have been the product of the uncertainty—of a lifetime of uncertainty behind the bluster and the posturing, a lifetime of terror indissoluble in alcohol and action, a lifetime of fearing the leap out of the dark, never allayed no matter how many beasts he brought down in bush or boondocks.

It was only 9:30 A.M. but, after a longer than customary lapse in our talk, Hemingway broke out a bottle of wine to help ease us all. "Tavel—a fine little wine from the Pyrenees," he said, without, apparently, any defensive irony or even any sense of the comic overtones of the cliché. Silence and platitude. Platitude and silence. This was the pattern of what never became a conversation. And I felt, not for the first time, how close Hemingway's prose style at its best was to both; how it lived in the meager area of speech between inarticulateness and banality: a triumph wrung from the slenderest literary means ever employed to contrive a great style—that great decadent style in which a debased American speech somehow survives itself.

"It's hard enough for me to wr-write much less—talk," he said twice I think, obviously quoting a favorite platitude of his own invention; and, only once, but with equal satisfaction, "I don't want to talk about literature or politics. Once I talked about literature and I got—sick." One could hear in his tone how often he must, in similar circumstances, have used both; but he meant the first of them at least. The word "articulate" became in his mouth an insult, an epithet. Of Norman Mailer, for instance, he said between pauses, quietly, "He's s-so— articu— late—" and there was only a little envy to mitigate the contempt. But he wanted to talk about literature really, or, more precisely, wanted to talk about authors, his colleagues and rivals. Yet his comments on them boiled down to two only: the first for writers over fifty, "Great guy, you should've known him!"; the second for those under that critical age, "That boy has talent!" Vance Bourjaily, I recall, seemed to him the "boy" with the most "talent." The one author he did not mention ever was himself, and I abided by the taboo he tacitly imposed, though, like him I fear, more out of cowardice than delicacy.

When I noticed in a particularly hard moment the *T.V. Guide* beside me open to the Saturday Night Fights, I welcomed the cue, tried to abandon Bourjaily in favor of Tiger Jones, though I really admire the style of the one not much more than that of the other. "Terrible what they make those boys do on television," Hemingway responded, like the joker next to you at the bar who baffles your last attempt at communication. And it didn't help a bit when Mrs. Hemingway entered to apologize in an attractive cracked voice for the state of the house. "If I had only known that someone was coming. . . ." But why was everyone apologizing and to whom?

It was the *politeness* of the whole affair which seemed somehow the final affront to the legend. Hemingway was like a well-behaved small boy, a little unsure about the rules, but resolved to be courteous all the same. His very act of asking us to come and talk during his usual working hours and at a moment of evident distress was a gesture of genuine courtesy. And he fussed over the wine as if set on redeeming our difficult encounter with a show of formality. At one point, he started to pour some Tavel into my glass before his own, then stopped himself, put a little into his glass, apologized for having troubled to remember protocol, apologized for apologizing—finally insisted on drinking to my next book, when I lifted my glass to his.

But what were we doing talking of next books when I could not stop the screaming inside of my head, "How will anyone ever know? How will I ever know unless the critics, foolish, biased, bored, tell me, tell us?" I could foresee the pain of reading the reviews of my first novel, just as I could feel Hemingway's pain reading the reviews of his later work. And I wanted to protest in the name of the pain itself that not separated but joined us: The critic is obliged only to the truth though he knows that truth is never completely in his grasp. Certainly he cannot afford to reckon with private anguish and despair in which he is forbidden to believe, like the novelist, inventing out of his friends and his own shame Lady Brett or Robert Cohn.

And I looked up into Hemingway's smile—the teeth yellowish and widely spaced, but bared in all the ceremonious innocence of a boy's grin. He was suddenly, beautifully, twelve years old. A tough, cocky, gentle boy still, but also a fragile, too-often-repaired old man, about (how could I help knowing it?) to die. It puzzled me a little to discover him, who had never been able to invent a tragic protagonist, so much a tragic figure himself—with meanings for all of us, meanings utterly different from those of his myth, meanings I would have to figure out later. . . . Yet he seemed, too, as we had always suspected, one who had been *only* a boy and an old man, never what the rest of us for too wearily long must endure being— all that lies between. I could not help recalling the passage where Gertrude Stein tells of Hemingway at twenty-three crying out that he was too young to be a father. And I could hear him now in my inner ear crying out that he was too young to be an old man. Too young to be an ancestor.

But he was not too young to be my ancestor, not too young for me to resent as one resents what is terribly there when he is born. I would not be able to say the expected kind things about him ever, I knew, not even after he was dead. And who would understand or believe me when I was ready to say what I could: that I loved him for his weakness without ceasing to despise him for his strength.

We had left Seymour Betsky's car in town, and as the four of us looked at each other now, more than ready to be done with our meeting, Hemingway and his wife offered to drive us back in to pick it up. He had to do some small chores, chiefly go to the bank. But it was a Saturday, as we had all forgotten; and Betsky and I stood for a moment after we had been dropped off watching Hemingway bang at the closed glass doors, rather feebly perhaps but with a rage he was obviously tickled to be able to feel. "Shit," he said finally to the dark interior and the empty street; and we headed for our car fast, fast, hoping to close the scene on the first authentic Hemingway line of the morning. But we did not move quite fast enough, had to hear over the slamming of our car door the voice of Mrs. Hemingway calling to her husband (he had started off in one direction, she in another), "Don't forget your vitamin tablets, Daddy."

—1962

Traitor or Laureate:

The Two Trials of the Poet

In the United States, poetry has been for so long not so much bought and read as honored and studied that the poet has grown accustomed to his marginal status. Unlike the novelist, he takes his exclusion from the market place as *given*, not a subject for anguish and protest but a standing joke, partly on him, partly on those who exclude him. Edmund Wilson was able to ask, as early as the Thirties, "Is Verse a Dying Technique?" and the mournful answer is implicit in the mournful cadence of the question. But Mr. Wilson did not, of course, pose the question for the first time; behind his concern there is a tradition of discovering the end of verse which goes back as far as Thomas Love Peacock's "Four Ages of Poetry" and the earliest impact of advanced technology on the imagination of the West.

Long before the poets of the United States had found an authentic voice, the survival of poetry itself had come to seem problematical; and certainly today there is no American poet who does not suspect that his own verse is likely to live (once his small circle of admiring friends has died) in the classroom and library, rather than in the hearts of men. Meanwhile, he is inclined to feel, he must somehow sustain himself on the long, difficult way toward academic immortality, and to do so he must choose between being subsidized by foundation grants and university sinecures, or earning his keep at some job completely unconnected with the making or reading of verse. Wallace Stevens was an actuary in, and then vice-president of, an insurance company; Robert Frost tried for a while to farm; William Carlos Williams was, all of his adult life, a family doctor; T. S. Eliot began his career as a bank clerk. Each choice is perhaps a metaphor for each poet's view of himself and his work: Stevens aspiring to the precision and objectivity of statistical analysis; Frost longing to root words in the soil; Williams thinking of himself as a healer and adviser to ordinary men in their daily suffering; Eliot viewing himself as the guardian of the treasury of culture. But all together, these choices surely reflect a common awareness of a common plight, the poet's inability to subsist on his poetry alone.

That plight, however, has sent more poets into the classroom than (with whatever metaphorical intent) into the great world of production for profit; even Robert Frost, for instance, ended up teaching, once he had discovered how little he could earn tilling the soil. It is not, I think, only the poet's aversion to a world of competition and economic risk which has led him more and more to seek refuge in the college, but a sense that there he is close to his own future, to the posterity for whom he writes. Certainly there he can, if he likes, tout himself and his friends, as well as abuse his rivals and detractors; and there he can set the captive youngsters before him the task of understanding and loving (or, at least, of seeming for a moment to understand and love) certain poems, including his own, more important to him than any of the goals—erotic, athletic, or technological—which those same youngsters pursue once out of sight. Sometimes he fears, in fact, that the *only* reading such poems will get in the world he inhabits is precisely this vicarious or symbolic one, between college walls and class bells.

All of the Southern agrarian poets from John Crowe Ransom to Randall Jarrell have ended up teaching at one university or another; and numerous other poets of quite different styles and persuasions from them and from each other (Delmore Schwartz and Robert Creely, John Berryman and Richard Wilbur, for instance) teach regularly if they can, irregularly if they must, or, best of all, enjoy the status and pay of teachers with a minimum of classroom duties. Even among the maddest of our poets, there are not a few to whom the academy seems the only real place preferable to the Nowhere that otherwise attracts their total allegiance. Sometimes, indeed, it seems as if the path which leads back and forth between the classroom and the madhouse is the one which the modern American muse loves especially to tread.

Yet the poet is finally aware that in the university he is expected not so much to write poetry, or even to teach it, as to be a poet: to act out a role which is somehow necessary to the psychic well-being of society as poems are not. And, similarly, it is the assumption of his poetic *persona* for which he is paid by grants and subsidies, and applauded at symposia and writers' conferences. After a while, it may even seem to the poet that he is being paid not to write; but this is not really so, and it is only a kind of desperate self-flattery which leads him to indulge in the conceit. In point of fact, our society does not really care whether he writes or not, so long as he does not do it on the time they ask him to spend in embodying publicly what they have rejected in themselves: a contempt for belonging and order and decorum and profit and right reason and mere fact; a love for exile and irrelevance and outrage and loss and nonsense and lies.

It is not merely himself that the poet is asked to play; if it were, there would be no temptation involved worth resisting. It is rather a *myth* of himself, or, more properly, perhaps, a myth of the poet in general which he is called on to enact. And he has, as a matter of fact, a choice of roles, for the morality play in which he is urged to assume a part demands, like all literature on the level of mass culture, heroes as well as villains, good guys as well as bad guys. But how can a poet be a hero? How can the projection of what the great audience rejects function for that audience as "good"? To be sure, we can imagine best-selling poets on the analogy of best-selling novelists, unequivocal spokesman for the mass audience and its values; but there is so steep a contrast between "best-selling" and "poet," between what the great audience demands and what verse, any verse, does, that the concept is soon abandoned.

At any rate, since the time of Longfellow at least, the largest public in the United States has decided it does not need such hybrids in the realm of verse. The fictionist, the journalist, and, more recently, the script-writer for movies or television, performs much more satisfactorily any tasks which could be imagined for them. The servile sub-poet does not cease to exist entirely, but he is barred from the place where poetry is chiefly read, judged, and preserved, the academy, and relegated to the world of commerce, where he produces greeting card mottoes, or to ladies' clubs, where he flatters vanity, or to the mass magazines, where he provides filler for the spaces between editorials and short stories. In return for such meager employment, he is asked to endure the indignity of being read, or listened to, without being noticed or remembered.

The "hero" of the popular socio-drama we have been discussing is not so simple and obscure a mouthpiece; he is, in fact, both problematical and ambiguous: a hero-villain, a good rebel, an admirable non-conformist. And what makes him good or admirable is his presumed attitude toward the great audience which notices him without ever reading him; for that audience, by certain mysterious processes of cultural transmission, comes, after a while, to know—or believe it knows—who in the realm of art is really on its side, who regards it without something less than contempt. The one thing it will never forgive a writer is despising its reading ability, which, to be sure, it does not usually get around to practicing. Such despite it regards as the ultimate treason, being willing, on the other hand, to forgive any challenge to its values or beliefs so long as that despite is not visibly present. As the critic at his best forgives a writer almost anything for writing well, the non-reader at his worst forgives him almost anything for writing ill—or simply for having the courtesy to *seem* to do so.

How can the great audience tell, after all, who is, in this

sense a friend and who a foe? The point is, of course, that they cannot really tell at all, that they are likely to be fooled by the most elementary sorts of duplicity, since all their judgments are rendered on the basis of a handful of lines quoted for the benefit of their immediate mentors (schoolmarms and leaders of P.T.A. discussion groups) in the columns of, say, the *Saturday Review*, the *New Yorker*, the front page of the *New York Times Book Review*, or the back pages of *Time*. As a matter of fact, the reviewers for such journals exist precisely in order to serve as prosecuting attorneys for the great public in its continuing case against the artist; and what they must establish in order to prove guilt is *that a given writer has produced passages which cannot be misconstrued or half understood without the reader's being painfully aware of his own failure.*

It is not, then, mere difficulty which constitutes the *prima facie* evidence of a writer's contempt for the mass audience, but *unaccustomed* difficulty, a difficulty different from the kinds long so familiar in the classroom that no one any longer expects himself to do more than recognize and label them: Shakespeare, Dante, Whitman, etc. Certain writers are, in fact, more flagrantly difficult than others, and sometimes they are deliberately so; but the public's consciousness of the writer's role in this regard does not always coincide with his own. As far as American serious poets are concerned, though all of them have known for generations that the onerous advantages of best-sellerdom are denied them, they have responded in two quite different ways: some of them writing *as if* for a very few, and some of them, nonetheless, writing *as if* for a popular audience.

What is, or at least, from any historical point of view, ought to be involved is rather a matter of stance than of genuine expectation; because in fact there is little correspondence between the poets' theoretical and actual audiences. Walt Whitman, for instance, theoretically popular poet that he was, had, at the time of publication and, I should guess, will have forever after, a much smaller readership than the theoretically anti-popular poet Edgar Allan Poe. Certainly school children, that largest audience of all, have never been urged to read Whitman as they have been urged to read Poe. Yet this has not kept certain later poets (irony breeding irony in the tangle of misunderstanding), dedicated to widening the audience of verse, from invoking Whitman as their model; while others, content to address an élite, have made their ideal Edgar Poe, at least as reinterpreted by the French *symbolistes*.

In the mid-nineteenth century, the great public needed neither Poe nor Whitman, having still at their disposal the respectable academic bard, Henry Wadsworth Longfellow, and not yet having acquired that fear of Harvard professors which now plays so large a role in political as well as literary matters on the level of mass culture. Both Poe and Whitman were, therefore, found guilty in the treason trial for which only Poe had braced himself: Poe of drunkenness and drug-addiction and the celebration of death; Whitman of blasphemy and obscenity and the celebration of sex. Poe, at least, knew always that he was on trial, while Whitman, more naïvely and more typical of the American writer, thought of himself as wooing an audience, which in fact saw itself not as his beloved but as his judge.

Essential to an understanding of the difficulties of the American writer (especially, but not exclusively, the poet) is an awareness of this conflict of imagined roles, the clash of metaphors on the border between art and life. The relationship of the poet to the audience in the United States is—in *his* consciousness—erotic or sentimental; the relationship of the audience to the poet is—in *its* consciousness—juridical. While the writer may fancy himself pleading a tender suit, or carrying on a cynical seduction, the reader is likely to think of himself as hearing evidence, deciding whether to say, not "no" or "yes," but "guilty" or "innocent": guilty of treason, or innocent by reason of insanity—or even, as in the case of Ezra Pound, *both* at once.

It is, of course, Pound who comes into our minds when we reflect on the trial of the poet. A century ago, it might have been still Poe or Whitman, but neither of these long-dead (and therefore for us inevitably sanctified and forgotten) figures is capable now of stirring passion in the minds of sub-literates, who have no memory. Each age must have its own, brand-new defendants, and the mass audience sitting in judgment in the middle of the twentieth century has tried and sentenced the poet once more, yet as if for the first time, in the person of Ezra Pound. Indeed, they have condemned him with what, from their standpoint, is perfect justice. I do not mean merely that Pound was, indeed, guilty of the charges of abetting anti-Semitism (and more recently anti-Negro feelings), praising Fascism, and condemning the best along with the worst in his own country; the popular mind in America has often regarded with favor enemies of democracy, Jews, and Negroes. I mean that all of the ambitious long poems of our time have been written under Pound's guidance or inspired by his example: Eliot's *The Wasteland*, for instance, and Hart Crane's *The Bridge*, and William Carlos Williams' *Paterson*: all of those fragmented, allusion-laden, imagistic portraits of an atomized world which have so offended the Philistine mind. And I mean, too, that in his *Pisan Cantos* Pound, driven by his tribulations beyond the circle of his bad literary habits and his compulsive political idiocies, has caught the pathos and the comedy involved in the relationship between artist and society in the twentieth century with absolute precision. Both the self-pity of the artist and the complacent brutality of the community that needs and resents him have been dissolved in irony only to be re-created as improbable lyric beauty. These are offenses hard to forgive for those convinced that they should judge and not be judged— certainly not by a mad poet.

Precisely the qualities, however, which have made Pound the prototypical enemy of the people in our time have attracted to him not only certain impotent young cranks who might have been successful Hitlers had time and circumstances conspired, but also the sort of disaffected young poet who turns out in the end to have written the poetry by which an age is remembered. Both kinds of Poundians wrote on the walls of bars and taverns "Ez for Pres," both dreamed him as their ideal anti-President in the time of Eisenhower, while Pound in fact still sat in an insane asylum in Washington—to which he had been remanded, just after World War II, by a jury of his peers, even more eager to find him nuts than to declare him a traitor. And what worthy living poet would such a jury not have found crazy enough to confine, whether or not he had made treasonable broadcasts for Mussolini?

The answer is easy: Robert Frost, through whose intervention Pound was finally released from the madhouse and allowed to return to the place from which he had once raged against his country. For Frost only could our whole nation have consented to parole Pound, just as for Frost only could it mourn officially and without reservations. Certainly it could not have mourned so for, say, T. S. Eliot, who, however sanctimonious in his old age, had once swapped citizenship; or for E. E. Cummings, who despised punctuation and the slogans of advertising; or for Wallace Stevens, who had obviously not even cared to be understood. Indeed, long before his death, the great audience had found Frost guiltless of the ultimate treason, the betrayal of what it defines as "sanity," and considers itself to possess in an eminent degree. Had certain poems of his not become so standard a feature of grade school and high school anthologies ("Mending Wall," for instance, or "Stopping by Woods") that one finally could respond to them no more than to yet another reproduction of the Mona Lisa? Were not other verses of his distributed every year as Christmas cards by his publishers, and were not still others quoted from station platforms and the backs of trains by candidates for political office?

Had he not even been invited by President Kennedy to read a poem of his own composing at the inaugural ceremonies, and had he not actually written one for the occasion, ending with the complacent boast that his appearance there itself inaugurated "A golden age of poetry and power/ Of which this noonday's the beginning hour"? Fortunately, fate fought for him against the adulation of politicians and the crowd, that kindly comic fate which protects great men from their own delusions; he could not read the text, the sun too bright in his aging eyes, and had to give up a television première in favor of more conventional modes of publication. But the damage had already been done; Frost had become in effect the first Poet Laureate of the United States, an honor and indignity no other American had ever endured. And the nation, which is to say, the mass audience, smiled at his discomfiture and applauded his honors.

But why did they feel so at ease in his presence? Was it merely that he had lived so long? There was enough in his career to dismay them, had they known or cared. He had begun as alienated from them as any poet they had ever cast in the role of utter villain; had fled to England already middle-aged and convinced apparently that he could make his American reputation only second-hand; had withdrawn from the pressures of getting and spending, as well as the obligations of citizenship, to sit alone in a back-country which its own inhabitants were deserting as fast as they could; had boasted all his life long of preferring loneliness to gregariousness, night to day, cold to warmth, melancholy to joy; had mocked in more than one poem the penny-saved-penny-earned philosophy of the American Philistine's laureate, Benjamin Franklin; had celebrated himself as a genius "too lofty and original to rage," and hinted that his message was not for everyone but hidden away "under a spell so the wrong ones can't find it."

In a long and, I suspect, not much read poem called "New Hampshire," Frost has spoken, for once, without defensive pretense or disguise, as an artist—though he assumes the mask of a novelist rather than that of a maker of verses—and has identified without equivocation the bitterness that underlies his vocation as a poet.

> I make a virtue of my suffering
> From nearly everything that goes on round me.
> In other words, I know where I am,
> Being the creature of literature I am,
> I shall not lack for pain to keep me awake.
> Kit Marlowe taught me how to say my prayers:
> "Why, this is Hell, nor am I out of it!"

He has spoken elsewhere quite as frankly of his audience, remarking, with the quiet and devastating irony that characterizes his best verse:

> They cannot look out far.
> They cannot look in deep.
> But when was that ever a bar
> To any watch they keep?

Yet reading this epitaph upon the grave of their fondest pretensions, the great public, which does not recognize irony, could see only what short words Frost used and how he respected both the syntax and the iambic measure which they had learned in school to honor, if not use. If he was "lofty and original," he did indeed keep it a secret, as he slyly declared, from the "wrong ones," from the very ones who made up his mass following, who hated all other living poets, but loved him because he seemed to them a reproach to those others who made them feel inferior with their allusions to Provençal and Chinese poetry, their subverted syntax and fractured logic, their unreasonable war against the iambic, their preference for strange, Mediterranean lands and big cities. Even if they themselves inhabited such cities, the Frostians knew that it was not fitting to write poetry about them; one wrote, like Frost, *not* Eliot or Pound, about hills and trees, streams and animals. Was this not what the Romantic poets, whom certain wiseacre moderns liked to mock, had written about; and did they not now venerate the memory of those poets whom they had despised, perhaps, in school, but who at a distance benefited by the illusion of attractiveness which attaches itself to terrors far enough removed: home, mother, the bad weather of our childhood?

Pound and Frost: these become the ideal antagonists of contemporary culture for the popular mind, which knows such myths better than any poems. The award of the Bollingen Prize for Poetry to Pound in 1949, while he was still a patient in St. Elizabeth's Hospital, made it all a matter of public record. First the intellectual community itself was rent by disagreement about the wisdom of honoring the verse of one whose ideas they condemned (at the high point, an eminent poet challenged to a duel a well-known editor who, alas, never realized he was being challenged); and then the great audience, which has never noticed before or since any other winner of a poetry prize, found a voice in Robert Hillyer and through him joined the debàte. In a series of articles for the *Saturday Review*, that second-rate poet vented his own frustration, as well as the public's rage, at the best poetry of the century, using Pound as his whipping-boy and Frost as his whip.

For this reason, then, we must come to terms with the legend of Pound and Frost, on our way toward a consideration of their verse. Indeed, not only the mass audience (to whom Pound is a curse-word in Hillyer's diatribe and a picture in *Life*, Frost an honorific in the same diatribe and a face on the television screen) but the poets themselves have been victimized by the myths mass culture has imposed on them. Under pressure, the poet tends to become his legend: Frost begins to believe he invented New England, and Pound to consider himself the discoverer of the Italian Riviera. And who is crude enough to remind the one that he was born in California, the other that he came from Hailey, Idaho? In the end, Frost almost succeeded in turning into the cracker-barrel philosopher from Vermont he played, spouting homely wisdom and affecting to despise the crackpot ideas of all intellectuals, while Pound came near to transforming himself into a caricature of the cosmopolitan esthete, a polyglot unsure before the fact whether the word trembling on his lips would emerge as Creek or Catalan or pure Mandarin.

Worst of all, Frost finally permitted himself to be cast— in complete contempt of his deepest commitments, which are to alienation and terror—as the beaming prophet of the New Frontier, court-jester to the Kennedy administration, even as Pound was content to mug his way through the role of traitor-in-chief to a nation, though he seemed more a clown in the entourage of Mussolini. And for accepting such public roles at the cost of scanting the private tasks imposed on them by their talents, these two chief poets of our time must stand trial in quite another court, the court of criticism. Before the tribunal of critics, they will not be permitted to plead that they voted right (or wrong), or even that they were in their writings comprehensible (or obscure)—only that, keeping faith with their gifts, they wrote certain lines which no literate American, perhaps no educated man anywhere, will willingly forget.

Similarly, the charges against them will not be that they voted wrong (or right), or that they were obscure (or comprehensible)—only that, pursuing their own legendary images, they wrote dull or trivial, arch or pedantic, smug or self-pitying verse; that, moreover, by their poses, they have made even their best work unavailable to certain readers: passionate liberals and sensitive Jews in the case of Pound, the disaffected urban young and a vast number of Europeans of all persuasions in the case of Frost; and that, finally, by a strange sort of retrospective falsification, they have seemed to alter the meaning, the very music of the lines in which they have, in fact, transcended the limitations of their roles and of the weaknesses in themselves out of which the mass mind created those roles to begin with.

How much time will have to go by before we are able to read either one of them without these prejudices? If there were, indeed, a justice in the world higher than that of the critics, as the critics' is higher than that of the mass audience, both Pound and Frost would be condemned to spend that time in purgatory—a single chamber in a shared purgatory, where Frost would say over and over to Pound:

> And lonely as it is that loneliness
> Will be more lonely ere it will be less—
> A blanker whiteness of benighted snow
> With no expression, nothing to express.
>
> They cannot scare me with their empty spaces
> Between stars—on stars where no human race is.
> I have it in me so much nearer home
> To scare myself with my own desert places.

while Pound would shout back ceaselessly:

> Thou art a beaten dog beneath the hail,
> A swollen magpie in a fitful sun,
> Half black half white
> Nor knowst' you wing from tail
> Pull down thy vanity
> > How mean thy hates
> Fostered in falsity,
> > Pull down thy vanity,
> Rathe to destroy, niggard in charity,
> Pull down thy vanity,
> > I say pull down.

The Death of the Old Men

It is with a sense of terror that the practicing novelist in the United States confronts his situation today; for the Old Men are gone, the two great presences who made possible both homage and blasphemy, both imitation and resistance. It is a little like the death of a pair of fathers or a pair of gods; like, perhaps, the removal of the sky, an atmosphere we were no longer aware we breathed, a firmament we had forgotten sheltered us. The sky we can pretend, at least, is Heaven; the space behind the sky we cannot help suspecting is a vacuum.

At any rate, both Faulkner and Hemingway are dead, a slow suicide by the bottle in one case, and a quick one by the gun in the other, as seems appropriate to our tradition; and we must come to terms with our surviving selves; yet first, of course, with them. Their deaths have made eminently clear what the passage of time had already begun to establish (and our sense of outrage over the awarding of the Nobel Prize to John Steinbeck merely emphasizes the fact): that these two writers represent to us and to the world the real meaning and the true success of the novel in America during the first half of the twentieth century.

Nevertheless, it must be added immediately that the moment of their world fame has not coincided with the period in which they produced their greatest work. In a sense, each received the Nobel Prize posthumously, though both lived long enough to accept it with thanks; and Faulkner, at least—perhaps Hemingway, too, though we still await evidence of this—continued to write to within months of his actual death. Yet each, in the last decade or so of his life, had published either second-rate imitations of his own best work (Faulkner's *The Town* and *The Mansion*, Hemingway's *The Old Man and the Sea*) or atrocious parodies of that work (Faulkner's *The Fable*, Hemingway's *Across the River and into the Trees*). Naturally, there are in all their books, even the worst, small local triumphs, flashes of something we wonder whether we perceive or remember; but we should not, in any case, deceive ourselves about either how bad their late books are or the way in which they are bad.

If Hemingway and Faulkner ended by parodying themselves, it is because their method was from the beginning actual parody or something (for which we have, alas, no name in the critical lexicon) which attained its effects by skirting the edge of parody. We should not forget what we are now in a position to see clearly, when polemics and envy no longer matter: that our two greatest recent novelists were essentially comic writers. We realize now that *The Torrents of Spring*, the Hemingway travesty of Sherwood Anderson, is not a trivial *jeu d'esprit* but one of his central achievements; and we have long been approaching the realization that the most abiding creation of Faulkner is the Snopes family, especially Flem Snopes, that modern, American, bourgeois, ridiculous version of Faust. We should not, then, be surprised that, having exhausted the worlds they began by caricaturing (and having succeeded in those very worlds at the same time), the two comic geniuses of our century ended by caricaturing themselves.

Despite their self-travesty, however, both Hemingway and Faulkner still continue to influence the fiction of younger men, and, even more deeply, the image of themselves as writers with which such younger men begin—the possibilities of success and failure they are able to imagine as they start their careers. The legend of Faulkner is a parable of success snatched from failure: the artist abiding, in loneliness and behind a smoke screen of lies, the day when the neglect of the great audience and the critics (everyone is aware that at the end of World War II no novel of Faulkner's was in print) will turn to adulation. There is something profoundly comic and satisfying in the notion of the great talent lying hidden, like Poe's purloined letter, in that obvious place which guarantees its invisibility, the place of its belonging and origin; of Faulkner safely concealed until the destined moment of revelation—in his home town, in the very Oxford, Mississippi, where, just after his death, Federal troops were deployed to insure the registration of a single, indifferent Negro student in a less-than-mediocre university. It is as if history itself were subscribing to Faulkner's view of the South—his notion of a baffled aspiration to the tragic, nurtured by dreams and memories, falling away always, in fact, into melodrama or farce. Surely Faulkner is involved as deeply in the legend of the South (which, indeed, he has helped create) as in the all-American morality play of success and failure. In a sense, he can be seen as the last of the old Southern writers, the final descendant of Edgar Allan Poe, the ultimate seedy Dandy, haunted by the blackness of darkness embodied in the Negro, and seeking in alcohol an even blacker darkness, in which the first may be, for a little while at least, lost. Unlike Hemingway's death, the death of Faulkner escaped both mythicizing and exploitation in the press, perhaps because the pressures which drove him to his last spree had already become a legend and certainly because they drive us all, so that no one need feel guilty of his death.

Faulkner died as the culture which sustained him was also dying, died in history, that is to say, rather than against it. For surely the Old South—as he foresaw and desired—cannot long survive him; and though we can applaud no more wholeheartedly than he the emergence of the New South, whose coming Faulkner projected in terms of the rise of the Snopeses, we can find in him a model for how best to hate it, along with the New North and the New West—how to hate any world to which we are bound by the accident of birth and a heritage of love. How to deal with Faulkner himself is another matter. We have already begun to teach him in the universities; and when, inevitably, Negroes come in large numbers to the classrooms of colleges even in the deepest South, he will be waiting for them there to show them how they, too, must learn to excoriate not the Other but themselves. Meanwhile, the tourist booths in his native Oxford are already displaying picture postcards of Faulkner's house; and when the plaque or monument to his memory is dedicated, as it must be soon, when speeches by fellow-citizens he despised are duly delivered, the joke he all along foresaw will be manifest. It is, of course, a joke we have heard before, yet a healthy one for young writers of fiction to be told over and over.

The legend of Hemingway is more commonplace: like the legend of Scott Fitzgerald, for instance, a mythic retelling of the failure of success; but, in Hemingway's case, the old story has somehow taken us by surprise. Only now has it become clear to all of us, for instance, what some of us have long suspected—that his truest strengths presented themselves all along in the guise of weaknesses, his most disabling weaknesses in the guise of strengths. Only the ultimate disaster was able to strip Hemingway of bravado and swagger and reveal behind the mask of the self-loved bully, which it pleased him to put on, the figure of the scared poet, which he hated to confess himself. He, who had lived for so long elsewhere, had come again to America, to the American West, to be stripped naked and to die, following, in a fated way, the path of Gary Cooper, with whose legendary image he had hopelessly confused himself by then. When Cooper died, Hemingway sent a strange telegram of condolence to the survivors, saying that he had never expected the actor to "beat him to the barn."

It was for the "barn," then, that Hemingway felt himself to be "headed" even before he pulled the trigger, a place of warmth and darkness where he could rest from the long day's posturing in the pasture. Enough of being the prize Bull, watched warily over the fence by idle onlookers! In the barn, perhaps, and just before sleep, Hemingway could become again the Steer he had originally imagined himself —not the doomed, splendid victim in the bull ring (this is the role of the celebrity rather than the writer), only the patient nudger of bulls on the way to the ring. In *The Sun Also Rises*, which seems now the greatest of his novels, it is the image of the Steer which possesses Hemingway, and this is appropriate enough in a book whose protagonist is impotent. Moreover, the castrated anti-hero of Hemingway's first novel is succeeded by the deserted anti-hero of his next, *A Farewell to Arms*; while beside these two stand the comic alter egos of Jake Barnes, Yogi Johnson of *The Torrents of Spring*, and, especially, Nick Adams, nearest thing to a frank self-portrait in Hemingway's work. Nick, who continues to reappear in the later fiction, is already set in those early stories which Hemingway gathered together in *In Our Time* —a harried, frightened boy, who can witness but not act, register but not influence events.

In the mouths of his early non-heroes, in flight from war, incapable of love, victims of history and helpless beholders of infamy, the famous Hemingway style seems suitable, really functional. Such anti-heroes demand anti-rhetoric, since for them there are no viable, new, noble phrases to replace the outworn old ones—only the simplest epithets, and certain short-breathed phrases, not related or subordinated to each other, but loosely linked by the most non-committal of conjunctions: *and . . . and . . . and . . .* In a world of non-relation, only non-syntax tells the truth as in a world of non-communication, only a minimal speech, the next best thing to silence, the equivalent of silence, gives a sense of reality. In the Hemingway style, so simple at first glance, a score of influences are fused: the sophisticated baby talk of Gertrude Stein; the passionate provincial stutter of Sherwood Anderson; the blending of poetry and dialect invented by Mark Twain; the laconic idiocy of upper-class British speech; the muttering of drunks at bars, and, most notably perhaps, the reticent speech of the American Indian and of the white frontiersman who imitated him.

Beyond a few deep, childhood memories of actual Indians, it is apparently through books that Hemingway learned to write Hemingway-ese—through the eye rather than the ear. If his language is colloquial, it is *written* colloquial; for he was constitutionally incapable of hearing English as it was spoken around him. To a critic who once asked him why his characters all spoke alike, Hemingway answered, "Because I never listen to anybody." Except, one imagines, to himself, to his own monologues, held, drunk, or sober, over a book or before a mirror, in the loneliness of his own head. He was, of all eminent writers, the most nearly inarticulate—garrulous, when garrulous at all, like the friendly drunk who claims your ear and at great length manages to say nothing. To the end of his life, "articulate" was to Hemingway a curse word, an epithet applied with mingled admiration and contempt to certain rival writers. And yet he, who spoke with difficulty, and surely wrote with more, managed to invent, without betraying his inarticulateness, one of the most imitated prose styles of all time.

What terror drove him to make speech of near-silence we can only guess; but whatever the spur, he made, with the smallest verbal means any major novelist ever had at his disposal, a dazzling success. What was in him he exploited fully, though too fully, too early in the game, perhaps. For the kind of perfection he attained was drastically limited, could only be reached once and for all, without the possibility of further development. Certainly, after the first two novels and the early stories, he was able only to echo, in the end parody, himself. But he was not, of course, his only parodist. In the conversation of the young, life frequently imitates art; and by a fitting irony, Hemingway, who listened to no one, was, after a while, listened to and emulated by all. He invented, scarcely knowing it, a kind of speech adequate to an age: the age of between-the-wars—when the young delighted in being told over and over (since they prized their disillusion as their sole claim to superiority over the past) that all was nothing, that nothing was all.

Hemingway's initial appeal, then, was as the exploiter of the self-pity of the first in a long series of American Lost Generations. But the feeling he evoked went deeper than mere self-pity, touched the depths of a genuine nihilism which may not have told the whole truth about existence, but which told a truth for which that generation hungered.

That he loved nothingness more than being, death more than his own life, and failure more than success, is the glory of the early Hemingway, which is to say, of the best Hemingway. His authentic work has a single subject: the flirtation with death, the approach to the void. And this subject he managed to treat in a kind of language which betrays neither the bitterness of death nor the terror of the void.

There is, however, a price to be paid for living always with the savor of one's own death on the tongue. One can sustain the mood of Ecclesiastes only in brief, ecstatic moments. The living experience of the void around us, like the living experience of God, is inevitably followed by what the Saints have called a dark night of the soul, doubly dark when the initial vision is itself of nothingness. And in the darkness, one is tempted to leave off one's death, to escape into suicide. To exorcise this temptation, to immunize himself against the urge toward self-destruction, Hemingway evolved a career of vicarious dying, beginning at the bull ring, and (so easily does the coin flip over) of vicarious killing in which lion and rhinoceros served as substitutes for the hunted self. In 1936, he wrote, speaking of himself—the only beast in view—in the third person: "If he had not spent so much time at shooting and the bull ring . . . he might have written much more. On the other hand, he might have shot himself."

But he did shoot himself in the end, losing finally the life for which he had paid so terrible a price. He became, in the course of time, the *persona* he had invented to preserve himself, became the hunter, the *aficionado*, the gusty, super-masculine, swaggering hero—in short, the Bull. Abandoning, first in life and then in art, the role of the anti-hero, the despised Steer, in whose weakness lay his true strength, Hemingway became first a fiction of his own contriving, then the creature of articles in newspapers and magazines, as unreal as a movie star or a fashion model. And it was the unreal Hemingway who wrote the later books, creating a series of heroes no more real than himself: men who sought rather than fled unreal wars, and who, in the arms of unreal women, achieved unreal delights. The boy, Nick Adams, who dreamed the first stories, the son of a failed father, proud only of his impotence, became himself a successful imaginary father, the legendary "Papa" of the newspaper columnists.

Beginning with the confusion of *To Have and Have Not*, rising to a climax in the fake nobility and sentimental politics of *For Whom the Bell Tolls*, and culminating in the sloppy self-adulation of *Across the River and into the Trees*, Hemingway betrayed again and again the bleak truth it had been given him to know, betrayed death and the void. Naturally enough, his anti-style went to pieces as his anti-vision of the world was falsified, becoming a manner, a tic, a bore. In *The Old Man and the Sea*, trying to recapture the spare horror of his early work, he produced only an echo, a not-quite-convincing counterfeit of his best. All this he must have known. Certainly, after *The Old Man and the Sea*, self-doubt overwhelmed him as the felt failure of his later work undermined his confidence even in the early, and the confusion about his identity (was he Papa? Gary Cooper? Nick? Jake Barnes?) mounted toward the pitch of madness. In his distress, he scurried back into his earlier life, seeking some self that might have written books worthy of survival. The articles on bullfighting in Spain which appeared in *Life* shortly before his death, the book on the 1920's in Paris on which he was working at the very end, are evidence of this search: a man without a future ransacking the past for the meaning of his career.

But the meaning of his career was there all the time in the authentic work of his youth, as the critics might have told him had Hemingway been able to read them less defensively. When he turned to the critics, however (and for all his pretended contempt, he was driven to them), he could find there, in his torment and self-doubt, only the reservations, the cruel judgments, the unkind remarks. And to whom could he have appealed for reassurance anyhow, having made himself the sole Papa of his world? At last, even the flesh betrayed him, the great, muscular body he had willed for himself shrinking beneath his handsome, old-man's head and his small-boy's beautiful smile. On the night before his death, we are told, he could not find a pair of pants he would wear, for even retailored to appease his vanity, they sagged around his skinny shanks. How to exorcise the demons, then, when not only art had failed him, but his body, too, and with it the possibilities of ritual killing, those vicarious deaths with which he had bought, for years, his own life?

He had long been unable to hunt big game, and after a while could no longer even shoot birds from cover, since he could not manage to crouch down. Now, perhaps, the moment had arrived when he would no longer be able even to fire walking. One quarry was left him only, the single beast he had always had it in his power to destroy, the single beast worthy of him: himself. And he took his shotgun in hand, improbably reasserting his old faith at the last possible instant, renewing his lapsed allegiance to death and silence. With a single shot he redeemed his best work from his worst, his art from himself, his vision of truth from the lies of his adulators.

In any case, both early and late, at his best and at his worst, Hemingway, like Faulkner, continued to influence the actual practice of the younger writers of fiction. Yet his influence has worked quite differently from Faulkner's. Hemingway, that is to say, has invented a style to which it is impossible for more recent American novelists not to respond, in one way or another; but he has not, in the United States at least, founded a school. Faulkner, on the other hand, whose style is impossible to imitate fruitfully, is the founder of an important school of fiction, which, in its several subdivisions, fills the pages of our magazines and books to this very moment.

There are, it is true, a few self-declared disciples of Hemingway: writers of "hard-boiled" fiction, who exploit a certain tough masculinity and a certain boyish ideal of heroism, neither of which quite successfully conceals a typical brand of sentimentality, an overriding self-pity. John O'Hara, for instance, or even Norman Mailer and Vance Bourjaily, make such claims; but, in the end, they are less like Hemingway than they think—or, perhaps, only assert. The one line of fiction which demonstrably descends from Hemingway is not quite literature: a special sort of vulgar, pseudo-realistic detective story, that grows progressively more debased as it passes from Dashiell Hammett to Raymond Chandler to Mickey Spillane to Richard S. Prather (the last sold exclusively in paperbacks and to the young, to the tune of some fifteen or twenty million copies).

On the level of art, Hemingway is a diffuse influence, found everywhere and nowhere, more often in nuance and inflection than in overt imitation, and especially in a language not merely written but spoken by two generations of young people, who may, indeed, claim to find him unsympathetic. No one these days, however, claims to find Faulkner unsympathetic. Such an assertion would be considered blasphemous by most literate Americans under, say, forty, especially by those with any pretensions to being writers themselves. Among them, he is a universal favorite; and everywhere his popularity increases, even among the aging, who despised him in the Thirties (for his presumed reactionary social content) only to make amends in the Sixties.

Moreover, there descends from him what has already become a tradition, a familiar kind of fiction which takes the South as its background, terror as its subject, the grotesque as its mode, and which treats the relations of black men and white as the chief symbol of the problem of evil in our time. Actually, three separate groups of writers have derived from Faulkner: the Southern Lady Writers, of whom Katherine Anne Porter is the most distinguished representative, and which includes Carson McCullers, Eudora Welty, Flannery O'Connor; the Effete Dandies or Homosexual Decadents, from Truman Capote to Tennessee Williams; and a one-man line of development, stemming from the popular and anti-feminine elements in Faulkner (so oddly transmuted in the first two groups), in the novels of Robert Penn Warren.

It is, perhaps, because the Negro question continues to be a pressing concern of contemporary America and threatens to become that of the whole western world that Faulkner has seemed a living influence in the sense that Hemingway has not. The mythology of bullfights and safaris and aggressive innocence seems to us, these days, less viable than that of slavery and war and the compounded guilts of segregation. Nonetheless, behind what is parochial and peculiar to him, Faulkner shares with Hemingway certain key experiences—experiences important not only in biographical terms but imaginatively as well—which make it meaningful to speak of both as members of a single generation, that of the Twenties, to which, of course, Scott Fitzgerald and Glenway Wescott also importantly belong, and against which the generation of the Thirties, as well as that of the Forties-Fifties, and that of the Sixties, have had to define themselves.

The New Mutants

A REALIZATION that the legitimate functions of literature are bewilderingly, almost inexhaustibly various has always exhilarated poets and dismayed critics. And critics, therefore, have sought age after age to legislate limits to literature—legitimizing certain of its functions and disavowing others—in hope of insuring to themselves the exhilaration of which they have felt unjustly deprived, and providing for poets the dismay which the critics at least have thought good for them.

Such shifting and exclusive emphasis is not, however, purely the product of critical malice, or even of critical principle. Somehow every period is, to begin with, especially aware of certain functions of literature and especially oblivious to others: endowed with a special sensitivity and a complementary obtuseness, which, indeed, give to that period its characteristic flavor and feel. So, for instance, the Augustan Era is marked by sensitivity in regard to the uses of diction, obtuseness in regard to those of imagery.

What the peculiar obtuseness of the present age may be I find it difficult to say (being its victim as well as its recorder), perhaps toward the didactic or certain modes of the sentimental. I am reasonably sure, however, that our period is acutely aware of the sense in which literature if not invents, at least collaborates in the invention of time. The beginnings of that awareness go back certainly to the beginnings of the Renaissance, to Humanism as a self-conscious movement; though a critical development occurred toward the end of the eighteenth century with the dawning of the Age of Revolution. And we may have reached a second critical point right now.

189

At any rate, we have long been aware (in the last decades uncomfortably aware) that a chief function of literature is to express and in part to create not only theories of time but also attitudes toward time. Such attitudes constitute, however, a politics as well as an esthetics; or, more properly perhaps, a necessary mythological substratum of politics—as, in fact, the conventional terms reactionary, conservative, revolutionary indicate: all involving stances toward the past.

It is with the past, then, that we must start, since the invention of the past seems to have preceded that of the present and the future; and since we are gathered in a university at whose heart stands a library[1]—the latter, like the former, a visible monument to the theory that a chief responsibility of literature is to preserve and perpetuate the past. Few universities are explicitly (and none with any real degree of confidence) dedicated to this venerable goal any longer. The Great Books idea (which once transformed the University of Chicago and lives on now in provincial study groups) was perhaps its last desperate expression. Yet the shaky continuing existence of the universities and the building of new college libraries (with matching Federal funds) remind us not only of that tradition but of the literature created in its name: the neo-epic, for instance, all the way from Dante to Milton; and even the frantically nostalgic Historical Romance, out of the counting house by Sir Walter Scott.

Obviously, however, literature has a contemporary as well as a traditional function. That is to say, it may be dedicated to illuminating the present and the meaning of the present, which is, after all, no more given than the past. Certainly the modern or bourgeois novel was thus contemporary in the hands of its great inventors, Richardson, Fielding, Smollett and Sterne; and it became contemporary again—with, as it were, a sigh of relief—when Flaubert, having plunged deep into the Historical Romance, emerged once more into the present of Emma Bovary. But the second function of the novel tends to transform itself into a third: a revolutionary or

---

[1] "The New Mutants" is a written version of a talk given at the Conference on the Idea of The Future held at Rutgers, in June, 1965. The conference was sponsored by *Partisan Review* and the Congress for Cultural Freedom, with the cooperation of Rutgers, The State University.

prophetic or futurist function; and it is with the latter that I am here concerned.

Especially important for our own time is the sense in which literature first conceived the possibility of the future (rather than an End of Time or an Eternal Return, an Apocalypse or Second Coming); and then furnished that future in joyous or terrified anticipation, thus preparing all of us to inhabit it. Men have dreamed and even written down utopias from ancient times; but such utopias were at first typically allegories rather than projections: nonexistent models against which to measure the real world, exploitations of the impossible (as the traditional name declares) rather than explorations or anticipations or programs of the possible. And, in any event, only recently have such works occupied a position anywhere near the center of literature.

Indeed, the movement of futurist literature from the periphery to the center of culture provides a clue to certain essential meanings of our times and of the art which best reflects it. If we make a brief excursion from the lofty reaches of High Art to the humbler levels of Pop Culture—where radical transformations in literature are reflected in simplified form—the extent and nature of the futurist revolution will become immediately evident. Certainly, we have seen in recent years the purveyors of Pop Culture transfer their energies from the Western and the Dracula-type thriller (last heirs of the Romantic and Gothic concern with the past) to the Detective Story especially in its hard-boiled form (final vulgarization of the realists' dedication to the present) to Science Fiction (a new genre based on hints in Poe and committed to "extrapolating" the future). This development is based in part on the tendency to rapid exhaustion inherent in popular forms; but in part reflects a growing sense of the irrelevance of the past and even of the present to 1965. Surely, there has never been a moment in which the most naïve as well as the most sophisticated have been so acutely aware of how the past threatens momentarily to disappear from the present, which itself seems on the verge of disappearing into the future.

And this awareness functions, therefore, on the level of art as well as entertainment, persuading quite serious writers to emulate the modes of Science Fiction. The novel is most amenable to this sort of adaptation, whose traces we can find in writers as various as

William Golding and Anthony Burgess, William Burroughs and
Kurt Vonnegut, Jr., Harry Matthews and John Barth—to all of
whom young readers tend to respond with a sympathy they do not
feel even toward such forerunners of the mode (still more allegorical than prophetic) as Aldous Huxley, H. G. Wells and George Or-
well. But the influence of Science Fiction can be discerned in poetry
as well, and even in the polemical essays of such polymath prophets
as Wilhelm Reich, Buckminster Fuller, Marshall McLuhan, perhaps also Norman O. Brown. Indeed, in Fuller the prophetic-Sci-
ence-Fiction view of man is always at the point of fragmenting into
verse:

> men are known as being six feet tall
> because that is their tactile limit;
> they are not known by how far we can hear them,
> e.g., as a one-half mile man
> and only to dogs are men known
> by their gigantic olfactoral dimensions. . . .

I am not now interested in analyzing, however, the diction and
imagery which have passed from Science Fiction into post-Modernist literature, but rather in coming to terms with the prophetic content common to both: with the myth rather than the modes of Science Fiction. But that myth is quite simply the myth of the end of
man, of the transcendence or transformation of the human—a vision quite different from that of the extinction of our species by the
Bomb, which seems stereotype rather than archetype and consequently the source of editorials rather than poems. More fruitful
artistically is the prospect of the radical transformation (under the
impact of advanced technology and the transfer of traditional
human functions to machines) of *homo sapiens* into something
else: the emergence—to use the language of Science Fiction itself
—of "mutants" among us.

A simpleminded prevision of this event is to be found in Arthur
C. Clarke's *Childhood's End*, at the conclusion of which the mutated
offspring of parents much like us are about to take off under their
own power into outer space. Mr. Clarke believes that he is talking
about a time still to come because he takes metaphor for fact;

though simply translating "outer space" into "inner space" reveals to us that what he is up to is less prediction than description; since the post-human future is now, and if not we, at least our children, are what it would be comfortable to pretend we still only foresee. But what, in fact, are they: these mutants who are likely to sit before us in class, or across from us at the dinner table, or who stare at us with hostility from street corners as we pass?

Beatniks or hipsters, layabouts and drop-outs we are likely to call them with corresponding hostility—or more elegantly, but still without sympathy, passive onlookers, abstentionists, spiritual cata-tonics. There resides in all of these terms an element of truth, at least about the relationship of the young to what we have defined as the tradition, the world we have made for them; and if we turn to the books in which they see their own destiny best represented (*The Clockwork Orange*, say, or *On the Road* or *Temple of Gold*), we will find nothing to contradict that truth. Nor will we find any-thing to expand it, since the young and their laureates avoid on principle the kind of definition (even of themselves) for which we necessarily seek.

Let us begin then with the negative definition our own hostility suggests, since this is all that is available to us, and say that the "mutants" in our midst are nonparticipants in the past (though our wisdom assures us this is impossible), dropouts from history. The withdrawal from school, so typical of their generation and so in-scrutable to ours, is best understood as a lived symbol of their rejection of the notion of cultural continuity and progress, which our graded educational system represents in institutional form. It is not merely a matter of their rejecting what happens to have hap-pened just before them, as the young do, after all, in every age; but of their attempting to disavow the very idea of the past, of their seeking to avoid recapitulating it step by step—up to the point of graduation into the present.

Specifically, the tradition from which they strive to disengage is the tradition of the human, as the West (understanding the West to extend from the United States to Russia) has defined it, Humanism itself, both in its bourgeois and Marxist forms; and more especially, the cult of reason—that dream of Socrates, redreamed by the Ren-aissance and surviving all travesties down to only yesterday. To be sure, there have long been antirational forces at work in the West, including primitive Christianity itself; but the very notion of literary culture is a product of Humanism, as the early Christians knew (setting fire to libraries), so that the Church in order to sponsor poets had first to come to terms with reason itself by way of Aquinas and Aristotle.

Only with Dada was the notion of an antirational antiliterature born; and Dada became Surrealism, i.e., submitted to the influence of those last neo-Humanists, those desperate Socratic Cabalists, Freud and Marx—dedicated respectively to contriving a rationale of violence and a rationale of impulse. The new irrationalists, however, deny all the apostles of reason, Freud as well as Socrates; and if they seem to exempt Marx, this is because they know less about him, have heard him evoked less often by the teachers they are driven to deny. Not only do they reject the Socratic adage that the unexamined life is not worth living, since for them precisely the unexamined life is the only one worth enduring at all. But they also abjure the Freudian one: "Where id was, ego shall be," since for them the true rallying cry is, "Let id prevail over ego, impulse over order," or—in negative terms—"Freud is a fink!"

The first time I heard this irreverent charge from the mouth of a student some five or six years ago (I who had grown up thinking of Freud as a revolutionary, a pioneer), I knew that I was already in the future; though I did not yet suspect that there would be no room in that future for the university system to which I had devoted my life. Kerouac might have told me so, or Ginsberg, or even so polite and genteel a spokesman for youth as J. D. Salinger, but I was too aware of what was wrong with such writers (their faults more readily apparent to my taste than their virtues) to be sensitive to the truths they told. It took, therefore, certain public events to illuminate (for me) the literature which might have illuminated them.

I am thinking, of course, of the recent demonstrations at Berkeley and elsewhere, whose ostensible causes were civil rights or freedom of speech or Vietnam, but whose not so secret slogan was all the time: *The Professor is a Fink!* And what an array of bad antiacademic novels, I cannot help reminding myself, written by disgruntled professors, created the mythology out of which that slogan grew. Each generation of students is invented by the generation of teachers just before them; but how different they are in dream and fact—as different as self-hatred and its reflection in another. How different the professors in Jeremy Larner's *Drive, He Said* from those even in Randall Jarrell's *Pictures from an Institution* or Mary McCarthy's *Groves of Academe.*

To be sure, many motives operated to set the students in action, some of them imagined in no book, however good or bad. Many of the thousands who resisted or shouted on campuses did so in the name of naïve or disingenuous or even nostalgic politics (be careful what you wish for in your middle age, or your children will parody it forthwith!); and sheer ennui doubtless played a role along with a justified rage against the hypocrisies of academic life. Universities have long rivaled the churches in their devotion to institutionalizing hypocrisy; and more recently they have outstripped television itself (which most professors affect to despise even more than they despise organized religion) in the institutionalization of boredom.

But what the students were protesting in large part, I have come to believe, was the very notion of man which the universities sought to impose upon them: that bourgeois-Protestant version of Humanism, with its view of man as justified by rationality, work, duty, vocation, maturity, success; and its concomitant understanding of childhood and adolescence as a temporarily privileged time of preparation for assuming those burdens. The new irrationalists, however, are prepared to advocate prolonging adolescence to the grave, and are ready to dispense with school as an outlived excuse for leisure. To them work is as obsolete as reason, a vestige (already dispensable for large numbers) of an economically marginal, pre-automated world; and the obsolescence of the two adds up to the obsolescence of everything our society understands by maturity.

Nor is it in the name of an older more valid Humanistic view of man that the new irrationalists would reject the WASP version; Rabelais is as alien to them as Benjamin Franklin. Disinterested scholarship, reflection, the life of reason, a respect for tradition stir (however dimly and confusedly) chiefly their contempt; and the Abbey of Theleme would seem as sterile to them as Robinson Crusoe's Island. To the classroom, the library, the laboratory, the office conference and the meeting of scholars, they prefer the demonstration, the sit-in, the riot: the mindless unity of an impassioned crowd (with guitars beating out the rhythm in the background), whose immediate cause is felt rather than thought out, whose ultimate cause is itself. In light of this, the Teach-in, often ill understood because of an emphasis on its declared political ends, can be seen as implicitly a parody and mockery of the real classroom: related to the actual business of the university, to real teaching, only as the Demonstration Trial (of Dimitrov, of the Soviet Doctors, of Eichmann) to real justice or Demonstration Voting (for one party or a token two) to real suffrage.

At least, since Berkeley (or perhaps since Martin Luther King provided students with new paradigms for action) the choice has been extended beyond what the earlier laureates of the new youth could imagine in the novel: the nervous breakdown at home rather than the return to "sanity" and school, which was the best Salinger could invent for Franny and Holden; or Kerouac's way out for his "saintly" vagrants, that "road" from nowhere to noplace with homemade gurus at the way stations. The structures of those fictional vaudevilles between hard covers that currently please the young *(Catch 22, V., A Mother's Kisses)*, suggest in their brutality and discontinuity, their politics of mockery, something of the spirit of the student demonstrations; but only Jeremy Larner, as far as I know, has dealt explicitly with the abandonment of the classroom in favor of the Dionysiac pack, the turning from *polis* to *thiasos*, from forms of social organization traditionally thought of as male to the sort of passionate community attributed by the ancients to females out of control.

Conventional slogans in favor of "Good Works" (pious emendations of existing social structures, or extensions of accepted "rights" to excluded groups) though they provide the motive power of such protests are irrelevant to their form and their final significance. They become their essential selves, i.e., genuine new forms of rebellion, when the demonstrators hoist (as they did in the final stages of the Berkeley protests) the sort of slogan which embarrasses not only fellow travelers but even the bureaucrats who direct the initial stages of the revolt: at the University of California, the single four-letter word no family newspaper would reprint, though no member of a family who could read was likely not to know it.

It is possible to argue on the basis of the political facts themselves that the word "fuck" entered the whole scene accidentally (there were only four students behind the "Dirty Speech Movement," only fifteen hundred kids could be persuaded to demonstrate for it, etc., etc.). But the prophetic literature which anticipates the movement indicates otherwise, suggesting that the logic of their illogical course eventually sets the young against language itself, against the very counters of logical discourse. They seek an antilanguage of protest as inevitably as they seek antipoems and antinovels, end with the ultimate antiword, which the demonstrators at Berkeley disingenuously claimed stood for FREEDOM UNDER CLARK KERR.

Esthetics, however, had already anticipated politics in this regard; porno-poetry preceding and preparing the way for what Lewis Feuer has aptly called porno-politics. Already in 1963, in an essay entitled *"Phi Upsilon Kappa,"* the young poet Michael McClure was writing: "Gregory Corso has asked me to join with him in a project to free the word FUCK from its chains and strictures. I leap to make some new freedom. . . ." And McClure's own "Fuck Ode" is a product of this collaboration, as the very name of Ed Sanders' journal, *Fuck You,* is the creation of an analogous impulse. The aging critics of the young who have dealt with the Berkeley demonstrations in such journals as *Commentary* and the *New Leader* do not, however, read either Sanders' porno-pacifist magazine or *Kulchur,* in which McClure's manifesto was first printed —the age barrier separating readership in the United States more effectively than class, political affiliation, or anything else.

Their sense of porno-esthetics is likely to come from deserters from their own camp, chiefly Norman Mailer, and especially his recent *An American Dream,* which represents the entry of antilanguage (extending the tentative explorations of "The Time of Her Time") into the world of the middle-aged, both on the level of mass culture and that of yesterday's ex-Marxist, post-Freudian *avant-garde.* Characteristically enough, Mailer's book has occasioned in the latter quarters reviews as irrelevant, incoherent, misleading and fundamentally scared as the most philistine responses to the Berkeley demonstrations, Philip Rahv and Stanley Edgar Hyman providing two egregious examples. Yet elsewhere (in sectors held by those more at ease with their own conservatism, i.e., without defunct radicalisms to uphold) the most obscene forays of the young are being met with a disheartening kind of tolerance and even an attempt to adapt them to the conditions of commodity art.

But precisely here, of course, a disconcerting irony is involved; for after a while, there will be no Rahvs and Hymans left to shock —antilanguage becoming mere language with repeated use and in the face of acceptance; so that all sense of exhilaration will be lost along with the possibility of offense. What to do then except to choose silence, since raising the ante of violence is ultimately self-defeating; and the way of obscenity in any case leads as naturally to silence as to further excess? Moreover, to the talkative heirs of Socrates, silence is the one offense that never wears out, the radicalism that can never become fashionable; which is why, after the obscene slogan has been hauled down, a blank placard is raised in its place.

There are difficulties, to be sure, when one attempts to move from the politics of silence to an analogous sort of poetry. The opposite number to the silent picketer would be the silent poet, which is a contradiction in terms; yet there are these days nonsingers of (perhaps) great talent who shrug off the temptation to song with the muttered comment, "Creativity is out." Some, however, make literature of a kind precisely at the point of maximum tension between the tug toward silence and the pull toward publication. Music is a better language really for saying what one would prefer not to say at all—and all the way from certain sorts of sufficiently cool jazz to Rock and Roll (with its minimal lyrics that defy understanding on a first hearing), music is the preferred art of the irrationalists.

But some varieties of skinny poetry seem apt, too (as practised, say, by Robert Creeley after the example of W. C. Williams), since their lines are three parts silence to one part speech:

> *My lady*
> *fair with*
> *soft*
> *arms, what*
> *can I say to*
> *you—words, words* . .

And, of course, fiction aspiring to become Pop Art, say, *An American Dream* (with the experiments of Hemingway and Nathanael West behind it), works approximately as well, since clichés are almost as inaudible as silence itself. The point is not to shout, not to insist, but to hang cool, to baffle all mothers, cultural and spiritual as well as actual.

When the Town Council in Venice, California was about to close down a particularly notorious beatnik cafe, a lady asked to testify before them, presumably to clinch the case against the offenders. What she reported, however, was that each day as she walked by the cafe and looked in its windows, she saw the unsavory types who inhabited it "just standing there, looking—nonchalant." And, in a way, her improbable adjective does describe a crime against her world; for nonchaleur ("cool," the futurists themselves would prefer to call it) is the essence of their life style as well as of the literary styles to which they respond: the offensive style of those who are not so much *for* anything in particular, as "with it" in general.

But such an attitude is as remote from traditional "alienation," with its profound longing to end disconnection, as it is from ordinary forms of allegiance, with their desperate resolve not to admit disconnection. The new young celebrate disconnection—accept it as one of the necessary consequences of the industrial system which has delivered them from work and duty, of that welfare state which makes disengagement the last possible virtue, whether it call itself Capitalist, Socialist or Communist. "Detachment" is the traditional name for the stance the futurists assume; but "detachment" carries with it irrelevant religious, even specifically Christian overtones. The post-modernists are surely in some sense "mystics," religious at least in a way they do not ordinarily know how to confess, but they are not Christians.

Indeed, they regard Christianity, quite as the Black Muslims (with whom they have certain affinities) do, as a white ideology: merely one more method—along with Humanism, technology, Marxism—of imposing "White" or Western values on the colored rest of the world. To the new barbarian, however, that would-be post-Humanist (who is in most cases the white offspring of Christian forebears), his whiteness is likely to seem if not a stigma and

symbol of shame, at least the outward sign of his exclusion from all
that his Christian Humanist ancestors rejected in themselves and
projected mythologically upon the colored man. For such reasons,
his religion, when it becomes explicit, claims to be derived from
Tibet or Japan or the ceremonies of the Plains Indians, or is composed out of the non-Christian submythology that has grown up
among Negro jazz musicians and in the civil rights movement.
When the new barbarian speaks of "soul," for instance, he means
not "soul" as in Heaven, but as in "soul music" or even "soul
food."

It is all part of the attempt of the generation under twenty-five,
not exclusively in its most sensitive members but especially in them,
to become Negro, even as they attempt to become poor or prera-
tional. About this particular form of psychic assimilation I have
written sufficiently in the past (summing up what I had been long
saying in chapters seven and eight of *Waiting for the End*), neglect-
ing only the sense in which what starts as a specifically American
movement becomes an international one, spreading to the *yé-yé*
girls of France or the working-class entertainers of Liverpool with
astonishing swiftness and ease.

What interests me more particularly right now is a parallel as-
similationist attempt, which may, indeed, be more parochial and is
certainly most marked at the moment in the Anglo-Saxon world,
i.e., in those cultural communities most totally committed to bourgeois-Protestant values and surest that they are unequivocally
"white." I am thinking of the effort of young men in England and
the United States to assimilate into themselves (or even to assimilate themselves into) that otherness, that sum total of rejected
psychic elements which the middle-class heirs of the Renaissance
have identified with "woman." To become new men, these children
of the future seem to feel, they must not only become more Black
than White but more female than male. And it is natural that the
need to make such an adjustment be felt with especial acuteness in
post-Protestant highly industrialized societies, where the functions
regarded as specifically male for some three hundred years tend
most rapidly to become obsolete.

Surely, in America, machines already perform better than humans a large number of those aggressive-productive activities which

our ancestors considered man's special province, even his *raison d'être*. Not only has the male's prerogative of making things and money (which is to say, of working) been preempted, but also his time-honored privilege of dealing out death by hand, which until quite recently was regarded as a supreme mark of masculine valor. While it seems theoretically possible, even in the heart of Anglo-Saxondom, to imagine a leisurely, pacific male, in fact the losses in secondary functions sustained by men appear to have shaken their faith in their primary masculine function as well, in their ability to achieve the conquest (as the traditional metaphor has it) of women. Earlier, advances in technology had detached the wooing and winning of women from the begetting of children; and though the invention of the condom had at least left the decision to inhibit fatherhood in the power of males, its replacement by the "loop" and the "pill" has placed paternity at the mercy of the whims of women.

Writers of fiction and verse registered the technological obsolescence of masculinity long before it was felt even by the representative minority who give to the present younger generation its character and significance. And literary critics have talked a good deal during the past couple of decades about the conversion of the literary hero into the nonhero or the antihero; but they have in general failed to notice his simultaneous conversion into the non- or antimale. Yet ever since Hemingway at least, certain male protagonists of American literature have not only fled rather than sought out combat but have also fled rather than sought out women. From Jake Barnes to Holden Caulfield they have continued to run from the threat of female sexuality; and, indeed, there are models for such evasion in our classic books, where heroes still eager for the fight (Natty Bumppo comes to mind) are already shy of wives and sweethearts and mothers.

It is not absolutely required that the antimale antihero be impotent or homosexual or both (though this helps, as we remember remembering Walt Whitman), merely that he be more seduced than seducing, more passive than active. Consider, for instance, the oddly "womanish" Herzog of Bellow's current best seller, that Jewish Emma Bovary with a Ph.D., whose chief flaw is physical vanity and a taste for fancy clothes. Bellow, however, is more interested in

summing up the past than in evoking the future; and *Herzog* therefore seems an end rather than a beginning, the product of nostalgia
(remember when there were real Jews once, and the "Jewish
Novel" had not yet been discovered!) rather than prophecy. No,
the post-humanist, post-male, post-white, post-heroic world is a
post-Jewish world by the same token, anti-Semitism as inextricably
woven into it as into the movement for Negro rights; and its scrip-
tural books are necessarily *goyish,* not least of all William Burroughs' *The Naked Lunch.*

Burroughs is the chief prophet of the post-male post-heroic
world; and it is his emulators who move into the center of the relevant literary scene, for *The Naked Lunch* (the later novels are less
successful, less exciting but relevant still) is more than it seems: no
mere essay in heroin-hallucinated homosexual pornography—but a
nightmare anticipation (in Science Fiction form) of post-Humanist
sexuality. Here, as in Alexander Trocchi, John Rechy, Harry Matthews (even an occasional Jew like Allen Ginsberg, who has begun
by inscribing properly anti-Jewish obscenities on the walls of the
world), are clues to the new attitudes toward sex that will continue
to inform our improbable novels of passion and our even more improbable love songs.

The young to whom I have been referring, the mythologically
representative minority (who, by a process that infuriates the mythologically inert majority out of which they come, "stand for" their
times), live in a community in which what used to be called the
"Sexual Revolution," the Freudian-Laurentian revolt of their
grandparents and parents, has triumphed as imperfectly and unsat-
isfactorily as all revolutions always triumph. They confront, therefore, the necessity of determining not only what meanings "love"
can have in their new world, but—even more disturbingly—what
significance, if any, "male" and "female" now possess. For a while,
they (or at least their literary spokesmen recruited from the generation just before them) seemed content to celebrate a kind of *reductio* or *exaltatio ad absurdum* of their parents' once revolutionary
sexual goals: The Reichian-inspired Cult of the Orgasm.

Young men and women eager to be delivered of traditional
ideologies of love find especially congenial the belief that not union
or relationship (much less offspring) but physical release is the end

of the sexual act; and that, therefore, it is a matter of indifference with whom or by what method ones pursues the therapeutic climax, so long as that climax is total and repeated frequently. And Wilhelm Reich happily detaches this belief from the vestiges of Freudian rationalism, setting it instead in a context of Science Fiction and witchcraft; but his emphasis upon "full genitality," upon growing up and away from infantile pleasures, strikes the young as a disguised plea for the "maturity" they have learned to despise. In a time when the duties associated with adulthood promise to become irrelevant, there seems little reason for denying oneself the joys of babyhood—even if these are associated with such regressive fantasies as escaping it all in the arms of little sister (in the Gospel according to J. D. Salinger) or flirting with the possibility of getting into bed with papa (in the Gospel according to Norman Mailer).

Only Norman O. Brown in *Life Against Death* has come to terms on the level of theory with the aspiration to take the final evolutionary leap and cast off adulthood completely, at least in the area of sex. His post-Freudian program for pansexual, nonorgasmic love rejects "full genitality" in favor of a species of indiscriminate bundling, a dream of unlimited subcoital intimacy which Brown calls (in his vocabulary the term is an honorific) "polymorphous perverse." And here finally is an essential clue to the nature of the second sexual revolution, the post-sexual revolution, first evoked in literature by Brother Antoninus more than a decade ago, in a verse prayer addressed somewhat improbably to the Christian God:

> *Annul in me my manhood, Lord, and make*
> *Me woman sexed and weak . . .*
> > *Make me then*
> *Girl-hearted, virgin-souled, woman-docile, maiden-meek . . .*

Despite the accents of this invocation, however, what is at work is not essentially a homosexual revolt or even a rebellion against women, though its advocates seek to wrest from women their ancient privileges of receiving the Holy Ghost and pleasuring men; and though the attitudes of the movement can be adapted to the antifemale bias of, say, Edward Albee. If in *Who's Afraid of Virginia Woolf* Albee can portray the relationship of two homosexuals (one in drag) as the model of contemporary marriage, this must be because contemporary marriage has in fact turned into something much like that parody. And it is true that what survives of bourgeois marriage and the bourgeois family is a target which the new barbarians join the old homosexuals in reviling, seeking to replace Mom, Pop and the kids with a neo-Whitmanian gaggle of giggling *camerados*. Such groups are, in fact, whether gathered in coffee houses, university cafeterias or around the literature tables on campuses, the peacetime equivalents, as it were, to the demonstrating crowd. But even their program of displacing Dick-Jane-Spot-Baby, etc., the WASP family of grade school primers, is not the fundamental motive of the post-sexual revolution.

What is at stake from Burroughs to Bellow, Ginsberg to Albee, Salinger to Gregory Corso is a more personal transformation: a radical metamorphosis of the Western male—utterly unforeseen in the decades before us, but visible now in every high school and college classroom, as well as on the paperback racks in airports and supermarkets. All around us, young males are beginning to retrieve for themselves the cavalier role once piously and class-consciously surrendered to women: *that of being beautiful and being loved.* Here once more the example of the Negro—the feckless and adorned Negro male with the blood of Cavaliers in his veins—has served as a model. And what else is left to young men, in any case, after the devaluation of the grim duties they had arrogated to themselves in place of the pursuit of loveliness?

All of us who are middle-aged and were Marxists, which is to say, who once numbered ourselves among the last assured Puritans, have surely noticed in ourselves a vestigial roundhead rage at the new hair styles of the advanced or—if you please—delinquent young. Watching young men titivate their locks (the comb, the pocket mirror and the bobby pin having replaced the jackknife, catcher's mitt and brass knuckles), we feel the same baffled resentment that stirs in us when we realize that they have rejected work. A job and unequivocal maleness—these are two sides of the same Calvinist coin, which in the future buys nothing.

Few of us, however, have really understood how the Beatle hair-do is part of a syndrome, of which high heels, jeans tight over the buttocks, etc., are other aspects, symptomatic of a larger retreat from masculine aggressiveness to female allure—in literature and the arts to the style called "camp." And fewer still have realized how that style, though the invention of homosexuals, is now the possession of basically heterosexual males as well, a strategy in their campaign to establish a new relationship not only with women but with their own masculinity. In the course of that campaign, they have embraced certain kinds of gesture and garb, certain accents and tones traditionally associated with females or female imperson-ators; which is why we have been observing recently (in life as well as fiction and verse) young boys, quite unequivocally male, playing all the traditional roles of women: the vamp, the coquette, the whore, the icy tease, the pure young virgin.

Not only oldsters, who had envisioned and despaired of quite another future, are bewildered by this turn of events, but young girls, too, seem scarcely to know what is happening—looking on with that new, schizoid stare which itself has become a hallmark of our times. And the crop-headed jocks, those crew-cut athletes who represent an obsolescent masculine style based on quite other val-ues, have tended to strike back blindly; beating the hell out of some poor kid whose hair is too long or whose pants are too tight—quite as they once beat up young communists for revealing that their pol-itics had become obsolete. Even heterosexual writers, however, have been slow to catch up, the revolution in sensibility running ahead of that in expression; and they have perforce permitted homo-sexuals to speak for them (Burroughs and Genet and Baldwin and Ginsberg and Albee and a score of others), even to invent the forms in which the future will have to speak.

The revolt against masculinity is not limited, however, to simple matters of coiffure and costume, visible even to athletes; or to the adaptation of certain campy styles and modes to new uses. There is also a sense in which two large social movements that have set the young in motion and furnished images of action for their books— movements as important in their own right as porno-politics and the pursuit of the polymorphous perverse—are connected analogically to the abdication from traditional maleness. The first of these is nonviolent or passive resistance, so oddly come back to the land of its inventor, that icy Thoreau who dreamed a love which ". . . has not much human blood in it, but consists with a certain disregard for men and their erections. . . ."

The civil rights movement, however, in which nonviolence has found a home, has been hospitable not only to the sort of post-humanist I have been describing; so that at a demonstration (Selma, Alabama will do as an example) the true hippie will be found side by side with backwoods Baptists, nuns on a spiritual spree, boy bureaucrats practicing to take power, resurrected socialists, Unitarians in search of a God, and just plain tourists, gathered, as once at the Battle of Bull Run, to see the fun. For each of these, nonviolence will have a different sort of fundamental meaning—as a tactic, a camouflage, a passing fad, a pious gesture—but for each in part, and for the post-humanist especially, it will signify the possibility of heroism without aggression, effective action without guilt.

There have always been two contradictory American ideals: to be the occasion of maximum violence, and to remain absolutely innocent. Once, however, these were thought hopelessly incompatible for males (except, perhaps, as embodied in works of art), reserved strictly for women: the spouse of the wife beater, for instance, or the victim of rape. But males have now assumed these classic roles; and just as a particularly beleaguered wife occasionally slipped over the dividing line into violence, so do the new passive protesters— leaving us to confront (or resign to the courts) such homey female questions as: *Did Mario Savio really bite that cop in the leg as he sagged limply toward the ground?*

The second social movement is the drug cult, more widespread among youth, from its squarest limits to its most beat, than anyone seems prepared to admit in public; and at its beat limit at least inextricably involved with the civil rights movement, as the recent arrests of Peter DeLissovoy and Susan Ryerson revealed even to the ordinary newspaper reader. "Police said that most of the recipients [of marijuana] were college students," the U.P. story runs. "They quoted Miss Ryerson and DeLissovoy as saying that many of the letter packets were sent to civil rights workers." Only fiction and verse, however, has dealt with the conjunction of homosexuality, drugs and civil rights, eschewing the general piety of the press which has been unwilling to compromise "good works" on behalf of the Negro by associating them with the deep radicalism of a way of life based on the ritual consumption of "pot."

The widespread use of such hallucinogens as peyote, marijuana, the "Mexican mushroom," LSD, etc., as well as pep pills, goof balls, airplane glue, certain kinds of cough syrups and even, though in many fewer cases, heroin, is not merely a matter of a changing taste in stimulants but of the programmatic espousal of an antipuritanical mode of existence—hedonistic and detached—one more strategy in the war on time and work. But it is also (to pursue my analogy once more) an attempt to arrogate to the male certain traditional privileges of the female. What could be more womanly, as Elémire Zolla was already pointing out some years ago, than permitting the penetration of the body by a foreign object which not only stirs delight but even (possibly) creates new life?

In any case, with drugs we have come to the crux of the futurist revolt, the hinge of everything else, as the young tell us over and over in their writing. When the movement was first finding a voice, Allen Ginsberg set this aspect of it in proper context in an immensely comic, utterly serious poem called "America," in which "pot" is associated with earlier forms of rebellion, a commitment to catatonia, and a rejection of conventional male potency:

> *America I used to be a communist when I was a kid I'm not*
> *sorry.*
> *I smoke marijuana every chance I get.*
> *I sit in my house for days on end and stare at the roses in the*
> *closet.*
> *When I go to Chinatown I . . . never get laid . . .*

Similarly, Michael McClure reveals in his essay, *"Phi Upsilon Kappa,"* that before penetrating the "cavern of Anglo-Saxon," whence he emerged with the slogan of the ultimate Berkeley demonstrators, he had been on mescalin. "I have emerged from a dark night of the soul; I entered it by Peyote." And by now, drug-taking has become as standard a feature of the literature of the young as oral-genital love-making. I flip open the first issue of yet another ephemeral San Francisco little magazine quite at random and read: "I tie up and the main pipe [the ante-cobital vein, for the clinically inclined] swells like a prideful beggar beneath the skin. Just before

I get on it is always the worst." Worse than the experience, however, is its literary rendering; and the badness of such confessional
fiction, flawed by the sentimentality of those who desire to live "like
a cunning vegetable," is a badness we older readers find it only too
easy to perceive, as our sons and daughters find it only too easy to
overlook. Yet precisely here the age and the mode define themselves; for not in the master but in the hacks new forms are established, new lines drawn.

Here, at any rate, is where the young lose us in literature as
well as life, since here they pass over into real revolt, i.e., what we
really cannot abide, hard as we try. The mother who has sent her
son to private schools and on to Harvard to keep him out of classrooms overcrowded with poor Negroes, rejoices when he sets out
for Mississippi with his comrades in SNCC, but shudders when he
turns on with LSD; just as the ex-Marxist father, who has earlier
proved radicalism impossible, rejoices to see his son stand up,
piously and pompously, for CORE or SDS, but trembles to hear
him quote Alpert and Leary or praise Burroughs. Just as certainly
as liberalism is the LSD of the aging, LSD is the radicalism of the
young.

If whiskey long served as an appropriate symbolic excess for
those who chafed against Puritan restraint without finally challenging it—temporarily releasing them to socially harmful aggression
and (hopefully) sexual self-indulgence, the new popular drugs provide an excess quite as satisfactorily symbolic to the post-Puritans
—releasing them from sanity to madness by destroying in them the
inner restrictive order which has somehow survived the dissolution
of the outer. It is finally insanity, then, that the futurists learn to admire and emulate, quite as they learn to pursue vision instead of
learning, hallucination rather than logic. The schizophrenic replaces
the sage as their ideal, their new culture hero, figured forth as a
giant schizoid Indian (his madness modeled in part on the author's
own experiences with LSD) in Ken Kesey's *One Flew Over the
Cuckoo's Nest.*

The hippier young are not alone, however, in their taste for the
insane; we live in a time when readers in general respond sympathetically to madness in literature wherever it is found, in estab-

lished writers as well as in those trying to establish new modes. Surely it is not the lucidity and logic of Robert Lowell or Theodore Roethke or John Berryman which we admire, but their flirtation with incoherence and disorder. And certainly it is Mailer at his most nearly psychotic, Mailer the creature rather than the master of his fantasies who moves us to admiration; while in the case of Saul Bellow, we endure the theoretical optimism and acceptance for the sake of the delightful melancholia, the fertile paranoia which he cannot disavow any more than the talent at whose root they lie. Even essayists and analysts recommend themselves to us these days by a certain redemptive nuttiness; at any rate, we do not love, say, Marshall McLuhan less because he continually risks sounding like the body-fluids man in *Dr. Strangelove.*

We have, moreover, recently been witnessing the development of a new form of social psychiatry[2] (a psychiatry of the future already anticipated by the literature of the future) which considers some varieties of "schizophrenia" not diseases to be cured but forays into an unknown psychic world: random penetrations by bewildered internal cosmonauts of a realm that it will be the task of the next generations to explore. And if the accounts which the returning schizophrenics give (the argument of the apologists runs) of the "places" they have been are fantastic and garbled, surely they are no more so than, for example, Columbus' reports of the world he had claimed for Spain, a world bounded—according to his newly drawn maps—by Cathay on the north and Paradise on the south.

In any case, poets and junkies have been suggesting to us that the new world appropriate to the new men of the latter twentieth century is to be discovered only by the conquest of inner space: by an adventure of the spirit, an extension of psychic possibility, of which the flights into outer space—moonshots and expeditions to Mars—are precisely such unwitting metaphors and analogues as the voyages of exploration were of the earlier breakthrough into the Renaissance, from whose consequences the young seek now so des-

---

[2] Described in an article in the *New Left Review* of November-December, 1964, by R. D. Laing who advocates "ex-patients helping future patients go mad."

perately to escape. The laureate of that new conquest is William Burroughs; and it is fitting that the final word be his:

"This war will be won in the air. In the Silent Air with Image Rays. You were a pilot remember? Tracer bullets cutting the right wing you were free in space a few seconds before in blue space between eyes. Go back to Silence. Keep Silence. Keep Silence. K.S. K.S. . . . From Silence re-write the message that is you. You are the message I send to The Enemy. My Silent Message."

The Naked Astronauts were free in space. . . .

—1965

Henry Roth's
Neglected Masterpiece

It would not be quite true to say that Henry Roth's *Call It Sleep* went unnoticed when it appeared in 1935. One contemporary reviewer at least was willing to call it "a great novel" and to hope that it might win the Pulitzer Prize, "which," that reviewer added mournfully, "it never will." It never did, the prize going instead to H. L. Davis's *Honey in the Horn,* which was also the Harper Prize Novel of the year and was even touted by Robert Penn Warren in the *Southern Review*—then still being subsidized by Huey Long. Not only the Southern Agrarians were looking elsewhere, however, when Roth's single book was published; almost everyone seemed to have his eye on his own preferred horizon, on which he was pretending to find his own preferred rising star.

The official "proletarian" party was busy hailing Clara Weatherwax for a desolately enthusiastic tract disguised as fiction and called *Marching! Marching! "Marching! Marching!"*—runs the jacket blurb—"is the winner of *The New Masses* contest for a novel on an American Proletarian theme, conducted jointly by *The New Masses* and the John Day Company—the first contest of the kind ever held." It was also the last such contest, partly, one hopes, because of the flagrant badness of the winner (the climax of Miss Weatherwax's book runs as follows: ". . . some of us thinking *Jeez! Bayonets! Machine Guns! They got gas masks on those bags around their necks on their chests—gas!* and others *For God's sake, you guys, don't shoot us! Come over to our side. Why should you kill us? We are your brothers"*)—but chiefly, one suspects, because a basic change in the political line of the Comintern instituted

211

in 1936 led to the substitution of the Popular Front novel for the Proletarian one.

John Steinbeck, the most sensitive recorder of that shift, was to publish his resolutely proletarian *In Dubious Battle* in 1936, but this reflects a lag demanded by the exigencies of publishing. *The Grapes of Wrath,* which represents the full-scale political-sentimental novel of the last half of the thirties, did not reach print until 1939. Meanwhile, Dos Passos and Farrell, the most ambitious talents of the first part of the decade, were closing out their accounts by putting between the covers of single volumes those fat trilogies *(Studs Lonigan* actually appeared in 1935; *U.S.A.* was that year in its last stages) which seemed for a while to the literary historians the great achievements of the period. And at the same time, Hemingway was preparing for his own brief fling at being a "proletarian" author, improbably publishing a section of *To Have and Have Not* in *Cosmopolitan* magazine during 1934.

To the more dogged proletarian critics, Henry Roth seemed beside Weatherwax or Dos Passos, Farrell or even Hemingway woefully "poetic" and uncommitted. "He pleads [prefers?] diffuse poetry to the social light . . ." the reviewer for the *New Republic* complained, adding rather obscurely but surely unfavorably that Roth "pinkly through the flesh sees the angry sunset." Actually, there was some point in chiding Roth for not writing a "socially conscious" book, since his dedication to Eda Lou Walton (his teacher, sponsor, and friend, who had identified herself clearly enough with the proletarian cause) indicated a declaration if not of allegiance at least of general sympathy. Certainly Roth did not take his stand outside of the world bounded by the *New Masses,* the *Nation,* and the *New Republic,* as, say, did John Peale Bishop, whose *Act of Darkness* was also published in 1935, or Thomas Wolfe, whose *Of Time and the River* was just then thrilling the adolescent audience for whom he had rediscovered *Weltschmerz* in *Look Homeward, Angel.* Nor was Roth willing to launch the sort of satirical attack on social commitment undertaken only a year later by another young Jewish writer, Daniel Fuchs, in *Homage to Blenholt.*

He was ideologically in much the same position as Nathanael West, whose *A Cool Million* appeared in the same year with *Call It*

Sleep, and whose technique, different as it was, also baffled the official "proletarians." Both had reached intellectual maturity inside a world of beliefs which they felt no impulse to deny but which they did not find viable in their art. West died inside that world and Roth apparently still inhabits it insofar as he retains any connection with literary life at all. At any rate, looking back from 1960 and the poultry farm in Maine to which he has finally withdrawn, that is the world he remembers. "Is Yaddo still functioning?" he recently asked an interviewer. "Whatever happened to Horace Gregory and Ben Belitt?" There is a half-comic pathos in the questions and the continuing faith from which they spring that a literary movement to which Roth never quite belonged must still somehow be going on.

But in Roth's novel itself there is little enough manifest social consciousness. Though his scene is Brownsville and the East Side of New York just after the turn of the century and his protagonists are a working-class Jewish immigrant family, there is small sense of an economic struggle. Jobs are gotten and lost because of psychological quirks and dark inner compulsions; money does not corrupt nor does poverty redeem; no one wants to rise like David Levinsky or fears to fall like the harried protagonists of Theodore Dreiser. If there is a class struggle and a revolutionary movement, these are revealed only in an overheard scrap of soapbox oratory at the climax of the novel, where they seem singularly irrelevant to the passion and suffering of Roth's child hero who is living through that climax.

> "In 1789, in 1848, in 1871, in 1905, he who has anything to save will enslave us anew! Or if not enslave will desert us when the red cock crows! Only the laboring poor, only the masses embittered, bewildered, betrayed, in the day the red cock crows, can free us!"

But even this prophecy uttered out of a "pale, gilt-spectacled, fanatic face," is turned into a brutal sexual jest, recast in light of the obsession which rides the book, its protagonist, and its author. "How many times'll your red cock crow, Pete, befaw y'gives up? T'ree?" asks a mocking Irish voice from the sidelines.

Perhaps it is this obsessive transformation of all experience into equivocations based on a hated and feared sexuality which put off the kind of reader who might have been expected to hail the kind of book Roth actually wrote. That the *New Masses* critics deplored him and the Southern Agrarians scarcely registered his existence is, after all, to be expected; nor is it proper to feel dismay over the yellowing lists of best-sellers in old newspapers, carefully documented testimony to what the largest audience was reading in 1935 *instead* of Roth. For some the whimsy, Anglophile or pseudo-Oriental, of James Hilton (both *Goodbye, Mr. Chips* and *Lost Horizon* topped the lists) seemed the specific demanded by the pangs of the Great Depression, while others found tranquillity in the religiosity of *The Forty Days of Musa Dagh* or in Mary Pickford's *Why Not Try God?* For those less serious or more chic, there was the eunuchoid malice and sentimentality of Alexander Woollcott's *While Rome Burns;* and the most nearly invisible audience of all (furtive high school boys standing at the circulating library racks in candy stores and their older sisters behind the closed doors of their bedrooms) were reading Donald Henderson Clarke's *Millie* and *Louis Beretti* —the demi-pornography which no library would think of stocking twenty-five years later.

But what of those specifically interested in Jewish literature in the United States, those who, picking up a first novel by a twenty-seven-year-old New Yorker, thought of Mary Antin's *The Promised Land* or remembered Abraham Cahan's breakthrough to the rich disorderly material of Jewish-American life? There is surely no more Jewish book among American novels. Though its young hero, David Schearl, for instance, goes to public school, that Gentile area of experience is left shadowy, unrealized. Only his home and the *cheder* and the streets between become real places, as only Yiddish and Hebrew and the poor dialects of those to whom English is an alien tongue are rendered as real languages. And yet those presumably looking for the flowering of a rich and satisfactory Jewish-American literature were not moved to applaud.

Some of them, on the contrary, protested against the unloveliness of Roth's ghetto images, the vulgarity and poverty of the speech he recorded—as if he had invented them maliciously. "Doggedly smeared with verbal filthiness," one such critic wrote.

"*Call It Sleep* is by far the foulest picture of the East Side that has yet appeared." It is, of course, the typical, the expected response to the serious writer by the official spokesmen of the community out of which he comes. Yet there was in Roth a special kind of offensiveness, capable of stirring a more than conventional reaction; for the real foulness of his book is rendered not directly but through the consciousness of an extraordinarily acute and sensitive boy of seven or eight. Its vulgarity, that is to say, is presented as *felt* vulgarity, grossness assailing a sensibility with no defenses against it.

The technique of *Call It Sleep* is contrived to make manifest at every moment that its real subject is not so much abomination in the streets as that abomination in the mind. Aside from a prelude, in which the arrival of David and his mother in America is objectively narrated, and a section toward the book's end which blends into a Joycean rhapsody the sounds of a score of city voices as overheard by some omniscient Listener—the whole substance of the novel is presented as what happens inside the small haunted head of David. It is only through him that we know the dark cellar swarming with rats whose door he must pass on his way in or out of the warm sanctuary of his home; the rage and guilt of his paranoid father or that father's impotence and fantasies of being cuckolded; his mother's melancholy, and her soft, unfulfilled sexuality; the promise of her body and the way in which it is ogled by others; the fact of sex in general as pollution, the very opposite of love. For David, the act by which he was generated is an unmitigated horror (in a dark closet, reeking of mothballs, he is initiated by a crippled girl, her braces creaking as she embraces him, "Between the legs. Who puts id in is de poppa. De poppa's god de petzel. You de poppa"); and he longs for a purity he cannot find in his world, a fire, a flame to purify him from his iniquity as he has learned in *cheder* Isaiah was once purified.

No book insists more on the distance between the foulness man lives and the purity he dreams; but none makes more clear how deeply rooted that dream is in the existence which seems to contradict it. It is, perhaps, this double insight which gives to Roth's book a Jewish character, quite independent of the subject matter with which he happens to deal. Certainly, it reveals his kinship to Nathanael West, also a novelist of the thirties, whose relationship to his own Jewishness is much more equivocal than Roth's, but who quotes in his earliest book an observation of Doughty's about the nature of Semites in general which illuminates his own work as well as Roth's: the Semite stands in dung up to his eyes, but his brow touches the heavens. Indeed, in Jewish American fiction from Abraham Cahan to Philip Roth, that polarity and tension are present everywhere, the Jew mediating between dung and God, as if his eternal function were to prove that man is most himself not when he turns first to one then to the other—but when he touches both at once. And who can project the awareness of this more intensely and dramatically than the child, the Jewish child?

It is possible to imagine many reasons for Roth's retreating to childhood from adult experience; for retreat it does seem in the light of his second withdrawal, after the publication of a single book, into the silence in which he has persisted until now. To have written such a book and no other is to betray some deep trouble not only in finding words but in loving the life one has lived enough to *want* to find words for it. A retreat from all that 1935 meant to Roth: from the exigencies of adult sexuality and political commitment alike—this is what *Call It Sleep* seems to the retrospective insight of 1960. The book begins in 1907, and though it jumps quickly some five years, never quite reaches the year of the Russian Revolution (the roster of splendid betrayals listed by the street-corner speaker stops at 1905) and the vagaries of Leninism-Stalinism; just as in coming to a close in a boy's eighth year it stops safely short of the point where "playing bad" becomes an act that can end in deflowering or pregnancy. In its world before the falls of puberty and the October Revolution, one can remember 1905 and Mama —play out the dream of the apocalypse and the Oedipal triangle in all naïveté.

Cued by whatever fears, Roth's turning to childhood enables him to render his story as dream and nightmare, fantasy and myth—to escape the limits of that realism which makes of other accounts of ghetto childhood documents rather than poetry. In its own time *Call It Sleep* was occasionally compared to Farrell's *Young Lonigan,* but one cannot conceive of such a foreword to Roth's book as that written for Farrell's by "Frederic M. Thrasher, Associate Professor of Education, New York University, Author of *The Gang.*" Roth's book aspires not to sociology but to theology; it is finally and astonishingly a religious book, though this fact even its latest admiring critics tend to ignore or underplay. Only in the account of a child's experience could a protégé of Eda Lou Walton (it would have been another matter if he had been sponsored by Mary Pickford) have gotten away with a religious resolution to a serious novel about ghetto life; and it was to a child's experience that he was canny enough to turn. An evasion of responsibility? A strategic device of great subtlety? It is not necessary to decide.

David Schearl, at any rate, is portrayed not only as a small boy and a Jew but also as a "mystic," a naïve adept visited by visions he scarcely understands until a phrase from the sixth chapter of Isaiah illuminates for him his own improbable prophetic initiation. Having just burned the leaven of the year in preparation for the Passover ("All burned black. See God, I was good? Now only white Matzohs are left"), David sits watching the play of light on the river and is transported ("His spirit yielded, melted into light. . . . Brighter than day . . . Brighter"). But he is awakened from his ecstasy by the tooting of a barge ("Funny little lights all gone. Like when you squeeze too hard on a toilet . . ."), thrust back into darkness until two Gentile hoodlums persuade him to drop a strip of zinc down into the third rail of a trolley line and he feels that in the dark bowels of the earth he has discovered the source of all light ("And light, unleashed, terrific light bellowed out of iron lips"). This light he identifies with the burning coal that cleansed the unclean lips of Isaiah, though his rabbi mocks him ("Fool! Go beat your head on a wall! God's light is not between car-tracks")—and in his joy he wets his pants.

For better or worse, the prophetic poetry reduced to an exercise learned by rote and beaten into unwilling boys has come alive in David, delivered him from fear so that he can climb the darkest stairway untroubled. ("Gee! Look! Look! Is a light . . . Ain't really there. Inside my head. Better is inside. . . .") Released a little from the warm bondage that binds him to his mother, he can climb now even to the roof of his house, where he meets for the first time the Gentile boy, Leo, a twelve-year-old seducer and eater of forbidden foods, beside whose absolute freedom David's limited release seems slavery still. And in Leo's house he finds new images for the inner light, the purifying flame, in a portrait of Jesus with the Burning Heart and a box bearing the symbolic fish, the name GOD. For the rosary that box contains, he agrees to introduce Leo to his sluttish cousin Esther, whose grimy favors Leo finally wins in the cellar beneath her mother's candy store.

As Leo and Esther squeal and pant in the darkness of one cellar shed, David crouches in another trying to exact light from the holy beads for which he has betrayed his family, his Jewishness, his very desire for cleanliness.

> Past drifting bubbles of grey and icy needles of grey, below a mousetrap, a cogwheel, below a step and a dwarf with a sack upon his back . . . sank the beads, gold figure on a cross swinging slowly . . . . At the floor of the vast pit of silence glimmered the round light, pulsed and glimmered like a coin. —Touch it! Touch it! Drop!

But the light eludes his efforts; and the other two, who have performed the act of darkness at the very moment he sought the light, emerge blaming each other as they are discovered by Esther's sister. "Tell 'er wut I wuz doin', kid," Leo blusters. "Yuh jew hewhs! We wuz hidin' de balonee—Yaa! Sheenee!"

AFTER such a denouement, nothing is possible for David but a plunge into hysteria, a hysteria which overcomes him as he is rereading the passage about the calling of Isaiah, betrays him into telling to his *rebbe* a story compounded half of his father's delusions, dimly perceived, and half of certain reminiscences of his mother, ill understood: his mother is not his *real* mother, he is a bastard, son of a goyish organist in an old country church, etc., etc. This fantasy the *rebbe* hastens to carry to David's home, arriving a moment before the horrified parents of Esther appear with their own scandal. And David, overwhelmed by guilt and fear, offers to his father a whip, grovels at his feet, the rosary falling from his pocket as if to testify to the truth of his illegitimacy, his contaminated blood. At this point, he must run for his life, his father's long rage at last fulfilled, presumably justified; and he runs where he must, toward God in the dark cleft, to the third rail, the coal of fire that can take away iniquity.

He snatches a ladle from beside a milk pail and flees to an obbligato of city voices, which from the girders of a half-finished building, a warehouse, a bar, a poker table speak with unclean lips of lust and greed, hatred and vengefulness. Only David dreams of a consummation that will transcend and redeem the flesh, finally thrusts the metal he bears between the black lips of the tracks and the awful lightning is released, his body shaken by ineffable power, and his consciousness all but obliterated. Yet his intended sacrifice redeems no one, merely adds a new range of ambiguity to the chorus in which one voice blasphemes against the faith of another and all against love. Himself dazzled, the reader hears again certain phrases he has before only half understood, listens again, for instance, to the barroom voice that mocked the street-corner orator, "How many times'll your red cock crow, Pete, befaw y'gives up? T'ree?"—notices the "three," the name "Pete," and remembers the other Peter who, three times before the cock crow, denied his Rabbi.

In the interplay of ironies and evasions the final meaning of the failed sacrifice, the private apocalypse (the boy does not die; the world is not made clean; only his parents are rejoined more in weariness than affection over his bed) is never made quite clear, only the transcendence of that meaning, its more than natural character. Turning the final pages of Roth's book, one realizes suddenly how in the time of the Great Depression all the more serious fictionists yearned in secret to touch a religious note, toying with the messianic and the apocalyptic but refusing to call them by names not honored in the left-wing journals of the time. The final honesty of Roth's book lies in its refusal to call by any fashionable honorific name its child hero's bafflement as he learns the special beauty of a world which remains stubbornly unredeemed: "Not pain, not terror, but strangest triumph, strangest acquiescence. One might as well call it sleep."

—1960

Master of Dreams:
The Jew in a Gentile World

If there were dreams to sell,
Merry and sad to tell,
And the crier rung the bell,
What would you buy?

T. L. BEDDOES

"AND JOSEPH DREAMED a dream," the Book of the Jews tells us, "and he told it his brethren: and they hated him yet the more." It is the beginning of a myth whose ending we all know, the opening of a larger dream which a whole community has dreamed waking and aloud for nearly three thousand years. But it is unique among communal dreams, this myth of Joseph and his descent into Egypt; for it is the dream of the dreamer, a myth of myth itself. More specifically (or maybe I only mean more Jewishly), it is the dreamer's own dream of how, dreaming, he makes it in the waking world; the myth of myth making it in the realm of the nonmythic; an archetypal account of the successful poet and the respected shrink, the Jewish artist and the Jewish doctor—hailed in the Gentile world, first by the Gentiles themselves, and as a consequence by their hostile brethren, their fellow-Jews.

I might have hit upon the meaning of the Joseph story in any number of ways, reflecting on the Biblical text itself, or reading Thomas Mann's true but tedious retelling of the tale in *Joseph and His Brethren;* but I did not. And only after I had begun my own ruminations did I come on Isaac Bashevis Singer's exegesis, in a little story called "The Strong Ones," in which he remembers the strange resentment of his childhood friends after he had first revealed to them his secret desire to become a writer: "And even though I asked how I had offended them, they behaved like Joseph's brothers and could not answer amicably. . . . What was it they envied? My dreams. . . ." But the archetypal beginning implies the archetypal ending; and just as mysteriously as they had rejected him, Singer's comrades end by asking his forgiveness: "It reminded me of Joseph and his brothers. *They* had come to Joseph to buy grain, but why had my friends come to me? Since I had not become Egypt's ruler, they were not required to bow down to the earth. I had nothing to sell but new dreams."

Actually it was a chance phrase in a most *goyish* poet which provided me with a clue to the meanings I am pursuing here, a verse in the Sixth Satire of Juvenal, where—describing the endless varieties of goods on sale in Rome, wares especially tempting, he tells us, to women—he remarks that "for a few pennies" one can buy any dream his heart desires "from the Jews." *From the Jews!* It was those few words which fired my imagination with their offhand assumption that dream-pedlary is a Jewish business, that my own people have traditionally sold to the world that commodity so easy to scorn and so difficult to do without: the stuff of dreams. And I found myself reflecting in wonder on the strange wares that have been in the course of Western History Jewish monopolies, real or presumed: preserved mummy, love philtres, liquid capital, cut diamonds, old clothes—Hollywood movies; which brought me almost up to date.

Moving backward in time, however, in reversion from such uncomfortable contemporaneity, I found myself in *Mizraim,* face to face with the archetypal ancestor of all Jewish dreamers, with that Joseph whom his brothers hailed mockingly, saying, "Behold, here comes the Master of Dreams," and whom they cast into the pit, crying out, "And then we shall see what will become of his dreams." But we *know* what, in fact, did become of those self-flattering dreams of that papa's spoiled darling. And how hard it is to believe that there was ever a *first* time when the envious brothers did not know in their deepest hearts what the event would be: how

Joseph, after he had ceased to dream himself, would discover that his own dreams of glory had prepared him to interpret the dreams of others, and how, interpreting them, he would achieve the wish revealed in his own.

Not, however, until he had gone down into Egypt, becoming in that absolutely alien world an absolute orphan, a Lost Son. When the Jew dreams himself in the Gentile world, it is as the preferred offspring of Jacob, which is to say, of Israel—betrayed by his brethren, but loving them still, forgiving all. When the Gentile dreams the Jew in his midst, on the other hand, he dreams him as the vengeful and villainous Father: Shylock or Fagin, the Bearded Terror threatening some poor full-grown *goy* with a knife, or inducting some guileless Gentile kid into a life of crime. But Shylock and Fagin are shadows cast upon the Christian world by that First Jewish Father, Abraham, who is to them circumcizer and sacrificer rolled into one—castrator, in short.

In the deep Jewish imagination, however, Abraham is seen always not at the moment of intended sacrifice, but the moment after —releasing his (only ritually) threatened Son to become himself a Father, and the Father of a Father, to beget Jacob who will beget Joseph. Abraham *and* Isaac *and* Jacob: these constitute that paternal triad which possesses the mythic memory of the Jews. And beyond them there is for us no further Father, only Our Boy, Joseph, who never becomes (mythically speaking) a Father at all—only makes good, i.e., provides salvation for the Gentiles and *nachas* for his own progenitor.

The Gentiles cannot afford the luxury of *our* Joseph, however, having an archetypal Son of their own, who denies his actual Jewish father ("Let the dead bury their dead"), called—appropriately enough—Joseph, too. How like and unlike the figure of the first Joseph is to that Gentiles' Son of the Father, the mythicized Jesus Christ, whose very Jewishness is finally sloughed off in the exportable archetype he becomes. Not for *our* Beloved Son a crucifixion and a translation to glory only after death. Our Dreamer, too, may begin by leaving his father's house on a mission to the Gentiles; but the temptations he must resist are the temptations of this world not the next. Specifically, he must elude not the clutch of Satan but the grasping fingers of the Gentile woman who lusts for him; and survive the slander with which she punishes his rejection of her alien charms. And his reward for virtue is to become a success in this world, the unredeemed here and now (not some New Heaven and New Earth, where he will sit at the right hand of Power), ruled over only by the powers-that-be: those fickle Pharaohs whose favor depends on his providing for them the good dreams they cannot dream for themselves, and therapeutically explaining away the bad dreams they cannot keep from dreaming.

And this means that the archetypal Jewish Son, in whatever *Mizraim* he finds himself, performs not only the function of the artist but also of the Doctor. My Son the Artist, my Son the Doctor —it is the latter which the tradition especially celebrates, the bad jokes recall in mockery; but in the tradition, the two—artist and doctor—are finally essentially one. In life, however, they may be, for all their affinities, split into separate persons, distinct and even hostile: in our own era, for instance, Sigmund Freud, on the one hand, and Franz Kafka, on the other, which is to say, the Healer and the Patient he could not have healed, since he is another, an alternative version of himself. The voice which cries, "Physician, heal thyself!" speaks always in irony rather than hope. Yet both Healer and Patient are, in some sense, or at least aspire to become, Joseph.

How eminently appropriate, then, that Kafka (first notable Jewish Dreamer of a cultural period in which the Jews of the Western World were to thrive like Joseph in Egypt, but also to be subject to such terror as the descendants of Joseph later suffered at the hands of a Pharaoh who knew him not) should have called his fictional surrogate, his most memorable protagonist, by the mythological name of Joseph. This time around, however, Joseph is specified a little, becoming—with the addition of the author's own final initial—Joseph K., a new Joseph sufficient unto his day. This Joseph, at any rate, along with the fable through which he moves, embodied for two or three generations of writers to follow (real Jews and imaginary ones, Americans and Europeans, White men and Black) not only a relevant dream-vision of terror, but also the techniques for rendering that dream in the form that Freud had meanwhile taught us was most truly dreamlike: with a nighttime illogic, at once pellucid and dark, and a brand of wit capable of revealing our most arcane desires.

Yet despite the borrowed name of his surrogate-hero, Kafka could no longer imagine a Happy Ending for either that character or himself, since he no longer dreamed himself the Beloved of his father, but an outcast, unworthy and rejected. In what has become perhaps the best known, since it is, surely, the most available, of his stories, *Metamorphosis*, his Joseph protagonist becomes a vermin in his father's eyes. And we are left with the question: how did the lovely boy in his coat-of-many-colors turn into a loathsome insect, the advisor at the royal ear into a baffled quester, an outsider barred forever from the Courts of the Mighty? But the answer to this question Kafka's own works, whatever difficult pleasure or stimulating example they may provide, do not themselves render up —not even the private and agonized "Letter to My Father," nor that final story, in which Joseph is altered in sex, demoted to Josephine, the Songstress. And the relation of the mouse-artist to the Mice-Nation (i.e., the Jews) is treated with uncustomary explicitness: "But the people, quietly, without showing any disappointment . . . can absolutely only make gifts, never receive them, not even from Josephine. . . . She is a tiny episode in the eternal history of our people, and our people will get over the loss."

No, if we would really discover what went wrong with Kafka's relationship to his own father, which is to say, to Israel itself (he who never mentioned the word "Jew" in his published work) which that father represented, or more generally to his inherited past—to history and myth—we must turn back to another Master of Dreams: the Doctor who preceded and survived the Artist: a latter-day *Baal-ha-chalamoth* (in the sense this time of interpreter rather than dreamer), Sigmund Freud, or better, Dr. Freud. Only at this moment, as we pass into a regime of rulers who know not Joseph, have we begun to outgrow our own dependence on that Healer, to learn to see him stripped of his clinical pretenses and assimilated to the ancient myth.

And mythologically speaking, he is, of course, an *alter ego* of Franz Kafka—or more precisely, of Joseph K.—one who, like the Biblical Joseph and his namesake, descended into the abyss of ridicule and shame for the sake of his vision; then was lifted up and acclaimed a culture-hero: a Saviour of the non-Jewish world which had begun by maligning and rejecting him. Certainly, it is as a solver of dreams that Freud first attracted public notice, with that book born just as the twentieth century was being born, *The Interpretation of Dreams*. Like an artist, he himself tells us—though the comparison did not occur to him—he was granted in that book an unearned illumination, on which he was to draw for the rest of his days. "Insights such as this," he wrote much later, toward the end of his life, "fall to one's lot but once in a lifetime."

And publishing the first fruits of that illumination, he prefaced it with a quotation reflecting his sense of how monumental and monstrous a task he was beginning to undertake: "*Flectere si nequeo Superos, Acheronta movebo.*" If I cannot influence the Gods above, I will set the world below in motion—set Hell in motion, he means really, but he chooses to call it "Acheron," to draw on Classical rather than Hebrew mythology, perhaps because he realizes how Faustian, Satanic, blasphemous his boast finally is. And he further clarifies what he means by quoting, in the Foreword which immediately follows, Aristotle's dictum (once more the source is our other, non-Jewish antiquity) that "the dream is not God-sent but of demonic origin." But precisely in his turning from the supernal to the infernal interpretation of dreams, Freud declares himself a true modern, which is to say, quite another sort of Joseph; though the first Joseph, to be sure, began his journey toward success with a descent into the pit.

Unlike the original Joseph, however (for whom there could be no Happy Ending unless his father survived to relish his triumph), Freud could not begin his Acherontic descent until after the death of his father—called Jacob, too, by one of those significant "accidents" which Freud himself would have been the first to point out in the case of another, but on which he never commented in his own. He could not even make the preliminary trip down, much less the eventual trip up, until his darkest wish-dream had been, in guilt and relief, achieved: not to do his rival siblings down in the eyes of his father, but to be delivered of that father—his last tie to the Jewish past—and thus be freed to become an Apostle to the Gentiles, a counselor at the Court of his own doomed Emperor. Yet, before releasing his published book to the Gentile world, or even lecturing on its substance at the Gentile University of Vienna, Freud rehearsed it in one lecture at the Jewish Academic Reading Hall, and

two (however incredible it may seem) before that most bourgeois
of Jewish Fraternal Organizations, the B'nai Brith—tried out his vision, that is to say, before the assembled representatives of the
community to which his dead father had belonged.

Yet, despite the pieties with which he hedged his blasphemy
about, Freud's Acherontic "insight" failed at first to impress either
the world out of which he was trying to escape, or the one to which
he aspired. The handful of reviews his book got responded to it
condescendingly, lumping it with old-fashioned "Dream Books" for
the ignorant and the superstitious; and it sold, during the first two
years after publication, some 350 copies, scarcely any in the next
five. But this is hardly to be wondered at since, to Jew and Gentile
alike, Freud was proposing a radically new myth of the relation of
sons to fathers, of the present to the past: a myth whose inversion
of the Joseph legend never occurred to him in those terms at all.
What is involved is not merely the flight from Hebrew mythology in
general, which we noticed in regard to the epigraph and Foreword to
The Interpretation of Dreams, but something much more particular.

After all, one figure out of the Old Testament did come eventually to possess the imagination of Freud and to occupy him on the
level of full consciousness: the figure of Moses, whose very name
—as Freud carefully points out—means in Egyptian "Son," with
the patronymic suppressed and whose own fleshly father, Amram,
plays no part in his myth, is not even named at the center of the
tale. Surely Freud loved Moses because he would brook no father
at all, Hebrew or Egyptian or Midianite, killing the surrogate for
the Egyptian King who had fostered him, running off from Jethro,
the father of the *shikse* he had married, and—most reluctant of
Jews—refusing to have his own son circumcized until the Angel of
the Lord (so runs the apocryphal extension of the story) had swallowed him from his head down to his testicles. Joseph, however,
Freud does not ever mention; though as an old, old man, he wrote
once—to his own son naturally—"I sometimes compare myself to
the old Jacob whom in his old age his children brought to
Egypt. . . ." (And not even this time did he pause to note that in
becoming "Jacob," he was becoming his own father.)

In his great pioneering work, however, it is neither Jacob nor
Joseph nor Moses himself whom Freud evokes, but a mythological

goy, two mythological *goyim* out of the dreams of the Gentiles. How casually, how almost inadvertently he calls up King Oedipus and Prince Hamlet side by side in what purports to be a casual three-page digression. Compelling the deep nightmare of fathers and sons dreamed by the Western World from the fifth century before Christ to the seventeenth after his death to give up its secret: "It may be that we were all destined to direct our first sexual impulses toward our mothers and our first impulses of hatred and violence toward our fathers; our dreams convince us that we were. . . ." How calm and objective he keeps his tone, as if the "we" were more impersonal than confessional. Yet everyone knows these days that *The Interpretation of Dreams* was not the product of a sudden revelation alone, but also of a painful self-analysis, into which the death of his father had impelled Freud to plunge and from which he liked to think of himself as having emerged healed.

Unlike Kafka's *Letter to My Father,* Freud's great antipaternal work is a solution, not an exacerbation, or so at least he claimed. In him (it is his proudest boast, and we believe it), obsession is turned into vision, guilt into knowledge, *trauma* into *logos;* while in Kafka, the end is paralysis, a kind of lifelong castration, memorialized by the incomplete and bloody stumps of his most ambitious works. Freud's major works are finished—their completion as much a part of their final meaning as the incompletion of Kafka's was of his. Nonetheless, between them, Kafka and Freud, the crippled poet and the triumphant savant (for, finally, not even a measure of the worldly success of Joseph was denied to the father of psychoanalysis), have helped to determine the shape of Jewish-American writing in the first half of the twentieth century—the shape of the tradition from within which (at the moment of its imminent demise) I write of them both.

From the two, our writers have learned their proper function: to read in the dreams of the present the past which never dies and the future which is always to come; and they have, therefore, registered their vision in a form which wavers between the parable and the discursive essay, art and science. For though the means of the Jewish-American writers from Nathanael West to Norman Mailer are poetic and fictional, their ends are therapeutic and prophetic. Their outer ear may attend to the speech of their contemporaries, in the realist's hope of catching out life as it passes; but their inner ear hears still the cry of Freud: "I am proposing to show that dreams are capable of interpretation." And their characteristic tone is born of the tension between the Kafka-esque wail of *"Oi veh!"* and the Freudian shout of *"Eureka!"*

That tone is established once and for all in the work of Nathanael West, in whom begins (however little the critics may have suspected it in his own time) the great take-over by Jewish-American writers of the American imagination—our inheritance from certain Gentile predecessors, urban Anglo-Saxons and midwestern provincials of North European origin—of the task of dreaming aloud the dreams of the whole American people. How fitting, then, that West's first book—published in 1931, at the point when the first truly Jewish decade in the history of our cultural life was beginning —be called *The Dream Life of Balso Snell* and that it turn out to be, in fact, a fractured and dissolving parable of the very process by which the emancipated Jew enters into the world of Western Culture.

Balso himself gets in by penetrating through the asshole that symbol of tradition and treacherous conquest, "the famous wooden horse of the Greeks." West makes his point with some care, perhaps a little too insistently for subtlety's sake: not only is it the Trojan horse that alone gets us into the beleaguered city; but for us Jews, just to make it into the horse in the first place is a real problem—since, after all, it was built for Greeks. We do not need Balso to tell us that there are only three possible openings, three entry-ways into any horse, even the most fabulous of beasts; but which way is for us we do not know in advance, and this he is prepared to explain, reporting of his hero, our thirties representative: "The mouth was beyond his reach, the navel provided a cul-de-sac, and so, forgetting his dignity, he approached the last. O Anus Mirabilis!" It is a lovely, an inevitable pun—and not only in 1931, since in any age, the Jewish Dream Peddler must, like Balso, "forget his dignity" to get inside. Not for him, the High Road to Culture *via* the "horse's mouth," nor the mystical way of "contemplating the navel"; only the "Acherontic" Freudian back entrance: the anal-sexual approach. "Tradesmen enter by the rear."

For West's Balso, at any rate, the strategy works; in a moment, he is transformed from outsider to insider, but he does not like it after all. God knows what he had imagined would be waiting for him in the belly of the horse; what he discovers in fact is that it is "inhabited solely by writers in search of an audience," all Josephs and no Pharaohs. And the approval of other approval-seekers is exactly what he neither needs nor wants, though for a while he pursues one of their number, "a slim young girl" called Mary McGeeney, who has written a novel "in the manner of Richardson," the Great WASP Father of the *genre*. It is not as an author, however, that Balso lusts for Mary, but as the archetypally desirable *shikse*, who—at the very moment his tongue is in her mouth—disconcertingly becomes "a middle-aged woman, dressed in a mannish suit and wearing horn-rimmed glasses," which is to say, Potiphar's wife turned schoolmarm. Once revealed, however, Miss McGeeney proves even less of a problem to Balso than her earliest prototype to Joseph: "He hit Miss McGeeney a terrific blow in the gut and hove her into the fountain." After which, she stays inside the limits of his fantasy, returning "warmly moist" to make possible the sexual climax with which the book ends, turning a dry dream wet.

More troublesome to Balso than his Gentile foster mother (to whom he can play Joseph or Oedipus, turn and turn about, with no real strain) is a kind of archetypal Jewish father, who disconcertingly appears in the very bowels of the horse, a self-appointed *kibbitzer* in the uniform of an official guide, from whom Balso has finally to wrench himself "with a violent twist," as the paternal busybody howls in his ear: "Sirrah . . . I am a Jew! and whenever anything Jewish is mentioned, I find it necessary to say that I am a Jew. I'm a Jew! A Jew!" It is the last such explicit declaration of Jewishness anywhere in West's work, on the lips of a character or in the words of the author himself; for after the exorcism of *Balso Snell,* his dreamers dream on presumably free forever of their aggressively Jewish censor. But the dreams that they dream—of Sodom burning, of the destruction of ever purer Josephs by ever grosser Potiphar's wives—we must call Jewish dreams.

Even the madness which cues them, we must call (more in sorrow than chauvinistic pride) Jewish madness; for just such madness, cuing just such dreams, we discover in that other great novel of the thirties, this time frankly Jewish in language and theme, Henry Roth's *Call It Sleep.* How aptly the ending of that book manages to catch, more in the rhythm, maybe, than in their manifest content, the phrasing of the words, that ambiguous moment at a day's end when it is uncertain whether the spirit is falling toward sleep and a dreaming from which it will wake with the morning or toward a total nightmare from which there is no waking ever. The cadences of that close and their hushed terror stay in my head, more than thirty years after Roth first conceived them, a valedictory both to his child protagonist in bed and to his own career as a writer: "He might as well call it sleep. It was only toward sleep that every wink of the eyelids could strike a spark into the cloudy tinder of the dark, kindle out of the shadowy corners of the bedoom such myriad and such vivid jets of images. . . ."

We know, having come so far in the novel, what those images "toward sleep" were, and are, obviously doomed to be until death for Roth and his protagonist: the adoring mother, exposed in her nakedness before jeering kids; the terrible rage of an actual Jewish father and the guilty dream of a *goyish* spiritual one; the Jewish girl betrayed in abject love to a mocking Gentile; the spark out of the bowels of the earth, up from the third electrified rail of the streetcar, bright enough to redeem all from darkness and pain; and, weaving in and out of the rest, the cry of the Prophet: "I am a man of unclean lips in the midst of a people of unclean lips. . . ."

Joseph—the solver of dreams—has become confused with Isaiah in the terrible thirties, learning to talk dirty instead of speaking fair; and he moves, therefore, not toward recognition and acclaim in his own lifetime and his father's, but like West or Roth, toward premature death or madness and silence. If, at long last, posthumous success has overtaken Nathanael West, and almost-posthumous acclaim Henry Roth—this is because the forties and fifties learned once more to believe in the Happy Ending, which the writers of Genesis postulated for the Joseph myth, but which the thirties could imagine no more than Kafka himself. The lowering into the pit, the descent into Egypt or Hell was all of the legend which seemed to them viable; and trapped in the darkness, they looked not to Pharaoh for deliverance, but to the psychoanalysts, the heirs of that Jewish Doctor who had boasted that he could set very Hell in motion.

In our time, however, with benefit of analysis or without, Joseph has once more been haled into Pharaoh's court, once more lifted up in the sight of his enemies and brothers; once more recognized as a true Master of Dreams, under his new names of J. D. Salinger and Bernard Malamud and Philip Roth and Saul Bellow. But this is the achievement of an era just now coming to a close, a decade or more of responsibility and accommodation, in which those erstwhile outsiders, Freud and Kafka, became assigned classroom reading, respectable topics for the popular press: an age which, rediscovering West and Roth, celebrated its own sons who had grown up reading them, the age of the Jew as winner. But how hard it is to love a winner—to love Bellow, let's say, after the National Book Award and best-sellerdom—in this land of ours, where nothing succeeds like failure, and all the world loves a loser.

How much more comfortable we feel with those exceptional figures of the forties-fifties who did not quite make it, dying too soon and still relatively unknown, like Isaac Rosenfeld, or surviving dimly inside of their wrecked selves until they could disappear unnoticed, like Delmore Schwartz. I, at least, find myself thinking often these days of Rosenfeld, who might well (it once seemed) have become our own Franz Kafka and who perhaps *was* (in a handful of stories like "The Pyramids" and "The Party," dreams of parables or parables of dreams) all the Kafka we shall ever have. And even more often my thoughts turn, ever since his pitiful death anyhow—in the same black year for the Jews which also saw Lenny Bruce go—to Delmore Schwartz, with whom the forties began two years before the official opening of the decade.

It was only 1938, even before the start of World War II, when there appeared a volume of his short fiction and verse called, appropriately enough, *In Dreams Begin Responsibilities*—"responsibilities" for the age to come, "dreams" for the long tradition on which he drew. In the title story, at any rate, a young man on the eve of his twenty-first birthday, is portrayed dreaming a dream that becomes a movie (not in technicolor, or even in black and white, but in gray on gray, those authentic Schwartzian colors), the movie of a dream. Asleep, but already on the verge of waking, he watches his parents, sundered by rage and mutual incomprehension before his birth or conception. " . . . and I keep shouting," he tells us, "What are they doing? Don't they know what they're doing? Why doesn't my mother go after my father?' . . . But the Usher has seized my arm and is dragging me away. . . ."

It is a nightmare uncannily apt for the Age of the Cold War and Going-to-the-Movies—an era whose chief discovery was disillusion: this bad dream of the past as irrevocably given and of the impotence of the young in the face of enormities which they inherit (and even understand) but cannot control. Born in reaction, it is a counterdream to the Marxian vision of apocalypse and social change which moved the thirties and of the hysterical despair which underlay it, the paranoia which its myth of the Class Struggle at once nurtured and concealed. But for the antipolitical politics of the forties-fifties, too, there is an appropriate psychosis, as there is for all brands of politics: the conviction of impotence freezing into catatonia—the total paralysis of the will of those with no place to go except *up* into the Counselor's seat at the right hand of the leaders of utterly corrupt states. Both the thirties and the forties-fifties, however, merely *suffered* varying forms of madness bred by Freud's Oedipal dream and the failure of Marxian politics.

It was left to the sixties (which got off to an even earlier start than most decades somewhere around 1955) to *celebrate* psychosis; and to attempt, for the first time, not to pretend that schizophrenia was politics, but to make a politics of schizophrenia recognized for what it is: a total and irrevocable protest against Things-as-They-Are in a world called real. And behind this movement, too, there is a Jewish dreamer, yet one more Joseph sufficient unto his day. I mean, of course, Allen Ginsberg who has escaped the hang-up of finding or not finding the ear of Pharaoh, by becoming a mock-Pharaoh, a Pharaoh of Misrule, as it were. Think of his actual presence at the head of parades or his image looking down at us from subway hoardings—crowned with the striped hat of Uncle Sam.

Ginsberg, however, unlike the Joseph before him, is no father's darling at all, not even such a baffled aspirant for paternal favor as was Kafka. He is a terminal son, to be sure, like the others—but a mama's boy this time, unable to imagine himself assuming papa's role ever ("Beep, emit a burst of babe and begone/ perhaps that's the answer, wouldn't know till you had a kid/ I dunno, never had a kid never will at the rate I'm going"), or saying *kaddish,* that traditional Jewish mourner's prayer which becomes an endearing synonym for "son"—except for his mother, called Naomi, and identified in his mythological imagination with her Biblical namesake, and with Ruth and Rebecca as well, though *not* with Rachel, that favored second wife of Jacob. She was a life-long Communist, that mother who haunts Ginsberg, who died—lobotomized and terror-stricken—in the nuthouse: "Back! You! Naomi! Skull on you! Gaunt immortality and revolution come—small broken woman—the ashen indoor eyes of hospitals, ward grayness on skin."

But her post-Marxian madness, the very paranoia which persuaded her that she had been shut away at the instigation of "Hitler, Grandma, Hearst, the Capitalists, Franco, Daily News, the 20's, Mussolini, the living dead," becomes in her son vision and a program fostered by that vision: "vow to illuminate mankind . . . (sanity a trick of agreement)." And when his own insanity fails to sustain him, he turns to drugs, singing—on marijuana and mescalin, Lysergic Acid and laughing gas and "Ayahusca, an Amazonian spiritual potion"—a New Song, appropriate to a new sort of Master of Dreams, the pusher's pusher, as it were. He does not sell the chemical stuff of dreams directly, of course (was this, then what the Jews *did* peddle in the market place of Juvenal's Rome?), but sells the notion of selling them—crying out in protest: "Marijuana is a benevolent narcotic but J. Edgar Hoover prefers his deathly scotch/And the heroin of Lao-Tze and the Sixth Patriarch is punished by the electric chair/but the poor sick junkies have nowhere to lay their heads. . . ." or insisting in hope: "The message is: Widen the area of consciousness."

The psychedelic revolution, however, whatever its affinities with the traditional Jewish trade of dream-pedlary and its appeal to the sons of Jewish merchants engaged in handling much harder goods, belongs to a world essentially *goyish:* the world of William Burroughs and Timothy Leary and (however little he might relish the thought) J.R.R. Tolkien. For a contemporary Master of Dreams more explicitly Joseph-ian, which is to say, Jewish, we must turn to a writer who in his own fantasies is never more than half-Jewish, to Norman Mailer. Those who have read the successive versions of his *The Deer Park* (or have seen it on the stage), and who know his most successful and impressive short stories, "The Man Who Studied Yoga" and "The Time of Her Time," as well as the notes on these in that mad compendium of self-pity and self-adulation, *Advertisements for Myself,* are aware that Mailer once planned a Great American Dream Novel in eight volumes.

Each volume, he tells us, was to have represented one of the "eight stages" in the dream of a defeated Jewish writer (Mailer makes him only one-quarter Jewish, which is to say, minimally though essentially so) called Sam Slavoda, who, in his nighttime fantasy sees himself as a kind of Super-Goy called Sergius O'Shaughnessy. In the dream of Slavoda, O'Shaughnessy, his heroic *alter ego,* is portrayed as eternally struggling with a Jewish father figure (in the recent dramatic version, we learn that he is "half-Jewish—on both sides"), named Eitel, for the possession of a Gentile girl, daughter or mistress or wife (essentially, I suppose, somebody else's wife, i.e., Potiphar's Wife), called Elena. It is all —thanks, alas, to Freud—distressingly explicit; and I for one was not, am not, sorry that the project ended in shipwreck and a ten years' silence; since out of that silence Mailer emerged to write a book less like Kafka and more like Pop Art—more indebted, that is, to the immediate Jewish past (those post-World War II Masters of Dreams, Shuster and Siegal, who inventing Superman for the comics, invented a possible future for the dying novel) than to a remoter one no longer viable.

That book is, of course, *An American Dream,* in which dreamer and dream-actor have become one, Sam Slavoda plus Sergius O'Shaughnessy turning into Stephen Rojack—who is half-Jewish, since in the world of myth a quarter Jew plus a full Gentile equals a half-Jew. But he is precisely the half-Jew, the half of Joseph, that neither Kafka nor the great writers of the thirties could envision: Joseph *after* his recognition, the very archetype of the Man Who Has Made it. No protagonist has entered our recent fiction with so impressive a list of distinctions, for he is a Congressman, a decorated War Hero, the friend of a future President of the United States, the M.C. of a successful T.V. program; as well as a tireless cocksman, who can get away with murdering his own wife, then walk the parapet of a penthouse under the eye of his evil Fascist father-in-law, turn down that Bad Father's homosexual advances, and triumph finally over a Total Conspiracy—in which all of his Bad Brothers (transformed fashionably into members of the Mafia and the C.I.A.) have joined with that Father to destroy him.

Mailer's latest book is, indeed, in its very banality and vulgarity just such an American Dream as its title advertises it to be; but it is also a Jewish Dream: if not Joseph's own dream, at least our dream of Joseph, as well as a Jewish interpretation of the dreams of Pharaoh's (read "John F. Kennedy's") servants. Try as he will, therefore, Mailer cannot basically alter the shape of the myth he has inherited. How desperately he yearns to permit his Joseph (unlike the earlier Josephs from whom he descends) to have all that glory and Potiphar's Wife, too—in fact, all three of the Gentile women into whom Mailer has split the single figure of the original legend. But, in the end, Rojack has to reject them like the Josephs before him, so that his soul may live. Deborah Coughlin Mangravede Kelly he marries and kills, though—or maybe because—she is Pharaoh's Wife rather than Potiphar's. Mailer nowhere says outright, of course, that she is intended to be a portrait of Jacqueline Kennedy; but she reminds us of the mythological Jackie at least. And Rojack, introducing her, explains, "Forgive me, I thought the road to President might begin at the entrance to her Irish heart."

And the mistress once dead, he must destroy the maid who is her extension, too: penetrating all three of her entrances, one by one, but reaching his climax—and cheating her of her own—in the *Anus Mirabilis* (we are back to Balso Snell once more, and this time the identification is explicitly made between asshole and Acheron: "I had come to the Devil a fraction too late, and nothing had been there to receive me. . . ."). Buggery is the essential aspect of a sexual connection whose aim is annihilation not fulfillment; and buggery extorts from the red-headed German Ruta, the confession that she had been a Nazi: " '*Ja.*' She shook her head. 'No, no,' she went on. '*Ja,* don't stop, *ja.*' " After which Rojack is able to declare, "There was a high private pleasure in plugging a Nazi, there was something clean despite all. . . ."

But another third of Potiphar's wife remains to be dealt with; after the Irish aristocrat and the Kraut servant, the ultimately blonde, all-American Wasplet: the Happy Ending Girl, whose name, Cherry, declares, I suppose, that whatever befalls her flesh, mythologically she remains eternally virgin. Cherry, Rojack truly loves, but her, too, he leads to her death—involuntarily, but inevitably all the same; not, however, until he has won her in an archetypal battle with a *really* Bad Brother—a Negro junkie who comes at him with a knife. It is as if Mailer were trying to declare, or his fable in his despite: "Things haven't changed all that much, my colored brothers; a Jewish boy in good condition can still beat out you spade hipsters in the struggle for that archetypal blonde *shikse* who embodies the American psyche." Yet in the end, the spades who cannot keep her in life do her in; the friends of the hipster whom Rojack has earlier defeated, humiliated, in effect, *killed,* destroy our poor Cherry. And Rojack, guiltless of that murder, is released from the burden of actual love—releasing his author at the same moment from all obligations to realism: liberating him into the world if not of pure myth, at least of Pop Art fantasy.

As the book closes, Mailer asks us to believe, Rojack has stopped at a disconnected phone booth in the middle of the Great American Desert; and when he dials (sleeping or waking, we are not sure) the voice of his dead beloved answers—and why not, after all. "Why, hello hon, I thought you'd never call. . . . Marilyn says to say hello." At this point, Mailer's personal fantasy becomes once more our common fantasy, his dream girl ours, as Cherry blends into our own late, perhaps too much lamented, Marilyn Monroe; and somehow we are supposed to be, somehow we *are* at peace. It is a long way from the beginning of Mailer's book to the end: from his evocation of the dead Dream Boy of us all (the novel opens, "I met Jack Kennedy in November, 1946. We were both war heroes and had been elected to Congress"), whose death one crazy Jew, himself now dead, thought he was avenging—to the Dead Dream Girl of us all, of whose death another saner Jew has written a play to prove himself guiltless. But it is a way which leads from madness to sanity, from falling asleep to waking up; from the lunatic wish to be President and screw all the women in the world, to the modest hope of finding someone to love and the resolve to take time out for thinking things over.

"But in the morning," Stephen Rojack ends by saying, "I was something like sane again, and packed the car and started on the long trip to Guatemala and Yucatan." Maybe this, too, is only one more fantasy, the last madness of believing oneself sane; or maybe Joseph *is* sane again, at least as Mailer has re-imagined, re-embodied him; maybe, in exorcising himself of the American Dream, the American version of the flight from Potiphar's wife, Mailer has healed himself—demonstrating that artist and doctor can inhabit the same head. Didn't Freud himself assert (apropos of his own attempt along the same lines, the very book with which we began) that successful self-analysis is possible to one who is "a prolific enough dreamer"?

But even granting all this, we are left with the final question: what does this mean to *us*? What do Joseph's personal healing and his consequent success (after all, *An American Dream* did prove a best-seller, and more, a way back into writing again for its author) mean to those who have helped make that success, critics or readers or nonreading buyers of books? And the answer to that question I have been pursuing throughout—reflecting on how the Jewish Dreamer in Exile, thinking only of making his own dreams come true, ends by deciphering the alien dreams of that world as well; thus determining the future of all those who can only know what lies before them dimly and in their sleep. It is the essence of the myth I have been exploring that Joseph, the Master of Dreams, cannot lie; for dreams tell only the truth, and the Dreamer is also a Dream. But the final word on the subject has been said by Freud himself, in his peroration to *The Interpretation of Dreams:*

> The ancient belief that dreams reveal the future is not entirely devoid of truth. By representing a wish as fulfilled the dream certainly leads us into the future; but this future, which the dreamer accepts as his present, has been shaped in the likeness of the past by an indestructible wish.

Buffalo, N. Y.
—1967

The Higher Sentimentality

PRIMITIVISM IS THE large generic name for the Higher Masculine Sentimentality, a passionate commitment to inverting Christian-Humanist values, out of a conviction that the Indian's way of life is preferable. From this follows the belief that if one is an Indian he ought, despite missionaries and school boards, to remain Indian; and if one is White, he should do his best, despite all pressures of the historical past, to go Native. Ever since the oft-quoted observation of Crèvecoeur that there must be something superior in Indian society since "thousands of Europeans are Indians, and we have no example of even one of those aborigines having from choice become Europeans . . . ," White men in America have continued to echo that primitivist hyperbole, whose truth cannot be diminished merely by disproving Crèvecoeur's facts.

Crèvecoeur's own *Letters from an American Farmer* ends with a declaration that he is about to pack up his family and head out for a wigwam in the forest, a resolution which, once he had written it down, he felt quite free not to live. But this seems irrelevant; for, in theory at least, the rejection of Our Side and the identification with Theirs involved in purely literary renegadism ought to be as disturbingly real as the act, say, of Simon Girty going over to the redskin enemy.

Yet, in fact, most of the literature written by literary renegades affords us only the easy pleasure and secondhand self-righteousness once derived by Victorians from reading

about the tribulations of the poor. Even a symbolic deser-
tion to the Indians should seem an outrage, a blasphemy—
certainly not just another pious gesture, one more Good
Work. But precisely this sense of do-gooding mars for me
the would-be primitivism of certain authors who, in addition to loving Indians and propagandizing on their behalf,
lived with them and knew them intimately: Oliver La
Farge, for instance, whose *Laughing Boy* was once taken
very seriously indeed, and Frank Waters, whose *The Man
Who Killed the Deer* is once again in print twenty-five
years after its first appearance.

The pretense of writing from within the consciousness
of Indians intrinsic to such fiction leaves me always with
the sense of having confronted an act of impersonation
rather than one of identification, a suspicion of having been
deceived; and this is reinforced when the presumable wisdom of the alien Red Man turns out to be some quite
familiar cliché of our own culture—as when toward the
end of Waters' novel, Byers, his surrogate and spokesman,
thinks:

> We are all caught in the tide of perpetual change.
> These pueblos, these reservations must sometime pass
> away, and the red flow out into the engulfing white. . . .
> So both must sometime pass: the Indian with his
> simple fundamental premise untranslated into modern
> terms, and finally the white with his monstrous
> materiality.
>
> But perhaps there would still be time, thought
> Byers, to learn from these people before they pass from
> this earth which was theirs and is now all men's—the
> simple and monstrous truth of mankind's solidarity
> with all that breathes and does not breathe . . .

The book ends not on this relatively somber note, however,
but with a temporary Happy Ending, the postponement
of the Vanishing American's vanishing for one more generation, as the Sacred Lake is saved for the tribe, and yet

one more boy adopted into a kiva to be initiated into the old ways.

Despite such concessions to Hollywood taste, however, Waters' book has a continuing appeal to the young, whose disaffection from a life dedicated to work and success makes them susceptible to even the *kitschiest* evocations of the Indian alternatives. It would be hard to understand otherwise how such a conventional example of slick fiction as William Eastlake's "Portrait of an Artist With 26 Horses" (about an Indian who gives up living in the white man's world, believing this involves giving up his wife and son, only to discover that they are waiting for him, having learned on their own such bits of esoteric wisdom as "money isn't everything" and "it won't buy happiness") was included in a recent collection made by Donald Allen and Robert Creeley, calling itself *New American Story.*

A more considerable and impressive try at the same sort of thing is Peter Matthiessen's *At Play in the Fields of the Lord,* which recounts at its center the story of a college-educated, brainwashed North American Indian called Lewis Meriwether Moon by a romantic father who had loved the memory of that doomed explorer for having crossed the continent without—he had been convinced— killing a single Indian. Moon, a mercenary soldier with a patched-up plane as his stock-in-trade and a Jewish hipster for a partner, finds himself among still primitive South American tribesmen; appalled at the emptiness of his own life, the lovelessness of his own world, he makes it back to nakedness and mindlessness in the jungle mud.

There is much in Matthiessen's book that is palpably false (his hippy Jew from the Bronx is incredible, his white missionaries stereotypes out of Somerset Maugham); but he renders with real convincingness the downward progress of Moon: first detaching himself by will from one way of life, then falling by necessity out of another, until, in utter loneliness, he recapitulates the beginning or invents the end of man. And at that extreme moment, he mourns the passing of his people, even before he bewails himself:

. . . a well of sadness for things irredeemable and gone flowed over him. The Indian nation had grown old; he knelt down like a penitent and wept. He wept for Aeore and the doomed people of the jungle, and he wept for the last old leatherfaces of the plains. . . .

He felt bereft, though of what he did not know. He was neither white nor Indian, man nor animal. . . .

He thought, Am I the first man on the earth; am I the last?

Finally, such works depend upon a pathos too simple, a world-view too naive, to sustain a major literary effort, however adequate they may seem to the living needs of the young. I, at any rate, have never been as much moved by any of the fictions derived from nostalgic primitivism as by a letter written me just after the death of Hemingway and my own published responses to it. Composed by a young Montanan who had just attended a meeting of the Native American Church, an Indian peyote cult with fundamentalist Christian trimmings, it is a deliberate non-literary, even anti-literary document; and maybe this is part of the real point, since a novel in praise of the analphabetic past stirs more ironies than it can ever resolve. "I hope you will pardon this midsummer madness," the letter begins, and "madness" is the keynote, my correspondent continuing a little later:

> Since attending an all night prayer meeting with . . . the Cheyenne I am also mad on Indians. I expected to have hallucinations, I did not expect to encounter truths. . . . What one sees, and this has no meaning (I suppose) until one has seen it, is one's mirror image, the image everyone (especially Hemingway) is secretly searching for, the answer to the question "What am I *really* like?" . . .

If Hemingway obsesses the writer, it is because Hemingway seems to him what he in fact was—except in the facetious talking-in-his-sleep of *Torrents of Spring*—the inventor for our time of the False Western. Hemingway (along with books and the movies) lies; the Indians (along with drum-beating and peyote) tell the truth: this is the simple-minded thesis.

> The mental mirror of the conqueror cannot be found in the culture of the conqueror. The mental mirror of the conqueror can only be found in the eyes of the conquered, those people who do not read or write or leave histories or legends, but simply live and die unremembered. It took hours of fire watching and drumbeating and chanting and meditation before that deepest of liberal prejudices, that underneath the skin we are all alike, finally wore off. . . . We are bred and inculcated from childhood in the doctrines and belief of winners. We are conquerors, upmen, all of us, collectively and individually. (The Jews, being a traditionally conquered people, get off more easily, but only in a relative way.)

Perhaps the parenthetical comment suggests one reason why Jews have played so large a role in creating the New or anti-"Upman" Western Novel; though, as a matter of fact, they did not begin to do so until, in America and especially in the field of the arts, they began to move rapidly into the establishment, i.e., to go "up."

> I cannot think of a single Hemingway hero, who was not, in one way or another, a conqueror's hero. Brave, stoic, modest, essentially unanalytic, never grasping, dedicated to honor in the face of events which made honor meaningless. . . . We conquerors heroize Gary Cooper and Natty Bumppo, because by pretending that they are really like us, we are able to create a mirror image of ourselves that is pleasing. . . .
>
> The mirror image that the American public has loved to find for itself in the Hemingway novels is the opposite of the true mirror image of the American public. Those of us who have come close to the pio-

neers in Montana know . . . those great heroes of the west, eulogized Monday through Friday on TV, were the most selfish, ruthless, cunning, conniving, grasping bastards in the history of the World. And to cover this up . . . they imitated, mimicked, mocked and claimed for themselves the nature of the person they tortured and murdered, the American Indian. No wonder the only good Indian is a dead Indian. They give the lie to the frontier myth. . . . The frontier heroes were mock Indians. . . .

At this point, my correspondent might well have sat down to write just such a satire of the Old West as David Markson produced in *The Ballad of Dingus Magee*. But, remembering Hemingway, he turns in another direction:

Anyway, the thesis which I never got to is that Hemingway is the colossal literary upman, playing the winner's game all the way. Like all good Nazis (racial upmen) he went nuts at the end. The Indians are colossal downmen (they are too lazy to write). While we have been playing checkers they have been playing give away. As a result they have nothing but poverty, anonymity, happiness, lack of neuroses, wonderful children and a way of life that is free, democratic and in complete fulfillment of the American dream, the one Hemingway longed for.

And as a final note, an obvious afterthought, he adds (thus emboldening me to use his text as I have):

I personally have joined the Cheyenne and am never going to use this thesis. I'm playing give away.

Madness, drugs, caricature, and abuse: many of the essentials of the New Western are already present here; but the setting will not do, for finally the Reservation (half island in time, half ghetto in space) is as inadequate a West in the latter half of the twentieth century as the remembered forests of Barth and Cohen, or the remote ones of Matthiessen. La Farge and Waters and Eastlake and even my friend fresh from firewatching in Montana are seeking the West in a past which is not less lapsed because it has been preserved in a few enclaves, flanked by motels and souvenir shops, and connected by superhighways. If there still exists for us a Wilderness and a Place-out-of-Time appropriate for renewal rather than nostalgia, rebirth rather than recreation, that place must be in the Future, not the Past: that Future toward which we have been pointed ever since the Super-Guy comic books and the novels of science fiction shifted the orientation of Pop Art by one hundred and eighty degrees.

But the real opposite of nostalgic is psychedelic, the reverse of remembering is hallucinating, which means that, insofar as the New Western is truly New, it, too, must be psychedelic.

The term is embarrassingly fashionable and disconcertingly broad in application, including, in the field of fiction alone, examples as varied as science fiction itself, both in its classic form, and in such extensions as Burrough's *Nova Express*, Harry Matthew's *Tlooth*, and Anthony Burgess' *The Clockwork Orange;* metapolitical fables, emerging out of the wreck of Marxist ideology, like the story behind that astonishing movie, *Morgan;* and even such High Church Christian allegories, pretending to be fairy tales, as J. R. R. Tolkien's *The Lord of the Rings*. But no other name fits as well the New Western, which, like the Old Western at its most authentic, deals precisely with the alteration of consciousness.

Besides, many of the so-called "psychedelics" themselves, those hallucinogenic drugs, at least, found in nature rather than synthesized in the laboratory (marijuana, peyote, the Mexican Mushroom, Ayahuasca, etc.), are our bridge to— even as they are gifts from—the world of the Indian: the world not of an historical past, but of the eternally archaic one. And so, too, are those other once-magical plants, now long socialized and deprived of power, *yerba maté*, coffee, cacao, and, especially, tobacco, on which Shamans once saw visions—and which somehow still threatens us Whites, as our Big Medicine, whiskey ("The White Man's Milk," the Indians called it), still threatens the Indian. It is easy to forget how those first hippies of the Western World, Raleigh, Marlowe, and company, cultivated a life-style based on homosexuality, a contempt for Established Religion, and "drinking" tobacco; for all that survives of the first Indian-inspired Drug Cult are a handful of lyrics, apt to strike us as much more amusing than dangerous:

> The Indian weed withered quite,
> Green at morn, cut down at night,
>   Shows thy decay;
>   All flesh is hay:
> Thus think, then drink Tobacco.

Nothing in the seventeenth century compares in scope and avowed seriousness even with the literature of the nineteenth century Drug Cult (centered around opiates, and therefore implicated in the myth of an Absolute East rather than a Polar West), from Poe and Coleridge and DeQuincy to Baudelaire—much less with the prose and verse being composed now on, or in the name of, "pot." Certainly it is hard to identify a tobacco-style, as one can an opium-style, and even a marijuana (or, as we come to synthesize a Super-West of our own, an LSD) one.

In Cohen's *Beautiful Losers,* for instance, the sort of vision evoked by psychedelics, or bred by the madness toward which their users aspire, is rendered in a kind of prose appropriate to that vision—a prose hallucinated and even, it seems to me, hallucinogenic: a style by which it is possible to be actually turned on, though only perhaps (judging by the critical resistance to Cohen's book) if one is already tuned in to the times. Yet even he felt a need for an allegiance to the past as well as the future, to memory as well as madness—or perhaps more accurately a need to transmute memory into madness, dead legend into living hallucination; and for him the myth of Catherine Tekakwitha served that purpose.

For us, however, on the other side of a border that is religious as well as political, mythological as well as historical, her story will not work; and what we demand in its place is the archetypal account of no analogous girl (for us women make satisfactory devils, but inadequate saints), but the old, old fable of the White outcast and the noble Red Man joined together against home and mother, against the female world of civilization. This time, however, we require a new setting, at once present and archaic—a setting which Ken Kesey discovered in the madhouse: *our* kind of madhouse, which is to say, one located in the American West, so that the Indian can make his reappearance in its midst with some probability, as well as real authenticity.

Perhaps it was necessary for Kesey to come himself out of Oregon, one of our last actual Wests (just as it was necessary for him to have been involved with one of the first experiments with the controlled use of LSD), since for most Americans after Mark Twain, the legendary colored companion of the white fugitive had been turned from Red to Black. Even on the most naive levels, the Negro has replaced the Indian as the natural enemy of Woman; as in the recent film *The Fortune Cookie*, for instance, the last scene of which fades out on a paleface *schlemiel* (delivered at last from his treacherous whore of a white wife) tossing a football back and forth with his Negro buddy in a deserted football stadium. Similarly, in such sophisticated fiction as James Purdy's *Cabot Wright Begins*, the color scheme demanded by the exigencies of current events is observed, though in this case, the relationship has become overtly and explicitly homosexual:

> . . . His dark-skinned prey seated himself under the street-lamp and Bernie, more desperate by the moment, seated himself next to him, then almost immediately introduced himself.

His new friend accepted the introduction in the manner in which it was meant. They exchanged the necessary information about themselves, Bernie learning that his chance acquaintance was Winters Hart, from a town in the Congo. . . . Taking Winters Hart's left hand in his, Bernie held his friend's dark finger on which he wore a wedding-ring, and pressed the finger and the hand.

Far from being annoyed at this liberty, Winters Hart was, to tell the truth, relieved and pleased. Isolation in a racial democracy, as he was to tell Bernie later that night, as they lay in Bernie's bed together, isolation, no thank you.

The title of the chapter from Purdy's book from which this passage comes is "One Flew East, One Flew West"— referring, I suppose, to the two sexual choices open to men; but it reminds us of the title of Kesey's archetypal Western, *One Flew Over the Cuckoo's Nest*, which represents a third possibility of White transcendence: madness itself.

A myth in which the non-White partner for whom the European American yearns is Black rather than Red, we tend to interpret as a parable of an attempt to extend our sexuality, to recover our lost *libido;* while one in which the White man longs for an Indian, we are likely to read as signifying a desire to breach the limits of reason, to extend our consciousness. Mark Twain tried valiantly to reverse this in his two books involving Huck Finn, making Injun Joe rather than Nigger Jim the threat to white womanhood; but trying in *Pudd'nhead Wilson* to imagine the only really sexually desirable woman in all his works, he felt obliged to make her minimally and by legal definition Black. Moreover, future Jims all the way down to Purdy's Winters Hart have tended to become ever more frankly the objects of *eros.* And this is fair enough, since in the language of archetype the Negro stands for alien passion, and the Indian for alien perception. (Or perhaps this is only another way of saying that at the level of deep imagination the Indian is male and the Negro female; the former Yang, the latter Yin.)

In no case does the longing for a Negro companion represent in the male a temptation to escape society once and for all by the final expedient of going out of one's head. Ike McCaslin in Faulkner's "The Bear," seems at first glance an exception; but the Sam Fathers who initiates him into lifelong isolation remains quite ambiguous, being Negro and Indian at the same time, maybe more Indian than Negro in the heart of the wilderness, where the crisis of the tale is enacted. In Faulkner's later work, his boy-heroes are humanized by their Negro mentors, saved for society rather than persuaded to abandon it by those bland, resilient post-Uncle Toms like Lucas Beauchamp. To be sure, an occasional female in Faulkner may have her madness compounded by the Negro upon whom she projects it, like Joanna Burden in *Light in August,* infuriated rather than satiated by the sexuality of Joe Christmas, who may, indeed, be less a Negro than a pretender to Negro-ness.

Even the most nearly lunatic of Faulkner's projections of his youthful self, Quentin Compson, is pushed over the brink not by finding a Negro Companion, but by failing to find one. His suicide on the verge of manhood may have been precipitated in part by a lifelong obsession with the impurity of White women, symbolized for him by his sister Caddy's soiled underpants; but it is more immediately occasioned by the absence in Cambridge of anything closer to a true Uncle Tom than Deacon, who blasphemously camps the role. Finally, Faulkner can imagine no America without the Negro—and when he tries to imagine someone like himself imagining it, he conceives of him wigging out of that world completely. But his Indians (the old Ikemotubbe, for instance, of his short stories) are vanishing by definition, disappearing as fast as the forests of the American past.

Not so with Ken Kesey, whose novel opens with an obviously psychotic "I" reflecting on his guards, one of whom identifies him almost immediately, speaking in a Negro voice: "Here's the Chief. The *soo*-pah Chief, fellas. Ol' Chief Broom. Here you go, Chief Broom. . . ." Chief Bromden is his real name, this immense schizophrenic, pretending he is deaf-and-dumb to baffle "the Combine," which he believes controls the world: "Look at him: a giant janitor. There's your Vanishing American, a six-foot-six sweeping machine, scared of its own shadow. . . ." Or rather Bromden is the name he has inherited from his white mother, who subdued the full-blooded Chief who sired him and was called "The-Pine-That-Stands-Tallest-on-the-Moutain." "He fought it a long time," the half-breed son comments at one point, "till my mother made him too little to fight any more and he gave up."

Chief Bromden believes he is little, too, what was left in him of fight and stature subdued by a second mother, who presides over the ward in which he is confined ("She may be a mother, but she's big as a damn barn and tough as knife metal . . .") and, at one point, had given him two hundred successive shock treatments. Not only is Mother II big, however, especially in the breasts; she is even more essentially *white*: "Her face is smooth, calculated, and precision-made, like an expensive baby doll, skin like flesh-colored enamel, blend of white and cream and baby-blue eyes . . ." and her opulent body is bound tight in a starched white uniform. To understand her in her full mythological significance, we must recall that seventeenth century first White Mother of Us All, Hannah Duston, and her struggle against the Indians who tried to master her.

Hannah has represented from the start those forces in the American community—soon identified chiefly with the female and maternal—which resist all incursions of savagery, no matter what their course. But only in the full twentieth century is the nature of Hannah's assault made quite clear, first in Freudian terms and then in psychedelic ones. "No, buddy," Kesey's white hero, Randle Patrick McMurphy, comments on the Big Nurse. "She ain't peck-

ing at your *eyes*. That's not what she's peckin' at." And
when someone, who really knows but wants to hear spoken
aloud what he is too castrated to say, asks at *what*, then,
R. P. McMurphy answers, "At your balls, buddy, at your
everlovin' *balls*." Yet toward the close of the book, Mc-
Murphy has to be told by the very man who questioned
him earlier the meaning of his own impending lobotomy
at the hands of Big Nurse ("Yes, chopping away the brain.
Frontal-lobe castration. I guess if she can't cut below the
belt she'll do it above the eyes"), though by this time he
understands why he, as well as the Indian (only victim
of the original Hannah's blade), has become the enemy
of the White Woman.

In his own view, McMurphy may be a swinger, and in
the eyes of his Indian buddy an ultimate Westerner, the
New American Man: "He walked with long steps, too long,
and he had his thumbs hooked in his pockets again. The
iron in his boot heels cracked lightning out of the tile. He
was the logger again, the swaggering gambler . . . the
cowboy out of the TV set walking down the middle of the
street to meet a dare."

But to Big Nurse—and the whole staff of the asylum
whom, White or Black, male or female, she has cowed—
he is only a "psychopath," not less sick for having chosen
the nuthouse in which he finds himself to the work-farm
to which his society had sentenced him. And she sees the
purpose of the asylum as being precisely to persuade men
like him to accept and function in the world of rewards
and punishments which he has rejected and fled.

To do this, however, she must persuade him like the
rest that he is only a "bad boy," *her* bad boy, quite like, say
Huckleberry Finn. But where Huck's substitute mothers
demanded that he give up smoking, wear shoes, go to
school, she asks (it is the last desperate version of "sivili-
sation") that he be sane: "All he has to do is *admit* he was
wrong, to indicate, *demonstrate* rational contact and the
treatment would be cancelled this time."

The choice is simple: either sanity abjectly accepted, or

sanity imposed by tranquilizers, shock treatments, finally lobotomy itself. But McMurphy chooses instead if not madness, at least aggravated psychopathy and an alliance with his half-erased, totally schizophrenic Indian comrade—an alliance with all that his world calls unreason, quite like that which bound Henry to Wawatam, Natty Bumppo to Chingachgook, even Ishmael to Queequeg (that versatile Polynesian, who, at the moment of betrothal, whips out a tomahawk pipe, quite as if he were a real Red Man). And this time, the alliance is not merely explicitly, but quite overtly directed against the White Woman, which is to say, Hannah Duston fallen out of her own legend into that of Henry and Wawatam.

For a while, the result seems utter disaster, since McMurphy, driven to attempt the rape of his tormentor, is hauled off her and duly lobotomized, left little more than a vegetable with "a face milk-white except for the heavy purple bruises around the eyes." Whiter than the White Woman who undid him, white as mother's milk: this is McMurphy at the end, except that Chief Bromden will not let it be the end, will not let "something like that sit there in the day room with his name tacked on it for twenty or thirty years so the Big Nurse could use it as an example of what can happen if you buck the system. . . ."

Therefore in the hush of the first night after the lobotomy, he creeps into the bed of his friend for what turns out to be an embrace—for only in a caricature of the act of love can he manage to kill him: "The big, hard body had a tough grip on life. . . . I finally had to lie full length on top of it and scissor the kicking legs with mine. . . . I lay there on top of the body for what seemed like days. . . . Until it was still a while and had shuddered once and was still again."

It is the first real *Liebestod* in our long literature of love between white men and colored, and the first time, surely, that the Indian partner in such a pair has outlived his White brother. Typically, Chingachgook had predeceased Natty, and Queequeg, Ishmael; typically, Huck had been younger than Jim, Ike than Sam Fathers. Everyone who has lived at the heart of our dearest myth knows that it is the white boy-man who survives, as the old Indian, addressing the Great Spirit, prepares to vanish. Even so recent a novel as Berger's *Little Big Man* has continued to play it straight, closing on the traditional dying fall, as Old Lodge Skins subsides after a final prayer, and his white foster son says:

> He laid down then on the damp rocks and died right away. I descended to the treeline, fetched back some poles, and built him a scaffold. Wrapped him in the red blanket and laid him thereon. Then after a while I started down the mountain in the fading light.

But on the last page of *One Flew Over the Cuckoo's Nest*, Chief Bromden is on his way back to the remnants of his tribe who "have took to building their old ramshackle wood scaffolding all over the big million-dollar . . . spillway." And his very last words are: "I been away a long time."

It is, then, the "Indian" in Kesey himself, the undischarged refugee from a madhouse, the AWOL Savage, who is left to boast: *And I only am escaped alone to tell thee.* But the "Indian" does not write books; and insofar as Kesey's fable can be read as telling the truth about himself as well as about all of us, it prophesies silence for him, a silence into which he has, in fact, lapsed, though not until he had tried one more Gutenberg-trip in *Sometimes A Great Notion.*

It is a book which seems to me not so much a second novel as a first novel written (or, perhaps, only published) second: a more literary, conventionally ambitious, and therefore *strained* effort—for all its occasional successes, somehow an error. *One Flew Over the Cuckoo's Nest* works better to the degree that it is dreamed or hallucinated rather than merely written—which is to say, to the degree that it, like its great prototype *The Leatherstocking Tales*, is Pop Art rather than *belles · lettres*—the dream once dreamed in the woods, and now redreamed on pot and acid.

Its very sentimentality, good-guys bad-guys melodrama, occasional obviousness and thinness of texture, I find—like the analogous things in Cooper—not incidental flaws, but part of the essential method of its madness. There is a phrase which reflects on Kesey's own style quite early in the book, defining it aptly, though it pretends only to represent Chief Bromden's vision of the world around him: "Like a cartoon world, where the figures are flat and outlined in black, jerking through some kind of goofy story that might be real funny if it weren't for the cartoon figures being real guys. . . ."

Everywhere in Kesey, as a matter of fact, the influence of comics and, especially, comic books is clearly perceptible, in the mythology as well as in the style; for like those of many younger writers of the moment, the images and archetypal stories which underlie his fables are not the legends of Greece and Rome, not the fairy tales of Grimm, but the adventures of Captain Marvel and Captain Marvel, Jr., those new-style Supermen who, sometime just after World War II, took over the fantasy of the young. What Western elements persist in Kesey are, as it were, first translated back into comic-strip form, then turned once more into words on the conventional book page. One might, indeed, have imagined Kesey ending up as a comic book writer, but since the false second start of *Sometimes A Great Notion*, he has preferred to live his comic strip rather than write or even draw it.

The adventures of Psychedelic Superman as Kesey had dreamed and acted them, however—his negotiations with Hell's Angels, his being busted for the possession of marijuana, his consequent experiences in court and, as a refugee from the law, in Mexico—all this, like the yellow bus in which he used to move up and down the land taking an endless, formless movie, belongs to hearsay and journalism rather than to literary criticism, challenging conventional approaches to literature even as it challenges literature itself. But *One Flew Over the Cuckoo's Nest* survives the experiments and rejections which followed it; and looking back five years after its initial appearance, it seems clear that in it for the first time the New West was clearly defined: the West of Here and Now, rather than There and Then—the West of Madness.

The Westering impulse which Europe had begun by regarding as blasphemous (as, for instance, in Dante's description of Ulysses sailing through the Pillars of Hercules toward "the world without people"), it learned soon to think of as crazy, mocking Columbus and his dream of a passage to India, and condemning as further folly each further venture into a further West after the presence of America had been established (think, for example, of Cabeza de Vaca walking into the vast unknown and becoming, on his impossible adventure, a god to those savages whose world he penetrated).

It is only a step from thinking of the West as madness to regarding madness as the true West, but it took the long years between the end of the fifteenth century and the middle of the twentieth to learn to take that step. There is scarcely a New Western among those I have discussed which does not in some way flirt with the notion of madness as essential to the New World; but only in Leonard Cohen (though Thomas Berger comes close) and in Kesey is the final identification made, and in Kesey at last combined with the archetype of the love that binds the lonely white man to his Indian comrade—to his *mad* Indian comrade, perhaps even to the *madness* of his Indian comrade, as Kesey amends the old tale.

We have come to accept the notion that there is still a territory unconquered and uninhabited by palefaces, the bearers of "civilization," the cadres of imperialist reason; and we have been learning that into this territory certain psychotics, a handful of "schizophrenics," have moved on ahead of the rest of us—unrecognized Natty Bumppos or Huck Finns, interested not in claiming the New World for any Old God, King, or Country, but in becoming New Men, members of just such a New Race as D. H. Lawrence foresaw. (How fascinating, then, that R. D. Laing, leading exponent among contemporary psychiatrists of the theory that some schizophrenics have "broken through" rather than "broken down," should, despite the fact that he is an Englishman, have turned to our world and its discovery in search of an analogy; he suggests that Columbus's stumbling upon America and his first garbled accounts of it provide an illuminating parallel to the ventures of certain madmen into the regions of extended or altered consciousness, and to their confused version, once they are outside of it, of the strange realm in which they have been.)

Obviously, not everyone is now prepared, and few of us ever will be, to make a final and total commitment to the Newest West via psychosis; but a kind of tourism into insanity is already possible for those of us not yet ready or able to migrate permanently from the world of reason. We can take, as the New Westerns suggest, what is already popularly called—in the aptest of metaphors—a "trip," an excursion into the unknown with the aid of drugs. The West has seemed to us for a long time a place of recreation as well as of risk; and this is finally fair enough, for all the ironies implicit in turning a wilderness into a park. After all, the West remains always in some sense true to itself, as long as the Indian, no matter how subdued, penned off, or costumed for the tourist trade, survives—as long as we can confront there a creature radically different from the old self we seek to recreate in two weeks' vacation.

And while the West endures, the Western demands to be written—that form which represents a traditional and continuing dialogue between whatever old selves we transport out of whatever East, and the radically different other whom we confront in whatever West we attain. That other is the Indian still, as from the beginning, though only vestigially, nostalgically now; and also, with special novelty and poignancy, the insane.

If a myth of America is to exist in the future, it is incumbent on our writers, no matter how square and scared they may be in their deepest hearts, to conduct with the mad just such a dialogue as their predecessors learned long ago

to conduct with the aboriginal dwellers in the actual Western Wilderness. It is easy to forget, but essential to remember, that the shadowy creatures living scarcely imaginable
lives in the forests of Virginia once seemed as threatening
to all that good Europeans believed as the acid-head or the
borderline schizophrenic on the Lower East Side now seems
to all that good Americans have come to believe in its place.

Boxing the Compass

To BEGIN ANSWERING the first of these questions, we need only notice the fact, too obvious, perhaps, to have been properly observed or understood, that geography in the United States is mythological. From the earliest times, American writers have tended to define their own country—and much of our literature has, consequently, tended to define itself—topologically, as it were, in terms of the four cardinal directions: a mythicized North, South, East, and West. Correspondingly, there have always been four kinds of American books: Northerns, Southerns, Easterns, and Westerns, though we have been accustomed, for reasons not immediately clear, to call only the last by its name. Not all American books, of course, fit into one or another of these geographical categories, or even some canny blend of them; yet much of our most distinguished literature is thus mythologically oriented and can be fully appreciated only in this light.

The Northern tends to be tight, gray, low-keyed, underplayed, avoiding melodrama where possible—sometimes, it would seem, at all costs. Typically, its scene is domestic, an isolated household set in a hostile environment. The landscape is mythicized New England, "stern and rockbound," the weather deep winter: a milieu appropriate to the austerities and deprivations of Puritanism.

Here where the wind is always north-north-east
And children learn to walk on frozen toes . . .
Passion is here a soilure of the wits,
We're told, and love a cross for them to bear . . .

In the field of the novel, the Northern is represented, in
general, by books easier to respect than to relish, since there
is not much savor in them, books which could easily be
thought of as *belles lettres,* fit for readers seeking loftier
satisfactions than pleasure in a time when Christianity had
been replaced by the Religion of Culture. The *other* novels
of Harriet Beecher Stowe (*The Mayflower,* for instance, or
The Minister's Wooing—the sort of thing she wrote when
the demon which dictated *Uncle Tom's Cabin* deserted her)
are a good instance of the type, as is most of William Dean
Howells, a little of Henry James, and, supereminently,
Edith Wharton's *Ethan Frome:* a dismal lot on the whole.

The Scarlet Letter is an apparent exception to these
observations; it seems a *pre*-Northern, finally, describing the
mythological origins of a world which wholly contains the
later, true Northern. Actually, the Northern works better
in verse than in prose, as a rule: in the narrative poems of
Robert Frost, for instance, notably, say, "The Witch of
Cöos"; in much of Edward Arlington Robinson, whose sonnet on New England is quoted above by way of illustration;
and most recently in the work of Robert Lowell. One of its
classics, however, is a prose poem in the form of a journal,
Henry David Thoreau's *Walden,* which defines once and for
all the archetypal essence of the transplanted lonely WASP
in the midst of, or better, *against* the Massachusetts wilderness—in the course of which encounter, he becomes transformed into the Yankee. (But when he floated, somewhat
earlier, at ease and with his brother for a companion, on the
voyage whose diaries he made into *A Week on the Concord
and Merrimack Rivers,* it is a Western he lived and wrote.)

The Southern, though its name is not quite so standardly
used as that of the Western, is at least as well-known, per-

haps too familiar to need definition at all. Certainly it is the most successful of all the topological subgenres of the novel in America, as triumphant on the highbrow level—from, say, Edgar Allan Poe through William Faulkner to Truman Capote or Flannery O'Connor—as on that of mass entertainment—from another side of that same Poe to Thomas Dixon's *The Clansman* (which suggested to D. W. Griffith the plot of *The Birth of a Nation*) or Margaret Mitchell's *Gone With the Wind* (the movie version of which leads an immortal life). The Southern has always challenged the distinction between High and Pop Art, since not merely Poe, its founder, but such latter-day successors of his as Faulkner and Capote have thriven in the two presumably sundered worlds of critical esteem and mass approval.

Perhaps this is because the Southern, as opposed to the Northern, does not avoid but seeks melodrama, a series of bloody events, sexual by implication at least, played out in the blood-heat of a "long hot summer" against a background of miasmal swamps, live oak, Spanish moss, and the decaying plantation house so dear to the hearts of moviemakers. Indeed, until there were ruined plantations—which is to say, until the Civil War, defeat, and Reconstruction —there could be no true Southern (Poe, being ante-bellum, had to imagine the doomed mansions appropriate to his horrors in a mythical Europe). The mode of the Southern is Gothic, American Gothic, and the Gothic requires a haunted house at its center. It demands also a symbolic darkness to cloak its action, a "blackness of darkness" which in the Old World was associated with the remnants of feudalism and especially with the dark-cowled ministers and "Black Nobility" of the Church.

What the Church and feudal aristocracy were for European Gothic, the Negro became for the American variety, "the Black," as he is mythologically called, being identified by that name with the nightmare terror which the writer of Southerns seeks to evoke, with the deepest guilts and fears of transplanted Europeans in a slaveholding community, or more properly, in a community which remembers having sent its sons to die in a vain effort to sustain slavery. But projecting those guilts and fears out upon the Blacks, draining himself of all his vital darkness, as it were, the European in the South condemned himself to a kind of mythological anemia; he became "Whitey."

Without the Negro, in any case, there is no true Southern. And whoever treated the Negro in our fiction—until urbanization changed everything—tended to write a Southern, whether he thought of himself as doing so or not; unless, of course, like Mark Twain in *Huckleberry Finn*, he turned his Negro protagonist into a Noble Savage, i.e. an Indian in blackface. Only where Jim is really a "nigger," i.e. at the very beginning and end of the novel where he plays the comic darky, or at certain points on the raft where he "camps" the role, addressing Huck as his "young master," does *Huckleberry Finn* become anything like a Southern; most of the way it is something quite other which we still have not defined. And occasionally it even threatens to become an Eastern, or a parody of one, when the Duke and the Dauphin bring their European pretensions aboard the raft; for the Eastern deals with the American confronting Europe, and cultural pretension is as essential to it as tourism.

Customarily, the Eastern treats the return of the American to the Old World (only then does he know for sure that he *is* an American), his Old Home, the place of origin of his old self, that original Adam, whom the New World presumably made a New Man. Its season is most appropriately spring, when the ice of New England symbolically breaks and all things seem—for a little while—possible; and, as is appropriate to that erotic time of year, it deals often with love (*The Roman Spring of Mrs. Stone* is the prototypical title of one Eastern, the single novel of Tennessee Williams, who turned from his mythological South when he briefly forsook drama): the flirtation of the American, usually female, with the European, most often male. Sometimes, as in Henry James's *The Ambassadors*, the sexual-mythological roles are reversed, or, as in James Baldwin's *Giovanni's Room,* both are males, though one suspects Baldwin's Giovanni of being a Negro disguised as a European, and the book consequently of being a disguised Southern. In any event, the distribution of the sexes makes little difference in the Eastern, the encounter of European and American being doomed to frustration by the very nature of the case. This is so in part because the American turns out to be impelled by motives not so much truly erotic as merely anti-anti-erotic, and in part because, being not an émigré or a cosmopolitan but only a tourist (the Eastern is the form which defines the American precisely as a "tourist"), he—or, alternatively, she—has to go home.

It is Henry James (who may have sent his Lambert Strethers home, but who never returned to stay himself) whom we think of as the High Priest of the cult of the Eastern, or even as its Founder, though Nathaniel Hawthorne in *The Marble Faun,* and James Fenimore Cooper before him in *Homeward Bound,* were there first. Even so unadventurous a laureate of the middle classes as Henry Wadsworth Longfellow tried his hand at the Eastern, by implication in his verse translations and adaptations of European models, quite explicitly in such a novel as *Kavanaugh: A Tale.* But James began his career by asserting a claim to the form in *The American,* a claim which came to seem more and more exclusively his as he produced example after example (turning his hand to an occasional Northern like *The Bostonians* as a breather) until he could write no more. And with James—not so much originally as after his revival in the twenties—the Eastern became associated with that Culture Religion, so virulent in the United States between the two world wars.

Basic to that worship of High Art was the dogma that there are some books, in fiction chiefly those of James himself, an appreciation of which distinguishes the elect from the vulgar, the sensitive from the gross, and that those books can be known immediately because *a*) they are set in Europe, *b*) they mention other works of art, often so

casually that only the cognoscenti know them without the
the aid of footnotes, and *c*) they are written by expatriates.
Obviously, most of the poetry of T. S. Eliot and much of
Ezra Pound ("tourist" or Eastern poetry *par excellence*)
falls into this category, quite in the style of their long unsuspected counterpart in the mid-nineteenth century—bound
to them by many affinities besides a common love for Dante
and a preference for being "abroad"—Longfellow himself.

Not all Easterns, however, belong in intention or in retrospect to the realm of self-conscious High Art; if any book
which deals with the reaction of the American abroad (via
tourism or dreams belongs to the genre, Mark Twain was
one of its most assiduous practitioners, all the way from
Innocents Abroad to *A Connecticut Yankee in King Arthur's
Court.* And in our own century, we have had Scott Fitzgerald's *Tender is the Night,* a borderline case, perhaps, as
well as most of the novels by Hemingway, who thought of
himself, surely, as an emulator more of Twain than of James.
But not everything is what it seems to a superficial scrutiny;
and looking hard at Hemingway's *The Sun Also Rises* and
For Whom the Bell Tolls, we discover that certain characters
whom he represents as Spanish peasants seem mighty like
Montana or Upper Michigan Indians—and that consequently
he is actually writing, if not quite Westerns, at least
crypto-Westerns, since it is the presence of the Indian which
defines the mythological West.

The heart of the Western is not the confrontation with the
alien landscape (by itself this produces only the Northern),
but the encounter with the Indian, that utter stranger for
whom our New World is an Old Home, that descendant of
neither Shem nor Japheth, nor even, like the Negro imported
to subdue the wild land, Ham. No grandchild of Noah,
he escapes completely the mythologies we brought with us
from Europe, demands a new one of his own. Perhaps he
was only a beast of the wildwood, the first discoverers of
America reassured themselves, not human at all; and at the
end of the fifteenth century, Princes of the Church gravely

discussed whether, being undescended from Adam, the Indian indeed had a soul like our own. It was a question by no means settled once and for all when the Church answered "yes"; for at the beginning of our own century, Lawrence amended that answer to "yes, but—" Yes, a soul, but *not* one precisely like our own, except as our own have the potentiality of becoming like his.

And in the five hundred years between, how the Indian in his ultimate otherness has teased and baffled the imagination of generation after generation of European voyagers and settlers. How they have tried to assimilate him to more familiar human types, to their own mythologic stock-in-trade. The name "Indian" itself memorializes the first misguided effort of Columbus to assure himself that he was in those other, those *East* Indies, after all, and confronting nothing but types known since Marco Polo, like the inhabitants of Cipango or Cathay.

After that delusion had collapsed, after the invention as opposed to the mere discovery of America, there were new explainers-away eager to identify the Red Men with the Welsh, the Irish—and especially the Semites, the lost Tribes of Israel.

Only the minority group comprising "scientific" anthropologists have clung in our time to the delusion of Columbus, postulating a migration from continent to continent which makes our Indians kin to the subjects of the Great Khan after all. And only a handful of nuts have been willing to identify the Indians as survivors of quite another world, another creation—refugees from Atlantis or Mu. Lawrence was tempted to the latter alternative, hinting somewhat mysteriously of an affinity between the western Indians, at least, and the priesthood of the lost Pacific civilization, "the world once splendid in the fulness of the other way of knowledge."

"They seem to lie under the last spell of the Pacific influence," he says of the Redskins of Cooper's *The Prairie;* "they have the grace and physical voluptuousness . . . of the lands of the great Ocean." But the deep imagination of

Americans has sought stubbornly to link the Savages of the
New World with the once-Chosen People of the Old.

From those apostles to the Indians of the seventeenth
century who thought of themselves as penetrating the wilderness to restore the Old Testament to those to whom it properly belonged, through Fenimore Cooper in the early
nineteenth, recounting the adventures of just such a deluded
missionary in the form of Parson Amen in Oak Openings
(to whom the bewildered Redskins object that, being Indians, they can never be *lost*), to the later Mormons,
incorporating the wrong-headed myth in their homemade
scriptures, and the rancher of *Cat Ballou*, baffled at the
Indian who refuses to answer his Hebrew greeting of
"*Shalom!*"—the tradition has never died.

It is, in fact, carried from door to door even now by
missionaries for the Church of Latter Day Saints, who
leave behind them the *Book of Mormon*, complete with a
prefatory gloss that sends those eager to know the "Fate of
Indians" to the fourteenth verse of the thirteenth chapter
of *First Nephi:*

> And it came to pass that I beheld multitudes of the
> Gentiles upon the land of promise; and I beheld the
> wrath of God, that it was upon the seed of my brethren;
> and they were scattered before the Gentiles and were
> smitten.

This may be, to true believers, a sufficient mythological
explanation not only of the origin, but of the expropriation of
the Indians. To the Indians themselves, however, though
they may be in fact as stubborn and persistent witnesses
as the Jews, it remains inconceivable that they can be anything so familiar to the three thousand-year-old tradition
of the White West as mere children of Israel, that they can
be anything but their untranslatable selves.

Everything else which belongs to the Western scene has
long since been assimilated: the prairies subdivided and
landscaped; the mountains staked off as hunting preserves
and national parks; fabulous beasts, like the grizzlies and

the buffalo, killed or fenced in as tourist attractions; even the mythological season of the Western, that nonexistent interval between summer and fall called "Indian summer," become just another part of the White year. Only the Indian survives, however ghetto-ized, debased, and debauched, to remind us with his alien stare of the new kind of space in which the baffled refugees from Europe first found him (an unhumanized vastness), and the new kind of time through which, despite all our efforts, he still moves (a historyless antiquity). It is for this reason that tales set in the West seem to us not quite Westerns, unfulfilled occasions for myth rather than myth itself, when no Indian —"stern and imperturbable warrior" or lovely, complaisant squaw, it scarcely matters—appears in them.

The Western story in archetypal form is, then, a fiction dealing with the confrontation in the wilderness of a transplanted WASP and a radically alien other, an Indian—leading either to a metamorphosis of the WASP into something neither White nor Red (sometimes by adoption, sometimes by sheer emulation, but *never* by actual miscegenation), or else to the annihilation of the Indian (sometimes by castration-conversion or penning off into a ghetto, sometimes by sheer murder). In either case, the tensions of the encounter are resolved by eliminating one of the mythological partners —by ritual or symbolic means in the first instance, by physical force in the second. When the first method is used, possibilities are opened up for another kind of Western, a secondary Western dealing with the adventures of that New Man, the American *tertium quid;* but when the second is employed—our homegrown Final Solution—the Western disappears as a living form, for the West has, in effect, been made into an East.

But into what exactly is the transplanted European converted by the Western encounter when he resists resolving it by genocide? It is easy enough to name the aspects of Americans defined by the three other forms: the Northern, in which we become Yankees; the Southern, in which we

are turned into Whitey; the Eastern, in which we are revealed as Tourists. But the transformation effected in the
Western evades easy definition. Thinking of Natty Bumppo
(that first not-quite-White man of our literature, for all
his boasts about having "no cross in my blood") and his
descendants, we are tempted to say that it is the woodsman
which the ex-European becomes beside his Red companion:
the hunter, the trapper, the frontiersman, the pioneer, at
last the cowboy—or maybe only next-to-last, for after him
comes the beatnik, the hippie, one more wild man seeking
the last West of Haight-Ashbury in high-heeled boots and
blue jeans. But even as he ceases to be beatnik and becomes
fully hippie, the ultimate Westerner ceases to be White at
all and turns back into the Indian, his boots becoming moc-
casins, his hair bound in an Indian headband, and a string
of beads around his neck—to declare that he has fallen not
merely out of Europe, but out of the Europeanized West,
into an aboriginal and archaic America.

It is tempting, at this point, to take the dilemma as the
answer, and to settle for saying that, since this new kind of
man came into existence only with the West, he is best
called simply the "Westerner," that there is no way of moving
beyond this. But we know, too, that at the moment of looking into the eyes of the Indian, the European becomes the
"American" as well as the Westerner. And if we forget
it for a moment, there is the title of Henry James's early
novel to remind us: his account of a white barbarian from
San Francisco, actually called—with a bow to Columbus—
Christopher Newman. And who has more right than the
man from the farthest West to be called both new and
American, since before a single White man had set foot
on American soil, the whole continent had been dreamed
by Europe as "the West": a legendary place beyond or
under the ocean wave, a land of the dead or those who
rise from the dead. And it needed only the invention of the
name America to set up the equation *America equals the
West.*

Once the Atlantic was crossed, moreover, the name *West* was transferred, step by step, to whatever part of the continent lured men on just over the line of settlement, to the unexplored space behind the next natural barrier, past the Appalachians, the Mississippi, the Rockies. Vermont or Maine may define our North once and for all; Georgia, Alabama, or Louisiana may circumscribe our mythological South; the harbors of Boston and New York City, ports from which tourists embark for the adventure of returning to the Old World, can scarcely be thought of as anything but the East.

But where, geographically, is the elusive West? We know that first of all it was Virginia itself, the Old Dominion, then New England, Pennsylvania, Kentucky, Louisiana, Ohio, Missouri, Texas, the Oregon Territory, etc., etc.—always a bloody ground just over the horizon, or just this side of it, where we confronted *in their own territory* the original possessors of the continent.

So long as a single untamed Indian inhabits it, any piece of American space can become to the poet's imagination an authentic West, as the small Vermont town of Acton was transformed, even in the twentieth century, by the vision of Robert Frost's extraordinary poem "The Vanishing Red." Beginning with the lines: "He is said to have been the last Red Man in Acton. And the Miller is said to have laughed . . ." it ends by becoming a parable of the war to the death between White Man and Red, though Frost pretends, ironically, to refuse to tell it:

> It's too long a story to go into now.
> You'd have to have been there and lived it.
> Then you wouldn't have looked on it just as a matter
> Of who began it between the two races.

It is, however, only a desperate sort of Last Western, a hymn to the end of one more West, that Frost manages to write, as seems appropriate to our time. For, by and large, we have used up the mythological space of the West along with its native inhabitants, and there are no new places for which we can light out ahead of the rest—even Alaska being only a fiftieth state. Can we reestablish the West anywhere at all, then? This is the question that troubles certain of our writers, eager to dream the old American dreams. The earth, it turns out, is mythologically as well as geographically round; the lands across the Pacific will not do, since on the rim of the second ocean, West becomes East, our whole vast land (as Columbus imagined, and Whitman nostalgically remembered at the opening of the Suez Canal) a Passage to India.

Maybe the moon will serve our purposes, or Mars; maybe up and out will turn out to be a true archetypal equivalent to the Way West, as we have already begun to surmise, calling some of the literature of space adventure "space operas," on the model of "horse operas," which is to say, Westerns. But unless "stern and imperturbable" Martians await us, or lovely and complaisant lady Lunatics—as certain makers of science fiction have already tried to assure us —whom we can assimilate to our old myths of the Indian, Outer Space will not seem an extension of our original America, the America which shocked and changed Europe, but a second, a meta-America, which may shock and change us. On our shores, the myth of the West which had teased the European imagination up to the time of Dante—the myth of an unattainable and unpeopled world—was altered into one of a world open to "plantation," but inhabited by hostile aliens: a myth so deeply rooted in us that, in spite of scientific testimony to the contrary, we insist on imagining the New Worlds we now approach inhabited by natives, "savages" benign or threatening.

We have defined the "territory ahead" for too long in terms of the mythologies created out of our meeting with and response to the Indians to abandon them without a struggle. They have proved sufficiently adaptable to describe our relations with Negroes and Polynesians, with all colored peoples, in fact (Twain's Nigger Jim and Melville's Queequeg are mythological blood brothers, after all, to Cooper's Chingachgook); and we dream of taking those same terms with us into a future not quite so terrifying and unfamiliar as it sometimes seems, if only they will work there, too.

Cross the Border—Close the Gap

To DESCRIBE the situation of American letters at the end of the sixties is difficult indeed, almost impossible, since the language available to critics at this point is totally inappropriate to the best work of the artists who give the period its special flavor, its essential life. But precisely here is a clue, a way to begin: not with some presumed crisis of poetry or fiction, but with the unconfessed scandal of contemporary literary criticism, which for three or four decades now has vainly attempted to deal in terms invented to explain, defend, and evaluate one kind of book with *another* kind of book—so radically different that it calls the very assumptions underlying those terms into question. Established critics may think that they have been judging recent literature; but, in fact, recent literature has been judging them.

Almost all living readers and writers are aware of a fact which they have no adequate words to express, not in English certainly, nor even in American. We are living, have been living for two decades—and have become acutely conscious of the fact since 1955 —through the death throes of Modernism and the birth pangs of Post-Modernism. The kind of literature which had arrogated to itself the name Modern (with the presumption that it represented the ultimate advance in sensibility and form, that beyond it newness was not possible), and whose moment of triumph lasted from a point just before World War I until one just after World War II, is *dead,* i.e., belongs to history not actuality. In the field of the novel, this means that the age of Proust, Mann, and Joyce is over; just as in verse that of T. S. Eliot, Paul Valéry, Montale and Seferis is done with.

Obviously *this* fact has not remained secret: and some critics have, indeed, been attempting to deal with its implications. But they have been trying to do it in a language and with methods which are singularly inappropriate, since both method and language were invented by the defunct Modernists themselves to apologize for their own work and the work of their preferred literary ancestors (John Donne, for instance, or the *symbolistes),* and to educate an audience capable of responding to them. Naturally, this will not do at all; and so the second or third generation New Critics in America, like the spiritual descendants of F. R. Leavis in England (or the neo-neo-Hegelians in Germany, the belated Croceans in Italy), end by proving themselves imbeciles and naïfs when confronted by, say, a poem of Allen Ginsberg, a new novel by John Barth.

Why not, then, invent a New New Criticism, a Post-Modernist criticism appropriate to Post-Modernist fiction and verse? It sounds simple enough—quite as simple as imperative—but it is, in fact, much simpler to say than do; for the question which arises immediately is whether there can be *any* criticism adequate to Post-Modernism. The Age of T. S. Eliot, after all, was the age of a literature essentially self-aware, a literature dedicated, in avowed intent, to analysis, rationality, anti-Romantic dialectic—and consequently aimed at eventual respectability, gentility, even, at last, academicism. Criticism is natural, even essential to such an age; and to no one's surprise (though finally there were some voices crying out in dismay), the period of early twentieth-century Modernism became, as it was doomed to do, an Age of Criticism: an age in which criticism began by invading the novel, verse, drama, and ended by threatening to swallow up all other forms of literature. Certainly, it seems, looking back from this point, as if many of the best books of the period were critical books (by T. S. Eliot and Ezra Pound and I. A. Richards, by John Crowe Ransom and Kenneth Burke and R. P. Blackmur, to mention only a few particularly eminent names); and its second-best, novels and poems eminently suited to critical analysis, particularly in schools and universities: the works of Proust-Mann-and-Joyce, for instance, to evoke a trilogy which seems at the moment more the name of a single college course than a list of three authors.

We have, however, entered quite another time, apocalyptic, antirational, blatantly romantic and sentimental; an age dedicated to joyous misology and prophetic irresponsibility; one, at any rate, distrustful of self-protective irony and too great self-awareness. If criticism is to survive at all, therefore, which is to say, if criticism is to remain or become useful, viable, relevant, it must be radically altered from the models provided by Croce or Leavis or Eliot or Erich Auerbach, or whoever; though not in the direction indicated by Marxist critics, however subtle and refined. The Marxists are last-ditch defenders of rationality and the primacy of political fact, intrinsically hostile to an age of myth and passion, sentimentality and fantasy.

On the other hand, a renewed criticism certainly will no longer be formalist or intrinsic; it will be contextual rather than textual, not primarily concerned with structure or diction or syntax, all of which assume that the work of art "really" exists on the page rather than in a reader's passionate apprehension and response. Not words-on-the-page but words-in-the-world or rather words-in-the-head, which is to say, at the private juncture of a thousand contexts, social, psychological, historical, biographical, geographical, in the consciousness of the lonely reader (delivered for an instant, but an instant only, from all of those contexts by the *ekstasis* of reading): this will be the proper concern of the critics to come. Certain older critics have already begun to provide examples of this sort of criticism by turning their backs on their teachers and even their own earlier practices. Norman O. Brown, for instance, who began with scholarly, somewhat Marxian studies of Classic Literature has moved on to metapsychology in *Life Against Death* and *Love's Body*; while Marshall McLuhan, who made his debut with formalist examinations of texts by Joyce and Gerard Manley Hopkins, has shifted to metasociological analyses of the mass media in *Understanding Media,* and finally to a kind of pictographic shorthand, half put-on and half serious emulation of advertising style in *The Medium is the Massage.*

The voice as well as the approach is important in each case, since neither in Brown nor McLuhan does one hear the cadence and tone proper to "scientific" criticism of culture, normative psychology or sociology attached to literary texts. No, the pitch, the rhythms, the dynamics of both are mantic, magical, more than a little *mad* (it is a word, a concept that one desiring to deal with contemporary literature must learn to regard as more honorific than

pejorative). In McLuhan and Brown—as in D. H. Lawrence earlier, Charles Olson when he first wrote on Melville—a not so secret
fact recently hushed up in an age of science and positivism is candidly confessed once more: criticism is literature or it is nothing.
Not amateur philosophy or objective analysis, it differs from other
forms of literary art in that it starts not with the world in general
but the world of art itself, in short, that it uses one work of art as
an occasion to make another.

There have been, of course, many such meditating works of art
in the past, both fairly recent (Nietzsche's *Birth of Tragedy)* and
quite remote (Longinus *On The Sublime),* which make it clear that
the authority of the critic is based not on his skills in research or his
collection of texts but on his ability to find words and rhythms and
images appropriate to his ecstatic vision of, say, the plays of Euripides or the opening verses of *Genesis.* To evoke Longinus or even
Nietzsche, however, is in a sense misleading, suggesting models too
grandiose and solemn. To be sure, the newest criticism must be aesthetic, poetic in form as well as substance; but it must also be, in
light of where we are, comical, irreverent, vulgar. Models have appeared everywhere in recent years but tentatively, inadvertently as
it were—as in the case of Angus Wilson, who began a review of
City of Night some years ago (in the pages of an ephemeral little
magazine), by writing quite matter-of-factly, "Everyone knows
John Rechy is a little shit." And all at once we are out of the
Eliotic church, whose dogmas, delivered *ex cathedra,* two generations of students were expected to learn by heart: "Honest criticism
and sensitive appreciation are directed not upon the poet but upon
the poetry. . . . The mind of the mature poet differs from that of
the immature one not precisely on any valuation of personality, not
by being necessarily more interesting, or having 'more to say,' but
rather by being a more finely perfected medium in which etc., etc."

Unless criticism refuses to take itself quite so seriously or at
least to permit its readers not to, it will inevitably continue to reflect
the finicky canons of the genteel tradition and the depressing pieties
of the Culture Religion of Modernism, from which Eliot thought
he had escaped—but which in fact he only succeeded in giving a
High Anglican tone: "It is our business as readers of literature, to
know what we like. It is our business, as Christians, *as well as* read-

ers of literature, to know what we ought to like." But not to know that such stuff is funny is to be imprisoned in Church, cut off from the liberating privilege of comic sacrilege. It is high time, however, for such sacrilege rather than such piety; as some poets have known really ever since Dada, without knowing how to keep their sacrilege from becoming itself sacred; as the dearest obscenities of Dada were sanctified into the social "art" of Surrealism under the fell influence of Freud and Marx.

The kind of criticism which the age demands is, then, Death-of-Art Criticism, which is most naturally practiced by those who have come of age since the death of the "New Poetry" and the "New Criticism." But it ought to be possible under certain conditions to some of us oldsters as well, even those of us whose own youth was coincident with the freezing of all the madness of *symbolisme*-Dada-*surréalisme* into the rigidities of academic *avant-garde*. In this sense, the problem of the aging contemporary critic is quite like that of the no-longer-young contemporary novelist, which one necessarily begins to define even as he defines the dilemma of the critic.

In any case, it seems evident that writers not blessed enough to be under thirty (or thirty-five, or whatever the critical age is these days) must be reborn in order to seem relevant to the moment, and those who inhabit it most comfortably, i.e., the young. But no one has even the hope of being reborn unless he knows first that he is dead—dead, to be sure, for someone else; but the writer exists as a writer precisely for someone else. More specifically, no novelist can be reborn until he knows that insofar as he remains a novelist in the traditional sense, he is dead; since the traditional novel is dead—not dying, but dead. What was up to only a few years ago a diagnosis, a predication (made, to be sure, almost from the moment of the invention of the novel: first form of pop literature, and therefore conscious that as compared to classic forms like epic or tragedy its life span was necessarily short) is now a fact. As certainly as God, i.e., the Old God, is dead, so the Novel, i.e., the Old Novel, is dead. To be sure, certain writers, still alive and productive (Saul Bellow, for instance, or John Updike, Mary McCarthy or James Baldwin), continue to write Old Novels, and certain readers, often with a sense of being quite up-to-date, continue to read them. But so do preachers continue to preach in the Old Churches, and congregations gather to hear them.

It is *not* a matter of assuming, like Marshall McLuhan, that the printed book is about to disappear, taking with it the novel—first form invented for print; only of realizing that in all of its forms—and most notably, perhaps, the novel—the printed book is being radically, functionally altered. No medium of communication ever disappears merely because a new and more efficient one is invented. One thinks, for instance of the lecture, presumably superannuated by the invention of moveable type, yet flourishing still after more than five centuries of obsolescence. What is demanded by functional obsolescence is learning to be less serious, more frivolous, a form of *entertainment*. Indeed, it could be argued that a medium begins to be felt as entertainment only at the point where it ceases to be a necessary or primary means of communication, as recent developments in radio (the total disappearance, for instance, of all high-minded commentators and pretentious playwrights) sufficiently indicates. Students at any rate are well aware of this truth in regard to the university lecture, and woe to the lecturer (of whom, alas, there are many) who does not know it!

In any event, even as the "serious" lecture was doomed by the technology of the fifteenth century, and the "serious" church service by the philology of the eighteenth and nineteenth—so is the "serious" novel, and "serious" criticism as well, by the technology and philology of the twentieth. Like the lecture and Christian church services, its self-awareness must now include the perception of its own absurdity, even impossibility. Since, however, the serious novel of our time is the Art Novel as practiced by Proust, Mann, and Joyce and imitated by their epigones, it is that odd blend of poetry, psychology, and documentation, whose real though not always avowed end was to make itself canonical, that we must disavow. Matthew Arnold may have been quite correct in foreseeing the emergence of literature as scripture in a world which was forsaking the Old Time Religion: but the life of the New Scriptures and the New Time Religion was briefer than he could have guessed.

Before the Bible of the Christians and Jews ceased to be central to the concerns of men in Western society, it had become merely a "book" among others; and this, indeed, may have misled the Arnoldians, who could not believe that a time might come when not merely *the* Book ceased to move men, but even books in general. Such, however, is the case—certainly as far as all books which consider themselves "art," i.e., scripture once removed, are concerned; and for this reason the reborn novel, the truly new New Novel must be anti-art as well as antiserious. But this means, after all, that it must become more like what it was in the beginning, more what it seemed when Samuel Richardson could not be taken *quite* seriously, and what it remained in England (as opposed to France, for instance) until Henry James had justified himself as an artist against such self-declared "entertainers" as Charles Dickens and Robert Louis Stevenson: popular, not quite reputable, a little dangerous—the one his loved and rejected cultural father, the other his sibling rival in art. The critical interchange on the nature of the novel to which James contributed "The Art of Fiction" and Stevenson "A Humble Remonstrance" memorializes their debate —which in the thirties most readers believed had been won hands down by James's defense of the novel as art; but which in the dawning seventies we are not sure about at all—having reached a time when *Treasure Island* seems somehow more to the point and the heart's delight than, say, *The Princess Casamassima.*

This popular tradition the French may have understood once (in the days when Diderot praised Richardson extravagantly, and the Marquis de Sade emulated him in a dirtier book than the Englishman dared) but they long ago lost sight of it. And certainly the so-called *"nouveau roman"* is in its deadly earnest almost the opposite of anything truly new, which is to say, anti-art. Robbe-Grillet, for example, is still the prisoner of dying notions of the *avantgarde;* and though he is aware of half of what the new novelist must do (destroy the Old, destroy Marcel Proust), he is unaware of what he must create in its place. His kind of antinovel is finally too arty and serious: a kind of neo-neo-classicism, as if to illustrate once more that in the end this is all the French can invent no matter how hard they try. Re-imagined on film by Alain Resnais, *Last Year at Marienbad* speaks to the young; but in print it remains merely *chic,* which is to say, a fashionable and temporary error of taste. Better by far, and by the same token infinitely more pertinent is Samuel Beckett, who having been born Irish rather than French, finds it hard to escape being (what some of his readers choose to ignore) compulsively and hilariously funny.

Best of all, however, and therefore totally isolated on the recent French scene (except for the perceptive comments of that equally ambiguous figure, Raymond Queneau) is Boris Vian, especially in his most successful work of fiction, *L'écume des jours,* recently translated into English as *Mood Indigo.* Indeed, Boris Vian is in many ways a prototype of the New Novelist, though he has been dead for a decade or so and his most characteristic work belongs to the years just after World War II. He was, first of all, an Imaginary American (as even writers born in the United States must be these days), who found himself in total opposition to the politics of America at the very moment he was most completely immersed in its popular culture—actually writing a detective novel called *I Will Spit On Your Grave* under the pen name of Vernon Sullivan, but pretending that he was only its translator into French. In fact, by virtue of this peculiar brand of mythological Americanism he managed to straddle the border, if not quite close the gap between high culture and low, belles-lettres and pop art. On the one hand, he was the writer of pop songs and a jazz trumpeter much influenced by New Orleans style; and on the other, the author of novels in which the thinly disguised figures of such standard French intellectuals as Jean Paul Sartre and Simone de Beauvoir are satirized. But even in his fiction, which seems at first glance quite traditional or, at any rate, conventionally *avant-garde,* the characters move toward their fates through an imaginary city whose main thoroughfare is called Boulevard Louis Armstrong.

Only now, however, has Vian won the audience he all along deserved, finding it first among the young of Paris, who know like their American counterparts that such a closing of the gap between elite and mass culture is precisely the function of the Novel Now— not merely optional as in Vian's day, but necessary. And though most of the younger American authors who follow a similar course follow it without ever having known him, by a shared concern rather than direct emulation, he seems more like them than such eminent American forerunners of theirs as Faulkner or Hemingway (except perhaps in Hemingway's neglected early burlesque, *Torrents of Spring,* and Faulkner's self-styled "pot-boiler," *Sanctuary.)*

Vian, unfortunately, turned to the form of the Pop Novel only for the work of his left hand, to which he was not willing even to sign his own name, writing in *L'écume des jours* what seems superficially a traditional enough love story to disarm the conventional critics; though it is finally undercut by a sentimentality which redeems its irony, and reflects a mythology too Pop and American for neo-neo-Classicists to bear.

The young Americans who have succeeded Vian, on the other hand, have abandoned all concealment, and when they are most themselves, nearest to their central concerns, turn frankly to Pop forms—though not, to be sure, the detective story which has by our time become hopelessly compromised by middlebrow condescension: an affectation of college professors and presidents. The forms of the novel which they prefer are those which seem now what the hard-boiled detective story once seemed to Vian: at the furthest possible remove from art and *avant-garde,* the greatest distance from inwardness, analysis, and pretension; and, therefore, immune to lyricism, on the one hand, or righteous social commentary, on the other. It is not compromise by the market place they fear; on the contrary, they choose the genre most associated with exploitation by the mass media: notably, the Western, Science Fiction, and Pornography.

Most congenial of all is the Western, precisely because it has for many decades now seemed to belong exclusively to pulp magazines, run-of-the mill T.V. series and Class B movies, which is to say, has been experienced almost purely as myth and entertainment rather than as "literature" at all—and its sentimentality has, therefore, come to possess our minds so completely that it can now be mitigated without essential loss by parody, irony—and even critical analysis. In a sense, our mythological innocence has been preserved in the Western, awaiting the day when, no longer believing ourselves innocent in fact, we could decently return to claim it in fantasy. But such a return to the Western represents, of course, a rejection of laureates of the loss of innocence like Henry James and Hawthorne: those particular favorites of the forties, who despite their real virtues turn out to have been too committed to the notion of European high art to survive as major influences in an age of Pop. And it implies as well momentarily turning aside from our beloved Herman Melville (compromised by his New Critical admirers and the countless Ph.D. dissertations they prompted), and even from Mark Twain. To Hemingway, Twain could still seem central to a living tradition, the Father of us all, but being Folk rather than Pop in essence, he has become ever more remote from an urban, industrialized world, for which any evocation of pre-Civil War, rural America seems a kind of pastoralism which complements rather than challenges the Art Religion. Folk Art knows and accepts its place in a class-structured world which Pop blows up, whatever its avowed intentions. What remains are only the possibilities of something closer to travesty than emulation—such a grotesque neo-Huck, for instance, as the foulmouthed D. J. in Norman Mailer's *Why Are We in Vietnam*, who, it is wickedly suggested, may *really* be a Black joker in Harlem pretending to be the White refugee from respectability. And, quite recently, Twain's book itself has been rewritten to please and mock its exegetes in John Seelye's *Huck Finn for The Critics*, which lops off the whole silly-happy ending, the deliverance of Nigger Jim (in which Hemingway, for instance, never believed) and puts back into the tale the cussing and sex presumably excised by the least authentic part of Samuel Clemens' mind—as well as the revelation at long last, that what Huck and Jim were smoking on the raft was not tobacco but "hemp," which is to say, marijuana. Despite all, however, Huck seems for the moment to belong not to the childhood we all continue to live, but to the one we have left behind.

Natty Bumppo, on the other hand, dreamed originally in the suburbs of New York City and in Paris, oddly survives along with his author. Contrary to what we had long believed, it is James Fenimore Cooper who now remains alive, or rather who has been reborn, perhaps not so much as he saw himself as in the form D. H. Lawrence re-imagined him en route to America; for Cooper understood that the dream which does not fade with the building of cities, but assumes in their concrete and steel environment the compelling vividness of a waking hallucination, is the encounter of Old World men and New in the wilderness, the meeting of the transplanted European and the Red Indian. No wonder Lawrence spoke of himself as "Kindled by Fenimore Cooper."

The Return of the Redskin to the center of our art and our deep imagination, as we all of us have retraced Lawrence's trip to the mythical America, is based not merely on the revival of the oldest and most authentic of American Pop forms, but also projects certain meanings of our lives in terms more metapolitical than political, which is to say, meanings valid as myth is valid rather than as history. Writers of Westerns have traditionally taken sides for or against the Indians; and unlike the authors of the movies which set the kids to cheering at the Saturday matinees of the twenties and thirties, the new novelists have taken a clear stand with the Red Man. In this act of mythological renegacy they have not only implicitly declared themselves enemies of the Christian Humanism, but they have also rejected the act of genocide with which our nation began—and whose last reflection, perhaps, is to be found in the War in Vietnam.

It is impossible to write any Western which does not in some sense glorify violence; but the violence celebrated in the anti-White Western is guerrilla violence: the sneak attack on "civilization" as practiced first by Geronimo and Cochise and other Indian warrior chiefs, and more latterly apologized for by Ché Guevara or the spokesman for North Vietnam. Warfare, however, is not the final vision implict in the New Western, which is motivated on a deeper level by a nostalgia for the Tribe: a form of social organization thought of as preferable both to the tight two-generation bourgeois family, from which its authors come, and the soulless out-of-human-scale bureaucratic state, into which they are initiated via schools and universities. In the end, of course, both the dream of violence in the woods and the vision of tribal life, rendered in terms of a genre that has long been the preferred reading of boys, seems juvenile, even infantile. But this is precisely the point; for what recommends the Western to the New Novelist is pre-eminently its association with children and the kind of books superciliously identified with their limited and special needs.

For the German, brought up on Karl May, the situation is quite similar to that in which the American, who grew up with Cooper or his native imitators, finds himself. What has Old Shatterhand to do with Art, asks the one, even as the other asks the same of Chingachgook. And the answer is *nothing*. The legendary Indians have nothing to do with Art in the traditional sense, everything to do with joining boy to man, childhood to adulthood, immaturity to maturity. They preside over the closing of the Gap which aristocratic conceptions of art have opened between what fulfills us at eight or ten or twelve and what satisfies us at forty or fifty or sixty.

In light of all this, it is perhaps time to look again at the much-discussed "immaturity" of American literature, the notorious fact that our classic books are boy's books—our greatest novels at home in the Children's Section of libraries; in short, that they are all in some sense "Westerns": accounts of an idyllic encounter between White man and Non-White in one or another variety of wilderness setting. But suddenly this fact—once read as a "flaw" or "failure" or "lack" (it implies, after all, the absence in our books of heterosexual love and of the elaborate analysis of social relations central to the Continental novel)—seems evidence of a real advantage, a clue to why the Gap we now want to close opened so late and so unconvincingly, as it were, in American letters. Before Henry James, none of our novelists felt himself cut off from the world of magic and wonder; he had only to go to sea or, especially, to cross our own particular Border, the Frontier, to inhabit a region where adults and children, educated and uneducated, shared a common enchantment.

How different the plight of mid-nineteenth-century English writers, like Lewis Carroll or Edward Lear or George Macdonald, who had to pretend that they were writing exclusively for the nursery in order to enter the deep wonderland of their own imaginations. Even in our own time, a writer like J. R. R. Tolkien found it necessary to invent the Hobbits in a book specifically aimed at children, before he could release the fearful scholarship (another device foreign to American mythologies) and presumably adult magic of the Rings Trilogy. It makes a difference, after all, whether one thinks of the World Across The Border as Faerie or Frontier, fantasy or history. It has been so long since Europeans lived their deepest dreams—but only yesterday for us. And this is why even now, when we are at last sundered from those dreams, we can turn rotten-ripe without loss of essential innocence, be (what has become a model for the young of all the world, as Godard's *Weekend* testifies) decadent children playing Indians; which is to say, imaginary Americans, all of us, whether native to this land or not. But to be an American (unlike being English or French or whatever) is precisely to *imagine* a destiny rather than to inherit one; since we have always been, insofar as we are Americans at all, inhabitants of myth rather than history—and have now come to know it.

In any case, our best writers have been able to take up the Western again—playfully and seriously at once, quite like their ancestors who began the Revolution which made us a country by playing Indians in deadly earnest and dumping all that English Tea into the salt sea that sundered them from their King. There are many writers still under forty, among them the most distinguished of their generation, who have written New Westerns which have found the hearts of the young, particularly in paperback form; since to these young readers, for reasons psychological as well as economic, the hardcover book with its aspiration to immortality in libraries begins to look obsolete. John Barth's *The Sotweed Factor* represents the beginning of the wave that has been cresting ever since 1960 and that has carried with it not only Barth's near contemporaries like Thomas Berger (in *Little Big Man),* Ken Kesey (in both *One Flew Over the Cuckoo's Nest* and *Sometimes a Great Notion),* and most recently Leonard Cohen (in his extraordinarily gross and elegant *Beautiful Losers)*—but has won over older and more established writers like Norman Mailer whose newest novel, *Why Are We in Vietnam?,* is not as its title seems to promise a book about a War in the East as much as a book about the idea of the West. Even William Burroughs, expert in drug fantasies and homosexual paranoia, keeps promising to turn to the genre, though so far he has contented himself with another popular form, another way of escaping from personal to public or popular myth, of using dreams to close rather than open a gap: Science Fiction.

Science Fiction does not seem at first glance to have as wide and universal appeal as the Western, in book form at least, though perhaps it is too soon to judge, for it is a very young genre, indeed, having found itself (after tentative beginnings in Jules Verne, H. G. Wells etc.), its real meaning and scope, only after World War II. At that point, two things become clear: first, that the Future was upon us, that the pace of technological advance had become so swift that a distinction between Present and Future would get harder and harder to maintain; and second, that the End of Man, by annihilation or mutation, was a real, even an immediate possibility. But these are the two proper subjects of Science Fiction: the Present Future and the End of Man—not time travel or the penetration of outer space, except as the latter somehow symbolize the former.

Perhaps only in quite advanced technologies which also have a tradition of self-examination and analysis, bred by Puritanism or Marxism or whatever, can Science Fiction at its most explicit, which is to say, expressed in words on the page, really flourish. In any case, only in America, England, and the Soviet Union does the Science Fiction Novel or Post-Novel seem to thrive, though Science Fiction cartoon strips and comic books, as well as Science Fiction T.V. programs and especially films (where the basic imagery is blissfully wed to electronic music, and words are kept to a minimum) penetrate everywhere. In England and America, at any rate, the prestige and influence of the genre are sufficient not only to allure Burroughs (in *Nova Express*), but also to provide a model for William Golding (in *Lord of the Flies*), Anthony Burgess (in *The Clockwork Orange*), and John Barth (whose second major book, *Giles Goatboy*, abandoned the Indian in favor of the Future).

Quite unlike the Western, which asserts the difference between England and America, Science Fiction reflects what still makes the two mutually distrustful communities one; as, for instance, a joint effort (an English author, an American director) like the movie *2001: A Space Odyssey* testifies. If there is still a common "Anglo-Saxon" form, it is Science Fiction. Yet even here, the American case is a little different from the English; for only in the United States is there a writer of first rank whose preferred mode has been from the first Science Fiction in its unmitigated Pop form. Kurt Vonnegut, Jr., did not begin by making some sort of traditional bid for literary fame and then shift to Science Fiction, but was so closely identified with that popular, not-quite-respectable form from the first, that the established critics were still ignoring him completely at a time when younger readers, attuned to the new rhythm of events by Marshall McLuhan or Buckminster Fuller, had already made underground favorites of his *The Sirens of Titan* and *Cat's Cradle*. That Vonnegut now, after years of neglect, teaches writing in a famous American university and is hailed in lead reviews in the popular press is a tribute not to the critics' acuity but to the persuasive powers of the young.

The revival of pornography in recent days, its moving from the periphery to the center of the literary scene, is best understood in this context, too; for it, like the Western and Science Fiction, is a form of Pop Art—ever since Victorian times, indeed, the *essential* form of Pop Art, which is to say, the most unredeemable of all kinds of subliterature, understood as a sort of entertainment closer to the pole of Vice than that of Art. Many of the more notable recent works of the genre have tended to conceal this fact, often because the authors themselves did not understand what they were after, and have tried to disguise their work as earnest morality (Herbert Selby's *Last Exit to Brooklyn,* for instance) or parody (Terry Southern's *Candy).* But whatever the author's conscious intent, all those writers who have helped move Porn from the underground to the foreground have in fact been working toward the liquidation of the very conception of pornography; since the end of Art on one side means the end of Porn on the other. And that end is now in sight, in the area of films and Pop songs and poetry, but especially in that of the novel which seemed, initially at least, more congenial than other later Pop Art forms to the sort of private masturbatory reverie which is essential to pornography.

It is instructive in this regard to reflect on the careers of two publishers who have flourished extraordinarily because somehow they sensed early on that a mass society can no longer endure the distinction between low literature and a high, especially in the area of sex; and that the line drawn early in the century between serious, "artistic" exploitation of pornography (e.g., *Lady Chatterley's Lover),* and so-called "hard-core" pornography was bound to be blurred away. Even the classics of the genre straddle the line: *Fanny Hill,* for example, and de Sade's *Justine,* as do more recent works like John Rechy's *City of Night* or Stephen Schneck's *The Night Clerk,* whose sheer dirtiness may be adulterated by sentiment or irony but remains a chief appeal. This, at any rate, Maurice Girodias and Barney Rosset appear to have sensed; and from both sides of the Atlantic they have, through the Olympia Press and Grove Press, supplied the American reading public, chiefly but not exclusively the young, with books (including, let it be noted, Nabokov's *Lolita,* the sole work in which the pursuit of Porn enabled that emigré writer to escape the limitations of early twentieth-century *avant-garde)* exploiting, often in contempt of art and seriousness, not just Good Clean Sex, but sadism, masochism, homosexuality, coprophilia, necrophilia etc. etc.

The standard forms of heterosexual copulation, standardly or "poetically" recorded, seem oddly old-fashioned, even a little ridiculous; it is *fellatio,* buggery, flagellation that we demand in order to be sure that we are not reading Love Stories but Pornography. A special beneficiary of this trend has been Norman Mailer, whose first novel, *The Naked and the Dead,* emulated the dying tradition of the anti-war art novel, with occasional obscenities thrown in, presumably in the interest of verisimilitude. But more and more, Mailer has come to move the obscenity to the center, the social commentary to the periphery, ending in *Why Are We in Vietnam?* with an insistence on foul language and an obsession with scatology which are obviously ends in themselves, too unremitting to be felt as merely an assault on old-fashioned sensibility and taste. And even in his earlier Pop Novel, *An American Dream,* which marked his emergence from ten years in which he produced no major fiction, he had committed himself to Porn as a way into the region to which his title alludes: the place where in darkness and filth all men are alike—the Harvard graduate and the reader of the *Daily News,* joined in fantasies of murdering their wives and buggering their maids. To talk of such books in terms of Dostoevski, as certain baffled critics have felt obliged to do, is absurd; James Bond is more to the point. But to confess this would be to confess that the old distinctions are no longer valid, and that critics will have to find another claim to authority more appropriate to our times than the outmoded ability to discriminate between High and Low.

Even more disconcertingly than Mailer, Philip Roth has with *Portnoy's Complaint* raised the question of whether "pornography," even what was called until only yesterday "hard-core pornography" any longer exists. Explicit, vulgar, joyous, gross and pathetic all at once, Roth has established himself not only as the laureate of masturbation and oral-genital lovemaking but also as a master of the "thin" novel, the novel with minimum inwardness—ironically presented as a confession to a psychiatrist. Without its sexual interest, therefore, the continual balancing off of titillation and burlesque—his book has no meaning at all, no more than any other dirty joke, to which genre it quite clearly belongs. There is pathos, even terror in great plenty, to be sure, but it is everywhere dependent on, subservient to the dirty jokes about mothers, Jews, shrinks, potency, impotency; and Roth is, consequently, quite correct when he asserts that he is less like such more solemn and pious Jewish-American writers as Saul Bellow and Bernard Malamud, than he is like the half-mad pop singer Tiny Tim (himself actually half-Arab and half-Jew).

"I am a Jew Freak," Roth has insisted, "not a Jewish Sage"—and one is reminded of Lennie Bruce, who was there first, occupying the dangerous DMZ between the world of the stand-up comedian and that of the proper maker of fictions. But Bruce made no claim to being a novelist and therefore neither disturbed the critics nor opened up new possibilities for prose narrative. Indeed, before *Portnoy's Complaint,* the Jewish-American novel had come to seem an especially egregious example of the death of belles-lettres, having become smug, established, repetitive and sterile. But *Portnoy* marks the passage of that genre into the new world of Porn and Pop, as Roth's booming sales (even in hardcover!) perhaps sufficiently attest.

It is, of course, the middle-aged and well-heeled who buy the hardcover editions of the book; yet their children apparently are picking it up, too, for once not even waiting for the paperback edition. They know it is a subversive book, as their parents do not (convinced that a boy who loves his mother can't be all bad), and as Roth himself perhaps was not at first quite aware either. Before its publication, he had been at least equivocal on the subject of frankly disruptive literature; full of distrust, for instance, for Norman Mailer—and appears therefore to have became a Pop rebel despite himself, driven less by principle than by a saving hunger for the great audience, quite like that which moved John Updike recently out of his elitist exile toward best-sellerdom and relevance in *Couples.*

There is, however, no doubt in the minds of most other writers whom the young especially prize at the moment that their essential task is to destroy once and for all—by parody or exaggeration or grotesque emulation of the classic past, as well as by the adaptation and "camping" of Pop forms just such distinctions and discriminations. But to turn High Art into vaudeville and burlesque at the same moment that Mass Art is being irreverently introduced into museums and libraries is to perform an act which has political as well as aesthetic implications: an act which closes a class, as well as a generation gap. The notion of one art for the "cultured," i.e., the favored few in any given society—in our own chiefly the university educated—and another subart for the "uncultured," i.e., an excluded majority as deficient in Gutenberg skills as they are untutored in "taste," in fact represents the last survival in mass industrial societies (capitalist, socialist, communist—it makes no difference in this regard) of an invidious distinction proper only to a class-structured community. Precisely because it carries on, as it has carried on ever since the middle of the eighteenth century, a war against that anachronistic survival, Pop Art is, whatever its overt politics, *subversive:* a threat to all hierarchies insofar as it is hostile to order and ordering in its own realm. What the final intrusion of Pop into the citadels of High Art provides, therefore, for the critic is the exhilarating new possibility of making judgments about the "goodness" and "badness" of art quite separated from distinctions between "high" and "low" with their concealed class bias.

But the new audience has not waited for new critics to guide them in this direction. Reversing the process typical of Modernism —under whose aegis an unwilling, aging elite audience was bullied and cajoled slowly, slowly, into accepting the most vital art of its time—Post-Modernism provides an example of a young, mass audience urging certain aging, reluctant critics onward toward the abandonment of their former elite status in return for a freedom the prospect of which more terrifies than elates them. In fact, Post-Modernism implies the closing of the gap between critic and audience, too, if by critic one understands "leader of taste" and by audience "follower." But most importantly of all, it implies the closing of the gap between artist and audience, or at any rate, between professional and amateur in the realm of art.

The jack of all arts is master of none—professional in none, and therefore no better than any man jack among the rest of us, formerly safely penned off from the practitioners we most admire by our status as "audience." It all follows logically enough. On the one hand, a poet like Ed Sanders, or a novelist like Leonard Cohen grows weary of his confinement in the realm of traditional high art; and the former organizes a musical Pop Group called the Fugs, while the latter makes recordings of his own Pop songs to his own guitar accompaniment. There are precedents for this, after all, not only as in the case of Boris Vian, which we have already noticed, but closer to home: in the career, for instance, of Richard Farina, who died very young, but not before he had written that imperfect, deeply moving novel, *Been Down So Long It Looks Like Up to Me,* and had recorded a song or two for the popular audience.

Meanwhile, even more surprisingly some who had begun, or whom we had begun to think of, as mere "entertainers," Pop performers without loftier pretensions, were crossing the line from their direction. Frank Zappa, for example, has in interviews and in a forthcoming book insisted on being taken seriously as poet and satirist, suggesting that the music of his own group, The Mothers of Invention, has been all along more a deliberate parody of Pop than an extension of it in psychedelic directions; while Bob Dylan, who began by abandoning Folk Music with left-wing protest overtones in favor of electronic Rock and Roll, finally succeeded in creating inside that form a kind of Pop surrealist poetry, passionate, mysterious, and quite complex; complex enough, in fact, to prompt a score of scholarly articles on his "art." Most recently, however, he has returned to "acoustic" instruments and to the most naïve traditions of country music—apparently out of a sense that he had grown too "arty," and had once more to close the gap by backtracking across the border he had earlier lost his first audience by crossing. It is a spectacular case of the new artist as Double Agent.

Even more spectacular, however, is that of John Lennon, who coming into view first as merely one of the Beatles, then still just another rock group from Liverpool, has revealed himself stage by stage as novelist, playwright, movie maker, guru, sculptor, etc., etc. There is a special pathos in his example since, though initially inspired by American models, he has tried to work out his essentially American strategies in English idioms and in growing isolation on the generally dismal English scene. He has refused to become the prisoner of his special talent as a musician, venturing into other realms where he has, initially at least, as little authority as anyone else; and thus provides one more model for the young who, without any special gift or calling, in the name of mere possibility insist on making all up and down America, and, more tentatively perhaps, everywhere else in the world, tens of thousands of records, movies, collections of verse, paintings, junk sculptures, even novels, in complete contempt of professional "standards." Perhaps, though, the novel is the most unpromising form for an amateur age (it is easier to learn the guitar or make a two-minute eight-millimeter film), and it may be doomed to become less and less important, less and less central, no matter how it is altered. But for the moment at least, on the border between the world of Art and that of non-Art, it flourishes with especial vigor in proportion as it realizes its transitional status, and is willing to surrender the kind of "realism" and analysis it once thought its special province in quest of the marvelous and magical it began by disavowing.

Samuel Richardson may have believed that when he wrote *Pamela* and *Clarissa* he was delivering prose fiction from that bondage to the *merveilleux* which characterized the old Romances; but it is clear now that he was merely translating the Marvelous into new terms, specifically, into bourgeois English. It is time, at any rate, to be through with pretenses; for to Close the Gap means also to Cross the Border between the Marvelous and the Probable, the Real and the Mythical, the world of the boudoir and the counting house and the realm of what used to be called Faerie, but has for so long been designated mere madness. Certainly the basic images of Pop forms like the Western, Science Fiction and Pornography suggest mythological as well as political or metapolitical meanings. The passage into Indian Territory, the flight into Outer Space, the ecstatic release into the fantasy world of the orgy: all these are analogues for what has traditionally been described as a Journey or Pilgrimage (recently we have been more likely to say "Trip" without altering the significance) toward a transcendent goal, a moment of Vision.

But the mythologies of Voyage and Vision which the late Middle Ages and the Renaissance inherited from the Classical World and the Judaeo-Christian tradition, and which froze into pedanticism and academicism in the eighteenth and nineteenth century, have not survived their last ironical uses in the earlier part of the twentieth: those burlesque-pathetic evocations in Joyce's *Ulysses,* Eliot's *The Waste Land,* Mann's *Joseph and His Brothers* or the *Cantos* of Ezra Pound. If they are not quite dead, they should be, *need* be for the health of post-Art—as, indeed, Walt Whitman foresaw, anticipating the twenty-first century from the vantage point of his peculiar vision more than a hundred years ago.

> Come Muse migrate from Greece and Ionia,
> Cross out please those immensely overpaid accounts,
> That matter of Troy and Achilles' Wrath, and Aeneas'
>   Odysseus' wanderings,
> Place "Removed" and "To Let" on the rocks of your
>   snowy Parnassus,
> Repeat at Jerusalem . . .

Pop Art, however, can no more abide a mythological vacuum than can High Art: and into the space left vacant by the disappearance of the Matter of Troy and the myths of the ancient Middle East has rushed, first of all, the Matter of Childhood: the stuff of traditional fairy tales out of the Black Forest, which seems to the present generation especially attractive, perhaps, because their "progressive" parents tended to distrust it. But something much more radically new has appeared as well: the Matter of Metropolis and the myths of the Present Future, in which the nonhuman world about us, hostile or benign, is rendered not in the guise of elves or dwarfs or witches or even Gods, but of Machines quite as uncanny as any Elemental or Olympian—and apparently as immortal. Machines and the mythological figures appropriate to the media mass-produced and mass-distributed by machines: the newsboy who, saying SHAZAM in an abandoned subway tunnel, becomes Captain Marvel; the reporter (with glasses), who shucking his civilian garb in a telephone booth is revealed as Superman, immune to all but Kryptonite—these are the appropriate images of power and grace for an urban, industrial world busy manufacturing the Future.

But the Comic Book heroes do not stand alone. Out of the world of Jazz and Rock, of newspaper headlines and political cartoons, of old movies immortalized on T.V. and idiot talk shows carried on car radios, new anti-Gods and anti-Heroes arrive, endless wave after wave of them: "Bluff'd not a bit by drainpipe, gasometer, artificial fertilizers," (the appropriate commentary is Whitman's), "smiling and pleas'd with palpable intent to stay"—in our Imaginary America, of course. In the heads of our new writers, they live a secondary life, begin to realize their immortality: not only Jean Harlow and Marilyn Monroe and Humphrey Bogart, Charlie Parker and Louis Armstrong and Lennie Bruce, Geronimo and Billy the Kid, the Lone Ranger and Fu Manchu and the Bride of Frankenstein, but Hitler and Stalin, John F. Kennedy and Lee Oswald and Jack Ruby as well; for the press mythologizes certain public figures, the actors of Pop History, even before they are dead —making a doomed President one with Superman in the Supermarket of Pop Culture, as Norman Mailer perceived so accurately and reported so movingly in an essay on John F. Kennedy.

But the secret he told was already known to scores of younger writers at least, and recorded in the text and texture of their work. In the deep memory of Leonard Cohen writing *Beautiful Losers,* or Richard Farina composing *Been Down So Long It Looks Like Up to Me,* or Ken Kesey making *Sometimes a Great Notion,* there stir to life not archetypal images out of books read in school or at the urging of parents; but those out of comic books forbidden in schools, or radio and T.V. programs banned or condescendingly endured by parents. From the taboo underground culture of the kids of just after World War II comes the essential mythology which informs the literature of right now. As early as T. S. Eliot, to be sure, jazz rhythms had been evoked, as in "O O O O that Shakesperherian Rag—It's so elegant, So intelligent . . .," but Eliot is mocking a world he resents; and even in Brecht's *Three Penny Opera,* the emulation of Pop music seems still largely "slumming." In the newest writers, however, mockery and condescension alike are absent, since they are not slumming; they are living in the only world in which they feel at home. They are able, therefore, to recapture a certain rude magic in its authentic context, by seizing on myths not as stored in encyclopedias or preserved in certain beloved ancient works—but as apprehended at their moment of making, which is to say, at a moment when they are not yet labeled "myths."

In some ways the present movement not only in its quest for myths, but also in its preference for sentimentality over irony, and especially in its dedication to the Primitive, resembles the beginnings of Romanticism, with its yearning for the Naïve, and its attempt to find authentic sources for poetry in folk forms like the *Märchen* or the ballads. But the Romantics returned exclusively toward the Past in the hope of renewal—to a dream of the Past, which they knew they could only write, not actually live. And, indeed, there persists in the post-Modernists some of that old nostalgia for folk ways and folk-rhythms, curiously tempered by the realization that the "folk songs" of an electronic age are made not in rural loneliness or in sylvan retreats, but in superstudios by boys singing into the sensitive ear of machines—or even by those machines themselves editing, blending, making out of imperfect scraps of human song an artifice of simplicity only possible on tape. What recent writers have learned, and are true enough children of the Present Future to find exhilarating, is not only that the *Naïve* can be machine produced, but that dreams themselves can be manufactured, projected on T.V. or Laser beams with all the vividness of the visions of Saints. In the first wave of Romanticism, pre-electronic Romanticism, it took an act of faith on the part of Novalis to be able to say, "Life is not a dream, but it can be and probably should be made one." And echoing his German producer, in the pages of both *Lilith* and *Phantastes,* George Macdonald, maddest of the Victorian mad visionaries, echoes the tone of desperate hope. But to the young in America, who have learned to read Macdonald once more, along with his English successors, Charles Williams and C. S. Lewis and Tolkien, the declaration of faith has become a matter of fact.

The Dream, the Vision, *ekstasis:* these have again become the avowed goals of literature; for our latest poets realize in this time of Endings, what their remotest ancestors knew in the era of Beginnings, that merely "to instruct and delight" is not enough. Like Longinus, the new novelists and critics believe that great art releases and liberates as well; but unlike him, they are convinced that wonder and fantasy, which deliver the mind from the body, the body from the mind, must be naturalized to a world of machines—subverted perhaps or even transformed, but certainly not destroyed or denied. The ending of Ken Kesey's *One Flew Over the Cuckoo's*

Nest expresses fictionally, metaphorically, that conviction, when the Indian who is his second hero breaks out of the Insane Asylum in which "The System" has kept him impotent and trapped—and flees to join his fellows who are building a fishing weir on a giant hydro-electric power dam. The Dam and Weir both are essential to post-electronic Romanticism, which knows that the point is no longer to pursue some uncorrupted West over the next horizon, since there is no incorruption and all our horizons have been reached. It is rather to make a thousand little Wests in the interstices of a machine civilization, and, as it were, on its steel and concrete back; to live the tribal life among and with the support of machines; to shelter new communes under domes constructed according to the technology of Buckminster Fuller; and warm the nakedness of New Primitives with advanced techniques of solar heating.

All this is less a matter of choice than of necessity because, it has turned out, machine civilization tends inevitably to synthesize the primitive, and *ekstasis* is the unforeseen end of advanced technology, mysticism the by-product—no more nor no less accidental in penicillin—of scientific research. In the antiseptic laboratories of Switzerland, the psychedelic drug LSD was first developed, first tried by two white-coated experimenters; and even now Dow Chemical which manufactures napalm also produces the even more powerful psychedelic agent STP. It is, in large part, thanks to machines—the supermachines which, unlike their simpler proto-types, insist on tending us rather than demanding we tend them—that we live in the midst of a great religious revival, scarcely noticed by the official spokesmen of established Christian churches since it speaks quite another language. Yet many among us feel that they are able to live honestly only by what machines cannot do better than they—which is why certain poets and novelists, as well as pop singers and pornographic playwrights, are suggesting in print, on the air, everywhere, that not Work but Vision is the proper activity of men, and that, therefore, the contemplative life may, after all, be preferable to the active one. In such an age, *our* age, it is not surprising that the books which most move the young are essentially religious books, as, indeed, pop art is always religious.

In the immediate past, however, when an absolute distinction was made between High Art and Pop, works of the latter category tended to be the secret scriptures of a kind of shabby, store-front church—a religion as exclusive in its attempt to remain the humble possession of the unambitious and unlettered, as the canonical works of High Art in their claim to be an esoteric Gospel of art itself, available only to a cultivated elite. But in a time of Closing the Gap, literature becomes again prophetic and universal—a continuing revelation appropriate to a permanent religious revolution, whose function is precisely to transform the secular crowd into a sacred community: one with each other, and equally at home in the world of technology and the realm of wonder. Pledged like Isaiah to speaking the language of everyone, the prophets of the new dispensation can afford to be neither finicky nor genteel; and they echo, therefore, the desperate cry of the Hebrew prototype: "I am a man of unclean lips in the midst of a people of unclean lips."

Let those to whom religion means security beware, for it is no New Established Church that is in the process of being founded; and its communicants are, therefore, less like the pillars of the Lutheran Church or Anglican gentlemen than they are like ranters, enthusiasts, Dionysiacs, Anabaptists: holy disturbers of the peace of the devout. Leonard Cohen, in a moment of vision which constitutes the climax of *Beautiful Losers,* aptly calls them "New Jews"; for he sees them as a saved remnant moving across deserts of boredom, out of that exile from our authentic selves which we all share, toward a salvation none of us can quite imagine. Such New Jews, Cohen (himself a Jew as well as a Canadian) adds, do not have to be Jewish but probably do have to be Americans—by which he must surely mean "Imaginary Americans," since, as we have been observing all along, there were never any other kind.

—1970

Exhibit A:

On Being Busted at Fifty

"*Az m'lebt, m' lebt alles,*" my grandfather began telling me when *he* was fifty and presumably thought me old enough to understand, "if you live long enough, you live through everything." And, I suppose, justice being as imperfectly practiced as it is in our world, one could consider getting arrested as inevitable a function of aging as getting cancer. But some people I know would have to reach 150 at least before falling afoul of the law, and others have sat in their first cell by sixteen or seventeen: so there must be some other, more specific reason why I find myself charged with a misdemeanor just past the half-century mark of my life.

Where did it all begin, I keep asking myself, where did it really start—back beyond the moment those six or eight or ten improbable cops came charging into my house, without having knocked, of course, but screaming as they came (for the record, the first of their endless lies), "We knocked! We knocked!"; and producing only five minutes later, after considerable altercation, the warrant sworn out by a homeless, lost girl on whom my wife and daughter had been wasting concern and advice for over a year. It seems to me that the actual beginning must have been, *was* the moment I got up before the Women's Club (an organization of faculty wives and other females variously connected with the State University of New York at Buffalo) to speak to them of the freedom and responsibility of the teacher.

I have no record of the occasion (was it a year ago, two?), can remember no precise dates or names or faces—but I do

295

recall the horrified hush with which my not very daring but, I hope, elegantly turned commonplaces were received. I spoke of the ironies of our current situation in which a broad range of political dissent is tolerated from teachers, but in which no similar latitude is granted them in expressing opinions about changing standards in respect to sex and drugs. I invoked, I think, the names of Leo Koch (fired out of the University of Illinois) and Timothy Leary (dropped from the faculty at Harvard, I reminded my ladies) and ended by insisting that the primary responsibility of the teacher is to be free, to provide a model of freedom for the young.

Needless to say, tea and cakes were served afterward, and one or two members of the Program Committee tried hard to make conversation with me as I gallantly sipped at the former and politely refused the latter. But there was a growing space around me no matter how hard they tried, a kind of opening *cordon sanitaire,* that kept reminding me of a picture which used to hang in my grade-school classrooms, of Cataline left alone on the benches of the Roman Senate after his exposure by Cicero. That evening there were phone calls rather drastically reinterpreting my remarks (I had, it was asserted by one especially agitated source, advocated free love and "pot" for fourteen-year-olds), as well as—for the very first time—voices suggesting that maybe there was something anomalous about permitting one with my opinions to teach in the State University.

It was then, I suspect, that my departmental chairman as well as some officials in the loftier reaches of Administration began receiving hostile letters about me—not many in number, I would judge, but impassioned in tone. Still, though this constituted a kind of prelude, it all might have come to nothing had I not then accepted an invitation to speak to the High School Teachers of English in Arlington, Virginia, at the end of January of this year. It was an intelligent and responsive group to whom I tried to talk as candidly as I could about the absurdity of teaching literature, i.e., teaching a special kind of pleasure under conditions of mutual distrust and according to an outmoded curriculum.

I said many things both in my initial presentation and in

response to a considerable stack of written questions about what students should be asked to read in high school (essentially, I said, mythological material from Homer to Shakespeare, and similar stuff from the twentieth century, which they themselves prefer, e.g., J. R. R. Tolkien's *Fellowship of the Ring*); what they should *not* be asked to read (such old standards as *Silas Marner* and *Ivanhoe,* such splendid but currently irrelevant poets as Spenser and Milton, plus the stuffier verse entertainers of the nineteenth century like, say, Tennyson); and what the teachers themselves ought to be reading to have some sense of the group they are theoretically addressing (the obvious New Gurus: Buckminster Fuller, N. O. Brown, Marshall McLuhan, Timothy Leary, etc.)

A reporter for the Washington *Post* was present and moved enough to do a feature piece (marred by minor inaccuracies and odd conjunctions born in his mind rather than in mine) headed: COOL IT ON MILTON, TEACHERS ADVISED, which became, as the article was reprinted throughout the country: AUTHOR: STUDY LEARY, NOT MILTON. And under an even more misleading rubric (ENGLISH TEACHERS TOLD TO STUDY LEARY) the story appeared on the front page of Buffalo's morning newspaper, a journal dedicated to scaring itself and its readers about where the modern world is going, largely—I would gather—to keep mail from the Far Right rolling in. Such readers may not ever have read either Milton or Leary, but they know which is the honorific and which the dirty word. It was at this point, at any rate, that the notion of me as a "corrupter of the young" seems to have taken hold in Western New York at least—spreading as far as the State Legislature, in which a member arose within a couple of weeks (representing as I recall the Hornell District) to ask why my presence was being tolerated in a publicly supported institution of higher learning.

I did not at first pay much attention to all this, nor to the fact that in a pamphlet on pornography, prepared by the same body of New York lawmakers, the cover of a Nudist magazine advertising the reprint of a review I had once done of that unexpectedly amusing movie, *The Immoral Mr. Tease,* had been given a prominent position. On the one hand, the small local furor had got lost in the overwhelming response the garbled version of what I had said in Arlington brought from all over the country—offers to publish my remarks in publications ranging from *Fact* to the *Catholic World,* invitations to run seminars for grade-school teachers, and pleas to join such organizations as America's Rugged Individualists Spiritualistic Entity (ARISE) and the Friends of Meher Baba. On the other hand, I had come more and more to think of what I had to say about young people and where they were (all that had begun with my immensely ambivalent and much misunderstood article on "The New Mutants" in *Partisan Review*) as being directed *not* to the young at all.

To be sure, in spite of their publicly announced contempt for the opinions of the aging, those under thirty desperately desire reassurance and confirmation from those beyond that magical boundary; but it is weakness in them which makes them ask it—and I had resolved not to respond. No, it seemed to me that it was to my own peers that I had to speak, to explain, to interpret—translating for the benefit of teachers what their students were saying in an incomprehensible tongue, deciphering for parents what their children were muttering in a code they trusted their parents to break. What did I have to tell the young about themselves (about Shakespeare or Dante or even Melville and Faulkner I could talk with special authority, but that is quite another matter) which I had not learned from them? One of the things I had learned —something I might have remembered from the *Apology* but did not—is that the young cannot, will not, be "corrupted" or "saved" by anyone except themselves. Out of my own ambivalence, my own fear, my own hopes and misgivings before a generation more generous and desperate and religious than my own, it seemed to me I could make a kind of sense—at least what might be made to seem "sense" to those in whose definition of that term I myself had been brainwashed.

But I found an adult community more terrified than myself, more terrified even than I had then guessed, of the gap between themselves and the young; and therefore pitifully eager to find some simple explanation of it all, something with which

they could deal, if not by themselves, at least with the aid
of courts and cops. "Dope" was the simple explanation, the
simple word they had found (meaning by "dope" the currently
fashionable psychedelics, especially marijuana); and once that
was licked, the gap would be closed, the misunderstandings
solved, the mutual offense mitigated. For such a utopian solution, a few arrests on charges of possession and selling, a few
not-quite-kosher searches and seizures would be a small
enough price to pay.

Meanwhile, however, some among the young (and a few
out of the older generations as well) had begun to propa-
gandize in favor of changing the laws against marijuana, or at
least of investigating the facts with a view toward changing
those laws; and this seemed to the simple-minded enemies of
the young a new and even greater cause for consternation.
To legalize pot would be, it appeared to them, to legalize
long hair and scraggly beards for young men, new sexual
mores for young women, Indian headbands and beads and
incense for everyone: to sanction indiscriminate love in place
of regulated aggression, hedonism in place of puritanism, the
contemplative life in place of the active one. And everyone
knew what that meant! At this point, the fight against marijuana with the aid of the police and strategic lies began to
be transformed into a *fight against the freedom of expression*
(though only in the case of those interested in changing the
marijuana laws, to be sure) employing the same weapons.

At this point precisely—it was in March of this year—
I became Faculty Adviser to LEMAR, an officially recognized
student organization on the campus at Buffalo, dedicated
to employing all possible legal means to make the regulations
on the consumption of marijuana no more stringent than those
on alcohol—and which, incidentally, asked all of its members
to sign a pledge not to possess or use pot. I was asked to
assume the job, I gather, in large part because I was notoriously "clean," i.e., it was widely known that I (and my wife
as well) did not and had never smoked marijuana. Though
this may have been in the minds of some of the students who
approached me a purely strategic reason for their choice,
it seemed to me a principled reason for accepting the position.
I would, given the circumstances, be able to fight for the

legalization of "grass" not in order to indulge a private pleasure, but in order to extend freedom for everyone. Besides, the situation struck me as intolerable, with exactly the same discrepancy between the actual practice of a community (in this case the subsociety of those under thirty) and the laws which presumably regulated it, as had prevailed in respect to alcohol during the late Twenties.

The same considerations which had led to the repeal of Prohibition early in the following decade, seemed to me to demand a change in the laws controlling the consumption of marijuana in 1967. Certainly I felt this with special urgency as one committed to limiting rather than extending or preserving the possibilities of alienation, hypocrisy, and lawlessness for the young. Moreover, I was convinced that if the University could not provide a forum for the calm and rational discussion of the real issues involved, the debate about the legalization of marijuana would continue on the same depressing level of hysteria and sensationalism on which it had begun. Finally, even if I had disagreed totally with its aims, I would have become faculty adviser to any intellectually respectable group that found as much difficulty in persuading someone to take on the responsibility as LEMAR was apparently having.

As a matter of fact, it depressed and baffled me that a score of applicants for the post of faculty adviser had not already stepped forward; though the student leaders of the organization explained to me that there was real cause for fear on the part of reluctant faculty members that sanctions might in fact be taken against them. *But what sanctions,* I asked in my innocence, *could possibly be taken?* A few anonymous letters to the President of the University calling for dismissal? Another indignant "editorial" on T.V. or in the Press? I began to learn soon enough and in an odd way, when an application I was making for an insurance policy was turned down, though my health was fine and my credit good. The letter from the life insurance company was vague and discreet: "like to be able to grant every request . . . not always possible . . . many factors must be taken into consideration . . . I am sorry indeed. . . ." But private conversations with people involved made it quite clear that at the moment of associating myself with LEMAR I had become to the pious underwriters a "moral risk," unworthy of being insured.

While I was considering whether my civil rights had in fact been infringed, and whether I should make an appeal to the American Civil Liberties Union—the local head of the narcotics squad (a man more vain and ambitious than articulate) had been attempting to argue down the students in public debates organized by LEMAR, and had ended in baffled rage, crying out—according to the student head of LEMAR who was his interlocuter: "Don't worry kid—when we get you LEMAR guys, it's gonna be on something bigger than a little pot-possession," and "Yeah—there are some of those professors out at U.B.—bearded beatnik Communists. I wouldn't want any of my kids to go out there, but that's all right—they'll be gotten rid of."

The issues are clearly drawn—*not* criminal issues at all in the first instance, but differences of opinion and style felt to be critical enough to be settled by police methods, even if this requires manufacturing a case. After all, what other way is there to cope with an enemy who is bearded (i.e., contemptuous of convention and probably cleanliness as well), and "beat" (i.e., dangerously aberrant), and a Communist (i.e., convinced of ideas more liberal than those of the speaker, and—worst of all—a professor (i.e., too smart for his own good, too big for his britches, etc., etc.). Indeed, the case against one bearded professor at least was being "prepared" for quite a while. The statements quoted above were made on April 18 and April 20, and on April 29, the day of the arrest, a spokesman for the police was reported as having said that for ten days my house, watched off and on for "months," had been under "twenty-four-hour surveillance" —a scrutiny rewarded (according to police statements in the press) by the observation of "many persons, mostly young, going in and out. . . ." All of which seems scarcely remarkable in a household with six children, each equipped with the customary number of friends.

What is remarkable is to live under "surveillance," a situation in which privacy ceases to exist and any respect for the person and his privileges yields to a desire to "get rid of" someone with dangerous ideas. Slowly I had become aware of the fact that my phone kept fading in and out because it was probably being tapped; that those cars turning around in nearby driveways or parked strategically so that their occupants could peer in my windows, though unmarked, belonged to the police; that the "bread van" haunting our neighborhood contained cops; and that at least one "friend" of my children was a spy.

It was the police themselves who had released to the press (the unseemly desire for publicity overcoming discretion and reticence) the news that this "friend," a seventeen-year-old girl with a talent for lies, had been coming in and out of our house with a two-way radio—picking up all conversations within her range, no matter how private, and whether conducted by members of my household or casual visitors. She had the habit of disappearing and reappearing with a set of unconvincing and contradictory stories about what exactly had happened to her (she had been in the hospital for a V.D. cure; she had been in jail; she had been confined to an insane asylum; she had been beaten up by incensed old associates) —but always she seemed so lost and homeless and eager for someone to show some signs of concern that it seemed impossible ever to turn her out. For me, the high point—the moment of ultimate indignity—in the whole proceedings came at my last Passover Seder when, just after I had spoken the traditional lines inviting all who were hungry to come in and eat, the "friend' had entered, bearing (we now know) her little electronic listening device, to drink our wine and share our unleavened bread.

The ironies are archetypal to the point of obviousness (one of my sons claims we were thirteen at table, but this I refuse to admit to myself), embarrassingly so. I prefer to reflect on the cops at their listening post (in the bread van?) hearing the ancient prayers: "Not in one generation alone have they risen against us, but in every generation. . . . This year we are slaves, next year we shall be free!" I cannot resist reporting, however, that at the end of the evening, the electronically equipped "friend" said to me breathlessly, "Oh, Professor, thank

you. This is only the second religious ceremony I ever attended
in my life." (My wife has told me since that the first was
the lighting of Channukah candles at our house.)

Fair enough, then, that the first really vile note I received
after my arrest and the garbled accounts of it in the local news-
papers (made worse by a baseless reference to "trafficking in
drugs" in the initial release from the University concerning
my case) should have struck an anti-Semitic note, reading,
"You goddamned Jews will do anything for money." Though
I had not really been aware of the fact, anti-Semitism was
already in the air and directed toward the University of
which I was a member. (Hate mail from an organization
calling itself MAM, or more fully, *Mothers Against Meyerson*,
had already begun to refer to Martin Meyerson, the President
of our University, as "that Red Jew from Berkeley.") It was
all there, ready to be released: hostility to the young, fear
of education and distrust of the educated, anti-Semitism,
anti-Negroism, hatred for "reds" and "pinkos," panic before
those who dressed differently, wore their hair longer, or—

I should have been prepared by my experiences only a few
weeks before the police invasion of my home, by some of
the responses I got over the telephone when I had agreed
to explain the nature and purpose of LEMAR and to comment
generally on the culture of the young over one of those
three-hour question-and-answer radio programs which appear
to bring out all the worst in all the worst elements in any
community. The tone of the whole thing was set by the
letter of invitation in which the conductor of the program
ended by saying that he could not understand why a man so
often quoted by *Time-Life* would agree to act as faculty
adviser to LEMAR, or in his terms "would willingly take up
the posture of Pied Piper to those young louts. . . ."

Still I was not merely distressed but *astonished* when, just
as I was recovering from being mugged, fingerprinted, mis-
quoted, and televised, I received an anonymous letter purport-
ing to be from "a group of Central Park neighbors," which
began by assuring me that I and my children were "condemned to a ghetto life," went on to refer to their Negro

friends (two of whom were also arrested after the police broke into my house) as "the colored, thieving and prostituting for a rattish living . . ." and concluded: "If Myerson doesn't dispose of you and you leave our neighborhood in a reasonable length of time be assured of total harassment. . . ." What such "total harassment" involves has teased my imagination —though I begin to have a clue or two, since having received only recently a notice that our homeowner's insurance policy was being canceled out of hand (in the extra-legal world of the insurance companies, all men are presumed guilty until proven innocent), which would mean—unless we can replace it—the loss of our mortgage.

In this context of abject fear and pitiful hatred the actual arrest, the charges, the legal maneuvering and courtroom appearances seem of minor importance, however annoying and time-consuming they may be. The elements of enticement, entrapment, planting of "evidence," etc., involved in "the well-prepared case" of the police will be revealed if and when the matter comes to trial (it is now adjourned until September 5), and the charges against my wife and me, my children and their friends are, as they must be, dismissed. Meanwhile it seems proper and appropriate only to repeat a couple of paragraphs from a letter I wrote to *Time* after they had published an account of the events which seemed to me to verge on slander: a correction which they shortened and slightly altered:

When the police recently broke into my home in Buffalo, after weeks of unseemly surveillance, they did not dis-cover—as your columns erroneously reported—anything remotely resembling a "pot-and-hashish Party." They found rather my wife, my oldest son, my daughter-in-law and me at the point of setting out for the movies, and another son plus two friends at widely scattered places in a large and rambling house. That second son—absurdly charged with "possession of marijuana"—far from indulging in some wild orgy, happened to be in the process of taking a bath.

The context of your article suggested that university

students may have been involved in the events; this is untrue. It further seemed to imply that I was smoking pot. This is also without basis in fact. Neither my wife nor I has ever used or possessed an illegal drug, nor are we charged with this even in the case manufactured by the police. What we are accused of is "maintaining a premise" —i.e., keeping up the mortgage payments and maintaining in good repair our home in which other people are alleged to have been in possession of marijuana.

Beyond this, legal considerations forbid my going at the moment, though I suppose two items could be added without indiscretion. First, I was initially surprised and pleased that the cops did not tear my first-floor study apart after they had crashed in on me: I attribute their unlooked-for courtesy either to a lurking respect for professors (they were only really rough—as could have been predicted—with the two Negro boys in the house at the time), or to their being unnerved at finding themselves for once in so grand a neighborhood (one of them could not help exclaiming in awe, "You can bet this is the biggest house I ever seen!"). But I have learned since, alas, that their whole "search" of the premises was a perfunctory sham—except on the third floor, where their young agent had been sent in an hour before the bust to leave a "little present" of marijuana, and where, she had assured them (exiting just five minutes before), it safely reposed. And second, the movie we were headed for was *Casino Royale* —a spy and pursuit film which, for obvious reasons, we have felt no need to see since.

I do not mean to say that even the courtroom is not penetrated by the hysteria that affects the community; at our original arraignment, for instance, a respectable judge was disturbed enough to lose all sense of decorum and to lecture those attending the proceedings (quite as if he were speaking over the heads of a group of condemned criminals) on the folly of considering a university a place where one learns "through the sweat of marijuana smoke. . . . They are taught this is not habit-forming. The records indicate otherwise." There is, finally, little doubt that agencies entrusted with law-enforcement have in Buffalo become instrumental in creating an atmosphere in which not only I, but my wife and children are persecuted and chivvied (largely for the simple fault of being *my* wife and children), my whole life at home and at school harried—quite as if we were all living in a Nazi or Communist totalitarian state supervised by Thought Police.

Even my children's friends have had to pay for their friendship, as the police have diligently tried to shore up their shaky case. One of them, as a matter of fact, was arrested before the 29th of April in the company of the same teeny-bopper spy who swore out our warrant; though it remains unclear whether this was a rehearsal for her, or the occasion of recruiting her for "police work." Since our arrest, there have been a couple more: one of a girl who plays in the same rock-and-roll group as my youngest son—the most shameless frame-up of all, in which, according to her story, the police simply broke down her door, walked into the middle of her living room, plunked down a packet of marijuana on a table, and looking up with a smirk, said, "Hey, see what we found!" More publicized was the second, which involved the arrest in their farmhouse home of what the police called "the operator of an electronic-psychedelic nightclub" and his wife —along with two of my sons and my daughter-in-law who had just come to call.

Quite as interesting to the cops as a "loose substance which will be analyzed to determine if it is marijuana, and several tablets and pills which will also be analyzed" were such other dangerous materials, which they confiscated along with them, as a pack of Tarot cards, some jars of macrobiotic foods, and "a lot of psychedelic literature," i.e., several copies of a volume of short stories written by "the operator of an electronic-psychedelic nightclub." The local press found even more intriguing and, apparently, damning the exotic furniture of the place ("... there were mattresses on the floor, there were short-legget [sic] tables ... candles were burning and there was incense in the room ...") and the garb worn by those arrested ("a long white cotton robe ... a kimono ... a black and white mini-skirt with black net stockings ... "hippie-type" sportswear, including tight-fitting denim trousers ...").

That the "tight-fitting denim trousers" were nothing more or less than garden-variety blue jeans the magic word "psychedelic" concealed from the titillated readers of the *Courier-Express;* and the adjective "hippie-type" glossed it for others less literate but equally convinced that all who dress differently from themselves are guilty even though ultimately found innocent—*especially* guilty if devious enough to convince the courts that they are less insidious than their clothes declare them.

Yet this is not the whole story; for everywhere there is a growing sense (especially as the police in their desperation grow more and more outrageous) that not I and my family, but the police themselves and those backward elements in the community, whose panic and prejudice they strive vainly to enforce, are on trial. The ill-advised remarks of the police court judge at my arraignment, for instance, brought an immediate rebuke and an appeal to the local Bar Association for "appropriate action" from a professor of law who happened to be present. And my own University has stood by me with a sense that not only my personal freedom but the very atmosphere of freedom on which learning depends is imperiled.

When there was some talk at an earlier stage of the game of "suspending" me pending an investigation, my own department served notice that they would meet no classes unless I could meet mine; the Student Senate voted to strike in sympathy if the need arose, and the Graduate Students Association seconded them. In the end, the President of the University announced that, "on the advice of the Executive Committee of the Faculty of Arts and Sciences and after consultation with the State University attorneys and Chancellor Samuel B. Gould," *no* action against me was warranted. The ground for this decision was, he indicated, "the American heritage of fair play in which a man is considered innocent until proved otherwise"; and for the ground as well as the decision, he won the overwhelming support and admiration of his faculty—some of whom, however, were prepared to go just a little further and insist on the principle advocated by the American Association of University Profesors: "Violations of the civil or criminal law may subject the faculty member to civilian sanctions, but this fact is irrelevant to the academic community unless the infraction also violates academic standards. . . ."

Meanwhile, letters, phone calls, and telegrams had been pouring in to both President Meyerson and me (for the first forty hours after my arrest I received not a single hostile or malicious message) from the faculties of America's great colleges and from many schools abroad—all expressing solidarity and the conviction that at stake was the future of a major university and of higher education as well as my personal fate. Even in Buffalo itself I have begun to sense of late a considerable shift of opinion in my favor—not merely on the part of other teachers and those professionals closest to us, like clergymen and psychiatrists, but from every sector of the population; as it becomes clearer and clearer that the unendurably vague charge of "maintaining a premise" (what high school or university would not fall under it?) has been invented to justify the malicious persecution of dissenting opinion.

Needless to say, my awareness of this growing support lifts up my sagging spirits. I have no taste for martyrdom; I do not know how to find pleasure in suffering even for the best of causes; and I find it harder and harder to laugh at even the most truly comic aspects of my situation. But if the Keystone Comedy being played out around me can be turned into an educational venture (education being, hopefully, an antidote to fear itself) which will persuade the most abjectly prejudiced that everyone, even a college professor advocating a change in the law, is entitled to full freedom of speech— then the shameless invasion of my privacy, the vindictive harassment of my family, and the (perhaps inevitable) misrepresentation of all of us in the press will have been worth enduring.

Chutzpah and *Pudeur*

IF *chutzpah* and *pudeur* seem an ill-assorted pair of words, one of those mixed marriages (or unblessed acts of miscegenation) which everyone thinks should not and cannot last, but everyone knows most often do, this is because they are in fact such a mismatch; which is to say, made not in heaven but in the head of some perverse matchmaker, some misguided *shadchan*—in this case, me. I had never seen them consorting together on a printed page, the delicate French word, appropriate to a tradition of tact and learning, and the vulgar Yiddish one, so suitable to a countertradition in which arrogance and self-deprecating irony reinforce rather than cancel each other out.

Yet why should they not lie side by side in cold print, I found myself thinking, since they already lived side by side not only in my own divided self, but also in the general culture around me—in American literature, surely, ever since Nathanael West, whose first book boldly displayed its affiliations with the most cryptic, i.e., *pudique,* of French schools, surrealism; and whose last shyly confessed its link with Jewish *chutzpah* by introducing an Indian, called only, in a bad Yiddish joke, "Chief Kiss-My-Towkus," meaning kiss my ass.

Not to have made the conjunction public, once it had occurred to me, would have been to betray a lack of gall, nerve, *chutzpah,* to put it precisely; but not to have regretted it a little almost immediately, would have been to reveal so total an absence of decorum that the very notion of boldness would have lost all meaning. In either event, I would have confessed myself half a man, half an artist,

as these are defined in our oddly hybrid tradition, whose two poles
Matthew Arnold (being an Englishman at home) termed quite
catholically Hebraic and Hellenic, and Philip Rahv (being a recently arrived immigrant) renamed rather parochially Redskin and
Paleface; but which I feel obliged to call (feeling neither just arrived nor quite at home) *chutzpah* and *pudeur*. It is not merely a
matter of speaking in two tongues neither really mine, but also of
insisting on a modicum of irony—that highest academic form of
pudeur—and thus escaping from both the myth of Antiquity and
that of the West, though risking, I suppose, a fall into the equally
legendary present, into fashion rather than piety.

I am, at any rate, interested in exploring the basic polarity, as
well as the basic ambivalence behind it, which this pair of words
seems to me to define more suggestively than any other: a basic
polarity in our very understanding of what constitutes art and literature. I am not meaning to suggest that the peculiar Western tradition of art is explained wholly or even chiefly by the tension between *chutzpah* and *pudeur*—merely that this tension plays a large
part in determining our essential double view of what it is the artist
says or does or makes. I have, as a matter of fact, reflected earlier
on two other sets of polarities and ambivalences which also underlie
our definition of art: Archetype and Signature in 1952, Mythos and
Logos in 1958; and there is some continuity of a complementary if
not a developmental kind between those earlier explorations, especially the first, and the present one.

This essay is, in intent, however, complete—not a total explanation but a self-sufficient one: the working out of an extended metaphor or conceit which, in theory at least, should provide a
"model" for a large body of literature, otherwise difficult even to
see wholly, much less to understand. Yet it is with some regret that I
enter on this third (and, I promise myself, final) venture into literary theory. It is a literary form which I practice seldom and reluctantly, finding it a disconcertingly attenuated form of poetry, or
more specifically, I guess, prose fiction, in which neither horror nor
humor—two effects of which I am, perhaps inordinately, fond,
seems quite suitable.

All forms of literary criticism I take to be art forms, but general
or theoretical criticism is so genteel or super-*pudique* that it is

driven to pretending it is science or philosophy—something else and presumably better, truer, more dependable. It is, however, the very shamefastness of literary theory, its love of disguise, which gives the game away; for, after all, the very essence of literature, or what at least we have agreed to call "literature" in the Western World, is a special use of words which sometimes alternately, sometimes simultaneously, reveals and conceals, exposes and hides: a dialectic movement back and forth between what threatens to become arrogant narcissism and what trembles on the verge of bashful dumbness.

This dialectic can be fruitfully discussed either historically or psychologically: either as it is recapitulated in the experience of the child or youth who begins to define his craft and the image of himself within our tradition, at first feeling, living rather than knowing that tradition; or else as it has been reflected in the long, slow evolution of that tradition itself, in terms, that is to say, of that tradition as it has come to be known. I intend, for reasons which I hope will become clear, to be chiefly historical in my approach, setting the problem in the context of what I take to be history, though others more positivist in their approach might prefer to call it myth or mytho-history: a particular version of the past best suited to illuminate what concerns me in the present.

I cannot, however, resist insisting to begin with on what most readers must already know—on the way in which, even at the earliest stages of his career, a nascent writer may well keep a secret journal, complete with lock and key; but which he ("she" is more apropos here, perhaps, since, mythologically speaking, *pudeur* is female) leaves lying about, unlocked, to be discovered by the first passer-by, even that ultimate invader of privacy, the parent. In a recent article on child poets, for instance, which appeared in *The New York Times,* the caption under a shy-proud ten-year-old face reads: "They don't know I write them"—and the reference of the pronouns is clear; the duplicity involved betrayed by the fact that the phrase was presumably spoken to a reporter and into a camera.

But it is not quite as simple even as that; for the young writer of the locked-unlocked, concealed-revealed journal will probably have developed a not-quite-legible hand, or a system of more or less deliberate misspellings to baffle his hoped-for discoverer. And at the next stage, the almost ultimate one (some writers, indeed, get no further ever), the still virginal artist will have invented for himself a special style, opaque, oblique, overgarrulous, underarticulate— somehow *diversionary* in any case—out of a shamefast desire not to be understood, not to be caught out, even if read! Think of those artists fixated on one or another of these deeply ambivalent, regressive styles: the reticence of Emily Dickinson, the endless qualifications of Henry James, the playful assault on syntax and punctuation of e. e. cummings.

But what exactly does the would-be artist play at concealing so transparently, and why? What, after all, did he produce long before he could muster words, which he was taught he must in all decency hide? What was he, in fact, applauded and praised for doing *out of sight?* The answer is obvious, and explains why so often the bashful beginning writer asked to show his work will answer, "Ah, it's all hogwash or crap or shit." The toilet is in our tradition, the prototype of the hideaway workshop, atelier, studio: the single habitually locked room in a house, where one performs in theoretical secrecy what "they" know in actuality he must be doing.

No wonder the most *pudique* and secretive writers are such palpable monsters of anality: Swift with his still secret "little language," and his obsession with excrement; Gerard Manley Hopkins with his poems tucked away, as it were, in his guilty asshole; Mark Twain with his hoard of shameful manuscripts concealed until after his death, and the give-away clue in his piece of privately circulated pornography, which begins with an attempt to conceal the real author of a fart and ends with an old man peeing away an erection. But the example of Twain's *1601* adds a disconcerting new factor, since the place of love is, he reminds us, quite as St. Augustine had earlier, *intra urinas et faeces.* Indeed, our earliest as well as our latest erections may be caused not by lust but by the simple need to urinate. The locked bathroom is, finally, also a spot for masturbation—for fantasies if not actual works of love, as well as for flushing away shameful wastes; and between its antiseptic white walls, two guilts are compounded into one beside the potentially symbolic roll of blank paper.

If anality signifies shame and implies concealment, orality, on the other hand, is a source of praise and a school for showing off.

The child is urged not to hide the first sounds he learns to make through his mouth, but to repeat them for an audience; and though he is quickly taught to excrete in private, his eating is a public performance. The high chair and the grownup's table are the prototypes, therefore, of the spotlight and the platform from which one recites, prototypes of publication.

How tempting in view of all this to make the easy Freudian identification of the artist's two conflicting impulses, *chutzpahdik* and *pudique,* with the mythological orifices on either end of the alimentary canal; to think of them as biologically, physiologically determined and therefore inevitable, universal. Such an identification would, however, profit by being itself exposed to history, examined in time; a process which might remind us that Freud's basic mythology of oral and anal was, as it were, toilet-trained into him: the product of a Middle European, bourgeois, Jewish mother, crying, as her descendants have ever since, "Eat! Eat! Talk! Talk! But, remember, keep clean, do it in the pot!"—with an implicit "for me, for your mama!" after each injunction.

It would be amusing, therefore, perhaps even instructive, to imagine the son of a non-Middle European, nonbourgeois, non-Jewish mother, who taught her child to eat in private lest he bring shame on her, and to do all his talking to himself behind lowered shades; and who further insisted that the best way of proving his love for her was to crap as frequently and copiously as possible—preferably in the presence of guests. "Fast! Fast!," such a mother might say, "but remember, too, bigger bowel movements or you'll break my heart!" A rather contradictory set of instructions, one must grant, but what mother was ever quite consistent or what mythology ever logical. And one can surmise, in any case, what different symbolic values our two alimentary openings would have, as well as how different "poets" and "artists" might be in such a world: professing macrobiotics, no doubt, indulging in milk shakes only in secret, but boasting to their proud mamas (laconically—or in gestures) how profligately they had spent their seed, and before how many bystanders they had produced record-breaking stools.

For me, in any event, psychological explanations tend to end in fantasies like these, once history has, as it must, broken in on their purity; and I propose, therefore, to start with a mytho-historical approach and let psychology break in only when it can no longer be resisted. Let us* begin then at the Beginning, with the more or less mythological assumption that at that primordial moment, before history existed at all, every song was sung and every story told in a single holy language, *lashon-ha-kodesh:* an esoteric tongue belonging to priests and shamans. At that point, there was not, in our sense, any "literature" at all, only "Scriptures," which is to say, "Revelation": something spoken through and, after a while, even written down by those priests and shamans. But writing itself was a further mystery—not a means of communication, but only another sign of the supernatural origin of what was revealed, one more warranty that in fact (i.e., in myth) it had come from the God or Goddess, Jehovah or the Muse: some supernal authority outside and before the human self.

Such a state, mythology tells us, could not long endure; since before history began, in order for history to begin, there was a Fall, the *Second* Fall according to the Hebrew tradition: a Fall which occurs not in the Garden of Nature, where man can only eat what is given him, not eat what is forbidden; but in the City, in the very midst of what men build with their hands, at the very height, in fact, of their presumably unlimited erection. Unlike the Fall in Eden, which is a fall from grace into morality, the Fall at the Tower of Babel is from the Tongue into many tongues, from "Revelation" to "literature."

From this point on, there exist for every would-be writer two languages: the Holy Language, which he may not even know but inevitably knows *about;* and the secular or vulgar language, his own "mother tongue," as we have come to call it. Thus history and "literature" are invented at the same time; since "literature" as opposed to "Scripture" is first spoken, then written (in a kind of unwitting parody of the sacred texts) in the *mammaloshen,* the *lingua materna.* This means that in a world divided rather than united by language, each man comes to speak for himself, and to others who always may not, frequently do not, really understand him. And it further implies that writing itself ceases to be a Revelation of a

---

* The canny reader will note that with this "us," my paper begins to move from the *chutzpahdik* first person to the *pudique* third—thus illustrating in its own form the thesis it is presenting—or rather, *I* am presenting.

single truth to all mankind, and becomes instead Confession-Communication of a personal vision to those few, if any, who will hear and comprehend.

No longer is it possible for the poet to pretend that he is a sort of divine ventriloquist's dummy or holy conduit. The very formulas with which he introduces his message are profoundly altered. Invocations to the Muse, where they persist at all, are felt as mere metaphors; nor does any manipulator of words dare assert, like his prelapsarian ancestors, "Thus sayeth the Lord," or "It is written." Instead, he is likely to stammer, "What I mean is. . . ," which amounts to little more than "What 'I' means is," or "What I mean am, what I am means. . .": a series threatening continually to end in the whimper: "That is not what I mean at all." The game of words, in short, is played now not in the light of eternity, but in the world of mortality, where the winner achieves not salvation but only fame. What is at issue when one claims to speak for God is life and death; while the confession that one speaks only for himself means that nothing but honor and shame are at stake.

Yet occasionally, even after the fall to literature and history, some blessed Bard (self-blessed, to be sure, but that is good enough) will arise, convinced that the Universe is infinitely hospitable, after all—at least to him—and he will cry his message loud and clear, as if Babel had never fallen and his own language were that spoken in Heaven. We know the names of those serenely *chutzpahdik* Bards, Dante and Shakespeare, for instance; and reading them, we are almost convinced that if not in the Empyrean itself, at least in the Earthly Paradise, the guardian angels converse in Italian or English. But most writers since the Fall have imagined themselves inhabitants of a Universe something less than friendly, a universe threatening at every turn to publish the news which they surmised from the start: that they are *rejected*. Think of the bugaboo of the young writer and all that is implied by its metaphorical name, the "rejection slip." No wonder most poets begin on guard, creating protections against being shamed, even as they invent strategies for winning recognition.

It may well be, as William Faulkner observed of Albert Camus in a moving little obituary, that no author since Babel has ever wanted to do anything more (or less) than to write on the fallen walls of the world, "I was here" and to sign his name. Certainly,

Milton suggested much the same thing in his own language, on a similar occasion: "Fame is the spur." But if *chutzpah,* in the seventeenth century or the twentieth, urges that the worst event of all is to die unknown, *pudeur,* at either point in time, answers that "Shame! Shame! Everybody knows your name!" is the most terrible of reproaches. And so the writer tries to have it both ways at once, *can* have it both ways at once, since all that we call literature was invented with this in view. He writes his name on the already scribbled wall, writes it large and dark to compel attention. But he encrypts it, encodes it—thus emulating those wily prototypes of the artist, Ulysses and Huck Finn, who never tell the truth right away: never begin by giving their right name, or telling the real story of where they have come from, whither they are tending.

Yet if poetry is, after all—as Dante himself confessed, for all his show of assurance—a *bella menzogna,* most beautiful of lies, then the true name of the poet is revealed precisely by giving a false one; since his most secret and authentic title is Liar, Deceiver, Man of Many Devices. He will begin with the joke of a pseudonym, inscribing: KILROY WAS HERE. MARK TWAIN WAS HERE. GEORGE ELIOT WAS HERE—meaning SOMEBODY ELSE WAS HERE. NOT ME. Or, as the shoddiest of all jests has it, "Boss, there's nobody in here but us chickens." At the end, however, he is likely to be joking more seriously, kidding on the square, as it were, by insisting in his last extremity (once more like the prototypical Ulysses) that he is really *OU TIS,* NOBODY AT ALL. *Pudeur,* in short, drives the writer first to plot disguises, and next to dream invisibility; so that he may be heard unseen and unscathed.

Not only Nathanael Hawthorne, then—as Poe once commented in an unfriendly review—but *all* writers—as Poe certainly should have understood—write in invisible ink, on occasion at least. And why not; since with one eye they tend to see themselves as spies, secret agents in a world so unremittingly hostile, that even, perhaps especially, at home they are in enemy territory. And so they feel compelled to communicate with their unknown compatriots (how can they ever be sure who they are, or even whether they exist?) in a secret language, in code.

For this reason, therefore, proper literary criticism, which is to say, the analysis of what is really new or forever inexhaustible in the realm of art, must be in large part cryptanalysis. Insofar as the artist is an agent, the critic must be a counteragent, engaged in a special brand of detective work made easy because the criminal he pursues has taken pains to leave clues everywhere. In fact, the artist is precisely the kind of outlaw or traitor who wants his crime to be found out: found finally not to be a crime at all; but only an act of supreme virtue, a true act of love, though committed with all the show of guilt proper to a crime. Sometimes that strange guilt for love is manifested in the sneaking shamefastness of *pudeur,* sometimes in the brazen arrogance of *chutzpah;* but it is all the same, for they represent finally not two impulses but one: a genuine ambivalence rooted in a single basic response.

Of what, then, does the artist perhaps not quite fear himself guilty, but surely fear he may seem guilty to others, so that in their presence, finally even alone, he is driven to cringe or swagger? If a crime at all or a sin, writing is essentially a lonely crime or sin, an offense without victims; and in this respect it oddly resembles masturbation—constituting a kind of reversed or mirror image of it, in fact. Like onanism, the creation of "literature" is an auto-erotic act, accompanied by, or rather creating, maintaining, certain fantasies. But in the realm of "literature" the auto-erotic act itself remains invisible, existing only in metaphor, by analogy; while the fantasies, once they have been committed to writing, are quite visible, palpable, one is tempted to say, real. But this is, of course, quite the opposite of masturbation.

Even if we think of the act of writing as a kind of aggravated masturbation, which is to say, as exhibitionist auto-eroticism, practiced in the hope (and fear) of attracting an audience, which the writer hopes (and fears) will be stimulated to follow his example, the writer has displayed in public no living flesh of his own, only fantasies whose exposure is banned by no law of God or man. And should his act provoke widespread imitation, it would only make him a best-seller rather than a real seducer; since the masturbatory orgy set off by a work of art, however successful, is one in which no one assaults anybody but himself, and even that within the private chambers of his own head. Where then is the offense; and if any can be presumed to exist, who is the offended?

But once more we have been betrayed by analogy and introspection into the trap of fantastic psychologizing, from which only a return to history can deliver us. And, indeed, if the questions to which we have come can be answered at all, the answers must lie hidden in history itself: *real* history this time, which is to say, the actual records of the emergence of vernacular poetry in Provence toward the end of the eleventh century—the second beginning of "literature" in the Western world.

It is the essence of our culture that in it art was twice-born, poetry twice-invented, the first time in the Near East, the second in Southern France; and the living sense of that second time is preserved for us in the eleven surviving poems (one with its musical setting) by William, the ninth Duke of Aquitaine and the seventh Count of Poitou, sometimes known simply as William of Poitou. He was, his early biographer tells us, distinguished by his royal connections ("he had a daughter who was wife to King Henry of England, and mother of the young King . . .") and his skill at seduction ("he went about the world for a long time to deceive women . . ."). History remembers him, however, as one of the unquestioned firsts of literature: first vernacular poet of the modern world.

There is some indication, in fact, that certain traditions had already begun to gel before the time of William, though in poems which have not come down to us. But they could not have been long in existence, since the deep Middle Ages were hostile not only to the making of poems as such, but to any use of the vernacular in writing whose ends were not immediate and practical. Christianity had, as every schoolboy knows, begun by attacking the "literature" of Greco-Roman civilization—in part because it was hopelessly secular from the parochial point of view called in the Middle Ages "Catholic"; in larger part, perhaps, because its canon clearly constituted a kind of "Scriptures" for a rival, pagan faith. But the war of the church against, say, Ovid (who was bootlegged and preserved anyhow) was not so much a war against a poet or poets as one aimed at destroying the very concept of art which had sustained them.

The Saints who cried, "What has Athens to do with Jerusalem?" provided the ammunition for an onslaught against all culture after Babel, an attack on any kind of Confession-Communication opposed to a single Revelation. And the dream they inspired in the leaders of the Roman Church was a dream of a world reunified around a single canonical Book, *The Book,* as the Christian Scriptures were commonly called, translated into a single, universally understood tongue, i.e., a New Holy Language. Oddly enough from a mythological point of view, though understandably from the point of view of history, that language turned out to be neither Hebrew nor Aramaic nor Greek, in which the Old Testament and the New had originally been written, but Latin, through which the Caesars had tried to unify an empire. But to build with hands in history is to recreate Babel, and the Roman Catholic Tower of Babel, though presumably built on Rock rather than sand, fell like the Tower which was its prototype.

This time, however, the Confusion of Tongues occurred not in myth but in history, and its record can be read in letters and memorial inscriptions and casual graffiti. Not instantaneously as in legend, but slowly over the centuries, Latin became Italian and French and Provençal; so that finally even crying assent to the Christian God, the inhabitants of the old Roman realm heard themselves shouting out variously, "*Si*" and "*Oui*" and "*Oc.*" Small wonder they chose to address, feeling free for the first time, those lesser divinities, the women they loved, in those same divided tongues. It was, in fact, in the *langue d'oc,* the language of Rome's First Province, that "literature" was reborn; and William, to whom it was not even really native, picks it up, his lines trembling still for the sensitive ear—not only with the shudder of passion released, but with an additional tremor of delight at exploiting precisely what was *not* a Holy Language—the first vulgar tongue in which it had become possible to say again the personal "I," to write again a signed poem.

Over and over, his poems begin with slight variations on the single formula: *I will make a poem, a verse, a little song*—as if he can never exhaust the wonder and newness of his enterprise: the "I" singing, after long silence, its own vision of the world in the *lingua materna.*

> *Companho, faray un vers . . . convinen:*
> *Farai un vers de dreyt nien:*
> *Farai un vers, pos mi sonelh . . .*
> *Farai chansoneta nueva . . .*

Four times he manages the formula in the first line, then once in the second:

> *Pos de chantar m'es pres talentz,*
> *Farai un vers, don sui dolenz:*

And the repetition conveys finally something more, something other than a sense of joy and release. *Grand seigneur* that he was, William, one suspects, must have been a little scared—aware of what was dangerous, or would be found so by the Church, in his unprecedented venture. Yet how could he have known what lay ahead, what he was releasing in his playful or melancholy comments on his adventures with women?

Perhaps it is only our retrospective knowledge of the terror and beauty which followed him in history—the scores of poets who followed his example and the repression which ensued—that leads us to read an undertone of bravado and terror into his verse. It was not, after all, the poetry of William or any other *jongleur* that cued the Albigensian Crusade, but profound doctrinal differences, a conflict of religions. And yet when the culture of Provence was destroyed by the armies of the Church, not only the alleged Manichaean faith of the *Cathari* went down with it, but also the cult of *Joia,* of sexual pleasure, to which Provençal poetry was dedicated. That kind of poetry moved elsewhere, to be sure—into the languages of *oui* and *si* first of all; but it had died forever in the lovely tongue William once chose as specially suited to his needs. *"Qu'eu non ai soing d'estraing lati,"* he had written long before the blow fell, *"Qu'e m parta de mon Bon Vezi."* "I need no stranger's tongue, no alien Latin, which might separate me from my Good Neighbor."

Even with a shift into *"estraing lati",* which is to say, foreign vernaculars, William's example continued to impose itself; for he had somehow hit upon two poetic modes whose uses and possibilities have not yet been exhausted. Neither an especially subtle thinker, nor a very sensitive lover, nor an extraordinarily gifted technician, he managed somehow to invent, re-invent, find in the *langue d'oc* two forms appropriate to the two poles of the ambivalence about making verses which was to trouble his successors, if it did not already trouble him: the Enigma to express *pudeur* (in the poem beginning *"Farai un vers de dreyt nien"*), the Pornographic Song to register *chutzpah* (in the one opening *"Farai un vers, pos mi sonelh"*).

The Enigma or the Riddle is a genre which we are likely to associate these days solely with the nursery and the child's book, though it is closely related to an adult form much prized in recent decades—the Conceit, which is to say, the extended, farfetched metaphor as practiced pre-eminently by John Donne. If we had not been told, for instance, in the sixth stanza of the perhaps-too-often cited "A Valediction Forbidding Mourning" that the poet is describing "Our two souls . . . which are one"—and reminded again in the third line of the seventh—the pair of stanzas which follow would be a Riddle rather than a Conceit:

> If they be two, they are two so
>   As stiff twin compasses are two;
> . . . the fix'd foot, makes no show
>   To move, but doth, if th'other do.

> And though it in the centre sit,
>   Yet, when the other far doth roam,
> It leans, and hearkens after it,
>   And grows erect, as that comes home.

An Enigma is, in fact, nothing but a Conceit which conceals one pole of its similitude in its tail, instead of presenting it forthrightly at its head. Moreover, even as the Conceit tends to become the Enigma, which, in a sense, it was in the beginning; the Enigma aspires to become—teases us with the possibility, even occasionally succeeds in becoming—the meta-Enigma, or Ultimate Riddle, fit symbol of the mystery at the heart of our existence: the Question without an Answer. Surely many children, all children, perhaps, must feel (as I myself once did) that the "answers" to certain well-loved riddles are irrelevant, a delusion and disappointment, a grown-up hoax intended to persuade them of what they instinctively know to be untrue: *that there is an answer to everything* and that it is the function of language to reveal that answer in story and song.

No wonder the wise child loves so desperately, before he realizes quite why, such anti-Riddles as Lewis Carroll's "Why is a raven like a writing desk?", to which the proper response is silence, or even better, laughter. Wonderland is, indeed, the school in which he learns to respond for ever after to the meta-Enigma, whether proposed jocosely, as in *Finnegans Wake,* in the form of a dreamed pun, "Why do am I look alike two poss of porter pease?"; or proffered quite seriously, as at the opening of Thoreau's *Walden,* in the guise of a confession or anticonfession:

> I long ago lost a hound, a bay horse, and a turtledove, and am still on their trail. Many are the travelers I have spoken to concerning them, describing their tracks and what calls they answered to. I have met one or two who have heard the hound, and the tramp of the horse, and even seen the dove disappear behind a cloud, and they seemed as anxious to recover them as if they had lost them themselves.

In Thoreau the question mark by which we are accustomed to identify the Riddle has been ingested, as it were; and we are confronted not with the puzzle itself but with a narrative about puzzle-asking ("I have spoken . . . describing their tracks . . .") and the bafflement of those asked. And we are here very close to what is generally called—once more with connotations of the nursery—Nonsense, i.e., the unanswerable Riddle without even a mark of interrogation to tease us into believing that there are answers at the back of *somebody's* book.

Nonsense always trembles on the verge of the ridiculous, though sometimes its practitioners seem blessedly unaware of the fact, as was Edgar Allan Poe, along with his French translators and imitators, Baudelaire and Mallarmé. A case in point is the following excerpt from *Ulalume:*

> These were days when my heart was volcanic
> As the scoriac rivers that roll—
> As the lavas that restlessly roll
> Their sulphurous currents down Yaanek,
> In the ultimate climes of the Pole—
> That groan as they roll down Mount Yaanek,
> In the realms of the Boreal Pole.

And for those still unaware of how funny the last two lines are, a reading of the notes in a recent scholarly edition (explaining the "Boreal Pole" is *really* the South Pole; and "Yaanek" a name derived either from "an Arabic execration, . . . probably obscene" or a term "sometimes used by Polish Jews for an unkindly Christian.") will perhaps suffice to illustrate at least the joke of seriously trying to solve Nonsense, or even Non-Sense, no matter how grave its tone. But Edward Lear—whom W. H. Auden has described as Poe's sole real imitator *in English*—guessed the secret long before us, revealing it in poems clearly intended as comic Nonsense (as opposed to mantic Non-Sense), though echoing Poe in cadence and sound pattern and especially in the invention of exotic-ridiculous place names.

> And in twenty years they all came back,
>   In twenty years or more.
> And every one said, 'How tall they've grown!
> For they've been to the Lakes, and the Terrible Zone,
>   And the hills of the Chankly Bore';
> And they drank their health, and gave them a feast
> Of dumplings made of beautiful yeast;
> And everyone said, 'If we only live,
> We too will go to sea in a Sieve,—
>   To the hills of the Chankly Bore!'

But what a crew they are, after all, these not-quite-askers of insoluble riddles; what guilt-ridden evaders of the public eye, what deviously invisible or masked men: Lewis Carroll and Henry David Thoreau, Edgar Allan Poe and Edward Lear. What artful dodgers into the nursery or the Azure—where fantasies of pederasty or necrophilia or incest, of sexual transgressions dreamed rather than dared are barely glimpsed past the concealing devices suggested by extreme *pudeur*. Not much doubt remains in their cases, that the Enigma is the form to which a writer turns when his awareness of guilt inclines him toward the pole of *pudeur;* when he lays, as it were, his finger to his lips or sticks his thumb in his mouth, thus betraying what he cannot, will not confess: *"I am guilty as hell, but no one knows it or ever will;* for how can they suspect, accuse, convict an Angel in Exile, or a mere child in adult form, of ultimate iniquity.

I was a child and *she* was a child,
In this kingdom by the sea;
But we loved with a love that was more than love—
I and my Annabel Lee—

Finally, however, precisely the pretense that the Riddle is a child's game gives away the sexual secret it tries to conceal; verifying what we learn from other sources: that everywhere in mythology, the Enigma is associated with the threat of incest—as Claude Lévi-Strauss reminds us in a remarkable passage of his inaugural address at the Collège de France. "Between the puzzle solution and incest there exists a relation," he writes, "not external and of fact, but internal and of reason. . . . Like the solved puzzle, incest brings together elements doomed to remain separate. . . ." And he then goes on to explain that "the audacious union of masked words or of consanguines unknown to themselves . . . engenders decay and fermentation, the unchaining of natural forces . . ."; and therefore brings on "an eternal summer . . . licentious to the point of corruption," yet often chosen in history and myth over "a winter just as eternal . . . pure to the point of sterility. . . ."

The unsolved and insoluble Enigma, the Non-Sense Riddle, for which William provided the prototype, is quite another matter, however; since it represents averted rather than achieved incest, guilt without consummation. William's model opens, as a matter of fact, with a disavowal of all guilt, a disavowal of everything; but the order of that everything amounts to a backhand confession.

Farai un vers de dreyt nien:
Non er di mi ni d'autra gen,
Non er d'amor ni de joven,
Ni de ren au . . .

"I will make a poem of pure nothing," he begins; and we are reminded, a little absurdly, of the adolescent's answer in the old joke: "Where are you going?" "Out." "What are you doing?" "Nothing." But then he starts to specify, "It is not about me or anybody else; it is not about love or youth, or anything else." "*I* will make a poem," the boastful formula asserts; but by the second line the singer has begun to deny his singing self, the "I" released by the vernacular tradition. First the self, and then love and youth; these are the foci of his guilt—and what therefore his poem must aver is *not* his subject, though it cannot help naming them. And who can blame him, in any case, for what floats to the surface of his mind, since he has dreamed it all (he hastens to assure us next) "asleep and on horseback."

> *Qu'enans fo trobatz en durmen*
> *Sobre chevau.*

Why then is he trembling at the point of death a couple of stanzas later, afflicted by a malady of which he knows only "what they tell me"?

> *Malautz suy e tremi murir,*
> *E ren no*n sai mas quan n'aug dir . .*

He may assure us over and over that he couldn't care less about whatever is really at stake behind all his mystification ("I prize it no more than a mouse . . . I esteem it no more than a cock . . ."), but the note of melancholy and terror will not be exorcised; the counterpoint of *timor mortis conturbat me*. And lest we have forgotten, or never quite realized, that it is a Riddle we have been presented, the final line teases us with the hope of a solution, a key, *"la contraclau,"* that can only be provided by another, answering poem. *Fag ai lo vers,* the poet has assured us only five lines earlier, "and now my story is done." But, of course, it is not—since the meta-Enigma, the Riddle Without an Answer, is in essence endless, a tale without a conclusion.

"Every telling has a tailing," James Joyce was to insist more than eight centuries later, "and that's the he and she of it." But the Absolute Riddle has precisely no "tailing" *("Non er d'amor ni de joven"),* no "audacious union of . . . consanguines . . ."; and without consummation there is no conclusion. The unsolved puzzle like the taboo mother is Ever Virgin, never quite possessed. William, however, wrote not only of love as forbidden and therefore repressed, but also of passion as forbidden yet irrepressible—providing a prototype for the poetry of *chutzpah* even as he had for that of *pudeur.*

That other prototype, however, turns out to be quite simply the pornographic poem: the vaunt of potency, the boast of full genitality —delivered not from the crouch of shame with the finger to the lips, but with a sexual swagger, the hips thrust forward and the arms spread wide for an embrace. Whenever poetry, in fact, becomes *chutzpahdik* rather than *pudique,* in Walt Whitman, say, or Allen Ginsberg, it learns again to talk dirty. Before the arrogant poet can be loved he must first be condemned as "the dirtiest beast of the age," then, not cleared of that charge but found through it, loved for it, quite as in the case of Whitman. The shamefast poet, on the other hand, must first be blamed for his *obscurity,* then without being absolved, found through it and loved for it, quite like Gerard Manley Hopkins. Whitman and Hopkins—they seem ideal, almost allegorical opposites; and yet as Hopkins himself was driven to confess (shyly, his finger characteristically to his lips): "I always knew in my heart Walt Whitman's mind to be more like my own than any other man's living. . . ." It is as close to confessing the particular guilt that dogged him, the homosexuality he shared with Whitman, as Hopkins could come; but it is also a reminder of the sense in which *chutzpah* and *pudeur* are originally and finally one, two faces of a single ambivalence.

But William alone could suffice to remind us of this, since his most successful piece of pornography is about a *chutzpahdik* character (called once more quite simply "I") who managed by shamming the discretion of *pudeur* to achieve a kind of total sexual satisfaction: "Eight days or more" in a Provençal Pornotopia, with a pair of uninhibited women, who first feed him up on capons, white bread, good wine and "pepper in abundance," then almost screw him to death.

> *Tan las fotei com auzirets:*
> *Cen e quatre vint et ueit vetz,*
> *Q'a pauc no·i rompei mos corretz*
>   *E mos arnes,*
> *E no us puesc dir lo malaveg,*
>   *Tan gran m'en pres.*

"So much I fucked them," William sings, "as you shall hear: One hundred and eighty-eight times, so that I almost broke my braces and my straps; and I can't tell you what misery ensued, it was so great."*

In order, however, to attain that good, which, as he tells us in another poem, men desire more then all else in the world *("esta ben . . . D'acho don hom a plus talen")*, but which, as we learn from this one, can end in pain, the poet finds it necessary to simulate precisely the dumbness associated with *pudeur.* He is, in fact, the least faithful of all versifying lovers to the vow of secrecy theoretically essential to Courtly Love. Not only does he boast again and again in his *chutzpahdik* songs of his sexual prowess in general ("I've never had a lady at night who has not eagerly awakened me next morning. . . . I could have earned a living by my skill. . . ."), but he names names: denominating, for instance, the pair he fucked one hundred and eighty-eight times, first by their husbands' names, then by their Christian ones.

In the poem itself, however, he responds to their courteous-erotic greeting—delivered, as he puts it, in the vernacular of one of the ladies *("en son latin")*—in the nontongue of the deaf-mute: not *"but"* or *"bat"* but only *"Babariol, babariol, Babarian);* and says no more, though, to test him, they drag their long-clawed, vicious cat down his naked back. *"Babariol, babariol, Babarian,"* it is a nonsense poem, a riddling song—a way of saying nothing, of guaranteeing that he is constitutionally incapable of exposing what actual *chutzpah* lurks behind their superficial *pudeur.*

Once loose from the prison of their bedroom, however, the poet finds his shameless tongue; singing once more between waking and sleeping, though this time afoot and in the broad daylight, how lustful and wicked and guilty they were, women are—how sly and indefatigable and *innocent* he turned out to be, men always turn out to be. It is the typical stance of the *fabliaux,* not of the love songs of Provence with their pretense of male humility, their vows of discretion and silence; and suggests disconcertingly the sense in which much of that poetry might be, or at least can be, understood as

---

* In the standard scholarly text, *Les Chansons de Guillaume IX,* edited by Alfred Jeanroy, there is a running translation of the text into modern French, but this stanza is coyly represented (in a book revised in 1964!) by a row of dashes; nor does the verb *fotre* appear at all in the appended glossary—which is, I suppose, a case of academic *pudeur* at its most ignominious in vain combat with the artist's *chutzpah.*

mock-humble only, a strategy in the game of seduction. It is what comes of singing at the unguarded moment of falling asleep on the broad highway: "I will make a verse, since I am falling asleep, walking and taking the sun."

The poems of *chutzpah,* William's poetry suggests, are written on the verge of sleep, just as those of *pudeur* are composed in its very depths: the one in the reverie that prepares us for the fatal loss of consciousness, the other, at the moment when, disturbed, we must either dream or start awake. And how finally appealing they both are—the dirty story, so appropriate to the eternal adolescent in us, and the riddle, so suitable to the immortal child; the wet dream which we prepare for ourselves before we have quite lost consciousness, and the irrational sequence of the not-quite-nightmare, which our unconscious prepares for us to forestall a little the advent of guilt-ridden awareness; the fantasy of consummation without guilt, and its twinned opposite of guilt without consummation.

Neither, though, not even both together, served to keep William (representative in this respect of the Christian conscience of Europe) quite at peace, waking or sleeping. And he closes his career by inventing or perfecting a third prototype: the poem of recantation, which begins untypically: *"Pos de chantar m' es pres talentz"* —but in which the old formula *"farai un vers"* appears in the second line, this time qualified, however, with the word *dolenz,* sorrowful, mournful, melancholy. Yet even at this point, he cannot forgo a boast in retrospect, confessing—half ruefully, half proudly —even as he assures us that he wishes to surrender all for the sake of God and his own salvation, "I knew joy and pleasure, far and near and in my own domain." Nonetheless the recantation does in theory represent a disavowal of everything which the opening up of a vernacular, secular tradition had seemed to promise: a rejection of songs of joy in favor of songs of sorrow, of the celebration of self in favor of the denial of self, of poetry in favor of piety. But for piety, not the *"latin"* of Agnes, wife of *en* Guari, but that of the Church, which is to say, real rather than mock Latin is appropriate.

The tradition which William helped to inaugurate did not, however, disappear when he lost, or played at losing, his nerve. Men have, as every reader knows, continued to write in the *lingua ma-*

terna; and such writers, along with those readers, have tended ever since his time to divide their allegiances between his two proto-types. The majority have always preferred pornography, the poetry of sexual consummation and its celebration—though most often they have bowdlerized it, saying *amar* rather than *fotre,* out of re-spect for the *pudeur* of their lovers or their audiences or the official censors. But a considerable minority, all the way from the academy to the nursery, have opted for the Riddle—though this, also, has been bowdlerized, by those too proud or scared to confront the Total Enigma, the Question without any Answer at all.

Academics, especially, have proved *chutzpahdik* enough behind their masks of *pudeur* to prefer the quasi-Enigma, the Riddle insol-uble to the uninitiated many, yet decipherable by the tiny congrega-tion of the chosen: a symbol not of the opacity of all existence, but of the mystery of election. "Many are called but few are chosen," sing the poets of the quasi-Enigma; to which the quasipornog-raphers answer in chorus, "All the world loves a lover." And the Provencals had invented quite early names for both of these schools; calling the former *trobar clus,* which is to say, hermetic or private poetry, and the latter *trobar leu,* which means light or open verse.

Arnaut Daniel is the master of the *trobar clus,* "the greatest craftsman of *la lingua materna,*" according to Dante, who actually wrote eight verses in Provençal, the first of mother tongues and Daniel's own, to show his love for the earlier poet as well as the skill he thought he owed to his example. Moreover, Dante com-posed sestinas, too, imitating the difficult form Daniel had presuma-bly invented. Dante's grave and tormented poems, however, have little of the playfulness, the willingness to walk the brink of non-sense, which characterizes the Provençal poet, who set himself the task of ringing changes on the words for "fingernail" and "uncle" (in the *langue d'oc, "ongla"* and *"oncle,"* words which tease us with their closeness of sound, their dissonance of meaning) in his famous sestina; and whose boast was, in love as well as art, that he "yoked the ox and the hare" and "swam against the current."

What Dante did understand is that the poetry of *pudeur,* the true *trobar clus,* is no mere pastiche of rare words and rich rhymes but a kind of verse built to keep out rather than let in—a way of using words as if they were opaque: not as windows opening on the soul, but reflecting jewels which redouble whatever light we cast on them, and end by dazzling us, blinding us with their icy splendor. *Trobar clus* is the poetry of winter light and winter cold—celebrating, in fact, precisely that "winter just as eternal . . ." to which Lévi-Strauss alluded, "pure to the point of sterility. . . ." And this, too, Dante comprehended, beginning his own hermetic sestina:

> To small daylight and the great circle of shade
> I've come, alas, and to the blanching of the hills,
> The season when the color leaves the grass. . .

quite on the model of Arnaut Daniel, who opens one of his thorniest, most forbidding poems:

> The bitter air
> Makes branchy boughs
> Quite bare
> That the sweet made thick with leaves. . . .

The poets of the *trobar leu,* on the other hand, of whom Bernart de Ventadorn is the most eminent and best remembered (nearly fifty of his poems have been preserved, as opposed to eighteen by Daniel), set their songs against a landscape not white but green, not chill but warm. Spring is their symbolic season:

> The sweet paschal season
> With its fresh greening
> Brings leaf and flower
> Of diverse color . . .

Their weather is not quite Lévi-Strauss's "eternal summer . . . licentious to the point of corruption," of which, in some ways, William's overheated interiors inhabited by overstuffed lovers—that world of glowing coals and plenteous hot pepper— seems a nearer analogue; and certainly when William does take us outdoors, it is into a sweet springtime appropriate to a poetry of unabashed sensuality: *la dolchor de temps novel,* in which trees burgeon and birds sing, as if an eternal summer lay just ahead. Springtime represents, perhaps, a compromise, a withdrawal to the moment of promised rather than accomplished bliss, on the part of poets more timid than William, but not less committed finally to the cult of *joia*. And even when they seem to celebrate an eternal April without a June, an eternally retreating horizon, at least it is a benign one. Not, in fact, until the time of T. S. Eliot does any poet portray April as more cruel than kind; since only the tradition of "modernism" and the *avant-garde* permits, as it wére, the frozen winter of *trobar clus* to creep past the vernal equinox.

Yet the poetry of the Waste Land is not unprecedented in making the impossibility of love its central subject, innocence as a function of impotence its second theme. Nor is it different from the main stream of *pudique* verse in its resolve to be deliberately "difficult" or "obscure," i.e., in determining to encode its secrets in a language comprehensible only to those already in the know. What is new is the particular language it employs—that blend of allusion and demiquotation in a Babel of tongues, which represents at once the climax and dissolution of a linguistic experiment carried on ever since the Renaissance: the attempt to create a "glorified" or "illustrated" vernacular, a proper "poetic diction," different, on the one hand, from the Christian Holy Language, which was Latin, and, on the other, from the simple prattle of women and children. It was certain insecure academics who had learned to be ashamed of not speaking the languages of Classical Antiquity, and therefore speculated on the possibility of creating a kind of half-holy tongue by splitting their own *lingua materna* into two dialects: one thought fit for the refinements of Art and Love, the other considered appropriate only for the gross business of every day. But various early vernacular poets, from William to Dante, had been there first, creating out of *chutzpah* what the scholars would feel obliged to justify in the name of *pudeur*.

That initial *chutzpah*, however, soon ran out, even for the poets that followed; and, in any case, those who wrote in the "glorified" or subholy tongues could no longer pretend to speak—or even to translate, render at a second remove—the Word of God, but only the words of men, which is to say, of themselves. And though with the passage of centuries and the replacement of the Church by the University as the chief instrument of education, certain humanistic texts began to seem more orthodox than heretical, finally canonical, they constituted no real Scriptures; only pseudo-Scriptures sufficient unto that pseudo-Cult, the Art Religion according to Matthew Arnold—or, in its revised American form, the Great Books Religion according to Robert Hutchins or the New Critics.

It is characteristic of aggravated *pudeur* that it tries to disguise even itself, pretending it is piety rather than mere bashfulness and shame and guilt; but the hermetic tradition, as it has passed from Arnold to Eliot to Leavis and Cleanth Brooks, is revealed finally as mere gentility, i.e., *pudeur* utterly bereft of *chutzpah*. To be sure, our early twentieth-century gentility is more highfalutin, perhaps, than the middlebrow gentility practiced in the middle of the last by, say, Longfellow; but it is equally hollow in its pretenses, redeeming neither language nor souls. Without an adequate faith to justify it, any venture at defining a canonical literature, like any attempt to separate a sacred language from a profane is revealed as one more spasm prompted by the castrating shame which has been haunting Western Art ever since the first Western artist set out to sing of sex and the "I." The chill that freezes the marrow of worshippers at the altars of High Art is not just the cold that possesses all empty churches, but the zero weather of the Eternal Winter, which sets a new generation of readers to shivering even in our superheated classrooms and libraries.

What, then, is to be done? To deliver the Waste Land of our Universities from shame-ridden sterility, shall we swing to the opposite pole—woo the Eternal Summer in which the Bacchae can dance in the *Aula Magna,* as well as on the lonely peaks; and all distinctions of high and low, kith and kind will be melted away in ecstasy? There is always conceivable at least, if never quite possible, a third way eloquently described by Lévi-Strauss in the inaugural lecture quoted earlier.

> In the face of the two possibilities which might seduce the imagination—an eternal summer or a winter just as eternal, the former licentious to the point of corruption, the latter pure to the point of sterility—man must resign himself to choosing equilibrium and the periodicity of the seasonal rhythm. In the natural order, the latter fulfils the same function which is fulfilled in society by the exchange of women in marriage and the ex-

change of words in conversation, when these are practiced with
the frank intention of communicating, that is to say, without
trickery or perversity, and above all, without hidden motives.

"Never quite possible," I have written (and I return in conclusion to the first person, since that is what I must remain in the silence, the blank space that follows my final phrase), thinking of
communal life or even the psychic life of the individual; since in the
first "perversity" is the rule, and in the second "hidden motives"
are inevitable; and "equilibrium," therefore, in either case merely a
wish, a fantasy, a dream. Perhaps this has not always been so; but
certainly it is so now, when we no longer possess—in a world of
air-conditioning and travel so rapid that summer and winter are
hours rather than months apart—the inescapable pattern of "perio-
dicity" provided by the "seasonal rhythm" of the natural year.

Only in poems does man create the balance which Lévi-Strauss
proposes and himself momentarily achieves on the page: in the use
of language we call "literature," and which, keeping faith with both
poles of our ambivalence, relies upon "trickery" and is shaped by
motives hidden even from ourselves. Only at the moment of becoming a poet can the anthropologist create the ideal community, the
perfect marriage which as a citizen, lover, father, even teacher he
inevitably betrays; and he does so, ironically enough, by abandoning or transcending "the frank intention of communicating" in
favor of the deviousness of the artist.

It therefore matters not at all whether the poet is asserting the
possibility or impossibility of "equilibrium" in the world outside his
text. His success in the world depends not on his declared allegiance, but on his undeclared ambivalence. And this is equally true
if, like Lévi-Strauss, he is projecting the hope of such a solution, or,
like Euripides in *The Bacchae*, singing its inevitable failure: the terror of repression, the terror of release not complementing or fulfill-
ing each other, but only destroying turn and turn about those who
have committed themselves either way. In either case, the end is
irony; since in the former the equilibrium achieved in the lecture
hall is lost in the streets, and in the latter the equilibrium achieved
in the theater belies the message which is its occasion. Yet the second kind of irony seems more appropriate to a historical moment in

which not the long-term goals for which we demonstrate, but the short-lived Demonstration itself seems to provide all the community we shall ever have; and in which, therefore, not marriage—as for Lévi-Strauss—but the Orgy—as for the Bacchae themselves—becomes the key Utopian image.

Small wonder, then, that *The Bacchae* of Euripides is currently on everyone's mind, as it has been continually on mine in these reflections on the seasons of the soul; that it among the surviving plays of the Attic theater occupies for us the central position held for our immediate predecessors by Sophocles' *Oedipus Rex*. At one point, during the past year, there were playing in the major theaters of the Western world, five new adaptations, free, faithful, naked, clothed, of that play; and as I walk the corridors of my own university, I see posted on the wall just outside our graduate student lounge (itself recently decorated in the course of a "mind-fuck" with painted slogans: FEMINISM LIVES. EAT SHIT. FAR FUCKIN' OUT. TOUCH ME FEEL ME HEAL ME) a casting call for the chorus of yet another production of the same play.

Clearly not every director who revives the *Bacchae,* in this time of a major shift from the tyranny of *pudeur* to the reign of *chutzpah,* realizes that Euripides is singing the inevitable failure as well as the inevitable resurgence of the dream of Eternal Summer. But all are aware that we have somehow used up the personal-psychological myth of the son who knows all the answers, yet does not know he has murdered his father and married his mother; and stand in the need of one more communal-political: the archetypal tale of the repressive son who, in the name of the *Polis,* the State, imprisons his mother's God, only to be ripped apart by her hands for the sake of her *Thiasos,* the Pack that worships her God on the hills.

Both myths seem at a glance equally absurd, yet the first has proved amenable to rational analysis from Aristotle to Freud; while the second stubbornly resists rationalization, leading only to nonwisdom, the ironic tag with which Euripides chose to end this last of his plays, as he had earlier at least three others.

> What we look for does not come to pass;
> The God finds a way for what we did not foresee.
> Such was the end of this story

It is less elegant as well as less hopeful than Lévi-Strauss's peroration: an absolute conclusion beyond which nothing can be imagined, an ending which consumes all beginnings, past and to come. But perhaps it is, by that token, closer than any prophecy to the true myth of our history, though whether more *chutzpahdik* or more *pudique* I am at a loss to say.

Buffalo, New York
—1969

The Passionate Pilgrim

A T THE HEART OF any continuous body of work—the total production of an age, a school, a single author—there is always present a set of assumptions about the nature of man and, more particularly, about the limits of the human. Sometimes these assumptions are stated explicitly as ideas or themes, but more often they are projected in obsessive fables and characters, perceptible everywhere beneath the nominal plots and dramatis personae which may seem at first glance to vary completely from one work to another. Traditional criticism began by calling the kind of character who, for an age, a school, an author, embodies an ideal of the human, the "hero," and the kind who embodies its opposite the "villain"; but these terms have long since fallen into disrepute. And, in any case, there exists in all literature an archetypal figure who escapes both poles of the classic definition—appearing sometimes as hero, sometimes as villain, sometimes as clown.

That borderline figure, who defines the limits of the human —customarily from the farther side, though never without some ambiguity—has been named variously the "shadow," the "other," the "alien," the "outsider," the "stranger." And it is with the stranger in Shakespeare that this study is concerned: primarily with the stranger as woman in *Henry VI, Part I*, the stranger as Jew in *The Merchant of Venice*, the stranger as Moor in *Othello*, the stranger as New World savage in *The*

Tempest, but also with the Jew, the black, the "savage man of Ind" and, most especially, the witch as they appear in the complex web of the whole Shakespearean corpus.

Though related in some ways to what earlier critics have identified as the "odd man out"—to such characters as Mercutio, Falstaff, and the two Antonios of *The Merchant of Venice* and *Twelfth Night*, those equivocal lovers excluded from the happy endings Shakespeare felt it incumbent on him to provide—such strangers differ in one essential aspect. Whatever marginal ambivalence Shakespeare may have felt at their final discomfiture or defeat, in the main he subscribed consciously to the values of the popular audience, which demanded their symbolic casting out. Othello represents, perhaps, if not an exception to, a severe qualification of this general rule; but by and large, the affective resonance of women, Jews, blacks, and Indians is the same in the private mythology of Shakespeare and the public mythology of the world for which he wrote. And this is notably *not* so when he portrays men whose deepest affection is bestowed on those of their own sex, so that they will not or cannot make a satisfactory last act–last scene marriage.

Nor is the stranger quite the same as the "spoilsport" (also identified by earlier critics): the kind of bad boy who, irked by the rules of the game, wants to take his ball and go home—or failing that, will sit on the sidelines and sulk. The spoilsport appears frequently in Shakespeare—initially as a courtly mocker like Berowne in *Love's Labor's Lost* and "the melancholy Jacques" in *As You Like It*, perhaps also, vestigially, as Hamlet himself; and he reappears in surly and unregenerate form as Malvolio in *Twelfth Night* and Thersites in *Troilus and Cressida*. But, after a while, he is cast chiefly in the privileged role of the jester or fool, as Feste on scene and Yorick off; as that faithful companion of Lear, so oddly identified toward the play's close with the doomed Cordelia; and as the cosmic jester, Puck, to whom all mortals seem finally the fools he pretends to be for his master's sake and the plot's.

In the fool, the spoilsport is, as it were, institutionalized, taken into the game he begins by refusing to play; but outside that role, he blends disconcertingly into the odd man out, as in Falstaff, or even into the stranger, as in Malvolio and Shylock or, most ambiguously of all, Iago. Such role confusions must not, however, be allowed to blur the difference at the poles between the stranger and the spoilsport. And the figure of the mocker, in any event, seems not to belong to the deepest and earliest level of Shakespeare's fantasy, the private mythology which preceded any poem or play.

It is, however, precisely with that private mythology that any examination of the stranger in Shakespeare must begin, though obviously the communal mythology which he inherited from his sources, along with plot structures and casts of characters, must also be taken into account. Especially important is the body of myth implicit in those fairy tales, fabliaux, and novelle to which he turned constantly in search of story material and most especially, the Metamorphoses, which possessed his imagination from the time of his school days, making him in the profoundest sense, as his contemporaries already surmised, another Ovid, Ovid reborn an Englishman.

Even less obviously archetypal sources, like travelers' journals and historical chronicles, helped sustain the tension between private and public, personal and communal, that characterizes his work at the mythic level. Certainly, a study of such documents can illuminate such vexing, though apparently peripheral, problems as why a poet committed to propagating the Tudor myth (on which Henry VIII so largely based his claim to legitimate succession) and, afterward, the Jacobean (by which James I hoped to sustain his theories about the divine right of kings) almost entirely ignored the myth of the

Virgin Queen (sponsored by Elizabeth I to help maintain her delicate balance of power). It was, however, that final myth which fired the imaginations of his most distinguished fellow poets, including Spenser and Raleigh, since they found the celebration of woman congenial on a personal as well as a public level. Shakespeare, on the other hand, began with an antifeminist bias; and it is the private mythology bred by that bias which most directly influences his view of the stranger, as well as his over-all theories about the nature of love.

The very scriptures, the holy text, of that personal mythology is the *Sonnets*, and, in particular, Sonnet 144. In it is distilled Shakespeare's vision of Eros as good and evil, a vision so camouflaged in the sequence as a whole that for generations scholars took it for the most conventional of poems. This mistake his first publisher, that pirate-entrepreneur William Jaggard, did not make, selecting texts which illuminate what is at once most unique and universal in the *Sonnets*—the heart of their archetypal appeal. Jaggard's collection, with which we must begin, since it is, in fact, the beginning, appeared in 1599, a year after Francis Meres had first mentioned in print Shakespeare's "sugared Sonnets among his private friends."

Jaggard's volume, which he chose to call *The Passionate Pilgrim*, contained not only the sonnet presently numbered 144 but also 138. And it included as well three poems extracted from *Love's Labor's Lost*, along with four sonnets on the theme of Venus and Adonis and eleven other pieces of verse, among them "Live with me, and be my love." The last is by all odds the favorite poem of the age—written and rewritten by Christopher Marlowe, Sir Walter Raleigh, and John Donne, among others, and surviving into an alien age in the cadences behind the opening lines of Milton's *L'Allegro* and *Il Penseroso;* but it is not one ordinarily associated with Shakespeare. Yet Jaggard's collection carries Shakespeare's name on its title page, so that scholars ever since have felt obliged to wrestle with the problem of the authenticity of its contents. No one can finally doubt, however, that Jaggard's selection, whatever the sources of the individual poems, reflects Shakespeare's own view of what he was after, or, at least, that of someone from the circle of "private friends" in which the Sonnets had first circulated.

The title itself carries assurance that the compiler was aware of one key image in the sequence: the image of the poet whose unquiet mind, even from afar, travels toward the beloved, as in Sonnet 27, "For then my thoughts, from far where I abide, / Intend a zealous pilgrimage to thee. . . ." And finding in second place among the twenty poems which constitute Jaggard's collection Sonnet 144 is doubly encouraging, for this is one sonnet which explicitly joins the praise of the fair friend to the outpouring of self-torturing lust for the dark lady. As printed in *The Passionate Pilgrim,* its octave runs as follows:

> Two loves I have of comfort and despair,
> Which like two spirits do suggest me still,
> The better spirit is a man right fair,
> The worser spirit a woman colored ill.
> To win me soon to Hell, my female evil
> Tempteth my better angel from my side,
> And would corrupt my saint to be a devil,
> Wooing his purity with her foul pride.

If all the sonnets except for this were to disappear tomorrow, we would be left in possession not only of the story Shakespeare tries to tell but also of the moral it is intended to convey. Beginning as an account of one who would divide his love in two, directing all that is noble in it toward one object, all that is vile toward another, it ends with his discovery of the two in each other's arms—the noble contaminated by the vile. The significance is clear enough, since such a story becomes inevitably a parable concerning the ambiguity of passion. Moreover, Sonnet 144 contains also the unconventional symbols through which Shakespeare chose to project both plot and theme: friend and mistress, boy and whore.

Finally, fable, moral, and symbol are rendered in a special tone, sustained also in Sonnet 138, whose opening betrays under the show of easy cynicism a sense of deep disgust: "When my love swears that she is made of truth, / I do believe her, though I know she lies. . . ." And the pun barely suggested by the last word is picked up in the concluding couplet, more clearly in its revised form than in the earlier text used by Jaggard: "Therefore I lie with her and she with me, / And in our faults by lies we flattered be." In both sonnets, the doubleness of tone finds expression in the *double-entendre;* and reading them at the head of *The Passionate Pilgrim,* the reader will recall how many poems in the entire sequence are precisely of this kind.

Indeed, the brand of humor they exploit must have been a staple amusement for young noblemen, contrived on demand by such privileged entertainers as Shakespeare, who made the mistake in fact (or fancy) of falling (or imagining he fell) in love with one of his elegant benefactors and who thereafter made love rather than mockery his essential theme. There must have seemed at first no contradiction, for the love his heart compelled was directed toward a male, while the cynicism demanded of him by fashion was directed toward the female.

It is *woman's* sexuality that Shakespeare's puns excoriate with special fervor, the play on "lie" and "lie" in Sonnet 138 equating their facility at falsification with the ease with which they are bedded down, the two meanings of "hell" in the sestet of Sonnet 144 equating the vagina with the place of eternal punishment, and the quibble on "fire" attributing to the dark lady the power both to damn and venereally infect the youth.

> And whether that my angel be turned fiend
> Suspect I may, yet not directly tell,

> But being both from me, both to each friend,
> I guess one angel in another's Hell.
>> Yet this shall I ne'er know, but live in doubt
>> Till my bad angel fire my good one out.

In the dark lady segment of the *Sonnets,* similar puns abound, reaching one climax in Sonnets 134 and 135, which ring changes on the several meanings of "Will": not only the name of the poet and perhaps also the friend but also a word signifying "testament" and "volition" and "carnal desire": "So thou, being rich in *Will,* add to thy *Will* / One will of mine, to make thy large *Will* more." A second such climax comes toward the very end of the sequence, in a series of puns on the male's erection, the unwilled response to woman's "Will." The couplet which concludes Sonnet 150 first suggests the double meaning ("If thy unworthiness raised love in me, / More worthy I to be beloved of thee"), which is then made explicit in Sonnet 151 ("flesh stays no farther reason, / But rising at thy name doth point out thee / As his triumphant prize") and confirmed wryly in the final couplet ("No want of conscience hold it that I call / Her 'love' for whose dear love I rise and fall").

This kind of wit, trembling always on the edge of disgust, is, however, found also as early as Sonnet 20 (whose punning close has occasioned much soul searching among the critics), which, despite its position among the sonnets of praise, is quite as antifeminist as any specifically directed against the dark lady. Its sestet begins, "And for a woman wert thou first created, / Till Nature, as she wrought thee, fell a-doting. . . ," and it ends, "But since she pricked thee out for women's pleasure, / Mine be thy love, and thy love's use their treasure." Involved here is a play not only on the word "pricked," but also on "use," which in Shakespeare's lexicon means, besides "employment," "usury" or "interest" and also "the sex act."

On these meanings Shakespeare loves to quibble, speaking in *Measure for Measure* of the "two usuries," by which he means moneylending and copulation, and making throughout *The Merchant of Venice* an implicit contrast between the consummation of love and the extortion of interest. It is clear which usury Shakespeare would prefer, but it is also clear that ideally he would choose neither; for his peculiar wordplay tends to identify the carnal love of women with a commercial practice that his age still regarded as an "unnatural" sin. In Dante (more orthodoxly), it is homosexuality which is associated with usury, the sins of Sodom and Cahors being punished in the same circle; but in the *Sonnets,* there is a tendency to make heterosexual love seem guilty by association.

Indeed, if a third sonnet out of the sequence had been included in *The Passionate Pilgrim,* it might well have been Sonnet 20—and not on the grounds of tone alone; for in comparing the friend to women whose hearts are given to "shifting change" and whose eyes are practiced in "false . . . rolling," Shakespeare implicitly comments on the theme of the two loves. What the poet insists on in Sonnet 20 is the epicene character of "the Master-Mistress of my passion" ("passion" here meaning "song" *and* "suffering" *and* "libidinal love"), what he shares with women as well as what distinguishes him from them. What differentiates him from the despised sex, the poem explains, is double: the male organ (alas!) and purity of heart (thank God!); what makes him like them is his physical beauty, as "womanly," in this sense, as theirs.

Many contemporary readers find it a little difficult, perhaps, to empathize with the taste for a kind of beauty in males identical with that sought in females; and they are likely to be brought up short when in Sonnet 53 the youth is compared in a span of three lines to both Helen and Adonis. But the latter allusion provides a clue, suggesting that the roots of the epicene ideal must be sought in Hellenistic culture, which for Shakespeare means especially Ovid, a clue whose importance is underlined by the inclusion in *The Passionate Pilgrim* of four sonnets by a single hand retelling the story of Venus and Adonis.

Whether that hand was Shakespeare's remains still unclear, even though one of them had been claimed in 1596 by a certain Bartholemew Griffin; Shakespeare had treated the theme in a long erotic poem, which, we are tempted to think, should have been sufficient. On the other hand, the four doubtful sonnets combine, quite as does *Venus and Adonis,* certain elements out of Ovid's account of Venus's passion for Adonis with his version of the love of Salmacis for Hermaphroditus. And that combination constitutes a compulsively repeated Shakespearean theme, a private myth of great power: the encounter between a passive male and an aggressive female, between modest reason and shameless lust, symbolized respectively by a boy and a woman.

In *Venus and Adonis,* the poet who makes a triangle of this encounter in the *Sonnets* is lacking. And there are, therefore, strange equivocations, as Shakespeare, lacking another mask, is compelled to embody in Venus—whom he basically fears—his own desire for epicene beauty. He actually puts into her mouth the argument that great beauties have a special obligation to marry and reproduce ("Seeds spring from seeds, and beauty breedeth beauty"), which in the *Sonnets* he speaks through his mouthpiece. We may, indeed, agree with one editor of the poems that "there is more of Shakespeare himself" in Venus than in Adonis, as there is more of him in Cleopatra than in Antony, in Falstaff than in Prince Hal.

But we remember, too, that Venus remains for him as late as the time of *The Tempest,* "Mars's hot minion," supreme representation of all he most distrusts in naked passion. No wonder then, that the end of *Venus and Adonis* is a catastrophe more unmitigated than the conclusion of the *Sonnets,* involving not the mere corruption of a boy by a woman, but the death of that boy, a death which Adonis seems all along to have felt as preferable to seduction; and that it is followed by

Venus's curse on the kind of love she embodies: "It shall be fickle, false and full of fraud; / Bud, and be blasted, in a breathing-while. . . ."

In the four Venus-Adonis sonnets of *The Passionate Pilgrim*, the rich, almost cloying texture of Shakespeare's long poem and its tragic tone are replaced by a show of easy irony quite like that which characterizes the two sonnets with which Jaggard opened his collection. Their meanings are simple, the puns obvious and undisturbingly obscene—one is tempted to say childishly obscene. The last three lines will do by way of illustration, foreshadowing as they do the goring and death of Adonis, but all in the guise of a joke.

> "See, in my thigh," quoth she, "here was the sore."
> She showèd hers. He saw more wounds than one,
> And blushing fled, and left her all alone.

What terror or sexual queasiness is implicit in all this is not permitted to show, as it is not in Jaggard's poem VI, which tells of Venus's passion for the youth as he stands naked on the edge of a pool—a scene derived from Ovid's tale of the lust of Salmacis for Hermaphroditus. But this reminds us once more that if in order to understand the fair youth of the *Sonnets*, we must see what in him is derived from the myth of Adonis, we must also understand how much of Shakespeare's Adonis is Hermaphroditus, that son of Hermes and Aphrodite whose body was blended with that of the water nymph Salmacis when she perceived that only thus could she attain the union she desired.

In Ovid, it is *not* Adonis but Hermaphroditus who struggles against love, adamantly preferring his own beardless beauty to that of woman; and it is Hermaphroditus who becomes, in his final transformation, the prototype of the "Master-Mistress" in Sonnet 20.

And the two bodies seemed to merge together,
One face, one form . . .
So these two joined in close embrace, no longer
Two beings, and no longer man and woman,
But neither, and yet both. . . .

In the museums of half the world, there are yet to be found Alexandrian images in marble and alabaster of the boy-woman Hermaphroditus, images worked in love by the craftsmen of a culture which considered pederasty a grace of civilized living. The beholder who first comes on the mythical figure, sees him from the rear, half curled up as if in sleep; and noting the lovely sweep of back and flank, takes him for a woman, a mistake apparently confirmed when the beholder peers round the hyacinthine head into the beautiful face. But looking lower he discovers, surprised, that the body is "pricked . . . out for women's pleasure," and knows he has found the Hermaphroditus.

Just such an image seems to have possessed the imagination of the Renaissance, in Italy first, in England afterward; and it is this image which, projected in the theater by boy actors of women's parts, gave sensual substance to the cult of friendship and the literary tradition of the praise of lovely boys. That the Elizabethans had no suspicion of the homosexual basis of that cult seems unlikely, particularly since any grammar school boy of the time was likely to have parsed the legend of Hermaphroditus in class. He knew, therefore, that, like Shakespeare's version of *Venus and Adonis*, the story ended with a curse, a curse no less terrible, though somewhat different in form. It is Hermaphroditus who speaks, according to Ovid, after his transformation in the pool, crying out in "a voice whose tone was almost treble":

    . . . O father and mother, grant me this!
    May every one hereafter, who comes diving

Into this pool, emerge half man, made weaker
By the touch of this evil water!

It is hard to believe that the group of Shakespeare's poems which included *Venus and Adonis* and the *Sonnets* is not centrally concerned with this problem of unmanning, with the price paid for attempting to flee woman. And one's suspicions are further strengthened in turning from Book Four of the *Metamorphoses*, which contains the myth of Hermaphroditus, to Book Ten, in which the story of Adonis is told. Book Ten opens with the legend of Orpheus and Eurydice, which, as Ovid recreates it, serves chiefly as a preface to a group of songs sung by the bereaved Orpheus. Overwhelmed by grief for his lost wife, we are told, the poet disowned women and turned for love to boys.

His love was given
To young boys only, and he told the Thracians
That was the better way: *enjoy that springtime,*
Take those first flowers.

Orpheus is not content, moreover, merely to celebrate pederasty; he dedicates himself, too, to the vilification of women, invoking Jupiter, lover of Ganymede, to inspire him:

. . . for I would sing of boys
Loved by the gods, and girls inflamed by love
To things forbidden, and earned punishment.

Shakespeare's hermaphroditic revision of Adonis assimilates him to those "boys loved by the Gods," Ganymede and Hyacinthus and Cyparissus. And his version of Venus makes her just another of those "girls inflamed by love to things forbidden," like the "foul Propoetides," whom Ovid portrays as the first whores, and Myrrha, who, seducing her own father, begot the very Adonis doomed to die beneath the boar's tusk.

In his own time and among the "private friends" for whom

his nondramatic poems were written, Shakespeare surely assumed he could evoke by simple allusion any section of the *Metamorphoses.* So Marlowe seems to have assumed when, in the concluding speech of *Doctor Faustus,* he quotes a tag from the Ovidian account of Jupiter's night of love with Alcmene, *"O lente lente currite noctis equi!"* All the more so, then, might one in whom, according to his contemporaries, "the sweet witty soul of Ovid lives" feel free to evoke in passing an aspect of Ovid's retelling of the Orpheus myth which is commonly expurgated in a day which requires scholarly studies to make us aware of Shakespeare's indebtedness to a text we know only casually if at all.

The context in which *The Passionate Pilgrim* sets the *Sonnets* is not, however, defined entirely by Ovid and Shakespeare's most Ovidian long poem; it includes as well *Love's Labor's Lost,* from which *The Passionate Pilgrim* extracts three lyrics, two of them also in sonnet form. These two, in fact, alternate with the first two Venus and Adonis sonnets near the beginning of the collection, thus serving to remind us early on that further clues to Shakespeare's private mythology can be found in this eccentric early play, the freest, least source-bound and mass-audience-oriented of all his dramatic works.

The first poem from *Love's Labor's Lost* is attributed in the play itself to a minor character called Longaville; the second, to Berowne, its spoilsport *raisonneur;* and both represent shamefaced attempts at erotic verse by young aristocrats who earlier had abjured love and retired to a kind of Neoplatonic academy in the woods. In that ascetic, all-male community, they had planned to pursue fame through single-minded "study," thus triumphing not only over their own feeble flesh but also over "cormorant devouring Time." The actual poems (perhaps verses of his own which Shakespeare had come to find intolerable) are miserable enough, philosophically as well as formally, to deserve the scorn of Berowne, who says of Longaville's rhymes what he surely knows applies also to his own:

> This is the liver vein, which makes flesh a deity,
> A green goose a goddess—pure, pure idolatry.

Indeed, the tone of the play throughout is close to that of the more troubled sonnets; yet, though presumably written for a select rather than general audience, it is more circumspect and oblique than the poems composed to be read in private by an even-smaller group.

In certain scenes, however, particularly those in which Berowne pays begrudging and witty court to an equally reluctant Rosaline, a relationship is developed clearly analogous to that of the poet and the dark lady of the *Sonnets.* Quite like the deceived lover of the *Sonnets,* Berowne in *Love's Labor's Lost* insists on the blackness of his beloved, describing her as:

> A whitely wanton with a velvet brow,
> With two pitch balls stuck in her face for eyes—
> Aye, and, by Heaven, one that will do the deed,
> Though Argus were her eunuch and her guard.

And reading these lines, we remember "Therefore my mistress' eyes are raven-black" in Sonnet 127. But "pitch" is the operative word here, and it is picked up again when Berowne speaks of falling in love as "toiling in a pitch—pitch that defiles."

Finally, however, he decides to brazen out his capitulation to the dark Rosaline though the play has already reminded us (once more like Sonnet 127) that if one opposite of "fair" is "black," another is "foul." "No face is fair that is not full so black," he boasts; and the King is moved to answer, reflecting surely Shakespeare's own sense of the metaphorical resonance of the adjective which happened to suit the complexion of the woman whom he happened to desire:

> Oh, paradox! Black is the badge of Hell,
> The hue of dungeons and the school of night, . . .

But this re-echoes the key words of the closing couplet in Sonnet 147:

> For I have sworn thee fair, and thought thee bright,
> Who art as black as Hell, as dark as night.

And it recalls the reworking of the same pair of lines in Sonnet 152:

> For I have sworn thee fair, more perjur'd I,
> To swear against the truth so foul a lie!

"For I have sworn" becomes by a kind of ellipsis "forsworn," a leitmotif of both the dark lady sonnets and *Love's Labor's Lost*. But though Jaggard fairly represents in his sampling Shakespeare's concern with the fate of love in a world forsworn, and though, further, he does justice to the theme of youth and age, which also obsesses the poet, he scants the equally important contrast of fair and black. Yet this contrast, along with that of boy and woman, true and false, age and youth, serves centrally to define the two loves, good and bad, between which he sees man eternally torn. The darkness of the dark lady is of her essence; and fair and black turn out to mean, moreover (though this level of significance is not made manifest until the later plays), what we have come to call white and black, Caucasian and Negro. Indeed, *Love's Labor's Lost* contains allusions in jokes, asides, and casual metaphors to all three of the alien races, those ethnic strangers we shall be discussing later: the "Ethiope," the Jew, and the "savage man of Ind."

In Jaggard, however, the theme is represented only by the passing contrast of "a man right fair" and "a woman colored ill," which opens Sonnet 144, and is overwhelmed immediately by an insistence on the theme of self-betrayal and self-deceit: "Therefore I'll lie with love and love with me. . . ."; "If love make me forsworn. . . ."; "Though to myself forsworn. . . ." Yet this is, in one sense, just; since at the close (not end, there being no end, happy or otherwise) of *Love's Labor's Lost*, there rings still in the ear of the audience the melancholy couplet in which Berowne accepts on behalf of us all man's comic-tragic fate:

> We cannot cross the cause why we were born;
> Therefore, of all hands must we be forsworn.

What is added by that play to the myth of the two loves is, then, a new version of the Fall of man, in which woman and the serpent are identified with each other and Adam is condemned to leave the garden arm in arm with his temptress—if she will have him.

It is a variant form of a theme found throughout Shakespeare's work: men bound together by friendship are sundered by the love of woman (as in *Two Gentlemen of Verona*) and must somehow make another, more fragile compact or sadly learn to part. Sometimes there are political considerations which persuade a younger man to reject his older friend (as in *Julius Caesar* or *Henry IV*); but more customarily, what causes the rift is the intervention of the female. Certainly this is the case in *Love's Labor's Lost*, as in the *Sonnets* themselves, though in the former, the conventions of comic theater require that the conflict between friendship and passion be played out in lighthearted wit combats. Only in the darkest sonnets and tragedies (most notably *Othello* and *Lear*) do the hatred and fear of female sexuality pass over into hysteria, as in Lear's mad rant:

> Down from the waist they are Centaurs,
> Though women all above.

But to the girdle do the gods inherit,
Beneath is all the fiends'.
There's Hell, there's darkness, there's
     the sulphurous pit,
Burning, scalding, stench, consumption, fie, fie, fie!
Pah, pah!

In *Love's Labor's Lost* such shrillness is avoided, even though, as the play moves toward its anticlimax, it is the women who seem to have triumphed, the men who appear to have been made fools in a tangle of disguises and counter-disguises, quite Mozartean both in complexity and in lightness of tone. What is being mocked, it becomes clear, are male pretensions to immunity from passion, perhaps even a specific all-male academy, around whose members charges of atheism and homosexuality floated at the time, that circle of "soul-loved friends" which included Derby, Northumberland, and Sir Walter Raleigh, and which boasted as its poet laureate George Chapman, favored candidate for the role of rival poet in Shakespeare's sonnet sequence. Speculation about this circle consists largely of scholarly attempts to reconstitute history out of ancient gossip, and skeptics have argued that the whole thing is a fabrication of bored twentieth-century academics. It seems likely, however, that Shakespeare knew of some such group, finding it a suitable butt for satire, since it competed with the Southampton circle, in which he seems to have played the role presumably accorded Chapman in the other.

But caricaturing Chapman and the intellectual-dandies whom he served, inevitably Shakespeare also caricatured himself and the lords he admired—even the one lord he truly loved. That is to say, the ironies of *Love's Labor's Lost* are not all directed outward at detested others. Self-hatred is everywhere an undercurrent, reflected especially in the self-tormenting wit of Berowne, who seems often another version of the poet of the *Sonnets*. In neither the *Sonnets* nor this most high-

brow and personal of all Shakespeare's plays, however, is the
last word a cynical acceptance of the pre-eminence of passion,
the inevitable triumph of woman over men's vows of dedication
to study and chastity and each other. As the title of the play
declares, *no* kind of love triumphs in the end; for even as the
irrational desire for the female has driven out reason, so the
shadow of death cools irrational desire.

The play climaxes not, as it seems to have promised, in
a mass wedding, but in the departure of the ladies and the
imposition on their lovers of certain unforeseenly grim tasks.
Berowne, for instance, is commanded by his beloved to remit
his suit for a year and visit hospitals, where he is bidden "With
all the fierce endeavor of your wit / To enforce the painèd
impotent to smile." Not only is the evocation of pain and
impotence an odd antiending for what opened as a comedy,
but the suggested necessity of seeking an antidote to both
more effective than wit undercuts, as well as the character to
whom it is directed, the witty play in which he appears and
its jesting author. The net effect is that of a palinode, just such
a denial of love and joy as Shakespeare makes in Sonnets 129
and 146 and which appears four or five times over in *The
Passionate Pilgrim,* most notably in the single stanza it reprints from the answer to Marlowe's "Live with me, and
be my love," a poem originally signed "Ignotus" and more
usually attributed to Raleigh.

> If that the world and love were young,
> And truth in every shepherd's tongue,
> These pretty pleasures might me move
> To live with thee and be thy love.

If these lines are, indeed, not Shakespeare's but those of
a member of the rival group he presumably satirized in *Love's
Labor's Lost,* the fact should serve to remind us of how many
assumptions (imported from Italy, perhaps, and become the
mode) were shared by the antifeminist academies. Shakespeare

or Raleigh, it makes little difference; either might have spoken those hermetic words. "The words of Mercury are harsh after the songs of Apollo" reads the tag which closes *Love's Labor's Lost*. And this line, too, the scholars hesitate to give to Shakespeare, taking it instead for the comment of a reader distressed by the final turn of the play, in which its comic characters return after the failed happy ending to represent the debate of the cuckoo and the owl, a debate without a difference, in which spring is presented as the season which brings fear to married men and winter as a time presided over by red-nosed and "greasy" kitchen wenches.

There is one other major concern of Shakespeare's private mythology unrepresented in *The Passionate Pilgrim* though present in the sonnet sequence as a whole: the myth of the two immortalities. But the perplexity in response to which it is generated is, in fact, suggested by the "Ignotus" stanza and all the other selections which deal with the problem of youth and age. If love is based on beauty and beauty depends on youth, how can love survive in a world which, like ourselves, from moment to moment grows older? Beauty, the *Sonnets* begin by stipulating, since it exists in the flesh, must seek its perpetuity in the flesh, by begetting, or "breed," as Shakespeare prefers to say. But before he has gotten very far into the poem, he is also insisting that beauty can survive eternally if it is turned into art, recreated as a poetic image. In either case, love is the spur: either the love which attracts man to woman, body to body, thus ending in marriage and the family, or the love which draws man to man, soul to soul, thus ending in—literature.

Obviously, this is the doctrine of Diotima, as reported by Socrates in the *Symposium* of Plato. "What object do lovers have in view?" the prophetess asks, and answers herself, "The object . . . is birth in beauty, whether of body or soul. . . . Wherefore love is of immortality." The final phrase could stand as the motto of the *Sonnets,* and their meaning is further illuminated as Diotima continues, "Those who are pregnant in the body only, betake themselves to women and beget children . . . but souls which are pregnant . . . conceive that which is proper for the soul. . . . And such creators are poets. . . ." Here, then, is the second classic context for Shakespeare's personal mythology of love: the homosexual apologetics of the *Symposium,* derived via various Italian middlemen (Michelangelo, Bembo, Bruno, Florio) and already given, before reaching Shakespeare, an anti-Petrarchan or anti–courtly love cast.

Shakespeare is clearly not alone in his attempts at undermining the idealization of woman and the pseudosanctification of adultery which lie at the roots of courtly love. In his own country, both Donne and Raleigh had recorded cynical reservations about women and love not very different from his; and even Wyatt, who imported into England the courtly love mythos in its Petrarchan form, undercut from time to time the image of the adored lady as angel and savior. The convention and anticonvention grow up together, and neither necessarily arises from a deeper or more honest perception of the world. When Shakespeare writes the well-known bitter sonnet beginning, "My mistress' eyes are nothing like the sun," he is inventing nothing new, only providing an already expected titillation. Yet his *Sonnets* are unique, though not in this aspect of their antifeminism.

What is peculiar to Shakespeare's sequence is its attempt to preserve the mystique of courtly love and much of its tradional imagery by transferring them to a male beloved. Like the poets of ancient Provence, as well as their ironical codifier Andreas Capellanus, Shakespeare seems to have believed that love is "a certain inborn suffering," but a suffering which redeems. And like his predecessors, he seems also to have been convinced that *only* love redeems—makes a gentleman, perfects a poet, improves manners, and refreshes the soul—so that, like them, he pretends to find in the joy of loving a sufficient counterbalance even to the pain inflicted by the indifference of the beloved.

Like earlier theorists, too, he apparently discriminated between two kinds of love, *amor purus* and *amor mixtus;* though, once more like them, he believed even "pure" love to be necessarily physical, implying, besides the communion of souls, a sensual delight in the cheek, lip, all the lovely flesh of the loved one—so long as there was no actual penetration of flesh by flesh, no expenditure of seed. Finally, like his Provençal forerunners, Shakespeare thought of both the lower and higher kinds of love as existing outside of marriage, as being, in some sense, adulterous. No more than any love poet of the Middle Ages would he have considered addressing an erotic poem to his wife.

In language, too, Shakespeare emulated his great predecessors, referring to his beloved as a rose, a muse, an angel, a Helen of Troy; but, unlike them, he found his rose-muse-angel-Helen in a boy rather than a woman. There is no use pretending that such a procedure is, either in the history of literature or of society, merely "conventional." It is extraordinary, even a little disturbing; and there is something more honest in earlier attempts to bowdlerize the text by changing "he" to "she" than in the modern pretense of having proved by an analysis of Sonnet 20 that Shakespeare did not actually have physical relations with boys. The point is that the poet confesses to sleeping with women and considering it filthy, while chastely (but passionately) embracing an idealized male.

How was he driven, fictionally at least, to advocate so extraordinary a splitting of love, to endure so profound a division between sentimentality and desire? What ended as a division began as a dream of synthesis, the desire to reconcile the lesson of the Scriptures and the burden of vernacular poetry as written in Europe for some six hundred years; and to understand Shakespeare, we must first understand the way in which courtly love, which began as a pastime for idle courtiers, became a counterreligion irreconciliable with the reigning orthodoxy. Between the deification—half in sport, half in earnest—of woman and the Christian teaching that such adulation of any creature is idolatry, there can be no compromise; and even less tolerable is the view that human love, like the love of God itself, is a sufficient source of grace. *Amor purus* required the worship of a mistress remote and unattainable; the flesh demanded sexual consummation; the love of God required the renunciation of both. And in any case, the love of another man's wife remained adulterous, consummated or unconsummated; adding a pseudoreligious note merely aggravated the sin.

Yet beyond this nest of paradoxes the Provençal poets could not go, leaving the next step to Dante, who completed in the *Divine Comedy* what he had begun in the *Vita Nuova*. For every man, he suggests in the earlier work, there is somewhere a woman who is his personal mediator, a "miraculous" avenue to salvation. Dante cannot resist reminding us the name "Beatrice" means "she who beatifies," and he extends the pun until he seems to be hinting that Beatrice is, in some sense, the Christ! At this point, the Inquisition moved in to expurgate his little book, and Dante moved on to the allegory of the *Divine Comedy*, which turns the actual Beatrice into Divine Theology. It is a solution which, operating in the empyrean, leaves unresolved on earth the contradiction from which it began, thus bequeathing to the soul of the West an institutionalized schizophrenia.

Shakespeare's theory of the two loves, one angelic, the other diabolic, is at least a new way of stating the old problem, especially when he directs the first impulse toward a fair youth (loved as purely as any Italian poet of the sweet new style ever loved his lady) and the second toward the black woman (lusted after in self-hatred and disgust). Love as grace is attached to the homoerotic Beatrice, love as sin to the dark lady. This means that sentimental salvation is attributed to the male, passionate damnation to the female, thus resolving one age-old contradiction at least: that between the popular-orthodox conception of woman as temptress and the courtly view of her as savior. By loving a boy rather than a daughter of Eve, Shakespeare insists, one can find salvation.

But the taint of homosexuality clings to such a suggestion, and Shakespeare is painfully aware of the proverbial fickleness of boys, declaring through the Fool in *Lear*, for instance, that "He's mad that trusts . . . a boy's love, or a whore's oath." After all, he lived with boys in the theater, watched them offstage as well as on; and though he can praise his fair youth with a tenderness so genuine that generations of men have read his words to their mistresses, the fable of the *Sonnets* does not end on a note of tenderness.

The poet, troubled from the first, finally sees in dismay his two loves in each other's arms, the untainted boy betrayed into the embrace of a gonorrheal whore. "Boy" and "whore"— no wonder these two words have a special affinity in Shakespeare, for in his world, boy actors daily put on and doffed the allure of women, *played* women. And who can doubt that on occasion their blatant homosexuality travestied behind the scenes the pure and rational love of males he dreamed, as mincing little queens caricatured those ambiguous boy-girl heroines so essential in their transvestite loveliness to such plays as *As You Like It* and *Twelfth Night*. In the end, for him, too, there remains, therefore, the terrible cry, as old as Christianity itself: "The expense of spirit in a waste of shame / Is lust in action. . . ."

It seems to have become clear to him finally that the seed of corruption was in the friend from the start, already present in the "chaste" relationship between him and the poet; since there is no pure masculine principle, no male is immune to the evil impulse represented by the female. Only the legendary "he that was not born of woman," the motherless man, can break out of the trap of sin. The youth, however, is very much his mother's child; and the poet desiring him has no way of being sure that he has not desired in him what Posthumus Leonatus in *Cymbeline* calls the "woman's part," the "motion that tends to vice." The poet cannot even be sure that he has not himself played that "woman's part," has not been the Venus who, in fantasy at least, has assailed the virtue he loves. When the youth falls, the poet cannot help suspecting that he has willed that fall, somehow collaborated in it; for the dark lady is a projection of something in his deepest imagination, too, and he has been the link between her and the fair friend.

Certainly, in the plays which deal with analogous love affairs—in *Henry IV*, *Julius Caesar*, and *The Merchant of Venice*—there is not only a pervading sense of melancholy, a presen.iment that the relationship which joins youth and age, boy and man is doomed, but also a hint of guilt, the feeling that the relationship should never have existed. As Shakespeare imagines it, the older lover does not escape unscathed, but is condemned, as in *Julius Caesar*, to be stabbed to death; or destined, as in *Henry IV*, to be cast off to die of a broken heart; or permitted, as in *The Merchant of Venice*, to make the gesture which hands over his friend to woman forever. Shakespeare, at the moment of writing the *Sonnets*, could not condone in himself the highest love he could conceive, but foresaw its dissolution in betrayal and lust, felt it deserved to be thus dissolved. And so he falls back, as generations of poets had before him, into the Christian palinode.

In the myth of the *Sonnets*, the Uranian strategy will not finally work; and the poet in the end abandons the solution of the *Symposium*, the dream of Diotima, in favor of the Christian doctrine that there is no rebirth of beauty except in God, that here on earth all beauty must be yielded up in order to ransom it from time.

Buy terms divine in selling hours of dross,
Within be fed, without be rich no more.
    So shalt thou feed on Death, that feeds on men,
    And Death once dead, there's no more dying then.

In the plays, however, Shakespeare does not come to this point until, with *The Tempest,* he is approaching the close of his career; and it is the long foreground to Prospero's Christian Epilogue that must be examined first, beginning at the beginning.

The Rebirth of God and
The Death of Man

IT HAS, I assume, become clear at this point to almost everyone that the successful Cultural Revolution we have been observing over the past fifteen or twenty years—here in the United States at least, and perhaps generally in the Western World—the emergence of what has been called variously the "Counter Culture," or "Consciousness III," or "The New Mutants," or the "Present Future," has been in large part, even essentially, a *Religious Revival*: the unforeseen, unsung and often quite misunderstood beginning of a New Age of Faith. The prophets of that Cultural Revolution, whether candid secularists like Wilhelm Reich and Herbert Marcuse or crypto-Thomists like Marshall MacLuhan, have, for reasons of their own, not emphasized this aspect of the movement they helped to create. And warmhearted but superficial analysts and apologists after the fact like Charles Reich or Theodore Roszak have obscured the religious dimensions of the Counter Culture (along with much else) because of their commitment to chic journalistic vocabularies intended to sell rather than describe what must be made at all costs to sound Brand New.

To be sure, one French opposite number of such apologists, Edgar Morin, has recently declared his adherence to the New Movement, with the phrase: "I am joining the Children's Crusade!" But in context (M. Morin is a sociologist and ex-Communist, or rather, I suppose, meta-Communist) this sounded like a mere metaphor—demanding immediate translation into more secular terms. Looking backward from the end of 1972, however, it is possible to see (almost impossible to miss) what was, while it was happening, too obvious to be perceived: the fact that the recent

361

Cultural Revolution has nurtured and, in a certain sense, *established* a dedicated minority, felt by the larger society to be somehow representative, exemplary—even "sacred." It is further evident that the values of that minority, as embodied in a lifestyle celebrated or deplored daily (it amounts to much the same thing) by the popular press, are much like those traditionally associated with earlier exemplary minorities: lay clergy and cloistered religious, isolated hermits and utopian religious communities, sponsored or somewhat reluctantly endorsed by the established Churches.

I do not intend to discuss here the lifestyle in which these values are embodied, though certain aspects of this, too, provide obvious analogies into religious practises of the past. The actual garb of the New Communicants, for instance, these robes and sandals so appropriate to the pilgrimages in which they habitually engage, seem to me to be superficial and symptomatic rather than essential, as does the show of poverty which characterizes their way of life. Their pilgrimages may be merely a new form of bourgeois tourism or even of American cultural imperialism while their much vaunted poverty is, perhaps, more aptly described as conspicuous under-consumption. It is, therefore, at a deeper level that I propose to begin, by examining their value system, at the center of which is the conviction that, after all, the contemplative life may be preferable to the active life. But, of course, to choose Rachel over Leah at this late date, the second wife of Jacob over his first, constitutes a radical rejection of the position defended against Catholic monasticism by an earlier Cultural Revolution launched by the Protestant churches: a position notoriously exploited by the secular heirs of Protestantism, the present Masters of our World, Capitalist and Communist alike.

From this major premise follow the corollaries that salvation rather than success is man's proper goal, and that, therefore, one must begin by rejecting goods in favor of the Good or even social welfare, and learn eventually to prefer being good to being well—a shocking antipsychiatric position. Furthermore, once contemplation is valued more highly than action, Vision rather than understanding is proposed as the proper end of man's inner life, the life of the mind. Oddly enough, I first became aware of this revolutionary shift in values in the classroom, where I teach from time to time courses on Dante, having done so, in fact, over the past three decades. During the first two of these decades, I was vexed by the sense of having to explain a radically alien point of view to my students before they could have any notion of what the poetry of the *Divine Comedy* was really about. But since 1960, anyhow, there has been no need to spell out for students what "Vision" once meant to certain benighted believers, since it is a category of experience to which they aspire even if they have not yet attained it. Still less is it necessary to expound for them the significance of the "Voyage," or, as it has become more fashionable to call it, the "Trip" through time to timelessness.

Never mind that the salvation sought by the New Religious is instant, here and now rather than at the end of days. Not they alone have become convinced that eternity does not lie beyond time, but intersects it. Still less must we be put off by the fact that the New Celebrants seek Vision by the use of once forbidden drugs, revelation not just through fasting and prayer and spiritual exercise, but by psycho-chemical means as well. All religions have employed intoxicants to initiate the entry into the Way—the grape, perfumes, music to aid in the trip toward ecstasy, where those means as well as everything else once prized and exploited will have become meaningless. After all, is not the ancient and holy practise of fasting itself a kind of negative psycho-chemistry?

We may *finally* be saved by that which comes out of the mouth rather than that which goes in, but all religions have initially concerned themselves with what is eaten as well as what is spoken: honoring not just the Word but Bread and Wine as well, Dionysus and Ceres, the Gods poured out or consumed in honor of the other Gods. Besides, is there not implicit in the contemporary use of sacred drugs, of what is inadvertently sacred in the intendedly profane pursuits of Science, a commendable desire to democratize ecstasy, to make Mystical Vision no longer the privilege of a handful of adepts but of *everyone*. The New Religious are determined to be no inert congregation rehearsing the words of dead Visionaries and half-mythological Saints, but a living church of actual Visionaries and Saints. This constitutes, perhaps, a peculiarly American dream, in its most virulent form even madder than our dream of universal higher education, this dream of universal *Ekstasis;* but, by the same token, it is even more beautiful—not least because it may be finally impossible, a Way to Idolatry more often than a Door to Perception.

Less noticed, perhaps, than the redemption of the Contemplative

Life but almost as critically important, has been the Revolt against Romantic Love everywhere present within the ranks of the Cultural Revolution: the quite conscious attempt to liquidate the antireligion or quasireligion or burlesque religion of Love, which has possessed the Arts of Western Christendom and haunted the imaginations of all who have read its texts, or looked at its ikons, or listened to its quasiholy songs since Courtly Love and vernacular poetry were born together at the end of the eleventh century in Provence. That essentially godless religion has come to seem to the New Communicants especially distasteful in its late Protestant-sentimental forms: that Angel-in-the-House tradition, in which the mock worship of women has been detached from adultery and linked to monogamous marriage and the bourgeois family.

Sometimes it is Sex—naked *libido,* unmythicized and polymorphous perverse—which the New Believers oppose to Courtly or Romantic or Sentimental Love. Sometimes it is *agape,* Holy Love, Sweet Charity, a universal bond which, by making all men and women Brothers and Sisters, challenges the authenticity of those exclusive bonds which define us as Sons and Daughters, Mothers and Fathers, Husbands and Wives, and especially faithful and jealous lovers of other single humans. Sometimes, under the New Dispensation, undifferentiated *libido* and universal *agape* blend into one ambiguous impulse, capable of motivating the sort of sub-orgasmic orgies often called these days "Sensitivity Sessions" or "Encounter Groups," or, more pretentiously and equivocally, "Tribal Experiences."

A wide variety of sexual behavior is tolerated under the New Dispensation, ranging from the total sublimation of passion, through multiple marriages to communities in which all are available in all possible ways to all; sex has become, like everything else, communal property. In no case, however, is exclusive heterosexual Love proposed as a means of Education and Civilization, a way of converting men and women, still moved by passion as dumbly and helplessly as beasts, into Ladies and Cavaliers, Courtiers distinguished by Gentle Hearts and the Intelligence of Love. And certainly the possibility has been preempted from the start of a compromise between *eros* and *agape,* the lust of the body and the longing of the soul, justified by the kind of Romantic Theology which begins with Dante's *Vita Nuova* and ends in the Anglican apologetics of Charles Williams, or the anti-Puritan Puritanism of D.H. Lawrence.

In addition to its attack on Work, Success, and Romantic Love, the New Religion is marked by an onslaught against certain conceptions of the central importance of Literature in the humanizing of man, conceptions that had remained basically unshaken (despite the rivalry of Science) ever since the Renaissance recovered from the Classical Past the notion of Culture as Secular Salvation for an educated elite. It is not, as Marshall MacLuhan, for instance, has argued, that the New Communicants, being children of an age dominated by the post-Gutenberg media, have ceased to read. MacLuhan is simply wrong in this regard. I have never myself visited an Agricultural Commune which does not possess some books—a slim collection of highly prized and carefully read volumes. But these must not be thought of as constituting in any traditional sense a "Library". No, in their function and use, they are more like the household books of some pious seventeenth-century New England Puritan than the contents of nineteenth-century study shelves stacked with critically approved "Great Books," or an early twentieth-century parlor table, loaded with the latest selections of the book clubs.

In place of the Puritan's Christian Bible, however, plus Milton and *Pilgrim's Progress,* one is likely to find a motley (but at last somehow standard) selection of some of the following: The *Tibetan Book of the Dead, The Whole Earth Catalog,* and the *I Ching;* along with all three well-worn volumes of J.R.R. Tolkien's *Rings* trilogy, plus a macrobiotic cookbook, Kurt Vonnegut's *Cat's Cradle* or *Slaughterhouse Five,* Castañeda's *The Teachings of Don Juan,* a couple of Hermann Hesse novels, and a complete file of the latest Stan Lee comic books. And, as I had almost forgotten, there would also be some pornography: a "Head Comic" by R. Crumm, or a more grossly sadomasochistic one by S. Clay Wilson, or perhaps, *The Kama Sutra.*

The point is not merely that the Scripture of various alien cultures have been given equal—or even superior—status with the Holy Book of Christianity, but that *any books which are read at all are read as Scripture,* which is to say, not for information or "cultural enrichment," much less to pass an idle hour, but as Guides to Salvation, and that even masturbatory fantasies are thus canonized.

It does not matter, certainly, what the author of any particular text, chosen by some mysterious process associated with the market place and the mode, may have thought he was writing or why.

He may, like Robert Heinlein, for instance, when he corrected the last galleys of *A Stranger in a Strange Land*, have considered that he was producing just one more in a long line of Science Fiction novels, intended to provide entertainment and make a quick buck. After all, at that point Heinlein was already a long-established and well-rewarded, if somewhat pedestrian, Old Pro. But he could not stay the process which kidnapped his work for "sacred" ends, extracting from it a new "holy" verb ("to grock") and supplying the initial inspiration, as well as a passage or two for Charlie Manson's syncretic Black Ritual. And it does no good to protest later, as Heinlein has, along with that master of Porno-S.F., Philip Jose Farmer, whose *The Lovers* apparently inspired him, that that is not what he meant at all. That *is* what they both meant *in context*.

Furthermore, it is neither accidental nor irrelevant that Heinlein's book comes from the area of Popular rather than High culture, the world of joyous junk rather than that of solemn art; for the new religion is essentially *Pop*. Pop Science is also raided in the endless search for a Pop Scriptures—as in the case of Ohsawa's various works on dietetics. Or perhaps one should rather describe the texts of the founder of Macrobiotics as Pop Science plus Pop Theology: a little vulgarized Zen Buddhism, mingled with some Pop Reflections on Yin and Yang, plus some practical admonitions at the level of the Home Medical Advisor on how to cure gonorrhea and avoid cancer by learning to eschew milk. It does not matter that none of this makes rational sense. What does matter is precisely that it does *not* make such sense, thus providing occasions for true acts of faith. "I believe because it is absurd," the naive believer has always cried, scandalizing the more sophisticated who had placed their faith in the rational.

Certainly, the skeptical have not given pause to any devotee, however anemic and wasted, nor disturbed his resolution to go ten days on "straight grains" in quest of health more spiritual than physical. Mere medical statistics seem as irrelevant to such a believer as they did earlier to the followers of Wilhelm Reich who crouched naked in their "Orgone Accumulators" in quest of an orgasm pure enough to inhibit cancer. In an age of Underground

Faith, the underground faithful rejoice especially in those leaders the established call "charlatans," in those who *are*, by established standards, charlatans in fact: from Leary and Manson to Wilhelm Reich.

But it is not charlatanism alone which moves the faithful. What are we to make, for instance, of the vogue of *The Whole Earth Catalog*, the product not of showmen and hucksters, but of modest believers rather than arrogant Shamans, yet also a Pop, i.e., a commercial success? Is is not also a Bible for yet another Sect created in a time of Pop Science; and does it not reflect the teaching of yet another Science Fiction writer who has chosen life over art as his preferred medium: that odd blend of technocrat, guru and a nut inventor, R. Buckminster Fuller. To be sure, his doctrine has been oddly transformed by being translated from the Urban centers he loves to the New Mexico countryside by younger men, less sure than he that technology can solve the problems it has created by becoming supertechnology. It is a kind of subtechnology, which the editors of *The Whole Earth Catalog* prefer, a minimal technology, a technology of do-it-yourself. But they share his faith, his Religion of Gadgetry; and in 1972, their technocrat's Bible was given, scandalizing some and gratifying others, a National Book Award.

The judges who bestowed that award were merely attempting to certify as "literature" a somewhat pretentious collection of ads for goods still considered *Kosher* in a time of conspicious underconsumption. But the early admirers of *The Whole Earth Catalog* had already canonized it as "Scripture." So that even before the National Book Award, it had made its way on to the shelves of readers who would never use any of the products it advertised— having no desire to build supergeodesic domes or prefabricated Indian teepees, but merely to read or own a Holy Text.

How different has been the fate of the *Sears Roebuck Catalog*, its predecessor and prototype, which only came to be esteemed and preserved when it had grown obsolete enough to the advanced to seem proper "camp." To be sure, the *Sears Roebuck Catalog* evoked no holy names like that of Buckminster Fuller, no sacred theory like his. But this is not the real point; for in the declining twentieth century, what is most debased, most despised, most utterly vulgarized in the realm of para-literature, i.e., advertising, is all the more prized, so long as it can be used for presumed "sacred" ends:

turning on, returning to nature, dropping out, avoiding pollution, ripping off the Establishment. It has, in fact, always been true in the case of Pop Religions, in America at least: in that of Christian Science, for example, and Mormonism, that the low literary value of New Scriptures has been taken as a warranty of their sincerity and truth.

And here, precisely, is where the habit of reading literature as Scripture so essential to the New Dispensation differs totally from the elitist "Culture Religion" whose great apostle was Matthew Arnold. For Arnold, what made literature, some literature, Scripture, or rather a replacement for Scripture in an age of declining faith and The Death of God, was its excellence as literature, and its consequent critical immortality. On the other hand, what makes literature, some literature, available as Scripture in an Age of the Revival of Faith and the rebirth of the Gods is its doctrinal content, in the light of which the very nature of literary excellence, in esthetic or formalist terms, becomes not merely irrelevant, but offensive as well. Once more Faith drives out before it the criterion of Taste, which could only have flourished in its absence. It is not that literary excellence is felt as totally inimical to relevance or truth, for some of the canonical texts of the New Dispensation are worthy enough for formalist standards: Tolkien, for example, or Hesse, or Kurt Vonnegut. And yet even these contain a redeeming element of *schlock* or *schmaltz,* or at least *Kitsch.*

Beyond the rejection of the Puritan Ethos and Love and Literature, there resides at the heart of the current Religious revival a fourth rejection, not less noticed, perhaps, but certainly less clearly understood than any of the others; and yet without coming to terms with it, we cannot fully comprehend the meaning of the Cultural Revolution. This is the Rejection of the City, a flight from urban to rural, which seems at first glance merely a reaction (comprehensible enough, and even sympathetic) from the unseemly sprawl, the congestion and pollution, the antihuman pace and the aggravated offense against nature apparently inseparable from urban civilization. But the New Mutants in their agricultural communes cannot be understood merely as the last heirs of a tradition of revulsion which, over the past two or three centuries, has driven increasing numbers of sensitive souls to abandon the centers of large cities, and to create first the Romantic Suburb, then the Bourgeois Suburb, and finally, Exurbia: all bound still to the urban core by trains and buses and private cars, a network of two-way roads leading back and forth from markets and jobs and theaters at the center to gardens and bedrooms on the periphery. No, the agricultural commune is no ultimate exurb disguised as a rural slum, not even a cross between Exurbia and Bohemia. It is an outward and visible manifestation of an inward and invisible rejection not just of the *metropolis* and the *megalopolis* but of the *polis* itself: not just of New York and Berlin and Tokyo and London, but of Rome and Athens, Florence and Urbino, Vicenza and Weimar, Green Belt and Bucks County.

There has been a deep ambivalence toward the city apparent at the heart of our culture ever since the city was re-invented sometime around the twelfth century. In Dante, for instance, innermost Hell, the heart of the Inferno, is thought of as a "sorrowful city," *la città dolente*; but in the ultimate Empyrean, he remembers the Holy City, stronghold of Empire and Papacy. And we are, therefore, not surprised when he draws on his tourist's memories of Rome for the setting of his final vision, portraying the Saints gathered together in an arena which is simultaneously a Rose and the Colisseum, the perfection of natural beauty and urban architecture. It is not the redeemed, the Heavenly City, which the New Religious dream but a world without cities—a world before or after cities, a world in which the Idea of the City has not yet been conceived or has been long forgotten. This is because Dante is already a Humanist, as the New Religious no longer are.

The idea of Man central to Humanism is inseparable from the Idea of the City: the notion of a complex community based on the division of labor, the centralization of specialized services, plus a concentration of talent, a maximization of cultural interchange, as well as the storage and distribution of the most varied kinds of goods. The actualization of this Idea made possible the creation of theaters and supermarkets, libraries and museums, hospitals and cathedrals, courts of law and parliaments, and supereminently, the University, the center and shrine, as it were, of dialectics and of the conversion of *mythos* to *logos*, the Shrine of Humanism. The End of the City, the death of the polis means, therefore, the End of Man as we have defined him over the past two and a half millennia. I scarcely need remind you of the Aristotelian text which is a chief source of that definition. *Man is a political animal; outside the polis, he is a beast or a god.*

Nor is it necessary to do more than mention the literary work

which constitutes a kind of dramatic and still half-mythic prefigura-
tion of that text, since it is a work which has pre-eminently possessed
our imaginations over the past decade or so, becoming for us by all
odds the favorite, the most living of all classic Greek dramas. I am
referring, of course, to *The Bacchae* of Euripides, which renders with
total clarity, though without simplification of the ambiguities
involved, the crisis of the human which occurs when men grow
weary of the institutions that have nurtured their humanity; or
rather, perhaps, when those institutions rigidify to the point at
which creative sublimation becomes deadly repression, and *logos*
becomes madness both for those who remain behind in the dying
city and those who abandon the *polis* in favor of the *thiasos*, the
pack, the Dionysiac rout.

There is no other alternative; when we flee the City, we wake to
find ourselves on Cithaeron, which is to say, in a world without order
or tradition or law or distinction: the Dionysiac world, which it is
possible to glorify by expurgation *à la* Nietzsche as a source of
fertility and song (which it is), a place where madness has at least a
sanctified function. But, as Euripides confessed long ago, it is also a
world of ecstasy from which one awakens, inevitably, necessarily, to
terror: the Mother discovering that the bloody head she holds in her
hand is not that of some sacrificial beast, but of her Son who, refusing
to sanctify madness in the name of the human, himself becomes
simultaneously a beast and a God, though still somehow a mortal
who must suffer and be destroyed.

But here precisely is the essence of the thiasic as opposed to
political experience, of life in the pack as opposed to life in the city.
For in the *thiasos*, all those distinctions are lost which made possible
the play of dialectic and the reign of reason: between male and
female, god and man, god and beast, drunkenness and sobriety,
sanity and insanity, waking and sleeping, Yes and No. The realm of
indistinction is, however, the realm of the metahuman: a realm we
inhabit only in dreams, dreams in which, alas, we can no longer
remain forever, like our prehuman ancestors, but from which we are
doomed always to awake. This we tend to forget in the drunken roar
of Dionysiac release, at the Demonstration, the Orgy, the Rock
Festival, the child's Saturday matinee, at the movies, the adult's
Sunday afternoon in the football stadium, when speech yields to
noise (one name of the terrible God of the Pack is Bromios, the

Roarer). It is, of course, in this world, the world of noise, of static and antimessages, of overloaded circuits and amplifiers turned up to full that the New Religious live by choice, and the rest of us, willy-nilly, assaulted by record players or radios or the juke-box, bull-horns or the screaming of crowds.

Noise or silence—but not speech, dialogue, communication—are proper to the realm of the ineffable, the metapolitical, the divine. One pole of the possibilities inherent in the New Religions, the New Religiosity, is, then, defined by the legend of Dionysus, as the adaptation of Euripides' play by Richard Schechner, *Dionysus in '69*, made clear—involving the audience itself, when it worked best, in the updated, naked Dionysiac rout it recreated in a theater which ceased to be a theater as the beholders became participants, followers of the Impostor God, the actor whose very act of imposture was proof of his Dionysiac claims. The God who was not a God but a neighborhood freak, in a theater which was not a theater but unstructured space, displaying his sex before spectators who, if moved, knew they were not spectators but celebrants and victims (they had paid to be so trifled with, so transformed): perhaps this was as close as we could come in our time to the true orgy, thiasic release. But maybe it was as close as anyone—after the building of cities, whether Thebes or New York—could *ever* come; emerging inevitably to other noises, other silences: the roar of the traffic which bears us home, the silence of our own house before we turn on the T.V. to watch the late, late show, or alternatively, the blaring insistence of the music our children are listening to when we enter. "Turn it down," we are likely to yell, glad to have a noise level we can control—not off, but *down*, for we find total silence also an affront.

Not so those pledged to meditation, who pursue, through techniques adapted from Yoga—legs folded in the lotus position or pressed tight as they stand on their heads—what they learned to call (while Zen was fashionable) "the sound of one hand clapping." There is in our own Western tradition a myth of Silence equivalent to the Dionysiac Myth of Noise, which, I cannot help believing, is on the verge of moving once again to the center of our imagination. This is the Legend of the Holy Grail—that terrifying account of the destruction of a society based on chivalric valor and courtly love by the pursuit of what exists only outside of all communities, which is to say, Nowhere. The present age which has also turned its back on traditional notions of heroism and romance in its pursuit of vision should find this myth particularly sympathetic, yet there has been no contemporary adaptation of the Holy Grail story equivalent to Schechner's revision of *The Bacchae,* only children's stories and musical comedy versions of Arthurian story on the level of *Camelot,* or—more interestingly—infinite variations in search of a new classic form in Science Fiction, short or long.

In fiction and verse, however, the major attempts to reveal the relevance of the Grail symbol to a time of reviving Faith have been made by writers whose religion is nostalgic rather than prophetic and whose esthetic stance belongs to a moment when Modernism had not yet yielded to the post-Modern: John Cooper Powys in the *Glastonbury · Romance,* Charles Williams in *War in Heaven,* and especially Eliot in his incoherent *The Wasteland,* framed on the one side by Jessie L. Weston's scholarly study, *From Ritual to Romance,* and on the other by Bernard Malamud's *The Natural.* Yet there is scarcely anyone among the New Mutants who is unfamiliar, through one child's adaptation or another, with Malory's *Morte d'Arthur,* that melancholy account of the end of the Round Table, the death of Arthur, and the destruction of Lancelot and Guinevere by the pure Knight who comes from silence and disappears into silence, creating nothing, only laying waste the world. If *The Bacchae,* especially as interpreted by Richard Schechner, was appropriate to the mounting ecstasy of the sixties, the Legend of the Grail seems an oracular prophecy, awaiting an interpreter, of the desolation which has succeeded it at a moment when the Rock Festivals have passed into the hands of the commercial exploiters, when the legendary fraternity of the Beatles falls apart in squabbles over money or prestige, when Lenny Bruce and Janice Joplin are dead—and the most devout among us withdraw into silent meditation.

In the world of silence, as in the world of noise, worship is possible as well as ecstasy, but not theology. The New Communicants begin where Thomas Aquinas ended, crying of his own *Summa Theologica,* "It is all rubbish." They know from the start that theology belongs to the realm of *Wissenschaft*—an alternative way toward vision, perhaps, quite like, though less sympathetic to them than the use of intoxicants and like the latter tending to become an occasion for Idolatry when considered an end rather than a means.

And they sense somehow at this point that the Death-of-God Theology was the last theology of the West, since what it was talking about, what it foresaw was its own death: the death of a method rather than its subject.

We live at a moment when the God of the Science of God is dead, so that the Science of Religion, invented in the eighteenth century, has become as unviable as the Religion of Science invented at the same time. We must not be misled in this regard by the growing popularity of university courses in "Theology," courses crowded these days with precisely the New Communicants we have been discussing. Their uses of such courses are eccentric, illegitimate in fact from any "scholarly" point of view, since they enter them in quest of ecstasy and entertainment, more material to be stored in the do-it-yourself kits for salvation which they will take with them when they leave the University for the desert, the classroom for the commune. Instinctively, they know that they must translate an ancient symbolic language into Pop Mythology, like that elaborated in the Stan Lee New Apocalypse series of comic books, in which Christian eschatology has replaced Captain Marvel and the myth of the secular saviour bred in the modern city. To recover that ancient language they raid even classes in Theology, "spoiling the Egyptians," as the old phrase has it.

It must not be thought, however, that they share the rationalist or rationalizing motives of their teachers. Indeed, they stand on its head the humane and scholarly tradition which begins with the Socratic slogan, "The unexamined life is not worth living," and comes to a climax in the Freudian tag—inspired by Part II of Goethe's *Faust*, itself inspired by the secular triumphs of Dutch land reclamation: "Where *id* was *ego* shall be." The votaries of the noisiest of Gods and of the silence that follows his triumph have turned all that upside down—crying out in the rout (and minding not a bit if no one can really hear what they say): "Only the unexamined life is worth living," and, "Where *ego* is, *id* shall return!" No wonder, then, that the New Religious reject utterly not merely those churches of the West which have become hopelessly genteel but any which have compromised with Humanism. Christian Humanism, Judaeo-Humanism, any attempt to reconcile reason and faith, ecstasy and dialectic: this is the Enemy. "Dehumanize yourselves," cry the new anti-Humanists, "dare be more than human or less."

That is why, when they do not create for themselves homemade Churches out of Popular Science, they turn either to the religions of the original inhabitants of our own continent, or to those of those after whom they were named in error, the original Indians. The native American Church, that odd blend of Protestant fundamentalism and the ritualized consumption of peyote buttons, has been especially appealing, since it involves the use of hallucinogens, and was blessed in the beginning by Timothy Leary. And what could be finally more sympathetic to the supermarket syncretism of our times than devotees who pray to Jesus, Mary, and Peyote? But the East Indians have proved even more so, proving America once more, *still* the "Passage to India" which Whitman called it. Not only Whitman was moved in the nineteenth century to turn east in search of a new scriptures, but Emerson and Thoreau as well. Typically, however, the New Communicants resemble Whitman rather than Thoreau in that they tend to adapt rather than assimilate Indian religions, almost deliberately half-understanding them. In the end, therefore, whatever those religions may have meant to their original believers, to the New Religious in our midst they represent essentially what is least familiar in their world, most alien to their own believing ancestors: a polar opposition to Aquinas or Maimonides.

Typically, they respond to such religions in their shabbiest, their most vulgar forms: if Zen Buddhism, as in the late 50's, Zen as expounded by popularizers like Alan Watts. But it is more *lumpen* movements, like Krishna Consciousness, which they prefer, as anyone knows who has confronted on the street corners of the world in recent years those shaven headed youths clashing cymbals and crying for alms. So also they seek out the sect which developed around Meher Baba, that most Pop of avatars, who looked like the late great comedian, Jerry Colonna, loved movies and cricket, and died ("dropped his body") without breaking his decades of silence as his followers had been long promised he would—a last vaudeville gag. If the mythology of Christianity has been accepted, begrudgingly and belatedly, by the New Religious, it is in its most Pop American revivalistic forms, the so-called "Jesus Freaks" being notoriously closer to Billy Graham or even Billy Sunday than to Ellery Channing or even Cotton Mather. Similarly, it is latter day Chasidism which appeals to converts out of all the possible varieties of Judaism: the followers of the Lubovitcher *Rebbe* recruiting with astonishing success among the long hairs, hippies, and freaks by descending on American campuses chanting, P.O.T. means put on *tvillim* (phylacteries); L.S.D. means let's start *davan-ing* (praying).

But this is by no means the nadir or the acme of the New Crusade which has led also to a revival of Satanism and Witchcraft, limited most often to simple theatrics and the cry (without consequence): "Evil be thou my good!"; but occasionally eventuating in orgiastic Sabbaths and even (as the Manson affair made manifest) in ritual murder. Everywhere, however, the latest recrudescence of Black Magic has been essentially popular and democratic, sometimes downright shoddy and subliterate: a kind of Satanism for everyone—clearly distinguished from that elitist devil worship that appealed to an aristocratic few at the end of the last century and is memorialized in literary works intended for a highly educated audience, like Huysman's *Là Bas* or the poems of William Butler Yeats.

The New Diabolism reflects, in this sense, the redemption, so characteristic of the movement, of everything which Science and respectable Religion had agreed in labeling "mere superstition": alchemy, astrology, fortune telling, all that had long been relegated to certain charlatans on shabby back streets or the filler columns in the popular press and the *Farmer's Almanac*. It is precisely the disreputable, antirational aura of these subsciences or antisciences that moves the young in an age that prefers astrology to astronomy, alchemy to chemistry, magic to technology: an age in which, among the New Mutants at least, the question "What are you?" is typically answered not with, "A student, a priest, a scientist," or even "A man;" but with "A Pisces" or "A Scorpio." And each eventless day is likely to begin with a casting of the *I Ching* or a shuffling through the Tarot Pack.

Moreover, this double revolt of visionary youth against rational religion and science is matched in some sense, perhaps essentially embodied in the re-appearance among them of certain "plagues" once nearly subdued by the combined efforts of laboratory researchers and medical technicians, plus a code of personal hygiene propagated first by primary school teachers, and then by the pseudo-Doctors in white coats on T.V. ads for toothpaste or sanitary napkins. There is something repulsive to anyone committed to living in his physical body and remaining faithful to his animal inheritance in the compulsive American drive (most recently and hysterically joined by upwardly mobile Blacks) to scrub, cleanse and deodorize oneself out of all semblance of physical humanity. Only when touring the remotest corners of the "backward" world, or lost in the midst of combat, or taken by chance or conscience into the houses of the hopeless poor, does the modern Western bourgeois catch a whiff of man's ancient smell, the true odor of mortality.

The invention of the flush toilet, perhaps, began it all—concealing from him his own wastes and precipitating an early ecological crisis, as the residue of what we had eaten and digested no longer fertilized what was to feed us next. This was succeeded by the cosmeticising and deodorizing of the dead, as a whole culture re-invented mummification in an effort to hide from sight the inevitability of death and decay. And what has finally followed everyone knows who watches daytime television, in which the truly sacred dramas (interspersed by secular ones, called significantly "Soap Operas" or just "Soaps") are commercials dedicated to products guaranteed to remove mouth odor, body odor, kitchen odors, toilet odors, the natural smell of the genitals themselves: the basic scent of our dying bodies, without an awareness of which no religion seems necessary or possible.

No wonder the New Communicants have turned from this travesty-transformation of apocalyptic expectation into therapeutic hygiene, this attempt to create a redeemed and purified body Here and Now—along with the implicit Credo that cleanliness is not merely next to godliness but is all the godliness we need. No wonder they flee hot water and find pseudoscientific reasons for eschewing soap, insisting that what in one sense cleans, in another, deeper sense pollutes. No wonder they leave behind "sanitary plumbing" and shit on the beaches and wooded hillsides of our own wilderness areas or whatever remote land they reach in their ceaseless pilgrimages, which seem not so much voyages to Holy Places, as flights from an unholy one: from the tiled bathroom with its locked door and stock of required reading.

More, however, is involved than the rejection of commercialized hygiene. The true, the ultimate enemy is modern medicine itself, most despised of the antimagical sciences, most distrusted of the secular technologies. It is, in part, *institutionalized* medicine which the New Communicants fear, associating it, on the one hand, with that soulless totalitarian institution, The Hospital, especially its psychiatric wards, where ecstasy is labeled "madness," and "sanity" is enforced with shock treatments and lobotomies. On the other hand, they cannot separate it from the "Doctor," that $50,000-a-year A.M.A. member, bad enough in reality and worse in their paranoic vision of him as a racist, sexist, exploiter of his patients—dedicated to supporting "unjust" wars while resisting "just" causes like socialized medicine, free access to drugs, euthanasia and legalized abortion.

For a while, the New Communicants opposed to that bogey man certain "good" doctors of their own, most notably, the famous "Dr. Hip-pocrates," whose columns of irreverent and fashionable hip advice appeared in the underground press. But Dr. Hip-pocrates has passed from favor for pointing out, in an access of responsibility, the danger to life itself of the famous ten days "straight-grain" regime sponsored by the Macrobiotic Faith. It is quackery which they prefer, flagrant antiscience as preached by Ohsawa himself, or Wilhelm Reich (anyone who seems more Medicine Man than professional practitioner). To be sure, some medical practices seem acceptable to the New Religious, especially if they are sponsored by regimes on the Left: Acupuncture, for instance, which has been officially blessed by Mao-Tse-Tung. But perhaps even its appeal is based not so much on its acceptance in Communist China as on its rejection by official circles in the United States, its aura of unredeemable disreputability. After all, it was first advertised on the American Scene not in some Maoist journal but in the pornographic pop novel, *Candy*.

Basically, however, there has been a movement away from all medical treatment, public as well as private, in favor of do-it-yourself techniques ranging from therapeutic diets to the use of hand held vacuum devices for abortions. Birth control has posed, in fact, a special problem, since contraceptive pills and the "loop" represent final achievements of the hated medical technology and its market place *ethos*. Chastity and homosexuality seem more truly religious methods of population control, being more easily adapted to antitechnological myths; yet despite some talk of sexual abstinence and of *coitus riservatus* as practiced in certain Tantrist sects or among the Yogin, and the popularity in the Feminist movement of Lesbian unions, the major drift of the New Religious has been toward pansexuality and the Orgy—solutions which in a real sense presuppose modern contraception.

It is, in any case, infestation and disease that have tended to occupy the center of the rekindled religious imagination rather than purity or continence; so that even though no major sect has raised the cry, "Sickness is preferable to health" (except in the limited area of mental health), many new Communicants act *as if* this were an essential article of their faith. And their rejection of established modes of prevention and treatment have eventuated in the return to the universities and the bourgeois suburbs of certain minor nuisances, once believed gone forever, like head lice and crab lice, as well as major diseases like gonorrhea and syphilis and infectious hepatitis. But hepatitis can be checked by careful sterilization of hypodermic needles (the chief source of its spread), and the common venereal diseases were on the point of disappearing in the decade after World War II, which had seen the development of ever more powerful antibiotics. Indeed, there is no "rational" explanation for their failure to become as obsolete as diphtheria and smallpox, no emergence of an especially virulent strain of *gonnochi* or *spirochetes* (as is sometimes believed) immune to these new "wonder drugs." No, what is involved is simply a refusal to be diagnosed or, once diagnosed, to follow prescribed treatments: a refusal based on a quite conscious contempt for science and a half-conscious longing for disease as some ultimate symbol of liberation.

It is no surprise that the highest incidence of venereal disease has occurred precisely in the holy places of the New Religious: the Haight-Ashbury, for example, and the agricultural communes, where a few instances of plague have also been reported. The very universal love and emancipated sexuality which characterize the New Faiths at their best become a means of mutual infection and re-infection; while dirty needles used to inject ecstasy-producing drugs lead to stupor and coma and total collapse, as released bile invades the blood streams of the devout.

It is possible, to be sure, to put all of this in historical context, reminding ourselves that all Crusades, i.e., resurgences of religious faith leading to the breaking of old cultural boundaries, have resulted in similar outbreaks of pestilence. We can think, for instance, of how the late Medieval wars against Islam, presumably intended to repossess the Holy Land, brought back into Europe leprosy; or how the discovery of America, conducted by one who called himself the "Christ-bearing Dove" and sailed on a ship named after the Blessed Virgin, resulted in the first major outbreak of syphilis in the western world. To be sure, the Medieval Crusades were not fought solely, or perhaps even chiefly, to redeem Christian shrines; nor were the voyages of exploration primarily intended, as Roman Catholic apologists argued, to find a new source of souls as replacements for those lost to the Protestant Revolt. And one can read the body-wasting diseases that resulted as outward and visible signs of the impure motives, political and commercial, which underlay and undercut their avowed ends.

But perhaps it is better to understand such "plagues" as physical manifestations of profounder psychic events: the culture shocks resulting from an encounter with other societies based on differing concepts of the human and divine, as well as rival religions created to sanction such concepts. The current Cultural Revolution represents a movement in inner space rather than outer, a psychological rather than a geographical journey; but it, too, has resulted in an encounter with an alien type of man, the Barbarian inside of our old humanist selves. How appropriate, then, seems the re-invention of syphilis, a "disease" associated (quite like the natural hallucinogenic drugs) with the American Indian, in whom the New Mutants have found a model for their alternative lifestyle. No new Gods without new diseases seems to be the lesson of history; no resurgence of faith without new mortifications of the flesh at the unconscious or psychosomatic level, as well as on levels where reason and consciousness fully function. But this means, in the end, new definitions of "sickness" and "health."

We have known all along that when Dionysus comes he brings affliction to the spirit, "madness" in terms of the society he scourges. Why is it more difficult to accept the fact that he occasions afflictions of the flesh as well, "sickness" in the language of the world he teaches us to deny? And the same is surely true of the *deus absconditus* of the Grail Legend, that God who, unlike the Christian God, neither begets a Savior on the Jewish mother (the father of Galahad is Lancelot, which is to say, depraved and passionate man) nor reveals himself. In the end, the insufferably pure hero disappears from us, leaving the world a little worse than when he entered, since woman is bereft of her adulterous champion and the realm of its betrayed king. Even the symbols the Grail Knight *has* seen are symbols of infertility: Cup and Dish, Lance and Sword—the receptacles for Wine and Bread and the phallic weapons, one broken, one bleeding, eternally sundered from the female vessels. There is no Bible which follows such a revelation, only an unfinished, unfinishable popular poem by a hundred authors, and the pips on the Tarot deck, used first to tell fortunes and at last only to amuse the bored. How fitting that this myth survive among us chiefly in children's books and musical comedies, and finally in the literary texts (even Eliot's *Wasteland*) read only by scholars.

But he is a real God, though his name is never spoken, this God whose story begins in silence and failure only to end in silence and success. His unspoken name, I suppose, is death, *The Death of the King, Morte d'Arthur;* but he is nonetheless quite as genuine, as authentic as that other God whose names are many and cried aloud: Bacchus, Baccheus, Iacchos, Bassareus, Bromios, Evios, Sabazios, Zagreus, Thyoneus, Lenaios, Eleotheos, the Imposter, the Intoxicator, the Twice Born, the Phallus, the Ox, the Voice, the Pine Tree, Noise and Madness. When God is dead, a Christian theologian predicted not so long ago, the Gods will be reborn; or, to change the metaphor, once the Guardian at the Twin Gates of Dream, Ivory and Horn, has been removed, the undying Gods will re-appear. And why, then, would we hesitate to hail those who have opened the unguarded Gate, dancing at the head of a procession whose end no one can see, and shouting prophecies too loud to be heard? What if they scratch themselves, head and crotch, as they come; or even if the embrace they offer threatens infection and pain and death itself?

Not only have they performed the Hermetic function, turning themselves into *theopompoi*, heralds of the Gods. They have already begun to create a *cultus* appropriate to those Gods, as well as institutions to promulgate their faith and to preserve it in a hostile or indifferent world: The Demonstration, the Rock Festival, the Encounter Group. These variations on the Orgy (more like the American Revival Meeting, perhaps, than remoter Greek models), sublimated, half-sublimated, or totally desublimated, constitute their missionary institutions. And no vulgarization or commercialization can impugn them; for they are, by definition, vulgar and commercial, immune to "humanization" or polite piety. Nor does an eruption of violence, even murder, itself, such as "marred" the Rolling Stones' orgiastic moment at Altamont, undercut their effectiveness. Like the stoned-out kids or the exhibitionists publicly masturbating on flagpoles at Woodstock, Mick Jagger invoking death for unknown others is part of the meaning of it all: ugly, dark, dangerous, ambiguously suspended between *eros* and *thanatos* like the God himself.

Finally, however, it is their preservative institutions which seem the most vital and significant achievement of the New Age of Faiths: the asylums or refuges established for those already sanctified or in search of sanctity (or only tired and hungry and spaced out) in certain green interstices of our industrialized world: the Agricultural Communes. They have been sufficiently portrayed, in their bewildering variety and final unity, at all levels of scholarship and journalism; and the sense of their living reality has been rendered in fiction and verse as well as in film. There seems, therefore, little point in rehearsing either their virtues (the sense of community and peace, the possibility of non-medical therapy) or their faults (the equivocal role of the *gurus* who lead them, their instability, the hostility they engender in their neighbors). It is now clear that they are viable and that they will persist for better or worse, as we still say, in a world where few agree on the meaning of better or worse. But it is equally clear that they will persist in a larger world that will, by and large, not follow their example, but continue to emulate commercial, competitive, and even violent social models.

Yet, like the monasteries of the Middle Ages, they have already altered the meaning of everything done around them, even in contempt of all they represent. Our Era can, in fact, be described as a Religious one not because all, or indeed most of us, live by a code which honors Contemplation and Vision, but because a few men and women, chiefly but not exclusively young, are laying up in isolation a kind of spiritual capital for us all, by living a life which many outside of their retreats are even now beginning to yearn for, or wish they yearned for, or wish they wished they yearned for. Certainly, most of us already envy them their presumed indolence, their boasted sexual freedom, their unashamed nakedness, and their apparent deliverance from urban *ennui*. There is, consequently, little doubt in my mind that in the near future our presiding form of hypocrisy will be the rhetorical tribute our vice pays to their virtue.

At that point, the analogy will be complete; and we will have as much right to call ourselves Dionysiacs or Anabaptists or orgiasts or ecstatic polytheists as the men of the Middle Ages had to call themselves Christians, despite their wars and uncharity and daily desecration of their official faith. For just as those would-be Christians endured or tolerated, sometimes even supported certain cloistered religious who *lived* the faith they could not really abide, so we are learning to endure or tolerate, even directly or by indirection support the hippies and freaks who are ushering in a New Dispensation we fear.

Yet how can we bring ourselves to applaud without reservation a group of believers who offer us a kind of salvation, to be sure, a way out of the secular trap in which we have been struggling, but who are themselves ridden by superstition, racked by diseases spread in the very act of love, dedicated to subverting sweet reason through the use of psychedelic drugs and the worship of madness, committed to orgiastic sex and doctrinaire sterility, pursuing ecstasy even when it debauches in murder, denying finally the very ideal of the human in whose name we have dubbed our species *homo sapiens*? If this is the price of religious renewal, who would not choose even the "quiet desperation" of Death-of-God Capitalism or Communism, both committed, in theory at least, to maximizing our earthly goods, minimizing suffering and pain, extending life and organizing the relations of the sexes in some rational and stable way.

Even if we stand in need of salvation rather than success or social welfare (as the equal though quite different anguish of rich and poor, male and female, Black and White, old and young among us suggests we do), surely we must look for that salvation to some other quarter. And yet I myself have been moved to the very verge of ecstasy, over the lintel of joy in precisely such religious communities as I have been describing; so that finally I can, *must* cast a balance in the most personal of terms.

Let me cite two instances. When my first grandson was born some four years ago, I found that I wanted him to be circumcized like all of his male ancestors for three thousand years; but not medically, therapeutically only and not certainly in the mumbled ritual of a tongue and faith no longer comprehensible to most of those who would be present. I decided, therefore, that I would myself adapt the ancient formulae to my own sense of the times, presiding, though leaving the actual cutting of the foreskin to a doctor from some church-sponsored hospital in New Mexico, Baptist or Methodist, I am no longer sure. The doctor, however, though a proper white-coated technologist, too emancipated certainly to suck a drop of blood from the child's penis like a traditional *moel,* was at least a Jew. Not so the young congregation which assembled from a nearby commune called the Domes. They were, in overwhelming majority, *goyim,* though bearded and sandaled and robed quite like my own ultimate forebears: living great grandparents, as it were, a living past somehow grown younger than I. But is that not the way one remembers the grandparents of his grandparents, as he himself grows older in the trap of time which they have long since escaped?

There is one point in the ancient ceremony when the Celebrant says to the child, who actually bleeds in full view of all, his pain subdued by his first sip of wine, "*I say unto you, 'In your blood live!' Yea, I say unto you, 'In your blood live!'*" And the young man who stood behind me, blond-bearded and blue eyed, his gentile head half a foot above my own, responded, "Heavy trip, man!" and fainted. It was a response written in no prayerbook, but it was the right response. Because for once, for the first time in my fifty years of life, a *Brith,* a commemoration of our ancient Covenant with the God we thought dead was really *happening!* Before the ceremony was over, two other people had gone down, because (I was suddenly aware) they had learned again the meaning of Sacrifice and the required shedding of blood, beyond all rational talk of "symbolic wounds" or liberal horror at the persistence of cruel and archaic rites. Afterward, we drank and danced, like my own Chasidic ancestors, for how many hours I cannot say, since we were out of time. And, at last, intoxicated and worn out, we slept, waking to joy with the next day. God knows (some reborn God) precisely what it was in me that danced and slept and waked and rejoiced: the undying child, perhaps, or the unredeemed savage, the unrecorded Polish rapist, or the half-remembered wonder-*rebbe* who healed the lame and raised the dead—maybe all of them, all of me except my customary professional self, though, I suppose, that too. And why not?

So I danced again (I who cold sober never dance, know when I am cold sober that, whatever I remember, I really never *have,* except maybe in my head), as I had actually danced at Purim services a year ago, my second son by my side. Purim is an odd holiday in the Jewish year to begin with, a mad occasion of masking and carnival release in honor of a woman: a Jewish girl, presumably, who began by dancing named before a Pagan King, then married him, and ended saving her people from the destruction plotted by that King's evil prime minister. But Esther is finally no Jewish girl at all, her name a Hebrew variant of Ishtar-Ashtoreth-Astarte, just as the name of her presumed uncle, Mordecai, is another form of Marduk. She is, in short, the great Goddess herself smuggled into its imaginary history by the most patriarchal of faiths. But never mind, Jews have danced and sung in drunken joy life to her and death to her enemy, Haman (it is taught that on Purim a good Jew must get so drunk that he cannot tell Haman from Mordecai), for centuries now. And what better place to continue that tradition than in the converted clam bar which serves as a synagogue for that same Chasidic sect that cries on the campuses, "LSD means let's start *davan*ing." And *davan* we did, swaying and chanting in prayer, with a congregation consisting chiefly of half-converted long-hairs and freaks, though a few old men as well, and a handful of orthodox in their long black coats.

My son and I are joined in memory and love always, but seldom in pious practice. He is a food freak, a refugee from cities—who, while I am pounding my typewriter or opening my mail, will be crouched on the grass in lotus position or standing on his head bolt upright and stark naked in his lonely room. But for once we moved together in a common living present, joined by a magic to which, momentarily at least, we both subscribed. And our dead ancestors danced with us, at home with the bearded kids, high perhaps on grass, and the *chasidim* a little drunk surely on rye whiskey. We had for that little while resurrected the dead, our own dead, given life to those who gave us the gift of life, and to the Father of us all, whose name we still did not say even when we knew he was dead. But his names as many, after all, since he is Many as well as One, is reborn as One when he dies as Many, twice reborn as Many when he dies as One: Jehovah and Elohim, Dionysus and Bacchus, or, alternatively, Astarte and Leukothea, Ishtar and Aphrodite and Cybele, it makes no difference. The women, young girls chiefly, were confined to the back of the synagogue, behind a screen, but somehow they knew. Together we had created the gods who created our humanity, male and female created we them. A minute later, of course, we were awake, sundered from each other, the past and those gods. But that, too, didn't, doesn't matter; couldn't, as the colloquial phrase has it, matter less.

And knowing this, I know what I must answer when the Priests and Professors, to whose world I return from the *Brith* and the exclam bar, cry out (as my own ancestors first cried—for I am truly a Priest as well as a *chasid*—some two thousand years ago), "Can salvation come out of Galilee?" "Salvation always comes out of Galilee," I will answer out of the chasidic side of my mouth; which is to say, it comes out of the quarter from which we Priests and Professors had least expected it, the world we find it easiest to despise: not some Galilee of the past that we have sanctified and made safe for ritual and research, but a Galilee of the future which we still revile and fear.

But the dialogue, after all, is in each of our own heads, as well as in the community at large; and it cannot stop here. For even knowing and confessing that salvation comes out of Galilee, perhaps only knowing and confessing that piece of the truth, we are not delivered of our priestly and professorial obligations, not permitted to cry like some mindless gentile or wandering barbarian the matching slogan of contempt and terror, "Can wisdom come out of Athens or Jerusalem!!" Wisdom *always* comes out of Athens and Jerusalem, which is to say, out of worlds clean, healthy, reasonable and sane to the point of absurdity. Yet we dare not ignore the voice of wisdom when it insists, "The false prophet shall be put to death!" "The witch shall be put to death!" "The Messiah is yet to come!" "The Messiah is *always* yet to come!"

Only in the eternal tension of these two conflicting views, the irreconcilable dialogue of these two voices, Goyish and Jewish, prophetic and priestly, mad and sane, can the dearest of all possibilities be kept alive: the possibility (after the death and rebirth of the gods) of re-inventing Man.

Leslie A. Fiedler
Buffalo, New York
Yom Kippur 1972

In Every Generation

A Meditation on the Two Holocausts

FOR A LONG time now I have resisted all importunities to confront head-on in print the destruction by Hitler of six million Jews, what has come to be called the "Holocaust." It is in part this intrinsically theological name for an essentially secular atrocity that has put me off. Not merely has it become an instant cliché, but by employing it (as how can I not?) I predetermine, as it were, my own attitudes and the response of my audience. Think how different those attitudes and that response would be if I were to rise more neutral sociological terms like "genocide"; or even the Nazis' mythological one, the "Final Solution."

Moreover, I have always been afraid that in dealing with that subject I could not keep from seeming to suggest that I, who as an American was safely removed from the European catastrophe, have been, insofar as I am at least allegedly Jewish, in some sense its victim. It is true, of course, that Hitler would have considered me a Jew (whatever my own doubts about my identity); but this gives me, I am convinced, no right to exploit—rhetorically, politically, philosophically —the ultimate misery of those alien others with whom he would have lumped me. At any rate, both my Jewishness and theirs remain for me even now not a given fact but an enigma, elevated by their fate as victims and mine as an unscathed survivor (perhaps to some degree a victimizer) if not quite to the level of a full theological Mystery, at least to that of a modest lower-case "mystery." It is, in any event, this minor mystery that I propose to explore in the subtheological meditation that follows: a meditation on not just one Holocaust, but—for reasons I hope will become clear before I am through—two.

Unlike many religious thinkers (though I speak their language, it should be understood that what for them is revealed truth is for me myth and metaphor), I do not consider the failed total destruction of European Jewry a *novum*—an event not merely monstrous but unprecedented, unique, and, therefore, incomprehensible, ineffable. It seems to me in retrospect disconcertingly predictable: an occurrence, or better, perhaps, a reoccurrence in history of what already existed out of historical time; which is to say, an event that had long since become a myth, the key myth, indeed, of Jewish existence.

My maternal grandfather, who had before he was quite full grown fled the Eastern European world of pogroms and the threat of pogroms, when asked what was happening in the world, would usually answer (at least so I remember it), "Nothing new. *M'hargert yidd'n*. They're killing Jews. What else?" The first time I heard it, I was left wondering whether it was some strange kind of adult joke at which, if I lived so long, I would be able someday to laugh. But it no longer seemed a joke of any kind, when at age seven or eight I found myself reenacting in fact that myth of our history. I was then a student in a suburban New Jersey grade school, where my brother and I constituted half of the total Jewish enrollment. We felt ourselves, therefore, interlopers in a goyish institution, where, of course, all of our teachers were goyim and we had weekly school chapels, at which we were expected to repeat *their* "Lord's Prayer" and, at the appropriate seasons, sing hymns celebrating the birth and resurrection of *their* Christ.

All of this, however, had made me only a little uncomfortable, until one day in the schoolyard all hell broke loose. During recess and after class, when my fellow students gathered together to choose up sides for a game, more often than not they would end with Protestants on one side and Catholics on the other (for me it was a baffling distinction without a difference), then proceed to pummel each other in a kind of mock Holy War. On this occasion, however, for reasons I still don't understand, they noticed me slinking off alone, as I customarily did; and remembering that I was a Jew, which is to say, the legendary enemy of both, joined together to chase me all the way home, screaming, "You killed our Christ."

At that moment of sheer funk (I was sure that they meant really,

really to kill me), I learned not only that my grandfather's joke was not a joke at all, but the reason why Christians had long slaughtered us in earnest: their myth of the Jews. But, of course, I did not yet know how to say this even to myself, much less my pursuers. If I had been able to find breath for anything but running I would probably have shouted, "What, I killed your Christ? I wasn't even there." Certainly, I would not have had the chutzpah, even if I had the breath, to answer their charge of deicide with the defiant affirmation I was to hear years later on the streets of Jerusalem. It was in the midst of the turbulent sixties, when a band of irreverent young Israelis cried aloud to watching tourists, including me, "We did so kill him. We did so!"

But after all, those marchers were at home in a world of their fellows, while I (as I realized first back then in New Jersey) was a stranger in a strange land, and would remain so to the day of my death. No matter that I could already read the language of the land to which my forebears had fled, better, speak it better, write it better than my child persecutors, to whose ancestors it "belonged" as it did not to mine. As a matter of fact, this only made matters worse.

Perhaps it would have helped if I had been familiar with the Jewish countermyths explaining the hostility between us and the gentiles, myths invented before Jesus had claimed to be the Messiah, and had been condemned by the High Priest of Israel as a blasphemer, then turned over to the dubious justice of Rome. The key text is, of course, the passage in the Haggadah for Pesach, repeated annually by all who consider themselves still Jews: "for not one only hath risen up against us, but in every generation there are some who rise up against us: but the Most Holy, blessed be he, hath delivered us out of their hands." "In every generation," the threat warns us, looking forward to Hitler and Muslim terror as well as backward to Haman and the Pharaoh, "who knew not Joseph."

But it is not the final word, being followed by a promise of deliverance, which reminds us that not merely did six million Jews die in the "Holocaust," but more millions escaped alive to tell the tale. It is, indeed, their survival and subsequent fate that is for me the true, the final mystery. Before returning to it, however, I feel obliged to wrestle with the question of *why* the threat of annihilation and the promise of redemption have continued to be the pattern of our history. Here, too, there is a traditional text suggesting an answer: the cryptic Chapter 53 of Isaiah, in which the prophet imagines the kings of the gentiles confessing that only through the suffering they inflict on God's faithful servant, Israel, can they themselves be saved: "Surely he hath born our griefs, and carried our sorrows: yet we did esteem him stricken, smitten of God and afflicted./But he was wounded for our transgression, he was chastised for our iniquities; the chastisement of our peace was upon him: and with his stripes we are healed."

It was not, however, until I was approaching middle age that I became aware of those texts and their relevance to my own fate as well as that of my people; which is to say, not until after the defeat of Hitler, the revelation of the full horror of the concentration camps and the simultaneous loss of my earlier faith in socialism and the universal brotherhood of all mankind. I was a communist of the Stalinist persuasion at age thirteen, a Trotskyite before I was twenty. My holy books, therefore, were not the Torah and Talmud, but the collected works of Marx, Engels, and Lenin, which seemed to me then to teach the True Way: not just a way to make a better world but a way to escape the limitations of my ancestral religion. To be sure, those limitations were not very onerous, since neither my parents nor my grandparents observed the rules of kashruth, nor were they members of any congregation. But they had nonetheless preserved intact in the New World the parochialism and xenophobia that had been concomitants of Old World Judaism,

Though my grandfather no longer recited the morning blessings in which he thanked his Creator for not having made him a goy, when I behaved intelligently, he praised my *yiddisher kopf,* and when I acted stupidly, he reproached me for having a goyish one. For my grandmother, who kept none of her opinions secret, all gentiles were contemptible: the Irish, the Italians, and especially those from whose midst she had fled, the Poles, along with the *schwarzers,* the Negroes, who seemed to her their American equivalents. Even in the mouths of my native-born parents, the words *shegetz* and *shikse* were epithets of contempt; and I was not surprised to discover that the root meaning of these standard words for a gentile male and female is "abomination." Small wonder, then, that the parents of my favorite high school teacher, a Jew, sat *shiva* for him when he married a shikse, mourned for him as if he were dead.

To be sure, I was aware that such Jewish hatred and fear of their non-Jewish neighbors was reflexive, a reaction to generations of persecution in Eastern Europe—and that, of course, it was finally impotent as well, drawing not a single drop of gentile blood in return for the buckets of Jewish blood shed by the gentiles for so many generations. Yet it was, I knew, weakness rather than charity that had made my people in their long exile settle for calling upon their God to pour out his wrath on the goyim, instead of slaughtering them themselves as their ancestors had done, when moving into the Promised Land.

In any event, I was convinced in those days that until such mutual recrimination and hostility ceased, until anti-Semitism and anti-anti-Semitism alike were ended, there could be no social peace. Nor would it cease, I believed, until the International Soviet had become the human race, until in a world without poverty, exploitation, and greed there were no longer Christians and Muslims, Hindus and Buddhists—and, yes, no longer Jews. Though I did not then go on record, in the thirties my response to a question about the future of American Jewry would doubtless have been much like that of Henry Roth, who wrote three decades later: "I feel that to the great boons Jews have already conferred upon humanity, Jews in America might add this last and greatest one: of orienting themselves toward ceasing to be Jews."

Since one of the boons of the Jews to humanity to which Both was referring was clearly Marxism, I felt that in abandoning Judaism in favor of socialism I was merely swapping an earlier, lesser Jewish faith for a later, greater one. After all, I assured myself, Marx bad been ethnically Jewish; and from the start his doctrines had been especially appealing to his fellow Jews. Of this I became aware early on when my grandfather, wanting to teach me a little Yiddish, began by making me sound out in the *mammeloshen* the masthead slogan of the *Daily Forward: "Workers of the World Unite!"* My father, to be sure, was a violent anti-Marxist; but being as confirmed an atheist as he was an American patriot (he dreamed that I or mv brother would make it into West Point), lie brought me tip reading Bob Ingersoll and Tom Paine, to whom organized religion was also anathema.

The mythological Hebrew texts to which I alluded at the beginning of this meditation were therefore quite unknown to me until I was closing in on middle age and had become the father of three sons. It was at that point that, finding myself and them all the more strangers in a strange land in Missoula, Montana, I organized the first seder I had ever attended: a communal celebration for a handful of fellow Jewish exiles, most of them also teachers in the State University and, predictably enough, almost none of them married to Jewish women. It was in that congregation, at any rate, that I first heard ringing in my ears (in my own voice and, of course, in English) the warning that "in every generation there are some who rise up against us" and began to puzzle out its meanings.

Even earlier I had begun to wrestle with the second key text, when, just after the end of World War II, I spent a full semester in the Harvard Divinity School, studying the twelve mysterious verses that constitute that fifty-third chapter of Isaiah. I had gone there to learn Hebrew, but why I was not really sure. I was motivated perhaps by a desire to rediscover—or, more accurately, to invent for the first time—my Jewishness, though there was a certain irony in my attempting to do so in a Christian school, as there was also in my simultaneously joining a choral group preparing to sing Christmas carols on Beacon Hill. Or maybe what motivated me was shame at the fact that of all the languages I had been exposed to up to that point—some eight or nine, I guess—the only one I had failed to learn well was my own ancestral tongue.

I had actually been sent, shortly before I turned thirteen (over my father's scandalized protests), to be prepared for Bar Mitzvah. But I stubbornly resisted learning Hebrew—spending most of my lesson time haranguing the rabbi, who sought to instruct me, about Jewish discrimination against Negroes in America and Arabs in Palestine; or trying to explain to him why all religions, including his own, were the opium of the people. To all of this he would retort only that I read Hebrew "like a cossack"; which was, alas, true.

Indeed, I still read the Holy Tongue like a cossack, even after the valiant efforts of Robert Pfeiffer, the eminent biblical scholar who was my teacher at Harvard, and who did his best to teach us "proper" pronunciation, insisting over and over (for the benefit of the few Jews in the class) that "Hebrew was not a dialect of Polish Yiddish." It was, in any case, pronunciation, grammar, and lexicography in which he believed. Of the mythic import of the text he said little except that it was not, as Christian theologians insisted, a prophecy of Christ's vicarious atonement for the sins of mankind, and that the "Suffering Servant" was Israel—as should be clear to anyone who understood the tenses of the verbs.

But in what the myth of the Suffering Servant might mean after the rise and fall of Hitler, Professor Pfeiffer was not interested. I, however, was, having come begrudgingly and at long last to recognize the full scope and horror of the Holocaust, of which I had for so long remained at least half-deliberately unaware. Before America's entry into World War II, I had dismissed the skimpy, garbled newspaper accounts of the Nazi persecution and slaughter of European Jewry as propaganda: "atrocity stories," like those about the poor Belgians and the rabid Huns, which bad circulated during World War I—and intended, like those, to brainwash the exploited masses into supporting a conflict that would mean more profits for their exploiters and death for them.

Such imperialist wars, I continued to believe even after I had lost faith in Stalin's Soviet Union and had begun to entertain doubts about Marxism-Leninism itself, were the ultimate evil threatening humanity. I was therefore proud that during the thirties I had stood shoulder to shoulder with my fellow students at New York University, crying aloud the "Oxford Oath"; which is to say, vowing that we would never support our own country in any war. Moreover, even as we shouted our resolve, we hoped, believed, that simultaneously massed protesters were echoing our words not only throughout our own country and those of our so-called allies, but even in those lands that a hypocritical F.D.R. (promising peace, but plotting war) had labeled our "enemies." Really, however, we were convinced the "enemy" was the ruling class of one's own country. That is why we sang over and over as we marched the streets of our cities and towns in the years between the Great Wars:

> In seventeen we went to war,
> In seventeen we went to war,
> In seventeen we went to war,
> Didn't know what we were fighting for.
> Time to turn those guns the other way.

So too we stubbornly resisted the argument that Hitler's planned extermination of the Jews made possible a moral distinction between the capitalist Third Reich (where, after all, multinational corporations like Krupp continued to prosper) and the rival capitalist powers, including our own. To grant this, we believed, was also to grant that our imperialist war against Hitler was a just one. It was a notion that most American Jews found easier to believe than did their Jewish brethren in Russia, where anti-Semitism had long since become a weapon in Stalin's struggle for power, or in France, where the Dreyfus case was still a living memory—or even in England, where every schoolchild grew up haunted by the nightmare figures of Shylock and Fagin.

Consequently, those of us self-styled "revolutionaries" who were also Jewish Americans considered it important to keep pointing out that the Jews were merely one target of Hitler's campaign of extermination, which also included gypsies, Poles, homosexuals, the congenitally malformed, Jehovah's Witnesses—and, especially, especially, Communists. To contend otherwise, we felt, would be to play into the hands of the capitalist warmongers like those well-to-do allrightniks whom we had always despised: those former bootleggers and sweatshop owners, who sought to prove that they were good Americans as well as good Jews by simultaneously launching Liberty Bond campaigns and raising money on behalf of Zionism. Which was worse I would then have been hard put to say—their offensively blatant American patriotism or their equally egregious pledges of allegiance to a nation state that did not yet exist.

Even after I had ceased to be a Marxist, their Zionism seemed to me especially offensive, for the last thing an already atomized world needed, I was convinced, was one more nation state. Because of the blessing-curse of exile from their original homeland, the Jews, it seemed to me, had been peculiarly well-suited to play a leading role in the inevitable progress toward a world without borders, flags, and ethnic divisions. The dream of a return to Zion, translated from the mystical to the political sphere, could, however, only eventuate in a society in which there would be not only Jewish statesmen and bureaucrats, but Jewish cops and soldiers—Jewish cossacks, in short. That in turn (as it needed no prophet returned from the grave to foresee) would breed an answering nationalism in the Arab inhabitants of what was to them also the "Holy Land," whom the new settlers would have to dispossess or displace. And to the ensuing Holy War, with mythic roots on both sides, there would be no end.

For a while, as the ensuing drama of terror and counterterror unfolded, I was tempted—following the Communist and Trotskyist line—to side in that struggle with the Arabs, who preferred (like the American Indians, with whom I could not help identifying them) poverty, disorganization, even tyranny under a regime of their core-ligionists, to prosperity, law and order, and a modicum of democracy under the auspices of colonizers whose technology, culture, and myths were utterly alien to their own. But I have ended by crying out—without ever ceasing to wish that the remnant of Israel in the Middle East survive and flourish—a curse on both your houses; though, of course, I would prefer to wish on both the blessing of universal brotherhood.

Clearly this has not come to pass in the land of Israel, nor indeed anywhere in the world; and it does not seem likely to come to pass in the foreseeable future. Yet it has not been easy for me to confess that I, who in the first quarter century of my life was sure that (if I lived so long) I would live to see a global *oecumene* without ethnic distinction, have instead lived long enough to see, as I prepare to begin my fourth quarter of a century, a world that atomizes rather than unites: a congeries of self-imposed ghettoes, in which the chief sources of political dynamism are particularism, parochialism, and sectarianism.

Perhaps I surmised all this (though I did not yet have the words to say it to myself as early as 1942, when I enlisted in the war I had so long anticipated with fear and loathing. Let me be clear. I was not drafted but volunteered, though I was at that point married, with a first child and a second well on the way; and I kept volunteering until I finally ended up at Iwo Jima, in the midst of what not only I came to think of as the mythological culmination of that bloody conflict. But *why*? is the question I still cannot answer.

I was prompted not, I think, by an indifference bred of despair after my discovery that the world had turned out so utterly different from what I had expected. Nor did I act as I did because, as I some-

times told those who asked, I could not endure refusing pusillani-
mously to share the key experience of my generation. Perhaps it
was only that I wanted to escape from what I had begun to feel as
the restrictions of premature maturity. Or maybe I just wanted to
learn another language; and the program promised not only to make
me a commissioned officer in the Navy but to teach me Japanese.
This would, however, take me to the remote Pacific—which is to
say, at the farthest possible remove from the threatened Jews in
Europe. It was there, at any rate, I finally found myself, listening to
reports of what was happening on the other side of the world as if
they were events on another planet. Though I did listen to those
reports in Honolulu, on Guam, and in China, I could not help
wishing—I feel obliged to confess—for the defeat of our own expe-
ditionary forces and those of our Russian allies, unable to forget
what I had learned too well in my years of Marxist indoctrination:
that it was the defeat of the Russians in the First World War that had
helped make possible the first successful Socialist Revolution.

I did not, of course—like the defeated soldiers of the Czar—
turn my guns the other way: since without ever having fired a gun
in any direction, I ended up as one of the victorious. When, therefore, I found myself at the war's end, helmeted and in full battle
gear, marching down the streets of a "liberated" Chinese city, I felt
like some Hollywood version of a conquering Nazi entering Paris.
So, too, grilling terrified and filthy POWs, I seemed to myself more
like an SS interrogator than a Jewboy from Newark, trapped in a
war in which he did not believe; but never more so than when,
flanked by a pair of offensively trim commanding officers, I helped
capture an alleged "war criminal": a pudgy Japanese businessman
who (quite like, I could not help thinking, a Jew trying to pass as a
gentile to escape the gas chambers) had disguised himself as a Chinese. He had castrated a coolie, we learned from "a reliable in for-
mant," and had buried in his backyard a treasure in gold coins. But
there was, it turned out, no treasure of any kind, which led me to
suspect that the mutilated coolie might have been a fiction as well.

I went therefore to the prison to which my war criminal had
been taken to ask whether there might have been some mistake, and
I was told that the mistake was mine, that no such person had ever
been incarcerated, or indeed existed at all. It is an incident I have

never forgotten, though, quite as if, indeed, he had really never existed, I cannot recall his face. What has continued to haunt my dreams ever since, however, is the painted face of the little girl (his adopted "daughter," he assured us, as my Chinese companions smirked) into whose hands he thrust a farewell gift, breaking temporarily from our grasp, as she kept screaming his name—which I have also forgotten. Another scene from a wartime propaganda film, in which I am once more hopelessly miscast.

Small wonder that long before I was finally shipped home I had come to identify with the Japanese rather than my American comrades-in-arms, whom I had seen performing not only acts of valor that put me to shame, but also atrocities: brutally beating disarmed prisoners, for instance, or stopping long enough under fire of their living enemies to extract with their bayonets the gold teeth of those dying or already dead. I never doubted for a moment that had I seen the Japanese as victors I would have witnessed equally atrocious acts. But I encountered them only as victims: and as victims, all men, I came then to believe, are the suffering servants through whose stripes their victimizers are healed—are, in the mythological sense, Jews.

Real Jews, however, were as rare on shipboard and the islands of the Pacific as they had been in Montana; but when I finally got to China—which is to say, when my long westward flight from my ancestral past had reached the ultimate East—I encountered, to my surprise, genuine Jewish refugees from European terror. They had not fled the Nazis, though, these loudmouthed hustlers in tight-waisted sports jackets, with whom I chatted over Sunday morning bagels and tea at the Imperial Hotel in Tientsin. Nor had the more soberly garbed burghers-in-exile, like the soft-spoken old gent who invited me home to show off his dog, who understood Yiddish, and his Hebrew prayerbook autographed by Eleanor Roosevelt.

It was the Bolshevik Revolution from which they had run in 1917 and were running still, side by side with goyim, to whom the new regime was equally threatening. But the goyish and Jewish expatriates in Tientsin had almost nothing to do with each other, the former socializing with their own kind in the White Russian Club (some of their rebellious children had already split off to form a Red one), while the latter gathered in what they called, of course, the *Kunst*, the Art Club.

The only art practiced there, however, was—as far as I could tell on a single visit—money changing. But, after all, a Jew has to live; and what else was there to do for these stateless wanderers, except maybe peddle contraband on streetcorners or run on a shoestring some sleazy brothel-saloon. Nonetheless, I could not despise or condescend to—much less, God forbid, pity—these *luftmenschen* without a past or a future. Undefeated and undismayed, they were capable still of a kind of ironical acceptance of their fate that made me feel childishly naive in my alternating fits of euphoria and despair.

I shall never forget, for instance, the time I made the mistake of saying "thank you" to one of them, after be had given me in exchange for a single U.S. dollar several thousand *yuan*, or whatever the local inflated currency was called. For an instant he regarded me in astonishment, then, shrugging his shoulders and looking up at the heavens, shouted (in an accent that reminded me heartbreakingly of my grandfather's), "Look at him. He gives me good American money. I give him shitpaper, and he says thank you." At that point, I knew that I had still a *goyisher kopf*, perhaps would never be a real Jew.

Nevertheless, quite as if I were one, I joined in conversations with those who were about the persecution of "our people" by Russians and Ukrainians and Poles. As far as I can remember, however, we never talked about the atrocities inflicted by the Nazis on their fellows who had remained behind in the *shtetlach* from which they had fled. Perhaps, once more like my grandfather, they could associate such murderous violence only with their traditional enemies, the Slavs; or maybe what was happening in a Europe in which they could no longer quite believe had remained for them as invisible and unreal as it was for me.

It became realer, however, once I had returned to America, where the full horror of the Holocaust was, I soon discovered, being relentlessly documented in print, on stage and screen, radio and TV. There was, therefore, no way in which I could avoid becoming aware not just of that horror but of the shame it triggered in me for having for so long (deliberately? half-deliberately?) remained unaware of it. My first response, though, to that belated awareness was not pity or terror, but rage: a blind rage directed at first not—

consciously at least—at myself, but at all the people of Germany, living or dead. For a long while, I would scream at anyone who attempted, however innocently, to address me in German, "I do not speak the language of Hitler!" forgetting that it was also the language of Kafka, whose *The Castle* I had, at age seventeen, painfully read in the original, not knowing that it had already been translated into English.

That visceral, irrational anger was further exacerbated by the fact that a catastrophe that had been labeled in an instant cliché "unspeakable" was being not only spoken about everywhere, but packaged, hyped, and sold on the marketplace: Anne Frank's memoirs, for instance, became overnight a best-seller, and the Nuremburg Trials were translated almost immediately from the headlines to the movie screen. The motives of the publishers and producers were, quite obviously, crassly commercial, which was bad enough, but what prompted their paying audiences, both Jewish and gentile, was, I could not help feeling, something worse: on the one hand, a kind of sadomasochistic voyeurism, which they did not confess even to themselves; and on the other, a desire, which they have easily confessed, to assuage the guilt they suffered for their earlier blindness.

That covert relish of horror pornography I shared, as well as that guilt, plus the added shame of being, though a Jew, an unscathed survivor. Nonetheless, I stubbornly resisted seeing any of those films or reading any of those books, because, I told myself, the vicarious atonement they afforded was too easy, too cheap. I was afraid, moreover, that seeking in such secondhand fictions— only print on the page or images on the screen, no matter how "true to life"—a substitute for the experience I had never really shared would make that experience for me not more but less "real." For similar reasons, I also refused to confront the killers of my people (of all my family that had remained in Europe, I learned on my return, not a single member had survived) on their own home ground. My grandfather's admonition about the dog returning to his vomit had until the war kept me from Europe. But even when in the early fifties I did make the voyage back, eventually living in Europe for two years, I still did not venture into Germany or Poland. Some ten years later, however, convinced that my reluctance was foolishly perverse, I began lecturing and attending literary conferences in Munster and Wurtzburg, Heidelberg and Berlin, finally even Munich, the very heart of Hitlerdom. Inevitably, I was asked by the German academics I encountered, their guilts obviously deeper than mine, "Why did we do it? Only we Germans could have done it, no?"; to which I was able to answer at that point, almost, almost believing it, "if you could have done it, *anyone* could."

In smugly, offensively prosperous Munich, however, my rage was kindled once more; so that crying out (as my ancestors had for generations) "Why do the wicked prosper?" I fled to nearby Dachau. It was not tearful compassion or nauseated revulsion I experienced, however, visiting my first and last concentration camp—only a sense of anticlimax, so nearly comic that I came close to laughing out loud. The spankingly trim barracks and gas chambers, I soon discovered, were not the originals, where real Jews had really bled and died; but a scrupulously reconstructed ersatz—like the restorations of bombed-out medieval churches at which I had gawked earlier. Finally, in the midst of giggling school-children, shepherded by grimly serious teachers, and bored sight-seers just off the bus, I felt myself not a pilgrim to a place of mar-tyrdom but a tourist in some horrific Disneyland.

Consequently, I returned with actual relief to the conference on Postmodernism from which I had been playing hooky; though once back, I endured the indignity, as I had everywhere in Germany, of being regarded not just as a representative American but a token Jew. And why not, after all, since—however problematical my Jew-ishness may have seemed to me—it is as a Jewish-American spokesman for the Jewish-American Renaissance of the fifties and sixties that I have been invited to speak almost everywhere on the face of the globe over the past two or three decades. During those exhilarating years gentile readers in Italy and France, India, Japan and Korea, particularly the younger ones, had been reading Saul Bellow and Bernard Malamud, Allen Ginsberg and Philip Roth in preference to writers in their own languages, feeling somehow that they spoke more directly to them. And they called on critics like me to explain to them why—assuming, of course, that like those writers I was a Jew. Nor did I refuse to play that part.

But I have had a little more difficulty maintaining that role

when those who call upon me to bear witnesses are Jewish themselves. The first time, for instance, that I ever visited Israel was as
a participant in a symposium of Jewish writers, American and
Israeli, at the end of which David Ben-Gurion himself urged me to
make *aliyah*. Not only was my life in exile inauthentic, unreal, the
then premier told me, but "unless more Jews like you return," he
went on to explain, "*they* will eventually outnumber *us*." It was
clear that by *they* he meant the Sephardim, the "black Jews," and by
"*us*," the Ashkenazim, the "white" ones. Never in my life have I felt
less like a Jew, black or white. Nonetheless, I have gone back to
Israel five or six times over the years since, only to leave each time
further confused and dismayed.

On my latest visit, for example, without quite realizing that it
was the Sabbath, I stood outside my hotel to watch Jerusalem turn
golden under the setting sun and to smoke a farewell cigar in
peaceful meditation. My peace did not last long, however, since
almost instantly a group of ultra-Orthodox zealots gathered together
across the road to scream Hebrew imprecations at my blasphemy;
to which I screamed back, "Don't worship idols!"—unsure whether
this made me more or less Jewish than they. In any case, they understood my English as little as I did their Hebrew, which made it all a
sort of bad joke.

My other close encounter with the ultra-Orthodox, however,
was no joke, good or bad, though it too exacerbated my lifelong
identity crisis. I bad been invited in the early seventies to a private
audience with the Lubavitcher Rebbe, who, it was evident from the
first, assumed that I was a Jew. Certainly, it was as a Jew that he
gave me his message, which was "The house is burning. Save the
children!" Nonetheless, when he went on to ask me for my name, I
was confused enough to answer "Leslie Fiedler"; and only after he
had shaken his head rather ruefully did I confess that my Hebrew
name was "Eliezar," my mother's in the same tongue "Leah"—that
I was, therefore, as he understood reality, really, *really* Eliezar ben
Leah. Under that name, at any rate, he promised to ask a blessing
for me when he next talked to his predecessor, who had been dead
for twenty years.

I was not churlish enough to say, though I could not help
feeling, that I, Leslie Fiedler once more, believed in no blessings

from beyond the grave; and that in any case I needed no such blessing, since I had already been blessed by the living: by the gentiles among whom I have made my career. Like him, they had assumed I was a Jew; and, seeking to make amends for the Holocaust, they have opened up to me—along with other Jewish Americans of my generation—academic posts and cultural distinctions, access to which had earlier been barred to those descended from the Killers of Christ. I have, that is to say, profited from a philo-Semitism as undiscriminating as the anti-Semitism in reaction to which it originated. And to make matters worse, I have shamelessly played the role in which I have been cast, becoming a literary Fiedler on the roof of academe.

But in what sense, though, I am really the representative Jew for which I have been taken, I have long asked myself, and ask myself still at age seventy-plus. "It's hard to be a Jew," my grandfather used to tell me; and from childhood on I have taken this to be an essential aspect of Jewish identity. For me, however, after that single scare of my childhood, it has all been only too easy. Ever since, anti-Semitism has been something I read about in the papers, what happens to someone else. Even in this negative sense, therefore, I can lay no claim to being really Jewish; and even less can I lay a positive one, being bereft of all *yiddishkeit* and almost entirely ignorant of rabbinic lore. What I know of the Five Books of Moses I know in King James English. Indeed, English is not just my *mammeloshen* but my *lashon-ha-kaddish* as well. My Holy Books, though no longer *Das Kapital* and *What Is to Be Done?* as in my youth, or *The Waste Land* and *The Golden Bowl* as in my early manhood, are in my declining years not the Torah and Talmud but *Huckleberry Finn* and the *Collected Plays of Shakespeare*.

Moreover, I have never in my life put on tefillin or attached a mezuzah to the doorpost of my house. Nor have I ever joined a Jewish congregation or fraternal order. In this, to be sure, I am like my father and grandfather, who also rejected all outward signs and symbols of Jewish belonging. In fact, the only religiously observant member of my family I ever knew was my paternal great-grandfather, the first of my seed to have been buried in American soil. I had met him, however, only once or twice (neither of us understanding the language of the other) before his funeral, where an equally pious friend of his delivered—in their language, not mine—a graveside sermon that set the mourners to weeping and screaming.

What they were crying and screaming about, however, I did not learn until much later, when an aunt interpreted for me. What grandpa's friend had said, she explained, was that he had suffered the worst indignity a good Jewish father could endure, seeing some of his children die before him; and this was because he had permitted those doubly accursed children to abandon their ancestral faith in the heathen New World. That they had indeed abandoned that faith became ever more evident as the years passed. The funeral service, for instance, of my father's only brother, who had married not one but two shikses, was held in a Methodist church; and his son's sons do not even know that their ancestors were Jews. Small wonder then that the children and grandchildren of my brother, who has long since become a Lutheran, are similarly ignorant of their roots.

Moreover, not a single one of my own eight children has at the present moment a Jewish mate; nor, for that matter, do I. Most of those kids, it is true, still think of themselves as in some vestigial sense Jews. But of my six grandsons only three have been circumcised—and one of those primarily because such ritual wounding is a part of the ancestral traditions of his Ashanti father. In any case, there is no one to say kaddish for me when I die. I am, in short, not just as I have long known, a minimal Jew—my Judaism nearly nonexistent—but, as I have only recently become aware, a terminal one as well, the last of a four-thousand-year line. Yet whatever regrets I may feel, I cannot deny that I have wanted this, worked for it. From childhood on, I dreamed a world without ethnic or religious divisions, though I knew that this meant a world without Jews.

What I did not suspect was that, ironically, in my lifetime half of that dream would begin to come true, reminding me of an aphorism of Goethe I should not have forgotten: "Be careful of what you wish for in your youth, because you will get it in your old age." What I have lived to see is a world in which even as sectarianism and anti-Semitic violence flourish in certain gentile communities, an ever larger segment of Jewry is losing its ethnic identity. Such attrition through intermarriage and assimilation has not, of course, been confined only to my own family—or even just to the United States, in which we are far from atypical. It is evident wherever large numbers of Jews continue to live in exile: particularly, perhaps, in England and the Commonwealth nations, but also throughout Western Europe, South America, and the Soviet Union, where refuseniks are the exception rather than the rule.

But none of this excuses my own complicity in what those who deplore it most (those observant Jews, who, though a majority, feel threatened and defensive) call with deliberate malice the "Silent Holocaust." That pejorative epithet I cannot help resenting, preferring neutral terms like "acculturation" or "assimilation"—even "apostasy." Finally, however, I must grant that the implicit comparison of the "Final Solution" I have abetted to Hitler's is hyperbolic perhaps, but not entirely unjustified. Both propose, that is to say, all end to a separate Jewish identity, whether defined racially, religiously, or culturally.

To be sure, our "Holocaust" is not imposed from without by brute force but freely chosen. Moreover, it is not motivated by hatred (not even self-hatred, as is sometimes charged) but by love: a love of all humanity, including those who have long persecuted us. Finally, we unreconstructed assimilationists, unlike the Nazis, seek not to obliterate along with their bodies the very memory of the Jews, but rather to memorialize in honor the last choice of the Chosen People: their decision to cease to exist in their chosenness for the sake of a united mankind. Still in all, it cannot be denied that the future we have dreamed is, like that foreseen for the "Thousand-Year Reign," *Judenrein*. It is for this reason that I have found it impossible to reflect self- righteously on the Holocaust which left me unscathed, without alluding uneasily to that other which has left me feeling like a Last Jew.

Nonetheless, Last Jew that I am, I cannot resist confessing, in conclusion, that each autumn, though I do not, of course, go to shul, I dutifully observe the fast of Yom Kippur. So, too, each winter, I light the lights of Chanukah, more often than not beside an already lighted Christmas tree. And each spring, after dyeing Easter eggs, I gather my family together for a Passover seder—crying out to the God in whom I do not think I believe, "Pour out your wrath upon the goyim. . . ." My children somehow do not ever ask me why, perhaps because they are sure they already know. If they did ask, however, I would say to them, as my grandfather said to me, sneaking me off to some storefront synagogue on the High Holy Days, "Not because I believe, but so you should remember."

I remember.

Why Organ Transplant Programs
Do Not Succeed

PERSONAL STATEMENT

My presence in a volume of essays on organ transplants may seem surprising to readers who know me only as a literary critic and long-time teacher in departments of English. As a matter of fact, I too was a little astonished when I found myself accepting an invitation to join a three-year project intended to end in the publication of a book addressed primarily (or so I surmised) to medical professionals, bioethicists, and government bureaucrats.

I had, to begin with, never thought very much about organ transplantation at all. Certainly, I had never contemplated donating any body part of my own, much less signing a pledge to do so, living or dead. I had, to be sure, lost a couple of my organs to the surgeon's knife during my long life; but they have wound up in the garbage disposal rather than the body of some stranger.

In any case, there seems something shamelessly chutzpahdik *in my addressing as an amateur an audience of specialists on a topic so clearly in their area of expertise and outside my own. Yet after all, I keep reminding myself, I have done so before, several times over indeed, beginning in 1978. In that year, I had published a thick, copiously illustrated book called* Freaks: Myths and Images of the Secret Self, *in which rather than analyzing—as I am accustomed to do— literary texts for their mythic content, I reflected on the ways in which our culture has mythicized people with congenital malformations, including dwarfs, giants, Siamese twins, and intersexes.*

In my book, I explored how and why such anomalous human beings were originally worshiped in awe or killed at birth in terror; then displayed as curiosities privately in courts and publicly at side shows; and finally came to be treated as patients by doctors, who attempted to cure them by chemistry, hormones, or radical surgery. And I concluded by pointing out that, when such medical intervention is counterindicated, "nonviable terata" are allowed to die.

My implicit disapproval of such therapeutic infanticide, in particular, seems to have annoyed many members of the medical profession; one of whom, indeed, at the end of a particularly heated argument with me on this topic, disrupted an otherwise friendly cocktail party by hurling a martini glass at me, barely missing my head. Nonetheless, ever since, I have been repeatedly invited to talk before groups of physicians, nurses, and bioethicists, presumably because I share their interests if not their points of view. Consequently, since I am reluctant to pass by any opportunity to talk about what moves me, whatever the motives of my sponsors, I have ended up speaking as an outsider to insiders, not just on teratology, but on gerontology, genomes, and child abuse, as well as broader topics like "What babies shall live?" or the images of doctors and nurses in literature and the arts, and finally, of course, "Why Organ Transplant Programs Do Not Succeed."

My original invitation to contribute to the colloquium on this subject suggested that more specifically I concentrate on the treatment of transplantation in popular fiction. And almost without thinking, I took down from my shelf the well-thumbed copies of two of the most popular of all popular books, Frankenstein *and* Dracula. *Rereading them, however, I was plunged deep into an iatrophobic nightmare from which I and (I began to suspect) many others have never fully awakened. But was this not, I thought, a clue to the answer for a riddle that has long vexed the medical profession: Why, despite our avowals to the contrary, do so many of us not give the much touted "gift of life"? That troubling question, at any rate, I have sought to pose as provocatively as I know how.*

From the start, there have been two major obstacles to the success of organ transplant programs, both of which can be called by the single name *rejection*. Most often that term is applied to a host body's stubborn refusal to accept the organs of another as its own; and since such reactions are purely somatic, physiological, chemical, their solutions are sought and sometimes successfully found in the laboratory. In ordinary usage, however, *rejection* implies volition, a psychological response not soluble by mechanical means. Less metaphorically, then, it can be used to describe the failure of the majority of our population to become organ donors, which has caused the evergrowing gap between supply and demand that so vexes the sponsors of transplant programs. Especially vexing to them, it seems to me, should be the refusal of young males (the optimum field for organ harvesting) to pledge parts of their bodies for posthumous donation, or of their surviving family members to permit their dismemberment after death.

To deal with this sort of rejection involves making changes not in the soma but in the psyche. This would be difficult enough in any case, but what makes it especially so is that the attitudes which underlie it are rooted in fears and fantasies below the level of full consciousness. Clear evidence of this is to be found in the fact that, when asked by pollsters, 90 percent of the same population that resists organ transplantation indicates a willingness, even an eagerness, to become a donor. There is, that is to say, a puzzling contradiction between what most potential donors say they are prepared to do and what most of them end up doing.

This is not mere hypocrisy. Rather it results from a profound, though quite unsuspected, contradiction between the conscious acceptance and the unconscious repulsion many of us—perhaps, to some degree, all of us—feel when confronted with a presumably benign surgical procedure that challenges our most deep-seated, primal notions about life and death, the self and the other, body and spirit: a procedure, moreover, conducted without any of the consoling rituals traditionally accorded the cadavers of our beloved ones.

In light of this, the naive strategies of indoctrination currently used to persuade the young to become donors of their own body parts evidently will not work—certainly not the one I recently received through the mail, urging that required courses on the benefits of organ donation be given in all high schools as part of driver training. It is a persuasive technique equaled in its naïveté only by the Donor Award Patches currently being offered by the Boy Scouts of America to members who pledge to "give the gift of life." Both, moreover, use pious and humane metaphors presumably more effective in moving the general public than the horticultural ones, like *transplantation* itself and *harvesting*, employed by medical professionals talking to each other.

Yet though less dehumanizing, even these religioid figures of speech are likely to be greeted with skepticism by the streetwise disenchanted young men (many of them poor and/or black) who are the suicides or the victims of traffic accidents and urban violence, and who provide the eminently suitable *membra disjecta* for transplantation. Indeed, they are unlikely to persuade very many of any gender, race, or class at the deep psychic levels where instinctive rejection occurs and where what matters is not our conscious beliefs but the myths that possess the underminds of us all. It is, therefore, those myths—the unconscious grids of perception through which we see the world—that we must understand if we are to come to terms with the problem of psychological rejection. I say "come to terms with" rather than "overcome" because I am not sure that we can overcome this problem in the foreseeable future, if ever.

But where to find such myths is a question not easily answered. It is tempting to look for them in the creeds of the established churches, to which the majority of us at least nominally belong. This, however, turns out to be of little use, since, as the propaganda leaflet to which I earlier alluded proudly and truly asserts, "All the major religions support organ and tissue donation." Indeed, the many sects and denominations of America (including the Roman Catholic, as the latest revision of their official catechism makes clear) are less conflicted and divided on this issue than on such other ethically problematic medical procedures as euthanasia, abortion, and *in vitro* fertilization.

In any case, the myth systems to which we late-twentieth-century Americans pay lip service on whatever our sabbaths may happen to be are not those that determine our daily behavior. No more are the myths implicit in our politics, liberal or conservative, which—to make matters worse—tend finally to divide rather than unite an already heterogeneous, multiethnic society. The sole myth system that unites us all is found in popular culture, which constitutes in fact a kind of unsuspected secular scripture. Certainly we are exposed to the archetypal images that popular culture projects in print and postprint form for a much larger portion of our waking lives than we spend listening to sermons or political speeches. Moreover, precisely because we are not aware that we are being indoctrinated as we watch, listen, or read in quest of entertainment and escape, we are less apt to resist the implicit messages.

One subgenre of popular literature deals centrally with technology, including medical technology, and with the bioethical problems posed by its impact on our lives. This is, of course, science fiction, to which it is, therefore, tempting to turn first, especially since it is at the moment a favorite form of the mass audience. But science fiction did not come into its own until the late 1920s, by which time the basic myths that trigger psychological rejection had already received their classic expression. Moreover, only quite recently have writers in that genre felt able to confront head-on the new procedures that have made organ and tissue transplantation available to a large number of patients, and consequently a topic of general interest.

The stories, in any case, when they do not project juvenile fantasies about transplanted members taking control of their host bodies, tend to be more ideological than mythological. In fictions, that is to say, by highly esteemed writers in the genre (like Robert Silverberg's "Caught in the Organ Draft," or Larry Niven's "The Patchwork Girl" and "The Jigsaw Man"), transplantation is represented as a form of exploitation. Sometimes it is portrayed as being imposed on the powerless young by a dictatorial gerontocracy, eager to add to its other privileges that of indefinitely prolonged life. Sometimes it is described as a stratagem of the very rich, who seduce the desperately impoverished into selling their own flesh, or, where such sales are forbidden by law, hire criminals to rob the graves of anonymous paupers and kidnap, drug, even murder the living poor.

Both of these scenarios seem updated versions of familiar nineteenth-century tales about "resurrection men," the bodysnatchers who provided corpses for dissection in anatomy classes of medical schools and hospitals. This time around, however, doctors, though villains still, are portrayed not as the instigators of such atrocities but merely as accomplices after the fact. In any case, these latter-day tales of "organ-legging" serve to foster similar fears and resent-ment of the medical profession, feeding a preexistent iatrophobia, which ever since the 1960s has been endemic in our society. To make matters worse, these tales have passed into the lore of the streets, in which they are reported as having actually happened. Occasionally, indeed, they do—chiefly in Third World countries like India—but even when the reports are apocryphal, they make it into supermarket scandal sheets, where, though in due course denied and disproved, they are still believed by the credulous.

Nonetheless, no late-twentieth-century grave robber has as yet been mythicized like those of the last century—the notorious Burke and Hare, for instance. Nor, for that matter, have any of the charac-ters in more recent science fiction entered the communal night-mares that trouble our sleep. Such mythological status has, how-ever, been achieved by the protagonists of four popular novels, which still in reprints and new postprint versions attract the mass audience and continue to haunt the nightmares we all share.

The first of these, Mary Shelley's *Frankenstein*, was written when the nineteenth century had barely begun; and the other three, Bram Stoker's *Dracula*, Robert Louis Stevenson's *Dr. Jekyll and Mr. Hyde*, and H. G. Wells's *Island of Dr. Moreau*, appeared in the last decades of that century. All of them, that is to say, were pub-lished not only before transplantation had become viable but also before science fiction, that literary genre that anticipates the tech-nology of the future, had found a proper name and a distinctive identity. All four, though not quite science fiction, seem forerunners of that form at its most bleakly dystopian, but they more closely resemble a related though finally different genre, the horror story.

Beginning in the late eighteenth century with the Gothic romance or tale of terror, and imported into this country by Edgar Allan Poe, such fictions have remained favorites of American readers down to the present day, most notoriously perhaps in the super best-sellers of Stephen King. Earlier examples of the form, however, typically seek to make us shudder by evoking the occult and supernatural; whereas three of the mythic books we are examining deal solely with what is, though terrifying, naturally explicable, the fourth, *Dracula*, treats both the natural and the supernatural.

What all four try to frighten us with are primarily the new horrors that have come to haunt us after the Age of Reason had presumably laid to rest forever all traditional demons and bugaboos. These are, of course, the horrors created by modern science and technology, particularly in the field of medicine, whose procedures most of us sooner or later become all too familiar with at first hand. Driven by pain and fear we entrust ourselves to such healers, even though their methods for averting death and prolonging life challenge our most dearly held beliefs about mortality and immortality. Small wonder then that, in our most archetypal fictions, doctors tend to be portrayed as villains, who, having hubristically usurped the divine power to create and destroy, end by bringing disaster on themselves and those they hold most dear.

More specifically, Wells's Dr. Moreau is portrayed as attempting, with an utter disregard for the pain inflicted, to take the process of evolution into his own hands: turning beasts into men by vivisections, plastic surgery, and hypnosis. Stevenson's Dr. Jekyll, on the other hand, experiments only on himself, releasing by psychochemistry all the dark impulses we normally repress for the sake of civility—and simultaneously altering the fleshy envelope of his body, which his potion makes younger even as it turns it repulsive. In the end he is trapped in that body, becoming a serial murderer, whose last victim is himself.

Bram Stoker's *Dracula* seems at first glance anomalous in this regard: although there are two doctors in the major *dramatis personae*, neither is identified as a villain. The first, Dr. Seward, a psychiatrist, however ineffectual, is clearly on the side of good, while the second, Dr. Bram Van Helsing, is portrayed as the enemy of the villainous vampire. On closer examination, however, Van Helsing turns out to be a disconcertingly ambiguous figure, as much an alter ego as an antagonist of that villain.

To begin with, Van Helsing, too, is a stranger in a strange land, speaking English with a foreign accent. Moreover, though he is introduced as "one of the most advanced scientists of the day," having (as we learn eventually) "revolutionized therapeutics by the discovery of the continuous evolution of brain matter," the only scientific means he uses to thwart the vampire is blood transfusion. For the rest he depends on Old World charms and amulets like wreaths of garlic, crucifixes, holy water, and stakes driven through the heart.

As a matter of fact, although one of Dracula's cognomens is Vlad Teppish Mad the Impaler), it is the good doctor we actually see impaling the vampire, as well as presiding over a similar ritual mutilation of Lucy Westenra, Vlad's first female victim. In any case, Van Helsing, for the most part, quite like the foe he seeks to destroy, operates in the realm not of modern science but of ancient magic, black and white.

Even transfusion seems finally to belong to that realm, being like vampirism an attempt to prolong life (the vampire, after all, aims not to kill but to make "undead") by transferring vital fluids from one body to another. Additionally, the transfusions from multiple donors, including Van Helsing himself—which he sets up in his earlier vain attempts to save Lucy—end by making her in a sense polyandrous. As when Dracula later forces Mina (Lucy's friend and his second intended female victim) to drink from his veins, Van Helsing's therapeutic mingling of blood calls into question the sanctity of Christian marriage. He perpetrates, that is to say, a travesty of sexual union, which undercuts the orthodox belief that only a man and his wife can and should be made one flesh.

It seems to me quite evident, in any case, that Stoker's fantasy about the irruption of vampirism into the modern world was initially triggered by the invention of blood transfusion, which is, of course, the precursor of organ and tissue transplantation, along with the bioethical problems it poses. Stoker, however, does not deal with those problems as explicitly as Mary Shelley does in *Frankenstein*, which—prophetically, as it were—confronts head-on the dark side of harvesting the body parts of the dead to prolong life. Her hyperbolic "fairy tale" was suggested, she informs us in her introduction, by an overheard conversation about recent experiments in which inert matter was revivified by the passage of an electric current. But in her actual text she never describes the process by which a patchwork of cadaveric parts is transformed into a living being.

What she does depict is the horror of digging up graves and dissecting corpses. Indeed, she does this twice over: once when she relates the creation of the original male monster; and again when she tells how, in response to that monster's demand, Frankenstein begins to fabricate a mate for him. Though he rejects the first creation and never completes the second, Frankenstein pays dearly for both impious attempts to manufacture more-than-human creatures by what amounts to a total body transplant.

Nor does it mitigate his guilt that, as Shelley makes clear from the very start, his motives are benign and his methods scientific. Old-fashioned necromancy, we learn early on, he has long since abandoned as delusory as well as evil. It is therefore in the university laboratory rather than the lairs of magicians that he seeks to discover "the cause and generation of life." And in this sense he is the prototype of the modern white-jacketed surgeon transplanting hearts and livers rather than the heir of alchemists searching for the *elixir vitae*.

To be sure, Shelley never refers to Frankenstein as a doctor, calling him only Victor or Baron. But in the popular mind, he rapidly came to be thought of, and has remained forever, Dr. Frankenstein; his name without that honorific title has been attached instead to his monstrous creation, whom Shelley left nameless. It seems a little surprising all the same that *Frankenstein* so deeply moved its readers long before the hospital had become a major institution, the practice of medicine a prestigious and rewarding (though ambivalently regarded) profession, health care a large part of every national budget, and bioethics a subject of obsessive concern. But surely this is no more surprising than the fact that it has continued to move readers (as have the three other books with which I have linked it); none of them, in fact, has gone out of print to this very day, despite the changes of fashion in literature and lifestyle. After all, they are essentially mythic works, which is to say, they exist out of time, in the eternal now of the collective unconscious.

For the same reason, these books have been felt from the very start as being in the public domain: the property not of their nominal authors but of the mass audience worldwide. Shortly after publication, they were translated into other media: first stage plays, then horror films, TV shows, and eventually comic strips and comic books. Finally, they have escaped from all media and are transmitted by word of mouth—the cognomens of their sinister protagonists turned into common nouns, familiar even to those who have never encountered their stories on the page or on the screen. This is less true of *The Island of Dr. Moreau* than of the others, but *Frankenstein* and

Dr. Jekyll and Mr. Hyde have been thus transmogrified scores of times, while the versions of *Dracula* have reached the hundreds. At the moment I am writing this, indeed, a movie is being released called (a little misleadingly, I gather) *Bram Stoker's Dracula.*

More typically, however, in the course of such metamorphoses the names inscribed on their original title pages have been forgotten by most readers and viewers. Moreover, as only the few like me are aware, much else has been lost, added, or radically changed in the process—not just style and structure, which is inevitable, but theme, plot, and character. Finally, however, even we happy few have to grant that these tales (once again like all true myths) should be stripped by the popular mind of all that it instinctively senses is extraneous, even as it fills in what it feels to be blanks. First of all, subthemes of the original texts that are ideological or personal rather than archetypal and universal tend to disappear in the later recensions. Such subthemes include Bram Stoker's many allusions to new technologies of information storage and retrieval, as well as his references to the impact on traditional morality of the feminist movement of late Victorian times, Mary Shelley's repeated allusions to birthing and mothering, and R. L. Stevenson's reflections on the oedipal encounter of fathers and sons.

Meanwhile, characters absent from the original *dramatis personae* have come to play important roles in the everdeveloping myth. Especially notable among these are the sinister cripple, Igor, who serves as Frankenstein's lab assistant; the even more monstrous bride, who rejects his monster; and the various female characters who have been added to the initially all-male cast of *Dr. Jekyll and Mr. Hyde* to provide occasions for romance or titillating sexual assaults. In addition, certain characters included from the start have been drastically altered; the monster himself, for instance, whom Shelley imagined as fully literate and superarticulate in at least two languages, has become a stuttering analphabetic with bolts in his head.

What has remained untouched, however, or rather what has become ever more clearly defined thanks to such changes, is the mythological core of these tales. At the core, the archetypal doctor is portrayed as an enemy (all the more dangerous because of his good intention) of those traditional beliefs that long enabled us to live at peace with our fragile bodies and our sense of their inescapable mortality. Typically in a lonely setting, which symbolizes his alienation from the rest of humanity, that doctor creates out of himself or the scraps of his dead fellows a creature intended to be better than his imperfect self, perhaps even immortal. Inevitably, though, that creature turns out to be a monster, and his creator even more of one for having dared to usurp the prerogatives of a superhuman creator. That archetypal scenario will, of course, continue to be imagined and reimagined for as long as humanity continues to fear death, calls on science to forestall it, and resents it for doing so.

Moreover, just as the telling of that mythic tale has no foreseeable end, it has no discernible beginning. Indeed, one reason for the instant success of books like *Frankenstein* and *Dracula* is their readers' feeling that the tale they tell is one they have always known without quite being able to formulate it. Even in medieval and early modern times, when society still put its trust in magic rather than technology to conquer the ultimate horror of death, mythic stories embodying that horror and that trust were already being formulated. The best known of these is *Dr. Faustus*, which has come down to us in a play by Christopher Marlowe and a long epic poem by Goethe, along with later plays and operas based largely on them.

Faustus, an ill-fated experimenter, not only succeeded in rejuvenating himself but also created the homunculus, a living human being of miniature size. His methods, to be sure, were not medical (despite his title, he was a magus rather than an M.D.) but thaurnaturgic, beginning with evoking malign spirits and culminating in a pact with the devil. Closer to the techniques of present-day science were those of the alchemists, whose search for the elixir of life also became the subject of many-times-told tales. But though their art was the forerunner of modern chemistry, in their own time they, too, were also portrayed as black magicians risking damnation in a quest for forbidden knowledge.

In our time, however, when many of us have ceased to believe in damnation or indeed in any form of otherworldly life after death, the pursuit of immortality in this life has come to be regarded, on the conscious level, as a benign activity. On the one hand, research in cryonics and cloning is generously supported, and the moribund are provided, at great expense, with prosthetic devices, artificial life-support systems, and of course, transplanted organs, including the mythological heart itself. On the other hand, we are being constantly urged to avoid suspected carcinogens and foods high in cholesterol, including such long-time staples as tobacco and whiskey, coffee, sugar, eggs, and milk, even as we pop vitamin pills and rack our decaying bodies with dieting, jogging, and aerobics. It is as if we were secretly convinced (though we do not confess it openly) that with one more food forbidden, one more exercise regime required, one more miracle drug or surgical procedure perfected, we will all live forever.

Nonetheless, at a deeper level of the psyche, the dark side of our old ambivalence about the quest for immortality keeps suggesting that perhaps this whole strategy is wrong, misguided—finally monstrous; that forestalling death indefinitely is as impious as hastening it was traditionally thought to be; that, in the eloquent words of Shakespeare, "We must endure our going hence even as our coming hither. . . . the readiness is all." Surely, such a conviction underlies the covert rejection of transplantation—not despite but precisely because of its success in prolonging life. Or so, at least, the mythic tales I have been examining would seem to indicate.

Who's the Cowboy? Who's the Indian? The Slowest Gun in the West

As we approach the end of the century in the second decade of which I myself was born, I find myself intrigued and perplexed by the contradictory changes which have occurred during that relatively brief time in the behavior condoned by society and permitted by law. Concentrating on the most passionately debated and widely publicized of these changes—the legalization of abortion and euthanasia—it is possible to think of our age as one of ever-expanding freedoms.

But in a larger context this seems only half true; since though by and large liberals rather than conservatives have played the key role in determining what has been condoned and permitted, for every opening up in the traditional moral code they have sponsored there has been a matching or sometimes overmatching closing down. So, for instance, the consumption of alcohol is no longer prohibited as it was when, at age fifteen, I choked down my first shot of bootleg booze (I really did; I may be the only one in this room who can boast that he had a drink during prohibition in the United States), and the pressure mounts for a similar decriminalization of pot. But opiates like laudanum, once sold freely over the counter, now cannot be bought without a prescription.

In some quarters, moreover, benign stimulants like coffee and tea have also become taboo; and fanatic new prohibitionists have even sought to ban from the family dinner table beverages and foods like milk, cream, butter, eggs, and good red meat, once urged on them as children by their solicitous mothers. So, too, some left-wing puritans forbid their children ice cream, chocolate cake and other classic desserts with which their mothers rewarded them for having eaten up the more nutritious entrées.

To be sure, the only one of such newly nominated forbidden foods which has been accepted as taboo by more than a few of their fellow fanatics is meat—the scare campaign against which has been so successful that it is almost impossible these days to find a cafeteria or school lunchroom in which a diner gnawing a hamburger does not feel himself being stared at contemptuously by a group of self-righteous vegetarians, usually teenage girls.

Moreover, if he is moved to smoke at his meal's ending and is lucky enough to be in one of the rare places where this is still permitted, he is even more likely to attract the cold gaze of pious disapproval, along with, perhaps, a stage-whispered insult or two from a coven of equally self-righteous anti-tobacconists—most of them probably only recently delivered from an addiction to what was once America's favorite drug and now has become its favorite bugaboo.

The anti-nicotine crusade, moreover, shows no signs of letting up. It seems likely, indeed, that long after I am dead and gone—and perhaps the youngest among you as well—politicians will still be finding the noxious weed an occasion for speechifying and the press a source of headlines. Recently, however, another subject has been competing for top place on the agenda of both. This is, as you are of course aware, the uses and abuses of sex, a very old subject, indeed, since like smoking tobacco making love is rooted in a primal human appetite. But two newsworthy events have caused our interest in it to peak: the cosmic tragedy of the AIDS epidemic and the domestic comedy of Bill Clinton's erotic misadventures. Between them they have moved us to re-examine traditional notions of how, how often, and with whom we should ideally consummate that drive.

Since those I have been rather snidely calling the New Puritans were pioneers in this area, it has seemed to me useful to begin by evaluating the code of sexual behavior with which they have proposed to replace the traditional one. As an unreconstructed libertarian, I rejoice in their subversion of the Judaeo-Christian ban on pre- and extra-marital intercourse between consenting heterosexual adults and all intercourse between homosexuals of any age. But I am dismayed by their redefinition of formerly acceptable kinds of flirtation between men and women—the casual slap and tickle or erotic badinage—as "sexual harassment": a crime punishable under the law.

It does not excuse so blatant an infringement of First Amendment rights to argue that it was intended to end the humiliation of women; and no more does it justify the concomitant banning from polite discourse of pejorative names for women. Once started, such lexical cleansing is hard to stop; and indeed, the prohibition of palpably offensive epithets like "bitch" or "bimbo" has led to the banning of apparently neutral ones like "girl" or "lady" for reasons I find it hard to understand and impossible to accept.

Nor did such politically correct euphemizing end here. It has been extended to other beleaguered minorities like the sexually deviant and the physically disabled, as well as stigmatized ethnic groups, especially those of color. As a result, the ruder colloquial epithets by which their stigmatizers formerly identified them have been banned from use not just in books and on the screen, but in academic discourse and polite conversation, quite like what the generations before us called "dirty words"—meaning the once infamous Anglo-Saxon monosyllables, erotic and scatological, which, in my own childhood appeared only in hardcore pornography and the graffiti scrawled by naughty boys on backyard fences and the walls of men's rooms.

Indeed, well into the early years of my adolescence, prissy females still referred to the more horrific of these tabooed epithets coyly as the "F" word and the "S" word. But now, of course, they are spelled out in full in otherwise quite respectable journals and books, and have become, as it were, not just permissible but almost required in the dialogue of pop films and TV shows. Finally, they have made it into the classroom and the lecture hall; so that even aging, tenured professors like me do not hesitate to say, when this seems necessary to make the point, "fuck" and "shit."

It seems to me only mildly ironic (in a realm of discourse where for every zig there is a zag) that delivering the relatively few old dirty words from the censors' limbo was the work of those who at the same moment were consigning a much larger number of new ones to the realm of the forbidden. This turns out not to be the fair swap it might seem at first glance; since while, in the presumably "Bad Old Days," the disciplining of an academic for improperly using a tabooed word was kept strictly in house, in the presumably Better New Ones, the forces of Law and Order are called in from the outside to help. Formerly, the worst that could befall a student found guilty of using such then forbidden words as "ass" or "sonofabitch" or "condom" was the loss of his scholarship or suspension from school, while an instructor accused of a similar offense faced only a delay in promotion or tenure. But nowadays any academic who uses one of the newly forbidden ones like "crip" or "gimp," "fairy" or "faggot, "kike" or (God forbid!) "nigger," may be charged with the felony of infringing on someone's "civil rights"— and if convicted, be sentenced to a whopping fine or a long stay in the slammer.

Much more ironic, it seems to me, is the fact that in order thus to enforce the New Morality, the New Leftists have entered into an alliance with the cops and the courts, whom the Old Leftists hated and feared as understrappers of the oppressive state. Such an alliance, moreover, and the criminalization of all disapproved behavior moves us ever closer to becoming a truly totalitarian state, in which everything that is not forbidden is required and whatever is not required is forbidden. To be sure, though some of these attempts at criminalization have succeeded, sometimes even spectacularly as in the case of tobacco, others have failed. Such failures, however, have impelled those who failed to turn to strategies even more distasteful and dangerous, like guerrilla actions or downright terrorism.

A prime example of the latter is the campaign launched by the self-appointed champions of "animal rights" against the manufacture, sale and wearing of fur and leather garments. As far as I know, no law prohibiting these has ever actually been passed. But perhaps for this very reason, frustrated advocates of such legislation have attacked the wearers of the skins of dead animals, slashing to ribbons the minks or sables they proudly sport. So, too, the pro-animal activists have blocked the entryways to, and broken the show-windows of, shops that sell such wares, and smashed open the pens to free the beasts bred for their pelts.

Nor has the campaign of terror stopped there. Eventually, in fact, any place where creatures thought of as lower on the evolutionary scale are confined, exploited, tortured or killed by others who deem themselves higher up on that scale, is considered fair game. This includes not just zoos and experimental laboratories but slaughterhouses and butcher shops—and even those pastoral sites where hunters gather together to prepare for tracking down their prey. Predictably enough, then, the defenders of animal rights have also supported the banning of the weapons used in hunting, thus becoming, as it were, the fathers (and mothers) of gun control: a movement in which they have been subsequently joined by some who, though untroubled by the killing of pheasants of antelopes, are uneasily aware that those who wield those guns will eventually—both accidentally and on purpose—turn them not just on each other but on some who have never shot at, much less killed, anybody or anything.

With this, I have come at long last to the subject we have supposedly gathered here to discuss, but which I have felt it necessary to approach slowly and circuitously in order to make clear not just who it is that have been trying to classify the possession of guns as a crime, but why they have had so much trouble doing so. It is, I am convinced, because, unlike other problematical activities, like smoking tobacco or shooting dope or eating meat, the legitimacy of owning guns is written into the Law of the Land. That is to say, the right of all Americans to bear arms is guaranteed—presumably for-ever—by the Second Amendment to the Constitution of the United States, or so it is possible to read that Amendment. To be sure, it is phrased there so ambiguously that more litigious advocates of gun control have felt it possible to argue it really does no such thing. But anyone familiar with the long struggle of the rising bourgeoisie for equality, which climaxed in the French and American Revolutions, cannot doubt for a moment that this key passage in our Bill of Rights, like earlier revolutionary manifestoes, unequivocally demanded that along with such other privileges as the rights to vote and to learn to read, once reserved for the ruling class, the formerly oppressed classes should be granted the right to carry guns, which, appropriately enough, to this very day are called in the vernacular, "equalizers."

That egalitarian right, however, which they finally won and have long enjoyed, some Americans (chiefly though not exclusively lower class, politically conservative white males) fear is now threatened by the liberal sponsors of gun controls; and that, to make bad matters even worse, the government of the U.S.A., which they have supported loyally in peace and war (many of them are veterans) is doing little or nothing to protect that right. Consequently the more militant and hopeless of these malcontents—some actually neo-Nazis—have begun to organize themselves into quasi-military bands—marching in protest down hostile city streets; or withdrawing to more peaceful wilderness retreats where they have previously stockpiled weapons to prepare in secret for an inevitable Final Conflict and for survival in the ravished world it will leave behind. That ultimate conflict has not, of course, come and never will; but brushfire combats have already begun to break out, when state or federal troops—scared kids, really, not knowing what it's all about—have been ordered to silence or disarm them.

Reading lurid accounts of such shoot-outs in the press or watching even more lurid shots on TV, the advocates of gun control were not merely outraged but terrified as well, though, of course, they are sitting safety at home and, in any case, they are confirmed in the belief that they are beleaguered and threatened victims rather than heartless victimizers. In a sense, this is a paranoiac fantasy, but in another it is quite true; though, confusingly enough, the same can be said of their opponents' equal and opposite belief. Consequently, so that its own half-truth might prevail, each side has sought to convince some constituency with prestige and clout that their half is truer than the other's. Understandably, both sides turned first in this quest to their elected legislators, though in this area the anti-gun-controllers seemed to have an initial advantage since the well-heeled NRA had long been lobbying Congress on their behalf.

Finally, however, their edge proved to be only marginal, because by and large most lawmakers sided automatically along party lines: the Democrats supporting the purportedly liberal cause, the Republicans the one considered conservative. To escape that ideological stalemate, advisors for both sides seem to have urged that an attempt should be made to appeal more directly to the people, the shortest way to whose heads and hearts was the mass media. However, most of the movers and shakers of Show Biz, no matter how notoriously conservative in the past, are now, ostensibly at least, liberals—on all public occasions, for instance, deploring the anti-leftist black listings of radicals in the '50s, and in the '80s and '90s sporting red ribbons to show their solidarity with the bleedingheart cause of the moment. I was not surprised, therefore, when just as I was writing this (it was Prime Time in the midst of the last Sweeps before the Summer Lull), the most highly publicized show of the evening, a semi-documentary called *Incident on Long Island* (one of whose producers and chief financial backers was Barbra Streisand), turned out to be a piece of flagrant pro-gun control propaganda.

I had not realized before watching it that it would treat that subject at all; though I recognized that the incident to which its title referred was the messy attempt at mass slaughter perpetrated on a Long Island commuter train by a paranoid black racist all of whose intended victims were white. One of those he actually killed was in fact the husband, and one of the seriously wounded the son of Carolyn McCarthy, a white woman who eventually wrote the first person account from which the film was made.

What interested and disturbed me about that atrocity, however, had nothing to do with gun control. What it triggered in me was a meditation on the historical and psychosocial roots of the vicious circle of hatred and incomprehension, violence and counterviolence, in which black and white Americans have been trapped for so long—and from which it sometimes seems we may never manage to escape. It did not occur to me that the event had happened because a particular man had found it so easy to buy a particular weapon on a particular day; and that consequently it and other such catastrophes could have been avoided by the passage of stricter gun control laws.

So blithe a faith in preventive legislation seems to me incredibly naive, since we have long since learned that though prohibition may jack up the price of forbidden goods, it does not necessarily lessen their availability. But even more so, I found disturbing the blindness of the makers of this film to the role played by race not just in this but in many violent crimes. As a matter of fact, that subject is never raised at all in the TV script except in one short intruded film clip of William Kunstler speaking of "black rage," in an apparent attempt to exculpate the African-American assassin.

In context, however, that radical do-gooder lawyer is made to seem a minor villain and his comment irrelevant if not actually downright malicious. He is, in any case, like its other villains, major and minor, male in a book whose only true hero is female: a kind of superwoman, in fact, who meets the criteria of female virtue in both the traditional old and the revolutionary new moral codes. On the one hand, she is "An angel in the house," a good Christian wife and mother, competent housekeeper and nurse. On the other, she is a formidable presence the public arena (eventually elected to congress on the Democratic ticket) who fights the good fight for what is deemed politically correct, like "freedom of choice" and gun control, and against that which is not, like capital punishment, negative political campaigning and poverty.

That I ended up hating her cordially will surprise none of you already aware that I prize ambivalence more than self-righteous certainty, believing, like Melville before me, that all who say yes—especially to what is considered gospel in their own little world—lie! And, like William Burroughs, convinced that the world would be a better place if a toxin could be invented that would kill only those who think they are right. Still, I am occasionally moved to say, "Yes, but . . . ,"as I am about to do to the argument that no matter what its cost in terms of personal freedom, some measure of gun control is at this moment urgently, desperately needed to save the children. There has always been deep in my psyche a longing not just to snatch deadly weapons from the hands of kids—but also to calumniate self-righteously those who put them there.

So, for instance, I reacted back in 1970, when I visited Odessa in what was still the Soviet Union, and my patriotic guide proudly watched with me an array of twelve-year-old boys and girls marching in uniform and with guns on their shoulders past a monument dedicated to the sailors who had died in the second World War. "Is it not beautiful," she asked, "to see these youngsters honoring the fallen Naval Heroes of the Great Patriotic War?" To this I replied, "Though not yet fallen, I am also a 'Naval Hero,' but I think kids like these would be better off at home playing games or reading books with no guns in sight." At this she wept and I, I am ashamed to admit, smugly smirked—forgetting what surely I already knew, that given free choice the books they would have read would be accounts of bloody combat, and the games they played would be Russian versions of "Cops and Robbers" or "Cowboys and Indians." Certainly these were the choices made as a child and later watched my own children making. Unlike my more righteous friends and neighbors at the time, however, I did not lecture them for wasting time on such trash; instead, I sometimes joined them in acting out their gun-centered fantasies—and even on some rare occasions, I would bring out as an additional prop a forty-five caliber automatic pistol—a real gun I had acquired in a real war.

AND HERE IT IS!

At this point I had originally intended to bring out for you that forty-five and bang it down like a gavel to signal my coming out of the closet as a gun lover—or rather out of the sock and handkerchief drawer in which my wife had persuaded me to hide that weapon, which finally, of course, I was not brave or foolish enough to try to smuggle across an international border. You will therefore have to take my word for it that I have it still in my possession after more than half a century—having resisted an offers to trade it in for cash, and snatching it from the smoldering ashes of a fire that almost totally destroyed my home. So, too, you will have to accept on faith the fact that, after being so loved for so long, that gun is still virgin, which is to say, I have never fired it. Indeed, even though I have hundreds of times in the playground and in the back yard blasted imaginary enemies with toy revolvers, cap pistols, water guns, sticks, twigs and, when nothing else was available, my naked index finger (*"Bang Bang*, you're dead," my child's voice still cries in my remembering head and "the hell I am," the boy next door—in fact long dead—replies), I have never pulled the trigger of any honest-to-god firearm.

Before I grew too old to play out such masturbatory fantasies in the waking world, I had begun to live them in the world of dreams, in which we seem never to grow old. Quite soon, moreover, I discovered that for the price of admission to the local movie theater (in those days only a dime) I could attain what Thoreau called the most blessed of states, "to be in dreams awake"; that is, I could while booing and cheering and munching jujubes in my grubby native city also be riding and shooting in the mythological West of *The Virginian* (1929) or *Riders of the Purple Sage* (1931). Only much later did I learn that these classic films were based on novels by Owen Wister and Zane Grey; in which "the simpleminded plot of the shoot-out between the hero and the villain, both males, had been complicated and enriched by the addition of a female third character.

Beloved by the former, who eventually saves and marries her and threatened by the latter, who seeks to murder or rape her, she had not made it into the sexless games we played as pre-pubescent kids. But she had already become a standard feature of "adult" Western pulp stories, paperback books and radio and TV shows. In these she continued to play a major role well into the late 1960s— typically portrayed as a church-going schoolmarm skeptical about the macho code of the West: an advocate *ante lettera*, as it were, of what we have come to call "gun control." It is of course not in the name of liberal "political correctness" but of pacifist Christianity and bourgeois gentility that she pleads with her would-be protector not to shoot it out with the villain but to turn the other cheek.

Realizing, however, at the last possible moment that this in-advised strategy would mean the destruction of them both, she abjectly apologizes to her beloved for her female weakness and, by implication at least, disavows Christian morality. "Master, be merciful," she cries out, "you are a man. When you buckled on your guns I loved you then." At that point, not only is the doom of the villain sealed—but the ultimate establishment of lasting peace and, security for a well-armed America is assured.

Equally popular during the same period is another kind of Western (about which I have written at considerable length elsewhere) set in a frontier wilderness where even schoolmarm and the prostitute have not yet arrived. In that world without white women, the lonely white male is compelled to seek for an alternative "help-meet unto him," and finally he finds one—improbably enough—in a redskin warrior; a refugee from the tents of his enemy, as the pale face himself is from the settlements of his people.

Before the novels of Owen Wister and Zane Grey had appeared, James Fenimore Cooper had already described such an interethnic, homoerotic union in his *Leatherstocking Tales*, in which the white refugee from civilization abandons along with much else his white man's name. Though baptized "Natty Bumppo" he is re-named in Indian fashion at each critical stage of his life with descriptive

names like Deer Slayer, Hawkeye and *La longue Carabine* or Long
Rifle.

Of all these the last seems to me the most mythologically reso-
nant, suggesting that Natty and the long line of uniquely American
heroes created in his image not merely carry them but in some sense
are one with their weapons, which seem finally as vital a part of
their essential selves as their maleness or their American-ness.

It is, in any case, only on that weapon and themselves that such
uniquely American heroes can depend, when, at the moment of their
final showdown with the overwhelming forces of evil, they find
themselves absolutely alone: the Community they defend having
turned its back on them out of fear or indifference; and their few
true friends being—for one reason or another—simply not there.
Whenever, therefore, we come upon characters in this plight, we
recognize them as authentic re-embodiments of Natty-Long Rifle,
however much their superficial appearance has changed. Though
they sometimes these days still come on as woodsmen or cowboys,
they are more likely to assume the guise of undercover Narcs, street
cops, private eyes, spies, mercenaries or Marines. Even more confusingly they often wear the immediately recognizable faces of the
actors who play them; macho favorites of the moment like Clark
Gable and Gary Cooper, John Wayne or Clint Eastwood.

Consequently, such latter-day avatars of Natty are typically
found in, such not-quite-respectable pop genres as the Detective
Story, the Horror Novel, the Tale of Wilderness Adventure and the
War Story—as well as much Fantasy and Science Fiction—and, of
course, as always the Western. All these genres are aimed at the male
audience, in order to lure whom away from watching sports they are
set in a world of bloodshed and mayhem, with a constant rat-a-tat-
tat of guns on the sound track loud enough to drown out all polite
conversation. Occasionally a work glorifying the Killer with a Gun
makes it—in drag, so to speak—into Female pop, too; most notably
in that best known and most loved of Ladies' Romances, Margaret
Mitchell's *Gone with the Wind* (1939). In it, her heroine, Scarlett
O'Hara, experiences the full orgasm which she had apparently never
achieved in bed, when she shoots to death a Yankee Soldier.

Mitchell's all time best-seller was, however, ignored or savaged
by some elitist critics and self-righteous moralists. Nor was this, as

they claimed, but because like all pop it was slick and shallow—
less a work of art than a commodity packaged and hyped for quick
sale on the cultural supermarket. They seem also to have been
turned off by Mitchell's sadomasochistic portrayal of Scarlett as a
justified Killer. Certainly they have similarly vilified other works
which similarly glorified violence, and its practitioners, even when
they were clearly high art, intended from the start not for instant
commercial success but for preservation in the libraries of the
future. Their authors include such troubled and troubling but gifted
writers as Hemingway and Faulkner, Stephen Crane, and Jack
London, John Steinbeck and Norman Mailer.

Despite the critics, these highbrows live on not just in libraries,
as they desired, but disconcertingly also in the hearts of the mass
audience side by side with equally troubling but less gifted low-
brows like Rex Stout and John D. MacDonald, Louis Lamour and
Margaret Mitchell. Indeed, joined in this improbable alliance, such
highbrows and low-brows have created a mythic grid through
which certain key figures of our history have come to be perceived—or even have come to perceive themselves—as "Justified
Killers," no matter how ambiguous their motives and equivocal
their achievements. Included in their ranks are figures otherwise as
different from each other as Davy Crockett and Daniel Boone, Gen-
erals Custer and MacArthur, John Brown and Nat Turner, Theodore
Roosevelt and Buffalo Bill, Wyatt Earp and Malcolm X.

Most Americans find it possible to identify only with some of
these, few with none or all. But the composite archetype of the
Righteous Gunslinger, to which they add up, lurks somewhere in
the deep psyche of everyone of us—influencing at a level below
that of full consciousness our political attitudes, whether we are liberals or conservatives.

This is particularly true in the case of gun control. And realizing
this, its more ardent advocates have sought to prevent the circulation of all new works glorifying the Hero with a Gun. Being as contemptuous of First Amendment rights as of those protected by the
Second Amendment, such would-be censors do not hesitate to call
for their total banning particularly on the air. Failing this, they advocate attaching to such presumably dangerous matter warning
labels—and providing anxious parents with the technological

means for blocking their children's access to material thus labeled. Unwilling to confess that they despise freedom of speech, the gun controllers contend that their censorship is directed not against what they themselves consider "politically incorrect" but at what everyone finds intolerably "violent."

To be sure, everyone does so because it is in fact violent; but so also are the plays of Sophocles and Shakespeare—and, for that matter, much of the Old Testament. I must confess that I have a special fondness for works of art which, like them, are intended to move us to "pity and fear"; so that, for instance, I do not willingly watch on television any program rated higher than "R." Why then have I not taken advantage of this opportunity to condemn without reservation or qualification the holier-than-thou censors of violence and advocates of gun control? After all, in addition to everything else that inclines me to do so, is my long term opposition to any attempt to prohibit for any reason any previously permissible form of human behavior. Despite all this, I have continued to equivocate—in large part I fear, because I find the defenders of the Second Amendment often as smug and sometimes even more obtuse than those who seek to repeal it. This is, however, mere snobbery—and does little to explain why on the subject of gun control I am not just ambivalent, as I am about almost everything, but ambivalent about my ambivalence. A clue to why this is so is to be found, I am convinced, in the fact that while, on the one hand, I have treasured my deadly beautiful .45, on the other, I have not only never fired it, but never stripped, cleaned, or loaded it as well. The first part of this paradox is easily explicable in light of my long exposure to the archetype of the Lonely Hero with the Gun, but the second part is harder to explain. It is tempting to try to do so by talking a little about the kind of community in which I lived during the first twenty years of that exposure: its inhabitants petty-bourgeois, second generation East European Jews, all of whom could have boasted that like me they have never fired—and certainly never owned—a lethal firearm. Moreover, they did their best to continue that pacifist tradition—gifting their sons when they came of age, not with beebee guns or even Swiss pen knives, but fountain pens. To be sure there were tales of bloody combat told in those environs—some by my own grandfather; but in them the killers were not portrayed as

Heroes but as Villains: Cossacks and *pogromchiks*, whose victims were, of course, Jews.

Tempting as it is to attribute my encrypted desire to silence all guns to my upbringing in Newark, New Jersey, I find it a theory hard to sustain in light of the fact that my only brother, who grew up in the same milieu, became a decorated war hero and a lifelong covert agent for the CIA. Moreover, I, as soon as I could, fled westward ending up finally in Missoula, Montana, a goyish town in which no activities were suspended on Yom Kippur, but everything shut down on opening day of the hunting season—and there was no household without a well-filled gun rack. Yet though I finally did not leave Montana for twenty-three years, I never in all that time picked up a gun—in order perhaps to bug those of my neighbors whom I thought of as "the Cowboys"; since they wore the faces which I had encountered before only in my dreams: faces not made for sociability but only for gazing toward some distant horizon out of which an enemy would come. But this is also, of course, the face of Gary Cooper gazing down the railroad tracks, prepared for the final shoot-out in *High Noon* (1952), which triggered those dreams to begin with. Those cowboys were, in fact, descendants of the pure white pioneers who had stolen that beautiful land from the Indians, and my refusal to play cowboy with them did bug them, since occasionally one of them would take time enough from buying and selling and suing another to drop me an anonymous note, reading "JEW COMMIE FAGGOT GO, HOME!!!"

The response of the actual Indians, however, was quite different. Perhaps because they recognized me as a fellow outsider, or realized that I had smoked without shame or apology the Holy Weed they had given to the world, they took me in. The Blackfeet, indeed, finally adopted me, giving me the name of Heavy Runner: one of their most admired warrior-chiefs, who had, they informed me, "gone East and come back with the weapons of his enemy." *Go thou and do like we*, they seemed to imply. And this almost made me giggle; since I was about to spend a year's leave teaching at Princeton and could not help speculating about which venerable Ivy League academic I would despoil and what weapon I would strip him of. I never decided on my victim but knew immediately that what I robbed him of would be the PMLA, an unreadable scholarly journal called in our house "the deadliest of weapons" since we used it only for swatting flies.

For some reason it did not occur to me until much later that the implied Blackfoot prophecy had already been fulfilled; since on an earlier, longer leave taken after I had surprised everyone, including myself, by joining the Navy, I had gone east as far as China, and returned with a trophy weapon. It is hard, however, to think of any sense in which those from whom I took it could be considered my enemy. The official enemy in that war in the East was, of course, the Japanese, from whom I took nothing. Indeed, as a Japanese interpreter and interrogator of prisoners of war I was forbidden to loot or harm them—much less to slaughter them or suffer them to be slaughtered. Even when I found myself on the bloody beaches of Iwo Jima, where the order of the day on both sides was kill or be killed, I invested all my time and effort in keeping those on our side from killing those on theirs. Ostensibly, my intervention was intended only to keep those prisoners alive long enough for a proper interrogation, but neither side appears to have believed this. The Japanese saw me as a heroic savior who had rescued them from their cruel captors, bonding ever closer with me in the ensuing interrogation and crying out, when the time came for us to part, "I love you. Take me home with you."

To play my part properly in this scenario I actually felt it incumbent upon me not to carry a gun; but this, of course, only further exacerbated the distrust and hostility of those on our side who already believed I was a double agent, which—like all interrogators—I was.

When fighting on Iwo which it seemed would never end, finally did, I was shipped off to Guam, the last stage, we were told, before the invasion of Japan and for which we prepared by drinking ourselves insensible day after day, night after night. I therefore felt no pain when I was for the first time actually issued a gun and ordered to wear it, as I led a platoon of equally sodden enlisted men into the dark heart of a woods where a last hold-out Japanese soldier was reputed to be hiding. Fortunately for all of us, we never found him, and so this gun, too, remained unfired.

On the very next day, in any case, the Bomb was dropped, ending the war, and in the ensuing hubbub that gun was lost or stolen. But that scarcely mattered since though also a classic forty-five, it was not destined to be the one I have for so long preserved. That prize awaited me in China where we were routed now instead of to Japan. Though at first we were welcomed there like liberators, the cheers soon stopped: and the curious crowds that gathered still to gawk at us instead of shouting, "Hubba, hubba, Joe," yelled, "Yankee go home." At that point our cautious commanding officer decreed that none of us should walk alone in the street but in pairs, at least one of whom should be armed. Happily, my favorite partner at that time, a dapper and articulate marine, turned out to be an expert procurer who procured for us a brand new forty-five. But fearing the unsightly bulge it would cause in his tailor-made uniform, he urged me to carry it, since in my ill-fitting jacket, he assured me, one more bulge would scarcely be noted. And I complied, not realizing, of course, that once I had stowed away that weapon I would never part with it. Occasionally, I have been moved to thank that dapper donor for his condescending gift—but have had no opportunity.

I did in fact see him once in the ensuing years. But that was on TV which had caught him—a veteran congressman by then (and dapper still) in the midst of a speech in which he was contending that a fellow marine, adored by many as a hero, was in fact an arrant villain. But I am unable any longer to stand immersion in a realm of discourse where it is difficult to tell a hero from a villain, an ally from an enemy—even good from bad. So very quickly I switched him off and went channel hopping in search of an old-fashioned, Western—preferably one starring John Wayne or Gary Cooper—in which a gunslinger whom everyone knows is good shoots it out with one everyone knows is bad and the Good Guy wins, as everyone knows he will in the long lost land of Let's Pretend.

Introduction to
The Star Rover by Jack London

WHEN IT APPEARED in 1915, *The Star Rover* sold fewer copies than any of Jack London's previously published novels. Consequently, it was soon allowed to go out of print, and it remained in that limbo of lost books for more than half a century. Though reprinted in England in 1967, under the alternative title of *The Jacket*, it has never been reissued in America under any title. It was excluded even from the two-volume collected fiction and nonfiction of Jack London published by the Library of America in 1982. This was a predictable enough exclusion, since that book was aimed at the academic market where *The Star Rover* had long since become unsaleable. Certainly, in no literature class I ever attended has it been mentioned, much less assigned and studied. It has, moreover, been similarly ignored in that rival source of information and entertainment, the post-print media. Though apparently a movie was once made of it, the filmed version has never been shown on the tube—not even during the wee hours of the morning when other fictions stillborn in print are given a second life.

Finally, in areas where neither esthetics nor popular appeal but political correctness determines whether a book lives or dies, *The Star Rover* has fared no better. Yet I, growing up in a city where the chief communist-front cultural organization was called the Jack London Club, originally thought of him as primarily a left-wing political writer. And this seemed to me to be confirmed when walking past a grubby urban park one day (it was during the Great Depression, and I had just turned fourteen), I heard his name being shouted by a speaker invisible to me behind the heads of the small

433

group of idlers that had gathered to listen to him. Moving in closer, however, I discovered that he was an obviously drunken hobo reading aloud from a book he held in his trembling hand. That book was, of course (what else could it have been?) Jack London's *The Iron Heel*. Blunt, unsubtle, and as immune to doubt or qualification as a Fourth of July Oration or an Easter Sunday sermon, for that very reason it still sells today, even making it occasionally on TV and in the classroom.

It has succeeded, that is to say, in every place and every way that *The Star Rover* has not, making me realize that his later, wiser book is, of all London's works, the one least likely to be read by a radical hobo in the park. Yet just before it was due to appear, London may well have believed that it would win the approval of Marxist intellectuals and the love of the left-leaning rank and file. After all, many of its pages were devoted to impassioned propaganda on behalf of prison reform and tirades against capital punishment—backed up by scrupulously documented descriptions of the horrors encountered by the incarcerated in the corrupt jails of capitalist California. Yet that ill-fated book turned out to be as invisible to London's fellow socialists as it had to almost everyone else except me. But I keep asking, as London himself must have asked, *why?*

The Star Rover, though like all London's books, was written with one eye on the marketplace, was as serious and solidly structured as London could make it; since, as he surely sensed only two years from his early death, it represented his last chance to write the book about prisons and prisoners he had promised himself he would write ever since he was sixteen. At that age, he had been convicted of "vagrancy" and sentenced to thirty days in the Erie County Penitentiary; an experience he found so traumatic that he vowed that thenceforward instead of actually living the hobo life which had left him friendless and terrified behind bars, he would only write about it—and doing so get rich and famous.

He had apparently planned to begin his career as an author by publishing a book about the experience which had prompted it, but this proved to be much more difficult than he had imagined. Indeed, it was thirteen long years before he was able to deal at all with that subject—by which time he was, in fact, well on the way to

becoming a millionaire, thanks to bestsellers on quite different subjects, like *The Sea Wolf* and *The Call of the Wild*.

When his block broke in 1907 and he got at last to the subject
with which he had hoped to begin, what he produced was pretty
slim: two brief chapters in a short autobiographical book called *The
Road*, which, as its title indicates, deals mainly not with incarcera-
tion but liberation—the freedom of hobo life. What London does
have to say about imprisonment is presented apologetically—with
a warning to the reader written into the text itself: "I do skim lightly
and facetiously the surface of things as I there saw them." Nevertheless, though it is possible to learn a few additional facts from
records preserved in Erie County (that London gave his occupation
as "sailor," for instance, and his religion as "atheist"), all we know
about his time in jail is what he "lightly" tells us in *The Road*, plus
what we read between its "facetious" lines.

It all seems more comic than tragic or pathetic—from the
moment when young Jack walked unsuspectingly into the arms of
the local cops. He had come to Western New York with no intent
more criminal than sightseeing, since while following across the
country, as an observer rather than a participant, one wing of
"Coxey's Army" (a group of militant unemployed marching on
Washington to protest their plight), he had noticed how close they
were to Niagara Falls and decided to take off and see that natural
wonder. He thought of himself, therefore, as a tourist like any other
tourist; not realizing that his plan to beg his meals from door to door
and to sleep out in the open fields rather than patronizing the local
inns and restaurants, made him in the eyes of the Chamber of Commerce—hence of the courts—a criminal.

At any rate, since what we now call being "homeless" and consider a plight to be ameliorated, was then labeled "vagrancy" and
regarded as a punishable offense, London was arrested and sentenced to some thirty days in the pen—his naive ranting and raving
in the courtroom about "habeas corpus" and "trial by jury" simply
ignored or perhaps sniggered at behind his back. Though most real
hobos would have considered a guaranteed month of free food and
lodging something less than a total disaster, this was not how young
London saw it. To him it seemed an unbearably humiliating ordeal.
Yet even according to his own account the worst indignities he suf-

fered were being forced to march in lockstep with an oversized black fellow prisoner and having his newly sprouted first moustache forcibly shaved off. Some have assumed (and whispered gossip in Buffalo confirms their surmise to this very day) that being young and handsome, London must have been raped by his guards or other convicts. But, of course, he does not say so, only hinting that such abuses exist at all in prisons by vague allusions to "unspeakable" and "unthinkable" practices.

In any case, he remained in the vulnerable general population of the jail for just three days of his term, after which he was made a "trustee," one of the dozen or so privileged prisoners whose lives were made easier in return for helping the guards keep some five hundred other less privileged ones in line. To do so, they were permitted to use whatever "force" seemed necessary. How he enjoyed doing this, London reports in detail and with evident relish. Nor does he ever express any regret for his behavior, much less condemn the prison officials for thus turning the inmates against each other. Instead he adds insult to injury by calumniating in retrospect those he helped victimize and oppress. "The scum and dregs of society," he calls them, "a very nightmare of humanity. . . ."

If all of this makes London seem a not very admirable young man, the way in which he became a trustee in the first place makes him seem even less so. Streetwise beyond his years, he spotted immediately an old con who knew how to operate in the slammer and persuaded him to operate in his behalf by smuggling small gifts to him—and flirting with him as well. Making him his "meat," the phrase which London uses to describe their relationship, usually means becoming his lover. But London may have been able to get away with just teasing his older protector, promising him that after their release he would become not just his partner in crime on the streets but his ever-loving buddy for life.

Obviously London had never intended to keep this promise, and did not even risk meeting him at the pre-arranged time and place. Instead, when he hit the streets of Buffalo, he "copped a fast sneak" and a few minutes later was on his way back to innocence and respectability: which is to say, to his home-state of California, where he reentered the educational system out of which he had dropped the first time around, this time finishing high school and enrolling briefly in the university before beginning his career as a full-time freelance writer.

London was still in California when World War I began and he—by then a well-to-do land owner with a beloved second wife and two daughters by an estranged first wife—tried once more to write the hitherto unwritable book about life in prison born of his experience as a lonely, frightened boy. His immediate inspiration were the accounts then appearing in the popular press of the revelations by two actual convicts, Ed Morrell and Jake Oppenheimer, about the cruel and unusual punishments imposed on recalcitrant prisoners in the California jails. Chief among these were permanent solitary confinement and prolonged constraint in straitjackets.

Both of these tortures are prominently featured in *The Star Rover*, not because London ever endured them in prison, but because he had reached a point in life when his multiple ailments were creating in him a gradual loss of mobility and a growing sense of isolation that made him responsive to all images of constriction and loneliness. Similarly, since at least one of those ailments was fatal and his doctors may have therefore warned him of how little time he had left to live, London identified with the condemned men in Death's Row, who not only share the universal horror of knowing that some day they will somehow die, but endure the special torture of knowing when and how their deaths will come.

In any case, death by hanging is central to the plot of *The Star Rover*, in which, for instance, the real-life execution of Oppenheimer, to which he was sentenced for an assault committed while he was already a "lifer," is transferred to the first-person narrator-protagonist of the novel. If this mingling of reality and fantasy seems strange, even stranger is the fact that stripped of his actual fate, Oppenheimer is introduced into the novel as a character along with his friend Morrell, where both of them under their real-life names and with their "real life" prehistories are portrayed as interacting with purely imaginary characters.

It would be a mistake, however, to take too seriously the metaphysical implications of that mingling of fantasy and fact, which after all is an accepted convention in the most popular genre, the historical romance. Besides, London, more interested in money than in metaphysics, may only have been trying, by introducing these legendary superarticulate thugs into his new book, to win back his old-time fans who had recently been lured away by new macho writers like Zane Grey and Edgar Rice Burroughs.

But it did not work because what those disaffected readers wanted was one more familiar pop saga of physical courage triumphing over physical adversity in a wilderness setting—and, in any case, a straightforward page-turner with a proper beginning, middle and, of course, Happy Ending. And though this was what London intended to give them, the book that insisted on writing itself turned out to be an ambiguous psychodrama which moves every way but straight ahead.

To give a semblance of unity and coherence to what threatened to become an untidy tangle of ill-assorted stories, London enclosed them in a narrative frame like those used in Boccaccio's *Decameron* and Chaucer's *Canterbury Tales*. The enclosed tales in the latter two are told to each other by many different narrators brought together by chance. But *The Star Rover* is a soliloquy rather than a colloquy; since in it the stories told for the first time by different voices are retold by a single one belonging to Darrell Standing, who is also the novel's protagonist and the current avatar of a spirit of which the other narrators were earlier incarnations. Standing's unprecedented multiplicity of functions might have bewildered London's old fans, but in the end they would have forgiven or overlooked it. What apparently distressed them to the point of disaffection, however, was his "bourgeois-fication." How could they have identified, as they had with more typical London characters, with one who was not a miner or a sailor, a trapper or a fisherman, a boxer or a hobo; no kind of hard-working, hard-drinking, hard-punching prole, in fact—but, of all things, a university professor.

To make matters even worse, one of the first things Standing reveals about himself is that he has "no aptitude for fighting or war." To be sure, it helps a little when we realize he is telling us this not from behind a desk at the University of California, but through the bars of a cell in San Quentin State Prison where he had already spent eight years of a life-sentence for first-degree murder. He reveals only enough about his crime to create in us a hunger to know how and why a self-declared pacifist committed that ultimate act of violence.

That appetite, however, is never satisfied, since the only reference to his time at the university in Standing's recorded reminiscences has nothing to do with the murder or anyone involved in it. Instead he records having seen at one of his lectures an eleven-year-old girl with an obvious crush on him to which he never responds. No further reminiscences follow this puzzling account of a non-event, because the book is only a few pages away from its conclusion and Standing only a few hours away from his death by hanging.

Not only the frame story of *The Star Rover* but many of the stories it frames thus end with the death of the character with whom we are asked to identify. Though this is an ending which Standing feels is, in his case at least, a happy one, few of London's long-time readers seem to have agreed. Rather they apparently felt that London had betrayed them by breaching the contract that every would-be popular author implicitly makes with the popular audience to provide a "happily-ever-after" in which the Good Guy always kills the Bad Guy and sometimes gets the Good Girl.

As a matter of fact, somewhere in *The Star Rover* London subverted almost all current definitions of a proper Happy Ending. Lovers of *Robinson Crusoe*, for instance, who, like Defoe himself, believed it meant discovering that "WE ARE NOT ALONE," must have been appalled by London's brief travesty in which a stranded seaman waits and waits and waits on his desert island for a Friday who never comes.

Quite as dismayed also were the critics who initially had contended that despite his manifest faults London should be honored as a pioneer realist, one of the first to eschew sentimentality, idealism and fantasy in favor of telling the hard, cold truth. They were thinking when they touted him so highly of such earlier works as *People of the Abyss*, *War of the Classes*, and *The Iron Heel*, but *The Star Rover* they did not even deign to notice for reasons which they have left us to guess. It seems to me clear that what turned them off was the absence from the new novel of any hope for or foreshadowing of what they as socialist sympathizers considered the only true Happy Ending: the emergence of a classless society from the ruins of exploitative capitalism.

It is, indeed, true that though London devoted many pages of *The Star Rover* to detailing the horrors of the California penal system and the corruption of the political machine which sustained it, he never even hinted that both could be radically changed by organized resistance from within or without. Certainly, he nowhere displayed any sympathy for violent protests on the part of the prisoners. On the contrary, he seemed to travesty all such attempts in a long ironic description of a jailbreak which never happened because it was from the start a hoax perpetrated by an obnoxious convict-informer called Cecil Winwood, who hopes to shorten the time still left of the term to which he was sentenced for forgery by revealing to the warden the identities of the imaginary planners of that fictitious mass escape. To make his outrageous fabrication seem plausible, Winwood had persuaded forty particularly hard-nosed cons to go through the motions of preparing for such a break-out.

But they were, needless to say, caught in the act by the forewarned guards whom the warden ordered to beat them into insensibility, and was delighted when his orders were carried out with such gusto that many of the convicts were left life-long mental or physical cripples. The one thing he regretted was that Standing, whom he hated more than any of the other incorrigibles, had not also fallen into the trap. But Winwood, who at this point ceased being just another self-serving scoundrel and began to assume mythic dimensions as villain-in-chief of the novel and the fabulous enemy of Standing, proved more than willing to help out with a new set of lies. A stash of dynamite, he claimed, with which the failed escapees had planned to blow their way out, had not been captured with them but had been hidden in a place within the walls known only to Standing.

If this were indeed true, as the terrified warden seemed to believe, then the use of any means, however atrocious, to make Standing reveal its whereabouts was justified. Raising his level of torture therefore would give the warden both the self-righteous sense of doing his duty and the guilty pleasure of watching pain being inflicted on someone he envied and despised.

Aware that the warden's hatred, seconded by Winwood's, was the cause of his plight, Standing hated them both in return and dreamed of finding an appropriate response. This proved easy enough to do in the case of the dim-witted, barely articulate warden whose use of physical force could be answered by simply surviving and whose brutal threats responded to by employing a condescending irony, all the more effective because not even perceived. The sharp-witted, glib Winwood was harder to deal with, since he used not physical force but words as his weapon—feeling himself more skillful in their use than a mere professor, since he was a poet. So he styled himself at any rate and Standing did not challenge him, though in his mouth that word became pejorative rather than horrific—appearing as it did in the list of insulting epithets he directed at Winwood. A "snitch," Standing called him, "a coward," "a stoolie," and "a surly cur," and finally not just "a poet," but a "weak-chinned, broadbrowed degenerate poet"—meaning, of course, an unmanly man, all brain and no brawn and a sexual deviant to boot.

By resorting to such verbal abuse, Standing had implicitly accepted Winwood's choice of weapons; and in the ensuing war of words it was Winwood who won. The warden, that is to say, believed Winwood's elegant lying story about the jailbreak and the dynamite rather than Standing's homely true account. It was uncertain whether this was because of the forger-poet's greater skill as a teller of tales or simply because accepting Standing's version would have left the warden with no excuse for his earlier brutality. But Standing, believing the first, apparently vowed that given another chance he would avail himself of a more effective weapon than words.

For a while it seemed as if he would never be given such a chance, since Winwood had disappeared from the jail, presumably because his term had in fact been shortened as a reward for his treachery. At the same time Standing, who kept denying that the dynamite had ever existed, was condemned to permanent solitary confinement. There the only visitors allowed were the warden and his enforcers who would appear at irregular intervals to kick and pummel him—and more and more often to strap him into a strait-jacket, or sometimes two, which they learned to pull tighter and tighter. Such torture went on first for hours and then for days at a time, until finally it was hard to tell whether they intended to break Standing's spirit or to kill him.

In any event, he neither confessed nor died. Moreover, though his bruised and suppurating body withered and shrank, he continued to emerge from the jacket smiling insolently at the warden and his sadistic subordinates—or insulting them in terms too subtle for them to understand. No more did they understand how Standing had

survived an ordeal that should have killed him. But they did not
ever ask, content with the inane diagnosis of the prison doctor, who
informed them gravely that Standing did not die because he was a
"wooz," meaning a not-quite-human, a freak.

Had they asked and Standing deigned to reply they would have
only been more confused, since he would doubtless have repeated
the explanation that London attributed to him elsewhere in the book
of how he had learned to reduce his body to a death-like state in
which it felt no pain, while his liberated spirit moved freely through
space and time.

If that explanation seems finally incoherent and unconvincing,
it is not surprising, since London had never had any out-of-body
experience. Moreover, what little he knew at second hand he had
learned not from a respectable philosopher, psychiatrist or psychic
researcher, but from Ed Morrell, the same convicted felon from
whom he had learned about the straitjacket and solitary confinement. London acknowledged his indebtedness in *The Star Rover*, in
which he portrayed Standing, after having been instructed by Morrell himself, trying to find a way to free his spirit from his body, as
his teacher claimed to have done. But he wanted somehow to do it
better, since though Morrell's disembodied spirit had been able to
pass through walls and see what the people on the other side were
doing, they could not see much less interact with him. Moreover, he
was hopelessly entrapped in the time and the identity into which his
body had been born. To get beyond this, Standing felt, would
require a technique based on Morrell's, but both bolder and more
reliable.

Nothing he tried, however, seemed to work, until one day pain
so intense that it blocked out the primal fear of dying enabled him
not merely to endure but to *will* his death—or, more precisely, that
of his body. He did this inch by inch, moving slowly upward from
the tips of his toes to the mythic centers of life, the heart and the
brain—learning as he proceeded that such a voluntary "little death"
did not mean the end of everything forever but only the temporary
cessation of bodily activity and a consequent liberation of the
immortal spirit.

Thus freed, the disembodied self bypassed time and space in an
instantaneous passage to a host body in which it had previously

been incarnated. There it reassumed its old identity and relived whatever happened to have been happening at that moment. Though he had forgotten these events after sloughing off his earlier incarnation, Standing knew he would remember them this time. And so, too, he would remember what he relived in any future incarnations triggered by dying the "little death."

Since he did so die many times in his continuing flight from pain and fully recorded what had happened in *The Star Rover*, such accounts finally took up nearly half of the novel. Feeling this to be excessive and unwarranted, some critics have contended that these presumable accounts of out-of-body experiences are really old London stories which for one reason or another he could not otherwise get into print. Most of them are, indeed, so like his published realistic fiction, that this charge may well be true.

But two of them, the first and last, are utterly different—so fantastic and oneiric that they could only have been written when toward the end of his life, London discovered Freud and Jung; and realizing that he had always been a mythic writer without knowing it, he decided to become one in full consciousness. This switch from ideology to mythology is most evident in the description of a vision that came to Standing after he had successfully entered a trance-state for the first time. "I walked among the stars . . . ," he wrote retrospectively, "I was a child . . . clad in frail, fleecelike, delicately coloured robes . . . like the garb of young angels. . . ." We learn further that this creature (he or she? it is hard to tell) carries a glass wand with which, it is somehow aware, it must tap each passing star to avert a cosmic catastrophe.

Though this brief passage is clearly the source of the title which London finally chose for his novel instead of the jail-related alternatives, *The Jacket* and *The Collar*, Standing almost immediately warns us that what it describes is no more valid than a dream dreamed on opium or a snake seen in the throes of the DTs. "A ridiculous orgy of the imagination" was his final judgment. The reason for so summary a disavowal was not, as we post-Freudians are likely to believe, that this image of his protagonist as a prepubescent in drag betrayed doubts about his own masculinity which London sought desperately to conceal all his life long. It was rather, Standing insisted, that the disembodied spirit first seen walking among the stars never finds—as happens in all true stories of the out-of-body experience—a proper host in which it can reincarnate itself.

Standing, however, never disavowed the last account of such an experience though it, too, is disturbingly anomalous, since its deviance from the norm consisted in telling a tale with a whole host of incarnations rather than the customary single one—and many was apparently more tolerable than none. In any case, a multiplicity of embodiments seemed unavoidable in a tale set, as this was, in the primeval era, which is the end of the line for questing spirits, who can only move backward in time. Since it had, therefore, no place else to go, this stranded spirit sought to reembody itself not once but over and over in the creatures it found where it was—subhuman or almost-human though they might be. Faster and faster it moved until, in Standing's version at least, the world around it seemed to blur it to indistinction. Though finally it came to rest, it was in a larger-than-human scale host who seemed not just another incarnation but the Archetypal Ancestor of us all—which meant, to racist, sexist London, all Aryan males. "Blond, ferocious, a killer and a lover, a meat-eater and a root-digger," was the definition of that first true *Homo sapiens* which London put into the mouth of Standing, whom the word "Lover," somehow reminded of the sapient but passive other half of humanity for whose sake the active half digs and kills, creates and destroys.

In any case, Standing launched into a free-form rhapsody in praise of women, in the course of which he evoked first the names of such mythic avatars of the feminine as Ishtar and Eve, Sheba and Lilith and Cleopatra, then those of actual women he had loved in his many incarnations and finally that of a hitherto unmentioned "Dorothy," who turns out to be the eleven-year-old school girl who had sat at one of his lectures on agronomics with lust for him burning in her eyes. Though at the time he had made no response at all, he never forgot and much later wrote of her, "She was a woman child, but she was the daughter of all women . . . before her . . . the mother of all women after her." However little this tells us about the real girl thus mythicized, it reveals much—encoded in a way that would have tickled Dr. Freud—about Standing and the author who created him.

Though this was Standing's last out-of-body experience, it was not the final recorded act of his life; since when he returned to his body, he discovered that Winwood—a recidivist as well as a stoolie—was back in jail again. But this meant that it was possible to reach him and inflict on him in fact the slow painful death which Standing had kept dreaming of in his absence. First, however, he had to find the strength necessary to break out of his cell. Frail and weak as he had become, his lust for revenge—that dark eros of men without women—proved to be a source of enough energy to enable him to cut through his bars, though not enough to reach his enemy and crush away his life in a fatal embrace. Indeed, he never even got close enough to see his intended victim; since not only had forced starvation turned him into a barely mobile bag of bones, but long confinement in a space scarcely larger than a coffin had made him a hopeless agoraphobe.

Consequently, after Standing had taken a few tottering steps into the terrifyingly open space of the prison yard, he collapsed against the closest wall—unable to rise again. There he was spotted by a husky young guard who hurled his healthy two hundred pounds onto Standing's meager ninety-seven. Despite the discrepancy in weight, Standing somehow managed to struggle long and hard enough to draw a few drops of blood from his assailant's nose. So at least that assailant later claimed; and his story was backed up by some of his fellows who had—quite unnecessarily—come to his aid by self-righteously pounding an already subdued Standing into a bloody pulp.

Though he was the only one seriously hurt in the fracas, Standing alone was hauled into court, where after a show trial, he was sentenced to death by hanging. The law making an assault by a "lifter" a capital crime had been passed well after his initial imprisonment, and the *post-facto* proceedings were therefore invalid; but this troubled no one.

In any event, it seems fitting and proper that a comedy of errors which began with Standing not sentenced to be executed for having actually killed a colleague who in no way threatened him, should end with his being condemned to die for ineffectually striking out at a guard who was viciously attacking him. To compound the irony, moreover, if that guard had assaulted Standing after he had been sentenced to death, it is he who would have been considered a criminal, since a long-standing regulation required that all convicts on Death Row be kept alive and healthy lest the hangman be cheated. His new guards performed this duty so well that Standing was able to finish in peace and without pain the journal in which he hitherto had to scribble his entries surreptiously and in haste. His valedictory "last lines" begin in the affirmative with a declaration of faith: "There is no death. Life is spirit and spirit cannot die." He does not, however, leave it at that, but adds immediately as a kind of qualifying afterthought: "What shall I be when I live again? I wonder. I wonder. . . ." That he thus questions his fate after death and, finding no answer, fades out with the inconclusive punctuation of three dots (. . .) does not finally subvert his faith in immortality.

Yet he continued to wonder; and I wonder, too, though not about what Standing believed. What concerns me instead is the question of whether or not London shared his belief; and if—as I am inclined to think—he did *not*, why he wrote this novel with a sympathetic protagonist who *does*. Unable to find a satisfactory answer in the text itself, I turned for a clue to what London himself told correspondents who had asked him similar questions. But I ended up more confused than when I began because of the inconsistency of his responses.

After reassuring one anxious fan by writing that "the keynote of the book is 'The Spirit Triumphant,' he more disturbingly wrote to another, "I am hopelessly a realist and materialist, believing that when I die I am dead and shall be forever dead." Then he confessed to a third that he had only pretended to take seriously much metaphysical nonsense in hope of producing a book "accessible . . . to the Christian Science folks and . . . the New Thought folks . . . and the millions who are interested in the subject in the United States today. . . ."

By "accessible" he meant, of course, saleable. Yet though there were at that moment millions of Americans bent over tapping tables and communicating with the dead (as London well knew since his mother had been a practicing medium), fewer than two thousand bought *The Star Rover*. This was partly because converts to spiritualism, theosophy and the other then fashionable sects were typically too serious and elitist to seek enlightenment in fantastic pop fiction. For that they turned to scholarly essays, sermons and what purported to be New Scriptures. But they also had special difficulty in coming to terms with the politics and theology of London's novel.

Since they tended to be as genteel as they were serious and as conservative as elitist, they found unacceptable the way in which London combined an advocacy of spiritual enlightenment (which they thoroughly approved) with propaganda for making a socialist revolution (which, of course, they thoroughly abhorred). Moreover, a majority of those "folks" to whom London hoped his work would be "accessible" were, however unorthodox, still theists and so were appalled when they realized that in the cosmos imagined by London, though many paranormal phenomena once considered hallucinations or downright frauds were accepted as "real"—God simply did not exist.

It is unlikely that *The Star Rover* would in any circumstances become a long-term bestseller like *The Call of the Wild*; but it could, I am convinced, become permanently visible to many and cherished by a sizeable minority in a milieu where the audience which London dreamed not only existed but played a key role in the marketplace. For London's America, however, to become such a place would require a cultural revolution that radically changed literature and society—and especially the nature of their relationship. First of all, a new type of reader would have to appear, who preferred fantasy over other sorts of fiction—and had no prejudice against reading it in pulp magazines and mass-produced paperbacks. Such an audience, moreover, would judge literary works not on esthetic or ethical grounds but on their ability to alter consciousness; so that the highest praise for a book would be, "Man, it changed my life!"—or, more briefly, "Wow!"

Such an audience would also consider an interest in the occult not incompatible with but complementary to left-wing political activism. The same people, therefore, who at one moment were chanting, drawing up astrological charts or casting the *I Ching*, would be found, at the next, marching down the street shouting slogans in support of the abused convicts in Attica—or holding candlelight vigils to protest the imminent execution of some rapist or murderer, preferably poor and not white.

Finally, no matter how many new sects appear or old churches survive in that future culture, whether consciously or uncon-

sciously, new trendsetters and taste-makers in fashion and entertainment must espouse the Death-of-God mysticism which has no
other temples than the theaters and auditoriums in which they display themselves and their wares.

But that cultural revolution did in fact occur in the 1960s; and
we live now in a society where the changes advocated by those who
made it have—however institutionalized and commercialized—
been enacted everywhere. Certainly, they dominate the popular arts,
which they helped make the sole part of the culture we all share,
whatever our class, gender or generation. But this, of course, has
also made ours a world familiar with and sympathetic to much in
The Star Rover that its first readers found alienating and bizarre.

Why else at the moment is the eerie-scary *X-Files* one of the
most popular shows on TV? And why is the book in the hands of a
reader on a seat in the subway, a bench in the park, or a folding chair
on the beach more likely to be the latest shocker by Stephen King
than Joyce's *Ulysses* or Faulkner's *The Sound and the Fury*, on the
one hand—or on the other, the *New Testament, The Book of
Mormon*, or *Science and Health*? As I reflected on this some time
ago, it occurred to me that King's bestseller and the smash hit on
television have in common a quasi-religious theme, attempting to
describe which, I wrote: "They believe that they *really* believe that
God is dead. They pretend that they *only* pretend that Dracula—or
Big Foot or the Loch Ness Monster or Creepy-Crawlies from Outer
Space—do live." Then later, upon further reflection, it occurred to
me that the same theme was the subtext of *The Star Rover*, which is
one of the reasons that I think it should be republished *right now*.

So, too, though for other reasons, I believe it should be reborn
right here. It was, to be sure, both written and set in California, but
it never would have been conceived at all if London had not tried to
visit Niagara Falls and ended instead doing thirty days in the Erie
County pen. How appropriate, then, that I who am playing the role
of midwife at this rebirth once found myself locked into a newer jail
still called by that old name. Though I was not there for long, it was
long enough for me to be mug-shot and finger-printed—and to
remember from behind bars this book which, like almost everyone
else, I had forgotten while I was free.

Poetry

Momotaro, Or The Peachboy:
A Japanese Fairy Tale

I. THE FINDING OF THE PEACH

An old wood chopper
And his old, old wife
Lived in the forest
For all of their life.

And the name of the chopper
Was Chopper;
And the name of his wife
Was Wife;
And the name of the days
They lived was Day;
And the name of the nights
Was Night;
But the name of the sum
Of them all was Pain,
For they had borne no child
To bear their name.

Till crouched one day
By the bank of a stream,
Washing her wash
And dreaming her dream,
The old woman saw
A giant peach,

Afloat on the water
Just out of her reach.

Over and over,
It turned in the Sun
Singing a song
Or humming a hum:
"Domburi, Domburi
Reach out your hand;
What is born in the Water
May live on the Land!
What begins as a Peach
May end as a Man.
So wet your feet
And catch, if you can.

Like a Child,
She clutched it,
Clutched at the Peach.
Something to fondle?
Or something to eat?
Like a Child, she held it
Tight to her breast;
But knowing no Names,
How could she guess
What to call it, or
What would come next.

"Peach," she called it,
Carrying it home
To where the Old Man
Waited alone.

II. THE CUTTING OF THE PEACH

"I'll cut it," said the Old Man,
Since cutting was his trade,

"Let's eat what luck has brought us,
Why should we be afraid?"

But his Wife was lost in wonder;
And talk, though not her trade,
Was what she did when she was not
Hanging in a glade
Their wash or the wash of Others,
Or mending what was frayed.

"Hold off," she cried, "or let me,
Who've held it to my breast,
Draw the knife across its skin
As soft as a caress—
I've felt its heart against my heart,
And a mother's touch is best."
"A mother," he cried angrily,
For hunger gnawed his gut,
"What have you borne but empty words.
Be still and let me cut."

But even as they argued
The peach was split, uncleft;
Without a stroke from either one,
It parted right and left.

And there within its bloody heart
They saw a red-gold boy,
A child as red-gold as the fruit,
Whose cry drowned out their joy.

"The child I could not bear," she said,
"Was brought us by the river—
A token like a fallen leaf
For us to keep forever."

"Peachboy is his given name,"
She said, "We have no choice."

"*One* name like him is given,"
He said, "But I rejoice
Another name is ours to give,
And his to bear forever;
Since he is Peachboy Son of Us
Who fetched him from the river."

III. THE COMING OF THE DEMONS

He grew between the two of them,
Like some astounding tree,
Whose only blossom was his face,
Its stem and leaf both he.

Till Demons came one evil day
And blackened with their wings
The noontime sky above their heads
And hushed the birds that sing;
And breathed upon the burgeoning wheat
And turned the seed to dust,
And ate the living cattle up
And chased the maids in lust.

Then Peachboy rose up taller
So that his thrusting head
Split the thatch to let him watch
The demons as they fled.

"I know you now," he cried aloud,
"I know, too, who I am,
For until he has spied his demons
No boy can become a man."

"Bake Milletseed cakes, dear Mother,
Kibidango to fill my sack,
And I'll load your lap with treasure,
When I come riding back."

"But all the skills you taught me, Dad,
And all your sage advice,
Now turn to dirty water,
Like a sheet of rotten ice;
For I must become a father,
Though I was not born a Son
I will beget myself upon myself,
Before my tale is done!"

"Oh, I'll be rich, dear Mother,
When the demons all are dead,
And I will buy you a palace
And a beautiful silken bed.
And Dad will sit in a rocker,
And rust will nibble his ax;
And the house you live in will be my house,
When I come riding back."

"Please take my ax on your journey;
It has killed a thousand trees,
Taller by far than demons,
Lords of the earth and the breeze."

"No, no," said the boy, "dear Father,
I will take the houschold knife
You raised to cut the red-gold fruit
That fed my secret life."

"Take me with you, Peachboy,
Take me, if you can."

"Be still, for a dog or a monkey
Is more use than an old, old man;
A bird or dog or a monkey
More use than a dying man."

IV. THE JOURNEY

The sun behind, the dark ahead,
As if he fled the day,
He set out in search of evening
Along the Demons' Way;
And all the beasts of the forest,
Smelling them hot from the pan,
Longed for his *kibidango*,
The best in all Japan.

First the bird from the highest treetop
Called to him by name,
"Where are you going, Peachboy,
On what journey or quest for fame?"

"I go to the Island of Demons
To conquer their evil King,
And make my dream a story,
A song that the minstrels sing."

"Give me one *kibidango*
And I will fly with you,
Until on the Island of Demons
Your song and mine are through.
And I will call you Master
And serve your every whim;
For I, too, have dreamed a journey,
And know that we shall win."

"Take and eat and fly with me,
For it seems that I have heard
That no man can be a Hero
Until he has talked to a bird."

Then the monkey called out from hiding,
"Peachboy, let me eat, too,
And I will swing from the branches

To spy out the world for you.
And I will call you Master,
And serve your every whim,
For I, too, have dreamed a journey,
And know that we shall win."

"Come eat my *kibidango*,
For it seems to me I've heard
That the man who would be hero
Must be monkey as well as bird."

The inu-san-barked from the bushes,
The dog who has always served man,
"I smell *kibidango*, dear Peachboy,
The best in all Japan.
I will serve you for food not glory,
Since like others I have my own tale
Which I chase in the hope of an ending,
Though I know I will never prevail.
And I will call you master, too,
And serve your every whim,
Though I have dreamed another dream
And know no one can win."

"Take and eat and come with me,
For it seems that I have heard
That the hero must heed the bark of a dog
As well as the song of a bird."

"I love you all, dear brothers,"
The Peachboy said to the three,
"For teaching me here in the forest
That, unlike the fruit of a tree,
I must hide and whimper and scamper,
And chatter and scratch my fleas,
And nip and slaver and growl
And ride the tide of the breeze."

"No man can be a mother,
To this I am resigned;
But though I was born from the heart of a peach,
You three are born from mine."

V. THE DEFEAT

How easy to conquer the Demons
Once he had encountered the beasts.
They lay in a drunken stupor
After a round of feasts,
Lie always in drunken slumber,
And only dream of the feasts;
From which they arise without waking,
To pillage the poor in their sleep.

On the back of the dog he lay hidden,
Fording their moat at high noon;
And the monkey rode on his shoulder,
And the bird flew over the moon,
Singing, "Conquer them all, Momotaro,
While they lie in their beds in a swoon;
For they dream that they dream they are dreaming
In a dream not even their own:
Warp and woof are a web of your weaving,
The test you begged as a boon.
They'll die, if you like, without waking.
Fade out like the vanishing gloom."

But he cried a great cry to arouse them,
And they rushed from the hush in his head,
To fall one by one on the pavement
As the coming of the morning flushed red;
And red as the red of the morning
Were the drops of their blood that he shed.

Till their King alone loomed before him,
A mountain of motionless stone
Eyeless and bloodless, undying,
Unborn on his carved granite throne;
Enthroned for all time in carved granite,
With eyes of unseeing stone.
Then his knife dropped unused to the pavement,
And a chill froze the boy to the bone;
For the unseeing face of the mountain
Was his own flower face turned to stone.

Seeing which, the three beasts in panic
Scrabbled and scratched at his eyes,
Biting hard the soft flesh of their master,
As if he were the foe and the prize.

But "Enough!" cried a voice from the mountain,
"The battle is over and done!"
"Begone!" cried a voice from its caverns,
"What there is to be gained you have won!"

And the Peachboy woke at the roadside,
A league from the place he was born,
Astride a great horse with a scepter
And a spear and a shield and a horn,
And a crown on his head gold as sunrise,
And behind him a treasure was borne
On percherons, palfreys, and asses
And the backs of men better unborn;
While a crowd on both sides of the roadway,
Defined a path to his door,
Where his parents waited to greet him
Their heads bowed down low to the floor.

"Rise up!" he cried out in horror,
"You need not bow down to your son."
His voice was the voice of the thunder,
And his head darkened the disk of the sun,

So all fled save his father and mother,
Who lay dead as he roared, "But I've *won!*"

Child's Play

Only child's play can solve
The spill of birth.
Our lofty mothers let us fall
To pain and when they heard us bawl,
Smiled first.

The stone, the stillest animal
Crouches in the dirt;
There is no brown unlikely love
Can sell it short.

From stone to stone the children sprawl,
Mistake the meaning of their fall,
The insolence of earth.
Their mothers from high windows call,
"The stone, the *stone* is hurt!"

Call It Sleep

One must learn to kill; one betray:
Yang's anguish, the yielding of Yin.
Under the random evasion of play,
Where does the child begin?

A Bloody Husband

A bloody husband thou are because of the circumcision. Exodus, iv, 26

Now February's name is March;
The winds choose for us: flood or parch,
And bare the shoddy earth below
The soft irrelevance of snow.
The child's hand tears the leaf from leaf
To learn time's names and will believe
The boundaries of the calendar;
Though all the grievous blood demur
And flow from twenty-eight to one,
To cry, "The season's never done.
Time bides no circumcision!"

O love, I lay and could not weep
Between those bright angelic teeth,
Head, neck and chest, down to the balls,
For my God's sake and for the false
Delays, delays! You took the stone
And hacked the foreskin from our son
Till God's mouth freed me and I stood
In all that bleeding, free of blood;
Then cried, "O bloody husband!" and
Wept into your sullied hand,
Until the child began to weep,
And cast his flesh before our feet.

My Silver Nutmeg

My silver nutmeg, my golden tree
Pulse like a riveter's shadow,
Dance like a riveter's dream;
They remember over the sea
The silence before your name.

They think, like addled children,
That you are the Princess of Spain.

My silver nutmeg, my golden tree
Pulse like a riveter's shadow,
Dance like a riveter's dream;
They menace the haze of the sea
With the silence after your name.

They say, like boasting children,
That you are the Princess of Spain.

My silver nutmeg,
My golden tree.

Marguerite

Let me enter,
Pale to a sun's center,
Pale as winter,
Gold as wheat,
Fringed, discreet
Marguerite.
Patient power
Along this flower
The unkept hour
Greens to gold—
But cannot hold
For long the cold
Bleaching. How,
Lapped like snow,
And even now,
The petals ice,
Are old. O Christ,
Margaret, twice
We burn; burn center
Gold, and winter
Cold—Let me enter.

In Vain from Love's Preakness I Fly

Win, place or show, tired absolvers,
All day you have repeated the track,
Until now your knowing it quivers
In the dark whose virginity is no joke.

Let me kiss fatigue from your fetlock,
Having in God to love all lovers;
For the humped jockeys rode you today like fevers,
And your iron endings embarrassed the track,
And the wind's desire where your tail made black
Ambush was taken and foundered on the forgotten cock.

Hell,
We needed no programs to know who you were.
Running was what we payed for;
We were still.

Schlepfer's Cocks

God knows I honor Schlepfer's bees,
Who flirt with blossoms on our trees;
And down below our naked knees
Rape zinnias and peonies,
Or make light love to dying phlox;

But greater far are Schlepfer's cocks,
Who crow the barnyard daylight in
To candle eggs that bless their sin.
For if I find it hard at dawn,
Blame Schlepfer's cocks upon the lawn.

Who teach my bird thus soon to rise
And make my lady close her eyes
In something wittier than sleep,
Though just as sibilant and steep.

Dumb Dick

This fugue must be hummed, found
As the wind fumbles, all thumbs.
What drops toward the furred stones,
Founders? Here is a hole in the wind;
Here, nothing! But look, look at our loves
Hung over nothing, hung on the wind's
Rupture—oiled with ourselves, slick
In the sick fury of unselving, sick
On that fool's honey. Dear, only Dumb
Dick glistens, up early, early.
It is always early in that blunt head,
Early to learn, all thunder, all thumbs,
The diving to where we will be dead,
Although living.

Love seethes to suds, seed runs
Like whey in the ravelled vein;
Dumb Dick stands alone, or shrunken
Sleeps. No matter. More than the stunned
Wonder matters, more counts than who comes.
We stumble past coming toward colder
Turnings: the turning in the dark to wheeze,
The head turning as the penned blood stutters,
The cold floor under the spent wonder
Turning, and the learning we are old
Turning like returning thunder.
Love, I will not be done dying,
I will not play dead.

I and My *Mishigas*

I and my *mishigas* strolled by the river,
Watching the holes our stones made in the water.
"Why are we falling," he asked, "is it loving?"
I and my *mishigas* droll by the river.

I and my *mishigas* bawled by the river,
Watching the holes our tears made in the water.
"Why are we feeling," he asked, "is it leaving?"
I and my *mishigas* bold by the river.

I and my *mishigas* danced by the river,
Danced with the drums to bring in the morning,
Danced with the bones to banish the evening.
"Why are we fooling," he asked, "is it living?"
I and my *mishigas* dazed by the river.

"Later," I said, "you will lie down
And tell the man all about it."

"Will he leap from the smoke, ochre and vermilion,
The blood on his belly where the stone knife stuttered,
The grease of a beast on his haunches, rancid,
The face of a beast on his dumb face, screaming?"

"You will lie down and tell the man."

"Will we run with the swine to the lip of the river?
Will he name the Name, turning the Ring on his finger?
Will he come with crossed staves to invoke the Dominions?"

"You will just lie down."

I and my *mishigas* sprawled by the river,
Watching the holes our gods made in the water.

The Deer

The crust of snow sustains the deer;
The deer holds up the sky;
And I, athlete, must balance both
Upon my bloodshot eye.

The endless wind blows through the deer;
The deer steps through the sky;
And both must pass to live again
The needle of my "I."

The Whiteness of the Whale:
Bologna, 1952

Who bled to dry the color of this colonnade
The Bolognese will tell you, naming names;
Shame never dies in parlors where the dead
Once memorized in spite are cited to allay
A lust for conversation. Yet here I fed
As if to break the fast of ghosts, feasted
Till my eyeballs bugged and frozen sweat
Stood on the hot bulge of my brows, then drank
Till morning in a garden where the dead
Snails shrivelled in their pails of salt. "God bless
Begonias!" sang my host. "God bless," I said,
"My bile."
               Six weeks I lay in bed
At odds with life in love with death. Red
Cities turn us tallow-yellow, mallow-soft.
The knowledge of blood's color is forbid
To us whose fathers fled from blood, left
Colonnades like clots of serum for the shade
Of sheds, of lofts, of sidings white as scars.

Risen at last, I took my notes by rail
Back to Bologna, back to my liver's hell,
And lectured on the Whiteness of the Whale.

O Al!

O Al,
What does the heart compel
Where you,
Beyond the urgency of tense,
Eschew
The lie, leave insolence,
All imposition of the will?

O Al,
What does the tongue unspell
Where now,
Beyond the fear of innocence,
You stow
The gab, the mock of eloquence,
All paid performance of the will?

O Al,
What does the blood distill
Where
You, beside sleep's relevance,
Prepare
Beyond the tickle tease of sense
The hushed, dark holiday of will?

Song from Buffalo

In the evening they came to my cavern
Where I lay with the bones of the dead,
Saying: *Sing us a song of rejoicing*
Come out of the web of your head
But I listened to whispers from nowhere
And whispered my answer instead—

At nightfall they came to my cavern
Crying: *Sing us a song for the streets*
Sing a song without rhyming or heartbeat
Since only madness is sweet.

But I'd died on the ovens at Belsen
And killed where the black lava sand
Covered small yellow men I had murdered
And buried my own severed hand.

I cannot sing with my head in an oven
And my fingers awash in the sea
My head turned to ash in an oven
And the ghosts of old friends eating me.

Dear Allen, I remember your singing
By the edge of the algae-dark pool,
And Gregory casting the *I Ching*
And nodding out in his drool.
It was mud I toiled in he told me
And his mouth unwound like a spool . . .

Fiction

Nude Croquet

Don't you ever get tired of being right!" Howard snarled ritually, jamming the brakes down hard as the house rose up from a tangle of runty pines and bushes just where Jessie had said it would be. They had been arguing for twenty minutes about the last turn, he with all the desperate passion of a man without a sense of direction.

"Won't you ever learn how to stop a car!" Jessie snapped back automatically; then, counting the seven crazy turrets, castellated and masked with iron filigree, "Seven! Bernie wasn't exaggerating for once," and at last, "I'm so damn tired of being right, I could *puke!*" She stared miserably at the bats sliding down the evening sky over the slate roofs—her face very pale in the last light. "It'll be raining in half an hour," she added. "There goes your swim."

"Don't sound so happy," he answered, cutting the motor and putting an arm around her shoulder. "Look. Let's turn right around and go home. There's no point in this whole—I mean,

475

what do we have in common any more, Leonard and Bill and I, except our remembered youth—and that's only a reproach. It's just that— I—" He gave up finally, waving his free hand at the grounds before them: the offensive acres of plants and flowers that neither of them could have named, the lily-infested pond barely visible beside the porte-cochere, the untidy extravagance of the great house itself.

Jessie shook herself free of his arm, and pulling her feet up under her, knelt on the seat; she thrust her face forward viciously, almost into the mirror on the sun visor above her. "I look so old —so god-damned *old!*" She touched the creases on her cheeks that had once been dimples, the vein-raddled crescents under her eyes, the ungenerous mouth that had sunk inward, pulling her nose and chin closer together.

"You *are* old. We're old. Forty-three, forty-five—that's not young. What do you want?" Howard turned slowly to look at the face he seldom saw.

"At least my hair's a good color this time." She lifted a lock of it in her bony hand—very red against the white, a splendid red, quite dark yet shot with lights even at that dim hour, just the color Howard liked. "But *you* look like a baby. It isn't fair. A spoiled baby!"

"It's worth paying a little more to get it done right. That other woman was a moron." He tried to concentrate on her hair, but could not resist glancing a little smugly at his own face in the glass, baby-pink and white under the baby-yellow curls, luxuriant and untouched by gray. His face had always been plump and never handsome, but its indestructible youthfulness had managed finally to lend it a certain charm.

"A spoiled baby—and I'm the one who spoils you. I must *want* you to look young. Why the hell do I want that, Howard, when I look like a witch? I know why *you* like it; it makes other women feel sorry for you, yoked to such a hag! But why do I want it, Howard, *why?*"

"I don't know. You're just a good American girl, I guess. All American men look younger than their wives. It's unconstitutional the other way." In the silence that followed, he could hear the sea walloping the rocks, realized that he had been hearing it for a long time: *thump—thump—thump*. Like a man in an empty house, he thought sadly, banging a table, banging a table and shouting into the darkness that—

"Do I really look so old, Howard? *Do* I?" she interrupted. "What would you think if you just met me for the first time?"

He examined her for a moment with his careful painter's eye. "Yes," he answered at length, "you do." He was quite serious; after much devious thought, he always ended up telling the truth, the simplest truth. It was a kind of laziness. "I always tell the truth," he explained, trying to embrace her again. "It's a kind of laziness."

"A bon mot!" she cried bitterly, shaking off his encircling arm once more. "Save it! Save it for your friends and their twenty-year-old wives." She tried vainly to light her cigarette at the car lighter in an intended gesture of nonchalance; and he flipped a match with finger and thumb, offered it. "Thanks for nothing."

"Listen, Jess. I'm not kidding. Let's turn around. It's bound to be gruesome—six men who never loved each other to begin with, and two brand-new wives. Besides, you're upset. We can call up later and say I got lost. Everyone knows I always get lost. Let's keep going to Atlantic City; a man can't die without having been in Atlantic City and this may be our only chance. The kids in camp and— To hell with Bill Ward and his caviar. We can eat salt-water taffy instead. We've already seen the Castle of Otranto, and so let's—"

She had not even been listening. "I suppose you intend to play the fool again tonight the way you always do. That's the difference between you and an ordinary fool; you always plan it in advance. Which one will you make a pass at tonight? Which twenty-year-old? Which ingénue, Molly or Eva?"

"Ay-vah," he corrected her. "She says it 'Ay-vah' not 'Eva.' It makes Leonard mad when—"

"To hell with Leonard. He's a worse fool than you are. Giving up a girl like Lucille for a—"

"A *girl!*"

"All right, a woman. That's exactly my point. He turned in a woman, who incidentally, *just* incidentally, supported him for seventeen years, for a little—"

"Please, Jess, don't yell at me. Take it up with Leonard. I'm not the one who divorced my wife, I just said—"

"You just *said*. You just sit there preening in the mirror and thinking what-a-good-boy-am-I because you didn't divorce your wife like Leonard or Bill. Many thanks."

"You're welcome."

"Oh, no, you don't divorce her; you only make a fool of her by slobbering over somebody else's twenty-year-old wife, because you're too lazy and too spoiled and too irresponsible even to be the first-class kind of bastard Leonard is. But don't think you just make a fool out of me. You make a worse fool out of yourself. After all, you *are* forty-five, even if you do look only thirty—forty-five and foolish and fat, just like in the comic strips." She took the fold of fat over his belt between two fingers and pinched it hard. She was crying. "The shame of it is that it's such a pattern, so stupid, so *expected*. Everyone knows what Howard Place, boy abstractionist, is going to do at a party, and everybody watches and waits for him to do it. Who will it be tonight? Which sleazy bitch or celebrity-happy sophomore from Bennington? And how will his gallant wife take it *this* time, brave, brave Jessie Place. Just like that time I was pregnant, eight months pregnant and you had the nerve to—"

"For God's sake, Jess, that was fifteen years ago, fifteen. And we haven't seen some of these people since, Marvin, for instance, and Irving. How long do you think anyone remembers—"

"But I can't forget, Howard. *I* can't."

"All right, then, we'll—"

"All right, then, we'll *what?* You don't even bother to protest any more, do you? You won't even lie to me. At least, you used to swear that this time, next time it would be different—that *this* time you'd try. It's the last tribute you can pay a woman, Howard—to lie to her a little, to—"

"O.K., so we won't see the gold-plated johns and the fountain in the living room. Let's get out of here. It's not worth it." Clumsily and in anger, he began to slew the car around, spinning his back wheels on the sandy shoulders and crushing the bushes behind him.

But Jessie had changed her mood without warning, though her tears were not yet dry. "At least we can still argue. *That's* a good sign, Howard, isn't it?"

"It sure is." He kissed her tentatively.

"Then don't turn around. How can you be such a fool. Don't you think I want to see the inside of the house, too? I want it to be so vulgar and stupid that—that—well, you know—vulgar and stupid. And I can't leave without seeing that girl who's so much more 'sympathetic' than Elaine."

He heard the ironic quotes around "sympathetic." "Look, darling, I didn't mean that—"

"Oh, you poor, helpless bastard, just lie to me a little, that's all. I *love* you, you know." She leaned over to return his kiss—not very hard.

"That's just because I'm going to be in next year's Biennale. You don't want to lose a winner."

"It helps." She kissed him again, and he held her to him almost with passion.

"I love you, too, Jess. God have mercy on us." It was the simplest truth, and yet he was already thinking how Eva (Leonard's wife whom he had seen only once) and Molly (for whom Bill had left Elaine and whom he had not yet met) would be to touch or taste, their flesh not much more subdued by love or time than his fourteen-year-old daughter's. The sea grew louder and louder as he eased the car down the narrow, overgrown drive under a quarter-mile tunnel of rhododendron bushes. It was roaring now, not thumping, roaring like the coming of sleep or the reaching back to childhood. He had not swum in the Atlantic since he was twelve, only crossed it on the way to Rome or Madrid, chasing light like the lunatic he had been when he was younger. And now he lived so far inland that he could not even imagine the sea's noises: Painter-in-residence at a university on a city-straddled, dull river that did not even live like water.

"I love you," Jessie repeated.

"I heard you the first time," he said, touching her hair appreciatively, "but my wife warned me against celebrity hounds. Where the hell's the ocean?" He could see before him only a horizon defined by a line of dunes, shaggy where they met the sky. He felt suddenly lonely, an alien in this place created by the taste of the grandfather of Bill's rich wife—a piece of the world that, when he was a boy, had been labeled "Restricted." Except for the glare from the house itself, there was not a light in any direction as far as he could see, only the ragged unraveling of the dunes under a livid sky. Even the noise of the waves on the shore seemed to him all at once empty. He longed for the swarming beach of his own childhood: the Moxie bottles, the *knish* venders, the screaming of lost kids and old ladies bouncing in ecstacy on the ropes, the tangled lovers frozen by the sun and walked over carefully by the middle-aged or sprayed with sand by the feet of children. "*This* is the shore?"

"It must be over those dunes," Jessie assured him, sensing his melancholy. "But it's not *your* ocean. That's a hundred miles north and thirty years away. Poor Howard. For pity's sake, forget what I've been saying; it's only that I keep thinking of Lucille and Elaine. Enjoy yourself tonight. Take one of those young imbeciles, if she'll have you. How much longer can you even look at twenty-year-olds without being sadder than you are funny. I don't really care as long as I know that— It's just— Take her out by the ocean that isn't even yours and—"

"Shh!" he interrupted. "Holy cow! Look at *that!*"

The drive had led them circuitously past the two tennis courts and wound now beside the pond, around which they could see the white gleam of some fifty statues, shoulder to shoulder, emperors and fauns, athletes and nymphs, carefully mutilated to look like recovered antiques. This time Howard stopped so short that Jessie pitched into the dashboard, and leaped out of the door without even setting the handbrake. "My God, what do you think you're doing?" she screamed, reaching across to stop the car that slowly but inexorably rolled toward the pond.

"They're marble, real honest-to-God marble," he yelled back, fondling the hairy backside of a satyr. "No plaster casts in the Castle of Otranto." It had begun to rain, and over his shoulder

Jessie could see the slender, high-breasted Venus, who straddled a shell in the middle of the pool, glisten with the drops; her arms were stretched out and down in a strange pose, her head tossed arrogantly back. "Aphrodite at the gates. It's a good omen." Howard whooped helplessly, abandoned to laughter, while Jessie yelled, "For pity's sake, don't be a child. What's so funny? Get back in the car, you fool. You'd think you'd never seen—"

"I'm back," he said, settling in beside her, a little damp where he pressed against her arm. "It's only that I never— For God's sake, it's Bill himself. But look what prosperity has done to him."

It *was* Bill at the door—unmistakably Bill, playing squire between the carriage lamps—waving a martini glass in their direction and yelling what must have been a fond greeting.

"Four bedrooms, three baths and two Fords," Howard murmured pointlessly, laughing again until he could no longer drive, and they tumbled out of the car.

Three years (was it only three since they had sat in the Piazza del Popolo choking on Campari-soda?) had done something cruel and comical to Bill. It was not merely that he had grown fat; that could happen to anyone, but he had grown fat so ludicrously. He looked somehow as if he had been blown up by a kid with a bicycle pump: the skinny, bewildered face he could never shave properly still skinny but *inflated*, the half-starved body of the first thirty-five years of his life ballooned out under the unbleached linen jacket.

When he tried to kiss her, missing her cheek as always, Jessie was tempted to squeeze him hard, keep squeezing until the air was forced out and he had shrunk to size again.

"Well, I never . . . ," she managed to say finally, while Bill thrust a hand out under her arm to shake Howard's.

"You never did. You really never did." He stood back and patted his belly proudly. "I'm not rich for nothing. Imagine it, me rich." He raised a plump arm with visible effort to indicate his domain. "Turrets—ivy—Venuses—sixty-two bedrooms— We even have a ghost, but unfortunately it's Sunday, and on Sundays, ghosts don't—" He seemed to remember for the first time the dark-haired girl with the pale eyes who stood beside him. Everything about her was tiny except for her breasts, which, thrust forward by her sway-backed stance, gave her the overweighted air of an eighth grader who has not yet grown up to her body. "And this is the secret of my success, Molly-o, my wife." A deprecatory grin fought to take shape in the tight, round blank of his face. It was impossible to say if he changed expression when he added with scarcely a pause, "Did you know Irving's dead?"

Molly reached a hand toward Howard first, very brisk and businesslike, though her pale eyes fluttered coyly. They were green, he thought, if they were any color at all. "Why don't you make up your mind," he wanted to say—to the eyes not to her.

"Place," she said, greeting him by his last name, as if she were a man. "Delighted. I recognized you from the picture in *Harper's Bazaar*." She was wearing a black turtleneck sweater without sleeves and an oxford gray linen skirt, just the right outfit, Howard knew, to make Jessie feel overdressed and deliberately snubbed.

He touched her cheek lightly, ignoring the proffered hand. "Ward," he said, echoing her manner. "Delighted, too. I recognized you from the picture outside Minsky's."

"I said Irving's dead," Bill repeated mildly. He was scratching himself under the left buttock as always.

"Minsky's has been closed for years. She's too young to have heard of it," Jessie put in by way of information.

"For Christ's sake," Howard hissed.

"What do you mean 'for Christ's sake'?" Jessie turned on him, glowering, and ignoring the girl who was now pointing her breasts in her direction.

"I'm very pleased to know you, Mrs. Place. Why don't we all move in out of the—"

"The hell you are," Jessie said in a half-whisper, still looking away from Molly toward the invisible sea and the storm that moved toward them now like a blow.

"Pardon me?" Molly asked uncertainly. Her lids moved up and down, up and down frantically over the ambiguous green.

She must be awfully proud of those thick, dark lashes, Howard thought, poor kid! And he put an arm around her shoulders to reassure her.

"Oh, for pity's sake," Jessie exclaimed, looking at her at last; then grabbing her away from Howard, gave her a hug and a large kiss. "You're only a child. I love you, you know. I love all of Bill's wives. . . ."

"He only had *two*," Molly answered, moving uneasily in Jessie's embrace. "I mean, I'm the second, that is—"

"I said Irving's dead," Bill tried again. "Irving's dead. Irving's dead." He was constitutionally incapable of shouting, but he pounded Howard's back with a pudgy hand to claim his attention.

"She looks just like Elaine," Jessie whispered in her husband's ear. "It's obscene. She has no right . . ."

"I know he's dead," Howard answered Bill at last. "Irving's been dead for years. I keep telling him so. He never got out from under the influence of Hans Hofmann. Might as well cut off your arm at the armpit. But where the hell is he? I haven't seen—"

"No! No!" Bill insisted, dancing up and down in exasperation. "He really died two nights ago. A heart attack. He was supposed to be here tonight, with Esther—"

"Sarah, you mean," Jessie interrupted. "Sarah was the one who—"

"I thought it was Esther. I always get those names— To hell with it. The important thing is, he's dead."

"You mean *dead*," Howard yelled, registering at last. "Irving? Irving Posner? Dead?" Though he was talking to Bill, he had grabbed Jessie, digging his fingers into her shoulders hard enough to hurt.

"He died two nights ago, the fourteenth, at 7:30 P.M. in the arms of his wife of a heart attack." This at least, Molly obviously believed, was a solid fact to be hung on to, to be asserted in the midst of references that baffled her and slippery insults. This was what she knew, what she could tell the others.

But what does her voice remind me of, Howard asked himself, that polite, private-school New York voice, so unlike the voices

of anyone I ever knew or hated or slept with, the voice (he had it
at last) of F.D.R., a Fireside Chat!

In his distress, he had not noticed Marvin and Achsa, who were
just then coming toward them out of the house, Marvin as usual
carefully not looking at his wife, who followed him fiercely, like
a dog on a fresh scent—her eyes hot and bulging in the leathery,
shrunken face.

"Esther notified us that night. The funeral was to be held at
the Beth El Synagogue at—" Molly tried to continue; but Marvin
leaned down toward her from his immense height, almost touching her pony-tail with his chin.

"You sound like a newspaper," he said in his flat, unpleasant
voice, "the kind of newspaper I never read. You ask me how I
know what kind of newspaper it is, if I never read it; I answer
I know that you read it, and knowing you I deduce—"

"Excuse me, Mr. Aaron," Molly retorted with schoolgirl iciness, "I wasn't aware that you were eavesdropping." He had
withdrawn again to his full height, lifting his dark, melancholy
face back into its customary loneliness; and she had to tilt her
own head back perilously to glare at him.

"Why don't you call me Marvin," he said. "That would make
me more uncomfortable yet."

"For the love of Jesus, shut up, Marvin," his wife cut in.
"You're not even drunk." She was not much larger than Molly;
but she did not try to engage his eye, shouting instead with all
the hopeless rage of one whose worst enemy has remained out of
range for twenty years. At that moment, she caught sight of Jessie
and screaming her name, flung herself with equal though opposite
passion from her husband toward her friend.

"Achsa! Achsa! What have you heard from Lucille and Elaine?
You never write." Jessie did not lower her voice; she had not so
much forgotten Molly as not yet taken her into account.

"I have no time for writing. I'm working full-time again—in
the same office with Lucille. You should see her; she looks like a
ghost—skin and bones and eyes, that's all. For the first three
months she had shingles, while that bastard Leonard—" she
stopped to glare at Bill who scratched himself absently, then con-

tinued, "while her dear husband Leonard (the divorce hadn't even gone through) was on a Caribbean cruise, a premature honeymoon."

"No, no, no," Jessie protested. "He wouldn't dare."

"Oh, wouldn't he? But she's doing very well now—psychiatric social work. You remember that's what she was doing when we were all in Minneapolis—when Leonard was working on his first book, the proletarian one. Proletarian!"

"For Christ's sake, Achsa—Irving is dead. Have a little decency." Howard found he still had his arm around Molly, in a gesture of solidarity he had not really thought out.

"I know. Thirty-eight years old. A tragedy for the Jewish people. It couldn't be worse if we lost Sholem Asch. I never liked that little twerp Irving, and you know it, Howard. Why should I be a hypocrite now? The last time we saw him he was going to *shul*—couldn't even stop to talk. He's a faker, Howard, admit it. First a Marxist, then a Jungian, then an Orthodox Jew . . . What's the use, Howard; dead or alive, he was a fake!"

"How do you do, Achsa? I'm very glad to see you again after all these—"

"Ah, you see, he's offended because I didn't kiss him. Aren't you, Howard? Isn't that sweet! You always were a *much* sweeter fake than poor Irving." She pecked him meaninglessly on his nearest cheek, her eyes swinging feverishly from face to face.

"And you, Marv? How are you?" It was an idiotic thing to say out of his complicated feelings, but Howard could think of nothing else. It was Marvin who had first taken him to an art museum, Marvin who had made him read Marx, and now—

"Sufficiently lousy." He inclined his head wearily toward Howard, without visible affection. "But she's right after all, though God knows how." He avoided his wife's name, using the simple pronoun in referring to her. "A mountebank, a bankrupt comedian. At least you've learned to come to terms with your badness and be popular. To be a bad avant-garde painter is only ridiculous; it gives aid and comfort to the enemy. To be a producer of bad kitsch (is there any other kind?) is solidly contemptible, *solidly* contemptible."

"Thank you, Marvin," Howard answered, scarcely realizing that he imitated Marv's toneless Brooklyn voice as he spoke. "The tribute of your envy is worth more to me than being chosen for the Biennale." It was the simplest truth again, and he wished there were some way for Marvin to know it.

"Oh, please come *in*, everybody, come in and have a drink. Please. All you intellectuals I've read about all my life, and you don't know enough to come in out of the rain." Molly urged and pushed them inside, aided by Howard to whom her stupidity and her not-quite green eyes seemed equally charming. But he dropped behind to sit on the marble lip of the basin in the entry hall, out of which a thin stream of blue water rose and fell, balancing a crown of spume at the highest point of its thrust. Around the rim, there were potted palms, seventeen of them, and in the shallow pool, great slow golden carp hung as if asleep. He could see into it, but was not yet ready to enter the hundred-and-fifty-foot living room, with its balcony for musicians and the mirrored walls at either end that reflected back and forth into a haze of planeless images the ivory buddhas, the carved oaken bishop's throne, the twisted iron lamp stands, and the faces of Achsa, Marvin, Jessie, Bill Ward—so improbably there.

The rain banged stupidly against the leaded window panes with the inset coats of arms, not steadily but in irregular spasms, as startling as the lightning which exposed the shuddering pines and an agitated gray strip of sea. In the center of the room, a long black table, sustained by carved hamadryads, was covered with bottles and trays of canapes arranged in spokelike patterns chiefly yellow and red. The room was oppressive after the chill of the rain, full of smoke and dead air and rock-and-roll music, blaring mercilessly from a pair of speakers in opposite corners of the ceiling.

"Hi-fi," Bill said, waving toward the speakers, and "Plover's eggs, fried locusts," indicating the table. "Believe me, it's the hardest buck I ever made."

"It's too damn hot. I can't stand it!" Achsa screamed, and grabbing a Cinzano bottle, hurled it through one of the windows at the point where, above a scarlet shield, the motto read: *Ad astras per aspera.*

"Real vermouth," Bill commented, while Molly giggled, obviously feeling that this was more like what she had read about writers and painters in novels, more like a real party at last.

The sound of breaking glass brought Howard into the room and startled the couple on the other side of the table into turning around. They had stood clutched together heedlessly when the others first came in, not really dancing but making little rubbing motions against each other in time to the music. It was Leonard and his new wife, Howard knew even from the backs of their heads, his black and a little grizzled, hers blond, the hair hanging straight to her shoulders. She was very slim and a little taller than Leonard even in her flat ballet slippers; and when she whirled around, her eyes still large and her mouth a little open, a large gold cross swung lazily between her breasts. Leonard had grown a beard and looked handsomer than ever, almost masculine despite his short legs and tiny feet, his soft, girlish body.

"Disgusting!" Achsa said, not troubling to make clear whether she meant the cross, the beard, the public caresses, or all three; and in the confusion of kissing and greeting that followed, no one cared. It was a full ten minutes and a drink later before they could hear each other saying what they had all been unable to stop thinking: "Thirty-eight." "Poor Irving." "Dead."

"Thirty-eight," Jessie managed to make herself heard above the rest. "Thirty-eight! The youngest of us and the first with a reputation—the first one whose name anyone knew but *us*. We're all a little dead now. What are we doing here anyway? Why don't we lie down like good corpses and—"

"What else was there for him to do?" Achsa asked mercilessly. "A painter who couldn't paint any more. It's better than praying, isn't it, more honest to die!" Irving had been her lover once, Howard was aware, for a little while and for reasons never very clear either to them or anyone else, but whatever tenderness she may have felt had long since dissolved in her scorn. "You don't *have* to die from a heart attack. It's an act of cowardice. Look at Marvin. He's had three already, three attacks, but he doesn't die, and what kind of a hero is he?"

"You're kidding," Jessie cried out. "For pity's sake, you don't mean to say that—"

But at the same moment Howard was saying, "He wouldn't give you the satisfaction, Achsa. You're his life preserver." Turning to Marvin, he winked, but looked away again, seeing the sudden terror in Marvin's loosened lip and staring eye. "Old revolutionaries never die," he went on, just to keep talking. "If the last Trotskyite in America conked out from a twinge of the heart, it would be sacrilege or *lèse-majesté* or something. . . ."

"It's the difference between angina pectoris and a coronary," Molly said, blinking sagely at Marvin, who stroked his upper left arm and said nothing. "I used to work for a doctor and I—"

"Nuts," Achsa interrupted her. "It's the difference between Karl Marx and Moses Maimonides. Irving already had one head in the womb and that's as good as a foot in the grave. After the womb, the tomb! And what a womb he picked to crawl into, with a *mezzuzah* at the entrance and two sets of dishes. A womb with two sets of dishes!" She apparently found this very funny, barking in amusement, though no one joined her.

"In 1935, he was the most talked-about young painter in America. 'A way out,' they said, a way out of the Cubist academy. And for the last five years he never touched a brush—defeated!" Howard filled his glass again and gulped it down, feeling very sorry for himself. But why *himself*? He hated martinis and only drank them, too quickly and without restraint, when he wanted to humiliate himself. "I loved him." Perhaps that was it; everyone must feel somehow guilty at the death of what he loves. He could see Irving's pinched, dark-bearded face before him, peering out from behind the tortoise-shell glasses as from behind a mask; and playing whatever part he had temporarily chosen, sage or revolutionary or prophet or kindly old uncle, with all the furious commitment of a ten-year-old. "I loved him."

"Is it true that just before he died, he was so . . . so . . ."

Once into the story which she had heard but not really understood, though she had laughed when Bill had laughed, Molly

wanted to retreat, but could find no way out. "That he was so
. . . so *Jewish* that he wore a cap when he drank martinis."

Why did no one laugh this time, when the time before everyone had just about— They all looked at her in an absolute silence
that not merely reproached but annihilated her; and when she
searched for Bill's eye, he was pretending to be too busy with
Achsa's glass to have noticed either her gaffe or the silence which
followed it. "What I mean is—" she tried again, and quit.

"He had the dignity of failure," Marvin said suddenly, not to
rescue her, but because whatever causes moved him a head and a
half above the others had brought him to a point where it was
time to switch sides. "He had the dignity of failure. Nothing else
matters." He might have been addressing Howard more directly
than the others, but it was hard to be sure. At any rate, Howard
wished that he did not have to remember (what Marvin drunk
and more proud than distressed had confided in him one night
years and years before) that Marvin had paid for Achsa's abortion
when she had been pregnant with Irving's child. They had been
married only a couple of years then, and Marvin had gone off to
Haiti on a Guggenheim, his last public recognition, leaving Achsa
behind; when he had returned, Irving had a new girl and was
broke as always.

"The dignity of failure," Achsa screamed, closing in on her
husband as if she intended to bite him. She, at least, was drunk,
and her glass tilted as she moved, sending most of her just-re-
plenished drink over her dress front. "You should be an expert
on that, Marv, a real expert. But I don't understand it, not even
after twenty-one years of postgraduate study. Just how dignified is
it to be the only spokesman of failure, *pure* failure, in a room with
a painter who's going to be one of the five Americans in the next
Biennale—"

"Four," Jessie corrected her, while Howard winced.

"Plus the winner of the Prix de Rome for literature—the only
poet in America married to an escapee from a convent!"

For a moment, it seemed as if Eva's mouth were shaping a protest, but she contented herself with pressing it against Leonard's
sleeve, snuggling up to him even closer. She had not yet said a

word audible to anyone but her husband, only touched him from time to time incredulously, as if she were afraid he was not really there.

"Not to forget our host, the author of *All Buttoned Up*, which not only got the Drama Critics' Circle Award and has been running for sixty-seven weeks—but even won him as a special bonus Molly-o, complete with the highest class sanitarium in the marshes of New Jersey." She spilled the rest of her drink on Molly, bowing exaggeratedly in her direction.

"Hardest buck I ever made," Bill repeated, giggling. He obviously thought it a classic remark—and was resolved to find Achsa merely funny.

Molly could not resist adding, "And he would have had the Pulitzer Prize, too, except that one of the judges was Ed Shorr, who everyone knows is—"

"And what do *you* have to offer, Marvin, to this distinguished group of repentant Marxists on the make besides the purity of your principles? Twenty-seven years of being called 'America's most brilliant young critic' till 'brilliant' and 'promising' get to be open insults! Twenty-seven years of conversation everyone admires and no one remembers! Twenty-seven years of nail-biting and insomnia—including twenty-one years of me. Let's not forget that, Marvin—twenty-one years of *me*. No book. No prize. No new bride. Only me. How do you like me, Marvin? Am I a dignified enough failure for you?"

"You see what I mean," Leonard cut in with his shrill, somewhat fruity voice. He was not addressing the rest of them really, only Eva, continuing the one dialogue that was important to him. "Conjugal love. Punishing each other for punishing each other. Eating each other, because each one is sure the other's the only true poison. This is just what it was like with me and—"

"Say Lucille's name and I'll leave this stupid party!" Jessie cried out. "How did she poison you? How? By letting you sit year after year writing poems no one would print, while she worked for twenty-five lousy bucks a week. By letting you weep on her shoulder after each of your 'little affairs' and wipe away your tears until the next one. By—"

"Shh! Jessie, for Christ's sake," Howard hushed her.

"Why should I shh? We used to sleep in the same bed, Howard, don't you remember? The four of us, you and I and Lucille and Leonard. Now we can afford a bed apiece and we wouldn't fit anyway! You remember whenever we used to come to Minneapolis, we'd talk all night until we couldn't keep our eyes open, daring each other to believe we'd be famous some day, read and dreamed about by young kids like us lying four in a bed. This *is* some day, Howard. How do you like it? Leonard used to read his poems and we'd argue, scream at each other. Was she poisoning you then, Leonard, was she? What happened, for pity's sake? Maybe she couldn't look at you any more with such big eyes, as if you were a god, the way this poor thing looks at you now. Lucille *knew* you, Leonard, like you knew her, and what is there to do under such circumstances but forgive one another?"

"Forgiving is a poison, too, Jessie," Leonard answered mildly. "It's habit-forming. After a while, you get so you can't do—"

"Put down that poisoned toothpick, Leonard! Bernie's here and no one hurts my Jessie. At least, not without a marriage license!" They had not heard Bernie Levine's Cadillac pull up on the cinders outside or seen him and Beatie come through the open front door; but he bounded now from one to the other, the last guest, fat and bald and incredibly ugly, kissing Jessie, lifting Achsa high into the air, thrusting a finger into Bill's middle to see if it was real, patting Eva's behind. "What a *tuchas!* What a *tuchas!* You're a lucky boy, Leonard. What a poet can do with this, I don't know, but a cloak and suiter like me— When do we eat?" He was dripping wet with perspiration and rain, his hundred-and-fifty-dollar silk suit wrinkled hopelessly, his Panama hat with the multicolored band (that he had hung on an empty candle holder) sodden. "What a dive! Incredible, huh? I suppose you have gin in the fountain, no? And they call them poor fish! My God, the heating bill alone! Where's Beatie? I know I had some woman with me when I started, and she didn't hold the car door open for me when we stopped. It must be my wife. Ah, there she is—naturally, with that Howard."

Beatie had been standing behind him through his whole act,

grimacing and shaking her head back and forth in her cradled hands to express mock horror; but now she smiled the slow, sweet smile Howard remembered out of her too-big, noble head under its fashionably cropped gray bob.

"I'm tired. Four kids and it's the summertime. But you, Howard, you're just beautiful. And you're famous, my oldest son tells me, my fifteen-year-old, imagine it! He saw it in *Time* magazine. Kiss me already." Pulling her close, Howard saw the tears in her eyes; they had known each other since they were three. "It's terrible, no? And it'll be worse before it's over. What an idea!" She gestured with her head to indicate she meant the whole party. "What can you expect in such a house. No self-respecting ghost would haunt it. Absolutely. Ah, poor Howard—and Jessie! Jessie!"

They embraced warmly, not speaking. "I'm really tired, I didn't realize it. What a summer—my mother-in-law's been with me for three weeks. And wet—and hungry. Why *don't* we eat? Thanks. Thanks." She waved off Bill who approached with a glass. "We stopped on the way for a drink. To tell you the truth, for three drinks. That's why we're late."

"It's Beatie's fault," Bernie said. "She can't stay away from the stuff—it's an affliction. An unhappy marriage, and, unfortunately, her religion forbids divorce." He kissed her on the neck, ducking under her blow.

"Are we ready?" Bill asked, turning to Molly.

"Ready for what?"

"To eat. It's nearly half past nine."

"*Eat!*" She said the word with exaggerated contempt, and leaning toward Bill, whispered furiously into his ear.

"O.K., O.K.," he said soothingly. "It doesn't matter. I'll hold off the wild beasts. It's just a question of looking them in the eye, showing them which one of us is master. Listen, let's all have another drink."

"But I thought—" Molly began.

"Thought," Marvin repeated. "Make no extravagant claims."

"I thought we were going to— Why don't *you* urge them, Bill. They're *your* friends."

"Urge them?" he asked, scratching his behind again in a mild panic. "But what should I urge them to— What do you mean?"

"You don't even remember. And it was going to be the High Point!"

"The 'High Point'?"

"We were going to *swim!*" There were tears in her eyes, darkening the elusive green.

"But it's raining, sweetie," Bill protested, "and it's cold and late and—"

"It's *best* in the rain. Don't you have any spirit of adventure? I thought that—"

"What? What?" Bernie shouted. "She wants to swim? The young lady wants to swim? So let her swim; it's a constitutional right. I personally will grease her down. I have in the back of my car—"

"*You'll* swim with me, won't you, Bernie?" Howard found himself resenting the "Bernie" (he had been coldly "Place"), as he resented the way Molly-o snuggled up to Bernie now, one breast nudging his solar plexus.

"*Me?* You mean *me* swim? Excuse me, my dear, this is another question entirely. After all I just ate two olives in my last martini. According to all the best scientific thought, I'll have to wait at least an hour. Otherwise I'd be glad to oblige."

"Really, dear, it's out of the question," Beatie added with a heavily matronly air that even Howard could scarcely abide. "It *is* cold. It *is* late. Some of us have to worry about bursitis. Besides, we have no bathing suits. Bill didn't say anything when he called about—"

"But that's just it. We don't need any bathing suits. It's no fun if it's not spontaneous. We have a lovely private beach, and I thought we would all just slip out of our clothes and— It was going to be so *exciting!* I mean, I remember when I was in college, a bunch of us kids sneaked off to a quarry with a case of beer and— Oh, everybody was so beautiful that night, so free and beautiful in the moonlight! Don't you *see?*"

"Moonlight!" Howard could not help breaking in, though he did not want to seem to stand against her with the veteran wives and their scared husbands. "Just look at the moonlight!" He pointed through the splintered pane to the sky whose murkiness an occasional lightning flash showed without dispelling.

"It'll be wonderful! We'll be like ghosts in the lightning. *Nude* ghosts." Noo-oo-oo-oode, she said it, lingering dreamily over the vowel of what was for her a magic word. "Nude ghosts."

"And now *listen!*" Howard persisted, hushing them, so that they could hear the noise of the sea on the rocks, the blows so quick and frenzied that they made a single, unbroken sound. "The surf! It would tear you to pieces."

"Oh, how can you all be so *sensible!* I'll never be *that* sensible even if I live to be a hundred. You're not just old, you're dead, *dead,* all of you! I wish your precious Irving was here. At least, he *knows* he's a corpse!" and shedding clothes as she ran, she headed out the door into the rain and toward the roar of the ocean. Her brassière she flung back over her shoulder as she disappeared in a final, theatrical gesture.

"Bravo!" Marvin shouted, clapping his long, thin hands together, "Bravo!"

"What'll I do?" Bill asked, starting to follow her, and then, turning irresolutely back. "It's the first time we— Should I—"

"You can show me the silent-flush toilets I've been hearing about for three months," Beatie answered, taking Bill's arm. "Leave her alone. She'll be all right. Don't you men know *any-thing,* even the second time around?"

"I tell you Elaine was never like this, I mean—that is—" Bill stammered to silence, flushing and Beatie drew him off.

"Well, I can go wading at least, while my wife consoles abandoned husbands in bathrooms." Bernie had taken off his shoes and socks as he spoke, and was heading for the marble fishpond in the entry hall. "This is more my speed. Oy! it's cold!" He jumped out, then with a shudder back in again. "Look at me! Free and beautiful." His nose, broken once and never properly repaired, gleamed with sweat, and a stubble of the tough beard that refused to look shaved darkened his fat jowls. "Do the fish care that they have no bathing suits? Young fish—they should worry! They tickle. Come on in, everybody. Join me! Hoo-hah! I'm F. Scott Fitzgerald!"

But no one even listened. Leonard and Eva were necking again, she utterly abandoned to an inner rhythm of desire that had nothing to do with any event in the external world, he glancing up occasionally, vaguely troubled, in search of an O.K. from his old friends. It's insulting, Howard thought; bad enough the girl is so young, but he doesn't have to play the naïve bridegroom himself (with a beard!), force the rest of us into the roles of father or uncle, called on to approve or cast out. He leaned over to kiss the hair of his wife, who sat on a low hassock before him, her head bent forward onto her knees; but he felt self-conscious, aware that any public love-making between two middle-aged people, shrunken or bulging, must appear a parody—a little obscene.

At least he was not Marvin, Jessie not Achsa! Marvin, with no one to talk to, drank in silence, pacing the room nervously, and Achsa, drifting behind him without being aware she followed, matched him drink for drink, though neither said a word to the other and each kept his eyes averted. Suddenly, Howard realized that the darkness before the house to which he had pointed an instant before was blazing with light, through which the slowing rain ran stitches like a sewing machine gone mad. Someone (it must have been Molly-o through all her tears) had switched on a bank of floodlights under the eaves. But *why*, Howard wondered; and he pressed his face against the window, staring out into the pointless glare.

Molly had apparently not gone swimming at all, but was sitting quite naked on a stone bench just at the verge of the last dune. She was set in absolute profile, her knees drawn up before her, her arms braced behind, and her head thrown back so that her hair fell onto the stone seat. Howard had not realized that it was so long and full, caught up in the pony-tail she had worn. In that excessive light and at that distance, all color was bleached from her body, leaving her perfectly black and white. She appeared no more or less real than the marble Venus, which also stood in Howard's direct line of sight, naked above the lily-pads and under the faltering rain. Tintless and eyeless, without motion and with her hair down, Molly seemed the twin of the statue, another Aphrodite.

It came to Howard all at once (and he laughed aloud) that the statue must actually be a *portrait* of the girl, an advertisement, as it were, a forecast of coming attractions. Yet it was impossible to despise her; for once out of her clothes, she seemed not disproportionate at all, the line from instep to thigh to breast a flawless stroke expressing utter complacency. This planned and artificial pose beside her marble double was, Howard sensed, her answer to their condescension and scorn; and though he relished, he could not help resenting, too, the dumb, triumphant rebuttal of her young breasts and thighs. He knew she was aware of his watching her as surely as he knew his wife to be watching his watching; and he turned away with a sigh.

In ten minutes, Molly was back with them again, having apparently re-entered the house by another door. She had changed into riding breeches and a man's plaid shirt, but was barefoot. "Soup's on," she said, grinning, her recent tears quite forgotten; and lifting her arms over her head, she stretched until the shirt was taut from nipple to nipple. She could not have been wearing a brassière.

She led them into the adjoining dining room, where around a floral centerpiece the color of fresh blood fifteen-foot-high silver figures of hooded monks each held up a white candle whose light set the other silver winking and flashing. "That's Oswald," Molly said, tapping one of the monks on his tonsured head. "He's my favorite. Isn't he a darling!"

Dinner began eventlessly enough and was probably excellent; but everyone was too drunk to taste it and the food splashed and fell and slipped from their open mouths with almost demonic malignity, staining tablecloth and ties and the fronts of dresses. "Just *look* at you," Achsa kept hissing at Marvin, pointing across the table in horror at the sauce stains on his white shirt, while her own trembling spoon sprayed her with melted butter or her lipsticked wine glass dripped one more contribution to the purple blur in which it stood.

Only Eva did not drink, raising to their occasional half-mocking toasts ("The Critics' Circle Award!" "The Biennale!" "The Prix de Rome!") a large, depressingly white glass of milk. Bernie, who sat beside her, kept pretending to shy from the glass, raising one hand to his eyes as if to shield them from the glare. At one point he reached over and dipped her cross into the milk ("To see if it's real gold," he explained); at another, he tossed an olive surreptitiously into it "to take off the curse."

"Revolt!" he kept telling her. "This is the last symptom of Momism. Let go of the titty, Eva."

"Ay-vah," Leonard pronounced it for him, irked at the way Bernie kept kneading his wife's arm.

"As long as you're unhealthy!"

There was a different wine with each course, clumsily uncorked by Bill, who grew more itchy and silent as his embarrassment mounted. Over the vichyssoise and Chablis, he tried his favorite quip for a final time, but nobody even looked up to acknowledge it. "Hardest buck I ever made!"

Howard had managed to sit beside Molly; but she had unfortunately drenched herself with some almost acrid sandalwood perfume after her imaginary swim, and he was actually relieved (his head aching and his eyes watering) whenever she rose to go down to the kitchen in pursuit of something forgotten or overlooked. She walked with greater and more perilous dignity each time, until the trip which brought her screaming back with a bloody rag wrapped around the forefinger of her left hand.

"Oh, Bill, I cut it! I *cut* it!" she howled. "I'll bleed to death all because of your silly friends and their silly socialist ideas. Everybody *knows* we have help! What could one person do with a house this size, even just for a summer place. Why did I have to send Ellen and Janet to the movies? So I could chop my finger to pieces? It's snobbery, that's what it is, silly socialist snobbery. They *like* being servants and I like having them and I— Oh, Bill —it's all over my pretty shirt—I'm all *bloody*, Bill." Looking down at the red-stained rag she screamed again.

"Really, I— Really, I—" Bill's mouth opened and closed, opened and closed, as if he were trying to say something, though it became clear finally that he was only laughing soundlessly.

"Bill just sent them away to protect them from Bernie," Howard began, feeling somehow that what would surely seem a good joke when they were sober they might as well laugh at now. But Molly was crying again. "I can't help it if I need servants, can I? Don't make me send them away again. *Promise!* I'm just stupid, that's all. Oh, Bill!" She held her wounded finger under his mouth until he made kissing noises in its general direction, glancing all the while at Marvin to see how strongly he disapproved and making indistinct remarks about the superiority of Bandaids to kisses.

Marvin, on the other hand, looked happy for the first time that night; his long head moving up and down like a horse eating sugar from a child's hand, he began to speak. "Sending servants away, this is more than a symptom of insecurity; it is clearly a symbolic action—but symbolic of what? What is the objection to a maid from people who have sold out their principles, their former friends, their past. To make jokes for hire about everything you believed in once, this is apparently all right, as long as it's in verse." He bowed toward Leonard, showing his crooked yellow teeth in the nearest thing to a smile he could manage. "To sign a loyalty oath to a state with a law against miscegenation in order to keep a job teaching schoolboys to draw vases and plaster casts, this is kosher." He nodded at Howard. "To live off a stupid mother-in-law who believes in 'Art,' but fortunately does not know what it is—who would object? Not our host, who objects to servants, or should I say to displaying his servants to former comrades."

He leveled a finger at Bill, who half-rose to object. "Marvin, it's not that simple. This is a matter that—"

"Quiet!" Marvin said, and Bill bowed his head like a child rebuked. "Why not a servant? This is a G.I. reaction. In every petty-bourgeois conformist, there is a G.I. for a conscience; and what is a G.I.? A man who will kiss ass but not *salute!* And why not? Ass-kissing is a private transaction, but saluting is public, official; it means that you know your masters know that you know that they are your masters. Do you follow this?"

A chorus of "no's" answered him, though they had all stopped their buzz and clatter to listen. He was the only one of them able to compel the attention of the others.

"Still, there's something in what he says," Bernie added. "Personally, I—"

"Please, I'd like to say something," Bill interrupted, holding his hand up like a boy in school. He still had the corkscrew in his clenched fist. "Marvin, you don't understand. About the servants, I won't say anything because it's—well, I just won't. And as for my mother-in-law, whatever help she gave me and for whatever reasons, I don't need it any more. With what I made on *All Buttoned Up*, I'm independent—for five years now I can— Never mind. You know how many people have seen *All Buttoned Up*?"

"What difference does it make?" Marvin answered, smiling condescendingly. "I guarantee you more saw *Abie's Irish Rose*. You still have room to sink, Bill."

"But I didn't write any *Abie*, Marv. I won't say that most people who come to my play don't go out laughing at Roderick the revolutionary bum. But the gimmick is all the time I'm laughing at them for being sucked in. I get them coming and going, Marv, don't you see. I—"

"I won't stand for it," Marvin broke in, pounding the table before him with his loose, hairy fist until the glasses rattled. "I warn you I won't stand for it. I drank your toasts to the Prix de Rome, the Critics' Circle Award, but only on the understanding that no one plays games with me. You're petty-bourgeois conformists. You're whores. O.K., these are the facts. Now, I'm not too proud to sit with whores; I'll even let a whore buy me a drink. But only on the condition that he wears his identification ticket: I AM A WHORE—and underneath it, I LIKE IT! or How UNHAPPY I AM! This much is optional; but no *principles*, for God's sake! That's my department. You have everything else: money, prizes, new wives, admiring coeds. I don't resent it. Only admit what you are. I warn you, I won't stand for it!"

"What'll you do, Marv?" Howard asked mildly. "Write an article?" He pretended he could not hear Jessie who whispered at him from across the table, "The man is sick, Howard. For pity's sake, he's sick."

Marvin refused to dignify his challenge with an answer and Bill, nonplused, had sunk back into his seat, his mouth working soundlessly. The rest stared at each other, unwilling or unable to pick up the conversations they had dropped to listen to Marvin, when Eva's voice rang out astonishingly distinct in the hush. It was the first thing they had heard her say. "Do you understand all this, darling?" She blew into Leonard's ear, bit the lobe gently. She had refused to sit anywhere except beside him, despite Molly-o's outraged protest.

"Certainly."

"But it's ridiculous, darling."

"Of course, it's ridiculous, but that's not the point. This is a language for unhappy people—a way·of pretending that unhappiness is virtue. Once, I talked this language, too."

"But now you're happy and sensible, aren't you, Leonard? And lucky, too, because it *pays* to be happy in America, to give up crazy talk about classes and conformity and discuss the New Criticism or transsubstantiation or how many angels can dance on the head of a Thomist poet." Marvin glared first at Leonard, then at Eva's crucifix.

"Why do you all *listen* to him, then? Why do you sit there apologizing to him, as if he were a fuehrer or something?" Eva had risen to her feet, brushing a long, blond lock of hair out of her eyes with the back of one hand. She was very red, and her lower lip trembled as if she might break into tears at any moment. "Don't you see, he's not only silly, he's vicious—a diseased man tearing at everything that's healthy. I suppose you all read his asinine article 'Fanny Freud at the Harpsichord,' and snickered over it, and thought how smart he was and how smart you were for knowing it. Well, Leonard doesn't care a hoot for what Mr. Marvin Aaron says about his poetry. After all, Leonard writes it, and Marvin is just a mad dog baying at the—at the—*whatever* it is." Her voice, tremulous throughout, broke, and she retreated behind her glass of milk again, scarlet and trembling.

"Take a tranquilizer," Bernie advised her. "Beatie swears by them."

"Never mind," Howard said. "It's refreshing to find a wife ready to defend her husband. But Leonard needs no defense. Who reads what Marv writes any more? Not even us . . ."

He had, of course, read carefully through Marvin's attack on Leonard, as he read (and the rest with him) each rare piece he wrote, his writing obviously blocked now except when malice moved him to snarl at some younger and more successful friend. It had become clear to everyone long since that Marvin would never write the long epic poem on the Wobblies or the immense study of American culture in four volumes that he had talked about all his life. But how to explain this to the girl with her cross and her glass of milk; how to make clear the sense in which Marvin (though only two or three years older) had been the father of them all, the model for the insolence and involution that they had learned from him to think the hallmarks of the revolutionary intellectual. "Bodhisattva," they had called him when they were in high school; and they had quoted his remarks to each other, passing them from hand to hand until they were worn out—their chief inheritance.

Howard knew that Marv clung to the old counters still, the inviable clichés of Marxism, not because he believed in them, but because they had once been tokens of his power to compel love and respect. In a sense, he held them in trust for them all, their one-time papa, now the keeper of the museum of their common past. He felt an obligation to insult Marvin publicly, as Marvin in the first place had taught him to do, to respond to Marv's insults of him as if they mattered. It was the last possible gesture of respect; to have greeted his sallies with silence, would have been to reveal pity, and that Marvin could never have stood.

". . . Not that what Marv wrote wasn't true and in a way deserved. Anyone who can write

And I have dreamed of golden girls,
Whom seeing men forget they die . . .

is asking for the hatchet."

Eva started to rise again, boiling up toward speech, but Howard hushed her. "Never mind, dear. Drink your milk like a good girl. Who takes Marv seriously, a man who writes from rage and out of weakness in a magazine no one sees, except the wives and friends of the author he's giving the treatment. What do you call it again, Marvin, that journal for boys who never grew up? *Peter Pan, Boy's Life, Our Sunday Messenger?*"

"*Contempt,*" Achsa answered for her husband. "*Contempt,* you clown!"

"Ah yes, *Contempt, or the Fountain of Youth.* No forty-year-old ex-post-Marxist can read it without sobbing to his image in the mirror, 'They're playing our song!' Believe it or not, I think Marvin really knows that an attack from him under such auspices helps a book, and since he's fast becoming a kindly old man—"

"Listen, Howard—"

"Listen, Howard—"

"Listen, Howard—"

Marvin, Achsa and Leonard, all three beginning at precisely the same moment and in precisely the same way, collapsed in laughter, while Jessie groaned aloud. She thinks I'm showing off for Molly-o, Howard told himself; and maybe I am, maybe I am. . . . But Molly was not even listening, staring instead at her finger tips which were drumming the tablecloth beside her plate, apparently without her permission. Her fingernails like those of her toes were painted silver.

"Quiet, *please,*" Bernie announced into the hubbub, pounding his glass with a fork. "Everyone's too melancholy. I'm going to tell a joke!"

"I thought that's what Howard was doing," Jessie said, as Beatie murmured, half to herself, "Now they'll first get melancholy."

"Well, since you all insist, reluctantly I'll do it. It seems that one day Mendel meets his old friend Sidney on the street and says to him, 'Sidney, where've you been? For two weeks I haven't seen you in the office, on the street . . .' 'I've been on my honeymoon!' 'Don't kid me,' Mendel says, 'I personally know you've been married already for—' 'Twenty-five years,' Sidney finishes. 'A *second* honeymoon. To celebrate our twenty-fifth anniversary, we went back to the identical hotel in Atlantic City, took the identical room—' 'And how was it?' Mendel asks. 'How was it? It was *wonderful*, exactly the same as twenty-five years before. Wonderful.' "

"Wouldn't you say this is a little long, Bernie?" Achsa asked. "Couldn't you—"

"Sh! I guarantee you it'll be worth it. It'll take another five minutes and you'll love it. Where was I? So, Sidney says to Mendel, 'Mendel, it was perfect. Everything exactly the same. We had the same waiters; we ate at the same table, the same chopped liver, the same chicken soup, the same—' "

"Do you have to recite the whole menu?" Achsa broke in again.

"Excuse me, Achsa. You have no joy de veever, no *ding an sich*. 'Everything,' Sidney says, 'was the same. We went on the boardwalk in the same chair; we ate the same dinner; the orchestra played the same music; at the same time, we went back to the room, jumped in the same bed and—' 'Even that part was the same?' Mendel asks. 'The same as twenty-five years before?' 'Exactly!' says Sidney. 'With one little difference.' 'Nu, what was it?' 'Afterwards, instead of my wife sneaking in the bathroom to cry, I went.' "

"That's funny, I suppose?" Achsa inquired scornfully when Bernie stopped. "The sort of thing you tell your customers to get them in a mood for buying ladies' underwear?"

"I'm laughing," Bernie said; and he was, though the others sat looking at each other in dumb horror, except for Molly who rose, brushing the crumbs from her thighs. "It's just *silly*," she said. "I never heard a story with less point."

"If this is going to be a wake," Leonard put in, pale with anger, "and it seems only proper to have one now that we've all died laughing, let's make it a really low-down one. Improbable as it seems, I know a joke, too—even worse than Bernie's, but shorter at least."

"I can never remember them," Molly said. "I hear some really cute ones, but—"

"Please," Jessie protested, rising, too. "Enough is enough." She looked across at Howard for support, but he said nothing.

"What are you afraid of, anyway?" Leonard persisted. "I'm not going to give away any secrets, only tell a joke. Well, anyway, this man and his wife were in bed together, making love, when suddenly he says, 'Did I hurt you, darling?' 'No,' she answers, 'why do you ask?' 'You *moved!*' he says."

"Oh, Leonard, that's *nauseating!*" Jessie cried. "It's exactly what I knew you were going to—" Howard had the uncomfortable sense that she somehow felt as if she were protecting him. "What are you trying to—"

Even Eva was moved to whisper, "Oh, sweetie, *don't!*" burying her head between Leonard's neck and shoulder.

Howard felt obliged to say something, too, but he was oppressed by a coldness that sank from head to chest to loins. He could feel himself shrivelling as he sat there under the too-hard light, staring down at the cigarette butts ground out on the greasy plates and smelling the dying odor of Molly-o's perfume. To reassure himself, he patted her firm haunch gently as she stood beside him.

"This is the ghost at the feast, isn't it?" Leonard screamed suddenly after having seemed to subside. His voice rose even more shrilly, almost soprano now. "The specter that's haunting New Jersey—and Westport—and Paducah—and Brooklyn! Why are we kidding ourselves. We've reached the age where it's possible to lie beside a woman who's moved you every night for twenty years and feel nothing—*nothing!* This is the critical fact of our lives; but we don't tell, do we? Not in Bill's plays or my poems or Howard's paintings—only in Bernie's crummy jokes. Ha-ha!

"How can you write a poem about nothing? How can you even talk about it unless you're too drunk to know any better. Well, I'm drunk and I'm telling you. Irving isn't the only victim of heart failure. It's the disease of us all without benefit of doctors: failure of the heart, failure of the genitals, failure of love." Though he was standing now and Eva had slumped far back in her chair, he had kept holding her hand all the while he talked, palm pressed to palm like a couple of high school kids. She tried to pull him down when he paused for breath, tugging at him and saying, "Oh, hush, please, hush."

"I'll be damned if I'll hush and let them sit around for the rest of the night sniffing at you and me. They're *sniffing* at us, can't you see! What have we betrayed? We're happy, that's all, and they can't stand it, each with the evidence of his suffering at his side. For better or for worse, in sickness or in health, till death do them— My ever-loving wife! Well, I broke out of the trap and so did Bill; that's what they'll never forgive us for. That's why they're sitting there right now not saying a word but cooking up nasty little stories about us that will last through a whole year of parties. Am I right, Bill?"

Bill was sound asleep at the head of the table, his head cradled in his arms, and the corkscrew, symbol of authority, lying beside him. Achsa, who sat next to him, lifted his head by the hair to reveal a look of childlike bliss, then dropped it again scornfully.

"Hell's bells," Leonard continued. "I'm out of the trap, the not-so-tender-forty-year-old-hell-for-breakfast-every-morning trap. But you wouldn't know about it, would you? Oh, no, vaginal jelly wouldn't melt in your—"

"Please, Leonard darling," Eva implored him.

"O.K., I'll be through in a minute. Well, I know about it anyhow. I know what it is to lie side by side with a woman you've made love to so many times you feel sick and silly when you add up the total—and each of you dead to the other. Such things may not happen to you, Achsa and Marvin, or you, Jess and Howard, or you, Beatie and Bernie; for you the honeymoon may last twenty years. You'll just have to take it on faith that it happened to me, to me and Lucille, who—"

"I told you, Howard, if he mentioned my friend's name in the same room with that silly little girl, I'd—" Jessie wove around the table and stood behind her husband's chair, straddle-legged, her fists on her hips.

"What do you want me to do? Hit him? Should I knock him down for you, Jessie, because he offended divorced American womanhood?"

"She may not have been good enough for you, Leonard," Achsa

interrupted him impatiently, "but she's so much more of a woman than you'll *ever* be a man, that it's a scandal. You and your masculine-protest-type beard that doesn't fool anybody for one minute! She was a splint for your poor feeble masculinity, Leonard, a splint. Don't think that I don't know that before her, you couldn't even manage to—"

"Achsa, what's the point of dragging up all the bedroom gossip you ever heard? All I'm trying to say is—"

"I wasn't the one who started bringing up bedroom gossip, Leonard, but since you began it, I'll just finish. I'm sure this will all be very educational for your new wife, who's been getting your special version of things. I'm sure she'll appreciate knowing that without Lucille you couldn't even—"

"Hell's bells, I'm not trying to justify myself against Lucille, Achsa. I'm a bastard, I know."

"You can say that again," Achsa screamed triumphantly, working her way slowly around the table to put an arm around Jessie's waist. "Now tell us exactly what *kind* of a bastard you are. I have a few little anecdotes to contribute that you may have forgotten."

"All I mean is, what else can you do when—"

"You can shut up, Leonard. So much you can always do." Beatie moved as she spoke toward the other two women, finally taking up a position on the other side of Jessie, though not yet touching her—like a last reserve. "We love you still, Leonard, believe it or not; but don't you see what an offense it is to bring that poor, sweet girl here and sit smooching with her. I wish you a hundred good years with her and a dozen children, but only—"

" 'Poor, sweet girl', with that ridiculous voodoo charm around her neck. I tell you—"

"Never mind the voodoo charm, Achsa. We all have our idiocies and that's not the worst. Leonard, all I say to you is this: go sit in a corner like a good boy and hold your Eva's hand, but leave us grownups alone."

"Beatie, I can talk to *you*. You're no fishwife. What do you *do*, Beatie, when you lie side by side with somebody, two people seeing each other naked, knowing each other by heart, as they say, but without love. It's not tolerable, Beatie. What do you *do?*"

"Lie side by side with the dignity of failure. There is no love." Marvin rose at last with the air of one contributing the final wisdom; he spoke more slowly than any of the others and from his greater height, very pale above their heads.

"Marvin, I tell you right now that if you say 'failure' or 'dignity' again tonight, I'll—I'll throw a water pitcher at your head. I'll—I'll—" Beatie put an arm around Achsa now, soothing her, while Jessie on her other side squeezed her waist without a word. "All right," Beatie kept saying over and over, "all right, all right."

Coffee had been set before everyone, and tasting it now, they discovered it had grown cold. The cognac they dutifully swallowed without tasting, but no one was capable of getting any drunker. Suddenly they had nothing more to say, and they looked away from each other in pained silence, like Leonard's perhaps legendary husbands and wives, wondering what dead and irrecoverable passion had left them stranded in an association that without it was merely absurd.

"Oh, let's *dance!*" Eva cried at the top of her voice, sensing that only a shout could break so deep a silence. She made her way to the hi-fi set in the mirrored room, fiddling with the knobs until music assailed them again from the corners, even louder than before. It was Billy Holiday, singing without vibrato and in ecstatic pain:

Love's just like a faucet,
It turns off and on.
Love's just like a faucet,
It turns off and on . . .

It was as if not their images only, bedraggled and dim-eyed, but the sound, too, was reflected from glass to glass across the immense room. Bernie and Leonard had carried Bill in, sagging between them, to deposit him in the bishop's chair, where he rolled over once then sank back snoring. Jessie, Achsa and Beatie sat side by side on a sofa, leaning their heads together and whispering like conspirators, while Marvin pulled down book after book from the wall shelves, glancing briefly and disapprovingly in each.

Molly-o had flung herself flat on the floor, gazing meditatively down between her breasts, her back nestled down into a white bearskin rug. "I'm too warm—and too full—and I drank too much," she announced mournfully, unbuttoning two more buttons of her shirt and smoothing her breeches across the hips.

Bill once dropped, Leonard had taken Eva in his arms, and they were moving together again in their slow un-dance off in one corner. No one joined them.

Sometimes when you think it's on, baby,
It has turned off and goooo-ooone . . .

"We have squash courts in the basement," Molly said without much conviction, snuggling even more sensually into the white fur, "and ping-pong tables—and sixty-two bedrooms, if anyone is inclined to—"

"The only game that interests me is craps," Bernie said. "If some of you gentlemen—"

"What about Guggenheim?" Marvin asked.

"Guggenheim!" Achsa cried scornfully. "Next it'll be charades."

"I can't play any of those category games," Molly said, looking quite pleased with herself all the same. "I'm too stupid."

"The only thing I ever played in my life," Howard put in from the doorway, where he stood gulping the damp, cold air by way of therapy, "was croquet. I was at Yaddo in '49, and all the time we weren't at the race track, we were playing—"

"You mean that stupid game for children with wooden balls?" Achsa asked.

"I never knew a child with— Isn't there some danger of splinters—" Bernie began, whooping with delight, but Achsa cut him short with a glare.

"Were you at Yaddo *too?*" Molly-o inquired, slowly easing herself over, then rising to sit on her feet like a Japanese. She looked admiringly at Howard as if she had just discovered his most dazzling distinction. "Bill was there once. Long, long ago, in '38."

"That's not so long ago," Howard objected. "It was that year that the Museum of Modern Art bought my—"

"I was six years old," Molly said, casting her eyes down modestly.

"Oy! Oy! Oy!" Beatie cried out. "It's the only answer. Oy! Oy! Oy! Imagine it, six years old."

"Bill says that in '38, they used to play *nude* croquet!" Molly lingered over the vowel of the magic word again. "You know, at night when the middle-aged prudes were asleep. There were lots of interesting people there that year. I don't remember their—"

"Marianne Moore and T. S. Eliot," Marvin suggested. "They'd look good at nude croquet."

"And Henry James," Jessie added. "That long ago he was in pretty good shape—and Henry Wadsworth Longfellow."

"We have a croquet set somewhere, don't we, Bill?" In her mounting excitement, Molly ignored their quips. "Don't we? Don't we?" She ran over, silent on her bare feet, and shook her husband until he opened his eyes, staring at her unseeingly. "*Don't* we have a croquet set? We can play it *nude*, just like you used to do at Yaddo, can't we, Bill? You always told me how much fun it was. It'll save the whole party! Howard, why don't *you* go down into the basement and look just behind the steps. I'm sure you'll find it, in a big cardboard box that says—"

"Croquet, I'll bet," Howard finished for her, while Bill blinking sightlessly repeated, "Nude . . . nude . . . nude . . . " and fell back again onto the seat snoring.

"Oh, Bill!" Molly sighed, then turning once more to Howard, "Well, we'll just have to play without him. He'll be so sorry tomorrow to think he missed it!"

"It's raining again," Howard said by way of answer. He had been holding one hand outside the door, cupped under the dripping eaves; and he wiped it off now on Molly's plump cheek. "Wet! It's a bog out there. You'll have to make it water polo."

"Oh, we're not going to play out there, silly. We'll play in here where it's all comfy. Right *here!* Just move some of these chairs back—and turn off that ridiculous music, and we're all set." She snapped off Billy in the middle of a phrase:

When he starts in to love me, it's so fine and . . .

while Leonard and Eva stood gasping in the sudden silence, like a couple of sea creatures hauled out of their element. "Well, get it, please. Go and get it," she insisted, laying a hand on Howard's arm.

"Howard," Jessie warned him, rising to her feet. "Let's not commit ourselves to anything childish. Really, it's late already and we have a long way to go. I'm sure Molly will understand, and explain to Bill tomorrow, that—"

"It's only eleven-thirty-seven," Howard answered, consulting his watch. What he would have done if his wife had not intervened he was not sure; but there was nothing to do now but go after the croquet set and see what would happen.

He found himself wishing that it would not be there, but, of course, discovered it immediately (he who could never find anything at home) at the bottom of the steps where Molly had said it would be. He wrestled the clumsy cardboard box up the steep stairs, tearing a chunk of flesh out of the back of one hand on the door jamb and scarcely feeling it. "It's here," he said triumphantly, casting it down at Molly's feet and sucking the bleeding place. He liked the taste of his blood. "Strip already!"

He had thought he was joking, but before he could laugh or try to stop her, Molly had stripped off her shirt, leaving herself bare to the waist. "Think fast!" she said, tossing the checkered blouse at him and beginning to fumble with the buttons of her riding breeches.

Bill, still asleep, writhed on the oaken chair, calling out in a choked voice, "Please, please, please . . ." and Bernie rushed toward Molly-o in sudden panic, pulling off his jacket to put around her shoulders. "What is this? Minsky's?" he yelled, flushing and paling by turns. "We're not going to go through with this craziness, are we? What are we anyway, high school children who think you're only living when you take off your clothes? Howard, you tell her—you're an artist, naked women are your bread and butter. A joke is a joke, but I'm forty-four years old—*forty-four*— an underwear salesman."

"What are you getting so excited about?" Howard calmed him,

feeling superior to them all. "Let's be reasonable about this and—"

"Reasonable!" Molly flung Bernie's jacket contemptuously aside, and stepping out of her breeches now, confronted them in a pair of pale green pants (the color of her eyes), covered with tiny red hearts. "Well, what are we waiting for?" Her skin was smooth and tight, unmarred by child-bearing and unmarked even by the crease of brassière or girdle. On shoulder and thigh, breast and belly alike she was tanned the rich brown of one who turns patiently under the sun lamp, reading a fashion magazine and loving nothing more than her own flesh.

"Just because Bill married a *nudnick* who reads F. Scott Fitzgerald do I have to play the bohemian in my old age? Nude croquet! I don't know which is worse, the nude or the croquet! Listen, Howard, God knows we've got nothing to show each other by letting down our pants. Nothing we can be proud of. We're naked enough now, for Christ's sake!"

"Bernie's right," Marvin said, looking directly at Molly who had gone on undressing and stood now with her underpants hanging delicately from silvered thumb and forefinger; if he saw her, he registered nothing. "It would be more to the point to put on steel masks and lead drawers, to hide in all decency a nakedness we can no longer pretend is exciting or beautiful. All our compromises are hanging out, our withered principles dangling obscenely, our hairy ulcers worn on the outside. We can't even remember to button our flies!"

"My God, what *difference* does it make!" Achsa cried out. "Let's show what we can't hide anyway. Let these children look at what they have to become, what they are already, even if their mirrors aren't ready to tell them yet. I only wish I could take off my *skin*, too." Her dress and slip, her brassière with the discreet padding, the girdle she wore only to hold up her stockings, she had off in a moment, rolling them into a ball and heaving them at her husband's head. He did not even lift a hand to block them, but bowed as they went past him, smiling obscurely to himself. Achsa was almost completely breastless, skinny and yellow with strange knobby knees and two scars across her flat, flaccid belly.

"You've all gone nuts," Bernie protested. "Nuts! I'm getting out of here before I find myself galloping bare-ass like a kid. What are we doing, grown men and women? Maybe it's kiddie night in the bughouse! Beatie, come on." He had picked up his rumpled Italian silk jacket, stuck his Panama on the back of his bald head. "Well, come on!"

"I'm not coming, Bernard," Beatie answered quietly, bending over and beginning to unlace the arch-preserver shoes into which her solid, unlovely legs descended without tapering. "I'm going to stay."

"You're going to play nude croquet—*nude* croquet? Are you crazy, too?"

"No—only a little drunk. Nude croquet, nude pinochle! Achsa's right, what difference does it make. Listen, Bernie, I manage to get one night in three months away from the kids—away from a house of flu and measles and diaper rashes. Well, this is the night and here I am and so I intend to stay at least till I've done something I'm sorry for. Do you understand? Excuse me, Bernie, but tonight I don't go home early."

"You're not only drunk," he screamed, pulling her by the arm. "You're crazy, plain, ordinary crazy."

"So, I'm crazy. I'd have to be crazy in the first place to have four children, to have your mother in the house for three weeks —in the hottest weather of the summer. Just let go of me, Bernie. *Let go of me!*" She turned on him her usually mild gaze now coldly ferocious, staring at him until he dropped his hold, then bent down to pull off her stockings. "Oy!" she exclaimed, reaching a hand back to brace herself just over the kidneys. "It's not easy, believe me." On her right leg she wore an elastic bandage, which she removed now, holding it up before them all. "In these things it's hard to be crazy! But varicose veins or not, I'm going to play nude croquet. Go home, Bernie, and when you get there, wake up little David and tell him his mama says—tell him I say—'Merry Christmas.'"

Everyone laughed and Molly shouted, "Hooray!"

"I'm giving you one more chance, Beatie." Bernie stood at the door, his nylon shirt dark with sweat, his coat dangling from his hand. "Come now or walk home. I for one will not—"

"Oh, go already," she sobbed. "Go! Can't you see I'm licking honey. A real orgy." She flung her head down on to Jessie's lap, weeping, her shoes off and her stockings dangling around her ankles. She did not even see Bernie, when, a moment later, he stuck his head back through the door, glowered around the room and, crying, "To hell with you all!" disappeared for good.

"Why don't *you* go, too?" Achsa asked, whirling on her husband; the light glinted from the knobs of her wrists and ankles, the bony outcropping of her pelvis. But Marvin was already undressing without a word, placing his black shoes, his socks with the garters attached, his pants folded neatly on a bookshelf which he had cleared by throwing the books on the floor. His limp, usually almost unnoticeable, grew more evident as he stripped.

Beatie meanwhile had staggered to her feet again, her shoes in her hand, and was making her way to the door, yelling, "Wait, Bernie. I'm coming. Wait! What am I doing here?"

"He's gone," Howard said, stopping her and whirling her around. He was one drink past the simplest truth, and so he lied to her without thinking, though he could still see through the window the red gleam of Bernie's Cadillac, in which he must have been sitting in sullen indecision and self-pity. "Don't worry. I'll drive you home later. It'll do him good to spend a few hours imagining you in a game of nude croquet."

"I don't know what got into me," Beatie sobbed. "You don't understand, Howard. He's in trouble, bad trouble, and I should stand by him. What else can a wife do but stick with her husband. It's her duty, isn't it, no matter what? I just don't know what got into me. I—" She dissolved once more into tears, Howard patting her head uncertainly, until all at once she looked up and winked. "It's all a joke, right, Howard? 'Duty,' 'husband,' 'stand by'—a *joke!* That's what's so hard to remember." She sat sprawled on a gilt and brocade chair that looked frail and ridiculous under her, her legs spread wide and one hand on her heart. "I'm here and I'll play if it kills me. Jessie, come here and help unbutton me."

"Oh, *good,*" Molly shouted, clapping her hands. "Good for you. You're a real sport!"

"Some sport," Beatie responded ruefully. "Poor Bernie!"

"And what about those two?" Achsa pointed to one corner where Leonard and Eva stood staring at each other mutely, their hands clasped. Then, even as she spoke, they began to undress each other, still without a word, moving in a slow pantomime that converted each unbuckling or tug of a zipper into a caress.

"And you, Jessie?" Howard turned deliberately toward his wife, wondering exactly how angry she was. He had already taken off his shirt and his T shirt revealed his fat chest, the thick blond prickles which covered it.

"Whatever you say, Howard." She was apparently going to try the tack of patient submission. "If you want me to join in this—"

"Certainly. You're only young once."

"And that was twenty years ago. Well—" She sighed a little; she had never looked so haggard, so ugly—her granulated eyelids pink and on her lip a slight rash left by her depilatory. "Tell me, Molly, is there a room on this floor where I could undress. I'm in poor shape for climbing stairs."

"A room! To undress!" Howard protested, feeling the request as somehow an intended rebuke. "But we're all going to be playing in here together in a minute, without a—"

"What harm does it do you, Howard? I'm willing to stand naked side by side with these young things and let you make comparisons, since it amuses you to torture yourself in this way. But getting undressed is a private matter for me. For pity's sake, indulge me a little. You can stay here with your—"

"I'll come with you," Howard volunteered, not quite knowing why.

"There's a room in there," Molly-o said, shrugging her shoulders a little contemptuously so that her breasts bounced. She pointed a tapering, tanned arm toward a door on her right. "A music room we hardly use any more."

Howard followed Jessie into the darkness, though she had walked off without even looking back in his direction and he knew he would be able to find nothing to say to her. When he reached for the wall switch, Jessie put a hand over it to prevent him; but she had left the door open a little so that in the mitigated gloom he could make out a dozen or so spindly chairs hunched under dustcovers around the walls, a love seat also protected from the dust, a piano, and behind it a harp.

"It's a harp!" Jessie said wonderingly, touching the strings lightly until they responded with a tingling and humming that filled the shadowy room. "Let's go home, Howard. Let's get out of here. You said before—"

"A ghost of a harp. No. It's too late now. We have to stay." He hung his pants on the harp, muting the strings. "Oh Lord, now that we've decided to stay, I've got to go."

"There's another door on the other side of the room. I imagine that somewhere through there— Can you see all right in the dark? Please, Howard, couldn't we just—"

"No, no, no. I can see fine." But he lurched and stumbled in the darkness, nearly tripping over one of the hooded chairs, and staggered finally into a lighted corridor, flanked by the john. He was wearing only his underpants, the ones with the repeated print of the *Pinta*, the *Niña* and the *Santa Maria*, a present from his in-laws which he had begun by hating, but had ended finding a good joke. He had not realized that he was quite this drunk.

Coming out of the toilet, he almost walked into Molly-o, who flung her arms around his neck and kissed him briskly. Her breasts were astonishingly firm despite their size, the nipples, not brownish or purple but really pink as a child would paint them, hard enough to press uncomfortably into his soft flesh. Jessie's, he thought dimly, had never been like this even when she was quite young. "Oh, *thank* you, Howard," Molly said breathlessly. "You saved the party. I thought we were going to have to sit there and *talk* all night. I had you all wrong. I—"

He grabbed her again, returning the kiss hard, his hands slipping down her back until he held her around the hips. Her mouth fell open all the way under his and he could feel her knees bend, her body sag, though whether from passion or alcohol he could not tell. I'm just doing this to shut her up anyway, he told himself; it's so silly to let her betray those woman's breasts with her girl's chatter; I'm not even excited. . . .

He jumped suddenly under a resounding smack on his right buttock, and Molly skittered off smiling at him vaguely over her shoulder. Beatie stood behind him, grinning broadly and quite naked. "*Shmendrick!*" she said. "Big Brother is watching. Do you call this croquet?"

She had not called him *shmendrick*, Howard realized, since they were both fifteen and they had fumbled their way into what was the first affair for both of them, more like friends playing than lovers. Then Beatie had really fallen in love for the first time and —somehow thirty years had gone by! "Thirty years!" he said, perhaps aloud, but Beatie did not respond. He looked incredulously at her body, a girl's body when he had touched it last, now all at once full-blown, the muscle tone gone, the legs mottled blue-black with varicose veins—like someone's mother.

"I was just—" he stuttered. "That is—"

"Never mind," Beatie answered. "Before you lie to me, I believe you. Go find Jessie."

As he turned around confusedly, looking for a way back into the music room, Howard had the impression that the door through which he had come was closed softly, as if Jessie had been watching him, too, and was now withdrawing. But when he entered, she was lying face down on the love seat, her naked back rising and falling regularly.

"Are you asleep?" he whispered.

"Asleep!" she answered, rolling over. "You bastard, come here." She pulled him down on top of her, winding her arms around him with a ferocity that astonished him. She had not clung to him so desperately in years. "Oh, hold me, Howard, and for God's sake don't say anything. Tight, tight, *tight!*"

The love seat creaked under them, groaning in rhythmic protest; and the harp, set jangling by their movements, called a sympathetic response from under the top of the piano. The whole room buzzed and hummed and sang to the tempo they set, until the noises of their bodies and their breathing seemed a part of a musical performance. Maybe the love seat will break under us, Howard found himself thinking, absurdly pleased at the prospect of so triumphant a climax. And then he was able to focus thought no longer. He could hear himself beginning a moan that mounted slowly to a real cry, drowning the mingled endearments and curses of his wife—a wordless declaration of terror and pain that was also a victory. And then it was over.

When they rejoined the others, they discovered that someone had set the record player going again (perhaps, it occurred to Howard, to drown out the embarrassingly unambiguous noises from the music room), and that the overhead lights had been turned off. Only two huge gilded and twisted seven-branched candlesticks illuminated the big room now, one set before each of the wall-length mirrors; and reflected back and forth from glass to gleaming body to glass, the fourteen points of light were multiplied to thousands. Leather-bound folios, opened to the middle and set spine up, did duty for wickets, and the others were already bent over the varicolored balls, mallets in hand. They had begun to scream insults and encouragement at each other, at ease in the friendly dark that camouflaged their bulges and creases and broken veins, their bunions and scars and grizzled hair. Only the smell of their naked bodies, triumphing over the cologne and perfume, could not be disguised, a thick, locker-room aroma that assaulted Howard at the entrance of the room so that he almost turned away.

After a while, he could begin to make them out more clearly through the flickering shadows: Leonard, vaguely hermaphroditic, pudgy and white; Eva, her cross falling just where her pancake makeup gave way to the slightly pimpled pallor of her skin (there was the mark of a bite on one small breast); Jessie, whose body was astonishingly younger than her lined witch's face, but whose gray below betrayed the red splendor of her hair; Achsa, tallow-yellow and without breasts; Beatie, marked with the red griddle of her corseting and verging on shapelessness; Marvin, sallow and unmuscled beneath the lank black hair that covered even his upper arms. He dragged more and more wearily behind him a withered left leg, creased from hip to knee by a puckered and livid scar, testimony to the osteomyelitis that had kept him in bed through most of his childhood. Only Molly pranced and preened, secure in her massaged and sun-lamped loveliness. To each of the others nudity was a confession, a humiliation. Yet they laughed louder and louder, though no one knew precisely what he was doing; and the crack of mallet on ball punctuated their chatter.

Once, in the hubbub, Beatie drew Howard aside into the music room where he and Jessie had undressed. She was crying abandonedly once more, snorting and heaving and dripping tears that seemed somehow ridiculous above the expanse of her nakedness. "What's going to be with me and Bernie, Howard?" she asked, not in hope of an answer he knew, but because the question had to be spoken aloud. "He's in bad trouble, sicker than anyone knows—under analysis. Don't tell anyone, Howard, not even Jessie. He doesn't want— And I let him go away alone. He couldn't any more take his clothes off in front of these people, than—I don't know—than finish the novel he's been working on secretly since he was in high school. He weighs two hundred and seventy pounds, Howard—and he makes more and more money. He can't stand it! One of his things is he's got it in his head that he's smaller than other people, smaller than other men, I mean. You know what I mean, Howard." She pointed vaguely toward her own shaggy crotch. But why doesn't she say it out, Howard thought, annoyed and impatient; she's a little sick, too. "His doctor says it has something to do with being a Jew, circumcision, God knows what. And knowing all this, I let him go alone— alone! *Why*, Howard? Howard, *tell* me something."

What did he have to tell her, what wisdom for all his forty-five years? He may have kissed her then, for he had come always to kiss women when he was at a loss with them—another laziness. But he could never remember later, though the feel and savor of it remained with him, into whose mouth he had melted so deliciously in that room, hers or Molly-o's. For a little later he had taken Molly, too (or had he only wished it?), into the darkened music room, while Bill slept peacefully in the sacred chair and the rest howled around him.

All other episodes, however, faded into the confusion of the endless and pointless game, and into the mockery of Marvin which finally became its point. All the rest, varyingly drunk and skillful, slapped an occasional shot through an improvised folio wicket, or successfully cracked an opponent's ball away from a favorable spot; but Marvin, incredibly unco-ordinated, could do nothing. Sometimes, his leg buckling under him, he would miss the ball completely, denting the hardwood floor with his mallet or catching it under a Persian rug; sometimes the ball would skid off the edge of his hammer, trickle two or three inches to one side and maddeningly stop. Once the head of his mallet flew off at the end of a particularly wild swing, just missing Molly's eye.

After a while, they were all trailing after him, Achsa leading the pack, like the gallery of a champion golfer, roaring at every stroke, while Marvin said nothing, only more grimly and comically addressed the ball. The real horror, Howard felt, was that Marvin now *wanted* to smack the elusive object before him squarely through the wicket, to win the applause of his mockers. For all that he knew it to be nonsense, Marvin had been somehow persuaded that it *mattered*—reliving, Howard supposed, the ignominy of his childhood, when in the street and to the jeers of his fellows he had failed at caddy or stoopball or kick the can.

Drawing the stick back between his scarred and rickety legs, Marvin delivered a stroke finally with such force and imbalance that he toppled over onto his face. He lay there for a little while motionless, his pale, skinny buttocks twitching, while they all laughed and hooted and cheered. They could not afford to admit that it was anything but a joke.

Only Eva, who had screamed at him earlier, was moved to protest. "Oh, don't!" she cried, whirling on the rest with tears in her eyes. "Please, *don't!* Can't you see he's like a fallen king—a fallen king!" She took a step toward him, but could not bring herself to touch his pale, sweaty body, and ended covering her eyes with the hand she had reached out toward him in sympathy.

"A fallen king!" Achsa repeated contemptuously, sensing the others were slipping away from her, beginning to feel shame and pity. "Why don't you get up, your majesty, and say a few words about the dignity of failure?" She was hopelessly drunk and the efforts of Jessie and Beatie to quiet her only seemed to infuriate her the more.

"He likes it down there on the floor and in the dark," she continued. "Don't disturb him, my fallen king. He's working out canto twenty-four of the epic, volume three of the cultural history. Don't laugh so loud. You might wake him and American literature will suffer." She leaned over and tapped her husband lightly on the side of the head with the flat of her mallet. "Get up, Marvin, and try again. You're holding up the game. Get up!" He rose slowly into a sitting position, very pale and avoiding her eyes. "Maybe you'd like to make a statement," she insisted. "Maybe you'd like to—"

"Give me a hand, Howard," he said. "I guess I'm higher than I thought. I need a—"

"I'll give you a hand," Achsa screamed before Howard could move; and she held out the end of her mallet toward Marvin who made no move to lay hold of it. "Here, *take* it!" she cried in rage, drawing it back and smashing it full force across his left cheek. "How come you don't say 'Thank you,' Marv? Say 'Thank you' to the nice lady!" She hit him even harder this time on the other side of the head; and when he remained silent, harder and harder still, first right, then left, then right. She could hardly breathe. "Why don't you talk to me, Marvin? Why don't you *talk* to me? Say 'Thank you,' Marvin. Why don't you say 'Thank you'—"

Howard, who had stood by paralyzed with the rest, grabbed her under the arms, dragging her backwards with her feet in the air, and hanging on grimly though sweat had made her slippery and she leaned over to sink her teeth into the back of his hand.

"Smack her, Howard," Jessie advised him. "For pity's sake, slap her. She's hysterical." But he did not dare shift his hold, for fear of losing his purchase on her damp and squirming flesh.

Meanwhile, Marvin had risen very slowly to his feet, a thin trickle of blood running out of one corner of his mouth and down over his chin. "I—I—" he began twice over. "I—" then sank to his knees, moaning. "Achsa," he yelled in terror. "Achsa, for God's sake, the pills in my pocket—my right— It's another attack, another—" His words burbled away into incoherence; then, grasping his upper left arm in his right hand and lifting his chin into the air, he cried out in agony and triumph—a cry so like his own on the love seat with Jessie that Howard thought for a moment he was only remembering it. Marvin's mouth was drawn back, his teeth shown in what may have been a smile, and his wordless cry may have turned again into Achsa's name before he pitched forward on his face again; but Howard could not be sure.

"Let me go! Let me go!" Achsa begged him, kicking and scratching. "What are you doing to him? My Marvin! Let me go!" He finally released his hold at the moment the overhead lights were switched on again, fixing them all in their nudity and helplessness, caught for one everlasting instant as in a flashbulb still.

Molly had begun to scream, a single note, high and pure, that seemed as if it would never end; and whirling about, they all stared at her in the hard light, even Bill, startled back to awareness on his bishop's throne. One arm concealing her breasts, the other thrust downward so that her hand hid the meeting of her thighs, Molly-o confronted them in the classic pose of nakedness surprised, as if she knew for the first time what it meant to be really nude.

The Last Jew in America

A T FIRST Jacob Moskowitz said only, "It's for Louie. So
don't argue, come. How much longer does he have to
live? A week, maybe, or ten days? I won't even say
please. For his sake, come."

But they just stared back at him blankly, those so-called
Jews from the Faculty—with their gentile wives, their Ph.D.'s,
their button-down collars—answering him evasively, turning
away even before his plea was finished. Yet he spoke the
simple truth. Louis Himmerfarb was indeed dying in St. Cyprian's Hospital of all places: an old Jew, a life-long socialist,
a man who had once worked side by side with Sam Gompers,
consumed now by cancer and tended by nuns.

"It's *erev* Yom Kippur," Jacob tried next. "The Eve of the
Day of Atonement. For Louie, his last Yom Kippur. It's important to him." *And to me,* he added to himself, remembering
his own nearly seventy years. *How many more will I see?
Where will I be this time next year?* Aloud, however, he settled
for saying, "How many of us are there altogether in this God-
forsaken town? How many in the whole world after what happened to the Six Million? Let's make a *minyan* while we can,
one more *minyan*. These days it's quite an accomplishment."

Did they even know what a minyan was, he thought, *did
they remember that it took ten men, ten male Jews over thirteen to make a quorum, a legal congregation? And how many
of them would you need anyhow to add up to ten real Jews?*
"All right," he urged them, "what do you say—yes or no?"

522

But their eyes answered him even before their lying mouths —their goyish eyes, bloodshot from last night's cocktail party: "A *minyan* for what, for Christ's sake?"

"Pardon me," he retorted. "I thought you were Jewish. Okay, so never mind Louie, never mind Hitler. Skip Yom Kippur even. All I'm asking is what makes you think you have the right to drop out of history, to elect yourself the last Jew in America? That's hubris (do I pronounce it right, professor?), overweening pride, ain't it?" And pleased with his own style, he scarcely listened to their only too predictable excuses.

Naturally, one of them was giving an evening lecture on criminology to the local Police Force; another had to attend a CORE meeting, to send petitions to Mississippi since there were too few Negroes to matter nearby; another's youngest daughter was "flying up" in Bluebirds and he had to be present to pin on her medal, or tie her tie; while the oldest son of still another was playing football for the County High School.

"He's the star," the proud father explained. "They're all depending on him." And on which night in the year would it not have been the same story?

"To hell with . . ." Jacob yelled, filling in the blank appropriately in each case, ". . . the Police . . . the Negroes . . . the Bluebirds . . . the goddamned High School. Just come!" And, "Bring your son," he added the last time around. "It wouldn't kill him either. Remember. In the Hospital. Louie's room, number 1303. I'll bring the Torah."

Unfortunately he could bring no more than the Scrolls of the Law, since his single child, a daughter, had died of peritonitis at the age of twelve, some thirty years before. Even the little cemetery in which she lay buried had ceased to be Jewish, having passed into the hands of the City Council with the death of his wife's father, who had been the last of the old Congregation, to which the Torah Jacob now offered had originally belonged. "We'll make it really *kosher* this time," he finished in self-contempt. "A Jewish Torah and a Catholic Hospital."

But his irony was wasted, the notion of *Kol Nidre* among the nuns seeming to his victims neither absurd nor disquieting.

Only the football player's father, who taught Anglo-Saxon and wore cowboy boots and a string-tie, seemed a little embarrassed. "Look," he said, "maybe tomorrow morning I could persuade him to—oh, hell, who am I kidding anyhow. You know the kid, I can't even get him to read Yeats or Joyce, much less Rashi or whatever. He's a real outdoor type, like his mother's family, and he got a brand-new shotgun. But my daughter, on the other hand, is always asking me about—"

"Who needs your lousy daughter?" Jacob cried, the violence of his response surprising him. Would he not have wanted his own daughter by his side, if things had worked out differently? "Bring sons or nothing. Sundown. Sharp."

"My God, at least I named him Abraham," the Professor of Anglo-Saxon said, lifting a hand not toward Jacob exactly but to some point just above his head. "Abraham—over my wife's dead body. What more could I do?"

And if this one turned out to be the last Jew in America, Jacob could not help thinking, as he watched him slap his broad-brimmed hat against the tops of his boots in an ecstasy of shame, *what a catastrophe, what a joke.* But he was not sure what it meant finally that the last catastrophe of the Jews be a joke.

Of one thing he thought himself sure, however, and crying, "Thank God!" aloud, congratulated himself on not being a professor at least, not really a faculty member at all. Still, he had been pleased when the students at the College had begun some years before to call him "Doc" and to invite him to lecture before their fraternities and their church groups on Nietzsche or Marx or Freud—whatever they knew him to be reading at the time. He realized that in part they found him a clown, with his comic accent and outlandish gestures; but maybe a clown was exactly what they needed to deliver them from the bloodless wisdom of their parents and teachers.

"Look," he would begin, after the embarrassed introduction, "you thought you were getting, I don't know, Pagliacci, Falstaff —and instead you're dealing with Socrates. Go do me something." And they would laugh and laugh, these sons of ranchers and miners and real estate salesmen and used car dealers, adding one more story to the legend of Jacob which they had inherited from students before them.

Certainly- they had all heard, if they had not themselves witnessed, how he would prowl the crowded gymnasium during Registration Week—arms behind his back, the knuckles of one nervous hand in the palm of the other—to demand of some young and unsuspecting instructor, a first-time "advisor," "So tell me, Professor, what course should I take . . ." (he would pause, his comedian's voice grown loud enough to be audible everywhere) ". . . to find out what is the good life and how should I lead it?"

He had learned nothing as a student himself, not even finishing his first year in the Ag School to which he had been sent by a rich Jewish benefactor, interested in persuading immigrant boys to go to the land rather than huddle in cities; since he had despised his instructors for their obtuseness, and himself even more for the difficulties with English which had got in the way of his showing them up. In any case, school had interfered with his reading, which had seemed then the whole meaning of his life, and so he had got out, bearing his questions with him. *What is the good life and how do you lead it?* he would ask himself aloud, leaning on his shovel in the remote forest where he found work after his escape; and though nobody had answered, no one had laughed, either.

Except, perhaps, whatever demon it was that had brought him out of the woods to the Lewis and Clark campus, where—looking up one day in astonishment—he discovered he had passed three decades, expecting each day to move on to something else. What he was, what he had been for nearly thirty-five years, was the animal man in the Zoology Department, a tender of guinea pigs and weasels and wild cats, a cleaner of cages.

Yet he drew more books out of the College Library, read more current magazines in the half-deserted Periodical Room, heckled more inspiredly at dull public lectures than any of his "colleagues" in Philosophy or Literature or the Behavioral Sciences. And for fifteen years he had held the nominal rank of Assistant Professor, thanks to a Dean who had shared his enthusiasm for *Evgeny Onegin*—on the basis of which his wife Leah had joined the Faculty Women's Club, even the American Association of University Women, where no one had thought to challenge her non-existent credentials.

Yet Leah had never felt really accepted by the women in whose midst she had sat for so many years, her hats, like her opinion of her husband, identical with theirs; since she could never forget that her father had been the local pawnbroker and —in the unproved opinion of everyone in town—a fence. Certainly Jacob had not helped her quest for respectability with his loudly professed political heresies, his stubbornly unfashionable clothes, and his refusal to unlearn his ghetto inflections and gestures. Her own voice had grown quieter and quieter, her motions of hand and head more restrained and minimal, until one day she had disappeared: dead finally, Jacob had not been able to deny even to himself (the confused doctors offering him no credible alternative), of a broken heart. But he had never heard of one breaking so slowly, over thirty or forty years anyway, perhaps over the full sixty-two which Leah had accumulated before sneaking away into death one night, without even a sigh.

At any rate, Jacob had been a widower for nearly three years now, a footloose and melancholy man, wandering from office to office, prowling the stacks of the Library, dawdling on the steps of the Administration Building, sitting hopefully hour after hour in the Cafeteria, in quest of a companionship that forever eluded him, a commitment—for half an hour, five minutes even—as total as Leah's had been, despite all their differences, for over four decades. But behind every Jewish male whom Jacob trapped, lurked the unseen presence, the threat of that man's wife, usually a gentile, so that their encounters smacked inevitably of a tryst, an indiscretion, an extra-marital affair without status or future; and each ended, therefore, in mutual ·recriminations and anger.

Finally Jacob had come to begin with the insults to which he knew he would be driven in the end, pouring out his accumulated rage on his newest interlocutor, who would stare at him in bafflement or incontinently flee. "My God, what a pest," he would hear him say, presuming on Jacob's deafness; and there was no use trying to kid himself. He *had* become a pest, a plain and simple pest, though not, thank God, quite so unmitigated a pest as Louie.

Louie had been a bachelor, which had made it worse, without even a wife to annoy or remember. So what had been left for him to do, after he had been voted out of office by the State County and Municipal Workers Union, whose business agent he had been since before Jacob had known him, except to become a one-hundred-percent professional Jew. His moderate socialism had long since been absorbed into New Deal pieties, and his allegiance to labor had not survived his rejection by those for whose sake he had endured being framed into two years in jail without a word of public protest or explanation.

To make matters worse, his enemies among his fellow workers had exploited precisely his most sacrificial action on their behalf. "A jailbird," his rival had called him from the platform during the union election that unseated him; and, "A crooked Jew," that rival had added in private, "he's got plenty of your money soaked away in the bank, and don't forget it for a minute. They always know what side their bread is buttered on. The Chosen People!"

So Louie had spent his last years in fund-raising for the United Jewish Appeal, arranging meetings for visiting Israeli speakers, and bullying the reluctant not-quite-Jews of the community into desultory Seders and Purim celebrations. "For the children," he had invariably explained to the bored planning groups, crowded uncomfortably into his rented room, where the only things that had been really his own were a handful of books and a giant hand-tinted portrait of Franklin Delano Roosevelt, hung between a pair of hunting scenes in the snow. "You owe it to them," he had customarily concluded, "whether you know it or not, whether you want to admit it or not. So eat, don't argue."

He would indicate then the snack he always prepared as a kind of unanswerable final argument: a bowlful of Mother's

Gefilte Fish, right out of the jars he had persuaded the local supermarket to stock; a loaf of rye bread with *kimmel,* flown in from Seattle; a gallon of Mogen David wine, bought at the bar of the Mint, which stocked it for the winos off the freights. "Eat, drink. Don't stand on ceremony. You're among *landsmenner* here."

Even Jacob had come to avoid Louie at last, slipping across the street or into the convenient shelter of a nearby store whenever he had seen him approaching—to avoid being reminded of some unpaid pledge, some unredeemable obligation to history and the dead. "And am I now in the Louie-position?" he asked himself bitterly, preparing to leave the campus for his final interview. "Have I become the town Jew for the rest of my life, a professional conscience for the conscienceless? I who fled the *shtetl* and the graves of my ancestors to be a new man in a new world. What do I think I'm doing? Who do I think I am?"

But he could not leave off what he had begun—not at that point anyhow; and the campus, he knew, really, was the easiest part of the job. Here, in some sense at least, he was at home as he never was in the "down-town" that still remained to be canvassed: an utterly alien place inhabited by the handful of non-academic Jews in Lewis and Clark City, with most of whom he had exchanged over the years no more than a dozen words—an underwear salesman, an aged lady librarian, the owner of a shoe shop, two lawyers who did not speak to each other, but neither of whom would deign to ask him if the other had been invited; and last of all, Max Shultheis the jeweler, the second (or was it only the third?) richest man in town.

But after all, it was not so hard, no harder than shoving his way among the cowboys, the Indians, the merchants (all equally wooden-faced and thin-lipped) to buy, say, a pair of socks or to get his hair cut. To each of his fellow Jews, scarcely distinguishable from their gentile neighbors except for their tell-tale names, he made his standard speech, occasionally embroidering it a little to keep from boring himself too much, and not caring certainly whether any of them quite understood what he was saying.

Yet he grew somehow more and more indignant with each repetition, until he came to feel himself more prophet than *nudnik*—speaking not with his own querulous voice but in the thundering tones of a God in whom, of course, he did not—he made no bones about it—believe. "What makes you think you have the right to be the last Jew in America? Five thousand years of history you have no right to cancel out unilaterally."

"What did I say? What did I do?" the underwear salesman, a great kidder, whom Jacob had caught packing his fishing gear into the trunk of his Chrysler, cried, backing off in pretended alarm. "You don't have to make a federal case out of it. I'll come."

Max, however, was another matter, and not merely because of his big mouth, and his shameless relish of his own success, for which Jacob cordially hated him; but because Max, knowing Jacob the way it is painful to be known even by those who love you and not loving him one damn bit, might laugh. In fact, he always laughed at Jacob when he was not bawling him out, thumping him on the back with hearty condescension, and crying, "Listen to the Professor, the *chochem*. He knows. Congress don't know, the League of Nations don't know, the Pope himself don't know, but Jacob Moskowitz knows. Only how to blow his nose he don't know, how to put a dollar in the bank, the *chochem*."

And in any case, Jacob's last argument, his clincher, would not work with Max; for Max had already chosen to be a last Jew, marrying a Catholic woman, a scarcely articulate peasant from the Ukraine, barely touched by her years in America. And he had been genuinely pleased that his six sons—scattered now across the whole breadth of the land—had married *shiksas*, too. "Why not?" he would bellow when challenged. "All the good Jews are dead. My six bad Jews should live a hundred and twenty years and die in bed. Knock wood."

On the other hand, Max had made a contribution to the United Jewish Appeal every year since the establishment of the State of Israel: twenty-five hundred dollars right on the line—more than twice the amount given by all of the Jewish professors added together. But Yom Kippur was not Israel, no headlines in the local paper, no seat in the U.N., no victories to celebrate. Besides, it was he, Jacob, who was going to do the inviting; and it was doubtful whether Max would have come to his own birthday party on Jacob's request.

Never mind, he reassured himself. *Ask. What can he do, eat you?* But standing with his hand on the knob of the front door of Max's store, the Sacajewea Hotel behind him, and the image of his own face on the glass before, Jacob could not help imagining the whole scene in advance. It was his habit, his curse, to live through everything three times—before, during, after.

Without even troubling to rise from the desk in the back room into which he would call Jacob, Max would pull a drastically chewed cigar from between his ill-fitting false teeth and laugh in his face. Not the slightest doubt about it. And who could blame him anyhow, since Max, who forgot nothing that might some day give him an advantage, would not have forgotten the story of Jacob and his mother and that other Yom Kippur long, long before.

But that story at least, Jacob assured himself, he would not recall, not here anyhow in the crowded street, and before the door of Max. Why, then, had he not held his tongue in the first place? He always told Max too much, Jacob had realized even at the moment of spilling everything; but how could he have resisted, things being as they were. He had been lonely, that's all, plain and simple lonely. And to talk in his own tongue even about what was most painful to him, especially what was most painful to him, had been a kind of consolation.

There had been only the three of them during the early days, in a town of nearly twenty thousand: three lonely Russian Jews jostled by a hybrid horde of Baptists, Presbyterians, Methodists, Episcopalians, Catholics, Lutherans, Jehovah's Witnesses, God knows what all—he and Louie and Max. To be sure, there was also Leah, whom Jacob eventually married, but she had scarcely seemed to count, having been born in the United States, in Lewis and Clark City itself.

And her father, stiff-faced and speechless in his wheelchair by the time Jacob had arrived, had been merely a silent witness: sole survivor of an older generation of Jewish tradesmen, who had strangely faded away before the influx of Jewish faculty into the University (then still an Ag School) had begun. He had seemed as vestigial and meaningless as an Indian—indeed, had looked like an Indian; his old, seamed face bronzed dark by the sun toward which he had insisted, in a sign language Jacob never understood, his daughter keep him turned all spring and summer.

So they had gathered together from time to time, just the three of them—invariably in Louie's house—to share memories of *cheder* and *shul;* of the difficulties of 1905 and the perils of avoiding the Czarist draft; but chiefly to speak Yiddish and to pass from hand to hand the current issue of the *Forwerts,* always a week old by the time it had crossed two thirds of a continent. They had been joint subscribers to that newspaper—Max, the cheapskate, insisting that the other two pitch in, though by that time he had given up the pretense of poverty to which he had clung for so long, and had moved from the clapboard bungalow down by the railroad tracks to the fourteen room mansion half way up the protected slope of Mount Heavyrunner.

Jacob, who had then still been a more or less faithful Stalinist, would have preferred to subscribe to the Communist *Freiheit,* not only because of its sympathetic politics but also for the sake of its superior Yiddish. The half-English jargon of the *Forwerts* had offended him even more deeply than its centrist hypocrisy, symbolized in a slogan which still called on the "Workers of the World" to unite, though its editors had long since abandoned all Marxist principles. But what use would it have been to argue his position with either of his Red-baiting companions? To both of them, the Social Democrat as well as the Republican, the term "Communist" had become merely one more dirty word, a contemptuous designation of the enemy; and they had never ceased to regard even him with suspicion—as if at any moment he might throw off his disguise as Jacob the Animal Man, and reveal himself in his true colors: a Sunday Supplement Secret Agent, loaded down with Moscow Gold.

As a matter of fact, Jacob had been sent to his improbable place of exile by the Communist Party, or at least by certain functionaries of the Party convinced that this scrawny Jew was intended by fate to lead the cowhands and apple-growers of the Mountain West toward a free and peaceful Soviet America. Had he not entered the United States via Galveston, Texas, worked his way up the very center of the country, then followed the Missouri back up its course toward the Rockies, like Lewis and Clark before him—finding odd jobs on cotton plantations and wheat ranches, in fruit orchards and cowbarns? Had he not even judged hogs once at a fat stock show? And did he not therefore speak the language of the people in that unimaginable hinterland?

Despite the cogency of this argument, Jacob had gotten nowhere fast attempting to bore from within at Grange meetings, or hopefully button-holing poor farmers at square dances and old-time fiddling contests. Everywhere he had seemed a stranger—more comic perhaps than malign, more endearing than threatening, but an outsider all the same. He had not finally been able to organize even the janitorial and grounds crew at the University, though individually its members had come to him for advice and small loans.

And meanwhile he had been growing more and more appalled at the ignorance of the handful of other local Party people and their petty contests for power, as well as their wife-swapping and hard drinking, before which his puritanical Jewish conscience and his queasy Jewish stomach had both quailed. It had not been until the Hitler-Stalin pact, however, until public scandal had seconded private distress, that he had spoken his doubts aloud and had been booted out of the Party as an infantile leftist. But by that time, he had become for most of his fellow townsmen, including Louie and Max and his own wife, a hopeless trouble-maker, an unredeemable fool. Yet a permanent fixture all the same, a part of the life of the community as irreplaceable as the bad roads, the high price of gasoline or any of the other minor annoyances without which all conversation might have faltered and died.

Certainly, during the early years, he had confessed none of his reservations about the Soviet Union and the Party either to Louis Himmelfarb, who had still continued to talk Norman Thomas though already voting F. D. R., or to Max Shultheis, who would rehearse without shame the foulest anti-Semitic slanders of Roosevelt, even, from time to time, defend Father Coughlin himself. Infuriated, Jacob would defend in return anything that Max opposed, right down to Russia's support of the Arabs in Palestine and the assassination of Trotsky. "Who needs them?" he would holler when the Zionists were brought up. "Agents of British Imperialism! Social Fascists!"

More often than not, therefore, their sessions would end with each of them attempting to scream the others down in rage and anguish; until, able to bear no more, Jacob would bolt out into the night, leaving Natasha Shultheis to mourn over the unconsumed pastry she had prepared especially for him. Unlike Louie, he had not had to worry about gout (ridiculous disease for a labor leader); and unlike Max, he had no tendency to grow fat, so that he had been able to indulge his sweet tooth untroubled by anything except anger. It was for this that Natasha had loved him, occasionally intervening on his behalf with her husband of whom she was terrified. "He don't mean it. He don't know what he's saying," she would plead. "Why do you even listen to him? Remember your pressure, your heart."

"Exactly what I'm telling him," her husband would answer. "So why don't he shut up and listen? And why don't you give him an example? Maybe you ain't got enough to do around the house." And having turned on her, he would forget about Jacob.

Once, however, after a particularly vicious hassle over the role of the Communists in Spain, even her mediation had failed; and for more than two years (*had she stopped baking the whole while?* Jacob had wondered) he and Max had ceased speaking completely, passing each other on the street with sidelong glances and snorts of contempt. He had never been more content with himself, Jacob came to realize later, than when he had been able wholeheartedly to despise the fellow Jew who was, in fact, the enemy of all in which he most deeply believed. But what had he been able to do, after Max had embarrassingly come to his rescue?

It had been in the worst of the McCarthy days, when it had looked as if Jacob was really going to lose his job, when his name had actually been mentioned on the floor of the legislature, and almost every mail had brought an anonymous postcard saying JEW COMMIE GO HOME! that had set poor Leah to trembling. He had been taking pills, unable to sleep and baffled in his feeble attempts to begin drinking seriously, by the time Max had intervened. It had not surprised Jacob, of course, that Louie had stood by him from the first, bullying his timid fellow unionists into issuing statements of support, even organizing a raggle-taggle parade before the Governor's Mansion at one point; but it had astonished and dismayed him that Max had rallied round, too—in the end, probably saving his skin.

He had scarcely recognized Max's voice at first, the phone rousing him from a troubled sleep at two one morning just when everything had seemed most hopeless; and trembling, afraid of God knows what, he had placed the receiver to his ear. "Listen, professor," Max had begun, "and don't say a word because I guarantee you it'll be the wrong thing."

"But who?" Jacob had answered. "Who is it? What—"

"You see," the voice at the other end had cut him off, "exactly what I expected. *Who*, he says."

"Max?"

"Who else? Listen, this is just between you, me and the lamp post, but you got nothing to worry. I done a little leaning where it counts. I won't mention names but you could guess maybe. After all, you're the *chochem* not me. Anyway, you're all right. Everything's all right. You understand?"

"I understand," Jacob had said, still bewildered and only half-awake. "Only I—thank you, thank you."

"What's the use to say thank you, when you'll do the same thing next time, am I right? The same thing."

"Well, I—"

"Never mind, never mind. With these *goyim* you have to know how to deal. *I* know. So sleep easy. You got nothing to be afraid."

There had been no love in his voice, however, not even pity —only condescension and contempt, plus a begrudged acknowledgment of some presumed obligation of Jew to Jew which Jacob had found especially offensive, as Max must have found all his presumptions offensive. "Don't do me any favors," he had shouted back finally. "I don't need anything from you, not now, not ever!" But Max had already hung up.

It was for Louie's sake that Max had acted, anyhow, Jacob had been sure even then, Louie whom Max had not only loved but even respected—for Louie, being an old time lobbyist, had called by their first names all the bigwigs whom Max resented and admired: state legislators, judges, officials of the Power Company, even the senior United States Senator, an anti-Semite and America Firster from way back. Moreover, Louie had served time, meaning to Max that he, too, was a crook like those bigwigs themselves.

The solid citizen and the *gonif,* these two types Max Shultheis understood and looked up to, since he saw himself as both. Twice President of the Lewis and Clark City Chamber of Commerce, he had hung on to his interest in the last functioning skid-row whorehouse out of some conviction that mere respectability was not enough to assert and prove power, not in the world of the gentiles. And if he had believed for one moment that Louie had all along been innocent of the charges on which he had been jailed, a victim of others slicker than he, Max would have despised him as he had always despised Jacob; since it had not been as a Red but as a fool that Max had held Jacob in contempt—as a fall-guy for the Soviet Union, a dupe of Stalin—for whom Max had had the sneaking admiration of one bully for another.

And what had Jacob been, after all, defending for so many years that monster, that *antisemit* in the Kremlin? About that, at least, he had to admit, Max had been right all along. *Not right,* he amended his own conclusion, *only correct, which is a horse of a different color. Never, never right.* So how could he talk to him about Louïe Himmelfarb's Yom Kippur, invite him and be refused, run the risk of being laughed at, reminded in shame of his past.

No, he decided, walking rapidly away from the jewelry store, back across the bridge and toward the western rim of the circle of hills that enclosed the town, no, he would not confront Max face to face, he would call him up. Over the telephone all things were bearable, even Max sniggering as he recalled in malice the story Jacob had told him in trust: the story Jacob had always to tell someone this time of the year, and that he now told to himself despite his earlier admonitions to himself not to remember it.

How young he had been, no more than fourteen at most, and still in the little town of Verenskaya, the place in which he had been born and had never up until that moment managed to leave. Yet he had already begun to dream of escaping to America; for he had known that the pious householders who sustained him would catch up with him soon: those gullible old Jews who had been supplying him with "days," putting food into his mouth, turn and turn about, on the understanding that he was continuing his study of the Torah.

"A boy who knows," the oldest and kindliest of them, a rich lumber merchant, childless himself, had liked to say, pinching Jacob's cheek hard, "a boy who remembers. 'He who remembers hastens the coming of the Messiah.'"

But what had the young Jacob been remembering in fact, and the coming of what demon had he been hastening—slipping off more often than not from the *beth midrash* to read *Werther* and Heine's poems, and, worst of all, *Sanine.* He had not been alone, Mendel, the boy from next door carrying in his pocket a vial of what he had claimed was poison to show himself ready for suicide, but he had been the worst of the lot: a full-fledged traitor already to everything in which his fathers believed, though a grubby little boy still. And to make matters worse, he had not even been ashamed, justifying himself to himself with fantasies of recognition and acclaim in the great gentile world outside.

He had not been outside at all, however, not in Vienna or Paris or New York; but still inside in Verenskaya, among those he loved and pained—not yet the great rebel he fancied himself, only a nasty little sneak. That year, at least, he had openly refused for the first time to accompany his father to *Kol Nidre,* sending him off to *shul* in tears, and sitting home over a copy of George Eliot's *Daniel Deronda* in Hebrew translation.

Dreaming of himself, as he idly scanned the pages, as a rich and handsome aristocrat, pursued by blonde Englishwomen but preferring to any of them an unfortunate daughter of his own people (oddly like, in his fantasy, the little girl he had passed often on his way to and from the single toilet in the courtyard, but to whom he had never dared say a single word), he had been suddenly overcome by a hunger more imperative than his still theoretical lust. And repeating to himself the line from the Yom Kippur service which only a year or two before his elders had laughed at him for repeating with such fervor, "For the sin which we have sinned before thee by unchastity . . . ," he had ransacked the house until he had turned up a hard heel of bread.

Leaning over his book, still open to the picture of Daniel sadly contemplating the beautiful Gwendolen Harleth at the gaming tables, Jacob had bitten into the bread ravenously. He had been aware the whole time that it was a fast day, the most solemn of fast days, but he had continued his chomping all the same, having known that it did not matter in a world where the God of his fathers was dead and the heritage of his fathers lost forever. In a way, it had been as if he was already leaving Verenskaya, stepping off the gangplank of a ship in New York.

Even after he had become aware of his mother in the doorway, watching him in horror, one hand to her heart, he had not stopped; but had turned to her straight on, his jaws moving still, his teeth grinding into the forbidden food. *"Nu,"* he had said brazenly, "so I'm eating."

"Shegetz," she had cried, "it's Yom Kippur. What are you

doing? What are you thinking? Murderer, you're killing me, you're killing your own mother, the only mother you'll ever have. My blood will be on your hands. Esau."

But she had not died of Jacob's broken Yom Kippur, of course: living, as a matter of fact, through his flight to America, his marriage and the death of his daughter in that strange land—or rather through the shadows of those distant events transmitted in scanty letters and poor snapshots; living to the age of 93 or 94, which was to say, long enough to have been gassed—along with Jacob's father, his two sisters, the lumber merchant who had loved him and the girl in the courtyard to whom he had never managed to talk—in the ovens of Belsen; her blood, like that of all the rest, on someone's else's hands.

And that story Jacob, fool that he was, had had to tell to Max, not in Verenskaya which was no more, but in Lewis and Clark City in which he walked now the block and a half to Hank Allen's Save-More Drugstore, between Hazelbaker's Buick showroom and the big Penney's store. *I'll call him,* he reassured himself once more, leaning against the wall of the phone booth and dropping in his dime. *What's to be afraid. If he asks where I am, I'll tell him I'm home sick in bed.*

But Max's voice startled him all the same, booming out of the receiver. "What? What? Spit it out already." *Had he been banking the whole time on not finding Max in, on escaping scot free?*

"I'm in a drugstore phone booth," Jacob said at last into the instrument before him, unwilling really to begin. "This is Jacob Moskowitz."

"I know. I know. How many accents like yours do we have in Lewis and Clark City? Thanks God, not many." He bellowed so loud at his own intended joke that Jacob had to move the receiver away from his ear.

"It's—it's about Louie," he managed to say at last. "I'll make it short and sweet. I know to you time is money."

And then he was into it, Max groaning and blustering and guffawing as his tale unfolded, but unable to cut him off before he finished. "So come," he concluded with a sigh, "just come."

"The answer is no," Max roared in reply. "N—O—, no!

This is superstition, my friend, plain craziness. I won't have no part of it. I won't touch it with a ten-foot pole. I won't be responsible. So what the hell is Yom Kippur with you all of a sudden? A few years ago you had it all figured out—a medieval hangover, a—a—I don't know *what*."

"Never mind what I thought a few years ago, what I think now," Jacob protested. "Louie wants it this way. That's good enough for me."

"Louie wants, Louie wants—a dying man, out of his head. What's *good* for him, that's the question, not what he wants. And what's good for him is rest, absolute quiet. So put your foot down, be a man not a jellyfish. Say *no!* If not, I'll call the hospital myself, I'll speak to his doctor personally, I'll do everything in my power to—"

But Jacob could stand no more, and he clicked off the connection, saying into the dead phone, "To hell with you and your power!" He was through with Max, he assured himself, this time for good. Through with his big mouth, his stupidity, his arrogance.

Even at the moment of thinking it, however, he knew it was a lie, one more lie that made it possible for him to move from the unbearable day he lived to the unbearable day to come. And burning with baffled rage, he walked past the racks of deodorants and perfumes and candy boxes and cough-medicines and paperback books, all decorated with pictures of what seemed to him the same half-naked girl, and all equally a travesty of everything he had ever dreamed for the world. For an instant, he contemplated stumbling deliberately into one of the overstacked racks, bringing the whole display down around him; but contented himself instead with slamming the glass front door of the drugstore hard enough to startle the clerk behind the prescription counter out of his late afternoon doze.

"Hey, man," a voice said at his ear, as he pushed between a couple of passersby toward the curb, "Where you going so fast anyhow?"

"Me?" Jacob asked, startled, and pointing uncertainly at his own chest.

"Like you, Doc," the voice continued, "long time no see."

And looking up, Jacob recognized the colored bartender from the Flame, Ned-what's-his-name. "I mean where you *going?*"

"Out," Jacob said in return, "what do you think."

"Never knew you was *in,* man," Ned replied, laughing and moving quickly away through the throng of shoppers in what seemed to Jacob more like a dance than a walk. "You come by now and have a drink on me."

"Certainly. Right away. Tomorrow first thing," Jacob cried at Ned's back, then moved off himself toward the Courthouse Square. *'Doc,'* he thought bitterly, *The Animal Man he calls 'Doc.' Well, listen, what does he give a damn. A schwarzer and he's right at home, owns the world. Him they can't shove around, but me—* He stepped off the curb to avoid three crew-cut high school boys, who, arms linked and heads down, were plowing ahead as if the crowded sidewalk were a football field. "Why don't you watch where you're going?" he yelled after them futilely, "why don't you—" But what was the use?

Still, the outside was a little better than the drugstore had been: the west side of the Courthouse and the lawn before it shadowed heavily now, as the sun declined, by the lofty double row of cottonwoods which surrounded it; and the faces of shoppers and businessmen almost peaceful as they hurried toward home. *But I am a stranger here still, an alien after all these years,* Jacob found himself reflecting, his back braced against the white and green bandstand, his eye idly scanning the statue of Captain Lewis and Sacajewea and the Negro Slave who had travelled with them into the West. *To what home can I return?*

All at once he felt himself really in America, as a man is aware of himself in a prison or a deserted house: at the dead center of a square town, in the very middle of a square state (no meandering river or jagged mountain range, but only the surveyor's plumbline having defined its boundaries), tucked away between Montana and Idaho, the cold wastes of Canada immediately to the north and a vast semi-desert to the south. He evoked in his head a map of North America, blocked out in red and yellow and green, with black diagonals raying out from the point where he stood toward the four corners of the continent, north-east, north-west, south-east, south-west: New-foundland, Alaska, Florida, Baja California.

And how many Jews, he asked himself, would such lines intersect on their various ways to the sea? If you meant *real* Jews, Jews like his father or his father's father, none, he supposed, not a single one. And even making the definition broad enough to include, say, Max, Louie, himself and the Professor of Anglo-Saxon, how many? A dozen? Twenty? His heart dropped, and he could taste his bile even as he raised a hand in heedless greeting to some passerby who hailed him, a clerk from a store, perhaps, or a teller in the bank, calling out his name in accents so alien his own mother would not have understood it. "Howdy, Jake. How's tricks?"

He tried to imagine across which of his fictional trajectories his own daughter would be moving now, had she lived—running to answer a phone, maybe, or to still a baby's crying, or to turn down the flame under a pot. But what kind of a Jew would she have been in any case, a *status quo* kid from her first day in school—begging to be allowed to go to the Episcopalian Church for dancing lessons, to the Lutheran Church for the meetings of some girls' club; secretly writing (and winning first prize, of course) an essay for the American Legion Contest on "Why I Am Proud to Call Myself an American."

It had been partly his own fault, he knew, for having started off on the wrong foot by permitting Leah to name their daughter Catherine rather than Rachel: a Saint's name rather than his grandmother's. And who would she have fooled, anyhow, with Moskowitz for a last name, unless, God forbid, she had ended up marrying a gentile. But worse than anything he had done, was what he had been—himself, Jacob Moskowitz.

Unbidden and unwelcome, a memory assailed him. He had been coming home from the Animal House, tired but uncustomarily elated for reasons he could no longer recall—perhaps only because of a certain slant of light through the leaves of the maple trees along their street. And then he had seen Catherine walking toward him (*how old could she have been? nine? ten?*), arm in arm with two other girls, gentiles naturally, but she as blonde as either of the others (*and how could that have been, his daughter blonde?*) and laughing quite as mindlessly (*but why not, since she was not really a Jew*). "Life is beautiful, ain't it?" he had wanted to say to her, just that, no more.

When, however, catching her eyes, he had stretched out his arms in preparation for an embrace, she had quickly pulled her companions around a corner to avoid him.

"Hey," he had heard one of them yell, "this is the wrong way," and his daughter had answered, "It's a short-cut."

He had never mentioned the incident to her, of course, but she had known that he knew; and he had been ashamed of the shame she obviously could not help feeling at his speech, his gestures, his unredeemable foreignness. Yet there had been some people, perfect strangers, *goyim,* who said he resembled Albert Einstein. But what had she known about Albert Einstein? Had he ever mentioned the name to her, ever really talked to her about anything important to him at all, about Marx, about Freud, about his own parents?

He had only demanded of her: *Love me! Love me!,* as if he were a father like the fathers in her schoolbooks, like the father of Dick and Jane, who plays baseball with his kids, who owns a dog and drives a car. He had never thrown a baseball, he hated and feared dogs, and had never learned to drive, relying on Leah. So what had he expected? What had he deserved? Yet when Catherine had failed to love him enough and had run around a corner to hide, he had only sulked, reproaching her with silence—he who found words for whatever he needed except in his own house.

Even Catherine a word might have helped, a word he had not known, or had been unable to speak. It would not have kept her alive, he wouldn't kid himself about that at least, but still . . .

Raising his arthritic fingers to his face, he could feel it burning after all these years; and he soothed himself, as if the man inside the face were someone else, as if only the gnarled fingers with which he touched it were really he. "What was so terrible?" he demanded of himself. "She ran around a corner. She was only a child." But it was not for the dead girl that his face burned in the autumnal cold.

"Fool," he said to himself aloud, remembering how often Leah had reproached him precisely for this ("People turn around in the street, like you're a show or something!"). "Why are you spanking yourself? For what? For being too strong to die? For being alive?"

He was glad to be alive, really, proud to feel how his muscles responded as he slapped his arms together across his chest, doing double time in place, and ignoring the kids who stopped to stare at him. "The constitution of a man of forty," he reassured himself, "never mind the hands." And he thought with satisfaction of the daily regime by which he had turned the frail body of a *chederbocher* into the gnarled frame of a tough old man: the cold shower to begin with, then the glass of hot water and honey, the five laps around the half-mile track, the fifty tosses from the free-throw line (and how few shots missed!), all before his day's work had started.

Not like Max, he told himself, *with his two heart attacks and his doctor's orders to quit smoking. Or Louie dying by inches in a hospital bed. At least I'm alive. All things are possible still, even at seventy.* And he headed for St. Cyprian's quickly, quickly, avoiding all further thought.

Even before he had reached Louie's room, averting his eyes from the starched nun in white who fingered her rosary at the reception desk; hunching in on himself in the elevator to avoid contact with the ranchers in uncustomary neckties, their strangulated red faces looming far above his; pressing against the back wall to escape their inadequately girdled wives, whose bulging flesh left him scarcely room enough to stand in and whose cheap perfume made his head reel; trying hard not to breathe the air of the corridors, whose antiseptic sweetness seemed to him to emanate from the holy pictures hung along them: the insipid Virgins and the incandescent hearts—Jacob knew that everyone would be there.

He had spotted, before entering the downstairs doors, the Lincoln Continental of the underwear salesman parked at the curb along with the green Jaguar of the Professor of Clinical Psychology and the Volkswagens (naturally!) of three other faculty members. And by the time he had fought his way out of the elevator, he could hear the cries of those already inside the room, over the buzzing and humming of the student nurses who clustered about the door of 1303, craning to look in every time that someone entered—as if (Jacob thought a little bitterly) an *auto-da-fe* were about to begin or a visiting tribe of Watusi about to perform native dances. Yet the smiles they gave him as he edged through their midst, these fresh-faced girls with their impossibly white teeth and their scarcely existent noses, were more congratulatory than curious, much less hostile.

"Good work," they seemed to be trying to say to Jacob, "good show, good scene!"—gratified, perhaps actually relieved, that the Jews who ordinarily moved among them in complete anonymity were being at last candidly and recognizably *Jews*.

He was not even surprised to find the lady librarian present, her two canes leaning against Louie's bed (*and was her hearing aid on,* he wondered, *would she turn it on at all?*); or to discover, gathered together at the furthest possible remove from that bed, four large boys of fourteen or fifteen, who later would glare across the room at their fathers, or, looking at each other covertly, barely suppress laughter. They were just the age, he could not help reminding himself, that his grandsons would now be, had his daughter lived, married and borne male children. *Some grandsons!* he thought (though not without envy all the same), noticing the crew cuts of three of them, the long untrimmed hair, collar length, of the other; the athletic sweaters, complete with high school letters, of two; the shameless shirt-sleeves of a third and the black leather motor-cycle jacket of the fourth; the simian crouch and slack Marlon Brando mouths of them all.

"Well, look who's here," he found himself saying in their general direction. "You thought maybe there was a ball-game or the Beatles on television?"

To which one of them responded (Jacob could not even tell who in the surrounding hubbub), "HA-HA-HA! Big joke."

He *had* been astonished, however, at the presence of Miles

Standdish, Professor of Cost Accounting, Administrative Assistant to the President of the University and Lieutenant-Colonel in the Air Force Reserve—a man who had never before confessed to being a Jew, and whom Jacob had certainly not invited. He and Standdish would pass each other sometimes on Sunday mornings: Jacob out for a little air, in sweat shirt and logging boots; Standdish with Homburg hat, impossibly pointed shoes, and a daughter clinging to either hand—on the way, Jacob had learned, to the Methodist Sunday School. The brief greetings they had exchanged on such occasions had been their only communication up to that moment; and, indeed, Jacob had always suspected that Standdish was the author of the anonymous letter to the Majority Leader of the State Legislature which had prompted the investigation that had almost cost him his job. Certainly, he wrote letters to the paper from time to time, urging the teaching of Americanism in the High School.

But Jacob had never had any real proof that Standdish had been the chief informer; and suddenly here he was, taking Jacob warmly by the hand and crying (his eye on Louie, who still sat propped up against his pillows in bed), "A solemn event. Wouldn't have missed it for the world. Almost brought my daughters along, but they're a little too young yet, I'm afraid."

Oich mir a Yid, Jacob had wanted to cry out, *everyone wants to get in on the act.* But he chose silence instead, striking the grizzled side of his head with the heel of his palm, and thinking, "Of course, Miles Standdish with two *d*'s. How could I have missed it? A dead giveaway." And with those dark eyes, that long melancholy nose, what had he thought Standdish was anyhow—an Indian?

"Would you be kind enough to introduce me?" Standdish asked then, taking Jacob by the elbow and guiding him to the foot of Louie's bed. "I've never had the pleasure."

"Certainly," Jacob answered. "Why not? It's a free country." But he had not really wanted to confront Louie close up, he realized as he approached, had not really wanted to learn how much more wasted his friend had grown in the two days since Jacob's last visit. Yet he looked now without flinching into the dimness of Louie's pale eyes, at the flaccidity of Louie's grey jowls and the grey stubble that covered them, at the pallor of his hairy nostrils and ears, the tenuosity of the fleshless cords in his neck; and he thought: *You will be like this, Jacob, my life's companion, in how long? Another five years, ten at the most.*

Aloud he said, "Louie, how do you feel? How are you? Tell me the truth." But without waiting for an answer (what could he have done with the truth?), only lifting briefly between his the cold hand that lay on the coverlet, trembling as if it wanted to rise and could not, Jacob continued. "This is Miles Standdish, Louie. Miles Standdish. Louis Himmelfarb." He was speaking too softly, he knew, to reach what spirit survived behind the wreck of Louie's eyes; yet he could not bring himself to shout.

"What?" Louie asked weakly. "Jake, what are you saying?"

"Miles Standdish," Jacob repeated, forcing himself this time to yell. "MILES STANDDISH."

"It's Yom Kippur," Louie responded, as if his friend had been making a bad joke. "Have a little respect."

"You see," Jacob said to no one in particular, turning away as he spoke, first from Louie, then from Standdish, who giggled nervously. "You see how it is."

Yet a few minutes later, Louie Himmelfarb was on his feet ("The Age of Miracles is not over,". Miles Standdish whispered, leaning to Jacob's ear. "I only wish I had brought my daughters after all"), supporting himself with the lightest of pressures—thumb and fingertips barely touching the surface of the improvised altar: a bedside table on which the scrolls of the Torah had been set in their jacket of blue and silver, and a prayer book had been spread out, open to the proper page. His narrow shoulders were wrapped in an immense prayer shawl, its white yellowed with age; and a tiny *yamelke* sat on the very back of his pointed skull.

But it was the sight of his legs that moved Jacob especially: his thin bare legs descending from a too-large plaid bathrobe into too-large furtopped slippers, and giving somehow the impression that they were connected neither with a real body nor with real feet: that only these two frail tubes, these tallow-yellow stalks joined the trembling head which sang with the earth from which it had come and to which—soon, soon—it would return; that Louie had ceased, so close to his death, to be a man and had become a flower, or rather an unlovely weed, a weed that sang. For sing he did, his voice rising out of and falling back into the confused hum that surrounded him—the whispers and throat-clearings, the titters and coughs —in the traditional cadences of the opening lines of *Kol Nidre*.

Louie did not begin the chant itself, however, until he had drawn to his side Jacob and the underwear salesman, who could limp along, at least, always a syllable or two behind the others, in the Aramaic, to repeat with him the traditional preliminary prayer.

> *In the tribunal of heaven and the tribunal of earth, by the permission of God, Blessed be He, and by the permission of this holy congregation, we hold it lawful to pray with the transgressors.*

Once perhaps it had been fitting and proper, Jacob thought, to make such a declaration for the sake of certain returning Marranos, apostate Jews who, on the Days of Awe, would slip secretly into the synagogues to beg God's forgiveness beside their publicly abjured brethren. What avail was it now, however, when not a few interlopers but the whole congregation were apostates, and no God sat in the empty courts of heaven to forgive or to blame?

Better to listen than to speculate, Jacob told himself; for Louie had already begun to chant: his voice moving up and down, in and out and around the first two words of the ancient plaint whose sense barely survived the elaboration of the song. *And what did the sense matter anyhow?* Jacob could not help asking himself, despite his resolve to listen without thought. *Who could make head or tail really of this involved legalistic quibble, this fuel for anti-Semitic fires?*

Kol Nid................ ....*re. Ah*..
Kol Nidre................ ....*Ah*..
Kol ....*nid*................*re*................
Ah   ....*Kol Nidre*........

On the final *Nidre* Louie stopped mid-course, his voice quavering to a break, squawking into silence, and his finger pointing to the wall over the bedside table-altar. "Who—" he began once, then "What"— and finally, "Take it down," he said dramatically. "Get it out of here. Somebody do something."

The "it" he could not bring himself to name was a crucifix, which Louie, tilting his head back in the fervor of his prayer, had just noticed for the first time: a particularly garish Christ on the cross, carved in wood, and painted so that each of his five wounds was defined in a color redder than any blood ever shed in fact for his sake or in his name.

How stupid of me, Jacob thought, taking the idol of the gentiles into his arms (for only he had moved at Louie's behest, the younger men standing about speechless, shocked, perhaps, or amused, as he had clambered first on to a chair, then the bed itself to reach the crucifix), *how benighted to tremble touching the statue of a dead Jewish boy—or a dead Jewish myth, what difference did it make. To be sure, other Jews had died at the hands of goyim carrying this image; but there was always some excuse for killing Jews, was there not?* "Enough," he admonished himself half-aloud, unable to stay the quaking of his terrified flesh.

"In the bathroom," Louie said then, spitting contemptuously into the air without looking around, though knowing somehow that Jacob stood right behind him, locked still in an ambiguous embrace with the wooden cross. "Through there." He indicated the direction with a jerk of his shoulder. "Lay it down on the floor. Cover it up with a towel."

A couple of the boys had started to giggle, and someone (the Professor of Anglo-Saxon?) was beginning a protest which trailed away into silence. "What kind of abysmal nonsense is this?" he was saying. "What sort of primitive—"

But before he could finish or Jacob cry out in disingenuous

response, "From this 'abysmal nonsense' we've been dying for two thousand years," Louie was insisting again, "The bathroom. Right over there. Hurry up already. It'll be *shevuos* before you're through."

"I'm hurrying," Jacob answered, feeling the awkwardness of his crippled fingers. "I'm hurrying as fast as I can. But why doesn't somebody give me a hand?"

Only Standdish had come forward, however, even then; and he had been more trouble than help really: wedging his arm of the crucifix against the doorjamb, stumbling over the sill, crying out unnecessary encouragement and useless instructions.

Inside the bathroom, he had taken out a handkerchief to mop his forehead. "Phew," he said. "This is what I call hot work." His face was almost purple, his eyes shiny as if with fever.

"So why am I shivering?" Jacob asked, bending to the cross with a concealing towel. "Answer me that."

But Standdish ignored the question, perhaps never even heard it. "Just like my father," he went on instead. "He reminds me of my father. The spitting image. Unbelievable." He wagged his head incredulously.

"What's unbelievable?" Jacob responded, genuinely bewildered. "Who reminds you of your father? This one maybe?" He touched with the tip of one toe the horizontal and swathed Christ at their feet, peaceful as a sleeper or a corpse beneath the blanket of toweling.

"What one?" Standdish cried, obviously offended. "What are you talking about? I mean Louie. Louis Himmelfarb reminds me of my father."

"You mean your father couldn't read Hebrew straight either?" True enough, Louie was making a hash of the traditional text; but what reason was that for being so bitter to this poor fool, this nothing? *What's eating me anyhow?* Jacob asked himself. *What do I want from this day?*

"All right," he said aloud, "it's covered up, no danger of infection. So let's go back in."

But there was no answer from Miles Standdish; and looking

back in his direction Jacob could see that the Professor of Cost Accounting was rushing toward the booth that enclosed the toilet, a hand over his mouth.

"Oh, God almighty," he moaned, "Oh, Jesus Jumping J. Christ."

"To tell you the truth," Jacob said, limping reluctantly after the stricken man, "they moved away, both of them. So forget it."

Before Jacob could touch him, however, Standdish was inside the booth, staggering so that first one shoulder and then the other banged against its metal walls. "My liver," he said, sinking to his knees. "I have trouble with my—"

"Hey, what's up," a voice interrupted him from the outer door. "What's with you guys anyway?" It was the boy in the black leather jacket, sent in, perhaps, by his father, or, who knew, by Louie himself.

"What's the matter?" Jacob answered. "You haven't got eyes in your head? We're playing leapfrog. So go away and leave us in peace."

"I just thought—" the kid tried again, obviously troubled.

"Don't think," Jacob shouted. "Just get the hell out."

And as the boy, shrugging, turned on his heel to leave, Standdish began to retch, his shoulders heaving, and his arms limp at his sides. "Oh God," he said finally, trying to rise. "I feel empty now, but better—much better. It's the only thing that helps."

"Better!" Jacob cried, astonished at how much rage his voice betrayed, how little pity. "Don't kid yourself you can get it off your chest as easy as that."

"Please," Standdish responded, on his feet at last but swaying a little as he turned to face Jacob, "please." He held a hand out toward the old man. "It's my liver," he explained aloud. "I shouldn't drink. I can't take it."

But Jacob was already on his way out, letting the spring-door bang shut behind him, and crying as he moved toward the improvised altar, "So what are we waiting for. Everything's O.K."

Actually no one had been waiting at all; certainly not Louie, who had begun again. Louder this time—the beads of perspiration standing out, distinct and silvery on his pale forehead; and if he swayed like Standdish, it was not from side to side in weakness; but forward and backward as his ancestors had always done in the urgency of prayer.

He was, perhaps, not so much actually praying as acting praying: imitating the style of the famous cantor Yussele Rosenblatt, or still worse, of Al Jolson in *The Jazz Singer*; yet it did not matter. The words were said, however approximately, the tune rendered, however inadequately.

> *All vows, obligations, oaths and anathemas, whether*
> *called konam, konas, or by any other name, which*
> *we may vow, or swear, or pledge, or whereby we*
> *may be bound, from this Day of Atonement until the*
> *next (whose happy coming we await), we do*
> *repent . . .*

From what vows, however, subscribed to in anguish and terror, from what compelled apostasies and desperate baptisms did this overfed and contented crew need a God to deliver them, Jacob wondered, watching his fellows in the waning daylight. Self-conscious under the little black skull caps and in the fringed prayer shawls Louie had forced on them—bending painfully to a cardboard box under his bed—they fingered the pages of their prayer books vaguely, in half-hearted search of the right place; or reached out to embrace their squirming sons in an act of reassurance in which neither party believed; or simply shuffled and stared like the members of a guided tour coming on real worshippers in a double-starred church.

He would translate *Kol Nidre* for them, Jacob decided, not into the equally alien English of the versions they held in their hands, but into their own real tongue; he would pray for them secretly in a brand-new service of his own—chant silently the *Kol Nidre* according to Jacob Moskowitz, which, not quite foreseeing the end, he began:

> *From the mortgages on their ranch-style, split-level*
> *houses; from their sales contracts for washing ma-*
> *chines, T.V. sets, garbage disposal units, air-condi-*

*tioners, electric lawnmowers, new cars and heated
swimming pools; from their oaths of allegiance to
Kiwanis and Rotary, the Masons and the state that
pays them their salaries; from their unpaid dues to
the N.A.A.C.P., the A.D.A., the League of Women
Voters, the American Civil Liberties Union and the
American Association of University Professors; from
their pledges to the U.J.A., the Community Chest
and all funds for the Victims of Polio, Heart Disease,
Muscular Dystrophy and Tuberculosis, plus other
afflictions too numerous to mention—from all these,
Oh Lord, deliver them. Oi Gottenu, deliver me. Let
them be null, void, and of no effect. Amen.*

Looking up, Jacob saw that Louie's mouth no longer moved,
that both their services had ended at the same moment; and
that Louie—all the false strength he had mustered suddenly
failing him—was sagging now against Miles Standdish's arm,
on his way back to bed. Meanwhile the others were preparing
to leave, calling out farewells in absurdly hushed voices, pushing forward to touch Max's hand, bending to deposit caps and
shawls in the cardboard box from which they had come; and
on every one of their faces embarrassment was giving way to
relief.

It was only Jacob's eye that Louie's sought, however, only
Jacob he signalled to approach, once he had tucked himself
painfully back into bed. And drawing Jacob down to him (his
breath thin and sour), he whispered, "Get him out!" Meaning,
of course, Standdish, who lingered and lingered, as if eager to
say what could under no circumstances have been spoken.

"I'm leaving right now," Standdish said, having overheard
Louie's urgent request. "I can take a hint as well as the next
guy." Then, abandoning all show of resentment (*how dapper
he looked,* Jacob thought, *how possessed, no trace left of his
crisis in the bathroom*), he added, "God bless you and thanks."

"For what?" Louie muttered. "For what is he thanking
me?" And only after Standdish was through the door, the
door closed behind him, did he manage to say, speaking with
difficulty now, "They'll remember, Yankel. They'll never forget."

For one troubled moment, Jacob believed his friend had

intended an assertion, a boast; but Louie's weakly lifted hand indicated the question, the plea his voice had not been quite able to register.

"They'll remember," he tried again. "They'll—" this time failing even to finish the phrase, much less attain the pitch of interrogation.

And now Jacob answered, "Certainly, they'll remember. Who could forget." Then, as if even this were not enough to make amends for his momentary doubts, he added a second lie to the first, shouting it from the doorway. "Tomorrow. I'll see you tomorrow, Louie. Right after work."

Daring to touch his own face only when his back was turned on Louie, Jacob learned that he wept.

But now the nurses were hustling into the room, bearing a bedpan and charts, a thermometer and opiates; switching on lights (*how had it grown so dark,* Jacob wondered, *without his having noticed?*); cranking down the head of the bed and plumping up the pillows under the dying man. "Sh!" they hissed at Jacob, an admonitory finger held to each pair of lips, as he tried to speak to his friend once more through the open door, and "Sh!" their starched skirts repeated the sussuration.

"But I still have to—" Jacob began, not sure how he intended to finish.

"No!" the youngest of the nurses whispered, "not now." And moving on noiseless rubber soles, she silently closed the door in his face.

Thank God! he thought, *just in time,* for at that very instant he saw Max Schultheis pumping down the hall toward him on short, thick legs—his jaw, blueblack with unshaveable beard, bobbing against the cushions of his lower chins; and his beaked nose cutting the air before him like the prow of a warship. *A caricature out of "Der Stürmer,"* Jacob told himself,. ashamed all the same at the revulsion that rose in him, *an insult to the Jewish people, he ought to be locked up, hidden away at least until the last anti-Semite is dead.*

Max, however, was already bellowing, with complete disregard for his surroundings, the little signs everywhere which read: SILENCE PLEASE, "You're proud of yourself, I suppose. You had to go through with it, even if it killed him. For what, that's all I'm asking you, for *what? Nu, chochem,* answer me!"

Surely his own accent was not so gross, Jacob assured himself, so essentially comic; surely, everything did not become in his mouth, too, a burlesque routine. And he tried to listen to himself answering, "Nobody's dead, so why are you yelling?"

"Nobody's dead," Max repeated scornfully, his voice dropping a notch. "But Louie's dying, am I right, as good as dead. That's what they told me at the desk only two minutes ago. They didn't even want to let me up to see him—*me,* his closest friend."

"Louie's been dying for six months, ain't it?" Jacob demanded, aggrieved. "So why all of a sudden is today the day to get excited. Are you accusing somebody of something, or what? Go blame the cancer, his *mazel,* his genes. But leave me alone, do you hear. I've had enough for one day, even Yom Kippur. I want to go home." Pressing himself against the wall, Jacob attempted to squeeze past Max, who stood between him and the elevators, legs spread wide, elbows crooked, fists at his hips.

Max would not let him go by, however, but grabbed him by the shoulders and whirled him around, hollering, "Listen to the *chochem* now. He wants to go home. Home. Can Louie go home, answer me that. Can he even get up out of his bed to pee, can he lift his head up from the pillow? I'll tell you the answer, *chochem.* No! And why not?" He pointed his stubby finger at a spot between Jacob's still inky-black eyebrows and his ruff of grey hair. "Because you had to have your goddamned Yom Kippur. The sage of Lewis and Clark City. A new prophet in Israel. Well, you had it. And you killed him. You and nobody else."

"Me?" Jacob asked mildly, astonished now out of all rage. "*My* Yom Kippur? *I* killed him?"

Yet why should he have been surprised. It was the story of his life, was it not, to be always on trial and always accused of the same crime—of murder, to be exact? And where there was so such smoke, surely there must be a little fire.

That he had killed somebody, everyone agreed, differing only on the question of who had been his victim. According to his mother it had been herself (*why had he bitten into that heel of bread?*); according to his wife, his own daughter (*why had he not been earning more money, so they could have called in a specialist?*); according to his own conscience, his wife (*why had he never learned to talk to her, how to touch her in bed?*); according to the whole gentile world, God himself in human form (*why had he not cried out against the Rabbis while there had still been time*)? But Louie at least was still alive, was he not? This charge certainly he did not have to endure.

"Louie's alive," he shouted into Max's face, "so what are you talking about? Why am I even listening to you?"

"Alive," Max echoed him mockingly. "Everything is called alive. You stick in the thermometer, it says ninety-eight point six—he's alive. But for how much longer, professor, that's the question. Five minutes more maybe? Ten?"

"Let's say five minutes," Jacob agreed. "But instead of what? What could he expect at the best? Two days? Three? Make it a lot, make it a week. He said *Kol Nidre*, he lost a week. To him it was worth it. To me it's worth it, too. Hell's bells, what's a *week?*"

"Everything," Max answered, resting one hand on the layer of fat that girdled his faltering heart. "I'm not a well man myself and I know a week of life is worth everything."

But now it was Jacob's turn to take up the word scornfully. "Life," he said. "You call it life to come home to a lonely room, to lay in bed until a bell rings on a clock; to get up, to sweat for a few lousy dollars, to sit in front of the T.V. set until it's time to lay in bed again—day after day for seventy-five years. Then one day you wake up screaming, you go to the doctor—cancer! That's life according to you?"

"That's all there is," Max said, wagging his head until his jowls trembled. "You want your money back? Or maybe you got something better to recommend—a superior article?"

"There's always the World-to-Come," Jacob answered him. "Worse than this one it couldn't be." But how had that phrase ever occurred to him: the World-to-Come, a word out of his father's vocabulary, a concept out of another time? He knew as well as anybody, did he not, that a man lived only once, and that once was more than enough. But in an argument you could end up saying anything, even this.

Max, however, had picked up the phrase immediately, would never let him forget it. "The World-to-Come," he kept saying over and over, "the World-to-Come!" meanwhile laughing and beating his thighs with the flat of his palm. "I'll be frank with you, my friend, for ten cents I'd sell you my share—free and clear, no strings attached."

"Make it a nickel," Jacob replied, feeling that coin between his fingers as he thrust his hand deep into the pocket of the over-sized hound's-tooth sport jacket he wore, a hand-me-down from his wealthy brother-in-law, "and you've got yourself a deal."

"Done," Max cried, holding out a fat palm for the money; and when Jacob had smacked the nickel hard down into it, "Believe me," he said, "it's the first profitable piece of business I've done all week. You'd think somebody put up a measles sign in front of the store. But here in St. Cyprian's Hospital, I've got myself five cents in good American money, and you, Professor, you've got—" He could not finish for laughing, almost losing the coin as he raised his hand to wipe his tearing eyes.

"I've got your share in the World-to-Come," Jacob finished for him, "invisible but guaranteed."

And that was the end; for an irate nurse had already been herding them toward the elevator, which they rode together to the ground floor—heads averted, eyes cast down, not speaking a word.

Jacob had never felt lonelier than he did that night after getting home, and—having turned on the gasflame under a pot of Campbell's chicken noodle soup—settling back into the single easy chair in his tiny living room, his shoeless feet on the hassock piled high with a week's worth of unread news-papers. His rented house had always depressed him, even be-fore Leah had died. A three-room bungalow, more suitable for a vacation than for a whole life, it squatted at the back of an ill-kept yard behind a larger brick house: an after-thought of the improvident owners, one more way to eke out a living without really working. It did not even have a proper path to its front door, or a proper number for its address.

What a disgrace to have lived for over twenty years at 769½ Mountainview Avenue, a half-man in a half-house. Even in his happiest days it had always depressed Jacob; and without the familiar noises of Leah in the kitchen, without the smell of food already cooking to greet him at the day's end, Jacob could sustain no sense of elation within its flimsy walls. Yet here he was, a man with not one but *two* shares in eternity, two portions in the World-to-Come.

"Well, let it come then," he said aloud, hugging himself against the drafts that seeped from every direction through the uninsulated plasterboards into which he could not even drive a nail. "I'm more than ready."

He should really have turned up the space-heater, he sup-posed, or at least lit the living room lamp under the beaded shade of which Leah had been so proud, to help dissipate the gloom. But the dim light that leaked in from the kitchen illu-minated sufficiently what he was not eager to see in any case: the shabby rug, worn through to the floorboards in a couple of places; the shabbier furniture, which he dusted all the same twice a week; and, just below the curtainless window with its cracked green shades, a box of Louie's treasures—entrusted to him over a month before, but still unpacked, unexamined.

Jacob was sure without looking that he knew what it con-tained: a few albums of seventy-eight r.p.m. records, most of them scratched or cracked: some once-celebrated *chasan* sing-ing *Eli, Eli;* Molly Picon doing a forgotten song from a for-gotten Jewish musical comedy; a handful of jokey dialect rec-ords, "Cohen on the Telephone" among them no doubt; a few dusty books: two or three volumes each out of the col-lected works of Peretz and Sholem Aleichem, a half-dozen

army-issue Hebrew Prayerbooks in paper covers, a life of
Chaim Weizmann and perhaps of Abba Eban as well; some
stray paraphernalia of Jewish Holidays: a *dredel,* an eight-
branched *menorah* manufactured in Israel, maybe even a *shofar*—a ram's horn, polished and scalloped on the edges, to
blow in the New Year.

Pitiful enough, this jetsam left by the ebbing of a great
faith, the death of a heroic people; but how could he afford to
despise it, Jacob asked himself, when in the bookcase behind
him were preserved the equally trivial remnants of another
chosen people, another religion that had shaken the world and
moved for three, four, five decades his own hungry heart: John
Strachey's *The Coming Struggle for Power,* Maurice Hindus'
Red Bread and Emile Burns' *Principles of Marxism;* an anthology called *Proletarian Literature in the United States* and
Clara Weatherwax' *Marching! Marching!,* winner of the first,
and only, *New Masses* award for fiction. His collected Lenin,
Leah had burned in their own furnace during the worst of the
McCarthy days.

"But what are you doing?" he had cried, catching her on
the basement steps with the second load in her arms. "What's
to be afraid?"

"You don't see them," she had said, putting the books down
on the step where he confronted her, and touching a hand to
her untidy hair. "They keep walking back and forth past the
house and looking in the windows. You don't know."

"So what's to see in this house—dirt under the couch?"

"What's to see they'll see," she had answered, pointing
portentously down toward the books. "You don't understand
how people are in the West, how they think, what they can do.
I grew up in this town, Jacob. I watched my own father suffer."

"So, I'll suffer. It won't be anything new. What do I have
to lose, Leah, that's what I'm asking you, what do I have to
lose?"

"Your job, that's what you have to lose. Maybe to you it's
not important, but to me—"

"My job. *Ah groisse metziah.* Anyhow, books you don't
burn, like Hitler, like, like—"

"Jacob, for my sake."

"For your sake," he had responded ironically, but had shrugged and turned away, letting her burn them, giving his silent approval.

"*Oi veh,*" he groaned aloud, remembering and lifting his hands into the air. Stretching and bending his crooked fingers, he thrilled to the delicious pain that shot through him from their calcified joints. "*Rebbenishe!* I let her burn them."

He walked slowly into the kitchen, turned off the light under his boiling soup; then, without even tasting it, returned to his chair. "Enough remembering," he admonished himself. "Live."

He should not sit here alone, of that he was certain, calling up the past, feeling sorry for himself. Of this, he knew, you died, if, indeed, it was not death already. Beginning soon, immediately, the first of the week, he would walk the streets right after supper (but first he would have to start eating supper again—*that* at least); he would ring the doorbells of his so-called Jewish colleagues, brave the anger of their gentile wives; he would sit and talk to someone for a change, become human once more. And why not; for he had something to give as well as to demand—especially in the households with little children. In a country that hid the old away in Centers for Senior Citizens, a world without grandfathers, he would become a kind of portable grandfather, a door-to-door link with the past.

He cast up in his mind an inventory of what he could offer the children, what he could teach them that they would not find at the Y or the Boy Scouts or the Little League. He knew how to play *pishe-paishe* to begin with, best of all card games for the very young; he could run the whole gamut of Cat's Cradle from the Cradle itself to the Spider; make with a handkerchief a rabbit that would jump; do tricks with a piece of string on his fingers, around his neck, in his buttonhole; tickle the palms of small hands to the tune of *miezele-mazele-tik-tik;* tell a version of "The Princess on the Glass Hill" that he had heard from his own grandfather in the Old Country, another world. But best of all, he could be for the descendants of vanished, incredible Jews a Jew in real life, a terrible fact.

Next week, he promised himself, trying desperately to believe it, *the first of the week, I will start. Absolutely.*

And just then the phone rang, loud in the almost empty house, rang once, twice, three times—Jacob's heart leaping with each peal of the bell. *It's about Louie,* he thought. *It's the Hospital to say that Louie is dead.* But when, lifting the receiver to his ear, he heard Max's voice, he knew that it was not a word about Louie at all but about something quite different, for which (without daring to confess it to himself) he had been waiting the whole time, hushed in the cold and the dark.

Max must have talked to his wife, as Jacob had, in secret even from his conscious self, foreseen; must have told her in intended jest about the bargain he had struck with Jacob, the fool; must have laughed and laughed, until, looking up, he had seen the horror in her slack mouth, her watery eyes—seen her hand helplessly sketching on her breast the sign of the cross, which he had forbidden her ever to make in his presence. "On your own," Jacob had heard him yell at her more than once, "in private, do what you want. Who cares. Go to church even. But when I'm around, positively no!"

In his inner ear, Jacob could hear how she must have pleaded with Max, wringing her puffy hands, looking down at her puffy ankles. "For God's sake, husband, not with your eternal soul. It's not a joke, Max, not to me. So for my sake, if not God's or your own, I beg you, buy it back. To humor me. Now. Tonight. Jacob will understand. He yells but he has a good heart." She would have been talking Russian, of course, as always when frightened or deeply moved; and in Russian she seemed less a stuffed dummy, almost human.

"I do have a good heart," Jacob wanted to cry out in answer to her imagined praise. But he was finally not so sure; for he fancied himself next listening to Max, who, overwhelmed by God knows what surge of superstitious terror from what buried depths of his soul, would have answered, also in Russian—his own uncertain Russian, lapsing always into Yiddish: "All right. Agreed. I'll make him an offer, 'It was a joke; it went too far. Come in the office, take back your nickel. Finished.' But if, with his good heart, he tries to make a *tzimmes,* if he says one word, I'll hang up in his ear. That I promise you. Because, mind you, to me this whole thing is foolishness—World-to-Come, eternal soul, complete *mishigas.*"

On all this, however, Jacob had only eavesdropped in fantasy, hearing in reality nothing but Max's voice on the telephone insisting over and over, "This is Max. Max Shultheis. Are you there? Can you hear me? This is Max. Are you deaf or something?"

"Certainly I'm deaf," Jacob answered at last, ready for the world he imagined and the world he lived to come together, for the comedy to be done. "Where have you been all these years? But you at least, I can hear. And I recognize the voice. So what do you want?"

"You know damn well what I want, Professor," Max bellowed. "Do I have to dot the 'i's' and cross the 't's'?"

"I'm not a mind-reader," Jacob answered. "If you want something spit it out."

But he had already set the receiver down on the hassock before him, pulled on the lamp above his head, and spread out yesterday's newspaper on his knees; for he knew now not only what Max would ask, but also what (when the squawking on the other end of the line had ceased) he was going to say in return.

Nobody Ever Died from It

There is no use beating about the bush. Not only will I never write the story of Abie Peckelis that I have begun a hundred times, but I am no longer even a writer. My novel, once within an ace of being published, lies untouched and dusty on a shelf; and tomorrow I will open my own shoe store: The New Bon-Ton Home Bootery, Hyman Brandler, Proprietor. Imagine it!

I tell myself that in two years at the outside I will be bankrupt, but it is no use. Store or no store, I am what I am. Each day when I shave, I look at the middle-aged shoe salesman under the lather, and suddenly I want to weep or giggle—I hardly know which. Here is the face of a man who at thirty-five has published nothing, who owns his own store, who has even sent himself a floral horseshoe inscribed: Success!

What am I doing shaving such a face, I who from the time I was twelve was sure that I would become a great writer. I could not sleep at night because of the fury of my ambition; and I would walk the floor sick with impatience for the future, until my mother would call out in fear, "Who is it? Who? What? What?" Please understand me, I am not whining. God forbid! I know well enough that the only answer is to laugh. Why do you suppose that every year I apply for a Guggenheim Fellowship in writing, listing as references my grocer; a whore in Jersey City, the sister of a close friend; and my third-grade teacher now ten years dead!

Sometimes, I must confess, I catch myself hoping that by some quirk I will be granted a Fellowship after all; but each year I am refused, of course—as I should be. And yet, who can tell, given the chance, the three thousand lousy bucks, a little house in the country not too far from New York, could I not write a comic novel that would define the sensibility of a whole generation, become the Rabelais of the shoe-dogs?

At least I could write the story of Abie Peckelis and the Quick Christmas Eve. I have no trouble, you understand, in telling the story by word of mouth. At parties, my friends who have heard the story a hundred times invariably turn to me at the point in the evening when one must laugh or go home. "Hy," they plead, knowing I will not fail them, "tell us about Peckelis." And if there is a newcomer present, it becomes a test. Woe betide him if he sits there straight-faced or only snickers politely. He is written off forever as a *shmuck*.

I do not think that my friends really believe the story; they think of it rather as something that I have invented especially for them; and it has become part of the ritual of our get-togethers, as essential as the jokes about waistlines and baldness and numbers of children. Such things are important to us, now that some of us have reached forty. Forty! A moment ago it was the age of our parents.

I begin always by describing Peckelis: the identical oily ridges of his marcelled hair, and sullen droop of his fat lips, the eyelids as heavy as if hewn in stone. I think of his face in profile—despite the blueness of his beard, the face of a wicked queen in an Assyrian bas-relief; a face ravaged by passions it does not understand—and set anomalously on the flabby body in the draped jacket, the peg-top pants. It is an ugly body, uglier because borne with such outrageous assurance of its allure: the swollen female breasts visible beneath the sag of the coat from the padded shoulders, the movement of the hips a parody, savage and tender, of womanly charm.

I was fourteen then, a stock boy at my first job, in my first shoestore. Fourteen! A child born in that year would be ready to vote in November; and even my memories of that time can be said to have attained their majority. I worked then only on Saturdays, thinking of those twelve hours in a shoestore as a parenthesis in my life. I remember myself on the way to work, the only one it seemed to me then fully awake among the half-sleeping adult workers on the streetcar. I can still feel my eagerness and my fear; and for the moment I seem to be jolted again on the straw seat, my hair damp and unnaturally plastered back. I am wearing knickers; I have never shaved. Suddenly, I am on the sidewalk, the sun dazzling after the gloom of the trolley; and there is the store-front, the orange neon sign blinking its simpleminded assertion over the doorway: FIVE DOLLARS—$5—FIVE DOLLARS.

Once inside, the smell of the store assails me: a dead female odor of sweat and leather, perfume and dust. It has been all of fifteen years since I entered that store, but I feel myself once more walking down the long aisle, past the six mirrors, past the unoccupied stools before each row of chairs, the seats of which have not yet been turned down for the business of the day. I enter the back room to set down, beside the bottles of shoe dye, the extra sock linings and the stacks of cork inner soles, my bag of lunch, which I have carried nonchalantly under my arm, the spot of grease concealed against my side. I hope no one has noticed the package, for I consider it degrading to be forced to eat sandwiches instead of going out to a cafeteria.

Delivered of the lunch, I walk the length of the store in reverse, saying good morning to the blue denim back of George, the porter, bent over his mop; good morning to Mr. Z., the manager, reading the day's directives in the cashier's cage; good morning to the hose girls moving stockings from boxes to the display cases. I try to walk like a real shoe-dog, banging my heels down hard, smiling broadly when I "give the time of day," as Mr. Z. has urged me; for I hope that at sixteen I will be given a job as salesman, be able to work my way through college.

It is hard to believe that a few weeks after I had gone to work, after I had already met Peckelis, my mother, silent and embarrassed, put into my hand a little book about sex and procreation. It was only the Saturday before, I remember, that the hose girls had given me a package for Abie Peckelis, a birthday present done up in our fanciest gift wrapping.

Those hose girls! They did not deliberately mock me, I am sure, for they were from the first a little afraid of me, aware that I was writing a novel about the store; and the manager, who was our next-door neighbor and had given me the job as a favor to my parents, must have told them by then that I was a "genius." "That Herman," he would say. "At his age, he's already a writer. Some day we'll be proud to say we worked with him in the same store." Which did not prevent him from using the word genius as a term of abuse when my shyness or clumsiness annoyed him. And, as you should already be aware, my name is "Hyman" not "Herman"—a fact of which I was never able to convince Mr. Z. or any of the rest of the crew.

I would have given a lot to be able to kid with the hose girls as some of the salesmen did; but though in my bed at night I often thought of offhand cracks to set them giggling, my actual conversation with them usually boiled down to a noncommittal grunt in answer to the occasional question, "How's the book coming, kid?" And so I was proud to be the messenger boy between them and Abie.

When I handed him the package, he shook it cautiously, smelled it, then tucked it coyly into his bosom. "I'll look later. Maybe it's something private. After all, I'm only sixteen!" But when we all protested, he opened the wrappings and drew out two round red Christmas tree ornaments attached to a limp hotdog. He performed his delight as we all expected him to: hugging himself, squealing with pleasure, even doing a little dance —one finger wagging in the air, his butt out, and his pointed suede shoes sliding on the waxed floor, what was then called "trucking."

Finally, dangling the thing before him, he gurgled, "OOOOH, daddy, I love it!" while the whole crew (we had just closed the store and were beginning to drop the stock) rocked with laughter. Only I did not laugh. I wanted to, you understand, but I choked on the first forced guffaw. Why did I not laugh, I who was to make my friends laugh over this very event so many times? It is no use asserting, as I did to myself then, that it was because I had read Freud and understood such matters. Embarrassed and even (it costs me nothing to admit it now) blushing, I pretended to be thirsty, rushing back to the water cooler, so that no one would notice me.

For reasons which I do not understand even yet, Abie felt it necessary to explain himself to me. "Don't get the wrong idea," he would hiss damply into my ear. "I only make fun for the boys. I only make fun!" and he would wriggle his buttocks in sheer earnestness. Or he would catch me sometimes by the water cooler or outside the can and clutch me by the shoulder. "You're my friend," he would insist, as I tried not to flinch under his too-clean hand. "You got a education, a brain in your head. You got *sechel*. Not like these other dogs." He would pretend to lower his voice, putting his powdered jaw within an inch of mine and spraying me with spit. "False! False! They're all false. Only you understand. Four walls!" He would regard me hopefully out of his moist cow eyes. "You understand? Four walls." And I who understood nothing for all my Freud and could never say a word to him, would nod dumbly.

"A education!" he would continue, sighing ruefully. "Me—I never got past the third grade." Then pulling himself erect in a sudden change of mood, he would slap his own face hard so that each finger left a distinct purplish welt. "Abie Peckelis, stand up! How much is two and two?" A pause, and then triumphantly, "Eleven!" "What's the capital of Philadelphia?" This time, he would step back as if baffled, hang his head for an instant, and then glowing, "Boh-livier? Right?" And in sheer self-congratulation, he would hit himself again, twice, three times.

I met him only once outside of the store, when he sat down next to me on the bus I was riding home from high school. I had a pile of books in my lap and he picked them up one by one, thumbing through them without really looking at them. "Al-ge-bra," he said proudly, pleased with himself for being able to pronounce the word. "Study! Study! So you shouldn't be a bum like poor Peckelis. Make from yourself something. Be a some-thing not a nothing like me." All at once he seemed overwhelmed with self-pity. "Poor Peckelis," he screamed at the top of his voice. "Poor Abie! Poor Florence!"

"Florence?" I asked, glancing up uneasily at the smirking faces around us, and wondering how soon I dared get off.

"Certainly, Florence! Only my dear friends call me that. A joke. I make fun for the boys." By that time, everyone on the bus was turning to crane at us and I, writhing in my seat, was trying to disappear inside the collar of my overcoat. But Peckelis, un-abashed, wheeled on the eavesdroppers, crying out more shrilly than before, "Dogs! What are you listening to? Come closer, you might miss something. Garbage!"

"Believe me," he continued, patting my shoulder, "stay in school. Study. What's more important? Diamonds isn't every-thing! Look at me. I didn't go to school." He put the sleeve of his beige polo coat into my hand. "Feel it! What are you afraid of? Two hundred and fifty dollars! But what am I. A bum in a two-hundred-and-fifty-dollar coat. A no-good. Could a mama be proud of Abie Peckelis? Tell the truth!"

Without waiting for an answer, he went on to tell me about how he had been in jail twice. Once he had been picked up for impersonating a female; but they had not even held him over-night, for he had screamed so loud in the men's cell block, the scream of a woman frantic to be had, that they had thrown him out. "The prisoners are going crazy," they had told him, "beat it!"

"But I like it in here," he had protested. "I got no place to go." As they had hustled him out the door, he had cried back over his shoulder, "At least you could say *please!*" Later, he had been picked up again, this time on a dope charge, though he had only, he assured me and the openly listening bus, been holding the stuff for a dear friend. "When you don't have a education, who believes you?"

After his first night in jail, he had come home to find his bags packed and thrown into the alley beside his house. His mother ("A beautiful woman, she should drop dead, big around like a barrel!") had locked him out, refused even to talk to him through the closed door, until he had screamed up at her from the street so loud that the neighbors had come out to cheer him on. "False!" he had accused her. "False! Your own son you're killing. What's the matter, I don't give you twenty-five dollars a week for board?"

Finally, she had thrown up a second-story window, stuck out her broad rump at him, waving a hand on either side in a gesture of contempt, the way a small boy thumbs his nose. Abie rose out of his bus seat to imitate the gesture for me, putting aside his blond overcoat, pulling up the skirts of his long, draped jacket, and bending over as if in a doctor's office. When a woman standing next to us in the aisle tittered, he interrupted himself only for a minute. "Excuse me. Lean over a little further—maybe you'll fall over on that face. It could only be an improvement."

He turned back to me slowly, very solemn now. "You're good to your mama, Herman?" I managed to nod. "Good, good. Be good to your mama. You have only one. My own, God rest her soul, she was not such a good person, but—mamas you can't buy. The important things you can't buy. Am I right?"

"No," I answered stupidly. "Yes. I mean—"

"Two-hundred-and-fifty-dollar coats you can buy. But a education, a mama—" He clasped my hand as I rose to get off, two stops before my own. "You're a smart boy with a golden heart. You understand. I only make fun for the boys."

It was that night that I began to put down the notes that have become the story I cannot write. I read Krafft-Ebing, Stekel, even Proust; and I would pump the other salesmen for Peckelis stories, even resist the queasy temptation to slip away when Abie himself came to confide in me his contempt for the others, his loneliness, his faith in my understanding. I sit now with the old, hand-written sheets before me; but I cannot bear to read

again my callow comments, and I do not need their prompting to
evoke Abie.

I can see him now stopping abruptly in the middle of the long
aisle (it is, let us say, four o'clock in the afternoon of the Saturday before Palm Sunday, and every woman who can walk is
in search of a new pair of shoes) and grabbing himself between
the legs, dropping whatever he is carrying to the floor. "Ooooooh,"
he would scream in an anguished falsetto. "Oh! oh! oh! I thought
I had it, but I lost it!" And he would look roguishly over his shoulder to see if he were being heard and appreciated.

But stretching a pair of shoes was always the true climax of his
day. As he thrust the stretcher in under the protesting vamp,
screwing it tight so that it spread the leather to the snapping
point and banging the distended shoe on the wrapping counter,
he would cry at the top of his mad voice, "Take it out, daddy, it
hoi-oi-oits!" Then, twirling the shoe frantically until it fell from
the shrunken stretcher, moan in sudden regret, "Oh, put it back,
daddy, I lo-o-o-ove it!"

Meanwhile the customers would swirl around him, listening in
astonishment or pretending to ignore him. Sometimes he would
whirl abruptly, catch some petrified girl staring at him incredulously, and "Dog!" he would scream, "Spy! What are you looking at? From Montclair you had to come to watch me! When
you start with me you start with the wrong one."

Yet he was never bawled out by Mr. Z., who hounded me
every minute of the living day—for too many lost sales, for un-
shined shoes, for being myself. Abie, you must realize, made more
sales than any two men in the store. "Naturally," Mr. Z. would
explain, "he thinks like them. He understands their Psychology."
And later he would add, glancing at me coldly, "Better than some
geniuses who study it in school."

Often Abie would drag an unsuspecting customer into his act.
He preferred for stooges large Negresses, who would roll their
eyes shyly; middle-aged matrons with foreign accents; or the
very old, the half-deaf, the obviously genteel. But in a pinch anyone would do. "Let me tell you, lady," he would begin in the
special tone that indicated "fun," while the rest of us began to

gather around his section on pretended errands, "this is the assblaster model—ASSBLASTER!" He would pause dramatically to shake a wire brush for cleaning suede shoes under the nose of his victim, at the same time smiling up at her his blandest smile. "Good for the hair around the hole."

And if, not believing her ears, the customer were foolish enough to ask what he had said, he would half rise from his stool, one hand on each fat thigh, his face thrust so close to his victim that she could feel the spittle from his purple lips on her cheek. *Dog! I said it's good for the hair around the HOLE!*" He would scream the words at her in pretended rage, then patiently repeat them over and over as if to an idiot or a child. Finally, he would dissolve into silent laughter, trembling with joy on his stool; and turning to us quickly, stick out his tongue in an infantile gesture of satisfaction with himself and contempt for the whole female world. Yet there were customers who would allow themselves to be waited on by no one but the "funny man," and who would begin to giggle in anticipation as they sat down. "False," Abie would say, settling down on his stool, "at what are you laughing already? Who died?"

And then, Christmas Eve—my first Christmas in the store. The feather-fringed mules on the special gift table were reduced to three or four soiled mismates, and we had finished tightening up the stock to make room for the gold and silver evening slippers to dance in the New Year. We closed early that night, I remember, a few minutes before six, though it was a Saturday; and Mr. Z. himself chased out the final customer without a pair of shoes. It was unheard of, to let a *schlager* walk out without a sale, but as Mr. Z. reminded us, "Christmas comes but once a year."

Though only twelve or thirteen of the crew had remained, he had set out six bottles on top of the water cooler. It was his treat, not only the whisky but also the corned beef and potato salad which no one ate; and he had draped himself in a piece of red cloth to suit the occasion, pasted on a false beard made of the absorbent cotton we used for swabs in dyeing shoes. With his stomach, his extra chin and his habit of false joviality, he made a convincing enough Santa Claus; and betrayed by his role into real affection, he even put an arm around me for the first time. "Herman," he said, "you're a fine boy. Now get the hell out of here. Merry Christmas." And Abie, who stood next to him, his eyes half-closed and his hands folded over his belly, nodded in confirmation. "Go home to your mama. With such dogs you don't have to stay after business."

Meanwhile, George, the porter, had pulled down the shade on the front door and locked all the windows in the back room, slowly, carefully, as if it were an ordinary night. He was a cautious man and he liked me; but he, too, warned me, wagging his solemn head, "Boy, you go home. This ain't gonna be for you." After so much advice, I had no choice. I had to stay.

It was to be a quick party—that was understood. At eight o'clock, everyone would be gone: to other parties, to trim Christmas trees, to finish getting drunk at a bar, it didn't matter—only the fact that it must be over at eight, that it must be *quick!* Mr. Z. teed off with a little speech beginning, "I'm no good at speeches," and ending "Merry Christmas." But before he was finished, he had downed his first paper cup full of whisky and the others had followed his cue. There was not much of a middle to his remarks, something about all of us becoming one big happy family; but his own sentiments brought tears to his eyes, and all the others nodded approvingly, even Abie whose eyes were mere slits now and whose lips were pursed as if he were about to whistle. But as the group dissolved, one of the salesmen called Max, a man with whom I had never exchanged more than three words, whispered into my ear, "Don't think I believe this shit."

Then Mr. Z. noticed me again and said, "Herman, you're too young. Go home!" He had opened his vest, his collar, loosened his belt, as if the expansion of his spirits demanded an equal expansion of the flesh. "You tell him, Abie," he added, as I stood there undecided. "He's your pal." At the word "pal," Max snickered and, flushing, I went into the back room to put on my overcoat, stopping only long enough to shout at the bottles of shoe dye, "My name's *Hyman*, not Herman."

When I came out, everyone began to yell at me, "Herman, go

home!" laughing as if it were the greatest of jokes; but Max, who was drunker than the rest (he was always half-drunk), put an arm around me, whispering, "You stay, kid, we'll show these boozhwahzee bastards." The word bourgeoisie seemed unlikely enough in the mouth of Max, whom I had known only as the most dapper and insolent of the salesmen. He was a small man, scarcely taller than me at fourteen, with thickly pomaded hair and a sly little mustache, and drunk or sober, he was most weeks second only to Peckelis in "production." He had never spoken to me before except mockingly, but now he leaned toward me earnestly. "Stay for the laughs, kid, this'll educate you. You've never seen anything like these jibeebees outside a zoo."

And so I stayed, sweating inside my overcoat beside the water cooler and the wastebasket full of crumpled paper cups. At first everyone was cutting the liquor with a little water; and as they came to the cooler one by one, I would note how their hands grew more unsteady, their greetings to me heartier and heartier. "You still here, shorty?" they would ask in mock surprise. "Go home. Don't you want to see Santy Claus?" Or later, still pretending, you understand, but not having to try too hard, "Christ, kid, where'd you get the brother? *Both* of you go home!" But after a while, they skipped the water, and I was forgotten.

I could scarcely believe the speed with which the whisky disappeared, the urgency with which they plunged toward drunkenness. What were they after? What did they want? It was oppressively hot, I remember, the heat dazzling in the bright, empty store, but I did not think of taking off my overcoat, only stared and listened. The silence of it all was a special puzzle to me. They scarcely spoke to each other, just drank; though occasionally two or three of them would join their voices in a carol, or a girl scream when old Greenie pinched her butt.

Greenie was the first to collapse (altogether that evening six passed out cold), the oldest man in the store, for eleven weeks running low man in findings, buckles, opera pumps and hosiery sales. It was clear to everyone that he would be fired inside of a month or two. The store was too fast for his old legs, the stock too hard for his weak back; and though he would sing bravely, when the younger men teased him about his potency, "It takes the old man a little longer, but he gets there just the same . . ." he did not really care any more.

His only remaining passion was a nostalgia for strength and beauty; with the same abstract, reverent air, he would pinch a girl's ass or feel the arm of some embarrassed, husky youngster. "What an arm," he would say, shaking his head ruefully, "like my leg!" and he would pluck some passing salesman by the sleeve to be his witness. "Look," he would insist, first pulling the pants leg tight around his own withered thigh, then attempting to span the biceps of the boy, "with both my hands I can't get around it— like my leg!" Max and I carried him, limp and almost weightless, to the back of the store, arranging him neatly behind the last row of seats.

"I used to work for an undertaker once," Max told me. "You don't believe me?"

"I believe you."

"Laid out many a stiff."

I took off Greenie's glasses and put them in his pocket. Wearing glasses myself, I realize how hard it is when they are broken. Greenie's eyes, naked and shadowed, were like black holes in his skull.

At this point, they began offering me drinks, the hose girls first of all. "Try a little sip, kiddo, it won't hurt you. Nobody ever died from it!" I would pretend to drink and, "Good boy," they would say with apparent relief. "You're no genius!"

By the time the cop entered, the hose girls had left on the arms of three indistinguishable gents, in black overcoats with velvet collars, who at five-minute intervals had rattled the locked front door until I let them in. They had each refused a drink, grunted something that might have been "Merry Christmas" though you could not have proved it against them in court, and had disappeared with the girls. Only the cashier, four salesman (including Abie and Max), the manager and I were still there and conscious. Max and I lugged two other bodies to what he kept calling "Shadyrest." Max was still walking fairly well, though his end of the stiffs dragged lower and lower, and he insisted on sprinkling each one of them with "embalming fluid" out of a gin bottle.

Not much liquor was going down anyone's throat any more, though the motions of drinking continued. I could see the whisky slosh, as if of its own accord, over shirts and down the front of dresses. I should say, I suppose, dress—singular—since the cashier was the only remaining woman. Ordinarily a reserved and un-friendly girl (everyone suspected her of being an anti-Semite, for she came from a fashionable suburb), she kept trying to sit on the manager's scarcely existent lap and ending up on the floor.

I opened the door for the cop, no one else by this time being willing to make the long trip to the front of the store, but I did not answer him when he asked hopefully, "What's going on in here?" At fourteen I was a regular reader of the New Masses and hated the police with a passion purer than any I have left.

"It's a raid!" Mr. Z. cried in pretended fright, letting the cash-ier slide to the floor again; and all at once, everyone was shout-ing, "Murphy, have a drink!" except for Max who whispered in my ear, "Damned Cossack!" I could not tell whether he was kidding.

In a few minutes they began to sing, "When Irish eyes are smiling . . ." and Abie, who had not even looked in my direction all evening, was rubbing up against Murphy's blue broadcloth like a cat. He had snatched the night stick away from the cop, and fondling it incredulously, kept repeating, "Oh, daddy, what a big one you got. Oh, daddy!" Though he had drunk nothing, his face had grown redder, his lips looser, his eyes more moist, and he was sweating with pleasure.

Murphy, knowing, by God, a good joke when he heard one, roared with delight, nearly choking on his drink in the process. Blowing and snorting, he wiped his mouth with the back of one hairy hand and jabbed Abie in the ribs with the other. "Ah, go on with yez," he shouted playfully (I swear to you that was what he said—what can I do!) at Abie picking himself off the floor and brushing the seat of his pants tenderly. "Oh, be careful, daddy," Abie said. "Don't break it, daddy." Then, so quickly I could not be sure it was aimed at me at all, he sent a wink in my direction, mouthing soundless curses in Yiddish as he put one arm around the cop.

A little later they were dancing together, Murphy's thick arm around Abie's shoulder, Abie's oiled head resting blissfully on the cop's chest, as the others stood around in a circle, clapping and stamping in time to the tune of "*Oi, oi, oi, oi, mazeltov!*" a song of rejoicing sung at Jewish weddings. Even the presumably anti-Semitic cashier was beating time on the top of Mr. Z.'s bald head, while George the porter, who had suddenly appeared from God knows where, danced slowly in place beside her.

I still stood apart from the rest, a witness beside the water cooler, when Max joined me again. "Feeling pretty *superior*, ain't you, snotnose. Su-per-i-or, that's a fancy word for a shoe-dog."

"No, look—really—I—"

"You think I'm like these other ignorant jimokes—stupid—nothing but a god-damned shoe-dog."

"I never—"

"Just a stupid shoe-dog, is that it?"

"Really, I—"

"Shut up! I know what you think. Think you're a radical, don't you, a radical."

I had never talked politics in the store that I could recall, but I would not deny it. "Yes, I—"

He made a meaningless gesture. "Oh, you know the score all right! We're just wage slaves, white-collared, yellowbellied boozhwahzees. Ain't that right, Comrade Genius?"

"You don't know what you're—"

"How old are you?"

"That don't make any—"

"Shut up!"

That was easy, because I had never really said anything; so I just looked at him, while he tried to stare me down. Finally, I turned my eyes away in weariness. I could see it pleased him; he thought he had proved something, God knows what.

"Listen," he said, grabbing me by the lapels of the overcoat (it was too big for me, a hand-me-down from my father, with large checks—"the horse-blanket," the kids in school called it), "listen. I was a union man once. You don't know a god-damn thing about—I suppose you read *Das Kapital*—"

I nodded.

"Christ, I read it before I was—" He stopped suddenly as if he had read something offensive in my glance. "You don't believe me?"

"I believe you."

"Ask John Harwood, Bella Biemoller. Ask Bill Smantz." Who were they? Where had the meaningless names come from? "Everybody knows—"

"I said I believe you!"

"Well, *sound* it! I was even a Yipsel. You know what that is, Comrade Genius?"

"Sure," I said. "Young People's Socialist League."

"That's right—Socialist. There were some pretty sharp youngsters in that outfit. You wouldn't know a guy by the name of— Jesus, no, you were working full-time filling your diapers then!"

"Well, then, why do you—why don't you *do* something, if you know so much, understand the principles of the class struggle. First of all, what you guys need is a union. Now I can get in contact with a representative of—" Class struggle! You see how it was. A minute before I had been bewildered, afraid, then suddenly—

"You talk about a union," Max said. "I was a business agent once for the undertakers' union. You think that's crap, don't you?"

"Look, if only—"

"A union man! Not like the rest of them, stupid, yellow boozhwahzees." He pointed toward Greenie, snoring slightly between the other two semi-corpses. "I was once a Yipsel."

"You said that," I told him. "Look, if we can get together with one or two others, even one other salesman, any night next week, I know a guy who—" Already in my mind the store was organized, and I was walking up and down on the picket line carrying a sign: UNFAIR TO—

"I used to be a union man myself—a Yipsel. You don't even

know what the hell that is." He walked over to a mirror, standing up to it in the old-fashioned socialist salute, the arm extended
up and out, the fist clenched. I stood up behind him, watching
his face over his shoulder, trying to see it as he saw it: the patchy
beard, the pimples, the hair streaked with gray under its shell of
pomade; but the face still of one who had been a Yipsel and a
union man. Softly he began to sing to the tune of "Maryland,
My Maryland," "The workers' flag is deepest red—The workers'—"
He could not get past the first line, and he turned to me for help.
"I don't remember. For Christ's sake, I don't remember any
more!"

I knew only one more line myself, but I sang it: "It shrouded
o'er our martyred dead," and together we sang the two lines over
and over, climbing up on to seats and down again in time to
the song, back and forth the entire length of the store. "The
workers' flag is deepest red—it shrouded o'er our martyred dead."

The cop, still dancing with Peckelis, the boss, still beating
his hands together and singing in parody, "Oi, oi, oi, oi,
mazeltov—the Rabbi has the whooping cough," paid us no heed.
Still we had the sense of shouting our defiance in the very teeth
of our oppressors: Mr. Z.'s belly sagging between the open
flaps of his vest, Murphy's brutal jaw—like a cartoon in the New
Masses.

I felt a special revulsion toward Abie, squirming in the arms of
a dumb cop and insulting him in Yiddish under his breath to
make the others laugh. "That god-damn fairy!" I said to Max as
we paused for a moment. "I hate his—"

But even as I spoke, Max tripped and fell. He rose again
quickly; but breathless and excessively pale, was barely able to
make it to a seat. "Gimme a minute, kid, just a minute." His
mouth was open and he held his hand to his heart like an old
man. I could hardly bear to look at him. As I turned away in disgust, I realized that not only our own singing had stopped; the
rest of the group still stood in a ring around Abie and the police-
man, but they were not even laughing any more. I pushed my
way curiously between the cashier and George, my head thrust
forward like a turtle's out of the shell of my foolish overcoat.

Finally I could see the cop with one arm still around Abie, though they were no longer dancing. He was goosing him with his night stick and Abie was making small squeals of pleasure, scarcely distinguishable from the noise of his quick, heavy breathing. His eyes under the half-closed lids were moist and dim; and his tongue, fat and foam-flecked, was going round and round, at the same time darting in and out of his open mouth.

I was fascinated by the erratic motion of the tongue, jerking crazily out of phase with his own breathing, as if moved by a will of its own, faster, faster, *faster*— Suddenly it stopped, and Peckelis' body, bent like a bow until a moment before, went limp. The cop, releasing his arm, let him drop with a thump to the floor and, standing over him, began to laugh, a huge contagious bellow that the others picked up, each in his own variation until the store echoed with laughter, billow on billow as if it would never stop. As Abie looked for a moment directly at me, I could read the Yiddish curses I could not hear: "May he swell up—may he be hanged; may he burn like a candle. . . ."

Things happened too fast from that point on. An instant later, George the porter had fallen over the railing into the basement below—breaking his leg, it was discovered much later, although at first no one would go down to look. "It's only a gag," Mr. Z. insisted. "All these jigs are first-class athletes—hard as nails." And when I kept protesting, he snapped impatiently, "Go down and look yourself if you're so worried."

But I did not go down, though George was my friend and would sit with me at lunchtime among the bales of old shoeboxes and the dusty china legs in the basement. It was pitch dark below and I feared the rats whom I could feel in my imagination nuzzling my ankles before I got the lights turned on. I could almost see them, fat and furry, sniffing at the pool of blood in which George lay—perhaps dying or dead.

I thought I had found an ally, when a few minutes later I saw the cashier leaning over the bannister above the cellar steps, as if peering into the darkness to see what had happened. But she was only puking into the shaft; and when I tried to draw her away, to tell her about George lying helpless below, she drew me to her damp, sour-smelling breast. "You're a fine boy—and you can call me Emma Jane. God bless you and a Merry Christmas to you and your family." She almost shouted the words, and suddenly everyone was repeating them. "God bless you and a Merry Christmas to you and your family," they cried to one another, exchanging kisses with sodden affection.

Only Peckelis did not join in, leaning against the wall now exhausted, and wiping first his forehead then his upper lip carefully with a large white handkerchief. I could imagine its sickly scent. "Christ is risen!" Emma Jane screamed. "Or is that Easter?" and she rushed back to the railing in a new spasm of nausea.

Even Max is better than this, I thought despondently; but I found him weeping in his chair, his head slumped forward until it almost rested on his knees. In his hands, he held a brown paper bag. "It's a baby doll," he explained, "for my little girl. For Christmas." He lifted the doll out, gold and pink and white, but it slipped through his clumsy fingers, fell to the floor at his feet. He was on his knees in an instant, scrambling to retrieve it, half-blind with tears.

I picked it up for him. "Look," I said, poking its belly so that it bleated maa-maa. "It's not even broken."

He snatched it from me in sudden anger. "You think I'm soft —a god-damn, no-good, sentimental boozhwahzee, don't you?" He was yelling at the top of his voice. "Nothing but a boozhwahzee."

"Listen," I said, "for Christ's sake."

"I'll show you who's a boozhwahzee! I used to be a Yipsel." He held the doll high over his head, standing as erect as he could manage, his legs straddled wide, though he listed dangerously. His fly was open. "Don't think this Christmas malarkey fools me one little minute. It's a boozhwahzee holiday!"

"Take it easy, you're drunk!" What did I know, a kid in a checked overcoat?

"I'll show you who's drunk!" He threw the doll to the ground, stamped on it, grinding the head to powder under his heel. "That proves it," he sobbed, "that proves it, God damn it, *don't* it?" But he passed out before making it clear just what he thought it proved.

I dragged him to the back of the store and laid him beside the others. As I tossed the crippled remains of the doll down beside him, he spoke without opening his eyes. His voice was low but surprisingly distinct. "Don't think harshly of me, kid," he said—a line from an old-fashioned melodrama. "Don't think harshly of me." But I was already on my way out.

And so in a way, I have got down the story, after all, though I have not had a moment's peace. As I have written, the phone has rung three times: the plumber, the landlord, the florist. What they asked I do not really know, answering them: yes, yes, yes— thank you—good-by. I do not believe in them, any more than in the Grand Opening tomorrow. If there are tears in my eyes, they are not for Hyman Brandler who is not a writer, who is thirty-five. I am fourteen again, and once more it is Christmas Eve.

I leave before the party is quite over, without looking back over my shoulder at Max, without daring to meet the eye of Abie, who is sitting now staring at the floor between his legs. I have forgotten George the porter, and no one cries "Merry Christmas" to my back; only Mr. Z. mutters thickly something about, "Go home!"

As I push open the front door, the carillon from the Public Service Building is playing "Silent Night, Holy Night" and the crowd at the trolley stop stamps in time to keep warm; their breaths are visible as they shout greetings and jocular insults to each other. Before my streetcar comes, Abie Peckelis thrusts past me, almost knocking me over.

I turn away from him, stare into the unlit display window, hoping he has not recognized me, afraid to be embarrassed before the holiday crowd. But he seems to pay no attention to me. "Dogs!" he screams back over his shoulder, shaking his fist at the group still left in the store. "Four walls! Diamonds isn't every- thing!" The people at the curb turn to watch him, grinning and nudging each other; and I grin with them.

He looks around him frantically, but the boy he was perhaps afraid had gone is still waiting, and coming out of the shadows, he links his arm with Abie's, looking down at him in dispassionate contempt. The boy is dark and heavily muscled but light on his feet, a boxer or professional golfer, and Peckelis snuggles close, patting his hair nervously into place. He has somehow the air of one resolving this time to be true.

Though he has not even glanced in my direction, and I huddle inside the shelter of my coat, my nose pressed to the glass, he has spotted me; and while the crowd listens in sudden silence, he turns toward me for a parting shot, screaming in unreasonable fury, "Dog! Don't try to hide. I know you already. False! You're like all the rest—*false!*"

"What a nut!" someone says out of the crowd and I smile smugly to myself at the nuttiness of Abie Peckelis—I who at fourteen believe I have never betrayed anything, and know that I never will.

What Used to Be Called Dead

We laid the Old Man on the pallet because he could not stand always on his feet as all men have now learned to do. Once all men had been like this Old Man, getting up and lying again as the sun also rose and went down. Until they lay down forever. Or so at least the Speakers who speak for all in the ritual tell us. The Speakers who gathered now about the Old Man make the Signs preliminary to speech.

IN THE BEGINNING, said the Speakers, the old man used to wake in the morning before the first hint of dawn and coil himself into the shape of misery at the side of the highroad, ready for the first passersby. He would place his hat beside his carefully twisted body, a gaping mouth waiting to be fed with coins. When someone, moved by his plight but penniless, would toss into it a crust of bread or a withered apple, he would throw them into a ditch as soon as the giver was out of sight. But the money he would take back with him at nightfall, piling it neatly at the bottom of the hole under the flat rock near the mouth of his cavern. God perhaps knew how much was there, as he did not—never counting it, much less spending it. And on what he lived, what he ate no one could tell; for he never went anywhere except along the short path (which grew longer day by day) that connected his cave to the road. It was along this road he had come by mistake, as it were, before the beginning. And it was here he had struck the viper with his knotted walking stick, breaking the stick and killing the serpent, brown and gold as it slithered across his path, bright as the daylight; but once dead black as night, though red, too, where its blood oozed and congealed. And up

582

from where it lay in the dust, a butterfly had risen, also black and red—or rather, red and black, coiling and uncoiling its flight until it disappeared into the sun.

Sometimes in the evening, the old man would think he saw the butterfly again at the heart of the glowing circle which was the horizon, and then he would know that it was time for him to leave the highroad and return to his cavern. Time to sleep. Even when he did not think he saw the butterfly, he would know when the moment of its coming had passed, and uncoiling himself begin his trek back along the path. To sleep.

And yet he knew that once he slept, the trees would begin their silent march toward the road, so that every morning would find them a little closer, the ribbon of sunlight that escaped their shade a little thinner. Often he would be waked in the night by their creaking, and he would open his eyes in terror knowing that there was nothing to see.

Even at high noon as he lay waiting for alms, he could hear the trees whispering, bending toward each other, tugging at their roots-preparing for that nighttime motion as slow and secret as the passage of years. But while he lay at the roadside they could not move, though he could feel their hatred, patient and dumb. And he could not halt their march, or hasten it. Only wait for the first hint of dawn, for another day.

His daughters, though they knew he dreamed, saw only an old man dozing in a rocker on the sunlit porch—until awakened by the creaking of his own rocking chair. They would be startled by the terror in his waking eyes, as they had been surprised by his age and lassitude, returning home from their various sorrows in search of a strength that was no longer there.

So they walked past him on tiptoe, speaking to each other in whispers; but their mother banged knife against knife in the sink, washing up with a clatter she must have intended to wake the old man. If only to quarrel with him. If only to break his dreaming. But the girls were busy dreaming him dreaming them. And so they did not see the old woman move stealthily from the sink to the porch and raise the knife high over the heaving breast of the old man, as if to plunge it deep toward the secret cavern where his heart slept in the hope of morning.

No one except the Old Man saw her move. No one. To every-one else she was still there at the sink, bent over the small noises of tidying up.

What we saw was the Old Man: a withered body that did not move, though its shlang *stood erect, swollen and purple. And this seemed to us a wonder; for what hung from the hairless juncture of our own legs, slept eternally. The Ritual, it is true, spoke of a time when the shlangs of all men rose and fell, even as their bodies did with the growing and fading of light, the going and the coming of the dark. For light then was not given and taken away as it is now, by the will of each of us. As food also is now given and taken away and the shape of the world. Then, the Ritual said, none had yet learned that each must become all. And there was pain.*

Which is why, the Speakers were saying, the knife changed in the hand of the old woman, turning before it fell into a serpent, a viper brown and gold, though growing black as it moved downward until its blackness was broken by red where the Old Man's blood oozed and congealed. And all the while the trees marched toward the high-road, though it was broad daylight, tugging at their roots, not whis-pering any more, but crying aloud as trees cry only at the center of a storm. Yet it was clear and no breeze stirred.

No matter. The Old Man lay in the bosom of his boyhood, crouched in a dark concrete chamber far underground. The city in which he lived for fifty more years had burned to the ground just before his fifteenth birthday, burning for two days and three nights. But what had started the fire no one could guess. The blacks perhaps, eager to destroy the rat-infested ghettos in which they lived. Or the whites, no longer able to abide the reproach of their misery. Or others, neither black nor white and more like trees than men, whom no one had ever seen in daylight, though both black and white dreamed them nightly. Or perhaps it had only been the long hot summer that had dried everything up: sidewalks and plateglass show windows, wood and stucco and brick and the streetside maples in their jackets of wire mesh, cats in back alleys and dogs breathless beside stone lions on the stone stoops—parching everything to a dryness that could grow no longer, only burn under the unremitting assault of the sun.

When it first started, he had been working (the old man, the boy) in a shoe store, as he always seemed to be working once he lay down in his bed, or—sitting or standing—dared to close his eyes. And the fire had raged with special fury in the store. But they had somehow escaped—he, Mr. Z, Max and Abie Peckelis—taking refuge in an abandoned concrete shelter of whose existence none of them had ever heard before. It lay under the Gutzon Borglum statue of the Wars of America, built God knows why and long since forgotten. But somehow they had found their way to it, bringing with them (but why, the old man wondered) a female dummy from their display window, three padded seats intended for customers, and three hard stools meant for crouching at their feet—as well as a whole wall of stock.

A whole wall of boxed shoes saved from the fire. And already they were beginning to open the boxes, tossing the empties to one side of the room and the crumpled paper they contained to another. As at the end of any day, they were preparing to tighten things down, to "drop the stock," to get ready for tomorrow. Business as usual. Why *not*? But he could see from the puzzled way in which Mr. Z and Max were peering inside each shoe, then turning to each other in bewilderment, that all the shoes were mismates. Not a matching pair in the whole batch. And they wept. Yet what difference could it possibly make, since they four (he suddenly knew) were the sole survivors, the city above them gone up in smoke and the ashes cooling under the rain.

After the Speakers had done speaking, the Singers came and the Dancers, for this is the way of the Ritual. But though the Singers sing alone, all dance to the words which are the heart of the mystery. And so we danced now about the pallet of the Old Man, not touching him or each other, and not moving so much as remembering, indicating movement. We did not have to look to know that his shlang *had fallen, nor listen to hear the Singers' words that had shriveled his flesh.*

> Give fire *back to the father*
> Give fire *back to the father*
> Give fire *back to the father*
> *We have given the fire back to the father*
> *And we no longer burn!*

The crackling of flames had ceased in the city of the old man's boyhood, and only the far-off sound of rain on the concrete blocks that sheltered him could be heard in the growing darkness. But where did the light he saw by come from, and why was it now starting to fade? And how could he hear the rain so clearly through all that thickness of concrete and earth and turf—but *not* the voices of Mr. Z and Max who still scrambled hopelessly among mismates at their feet and seemed to be screaming at each other in rage? Or maybe they were praying? He could not even hear the laughter of Abie Peckelis; though Abie, having undressed the display mannequin, stood before her blank nakedness, his fat hands slapping his plump thighs, and his marcelled head thrown back as if he bellowed in pleasure. It was from his greased head that the little light left must be streaming (the old man thought with a sigh) or from the stripped dummy or from somewhere between them.

And in the last light, was it a red and black butterfly that glimmered above them, banging itself against concrete in a vain effort to find the sun? No. It was not a butterfly. It was the old woman, or rather the mouth of the old woman opened slightly to kiss him as she bent over his rocker—no knife *or* snake in her hand after all. Only a damp dish towel bordered with red and black. Bent over to wake him, though his daughters protested (and why could he see them no longer? where had they gone?), crying, "Ma, let him sleep, for pity's sake." "Never mind," he thought he answered, knew that he could not wake—for he lay now in the heart of a strange domed city, a city without a sky.

He lay on a pallet that gave with every heave and thrust of his body, that caressed him like skin against skin. And over his head there was no sky, only a translucent vault, not glass or ice though likest to them, through which light came but no images. No shape of a cloud, no hint of the sun. And he told himself, not knowing what the words might mean even as he said them, that the sun had blown out and there was no longer a sky. "No longer," he repeated, this time, he was sure, half-aloud, *"No longer."* And he felt like a chill at the core of his bones a sense of the aeons that must have passed between the time out of which he had fallen asleep and the time into which he awoke: an endless desert of time, more like the vacuum of space than the small crowded cycle of life he had grown up expecting to live.

It did not surprise him, looking up, to discover that he could see no women at all, though he sensed somehow (but how?) that the area capped by the dome was all that remained of the world. He could not see everyone it held, of course; for it was vast, vast—and the crowd which stood shoulder to shoulder, belly to back, assembled he was sure just to watch him blurred to indistinction at the furthest limits. But he knew beyond doubt that they must all be males, as ageless and naked as the three men who now bent over him, probing his body with instruments for which he had no name; and bending close to his face their faces—not young, though unmarked by pain or sorrow or the passage of years.

Obviously, they were Doctors, or at least something more like what Doctors once were than anything else for which he had a name. And sensing their bafflement, he tried to speak but found he could not. Could not say a word or open his mouth or move. But had he not cried just a moment before, "No longer"? Or had he only dreamed it? Or was it something remembered from another life, another story? A life not yet lived, perhaps. Or a story still untold. The three Doctors seemed as dumb as he, or at least he could hear nothing, see no movement of their lips. Yet they appeared to communicate, even to quarrel with each other—or rather, gravely to disagree. Their eyes remained fixed on him, though they no longer touched him or even pointed in his direction; their hands flickering from time to time to indicate their own faces or the naked sex which hung from their hairless bodies like great gold and brown snakes. Limp and peaceful.

He could not help remembering then the serpent in his path that had been the beginning of it all, and he felt his own flesh stir as fear rose in him. But it came to him all at once, like a message from elsewhere or elsewhen, that these vipers could neither raise their heads nor strike, and that therefore they would not ever bleed or be killed. That the men who wore them like an ensign of some old victory or defeat could also never bleed or be killed. "They have paid the price," he found himself thinking, "and it is worth it." And "Let me, too," he tried to say, trying to rise, "let me pay, too."

If he really spoke they did not hear him, and if he rose they did not see him; for suddenly one of the three, ripping from the wall a tissue of black and scarlet, subtle as silk and warm as flesh, flung it over his body, all three averting their eyes. No—it was not *from* the wall they tore it, but *out* of the wall, leaving a wound that quivered and bled and closed in an instant.

And now a cry of horror arose from the ranks that encircled him. Or at least he seemed to hear as a word what was surely not spoken at all, *"Cover him! Cover him!"* For a little while the tissue hung in the air, weightless, fluttering. And before it fell over his eyes, sealing them, becoming one with the lids—flesh of his flesh— he could see that softie of the naked horde clustered about him appeared to weep. But even that was not yet the end; for under the cover which smelled of darkness and earth and himself, he could hear still like a voice what was surely no voice, crying, "He is *dead*. We remember now, he is what used to be called *dead*."

Even to the old man the word seemed an obscenity too gross to be spoken; but echoed from rank to rank of the watching crowd, it grew in volume like approaching thunder: "Dead. Dead. Dead. *Dead. Dead. Dead.* DEAD. DEAD. DEAD." Then, there being nothing else to do, they all laughed—out of shame or relief or in selfish pleasure he had no way of knowing, knowing only that they laughed, and that he was indeed what used to be called dead.